The Strict Liability Principle and the Human Rights of Athletes in Doping Cases

Partners of the ASSER International Sports Law Centre:

**LARRAURI &
LÓPEZ ANTE**

avvocati e commercialisti
d'impresa
studio associato

C/M/S/ **Derks Star Busmann**
ATTORNEYS AT LAW CIVIL LAW NOTARIES TAX ADVISERS

DE KEERSMAEKER VROMANS

WILKENS C.S.
TRANSLATORS & INTERPRETERS

T.M.C. ASSER INSTITUUT
ASSER International Sports Law Centre

The Strict Liability Principle and the Human Rights of Athletes in Doping Cases

Janwillem Soek

T·M·C·ASSER PRESS

Published by T·M·C·Asser press
P.O.Box 16163, 2500 BD The Hague, The Netherlands

<www.asserpress.nl>

T·M·C·Asser press' English language books are distributed exclusively by:

Cambridge University Press, The Edinburgh Building, Shaftesbury Road,
Cambridge CB2 2RU, UK,
or
for customers in the USA, Canada and Mexico:
Cambridge University Press, 100 Brook Hill Drive, West Nyack, NY 10994-2133, USA

<www.cambridge.org>

ISBN 10: 90-6704-226-9
ISBN 13: 978-90-6704-226-0

T.M.C. Asser Instituut - Institute for Private and Public International Law, International Commercial Arbitration and European Law
Institute Address: R.J. Schimmelpennincklaan 20-22, The Hague, The Netherlands; Mailing Address: P.O. Box 30461, 2500 GL The Hague, The Netherlands; Tel.: +3170 342 0300; Fax: +3170 3420 359; Internet: www.asser.nl.
Over thirty years, the T.M.C. Asser Institute has developed into a leading scientific research institute in the field of international law. It covers private international law, public international law, including international humanitarian law, the law of the European Union, the law of international commercial arbitration and increasingly, also, international economic law, the law of international commerce and international sports law.
Conducting scientific research, either fundamental or applied, in the aforementioned domains, is the main activity of the Institute. In addition, the Institute organizes congresses and postgraduate courses, undertakes contract-research and operates its own publishing house.
Because of its inter-university background, the Institute often cooperates with Dutch law faculties as well as with various national and foreign institutions. The Institute organizes *Asser College Europe*, a project in cooperation with East and Central European countries whereby research and educational projects are organized and implemented.

PRINTED IN THE NETHERLANDS

FOREWORD

I am very honoured and pleased to write the foreword to this book, whose title and contents are somewhat controversial – to say the least. The subject of doping and how to deal with it is a very important one to all those involved in sport as participants, members of governing bodies, sponsors and many others. Doping is the antithesis of everything that sport stands for – not least the need to protect the health of athletes and also to encourage and safeguard the fundamental principle of fair play.

And fairness is at the heart of this welcome and timely study by Dr Janwillem Soek, a leading expert and writer on doping issues in sport. His essential issue is whether the principle of "strict liability" – namely that an athlete is solely responsible for whatever substances are found in his/her body – is consistent with the human rights of the athlete, in particular the legal presumption of innocence until proved otherwise – rather than a presumption of guilt – and also the right to be heard, two of the most basic principles enshrined in the European Convention on Human Rights. These are not only edifying legal concepts to be debated by lawyers and academics, but their application also gives rise to very significant practical consequences for the athletes concerned, especially athletes who earn their livings from sport. Lengthy, not to mention lifetime bans can not only destroy an athlete's ability to practise his/her sport, but also have serious economic consequences too, such as loss of earnings and lucrative sponsorship and endorsements deals. Are such doping bans "restraints of trade" and, if so, are they legally enforceable or not? Another vital issue that this book tackles concerns how effectively are doping cases handled by the Court of Arbitration for Sport, which, under the World Anti Doping Code, is the ultimate "Court of Appeal" in such cases.

Doping and its consequences are not only matters that concern the athletes themselves and lawyers and academics, but are also of vital interest to the International Olympic Committee, of which I am a member, in its continuing fight to bring so-called "drugs cheats" to account. Sports administrators, such as myself in my capacity as Honorary President for life of the International Cycling Union (UCI), are of course only too aware of the continuing need to preserve the integrity of our sports. In fact, the UCI operates a rigorous anti-doping programme and is at the forefront of eliminating drugs from our sport. It is not, however, for me to debate here the pros and cons of operating a "strict liability" regime in sport and its interface with basic human rights that have the force of law or even attempt to discuss its legal limits – that is for Dr Janwillem Soek, who does so admirably in his book. Suffice to say, however, that without such a regime, the fight against doping in sport would be difficult, if not impossible, to carry out. It is – in this respect – of crucial importance that National Governments guarantee a non-infected food and drug production. If that is not the case, strict liability will make victims amongst innocent athletes.

That said, I have no hesitation whatsoever in recommending this book, which, as I said earlier, is both timely – witness the range of doping tests and novel situations that arose at the 2006 Winter Olympics in Turin – but also a welcome addition to the literature and continuing debate on doping in sport, which is a matter of great concern to us all.

Hein VERBRUGGEN
*UCI Honorary President for life
and IOC Member*

CONTENTS

PART I
SUBSTANTIVE LAW

Chapter 1

Chapter 2

Chapter 5
System of Sanctions

PART II
PROCEDURAL LAW

ABBREVIATIONS

AAA	American Arbitration Association
AC	Appeals Commission (or Committee)
ACF	Australian Cycling Federation
ACNO	Association des Comités Nationaux Olympiques
ADC	Anti-Doping Commission (Australia)
AER	Anti-doping Examination Regulations (UCI)
AFA	Argentinean Football Association
AIBA	International Amateur Boxing Association
AIOWF	Association of the International Olympic Winter Sports Federations
AIWF	Association of the International Olympic Winter Sport Federations
AlS	Australian Institute for Sport
AMA	Agence Mondiale Antidopage
ANOC	Association of National Olympic Committees
AOC	Australian Olympic Committee
ARA	The Amateur Rowing Association
ARISF	Association of Recognized IOC International Sports Federations
ASA	Swiss Arbitration Association
ASDA	Australian Sport Drug Agency
ASDTL	Australian Sports Drug Testing Laboratory
ASFGB	Amateur Swimming Federation of Great Britain
ASOIF	Association of Summer Olympic International Federations
ATF	Arrêts du Tribunal Fédéral Suisse
ATP	Adenosine trifosfaat
ATP Tour	Association of Tennis Professionals
BAE	Badminton Association of England
BBA	British Bobsleigh Association
BBBB	Nederlandse Basketball Bond
BBF	Belgian Boxing Federation
BCF	British Cycling Federation
BCU	British Canoe Union (B.C.U.)
BDR	Bund Deutscher Radfahrer
BEF	British Equestrian Federation
BFA	British Fencing Association
BJA	British Judo Association
BJP	Bulletin de jurisprudence pénale
BK	Berner Kommentar
BOA	British Olympic Association
BRF	Bundesfachverband für Reiten und Fahren (Austria)
BSSF	British Ski and Snowboard Federation
Bull. ASA	Bulletin de l'Association Suisse de l'Arbitrage
BverfG	Bundesverfassungsgericht
BW	Burgerlijk Wetboek (Civil Code, Netherlands)
CA	Cour d'Appel (France)
CAD	Commission Antidopage (UCI)
CAF	Commissione d'Appello Federale (Italy)
CAS	Court of Arbitration for Sport

CC	Civil Code
CC	Code Civil Suisse / Swiss Civil Code
CCP	Code of Criminal Procedure
CDI	International Disciplinary Court (of FIM)
CEDH	Convention européenne des droits de l'homme
CGA	Commonwealth Games Association
CGF	Commonwealth Games Federation
CHF	Francs suisses / Swiss Francs
CHIO	Concours Hippique International Officiel
CIA	Concordat intercantonal sur l'arbitrage
CIAS	Conseil International de l'Arbitrage en matière de Sport
CIO	Comité international Olympique
CMR	Fédération camérounaise d'athlétisme / Cameroon Athletics Federation
CNCDD	Comité Nacional de Competicion y Disciplina Deportiva
CNLD	Commission Nationale de Lutte contre le Dopage
CNO	Comité National Olympique
CNOSF	Comité National Olympique et Sportif Français
CO	Code (suisse) des obligations
COA	Canadian Olympic Association
COC	Canadian Olympic Committee
COC	Chinese Olympic Committee
Code	Code of Sports-related Arbitration
COE	Council of Europe
COJO	Comité d'Organisation des Jeux Olympiques
CONI	Comitato Olimpico Nazionale Italiano
CP	Code de pointage
CP	Code pénal
CSIO	Official International Show Jumping Championships
Cst	Constitution fédérale suisse
DAC	Disciplinary and Arbitration Code (FIM)
DBB	Deutscher Basketball Bund
DBF	Dansk Bueskytteforbund
DBSV	Deutscher Bob- und Schlittensportverband
DCF	Doping Control Form
DCR	Doping Control Rules
DCU	Danmarks Cykle Union
DCV	Deutscher Curling-Verband
DEB	Deutscher Eishockey Bund
DEG	Deutsche Eisschnellauf-Gemeinschaft
DFB	Deutsche Fußball-Bund
DHB	Deutscher Handball-Bund
DHB	Deutscher Hockey-Bund
DHEA	Dehydroepiandrotestorone
DIF	Danmarks Idræts-Forbund
DJB	Deutscher Judo Bund e.V.
DKV	Deutscher Kanu Verband
DLV	Deutscher Leichtathletik Verband
DM	Deutsche Mark
DR	Disciplinary Regulations (UEFA)
DRB	Deutscher Ringer-Bund
DRC	Dispute Resolution Chamber (of FIFA)
DRP	Doping Review Panel
DRV	Deutscher Ruderverband
DRV	Deutsche Reiterliche Vereinigung

DS/USA	Disabled Sports USA
DSB	Deutsche Sportärztebund
DSB	Deutsche Sportbund (German Sports Association)
DSV	Deutscher Schwimm-Verband
DTTB	Deutsche Tisch Tennis Bund
DTU	Deutsche Triathlon Union
DVV	Deutscher Volleyball Verband
EBBA	English Basket Ball Association
EC	European Community
ECA	English Curling Association
ECHR	European Convention of Human Rights
ECtHR	European Court of Human Rights
EEA	European Economic Area
EEC	European Economic Community
EFI	Equestrian Federation of Ireland
EHRR	European Human Rights Reports
EMRK	Europäische Menschenrechtskonvention
EOC	European Olympic Committee
EPO	Erythropoietin
ESF	European Sports Conference
ETTA	English Table Tennis Association
EU	European Union
EUR	Euro
FA	The Football Association
FCI	Federazione Ciclistica Italiana
FEB	Federación Española de Baloncesto
FEF	Federación Española de Fútbol
FEI	International Equestrian Federation
FEP	Federação Equestre Portuguesa
FFB	Fédération Française de Boxe
FFB	Fédération Française de Badminton
FFC	Fédération Française de Cyclisme
FFE	Fédération Française d'Escrime
FFF	Fédération Française de Football
FFG	Fédération Française de Gymnastique
FFH	Fédération Française de Handball
FFJDA	Fédération Française de Judo, Jujitsu, Kendo et Disciplines Ass
FFL	Fédération Française de Lutte
FFS	Fédération Française de Ski
FFSA	Fédération Française des Sociétés d'Aviron (FFSA)
FFT	Fédération Française de Tennis
FFT	Fédération Française de Triathlon
FFTT	Fédération Française de Tennis de Table
FFV	Fédération Française de Voile
FI	Fédération internationale
FIAL	Federazione Italiana di Atletica Leggera
FIBA	International Basketball Federation
FIBT	International Bobsleigh and Tobogganing Federation
FICK	Federazione Italiana Canoa Kayak
FIDAL	Federazione Italiana di Atletica Leggera
FIE	International Fencing Federation
FIFA	International Association Football Federation
FIG	International Gymnastics Federation

FIGC   Federazione Italiana Giuoco Calcio
FIH   International Hockey Federation
FIJ   Fédération Internationale de Judo
FIL   International Luge Federation
FILA   International Amateur Wrestling Federation
FIM   Féderation Internationale de Motocyclisme
FIN   Federazione Italiana Nuoto
FINA   International Amateur Swimming Federation
FIP   Federazione Italiana Pallavolo
FIP   Federazione Italiana Pallacanestro
FIS   International Ski Federation
FIS   Federazione Italiana Scherma
FISA   International Rowing Federation
FISE   Federazione Italiana Sport Equestri
FISI   Federazione Italiana Sport Invernali
FIT   Federazione Italiana Tennis
FITA   International Archery Federation
FITARCO   Federazione Italiana di Tiro con L'arco
FIVB   International Volleyball Federation
FLB   Fédération Luxembourgeoise de Basketball
FLF   Fédération Luxembourgeoise de Football
FLL   Fédération Luxembourgeoise de Lutte
FLNS   Fédération Luxembourgeoise de Natation et de Sauvetage
FLT   Federation Luxembourgeoise de Tennis
FLTT   Fédération Luxembourgeoise de Tennis de Table
FLVB   Fédération Luxemburgeoise de Volley-Ball
FPA   Federação Portuguesa de Andebol
FPB   Federação Portuguesa de Badminton
FPBB   Federação Portuguesa de Basquetebol
FPH   Federação Portuguesa de Hoquei
FPH   Federação Portuguesa de Halterofilismo
FPJ   Federação Portuguesa de Judo
FPR   Federação Portuguesa de Remo
FPT   Federação Portuguesa de Tenis
FPTA   Federação Portuguesa de Tiro com Arco
FRBPA   Fédération Royale Belge de Patinage Artistique
FRBPV   Federation Royale Belge de Patinage de Vitesse
FRBSE   Fédération Royale Belge des Sports Equestres
FRBT   Federation Royale Belge de Tennis
FRBV   Federation Royale Belge de Volleyball
FSSE   Fédération suisse des sports équestres
FTP   Federaçào de Triatlo de Portugal

GAISF   General Association of International Sports Federations
GBOHB   Great Brittain Olympic Hockey Board
GG   Grundgezetz (Constitution, Germany)
GISF   Grenada International Sports Federation
GNAS   The Grand National Archery Society
GOA   Grenada Olympic Association
GR   General Regulations
GW   Constitution (Netherlands)

HCL   Hockey Club Luxembourg
HFL   Horseracing Forensic Laboratory
HGH   Human growth hormone

Hof	Gerechtshof (Court of Appeal, Netherlands)
HR	Hoge Raad (Supreme Court Netherlands)
IAAF	International Amateur Athletic Federation
IAC	Intercantonal Treaty on Arbitration of 1969
IARU	Irish Amateur Rowing Union
IAWA	Irish Amateur Weightlifting Association
IAWA	Irish Amateur Wrestling Association
IBA	International Baseball Association
IBF	International Badminton Federation
IBU	International Biathlon Union
ICAS	International Council of Arbitration for Sport
ICC	International Chamber of Commerce
ICCA	International Council for Commercial Arbitration
ICD	Instance de Contrôle ei de discipline de l'UEFA
ICF	Irish Cycling Federation
ICF	International Canoe Federation
ICR	International Ski Competition Rules
ICU	Irish Canoe Union
IDTM	International Doping Tests and Management
IEC	International Electrotechnical Commission
IF	International Federation
IHA	Irish Hockey Association
IHF	Ishockeyförbundet
IHF	International Handball Federation
IICGAD	International Intergovernmental Consultative Group on Anti-Doping
IIHF	International Ice Hockey Federation
IJF	International Judo Federation
ILAC	International Laboratory Accreditation Cooperation
IOC	International Olympic Committee
IPC	International Paralympic Committee
IPRG	Bundesgesetz über das Internationale Privatrecht (Schweiz)
IR	Internal Regulations (FIBA)
IRMS	Isotope Ratio Mass Spectrometry
ISA	Irish Sailing Association
ISAF	International Sailing Federation
ISF	International Softball Federation
ISO	Independent Sampling Officers
ISO	International Organization for Standardisation
ISOD	International Sports Federation for the Disabled
ISSF-UIT	International Sport Shooting Federation
ISU	International Skating Union
ITA	Irish Triathlon Association
ITF	International Tennis Federation
ITTF	International Table Tennis Federation
ITU	International Triathlon Union
IUML	Institut Universitaire de Médecine Légale
IWF	International Weightlifting Federation
JEM	Jeux Equestres Mondiaux
JO	Jeux Olympiques
JT (JdT)	Journal des Tribunaux (Suisse)
KBBB	Koninklijke Belgische Boksbond (Royale Fédération Belge de Boxe)
KBGF	Royal Belgium Weightlifting Federation

KBVB	Koninklijke Belgische Voetbal Bond
KNASB	Koninklijke Nederlands Algemene Schermbond
KNAU	Koninklijke Nederlandse Atletiek Unie
KNBSB	Koninklijke Nederlandse Baseball en Softball Bond
KNGB	Koninklijke Nederlandse Gymnastiek Bond
KNHB	Koninklijke Nederlandse Hockey Bond
KNHS	Koninklijke Nederlandse Hippische Sportbond
KNLTB	Koninklijke Nederlandse Lawn Tennis Bond
KNRB	Koninklijke Nederlandse Roeibond
KNSA	Koninklijke Nederlandse Schutters Associatie
KNVB	Koninklijke Nederlandse Voetbalbond
KNWU	Koninklijke Nederlandse Wielren Unie
KNZB	Koninklijke Nederlandse Zwembond
KOC	Korean Olympic Committee
LAC	Latvian Antidoping Commission
LAD	Laboratoire suisse d'Analyse du Dopage
LBF	Latvian Bobsleigh Federation
LDIP	Loi fédérale sur le droit international privé (Switzerland)
LNDD	Laboratoire National de Dépistage du Dopage
LTA	Lawn Tennis Association
MC	Medical Code
MED	(FINA) Medical Rules
MPC	Model Penal Code
MS	Mass spectometry
MTB	Mountainbike
NA	Norandrosterone
NADO	National Anti-Doping Organisation
NAS	Commando Carabinieri per la Sanità
NBA	National Basketball Association
NBB	Nederlandse Basketball Bond
NBB	Nederlandse Boksbond
NE	Noretiocholanalone
NeCeDo	Nederlands Centrum voor Dopingvraagstukken
NESP	Novel erythropoiesis stimulating protein
NFL	National Football League
ng	nanogrammes
NGB	National Governing Body
NHB	Nederlandse Handboog Bond
NHV	Nederlandse Handbal Verbond
NIJB	Nederlandse IJshockey Bond
NOC	National Olympic Committee
NPC	National Paralympic Committee
NSkiV	Nederlandse Ski Vereniging
NTTB	Nederlandse Tafeltennis Bond
NWBA	National Wheelchair Basketball Association
NZ-SDA	New Zealand Sports Drug Agency
NZOC	New Zealand Olympic Committee
OC	Olympic Charter
OCOG	Organizing Committee of the Olympic Games
OG	Olympic Games
OJ	Loi suisse sur l'organisation judiciaire

OLG	Oberlandesgericht (Germany)
OM	Olympic Movement
OMADC	Olympic Movement Anti-Doping Code
OR	Obligationenrecht
ÖSV	Österreichischer Skiverband
PGDC	Procedural Guidelines for Doping Control (IAAF)
PIL Act	Swiss Private International Law Act
PJA	Procédure judiciaire administrative
Rb.	Rechtbank (District court, Netherlands)
RCAD	Anti-doping Examination Regulations, Réglement du contrôle antidopage
RD	Règlement Disciplinaire (UEFA)
RDS	Revue de droit suisse
rEPO	Recombinant Erythropoietin
RF	Riksidrotts Förbundet
RFEA	Real Federación Española de Atletismo
RFEBM	Real Federación Española de Balonmano
RFEC	Real Federación Española de Ciclismo
RFEDI	Real Federación Española de Deportes de Invierno
RFEF	Real Federación Española de Fútbol
RFEH	Real Federación Española de Hockey
RFEJYDA	Real Federación Española de Judo y Deportes Associados
RFEV	Real Federación Española de Vela
RIHF	Russian Ice Hockey Federation
RLVB	Royale Ligue Vélocipédique Belge
RNOC	Russian National Olympic Committee
ROC	Russian Olympic Committee
RPS	Revue pénale suisse
RT	Règlement technique
SA	Sampling Agent
SAAF	South African Athletic Federation
SAL	Skiing Australia Limited
SAT	Suomen Antidoping-Toimikunte
SBF	Svenska Boxingsförbundet
SFA	Scottish Football Association
SGF	Svenska Gymnastik Förbundet
SJZ	Schweizerische Juristen-Zeitung
SKF	Svenska Konstäkningsförbundet
SLOC	Salt Lake Organizing Committee for the Games
SOCOG	Sydney Organising Committee for the Olympic Games
SOV	Swiss Olympic Association
SpuRt	Zeitschrift für Sport und Recht
SRF	Swedish Riksidrotts Förbundet
SSF	Svenska Skridskoförbundet
SWF	Swedish Weightlifting Federation
T/E ratio	Testosterone/Epitestosterone ratio
TAS	Tribunal Arbitral du Sport (Court of Arbitration for Sport)
TC	Triathlon Canada
TF	Tribunal fédéral (Swiss Federal Tribunal)
TI	Tennis Ireland
TJA	International Tribunal of Appeal (FIM)

UBH	Union Belge de Handball
UCI	International Cycling Union
UCLA	University of California, Los Angeles
UDS	Urheilujärjestöjen Doping-Säännöstö (Finnish Anti-Doping Committee)
UEFA	Union Européenne de Football Association
UEG	Union Européenne de Gymnastique
UIPM	International Union for Modern Pentathlon
UIT	International Shooting Union
UNESCO	United Nations Educational, Scientific and Cultural Organization
URBSFA	Union Royale Belge des Sociétés de Football Association
USADA	United States Anti-Doping Agency
USATF	United States Track and Field
USOC	United States Olympic Committee
VAI	Volleyball Association of Ireland
VBL	Vlaamse Badminton Liga
WADA	World Anti-Doping Agency
WADC	World Anti-Doping Code
WBU	Welsh Badminton Union
WCF	World Curling Federation
WFA	The Football Association of Wales
WHU	Welsh Hockey Union
WTA	Women's Tennis Association
WTF	World Taekwondo Federation
WvSR	Criminal Code (Netherlands)
ZGB	Zivilgesetzbuch (Schweiz)
ZPO	Zivilprozessordnung (Code of Civil Procedure, Germany)

INTRODUCTION

This study concerns the legal position of the athlete in doping cases under the law of the regulations of national and international sports federations and how this legal position can be reinforced. The focus is particularly on the question of the acceptability of what is termed the "strict liability principle" which is currently also laid down in the World Anti-Doping Code.

Background of the study

In 2000 the growing importance of the fight against doping led the budgetary authority of the European Union to include a budget heading to finance pilot projects for campaigns to combat doping in sport in Europe. In this context a study on the "Legal Comparison and Harmonisation of Doping Rules" was commissioned by the European Commission, Directorate-General for Education and Culture to an international research group consisting of sports law experts from the University of Erlangen-Nuremberg, Germany, the T.M.C. Asser Institute, The Hague, The Netherlands, The Max Planck Institute for International and Comparative Criminal Law, Freiburg i.B., Germany, and the Sports Law Centre of Anglia Polytechnic University, Chelmsford, United Kingdom. The aim of this study was described as follows: "The current diversity of rules and regulations of sports organisations and of relevant legislation of Member States leads to ineffectiveness as well as a lack of public acceptance and legal certainty in the fight against doping in sport in Europe. Adequate sanctioning of doping offences must be achieved and procedural guarantees for the protection of the rights of the athlete under the responsibility of the sports organisations must be improved." Recommendations for improving the existing legal instruments would be based on inter alia the analysis and comparison of the doping rules and regulations of the international sports organisation and their national counterparts in the Member States of the European Union.

As far as the rules and regulations of the sports organisations were concerned, the recommendations were to include a catalogue of appropriate penalties for doping offences, in which account would also be taken of a checklist of procedural requirements (including rules of evidence) for the protection of the rights of the athlete.

The first three points of the brief description of the operation concerning the task of of the T.M.C. Asser Instituut, i.e. the task of the author of this book, included the following proposed methodology for the pilot study: (1) Analysis and comparison of the doping rules and regulations of the International Olympic Committee, the International Paralympic Committee, and the international (global and regional, i.e., European) sports federations (Olympic sports), as well as of the corresponding national sports organisations in all EU Member States, with regard to the following aspects in particular: the definition of doping; the purpose of the ban on doping; the rules of evidence; the fundamental rights of the athlete and procedural guarantees; the system of sanctions; the competence to impose sanctions; and the mutual recognition of sanctions. (2) Analysis and comparison of the application and interpretation of the rules and regulations of the organisations as mentioned above with regard to the aspects listed above; (3) Analysis of the decisions (arbitral awards and advisory opinions) of the International Court of Arbitration for Sport (CAS) on doping. One of the expected results of the operation was to create a detailed inventory of the "law" on doping of the international (global and regional/European) sports organisations and the corresponding national organisations (members of the international organisations) in the EU Member States.

For the pilot study the doping regulations of all international Olympic sports organisations and of 525 national sports organisations within the European Union (i.e. about 60/70% of all national organisations) were examined, which was considered to be a sufficient basis for an adequate analysis which could yield conclusions. The Final Report with the contributions of the four partners to the project was presented and discussed at an international conference, which was organised by the T.M.C. Asser Instituut with the support of the Flemish Ministry for Sports (Belgian EU Presidency), on 7 November 2001 in Brussels.[1]

A first superficial reading of the doping regulations gave the impression that they were greatly alike in respect of their structure. Further study however revealed that underneath this structure the image was much more varied. This variety mainly occurred with respect to subjects like the definition of doping, the description of the doping offence (including the references to the list of prohibited substances), the sanctions and the way in which the disciplinary doping proceedings were to be conducted. In addition, countless minor elements were regulated in different ways. This diversity existed not only between the different branches of sport, but also within these branches. In one sport, the analysis of a doping sample could lead to disciplinary proceedings against the athlete, while in another sport the athlete would not even be charged. For similar doping infractions, one athlete could be punished severely, while another athlete in a different branch of sport would be let off with a warning. This inequality in the law was always made much of by the media. The call for harmonisation at the end of the last century from both the sports community and politics was amply justified.

The aim of the abovementioned pilot study to an important extent was to provide a catalogue of the existing rules in the field of combating doping and to a lesser

---

[1] The conference was attended by representatives of international sports federations (Olympic sports) as well as sports ministries and national sports organisations of the fifteen EU Member States (Project No. C 116-15, Final Report, November 2001; restricted distribution on CD-ROM amongst national sports ministries as well as national and international sports organisations).

extent to compare these rules. Based on the outcome of the study, the researchers were to formulate recommendations. The pilot study was intended to contribute to the discussion within the European Union concerning the harmonisation of the different doping regulations. Its results and recommendations would be used in the framework of the Commission's proposals at the Community level with a view to better co-ordination and complementarity between national and European measures and actions. The materials collected for the purpose of the pilot study lent themselves particularly well to further examination of these rules which can impact so deeply on athletes' lives, i.e. to a study into the legal position of athletes who are suspected of having used doping.

Central question

An aspect that immediately came to the fore upon examining the doping regulations was the difference in the legal positions of athletes suspected of doping. Under some doping regulations the prosecuting sports organisations still had to prove guilt or intention on the part of the athlete, while under others guilt was considered established with the finding of prohibited substances in the doping sample, i.e. the strict liability rule. With this rule – which has also been laid down in the recent World Anti-Doping Code – the balance tipped completely in disfavour of the athlete. The central question of this book is whether the rule which presumes the athlete's irredeemable guilt after the finding of doping might not go against one of the most fundamental principles of the law, expressed in the adage "no punishment without guilt." In order to find an adequate answer to this question it must be examined whether a rule of a higher order such as that included in Article 6(2) ECHR applies to the doping procedure. In case this question needs to be answered in the affirmative, the next question would be whether the strict liability rule should therefore be considered *contra legem*.

Starting points

Disciplinary law in general is positioned on the crossroads between private law and criminal law. What is the position of disciplinary doping law in this respect? For the purpose of legal orientation we might use the criterion of voluntariness. The voluntariness of the submission of members of a group to doping law determines whether this law is rather more private law-orientated or criminal law-orientated. As the athlete's level of professionalism increases, the level of voluntariness decreases. Exercising the profession of professional athlete means complete submission to the doping rules applicable in that particular branch of sport. Given how relative the professional athlete's voluntary submission to the sports organisation is, it could be argued that the impact of the fundamental principles of criminal law should not only be substantial but should in fact be predominant. There must be no misunderstanding concerning the fact that disciplinary doping law is not criminal law and will never be criminal law, but in the framework of the law of associations it is a *kind* of criminal law, at least, a system of imposing sanctions that should have criminal law principles and concepts applied to it. Considering doping law as "the criminal law of private organisations" in which the principles of criminal law are especially present offers several advantages over the starting point that doping law is geared towards private law or governed by several fields of law at once.

The adoption of criminal law principles in doping law adds to the standing of this body of law rather more than does the arbitrary application of criminal law principles and private law principles. In Chapter 6, the argument in favour of applying the principles of criminal law in disciplinary doping proceedings is put forward. Not only do these principles have an advantageous effect on the interpretation of the procedural rules in doping regulations, they also offer added support in the interpretation of substantive rules. This would make the description of the doping offence the counterpart of the description of the offence in an indictment under criminal law. The similarities between the sanctions systems included in doping regulations on the one hand and in criminal (procedural) law on the other are too great to ignore. Criminal law terminology and the principles which have developed through the centuries in substantive and procedural criminal law have served as invaluable guidelines in structuring the subject matter discussed in this book.

Methodology

To reach Ithaca, one must call in at and explore many ports. Problems arising in these places have to be conquered before anchor can be lifted once more. As opposed to the ancient myth, in which the journey described was unpredictable for the mortals undertaking it, this book clearly marks the ports of call. The compass used in navigation is the same as that used in substantive and procedural criminal law, as was already expressed above. In addition, the criminal law compass is also used in this study to point out gaps in doping law and indicate alternatives to existing interpretations of the doping rules.

Where then does the compass lead us? In brief, in the first place the reasons will be sought on the basis of which sports organisations conduct their fight against doping and for which they have chosen to formulate a particular description of the doping offence. What makes the phenomenon such a threat that there is even talk of a "war on doping"?[2] Secondly, this description which makes the investigation of doping, the doping charge, disciplinary proceedings and the punishment of the athlete in question possible is discussed. This will not only include the objective elements of the description of the doping offence, but also the subjective elements. Thirdly, the penalties by which doping infractions are punishable are considered

---

[2] In the Communication from the Commission to the Council, the European Parliament, the Economic and Social Committee and the Committee of the Regions on a Community Support Plan to Combat Doping in Sport (1 December 1999, COM(1999) 643 final), one reads that "doping has always been at variance with the basic principles of sports ethics."

more closely. Finally, a detailed description and analysis is given of the rules apply-ing in disciplinary proceedings. This methodology not only reveals in abstracto the nature of the strict liability rule and its contextual framework, but also provides insight into the way in which the rules are used in practice. In this way, the relation-ship between the strict liability rule and human rights as they have developed in our culture may be demonstrated.

PART I
SUBSTANTIVE LAW

CHAPTER 1
THE PURPOSE OF THE BAN ON DOPING (ARGUMENTS AGAINST THE USE OF DOPING)

1. INTRODUCTION

If one wishes to say anything useful concerning certain aspects of the regulation of doping, one cannot do without a discussion of the objections which have been raised against the use of doping. For as long as people have played competitive sports, it appears that they have used some means to enhance their physical performance. In case those means consisted of the use of substances which altered the normal functioning of the body – or were at least thought to have that effect – their use has always been objected to. Why is that? Because – it is said – "doping practices have at all times been contrary to the fundamental principles of ethics in sport."[3] Nowadays, it is considered that "the widespread use of [...] [performance-enhancing] drugs has threatened the essential integrity of sport and is destructive of its very objectives. It also erodes the ethical and moral values of athletes who use them, endangering their mental and physical welfare while demoralising the entire sport community."[4] In their fight against the use of doping substances and methods the international sports federations have referred to several fundamental principles, among which principles which demonstrate concern for the concrete risks of doping use and principles which demonstrate concern for the threat doping poses to the ideological foundations of sport. In the first place, the argument has been raised that the mental and physical health of athletes using doping is endangered (paragraph 2 below). Secondly, the argument of the falsification of competitions through the use of doping is raised. Turning to this category – the category of ideologically orientated arguments – the first argument used is closely connected to the argument of falsification of competition, namely gaining an unfair advantage over athletes who do not use doping; in other words: the argument of fair play. Another ideologically orientated argument is contrary to ethics. Ethics are understood to include both the ethics of sport and medical ethics. The argument that doping jeopardises the integrity and values of sport is also ideological (Sections 3–6 below).

---

[3] Communication of the Commission to the Council, the European Parliament, the Economic and Social Committee and the Committee of the Regions – Plan for the Community contribution to the fight against doping in sport – Statement by Ms Reding in consultation with Mr Byrne, p. 3.
[4] De Pencier, "Law and Athlete Drug Testing in Canada," cited in John O'Leary, "Doping solutions and the problem with problems," in John O'Leary, ed., *Drugs and Doping in Sport* (London, Cavendish 2000) p. 167.

It was explained in an IOC document[5] that definitions of doping which from a philosophical point of view would be considered completely satisfactory still lost out to the legalist precision of the lawyers. When a description of a concept based on philosophical grounds is no match for the arguments of lawyers, there must be something wrong with the description. This not quite fair point of view in its elaboration became entirely disputable. In the eyes of the IOC the lawyers' activities were regarded as a "phenomenon that allowed the guilty to proclaim their innocence, to escape well-deserved sanctions, and even to make their fortune at the expense of trusting and naive organisations by means of morally unjustifiable damages."[6] This point of view, unfairly condemning an entire profession, caused the IOC to develop "a practical view on the situation," "by proclaiming the principles which, in its view, justified the fight against doping:

– protection of the athlete's health;
– defence of medical and sports ethics;
– an equal chance for all in competition."

Together with the list of prohibited substances, methods and manipulations these principles constituted the IOC's definition. "Any action that goes against these principles or infringes the banned list constitutes a doping case." Bette and Schimank recognised the sport organisations' problems where the reasoned underpinning of the prohibition of doping is concerned. "Verschiedene offene Flanken bieten einem advocatus diaboli Gelegenheiten, die mangelnde Trennschärfe einer Wesensdefinition von Doping zu demonstrieren."[7] The "Wesensdefinition" starts from the premise of a sound sport ethic and from the thought that there will be no need for it in everyday practice. "The definition lies not in words, but in integrity of characters."

It has been claimed that the use of doping substances in sport has to be placed within the wider framework of the general drug problem. One preamble of the International Olympic Charter Against Doping In Sport started out with the words: "Considering that doping in sport is part of the problem of drug abuse and misuse in society...."[8] It is, however, not that obvious that arguments be derived from the social drug abuse problem to apply in the fight against doping in sport. On the discrepancy between drug use and doping use Lüschen and Lüschen write: "Die gerade in den USA umfangreichen Ergebnisse aus der sogenannten Drogenkultur sind nur randseitig übertragbar, weil das Doping zwar auch abweichendes Verhalten ist, aber ungleich rationaler und mit deutlich anderer Motivation verfolgt wird. Rationalisierung dieses Verhaltens im Hinblick auf die Verfolgung höherer Ziele

---

[5] Olympic Charter against Doping in Sport, Preamble.

[6] Doping: An IOC White Paper, Part 1, p. 9.

[7] Karl-Heinrich Bette and Uwe Schimank, "Doping und Recht – soziologisch betrachtet" in K. Vieweg, ed., *Doping. Realität und Recht* (Berlin, Duncker & Humblot 1998) (Bette/Schimank 1998), p. 357 et seq.

[8] Preamble and principles, point C.

(Verein, Nation) ist für den dopenden Sportler immer möglich, während der Drogen-konsument in dieser Beziehung ganz auf sich allein gestellt ist."[9]

In the following the principles on which the sports organisations in the pre-WADC era waged their "war against doping" will be reviewed. Firstly, attention will be paid to the principles arising out of concern for concrete risks and secondly to the principles concerning the threat to the ideological foundations of sport.

2.   THE USE OF DOPING ENDANGERS THE ATHLETE'S HEALTH

Of all the arguments against doping that have been put forward, the argument that the use of doping substances endangers the user's health is used the most. The majority of international federations concentrate on safeguarding the mental and physical health of athletes in their particular branches of sport. The IOC, according to the IOC Charter's preamble, has declared this to be part of its mission and prom-ises to "take measures, the goal of which is to prevent endangering the health of athletes." In order to practise what it preached the IOC has established doping con-trols "as a deterrent to protect athletes from the potential harmful side effects which some drugs can produce." "The use of doping agents is [...] unhealthy [...] and it is necessary to protect the physical and spiritual health of athletes [...]," according to the International Charter against Doping. This wording is illustrative of the word-ing most federations invoking the health argument used. According to the ICF Dop-ing Rules, Rule 1, subsection 1(3): "doping is a threat to physical and mental health." The Doping Control Regulations for FIFA Competitions took this slightly further. "Doping [...] constitutes an acute or chronic health hazard to players with possible fatal consequences." The International Weightlifting's (IWF) Anti-doping Policy was a bit more reticent sub 1.1.1: "The use of banned substances and other doping methods [...] can endanger the health of athletes." Most federations' regulations carried a similar general provision, although some went beyond a general descrip-tion. For these, the potential health hazards prompted them to take an active stance in order to contain the risks. The IOC's position was already mentioned above. The Committee attempted to protect athletes' health by way of doping controls. A simi-lar position was taken by the IPC: "doping control is undertaken by IPC to ensure fair competition and also to protect the health of an athlete," by the International Fencing Federation (FIE): "En raison du grave danger que présente le dopage pour la santé des pratiquant(e)s licencié(e)s, le Président de la FIE ou toute autre personne habilitée à cet effet par la Fédération, peut, sous contrôle médical, faire effectuer à l'occasion de toute compétition organisée sous le contrôle de la FIE, un prélèvement sur les solides, liquides ou gaz absorbés ou rejetés par l'organisme des licencié(e)s

---

[9] Günther Lüschen and Leila Sfeir Lüschen, "Die Struktur des Dopings im Sport, seine rechtliche und soziale Kontrolle – Eine vergleichende Untersuchung über Frankreich und die USA" in: K. Vieweg, ed., *Doping. Realität und Recht* (Berlin, Duncker & Humblot 1998) p. 254.

aux fins d'analyse," and by the International Association Football Federation (FIFA): "The aims of doping control are based on three fundamental principles: (inter alia) protecting the physical and mental integrity of the player, in effect safeguarding his health [...]"

The International Baseball Association's (IBA) provision was structured differently in that it did not address the athlete when voicing its concerns as regards his health, but third parties. The Preamble of the IBA Anti Doping Rules read, among other things: "In order to protect athletes' health according to the provisions of the IOC Medical Code and the International Olympic Antidoping Charter, the IBA issues the present anti-doping Rules related to the prevention and repression of the use of pharmacological classes of doping agents or doping methods among athletes, coaches, trainers, umpires, medical staff, officials, during competitions, trainings and sports events organized by the IBA or by its member Federations." A similar rule was to be found – although in appearance it rather resembled a description of the doping offence – in Article 6.1, subsection 4 of the Regulations Governing Doping Control of the FIBA. "Any person who helps a player or encourages him to use banned substances or methods of doping shall be found guilty of endangering the health of the player [...]"

Within the framework of the health argument the rules of the (International Equestrian Federation (FEI) and the International Bobsleigh and Tobogganing Federation (FIBT) should not go unnoticed. The FEI rule of course concerned the doping of horses. The health argument against the doping of horses in this branch of sport was that the use of a doping substance would not only in all probability affect the horse's performance but might also – according to Annex IV of the Veterinary Regulations – "mask an underlying health problem." The rule in the FIBT Doping Control Regulations should not be left aside either, because it tackled a problem specific to sport. The use of doping substances is not only potentially harmful to the bobsleigher's own health but may also "[...] endanger the bobsleigh driver when descending." In Germany the *Bundesverfassungsgericht* at one point emphasised the protection of life and health as a special task of the legislative. How such protection should be afforded in individual cases was left to the competent legislator. Whether it is specifically also the duty of the state to protect individuals from self-harm (*Selbstgefährdungen/Selbstschädigungen*) is rather doubtful in a legal order focused on personal freedom. "Die Nutzung von Stimulantia in Prüfungen oder berufliche Streßsituationen etwa is schließlich auch nicht untersagt. Aus den Grundrechten eine 'Pflicht zu gesundheitsgemäßer Lebensführung' herleiten zu wollen, hieße, wie in der hiesigen Fachliteratur hinreichend deutlich artikuliert wurde, den freiheitlichen Charakter einer Gesellschaftsordnung diametral umzukehren," as Tettinger has considered.[10] Krogmann[11] has argued that a start to the resolution of the doping

---

[10] Peter J. Tettinger, "Die Dopingproblematik im Lichte der europäischen Grundrechtediskussion" in K. Vieweg, ed., *Doping. Realität und Recht* (Berlin, Duncker & Humblot 1998) (Vieweg 1998) p. 98.

[11] Mario Krogmann, *Grundrechte im Sport, Beiträge zum Sportrecht*, Band 2, PhD (Berlin, Duncker & Humblot 1998) (Krogmann 1998), p. 141.

problem could consist of penalising the use of doping substances through legislation. Although athletes often take medication at the initiative of third parties, such as their trainers or doctors, they are mostly aware whether or not they are taking substances constituting doping. Moreover, every athlete has access to information on whether certain medication contains substances featuring on the doping list. Justification of the penalisation of the use of doping is, however, not to be found in the state's duty of protection based on Article 2, subsection 2, first sentence of the German Constitution. "Gegen die Bestrafung von Sportlern, die Dopingmittel einnehmen, spricht, daß es sich hierbei um Fälle von bewußter Selbstgefährdung handelt. Die Selbstgefährdung steht jedoch ebenfalls unter grundrechtlichem Schutz. Jeder Einzelne besitzt im Rahmen der ihm zustehenden allgemeinen Handlungsfreiheit (Art. 2 Abs. 1 GG) bzw. Im Rahmen des ihm aufgrund seines allgemeinen Persönlichkeitsrechts (Art. 2 Abs. 1 i. V. M. Art. 1 Abs. 1 GG) zustehenden Selbstbestimmungsrechts grundsätzlich auch ein Recht auf eine 'risikobehaftete Lebensführung.'" Seeking out certain risks – for example, in the framework of hazardous sports – is part of the individual freedom of all persons. Legislative interference with this freedom with a view to fighting doping would only be an option if the interest served by protecting the athlete's health would be accorded more weight than the athlete's need for self-fulfilment or "*Dopingbedingter Selbstschädigung.*" This would not be the obvious choice. The individual is free to damage his own health, even if this involves taking doping, "um der Bedeutung der freiheitlichen Lebensgestaltung des Individuums angemessen Geltung zu verschaffen." Doping in this respect is no different from the use of nicotine and alcohol as far as risks to the user's health are concerned. The underlying philosophy of this view is that anyone is entitled to live any way they choose, even if this involves the use of stimulants in a manner which damages their body and/or mind. In Giltay Veth's[12] opinion, this view should be rejected completely. "It is not only contrary to both medical and sport ethics, but also to the foundations of our labour, health and social security law. There are a number of (Dutch) laws, such as the Factories Act (1919), the Opium Act (1928), the Driving Hours Act (1936) and the Medicines Act (1958), which protect the individual against himself, regardless of whether he is an employee or not. Nowadays, there is also extensive legislation in the field of working conditions to carry on this tradition."[13]

To doping users, the side effects and long-term effects of doping substances are usually nothing compared to the advantages they offer. "At the highest level the competitive instincts of many participants may blind them to the dangers," O'Leary

---

[12] Berry Bertels, "'Helicopter-view' met Prof. Giltay Veth over 'dopinglandschap'," (1998) *Sportzaken*, pp. 12-14.

[13] Scott J. in *Gasser v. Stenson* indicated that there are some examples of English criminal law sanctions, which are absolute as far as liability is concerned. Such an example is s. 58(2) of the Medicines Act 1968 "which provides that no person shall sell by retail specified medicinal products except in accordance with a prescription given by a medical practitioner." Another example is s. 5 of the Misuse of Drugs Act 1971 on possession.

thinks.[14] As opposed to German authors, O'Leary is not critical of the health argument by citing the individual constitutional freedom of any person to endanger his or her own health. His criticism is levelled from a purely human point of view: why do sport organisations feel they are entitled to assume such a patronising attitude towards grown-up athletes? Perhaps the situation is different if the substances are not used voluntarily? Athletes could be using doping substances because they are told that without them they do not stand any chance of success. This, however, takes O'Leary to his next objection: "This argument also forms the basis for another objection, that an athlete taking performance-enhancing drugs is coercing others into taking them for the same reasons. There are many training regimes which athletes may and do reject on the basis that they may cause long-term physiological damage, so it is difficult to understand why drug taking should be treated differently. Further, many young sportsmen and women undertake training routines or compete when injured, to their later physical detriment."

Based on various arguments, different authors have reacted against the rules in sport aiming to protect the athlete from himself. On the other hand, there have been proponents of these rules in the literature. Krogmann,[15] for example, has stated that "[...] mit dem Dopingmißbrauch in vieler Hinsicht massive gesundheitliche Risiken verbunden [sind]. Hiervon zeugen nicht zuletzt die nachweislich auf den Gebrauch von Dopingmitteln zurückzuführenden körperlichen Veränderungen, die bei Leistungssportlern zu beobachten sind und aus denen nachhaltige Schädigungen im gesamten Organismus resultieren können. In zahlreichen Fällen hat der Gebrauch von Dopingmitteln sogar schon den Tod von Sportlern nach sich gezogen."

3. THE USE OF DOPING LEADS TO AN UNFAIR ADVANTAGE

This argument which appeared in the anti-doping rules of various international federations derives from the assumption that doping substances are capable of enhancing athletic performance. However, it was obvious from the way in which this assumption was generally worded that the federations were not absolutely convinced that certain pharmacological substances were able to boost performance. Still, the possibility that they could had to be reckoned with, and it was already this possibility that had to be countered. A second assumption which followed naturally from the first one was that athletes who avail themselves of doping in order to enhance their performance thereby gain an unfair advantage over opponents who do not use these substances. This second assumption was often worded quite plainly. These two assumptions that, combined, make up the argument of falsification of competition concern a core element of sport. This core element roughly consists of the fact that the essence of sport is two or more athletes or two or more teams of

---

[14] O'Leary, in Simon Gardiner, Alexandra Felix, Mark James, Roger Welch & John O'Leary. eds. *Sports Law* (London-Sydney, Cavendish 1998) (Gardiner/O'Leary 1998) pp. 164-166.
[15] Krogmann 1998 (*supra* nt. 11), p. 134.

athletes competing in a sports context to establish who is the better athlete or which is the better team. A precondition for such a competition is that the athletes have prepared themselves for "battle" in a natural manner – i.e., through training. The use of doping upsets the natural balance between the athletes or teams.

3.1. Doping enhances athletic performance

The preamble to the IOC Medical Code spoke of "certain substances and methods intended to enhance and/or having the effect of enhancing athletic performance." From this wording it emerges that of certain substances and methods it does not need to be scientifically proven that they boost athletic performance. It is sufficient that these substances and methods are intended to create this effect. The Veterinary Regulations of the FEI, in Annex IV – Prohibited Substances, stated that "The use of a Prohibited Substance might influence a horse's performance." The International Biatlon Union's (IBU) Anti-doping, Blood Test and Gender Verification Rules, III, sub I spoke of "products and methods which [...] serve the purpose of artificially improving the performance of competitors in sports." The wording of Rule 1 of the International Ski Federation's (FIS) Doping Rules is very similar to that which was used by the IBU. In the Doping Control Regulations, 1. mention was made of "medicaments and the application of doping practices to augment the athlete's performance [...]." The rules cited above all took the substances and methods as the starting point. It is also possible, however, to take the athlete using performance-enhancing substances and methods as the starting point and focus on the athlete's intention when using doping. This was, for example, the case in the Preamble to the Doping Operating Procedure of the International Paralympic Committee (IPC), which dealt with "Drug-taking to enhance performance." In Chapter 1, 1.1. of its Anti Doping Rules the IBA also considered doping as "the use or the administration to athletes of pharmacological classes of doping agents or doping methods [...] in order to obtain an unfair advantage of the athletes performance during competition, training, or recuperation after competition or training." In Part XIV of the International Cycling Unition's (UCI) Antidoping Examination Regulations, Introduction, the UCI addressed cyclists "trying artificially to increase their performance." The difference between the rules taking the effect of the substance as the starting point and rules taking the athlete's intention in using doping as the starting point was not only textual. Rules focusing on the athlete also raised the question of whether they were sufficiently solid to serve as an argument against doping, given that they start from the mere intention of achieving a certain end. If an athlete is convinced that he is using a performance-enhancing substance but this substance is in fact not capable of having this effect there is at best – to use criminal law terminology – mens rea or negligence, but one essential element for the imposition of a penalty is lacking: illegality.

3.2. Athletes using doping gain an unfair advantage

Using doping substances which (might) enhance athletic performance is already objectionable in itself, but becomes even more so if their use disrupts the balance of equality between athletes. The time is long past when training was already frowned upon for unnaturally affecting equality between athletes. These days training is accepted and considered necessary to be able to play; training is inherent in sport. Improvements in equipment and nutrition are not achievements which are regarded as undesirable either. However, the situation is completely different when athletes attempt to enhance their capabilities by means of doping. This is understandable, as nobody can be forced to have substances which are alien to the body administered against their will. If the use of doping were to be made legal, athletes would in effect be so forced, if only to maintain competitive equality. The introduction to Chapter IV of the IOC Medical Code put this very aptly. "The IOC and international sports organizations initiated drug testing to protect athletes from the potential unfair advantage that might be gained by those athletes who take drugs in an attempt to increase performance." Although the IOC is spokesman for all international sports organisations, some organisations still repeated this rule in their own regulations. Section 1.1. of Chapter I of the Anti Doping Rules of the IBA considered that the aim of doping was "to obtain an unfair advantage of the athletes performance during competition, training, or recuperation after competition or training." In Rule 1, subsection 1(3) of its Doping Rules the ICF rejected the use of doping "as it is possible by means of doping to get an unfair advantage on other athletes." After having established in Annex IV of the Veterinary Regulations that horses taking part in a competition must be healthy and "compete on their inherent merits," the FEI voiced its fears that doping "could falsely affect the outcome of a competition." Rule 1 of the FIS Doping Rules will serve as a final example. It is phrased with great care: "as it is possible by means of doping to gain an unfair advantage over other athletes [...] doping is incompatible with the general standards of sporting ethics and is a contradiction of the rules and regulations of sport."

Banning the use of doping from sport must not be considered equal to a desire to ban any unfair advantages which athletes may hold. This would not only be impossible, it would also be undesirable. Competitive sports are there by the grace of inter-athlete inequality. "[...] it is desirable to have physiological and psychological differences between the participants" says De Pencier.[16] There are no objections against an athlete's stamina being heightened through an increase in red blood cells, if this increase is the result of high altitude training. The staying power of people who were born and raised at high altitude is in principle already greater than that of

---

[16] Cited in Gardiner/O'Leary 1998 (*supra* nt. 14), p. 167. "There are many advantages inherent in, for example, the nationality of an athlete. The skier raised in Austria or Switzerland has an advantage over one raised in Belgium; the runner living at altitude over the runner at sea level; the height advantage of the average American basketball player over the average oriental player; or the technological, training and dietary advantages of the rich nation over the impoverished third world county. All these are advantages and may be considered unfair in terms of sporting equality."

people living at or below sea level. The differences in muscle volume which exist between these people makes the one better equipped than the other to play a certain sport. These differences will not be challenged either. The same is true of increasing muscle volume through training. In sport such differences are not suppressed. Bette and Schimank countered the argument that doping results in an advantage over one's opponents by the following arguments: 1. already before they take up sport people are physically different; 2. a different training scheme or a different quality work-out gives different results; 3. good coaches can make all the difference; 4. in rich countries, athletes are able to benefit from better training conditions than they can in poor countries, and 5. training in high altitude countries is more beneficial than in lower-lying countries.[17]

What makes the difference is whether the advantage is the result of practices which are considered as going against the guiding principles of sport. But when should this be considered to have occurred? At what point can a result achieved by means of the physical characteristics or training methods described above be said to differ from a result achieved through the use of blood doping or the administration of growth hormones? "The obvious difference is that the advantages gained by blood boosting and HGH are achieved through the use of a (supplemented) substance. However if the basis of our objection is to be that using a substance is an unacceptable means to gaining an advantage, then the inconsistencies are more than apparent," according to Gardiner.[18] In sport, the use of substances is not entirely rejected. There are quite a number of permitted substances aiming to give the user an edge over his colleagues (amino acids, protein powder, creatine, vitamins, minerals, caffeine, drinks containing glucose polymers). Injecting with adenosine trifosfaat (ATP) (a naturally produced chemical substance which influences the functioning of the muscles)[19] is also permitted. The advantage which might be gained through these substances is not considered unfair. Only the use of prohibited substances would render the advantage unfair. "This being the case, it seems that some form of definitive criteria would have to be established in order to differentiate between permissible and prohibited substances. Yet, such criteria do not seem to exist," says Gardiner.[20]

4. THE USE OF DOPING IS CONTRARY TO FAIRNESS

In determining their position *vis-à-vis* the use of doping various international federations were persuaded by arguments with a moral content. One such argument is that the use of doping is against the principle of fairness. Everybody has some

---

[17] Bette/Schimank 1998 (*supra* nt. 7), p. 357 et seq.

[18] Gardner, "On Performance Enhancing Substances and the Unfair Advantage Argument", cited in De Pencier, who in turn is cited by Gardiner/O'Leary 1998 (*supra* nt. 14), p. 168.

[19] ATP molecules are in fact little batteries which move through the cell and provide energy for all processes.

[20] Gardiner/O'Leary 1998 (*supra* nt. 14), p. 167.

global notion of what fairness should be understood to mean, but it is not a clearly delineated concept. How one person chooses to interpret it need not correspond with how someone else would construe it. It is a vague concept, with friendly features. In the regulation of sport the concept is widely used, as it is in the regulations in the field of doping. In Article 7 of Byelaws II of the International Handball Federation (IHF) it was, for example, stated that this federation "shall be committed to fairness in sports and prohibit any attempts at unfair performance improvement." In the International Judo Federation's (IJF) Regulations and Procedure concerning Drug Tests it was established that the federation "condemns competitors' use of prohibited substances and prohibited methods for reasons of fairness and health." Closely connected, if not intrinsic, to the concept of fairness is that of fair play. This phrase is used even more often as a reason to combat doping in sports. In the preamble to Chapter 8.2, in which the IPC formulated the objectives of its anti-doping policy, the federation simply presupposed general familiarity with the concept. "The objective of this policy is to ensure a consistent and serious response to the use of banned drugs and practices in sport for the disabled which will deter those who might engage in doping and protect those who commit themselves to the practice of sport based on fair play." After having put into words what it considered to be doping in its Medical Rulebook, 1. the International Union for Modern Pentathlon (UIPM) informs the reader that "such manipulations [...] are in contradiction to the principle of "Fair Play" The principle was also to be encountered in Article 2.3.2 of Chapter 2 of the International Archery Federation's (FITA) Constitution and Administrative Rules. "The FITA medical provisions are essentially intended to safeguard the health of the athlete, and to ensure respect for the ethical concepts implicit in fair play [...]" In Appendix 4, 1 Doping – Preamble And Principles 1.1 the FITA again emphasised its position by pointing out that "doping is contrary to the values of sport and the principle of fair play." That one finds oneself in the realm of ethics when using the concept of fair play, emerges clearly from the preamble of the IOC Medical Code. The Code, which, despite its name, did not contain that many medical provisions, but rather aimed to limit the use of doping substances, was "essentially intended to safeguard the health of athletes, and to ensure respect for the ethical concepts implicit in Fair Play [...]"

A connection may be made between these fairness and fair-play arguments and the argument discussed above that doping results in an unfair advantage for those using it. The fairness argument was also used by the drafters of the various anti-doping rules to indicate that the equal opportunities of all athletes must be safeguarded. In the relevant rules of the International Skating Union (ISU) and the (International Sport Shooting Federation (ISSF) the concept of fairness was made somewhat less abstract. In Communication no. 956, 1.1 the ISU stated: "Doping or Doping Methods are contrary to the spirit of good and fair sportsmanship [...]" The Anti-doping Regulations of the ISSF "are based mainly on 3 principles: The defence of ethics, the protection of the health of shooters and ensuring equal chances for all shooters." Guaranteeing equal chances for all shooters may be regarded as the concretisation of the concept of fairness. Fairness and fair play are diffuse concepts which gain clarity when linked to the concept of "fraud." Fraud is the antithesis of sport.[21] According to O'Leary fraud includes unfairness. He writes that "on a philosophical level it is argued that taking drugs will give the taker an advantage over a competitor who has not taken drugs and is therefore cheating."[22] The cheating, in his view, is twofold, as it in the first place offers the athlete an "unfair advantage" compared to other athletes and secondly offers the athlete this advantage over sport.

5.   THE USE OF DOPING IS CONTRARY TO ETHICS

The ISSF rule quoted above also contains an ethical argument against doping. This argument is closely connected with the arguments invoking fairness and fair play, as appeared from, among others, the preamble to the IOC Medical Code. One of the essential objectives which the drafters of the Medical Code strove to obtain was "to ensure respect for the ethical concepts implicit in Fair Play." Elsewhere in the Medical Code this express connection with fair play was absent where it was stated that "the use of doping agents is [...] contrary to the ethics of sport." The concept of sport ethics was repeatedly used in the formulation of arguments against the use of doping in sport. Examples might be found in Article 6.1, subsection 4 of the Regulations Governing Doping Control of the FIBA: "Any person who helps a player or encourages him to use banned substances or methods of doping shall be found guilty of [...] acting against the principles of sport ethics." Rule 1, subsection 1(3) of the International Canoe Federation's (ICF) Doping Rules declared doping to be "incompatible with the general standards of sports ethics." The Doping Control Regulations for FIFA Competitions indicated that "doping contravenes the ethics of sport," and according to Rule 1 of the FIS Doping Rules "Doping is incompatible with the general standards of sporting ethics." Where ethics are the starting point, especially the ethics of sport, it is never entirely clear what this should be understood to mean. But if it is already difficult to form an opinion on the concept of the ethics of sport, things become even more complicated with the inclusion in the Medical Code of the concept of medical ethics. One phrase used in the preamble concerning doping substances and methods which enhance athletic performance was "such practices being contrary to medical ethics... ." And, if this is not sufficient indication of the part ethics play in the rejection of the use of doping, Chapter II of the Medical Code added that "doping contravenes the ethics of both sport and medical science." Basing an argument on the ethics of sport alone may drive a lawyer to despair, but if in so arguing medical ethics or the ethics of medical science are likewise invoked his mental abilities are even more severely tested.

---

[21] De Pencier, "Law and Athlete Drug Testing in Canada", cited in Gardiner/O'Leary 1998 (*supra* nt. 14), p. 167.

[22] Gardiner/O'Leary 1998 (*supra* nt. 14), pp. 167-169.

No distinction was commonly made between the various situations in which use can be made of prohibited substances. O'Leary establishes that "this results in decisions which are capricious and unfair and therefore athletes are dealt with inappropriately in terms of establishing guilt and punishments."[23] How the International Federations (IFs) punished the use of doping O'Leary can only make clear by applying the missing distinctions. These are: 1. intentional use of performance-enhancing substances; 2. unintentional use of such substances and 3. the use of social drugs. O'Leary concludes that either the IFs had been unable to distinguish between these situations or that they were unwilling to do so. Nevertheless, he found that the manner in which the intentional use of performance-enhancing substances which work over longer periods of time was punished was more consistent. "Therefore it would seem that sports governing bodies perceive an athlete who has failed a drugs test for performance enhancing drugs as cheating and subject to a lengthy ban for a first offence."[24] The way in which the use of social drugs was dealt with is more difficult to understand. O'Leary blames the desire of the sports organisations to expel all use of prohibited substances by athletes from their sphere of influence. He adds that the use of soft drugs generally does not give athletes an advantage. The penalties imposed for the use of soft drugs can, in his view, not be logically applied on the basis of fraud. In addition, these drugs only work for short periods of time.[25] O'Leary cites two cases where the use of social drugs was at issue. Roger Stanislaus, an English football player caught using cocaine, was suspended for one year by an Football Association (FA) disciplinary commission. An additional factor was that Stanislaus had used the cocaine within a period of two hours before the start of the match. Another footballer, Paul Merson, publicly declared that he was addicted to alcohol. The FA judged this case leniently and imposed six weeks' compulsory treatment in a rehabilitation clinic. Based on these two cases, O'Leary concludes that the use of social drugs is only punished when they may affect athletic performance and may therefore be labeled as fraud. O'Leary goes on to compare the cases of Stanislaus and Merson to that of cricketer Ed Giddins. Giddins was suspended for two years, after traces of social drugs were found during a routine check. It was not proven that Giddins played his match under the influence of drugs "[...] therefore the punishment seems excessively harsh if the objective of punishment is to prevent cheating."[26] American athlete Danny Harris was suspended for four years by the IAAF after having tested positive for the use of cocaine. Harris had had no intention of improving his athletic performance; he was simply addicted.

After he had come off the habit the International Amateur Athletic Federation (IAAF) once more allowed Harris to participate in competitions, even before his

---

[23] *Idem*, p. 194.

[24] *Idem*, p. 195.

[25] "Therefore unless tests prove conclusively that players were under the influence of the drug at the time of the performance then it cannot be 'cheating' in the sporting context," Gardiner/O'Leary 1998 (*supra* nt. 14), p. 195.

[26] Gardiner/O'Leary 1998 (*supra* nt. 14), p. 196.

term of punishment was up. The third category dealt with by O'Leary consists of cases of unintentional use. In the cases examined, the sports organisations all responded differently. The doctor treating Willie Johnston, a Scottish football player, prescribed some pills against a common cold, although the FA doctor had warned him that prescription drugs might show up in a doping sample. Johnston had not realised that the pills contained the prohibited substance fencamsamin but was still suspended. Rugby player Graham Steadman unknowingly imbibed a prohibited substance in a cough syrup. He was fined but not suspended. Linford Christie tested positive for the use of pseudoephedrine. He was able to sustain that he had used ginseng and had not realised that the substance was present in it. The charges against Christie were dropped and he could resume participation in competitions. "Sports governing bodies are able to achieve a level of consistency when the motive for drug consumption is deemed to be cheating. When wider issues are involved, such as the reputation of the sport but where the athlete has not been cheating, the diversity of responses has resulted in an undesirable lack of certainty," according to O'Leary.[27]

6. THE USE OF DOPING IS CONTRARY TO THE RULES OF SPORT

Some international federations included the argument that doping goes against the rules of sport in their anti-doping regulations, for example, the ICF and the FIS. Doping is "in contradiction to the rules and regulations in sports," according to Rule 1, subsection 1(3) of the ICF Doping Rules and Rule 1 of the FIS Doping Rules. Other federations claimed that doping undermines the values of sport. "The use of banned substances and other doping methods to artificially enhance performance [...] undermines the values of sport," stated 1.1 of the IWF Anti-doping Policy. Likewise: 1 of Appendix 4 – Doping Control Procedures of the FITA: "Doping is contrary to the values [of sport]." Finally, the federations governing tennis argued that doping impairs the integrity of the sport. "The purpose of the Tennis Anti-Doping Programme [...] is to maintain the integrity of tennis [...]," according to the Tennis Anti-Doping Programme of the International Tennis Federation (ITF) sub (A) and the Official Rulebook of both the Association of Tennis Professionals (ATP) and the Women's Tennis Association (WTA) sub A.1. In all these examples sport is regarded as coming under fire, whether by infringement of the rules of sport, the values of sport or the integrity of sport. However, it must still be pointed out that the federations using these phrases as a basis for their anti-doping efforts failed to indicate what they intended to cover. It has been contended in the literature that an athlete using doping is not so much cheating on his colleagues but on sport itself. As Gardner puts it "would allowing unrestricted use of steroids in the 100 metres be somewhat like providing the participants with motorcycles?"[28]

---

[27] *Idem*, p. 197.
[28] *Idem*, p. 168.

7. THE RATIONALE OF THE WORLD ANTI-DOPING CODE

The reasons for combating doping use in sport which have been enumerated above also underpin the World Anti-Doping Code (WADC), although here they are expressed more indirectly. One of the Code's objectives is to protect the fundamental right of athletes to participate in doping-free sport "[...] and thus promote health, fairness and equality for athletes worldwide." Further on in the introduction it is explained that the anti-doping programmes were created to maintain the intrinsic value of sport. "This intrinsic value is often referred to as "the spirit of sport"; it is the essence of Olympism; it is how we play true." This article of faith is followed by one of almost Olympic beauty: "The spirit of sport is the celebration of the human spirit, body and mind." The essence of the WADC is that "doping is fundamentally contrary to the spirit of sport." The entire structure of the WADC is actually based on an ideological concept whose content may be determined differently throughout time, namely that of "the spirit of sport."[29]

8. CONCLUSION

In the above, several arguments against doping in sport have passed in review. They were that:

- the use of doping endangers the athlete's health;
- the use of doping leads to an unfair advantage;
- the use of doping is contrary to fairness;
- the use of doping is contrary to ethics;
- the use of doping is contrary to the rules of sport.

These arguments, regardless of whether they were practical or ethical, remain no more than postulates. They merely allow us some insight into the motivating factors which incited the various federations to engage in the fight against doping. They did not, apparently, play any real part in that fight. If they had not been revealed, the fight would possibly still be fought in the same manner as it is now. Some 13 of the 39 federations examined did not offer any argument(s) on which to base their struggle against doping, almost as if they wished to prove to themselves and other federations that they could manage without arguments. Vieweg, when discussing the German situation in which not many federations cited reasons for wishing to eradicate doping either, writes: "The reasons for refraining from clarifying the purposes of the ban on doping can only be assumed. The fact that clarifica-

---

[29] According to the WADC the spirit of sport can be characterized by the following values: "Ethics, fair play and honesty; health; excellence in performance; character and education; fun and joy; teamwork; dedication and commitment; respect for rules and laws; respect for self and other participants; courage; and community and solidarity."

tion is necessary for the definition of doping and for the type and extent of the accepted doping controls including potential sanctions has obviously been ignored. It is of interest whether the courts of justice would accept the named purposes of the doping ban."[30]

The use of performance-enhancing substances is not prohibited in general. The prohibition extends to the use of certain – named – substances. Not all permitted substances may – euphemistically – be said to have a beneficial effect on the health of the person using them. The argument against doping starting from a health angle is not entirely convincing. The argument built around the falsification of competition has also lost force. However, all the reasons listed above returned in the WADC, albeit indirectly. What then constitutes the core argument on the basis of which a certain substance is declared to be doping and, for this reason, prohibited? O'Leary attempts to uncover the quintessence of the prohibition. First, he demonstrates that, on the one hand, not every tactical or technical deviation from the norm is prohibited and, on the other hand, that performance-enhancing substances are not intrinsically substances which are completely unrelated to the athlete's physical condition. His answer is sociologically orientated "[...] can a competitor truly claim victory if it is achieved with the assistance of drugs? Victory is inextricably linked to rules. It is questionable whether the drug-taking athlete has competed in the first place. Successful athletes are afforded a unique place in society. Sporting heroes are society's heroes. By heralding the success of a drugs-assisted athlete we are in danger of undermining society itself. Perhaps the most acceptable reason for prohibiting performance-enhancing drugs is that otherwise sporting competition fails to be a test of persons and therefore, drug taking is ethically indefensible."[31]

---

[30] Vieweg 1998 (*supra* nt. 10); Klaus Vieweg, "The Harmonization of Antidoping Rules and Regulations Different Approaches on the Basis of a Cybernatic Model," in Nathalie Korchia and Christophe Pettiti, eds., *Sport et Garanties Fondamentales*, (Paris, l'Institut de Formation en Droits de l'Homme du Barreau de Paris – Centre Louis Pettiti 2001) p. 433.

[31] Gardiner/O'Leary 1998 (*supra* nt. 14), p. 169.

CHAPTER 2
DEFINITION OF DOPING AND THE DESCRIPTION OF THE DOPING OFFENCE

1. INTRODUCTION

The sports organisations' opposition to the use of doping is based on the principles discussed in the previous chapter. In order to ensure that sportsmen (and of course sportswomen[32]) are "clean," i.e. not under the influence of some substance of which the organisations have declared that they consider it doping, and in order to take legal action against these sportsmen and women in case they are not "clean," the organisations have formulated legal norms which together constitute their anti-doping regulations. At a later stage in this book I will focus on the provisions concerning legal action against athletes suspected of doping. In this chapter, the focus will be on the rules defining certain behaviour as doping.

Only part of the rules which apply within associations may be considered legal norms. Enschedé[33] defines legal norms as rules of behaviour instructing citizens how to behave in accordance with the law in specific circumstances. The rules in question are *substantive* legal norms. "These legal norms are therefore *guidelines* for future conduct. But, when applied by the courts, they are also *standards* for judging such conduct after the fact." In addition, legal norms according to Enschedé have a third function, namely to act as "a source of *legitimate expectations* as to people's own behaviour and especially other people's behaviour" (Nieboer in this context uses the term actions).[34] The legal norms Enschedé refers to are plentiful in society in general and address the citizen. Within the disciplinary law of associations, the image outlined by Enschedé easily allows itself to be transformed into a collection of legal norms applicable within the association and addressing the mem-

---

[32] Where in the text below the term "sportsman" is used, that term must be understood to include "sportswoman."

[33] Ch.J. Enschedé and A. Heijder, *Beginselen van strafrecht* (Deventer, Kluwer 1974) (Enschedé 1974), pp. 13-15.

[34] The definitions in criminal law are very precise. The definition of concepts in the disciplinary law concerning doping are not as strict. Still, it is advisable not to stray too far from the descriptions which were developed in criminal legal science. Nieboer (W. Nieboer, *Strafrechtelijke zorgplichten*, in: Liber Amicorum Th.W. van Veen 1985, p. 259) considers the difference between conduct and actions to be of great importance. *Actions* he takes to mean human choices of position, which may be tested against norms. *Norms* in his view are rules, which people can break. The concept of *conduct* he describes as "human, animal or vegetable 'expressions' viewed from the aspect of patterns (automatisms, fixed patterns, pre-programmed modes of reaction, (un)learnable responses to stimuli, etc.)." In the following, however, I choose to use the terms conduct or behaviour and act, rather than action.

bers of that association. Within the scope of the disciplinary law of associations, the judicial function is exercised by institutions which, through the consent of the general assembly of the association, have been granted the authority to carry out disciplinary procedures and impose sanctions. The substantive norm prohibiting the use of doping will in most cases be found in the association's disciplinary law concerning doping. Practically all doping regulations include a provision corresponding to this substantive norm. In these regulations it is this norm that lies at the root of the description of the doping offence.

Misconduct in the sense of committing an act of doping is only punishable if it was expressly qualified as punishable beforehand in the regulations of the sports organisation concerned. The principle of legality is enshrined in criminal law.[35] In disciplinary sports law it entails that an act, however deserving of punishment it may be considered to be, can only be punished if a provision to that effect was included in the doping regulations prior to the commission of the act. The principle of legality can also be found in the description of the doping offence. Certain behaviour may only be qualified as deserving of punishment when this behaviour has been defined in the description of the doping offence. The disciplinary law of doping is not – as, indeed, criminal law is not – a system of substantive norms addressing the members of the association; it is a sanctioning system, determining the rights and duties of various officials of the association with a view to the enforcement of the substantive norms.[36] In the following, the substantive norm is therefore understood to mean a postulate, which declares the act of doping to be objectionable in general. A postulate such as "doping is prohibited"[37] constitutes the substrate of the description of the doping offence.

As was stated above, the substantive norm has three facets: it is a guideline for future behaviour, a standard for judging behaviour afterwards and a source of legitimate expectations. Doping regulations were drawn up in order to have a tool at hand by which to examine whether athletes abide by the substantive norm. They are the instrument allowing the initiation of disciplinary action against athletes who violate the norm.

It is an illusion to assume that doping regulations can eliminate the use of doping in sports.[38] If this illusion were cherished it could easily lead to zealotry and inqui-

---

[35] See *infra* Chapter 6.

[36] "In their basic form, rules *prohibiting* certain behaviour are not part of criminal law. *Punishable* are generally only those acts which the law *expressly* penalises. In order to protect the citizen against arbitrary government action this is done through a precise description of the behaviour deserving of punishment in the descriptions of the offence," see L.J. van, Reijntjes, J.M. Boon, P.J. Bergamin, R.J.B. (eds.) *Van Apeldoorn's Inleiding tot de studie van het Nederlandse recht* (Deventer, Kluwer 2000) (Van Apeldoorn 2000), p. 304.

[37] See *inter alia* IOC Medical Code, Ch. I, Art. 1; IAAF: Rules and Regulations, Art. 55: "Doping is strictly forbidden and is an offence under IAAF Rules"; FISA: Rules of Racing and Related By Laws, Rule 80: "Doping is strictly prohibited," FIBA: Regulations Governing Doping Control, 6.1.: "Doping is prohibited," etc.

[38] This illusion, however, is still cherished by the IOC. On the website on which the IOC has placed the new OMADC, it says: "This new Code considers that the complete elimination of doping from

sition. A more reasonable objective is for legislation to render the use of doping unappealing. Now that doping in sports is a very real phenomenon, which apparently cannot be called to a halt by appealing to athletes' own responsibility, rules have had to be established to counter it. With those rules, based on the substantive norm, the option of appealing to the athlete's own – ethical – responsibility has been abandoned in favour of the option of requiring compliance with these rules.[39] Ethical norms have weathered down and their place has been taken by norms of a legal character.

The international and national federations have all made the prohibition of the use of doping part of their policy (culminating in the substantive norm). In order to achieve their goal the federations have indicated in their doping regulations that the doping offence is an occurrence constituting undesirable and unlawful – and therefore prohibited – behaviour, whereby they have created the opportunity to act under disciplinary law. In order to be able to describe such an offence it is first of all necessary to put the objectionable – and therefore prohibited – human behaviour into words.

It needs to be added that the substantive norm, usually expressly laid down in the respective doping regulations, often lies behind the description of the doping offence, which in most cases is to be found in the doping definition. For it is oddly the case that the definitions do not indicate what doping as a phenomenon is to be understood to mean, but rather what the objectionable act that is called doping is to be understood to mean. The concept is hybrid not only legally speaking, but also linguistically speaking; it is not only understood to mean the substance itself, but also the use of that substance.[40]

Legally speaking, the definitions of doping already give the main elements of the doping offence, the "Tatbestand." "The [...] (descriptions of the doping offence) may, because they indicate when the transgression of a primary norm is punishable, be seen as the [...] relevant formulation (under disciplinary law) of that primary

---

sport is one of the fundamental objectives of the Olympic Movement." (www.Olympic.org/e/org/ medcom/ medcom_antid_aim_e.html).

[39] M. Budzisch, K. Huhn and H. Wuschech,: *Doping in de BRD – Ein historischer Überblick zu einer verschleierten Praxis* (Berlin, Spotless-Verl. 1999) (Budzisch 1999), pp. 14-15: "[...] der deutsche Biochemiker Manfred Donike kommentiert: 'Dieses Katz- und Maus-Spiel wird wohl weitergehen.' Jeder Sportler lernt unzweideutig, 'daß ihm niemand mehr eine moralische Gesinnung abverlangt. Eine äußere Verhaltenskonformität mit den rechtlich forcierten Verbotsregeln genügt bereits. Mehr noch: Jeder Sportler erfährt daß von ihm geradezu erwartet wird, seinen persönlichen Vorteil auch dadurch zu suchen, daß er findig mit den Verbotsregeln umgeht. An die Stelle der früheren Maßstäbe moralischer Skrupelhaftigkeit tritt immer stärker, wenn auch bislang noch selten ganz deutlich ausgesprochen, so doch hinreichend unmißverständlich suggeriert, die ebenso unerbittliche Forderung nach regelumgehender professioneller Schläue. Wer nicht all das tut, was er ungestraft tun kann, wer also Regellücken sowie die noch anzusprechenden Kontrolldefizite nicht konsequent ausnutzt, hat seine Niederlage gegenüber den raffinierteren Gegnern im Grunde selbst verschuldet'."

[40] "It is not easy to articulate conceptually what 'doping' actually is. [...] the only safe conclusion for present purposes is to maintain the narrow definition that 'doping' simply means a violation of particular disciplinary rules applying to the case under consideration," says Tim Kerr: "Doped or Duped? The Nandrolone Jurisprudence," *International Sports Law Review* (2001) p. 99.

norm; they are primary norms settled into concrete rules," freely rendered from Van Apeldoorn.[41] In this section – structured according to corresponding elements – the definitions of doping will be addressed.

In what follows the phrase "description of the doping offence" will be used exclusively to indicate the concretisation of the substantive norm. By testing the behaviour of an athlete against the substantive norm – which thus lies at the root of the description of the offence – it may be established whether his behaviour was illegal.[42] Illegality is one of the conditions for punishability. Couched in criminal law terms, a doping offence is a punishable act, consisting of a human act, which fits inside the framework of the description of the doping offence, is illegal and is imputable to guilt.[43] Especially the element of responsibility is important in the description of the definitions of doping. In this book the criminal law meaning of responsibility (guilt and intent) is used. Guilt (culpa) is understood to mean that the perpetrator *should have known, while intent is understood to mean that he knew*. In earlier definitions – and thus also in the descriptions of the doping offence – the guilt/intent element took up an important position, albeit implicitly. Over the past decade a shift has taken place from guilt to intent. Of the three aspects on which the punishability of the use of doping has to be based – the description of the offence, illegality (*wederrechtelijkheid*) and liability (*aansprakelijkheid*) – the constituent elements of the description take up a central position (see also Chapters 4 and 5 below).

The description of the doping offence is the *trait-d'union* between the substantive (material) law and adjective (procedural) disciplinary law on doping. With the *adjective* description the focus is on the act; this act is already contrary to the doping prohibition and punishable in itself. Such descriptions lead to a constitutive result. *Substantive* descriptions, by contrast, declare the result of a certain act prohibited and punishable.[44] On the one hand, the description impacts the practical effect of the principle of illegality. A disciplinary law sanction can only be imposed when the facts in a given case correspond to those which were previously described. Jonkers[45] calls this the *function of legal protection*. On the other hand, the description serves to indicate what evidence is required. The description of the doping offence, like the description of the offence in an indictment, "indicates what needs to be lawfully *proven* in order to be able to arrive at the conclusion of punishability," says Jonkers.[46] What is true for criminal law, namely that "everything con-

---

[41] Van Apeldoorn 2000 (*supra* nt. 36), p. 304.

[42] The question is whether the private law concept of "unlawfulness" [*onrechtmatigheid*] is the same here as the criminal law concept of "illegality" [*wederrechtelijkheid*]. Enschedé 1974 (*supra* nt. 33), p. 13, considered them synonyms. In order to avoid confusion, I have replaced "unlawful" with "illegal".

[43] Cf., Enschedé 1974 (*supra* nt. 33), pp. 128-129.

[44] *Idem*, p. 129.

[45] W.H.A. Jonkers, *Inleiding tot de strafrechtsdogmatiek: het schuldbeginsel, het legaliteitsbeginsel, de strafbaarheidsvoorwaarden, de poging en de deelneming*, Studiepockets strafrecht nr. 12, (Zwolle, WEJ Tjeenk Willink 1984) (Jonkers 1984), p. 22.

[46] *Idem*.

tained in the description of the offence in the indictment (and no more) [...] (must) be proven in accordance with the rules of the procedural criminal law of evidence," is also true for the description of the doping offence under the disciplinary law on doping. The adjective law function of the description of the doping offence will be dealt with in Part II of this book.

The various descriptions of the doping offence may be broken down into those involving the "offence of use" and those, involving the "offence of doping other than use."[47] In this chapter, the focus will primarily be on the "offence of use," i.e., the offence committed by the athlete through his own actions (Section 2 below). Doping offences other than use are offences committed by third parties who aid and assist in administering doping substances (Section 3 below). Finally, the various doping substances and methods are dealt with in Section 4.

2.   THE EVOLUTION OF THE DESCRIPTION OF THE OFFENCE OF THE USE OF DOPING

Within the description of the doping offence, the description of the act of doping (contained in the definition of doping) and the prohibition of that act (the prohibitory norm) are inextricably bound up. In the various doping regulations two methods appeared for expressing those two elements: they were either divided into two separate provisions, containing the definition and the prohibitory norm respectively, or both aspects were contained in one single provision. As the prohibitory norm – doping is prohibited – was a recurring feature in the various doping regulations, I will only deal with this norm here when it is part of the provision in which the doping definition has been laid down.[48]

In this section, a distinction will be made according to the nature of the description of the offence. A handful of national and international federations used to prohibit the use of unspecified doping substances and methods if such use was primarily *intended to enhance* athletic performance. A larger number of federations branded the *simple use* of certain specified substances and methods a prohibited act. Other federations prohibited the use of specified substances and methods *only if they did in fact enhance* performance. Finally, there were federations which penalised *the actual presence of specified substances* in an athlete's body (Section 2.1). In Section 2.2 various ancillary forms of the use of doping will be discussed and in Section 2.3 some related aspects are dealt with, namely offences committed by the doping suspect which do not consist of the use of doping.

---

[47] In the wording of the IPC, for example, there are "use infractions" and "infractions other than athlete use of banned substances and practices."

[48] However, the anti-doping provisions of the International Baseball Federation do not actually contain a prohibitory norm.

2.1. Main categories of the use of doping

2.1.1. *Doping is the use of substances and methods for a specific purpose*

As one of the first to do so, the *Deutsche Sportärztebund* in 1952 formulated a definition of doping: doping was understood to mean the taking of a drug – regardless of whether it was effective or not – with the intention of enhancing performance during the match.[49] In the definition of doping adopted by the Committee of Ministers of the Council of Europe on 29 June 1967 (1967 Resolution) doping is understood to mean

> "the administration to or use by a healthy person, in any manner whatsoever, of agents foreign to the organism, or of physiological substances in excessive quantities or introduced by an abnormal channel, with the sole purpose of affecting artificially and by unfair means the performance of such a person when taking part in a competition."[50, 51]

The Council of Europe had already produced a definition of doping in 1963 which largely corresponded to the 1967 definition. However, under the earlier definition psychological measures which could lead to enhancement of athletic performance were also considered doping.

> "Bei den 'psychologische Maßnahmen' – unter die so allgemein wie in dieser Definition gefaßt natürlich auch jede Motivationsarbeit des Trainers fiele – war vor allem an Formen von Hypnose gedacht."[52]

The 1967 definition included all the relevant components for a *Wesenbestimmung* ("essential" definition) of doping at the time the definition was drafted, but also for some time after that. Among other things, the definition included core concepts with ethical content, such as "unfairness" and "artificial." The latter concept was understood to mean "alien to the body" and "abnormal."

Although the Olympic Movement Anti-Doping Code (OMADC)[53] contained a provision rating the use of any substance or method towards the enhancement of

---

[49] "Die Einnahme eines jeden Medikamentes – ob wirksam oder nicht – mit der Absicht der Leistungssteigerung während des Wettkampfes eingenommen, is als Doping zu betrachten." Cited by M. Sehling/R. Pollert/D. Hackfort, *Doping im Sport. Medizinische, sozialwissenschaftliche und juristische Aspekte* (München 1989) p. 18, from Bette/Schimank 1998 (*supra* nt. 7), p. 358.

[50] The UNESCO still uses a similar definition: "l'Administration a un sujet sain, ou l'utilisation par lui-même et par quelque moyen que ce soit, d'une substance étrangère à l'organisme, de substances physiologiques en quantité ou par une voie anormale et ce dans le seul but d'augmenter artificiellement et de façon déloyale la performance de ce sujet à l'occasion de sa participation à une compétition. Certains procédés psychologiques créés afin d'augmenter la performance du sujet peuvent etre considérés étant du 'doping'."

[51] Resolution (67)12 – Doping of Athletes.

[52] Bette/Schimank 1998 (*supra* nt. 7), p. 359.

[53] Chapter II, Art. 2, sub 1.

athletic performance as doping, other provisions in the Code indicated that it was mainly the use of substances and methods which appeared on a list which should be counted as doping. Only the anti-doping regulations of one international federation, the International Fencing Federation,[54] carried an "essential" definition without reference to any kind of doping list.

> "Le dopage est l'usage ou l'application sous toute forme de produits étrangers à l'organisme et de produits organiques en dose anormale ou administrés par voie anormale, dans le but d'augmenter d'une manière déloyale les performances."

Pursuant to Article 2, 6° of the Belgian *Decreet inzake Medisch Verantwoorde Sportbeoefening* "doping practices" were, among other things, understood to mean the use of substances or the application of means with an eye to artificially enhancing the athlete's performance, when this might cause damage to his physical or psychological integrity and the use of substances or the application of means aiming to mask said doping practices. Various Belgian federations included similar definitions in their doping regulations[55] or simply referred to the Decree.[56]

Pursuant to Article 22 of the Belgian Decree the Executive, after hearing the advice of the anti-doping commission, has to determine a list of prohibited substances, where necessary accompanied by an indication of the prohibited dose, and prohibited means.

The doping regulations of the Belgian Boxing Federation contained a definition which was also pre-eminently based on the essence of doping and did not refer to any doping list:[57]

> "Doping is considered to be: the use of all substances and means intended to artificially increase results with a view to or on the occasion of the competition or the matches, and which may injure the ethics of sport and the psychological or physical soundness of the boxer."

The *Dansk Bueskytteforbund* (DBF) made use of the doping rules of the International Archery Federation (FITA). These rules[58] contained the following definition of doping:

> "Doping is:
> The use of an expedient (substance or method) which is potentially harmful to the athletes' health and/or capable of enhancing their performance."

---

[54] FIE Statutes – Titre Troisieme – Chapître I, para. 2, 93.
[55] Vlaamse Badminton Liga: Reglement Betreffende Medisch Verantwoorde Sportbeoefening, Deel I, Art. 1.
[56] Union Belge de Handball, 28. Anti-Dopingreglement; Federation Royale Belge de Volleyball; Federation Royale Belge de Tennis, VTV Huishoudelijk Reglement.
[57] Royale Fédération Belge de Boxe: Dopingreglement KBBB, 2. Begripsbepalingen.
[58] FITA Constitution and Rules, Appendix 4 – Doping Control Procedures, sub 1.4.

The *Deutscher Curling-Verband* (DCV) included the doping definition of the World Curling Federation (WCF) in its doping regulations:[59]

"Doping
Die Einnahme leistungssteigernder Medikamente is verboten, unabhängig davon, ob die Einnahme wissenlich erfolgte."

The doping regulations of the *Real Federación Española de Balonmano* (RFEBM)[60] stated that:

"El Dopaje es el uso o administración de sustancias o empleo y aplicación de métodos destinados a aumentar artificialmente las capacidas fisicas de los deportistas o a modificar los resultados de las competiciones deportivas."[61]

The doping regulations of the *Federação Portuguesa de Basquetebol* (FPBB)[62] contained the following provision:

"É considerado dopado qualquer praticante em relação ao qual o respectivo controlo antidopagem acuse a administração de substâncias ou produtos, ou a utilização de outros métodos, susceptiveis de, por qualquer forma, alterarem artificialmente o seu rendimento desportivo, quer essa alteração ocorra efectivamente ou não, quer em competição, quer fora de competição, e que sejam interditos nos termos deste regulamento ou seus anexos."

The French law of 1999 concerning the protection of athletes' health and the fight against doping[63] also includes an "essential" definition of doping. Notwithstanding the fact that the French legislator refers to further legislation which had to describe the prohibited substances and methods in further detail,[64] the provision in question still describes the aim of the use of doping.[65]

---

[59] Durchführungsbestimmungen Saison 2000/2001, 5. Spielregeln, 16. Doping.

[60] RFEBM Estatutos y Reglamentos, Reglamento Control de Dopaje, Art. 2.

[61] Cf., Real Federación Española de Hockey, Reglamento de Control del Dopaje, Titulo Primero, Disposiciones Generales, Art. 2. It must be noted, however, that Art. 1 of the regulations mentioned "las sustancias y métodos prohibidos en el deporte a que se refiere el Titulo VIII de la Ley 10/1990, de 15 de octubre, del Deporte."

[62] Regulamento Antidopagem da Federação Portuguesa De Basquetebol, Capítulo I – Âmbito de aplicação, Artigo lo, sub 2.

[63] Loi no. 99-223 du 23 mars 1999 relative à la protection de la santé des sportifs et à la lutte contre le dopage, Titre II B De la prevention et de la Lutte contre le dopage, Section 2 Des Agissements interdits., Art. 17.

[64] "Les substances et procédés visés au présent article sont déterminés par un arrêté conjoint du ministre chargé des sports et du ministre chargé de la santé."

[65] In the "Annexe – Règlement Disciplinaire type des Fédérations Sportives agréées relatif à la Lutte contre le dopage", Art. 2 of the "Décret no. 2002-36 du 11 janvier 2001 relatif aux dispositions que les fédérations sportives agréées doivent adopter dans leur règlement en matière de contrôles et de sanctions contre le dopage en application de l'article L.3634-1 du code de la santé publique" Art. 17 of the law of 1999 was repeated verbatim.

"Il est interdit à toute personne, au cours des compétitions et manifestations sportives organisées ou agréées par des fédérations sportives ou en vue d'y participer: d'utiliser des substances et procédés de nature à modifier artificiellement les capacités ou à masquer l'emploi de substances ou procédés ayant cette propriété [...]."

Various French federations included the doping definition of the 1999 law in their doping regulations.[66] Other federations simply referred to the 1999 law in their doping regulations.[67]

The rules establishing that doping is the use of certain, specified substances and means with a view to a certain objective will be further dealt with in a separate section below. In the present section, the focus is on definitions prohibiting the use of certain unspecified substances and methods with the intention of enhancing athletic performance. Various regulations of federations in various EU countries may be cited as points in case. The anti-doping provisions of the Hellenic Football Federation,[68] for example, contained an "essential" definition of doping without reference to a doping list.

"The use or taking of any substance that is able artificially to alter the natural playing efficiency of a player is prohibited as is the use of any physical or nervous stimulant according to the specially stipulated provisions in the legislation in force."

The relevant rules of the Hellenic Volleyball Federation[69] were largely identical and did not refer to prior prohibitions of certain substances either.

Although this does not expressly become clear from the doping definitions mentioned above, it must still be assumed that the doping substances and methods targeted by the respective legislators did appear on some doping list. The doping regulations of the EU Member States were mostly enacted so as to comply with the Anti-Doping Convention of the Council of Europe which does contain a list. The definitions which go to the essence of doping and in addition refer to lists of specified, prohibited substances and methods will be dealt with in Section 3. The difference between the definitions in this section and the ones discussed in Section 3 is mainly editorial. The first group stresses the "essence" of doping while the second group includes the "essence" more or less into the bargain.

Lawyers would complain that the concepts used in the "essential" definitions suffer from legal vagueness. Bette and Schimank have also highlighted this weakness:[70]

---

[66] Fédération Française des Sociétés d'Aviron (FFSA), Réglementation Antidopage, Principes, 1.3. Agissements interdits.; Fédération Française de Boxe, Règlement Féderal d Lutte contre le Dopage, Titre I – Dispositions Générales, Art. 1.

[67] *Inter alia*, the Fédération Française de Badminton.

[68] Art. 32 – Protection of football players' health – excitation through drugs, sub 3.

[69] General Regulations of the Championships' Organisation and Conduct.

[70] Bette/Schimank 1998 (*supra* nt. 7), p. 359.

"Damit hängt für eine – insbesondere auch rechtliche – Handhabbarkeit dieser Art der Dopingdefinition alles davon ab, inwieweit sich in sachlicher Hinsicht hinreichend präzise und umfassend, in zeitlicher Hinsicht hinreichend dauerhaft und in sozialer Hinsicht hinreichend intersubjektiv einheitlich bestimmen läßt, welche Art von Handeln sich als 'unnatürliche' sportliche Leistungssteigerung begreifen läßt. In dem Maße hingegen, wie genau diese Spezifizierungen nicht gelingen, erweist sich eine Wesensdefinition des Dopings als unbrauchbar. [...] 'Unnatürlichkeit' enthält als semantisches Konstrukt mehrere gravierende, kaum ausräumbar erscheinende Uneindeutigkeiten. Um sie herauszuarbeiten, nehmen wir gegenüber den verbreiteten Versuchen, die 'Unnatürlichkeit' des Dopings zu bestimmen, die Haltung eines advocatus diaboli ein."

2.1.2. *Doping is the use of certain, specified substances and methods*

As the stakes in the business of sport increased, both commercially and in terms of prestige, and lawyers began to act as counsel to athletes who were suspected of the use of doping, descriptions of the doping offence along the lines of the 1967 Resolution were no longer sufficient. The vagueness of the concepts used meant that they were no match for the legal profession.[71] The sports organisations were perhaps still able to prove that an athlete had used "agents foreign to the organism, or physiological substances" and that they had done so "in excessive quantities or introduced by an abnormal channel," but they often failed to prove that the athlete had used these substances in the manner described "with the sole purpose of affecting artificially and by unfair means the performance of such a person when taking part in a competition." The sports organisations needed to come up with a new design for the description in order not to be given the go-by in every doping trial. The new direction in design was found with the drawing up of lists specifically naming the substances and methods that were prohibited in the business of sport. The IOC was the first to introduce a doping list in 1968.[72] Doping was now under-

---

[71] Budzisch 1999 (*supra* nt. 39), p. 14: "Denn unter Erfolgsdruck stehende Sportler werden immer stärker dazu neigen, im Zweifelsfall stets erst einmal den eigenen Vorteil zu sehen und dementsprechend die Diffusität der Wesensdefinition zu eigenen Gunsten auszulegen. Versucht man den Athleten dann aber in rechtlichen Auseinandersetzungen mit Hilfe der Wesensdefinition zu sanktionieren, wird schnell offenbar, daß deren mangelnde Trennschärfe Kriterien der Rechtssicherheit in keiner Weise genügt. Nach dem Grundsatz 'in dubio pro reo' hätten die Verbände daher kaum Handhaben gegenüber sich dopenden Sportlern gehabt. Deshalb war schnell absehbar, daß die Sportverbände in dem Moment, wo Doping zu einem ernsthaften Dauerproblem vieler Sportarten wurde, von Versuchen einer Wesensdefinition abgehen und eine andere Art von Dopingdefinition linden mußten."

[72] Thomas Summerer, *Internationales Sportrecht vor dem staatlichen Richter* (Munich, Verlag V. Florenz 1990) (Summerer 1990), pp. 144-145: "Als Sanktionstatbestand muß der Begriff des Doping dem Bestimmtheitsgebot genügen. Die medizinische Kommission des IOC hat davon Abstand genommen, eine allgemeine, ethisch begründete Definition zu geben, wie sie beispielsweise in den DSB-Richtlinien zu finden ist. Es gilt der Satz: 'Doping ist die Verwendung von Substanzen aus den verbotenen Wirkstoffgruppen und die Anwendung verbotener Methoden. Diese pragmatische Definition bietet den Vorteil, daß neue pharmakologische Wirkstoffe, die speziell für Doping-Zwecke synthetisiert sein mögen, automatisch wegen ihrer zugehörigkeit zu einer solchen Wirkstoffgruppe verboten sind'."

stood to mean the use of substances and methods appearing on the doping list. It no longer needed to be proven that a certain substance resulted in enhanced performance; through reference to the doping list the sports organisation could, after a listed substance had been found in an athlete's urine, convincingly maintain that the athlete had made use of a performance-enhancing prohibited substance. A number of IFs made swift and thorough changes to their doping regulations by introducing a description after the latest fashion, referring to their own doping list or that of the IOC.

The Olympic Charter against Doping – which was in force until 1 January 2000 – declared that:

"doping, as defined and adopted by the International Olympic Committee (IOC), is the administration or use of prohibited classes of drugs and of banned methods."

Those prohibited classes of drugs and banned methods were and are placed on a list drawn up by the IOC Medical Commission. Various *international* federations used similar descriptions and referred to the list of the Medical Commission,[73] or to doping lists of their own.[74] A great many *national* federations in the EU countries in

---

[73] IBA: Anti Doping Rules, Chapter 1 sub 1.1. "[...] the use or the administration to athletes of pharmacological classes of doping agents or doping methods banned by the I.O.C." FIBA: Regulations Governing Doping Control. Art. 6.1, subsection 1: "Basketball players are prohibited from doping, namely from using doping substances and methods, as well as substances subject to certain restrictions. Prohibited substances and methods are classed by the IOC and the lists are amended regularly. It is the player's responsibility to keep himself informed of the current lists." IJF: Regulations Concerning Dope Tests, 2: "Doping is defined as a competitor's use [...] of one of the forbidden doping substances contained in the list drawn up by the IOC Medical Committee." WTF: Competition Rules, Art. 4, subsection 3: "The use or administration of drugs or chemical substances described in the IOC doping by-laws is prohibited." ICF: Doping Rules, Rule 1 – Doping, subsections 1-5: "Doping is defined as the administration or the use of prohibited classes of drugs and of banned methods. As it is possible by means of doping to get an unfair advantage on other athletes, and because doping is a threat to physical and mental health, doping is incompatible with the general standards of sports ethics and is in contradiction to the rules and regulations in sports. The ICF declares that doping is strictly forbidden and is an offence under the ICF rules for all athletes affiliated to National Member Federations. The ICF recognises the IOC list of doping classes and methods. This list is normally revised in April every year. The offence of doping takes place when a prohibited drug is found to be present within the athlete's body tissue or fluids, or an athlete uses a banned method, or an athlete admits having used a prohibited drug or a banned method on the IOC list of doping classes and methods." FIG: Doping Control Regulations, 1. General Principles, preamble and subsection 1: "Doping is forbidden. This prohibition is not limited to the competitions, but also applies to all training periods, both during and periods. The list of products / drugs prohibited by the FIG is available to Federations. Except for where duly indicated, the list is identical to that of the IOC. Whenever the IOC revises its list, account must be taken of the fact that their decisions apply, at the same time, to the FIG."

[74] UCI: Antidoping Examination Regulations, introduction to Part XIV: "The UCI definition of drug abuse ('doping'), as that of the IOC Medical Commission, is based on the principle that the use of all substances belonging to the pharmaceutical categories mentioned in the Regulations shall be strictly forbidden." FIS: Doping Rules, Rule 1: "Doping is defined as the administration or the use of prohibited classes of drugs and of banned methods (see list of doping classes and methods)." FIBT: Doping Control Regulations: Doping Control Regulations: Doping is "the use by athletes of certain substances mentioned under item 3 of the FIBT Doping Control Regulations as banned substances as well as the application of forbidden practices."

their doping definitions also referred to lists of prohibited doping substances and methods, which could be either:

- the list of the corresponding international federation;[75]
- to the list drawn up by the relevant national authorities;[76]
- a list drawn up by a national anti-doping committee;[77]
- the IOC list;[78] or

---

[75] *List of internationale federations*
Austria Österreichischer Skiverband
Belgium Federation Royale Belge de Patinage de Vitesse; Royal Belgium Weightlifting Federation
Germany Bund Deutscher Radfahrer e.V.: Dopingkontroll-Reglement, 1. Einführung, 1.1 Definition; Deutscher Curlingverband e.V.
France Fédération Française de Voile
Gr. Britt. National Ice Skating Association of UK; The Royal Yachting Association
England English Curling Association
Greece Hellenic Table Tennis Federation.

[76] *List of national authorities*
Belgium Vlaamse Badminton Liga: Reglement Betreffende Medisch Verantwoorde Sportbeoefening, Deel I, Art. 1 – Doping; Union Belge de Handball: 28. Anti-Dopingreglement; Federation Royale Belge de Volleyball; Federation Royale Belge de Tennis: VTV. Huishoudelijk Reglement
Spain Spanish Swimming Federation; Real Federación Española de Judo y Deportes Associados (RFEJYDA), Reglamento de Control de Dopage, Capitulo I – Disposiciones Generales, Sección 1a – De la normativa; Real Federación Española de Deportes de Invierno: Reglamento de Control Dopaje, Titulo I – Disposiciones Generales
France Fédération Française des Sociétés d'Aviron (FFSA): Réglementation Antidopage, Principes; Fédération Française de Badminton; Fédération Française de Handball, Lutte contre le dopaje; Fédération Française de Lutte; Fédération Française de Tennis: Annexe III – Règlement relatif à la lutte antidopage; Fédération Française de Tennis de Table; Fédération Française de Triathlon; Fédération Française de Ski: Réglement Interieur Particulier, "De Lutte contre le Dopage," Chapitre 1: Dispositions Générales; Fédération Française de Boxe: Règlement Féderal d Lutte contre le Dopage, Titre I – Dispositions Générales, Art. 1; Fédération Française de Judo, Jujitsu, Kendo et Disciplines Associées: Règlement Intérieur de la FFJDA – Annexe 4, Règlement Particulier de Lutte contre le Dopage, Titre 1 – Dispositions Générales, Art. 1.

[77] *Anti-doping committee list*
Germany Deutscher Baskettball Bund e.V.: Anlage zur Satzung para. 7 Doping Abs. 1; Deutscher Kanu Verband: Anti-Dopingbestimmungen des Deutschen – Kanu-Verbandes e.V.: 1.Teil – Aligemeines, para. 2 – Begriffsbestimmungen; Deutsche Reiterliche Vereinigung: Abschnitt C III: Ordnungs-maßnahmen, para. 920 – Verstöße; Deutscher Bob- und Schlittensportverband; Deutscher Eishockey Bund e.V.
Spain Real Federación Española de Vela: Reglamento Anti-Dopaje, Disposiciones Generales, Articulo 5.
Luxemb. Fédération Luxembourgeoise de Basketball: Mesures contre le dopage, Art. 1; Hockey Club Luxembourg: Mesures contre le dopage, Art. 1; Fédération Luxembourgeoise de Lutte: Statuts, VII – Du Dopage, Art. 2; Federation Luxembourgeoise de Tennis: Chapitre XIV – Mesures contre le dopage, Art. 1; Fédération Luxemburgeoise de Volley-Ball: F.L.V.B. Règlement D'ordre Intérieur, 4.6. Mesures contre le dopag; Fédération Luxembourgeoise de Natation et de Sauvetage: Mesures contrele dopage, Art. 38.

[78] *IOC list*
Germany Deutscher Ringer-Bund: Richtlinien des Deutschen Ringer-Bundes e.V. zur Bekämpfung des Dopings (RZBD), Erster Abschnitt: Doping-Verbot, para. 2 Begriffsbestimmungen; Deutsche Triathlon Union (DTU), D) Antidopingordnung der Deutschen Triathion Union (AdO)

– the lists of the different institutions mentioned above.[79]

Spain Real Federación Española de Ciclismo: Reglamentos Técnicos y Particulares del Ciclismo, 10 de diciembre de 1999, 5. Reglamento Nacional del Control del Dopaje, Capítulo 1 – Disposiciones Generale Art. 3.
Gr. Britt. British Fencing Association: Modified Proposal, Chapter 6 – Anti-Doping Code, t.129; The Grand National Archery Society.
England English Table Tennis Association, Rules, 32.14. Doping.
Wales Welsh Hockey Union, Appendix on Doping Control.
Greece Greek Boxing Federation.
Italy Federazione Pugilistica Italiana: Regolamento Federale Antidoping, Titolo I – Principi Generali, Art. 1 – Definizione del doping nello sport; Federazione Italiana Giuoco Calcio: Regolamento dell'Attività Antidoping, Titolo I – Principi Generali; Federazione Italiana Sport Invernali: Nuovo Regolamento Antidoping FISI, Titolo I – Principi Generali; Unione Italiana di Tiro a Segno: Regolamento Antidoping Federale, Titolo 1 – Principi Generali, art. 1 – Definizione del doping nello sport; Federazione Italiana di Tiro con L'arco (FITARCO): Regolamento Antidoping; Federazione Italiana Canoa Kayak: Título I – Principi Generali, Art. 1 – Definizione del doping nello sport; Federazione Italiana Nuoto: Regolamento dell'attività antidoping, Titolo I – Principi Generali, Art. 1 – Definizione del doping nello sport; Federazione Italiana Tennis: Regolamento dell'attività antidoping, Titolo I – Principi Generali, Art. 1 – Definizione del doping nello sport; Federazione Italiana Pallavolo: Regolamento Federale Antidoping, Titolo I – Principi Generali, Art. 1 – Definizione del doping nello spor; Federazione Italiana Scherma: Titolo I – Principi Generali, Art. 1 – Definizione del doping nello sport; Federazione Italiana di Atletica Leggera: Regolamento dell'attivitá antidoping, Titolo 1 – Principi Generali, Art. 1 – Definizione del doping nello sport; Federazione Italiana Sport Equestri (FISE): Regolamento Antidoping Cavalieri 2000, Titolo I – Principi Generali, Art. 1 – Definizione del doping nello sport; Federazione Italiana Pallacanestro: Regolamento Antidoping Cavalieri 2000, Titolo I – Principi Generali, Art. 1 – Definizione del doping nello sport.
Ireland Irish Cycling Federation: Anti-Doping Regulations
Portugal Federação Portuguesa de Badminton: Regulamento Anti-Doping, Regulamento de Controlo Antidoping, 20 – Dopagem; Federação Portuguesa de Judo: Regulamento de Controlo Antidopagem, sub 1 en 3; Federação Portuguesa de Tenis: Regulamento de Controlo Antidopagem, sub 1 en; Federação Portuguesa de Halterofilismo: Regulamento Antidopagem, Artigo 3o – Definições
Sweden Riksidrotts Förbundet: Dopingregler, 13 kap, RF:s stadgar, 1 para. Doping; Svenska Gymnastik Förbundet; Svenska Konstäkningsförbundet/Svenska Skridskoförbundet: Riksidrottsforbundet, Chapter 13 – Doping Rules, 1 para. – Doping; Svenska; Ishockeyförbundet: RF:s Stadgar, 13 kap Regler mot doping, 1⁰ Doping.

[79] *Various lists*
Germany Deutscher Judo Bund e.V.: Wettkampf-Ordnung, E. Anti-Doping-Bestimmungen, para. 3 Dopingbegriff; Deutscher Volleyball Verband, Anti-Doping-Ordnung, Erster Abschnitt – Dopingverbot, 2. Begriffsbestimmung; Deutsche Eisschnellauf-Gemeinschaft e.V.: Satzung, para. 21 Doping, 1 Grundsätze
Wales Table Tennis Association of Wales; The Football Association of Wales: Memorandum on the use of drugs; Welsh Badminton Union, Positive Dope Test Protocol, Section One – Regulations.
Portugal Federação Equestre Portuguesa: Regulamento de Controlo de Antidopagem de Cavaleiros/condutores, Capitulo 1 – Disposições gerais, Artigo 20 – Definição de dopagem; Federação Portuguesa de Andebol: Regulamento Geral da Federação Portuguesa de Andebol e Associações, Titulo 9 – Regulamento de Controlo Antidopagem, Capitulo I – Disposições gerais, Artigo 20 – Definição; Federação Portuguesa de Judo: Regulamento de Controlo Antidopagem, sub 3.1.; Federação de Triatlo de Portugal: Regulamento Anti-Dopagem, Título I – Parte Geral, Capítulo Único – Disposições e Princípios Gerais, Artigo 20 – Definições; Federação Portuguesa de Remo: Regulamento do Controlo Antidopagem, Capitulo I – Disposições gerais, Artigo 30 – Definição
Sweden Swedish Weightlifting Federation: 17. Antidoping-Policy och Regler, 17.1 RF:s dopingregler; Svenska Boxningsförbundet
Finland Suomen Purjehtijaliitto; Finnish Table Tennis Association, 3.3.7 Antidoping.

In some cases a doping definition would mention prohibited substances and methods but would not actually refer to a doping list.[80]

Technically speaking, the French laws of 28 June 1989[81] and 23 March 1999[82] and the decrees of 30 August 1991, 1 April 1992[83] and 11 January 2001[84] did not contain a definition of doping. These laws and decrees to which the majority of doping regulations of the French federations referred determined that:

> "Il est interdit à toute personne, au cours des compétitions et manifestations sportives organisées ou agréées par des fédérations sportives ou en vue d'y participer:
> – d'utiliser des substances et procédés de nature à modifier artificiellement les capacités ou à masquer l'emploi de substances ou procédés ayant cette propriété;
> – de recourir à ceux de ces substances et procédés dont l'utilisation est soumise à des conditions restrictives lorsque ces conditions ne sont pas remplies.
> Les substances et procédés visés au présent article sont déterminés par un arrêté conjoint du ministre chargé des sports et du ministre chargé de la santé."

The situation in Sweden was comparable to that in France. The *Dopingregler* of the *Riksodrotts Förbundet*[85] lacked a "proper" doping definition. Instead, they provided that doping was considered the use of substances and methods designated as doping by the IOC. Most Swedish federations followed the *Dopingregler*; only the *Svenska Gymnastik Förbundet* (SGF) steered a course of its own by adopting the IOC Anti-Doping Code. The Swedish Weightlifting Federation (SWF) and the

---

[80] *Unknown list*
Germany Deutscher Schwimm-Verband: DSV-Antidopingbestimmungen, para. 3 Dopingverstöße.
Gr. Britt. Great Britain Olympic Hockey Board, Bue-law 1, Doping Policy, 1.
England English Basket Ball Association, Doping Control (EBBA regulation 26)
Scotland The Scottish Football Association, Doping Charter, 4.
Ireland Irish Sailing Association: Doping Control Policy, 2.2. Doping Offences
Portugal Federação Portuguesa de Hoquei: Regulamento Antidopagem, Título 1 – Da Antidopagem, Capítulo 1 – Disposições Gerais, Art. 20, Proibição e Noção de Dopagem, sub 3; Federação Portuguesa de Futebol: Regulamento do Controlo Antidopagem, Artigo 1o. In this regulation one finds a reference to Decreto-Lei no. 183/97, de 26 de Julho e na Portaria 816/97, de 5 de Setembro; Federação Portuguesa de Tiro com Arco: Regulamente do Controlo Antidopagem, Capítulo I – Disposições Gerais, Artigo 3o – Listas de substâncias ou métodos de dopagem ("As listas de substâncias ou métodos de dopagem que sejam considerados dopantes figuram em anexo e são revistas anualmente ou sempre que as circunstâncias o aconselhem nos termos da legislação em vigor; sendo sempre publicadas em Comunicado Oficial da Federação Portuguesa de Tiro com Arco.").
[81] Loi 89/432.
[82] Loi no. 99-223 du 23 mars 1999 relative à la protection de la santé des sportifs et à la lutte contre le dopage: Titre II B De la prevention et de la Lutte contre le dopage, Section 2 Des Agissements interdits, Art. 17.
[83] Decrèts nos. 91/837 en 92/381 betreffende "la prévention et à la répression de l'usage des produits dopants à l'occasion de compétitions et manifestations sportives."
[84] Décret no. 2002-36 du 11 janvier 2001 relatif aux dispositions que que les fédérations sportives agréées doivent adopter dans leur règlement en matière de contrôles et de santions contre le dopage en application de l'article L.3634-1 du code de la santé publique: Annexe – Règlement Disciplinaire type des Fédérations Sportives agréées relatif à la Lutte contre le dopage, Art. 2.
[85] 13 kap, RF:s stadgar: 1 para. Doping, 2nd section.

Svenska Boxingsförbundet (SBF) referred not only to the IOC list, but also to the lists of their respective international federations (the International Weightlifting Federation (IWF) and the International Amateur Boxing Association (AIBA)).[86]

"Med doping avses användning av medel och metoder som förbjudits av Internationella Olympiska Kommittén (IOK) eller därutöver av vederbörande internationellt specialidrottsförbund."[87]

The Portuguese law of 1997[88] also followed the parameters discussed in this section. It gave a definition of doping and then referred to a list of prohibited substances and methods, namely that of the IOC.

"Article 2 – Definitions
1. For the purposes of this statute:
a) 'Doping' means the administering to sports practitioners or the use by them of those pharmacological classes of substances or methods which appear on the lists approved by the competent national and international sporting organisations;
[...]
2. The lists referred to in this article shall be organised in such a way as to conform to such lists established within the framework of the international conventions on doping in sport as Portugal is or shall become a party to in the future, or, in the absence of such lists or conventions, to the most comprehensive list established by the International Olympic Committee or by the competent international federation respectively."

Various Portuguese federations have included the provisions of the 1997 law in their doping regulations.[89] Some federations referred to lists which had been approved by national and international organisations.[90] Such references read as follows:

"Considera-se dopagem a administração aos praticantes ou o uso por estes de classes farmacológicas de substâncias ou de métodos constantes das listas aprovadas pelas organizações desportivas nacionais e internacionais competentes."[91]

Or, as the case may be, as follows

"Lista de classes de substâncias, produtos ou métodos dopantes
A lista oficial das classes de substâncias, produtos ou métodos dopantes corresponderá

---

[86] Swedish Weightlifting Federation: 17. Antidoping-Policy och Regler, 17.1 RF:s dopingregler, Svenska Boxningsförbundet (no source cited).

[87] Doping means any use of preparations or methods which have been banned by the IOC or additionally by the appropriate national specialist body.

[88] Statute Law no. 183/97 of 26 July 1997.

[89] *Supra* nt. 79.

[90] *Supra* nt. 80.

[91] Federação Equestre Portuguesa: Regulamento de Controlo de Antidopagem de Cavaleiros/condutores, Capitulo 1 – Disposições gerais, Artigo 20 – Definição de dopagem.

às que forem estabelecidas no quadro de convenções internacionais sobre a dopagem a que Portugal venha a aderir ou, na sua ausência às listas mais exigentes estabelecidas, respectivamente pelo Comité Olímpico Internacional pela Federação Internacional de Judo ou pela União Europeia de Judo."[92]

Still other Portuguese federations referred to their own list of prohibited doping substances and methods, annexed to the doping regulations.[93]

"Consideram-se dopantes as substâncias constantes da lista que constitui o anexo 1 do presente Regulamento."

2.1.3. *Doping is the use of certain, specified substances and methods for a specific purpose*

As appears from the above, some international and national federations merely referred to a list of prohibited doping substances and means. Others did the same, but, as the descriptions they used reveal, were not entirely convinced that they were doing the right thing. In the doping regulations of the latter group references could also still be found to the essence of doping. What should we make, for example, of the description of the doping offence of the International Amateur Wrestling Federation (FILA): "The absorption of any substance intended artificially to improve the performance of the athlete is strictly prohibited. The IOC's official list is authoritative."[94] Six other international federations used such dual descriptions.[95] It

---

[92] Federação Portuguesa de Judo: Regulamento de Controlo Antidopagem, sub 3.1.

[93] Federação Portuguesa de Hoquei: Regulamento Antidopagem, Título 1 – Da Antidopagem, Capítulo 1 – Disposições Gerais, Art. 20, Proibição e Noção de Dopagem, sub 3.

[94] Constitution, Art. 10.

[95] IBA Anti Doping Rules, Chapter 1 sub 1.1 "[...] the use or the administration to athletes of pharmacological classes of doping agents or doping methods banned by the I.O.C. or having either adverse effects on the health of those who take them, or of pharmacological classes of agents or methods masking the use of substances or methods having this property in order to obtain an unfair advantage of the athlete's performance during competition, training, or recuperation after competition or training." FIVB Medical Regulations, 2. Antidoping Control Regulations, 2.1. General Indications: AThe use of certain drugs for the improvement of sports performance through stimulation on the muscular and the nervous systems (see Art. 2.5) is strictly prohibited. This prohibition is based on essentially ethical reasons and also because of their detrimental effects on athletes. Doping goes against both the ethics of sport and of medical science, Doping is: 1) to administer substances belonging to classes of forbidden pharmacological substances and/or to use various forbidden methods." FIFA Doping Control Regulations for FIFA Competitions (except for FIFA World Cup), I. Definition: "Doping is any attempt by a player himself, or at the instigation of another person, such as the manager, coach, trainer, doctor, physiotherapist or masseur, to enhance his mental and physical performance unnaturally or to treat ailments or injury when this is medically unjustified for the sole purpose of taking part in a competition. This includes using (taking or injecting), administering or prescribing prohibited substances prior to or during a competition. These stipulations are also applicable out of competition for anabolic steroids and peptide hormones as well as substances producing similar effects. Other prohibited methods (e.g. blood doping) or manipulation of the doping samples are also classified as doping. Doping contravenes the ethics of sport and constitutes an acute or chronic health hazard to players with possible fatal consequences. Prohibited substances in the context of these regulations are included as

was often difficult to decide on the basis of such a description whether it was intended to stress once more that the substances on the list were listed because they enhanced performance, or whether an extra requirement was intended.[96] If intended as an extra requirement, the advantage gained by introducing the possibility of referring to a list would be lost, as it would still have to be shown that the athlete aimed to enhance his performance when he used the substance in question.

In the following, I will simply cite the "essential" definitions cited, but in all these cases a doping list was also referred to.

Rahmen-Richtlinien des Deutschen Sportbundes zur Bekämpfung des Dopings:[97]

"Doping ist der Versuch der Leistungssteigerung durch die Anwendung (Einnahme, Injektion oder Verabreichung) von Substanzen der verbotenen Wirkstoffgruppen oder durch die Anwendung verbotener Methoden (z. B. Blutdoping)."

---

appendix B. Players are also prohibited from using (taking, injecting or administering) any of the substances listed on appendix B, even for medical purposes, while they are taking part in a competition. The only exception to this is local anaesthetics to combat pain (excluding cocaine)." IWF Anti-Doping Policy, 1. Position Statement, Arts. 1.1 and 1.2: "The sport of weightlifting involves physical health and fitness, mental application and dedication to training. The use of banned substances and other doping methods to artificially enhance performance can endanger the health of athletes and is unethical, contrary to the concept of fair play and undermines the values of sport. The International Weightlifting Federation (IWF), condemns the use of banned substances and doping methods. Doping is forbidden. No person who is subject to this Policy shall engage in a doping offence or assist, encourage or otherwise be a party to a doping offence." ITTF Anti-Doping Regulations, 1.1 Medical Code, 1.1.1 and 1.1.2, and the Regulations for International Competitions, Arts. 3.5.3.1. and 3.5.3.2. respectively: Definition of doping: "any use of doping substances or methods by a player and/or application of doping substances or methods to a player by an attending person (team leader, physician, coach, trainer, physiotherapist or other attendance) to increase the player's performance shall be considered as doping. Doping substances and methods, including substances and methods which alter the integrity and validity of urine samples used in doping controls, are those confirmed by the International Olympic Committee (IOC). There shall be no doping before or during play in any competition. For the purpose of this regulation, doping is the introduction into the body of a prohibited substance with the object of improving performance; a list of prohibited substances is available from the Secretariat." FITA Appendix 4 – Doping Control Procedures, 1 Doping – Preamble and Principles, Arts. 1.1-1.3.: "Doping is contrary to the values of sport and the principle of fair play. FITA takes appropriate steps for organizing fair competitions, free from doping. Doping in archery is strictly forbidden. Doping is the administration or the use by an athlete of any substance and/or method banned by the IOC Medical Commission and the FITA Medical Committee which increases in an artificial and unfair manner his/her performance in competition."

[96] Summerer 1990 (*supra* nt. 72), p. 145: "Die IOC-Bestimmungen werden von vielen Weltfachverbänden sinngemäß angewendet. Sowelt die IFs auf sie nicht ausdrücklich verweisen, sondern sich mit einem pauschalen Doping-Verbot begnügen, bestehen im Hinblick auf das Bestimmtheits- und Transparenzgebot erhebliche Bedenken. Zwar soll nach einer verbreiteten Auffassung das strafrechtliche Bestimmtheitsgebot im Vereinsrecht nicht gelten. Diese Auffassung ist jedoch abzulehnen, soweit, wie bei Doping, mehrjährige bis lebenslange Sperren verhangt werden, weil diese den Täter mindestens genauso, meist sogar schwerer treffen als eine vom Strafrichter verhängte Geldstrafe. Hier sollten die Weltfachverbände im eigenen interesse Klarheit schaffen und sich mit dem IOC sowie untereinander zugunsten einer einheitlichen Verbotsliste abstimmen."

[97] Erster Abschnitt – Dopingverbot, para. 2 Begriffsbestimmungen, sub 1. *Idem:* Deutscher Basketball Bund, Anlage zur Satzung para. 7 Doping Abs. 1; Deutscher Judo Bund e.V.: Wettkampf-

Deutscher Fußball-Bund (DFB):[98]

"Unter Doping versteht man jeglichen Versuch eines Spielers, selbst oder auf Anstiftung einer Drittperson, wie z. B. dem Manager, Trainer, Arzt, Physiotherapeuten oder Masseur, seine mentale und körperliche Leistungsfähigkeit auf unnatürliche Weise zu erhöhen [...]."

Deutscher Eishockey Bund (DEB):[99]

"Doping ist der Gebrauch (Einnahme, Injektion oder Verabreichung) oder die Verteilung von gewissen Substanzen an einen Spieler. Diese können die Auswirkung haben, künstlich die körperliche und/oder geistige Beschaffenheit zu verbessern und somit seine sportliche Leistung zu steigern, jedoch seiner Gesundheit Schaden zuzufügen."

It is true that in the Spanish Decree of 1996[100] the essence of doping was referred to, but the wording used did not give rise to the question of whether there was an extra requirement involved, which had to be met in order to establish doping.

"Se consideran como infracciones muy graves a la discipline deportiva las siguientes: La utilización de las sustancias y grupos farmacológicos probibidos, asi como de métodos no reglamentarios destinados a aumentar artificialmente las capacidades fisicas de los deportistas o a modificar los resultados de las competiciones. [...]"

The *Real Federación Española de Ciclismo* (RFEC)[101] adopted the same approach, put slightly differently:

"El Dopaje es el uso de un artificio (sustancia o método) potencialmente peligroso para la salud de los atletas y susceptible de mejorar su rendimiento o la presencia en el organisme del atleta de una sustancia o la constatación de la aplicación de un método que figure en una lista anexa al código antidopaje del movimiento olimpico. Semejante práctica es contraria a la ética deportiva y médica, al espiritu del juego limpio y a los principios fundamentales que constituyen la base del movimiento olimpico, que preconiza la salud de los atletas, asi como una seria violación de las

---

Ordnung, E. Anti-Doping-Bestimmungen, para. 3 Dopingbegriff; Deutscher Bob- und Schlittensport-verband; Deutscher Volleyball Verband: Anti-Doping-Ordnung, Erster Abschnitt – Dopingverbot, 2., Begriffsbestimmung, sub 2.1; Deutsche Eisschnellauf-Gemeinschaft: Satzung, para. 21 Doping, 1 Grundsätze, sub 2.

[98] Durchführungsbestimmungen – Doping, para. 1 – Dopingbegriff.

[99] Anti-Doping Regularien für den Bereich des DEB und der DEL, Einleitung, sub b).

[100] Real Decreto 255/1996, de 16 de febrero, por el que se establece el régimen de infracciones y sanciones para la represión del dopaje, Titulo 1 – Régimen Disciplinario del Dopaje, Art. 1 – Tipificación de las infracciones, sub 1. *Idem:* Real Federación Española de Fútbol: Estatutos, Título VIII Del Régimen Disciplinario y Competicional, Capítulo 3 – De las infracciones y sus sanciones, Sección 4a – De las infracciones especificas en relación con el dopaje, Disposiciones generales, Articulo 143.

[101] Reglamentos Técnicos y Particulares del Ciclismo, 10 de diciembre de 1999, 5. Reglamento Nacional del Control del Dopaje, Capítulo 1 – Disposiciones Generales, Art. 3.

leyes deportivas promulgadas por el COI, las federaciones internacionales y los Comités Olimpicos Nacionales que rigen el deporte de competición."

Although the *Real Federación Española de Atletismo* (RFEA) included an identical provision to the one in the abovementioned law in its doping regulations, the clarity of that provision was partly cancelled out by the provision preceding it:[102]

"El Dopaje es el uso o administración de sustancias o el empleo y aplicación de métodos destinados a aumentar artificialmentelas capacidedes físicas de los deportistas o a modificar los resultados de las competiciones deportivas."

The doping regulations of the *Federación Española de Baloncesto* (FEB) and the *Real Federación Española de Vela* (RFEV) only included the above definition which was, however, preceded by a reference to Title 8 of Law 10/1990 of 15 October.[103]

The statutes of the *Fédération Luxembourgeoise de Tennis de Table* (FLTT)[104] again contained a combined definition (essence of doping and designated doping substances/means), but from the wording of the provision in question it might be concluded that the emphasis was on the listed substances and means.

"Unter Doping versteht man den unerlaubten Gebrauch durch einen Spieler von Mitteln die seine sportliche Leistungsfähigkeit sowie seine Leistung selbst beeinflussen ('Dopingmittel') und die auf der diesbezüglich vom internationalen Olympischen Kommittee erstellten Liste der Dopingmittel ('Dopingliste') als solche gekennzeichnet sind."

2.1.4. *Doping is the presence of a prohibited substance in the body of an athlete (strict liability)*

In practice and over time the "referring" description proved to be inadequate. Problems of an evidentiary nature were constantly causing trouble for the federation having to prove that the athlete was guilty of the act of doping. It became clear that in order to conclude that the act of doping was punishable it was not enough to show through doping analysis that that act had taken place. An additional shortcoming of the first generation descriptions of the doping offence, namely that the guilt or intent of the athlete had to be proven, remained unaddressed in the referring description of the doping offence. A description needed to be found which would make things easier from an evidentiary point of view for sports organisations that were involved in doping trials. The solution that a number of IFs came up with

---

[102] D) Reglamento de los Controles de Dopaje de la Real Federación Española de Atletismo, Capitolo I – Disposiciones Generales, Art. 2.

[103] Reglamento Contro de Dopaje: Titulo Primero – Disposiciones Generales, resp. Reglamento Anti-Dopaje, Disposiciones Generales, Arts. 1 and 2. See also Real Federación Española de Balonmano: RFEBM Estatutos y Reglamentos, Reglamento Control de Dopaje; Real Federación Española de Hockey: Reglamento de Control del Dopaje, Titulo Primero, Disposiciones Generales, Arts. 1 and 2.

[104] Statuten, 5. Offizielle Spielordnung, 5.1. Allgemeines, Art. 5.1.151.

consisted of moving the gravamen in the description of the doping offence. Where the gravamen of earlier descriptions consisted of the act itself, it now came to consist of the discovery of the prohibited substance. The presence of a prohibited substance in the sample had to demonstrate that the athlete had committed an act of doping of which he was guilty *prima facie*. The description of the doping offence (e.g. the description used by the international athletics federation)[105] which applied until the acceptance of the WADC, for example, stipulated that "the offence of doping takes place when a prohibited substance is found to be present within an athlete's body tissue or fluids" and that the athlete was presumed guilty of the offence of doping, if the analysis showed a positive result. This was not the end of it, however, as this description still gave rise to numerous evidentiary problems.[106] As Bette and Schimank[107] put it:

> "Bevor ein Handeln als Fehlverhalten bestraft werden kann, müssen Verstöße gegen sportinterne Verhaltensstandards zunächst als solche genau markiert und damit in eine justitiabele Form gebracht werden. [...] Weder die eine noch die andere Voraussetzung ist bisher befriedigend gelöst worden. Doping bleibt deshalb ein Thema, das auch weiterhin durch Definitionsprobleme und Kontrolldefizite den öffentlichen Diskurs über den Sport in maßgeblicher Weise bestimmen wird."

The strict liability definition causes the athlete involved to be found guilty *prima facie* whenever a prohibited substance has been shown to be or have been present in his body. However, as it not possible to conclude from the presence or absence of certain prohibited substances that a certain prohibited method or technique was used, this element of the description of the doping offence remained within the regime of fault liability. For this reason, a large number of international federations decided to no longer take the use or administration of certain substances as a starting point in their doping definitions. For these federations, doping was only the presence in an athlete's body of prohibited substances.[108]

---

[105] Rules and Regulations, Rule 55, subsection 2.

[106] See also E.N. Vrijman "De IOC Conferentie 'on Doping in Sport', doorbraak of mislukking?" (1999) *Sportzaken*, pp. 78-80. "The current definition of the concept of 'doping', as far as the contents of the current international regulations on doping, still constitutes a continual source of concern. Although many (international) sports organisations no longer define doping as Athe use of or administration to an athlete of substances and/or means which are capable of artificially and unfairly influencing the performance of athletes' and instead now use a definition on the basis of which the simple fact that a prohibited substance and/or method is present in the athlete's body in principle constitutes sufficient grounds for establishing an offence, this does not imply that hereby all (evidentiary) trouble has come to an end."

[107] Bette/Schimank 1998 (*supra* nt. 7), p. 357.

[108] FISA Rules of racing and related By Laws, Rule 80, para. 1: "Doping is strictly prohibited. Doping consists of the presence, above the permitted concentration, in an athlete's body [...] of one or more prohibited therapeutic substances appearing on the International Olympic Committee's list of prohibited substances valid at the time at which the sample was taken, or of blood or blood products, and/or pharmacological, physical or chemical manipulation aimed at making these substances difficult to detect." IWF Anti-doping Policy – 5. Doping Offence, 5.1.: "For the purpose of this Policy a Doping

Only a limited number of national federations and central doping committees proceeded to include a definition of doping in their doping regulations which established strict liability upon testing positive.

In Denmark there was strict liability for all athletes, whichever Danish federation they belonged to, as the *Danmarks Idræts-Forbund* (DIF) (NOC and Sports Confederation of Denmark)[109] determined:

"Ved doping forstås tilstedeværelse i den menneskelige organisme af stoffer, der er forbudt i henhold til den Internationale Olympiske Komites og/eller den pågældende medlemsorganisations internationale liste over forbudte stoffer."

From the doping regulations of the federations competent to regulate for the entire territory of Great Britain it appeared that strict liability was prevalent there. The doping definition of UK Athletics stated that:[110]

Offence is: 1. the presence of a prohibited substance or metabolite, [...]." FIH: "Doping Policy: [...] Doping is defined as the presence in the athlete's body of one or more substances in the prohibited therapeutic categories (appearing on the IOC List of Prohibited Classes of Substances at the time of the test), of re-injected blood or its derivatives and/or any pharmaceutical, physiological or chemical manipulation intended to make these substances difficult to detect, above the allowed concentration, whether intentional or due to negligence or even innocent or unknowing use. The presence of such substance in an athlete's urine or blood entails presumption of voluntary use." FINA: Doping Control: DC 1.2 and Guidelines for Doping Control. "The offence of doping occurs when: (a) a banned substance (see DC 2) is found to be present within a competitor's body tissue [...]." IBU: Anti-doping, Blood Test and Gender Verification Rules, I. Doping controls, 1. Principle. [...] "The offence of doping takes place when a prohibited drug is found to be present within an athlete's body tissue or fluids [...]." ISF: Doping Control and Testing as Established by the ISF Medical and Doping Commission: "It should be noted that the presence of the drug in the urine constitutes an offense, irrespective of the route of administration." ITF: Tennis Anti-doping Programme – (c) 2. "Under this Programme the following shall be regarded as doping offences: A Prohibited Substance is found to be present within a player's body [...]." ITU: Doping Control Rules and Procedural Guidelines, preamble and 2. Definition of Doping: 2.2. "[...] For the purpose of these Rules, the following are regarded as doping offenses: – the finding in an athlete's body tissue or fluids of a prohibited substance [...]." ISAF: Medical Regulations – 2. Antidoping Control Regulations, 2.1. General Indicationsand the 1998 ISAF Regulations – Medical Code (Old 17) respectively: "[...] It should be noted that the presence of the drug in the urine constitutes an offence, irrespective of the route of administration." ISU: Communication no. 956 – Doping: 1.2 Definitions: 1.2.1.: "Doping – is the detection of any substance contained in the current International Olympic Committee's list of doping classes by the competitor or the administration [...]." FIS: Doping Rules – Rule 1 – Doping: 3: "The offence of doping takes place when a prohibited drug is found to be present within an athletes body tissue of fluids [...]."

[109] Dopingkontrolregulativ, para. 1, Stk. 1. "Doping is defined as the presence in the human body of substances which are prohibited according to the lists published by the International Olympic Committee and/or the international organization of the member organization concerned."

[110] UK Current Doping Rules and Procedures, Rule 24 Doping, sub (5). *Idem:* British Cycling Federation: Anti Doping Regulations, Principles, sub 1a); British Judo Association: By Laws relating to Drug Abuse, Anti-Doping Control Regulations of the British Judo Association, A.2.; British Bobsleigh Association: Rules for Doping Control, 2. Doping Offences, 2.2; The Lawn Tennis Association, LTA Rules, Appendix 4 – Tennis Anti-Doping Programme, A. General Statement of Policy, 2; Amateur Swimming Federation of Great Britain: ASFGB Doping Control Rules and Protocols, 3. Doping Offences, 3.1.1.

"The offence of doping takes place when: a prohibited substance is found to be present within an athlete's body tissue or fluids [...]."

This provision was subsequently taken over by a large number of British federations. This definition also resounded with the federations exercising jurisdiction over parts of Great Britain only, such as the Badminton Association of England (BAE)[111] and the Football Association (FA).[112] The English Table Tennis Association (ETTA)[113] opted to rephrase the definition so as to read that:

"32.14.1. A Member must not use any of the substances specified in the List of Banned Substances contained in Appendix 'P' to these Rules (such use being the offence of Doping).

[...]

32.14.3. For the purposes of Rule 32.14.1 use shall be conclusively established by -

32.14.3.1. in the case of an endogenous banned substance the presence in a body fluid, established by quantitative analysis, of more than the amount specified by the International Olympic Committee's Medical Commission as the amount the presence of which is the minimum necessary to show that the quantity present could not have occurred naturally

32.14.3.2. in the case of any other banned substance the identification in a body fluid of it and/or one of its metabolites."

The doping regulations of six Irish federations contained a strict liability definition of doping identical to that of UK Athletics.[114]

In the Netherlands, most federations also opted for a doping definition starting from strict liability. Unlike the British federations mentioned above, which assumed that a doping offence had taken place if a prohibited substance or its metabolites were found in a urine sample, the Dutch federations only considered the use of doping likely upon such findings.

The *Koninklijke Nederlandse Atletiek Unie* (KNAU),[115] for example, stated in its regulations that:

"It is likely that an athlete has used doping when after a doping test the urine or blood of the athlete involved is discovered to contain:

---

[111] Doping Control Rules for the Badminton Association of England, Appendix A – Doping Offences, 2.

[112] Drug Testing Programme, Memorandum and Procedural Guidelines for the Conduct of Drug Testing, Season 2000/2001, Memorandum, Drug Testing, 1.

[113] Rules, 32.14 Doping, sub 32.14.3.2.

[114] Irish Canoe Union: Irish Canoe Union Doping Control Regulations, 6.00 Offences, 6.01, sub (a); Equestrian Federation of Ireland: Model Doping Control Policy for National Governing Bodies, 2. Doping Control Policy, 2.2 What is a Doping Offence?, sub 2.2.2. (a); Tennis Ireland: Doping Control Policy, 2. Doping Offences, sub 2.2. (a); Irish Triathlon Association: Doping Control Policy, 2.2 What is a Doping Offence?, sub 2.2.2 (a); Volleyball Association of Ireland: Doping Control Policy of the Volleyball Association of Ireland, 1.2 The Doping Offence, sub 1.2.2.a.; The Irish Amateur Wrestling Association: 2 Doping Offences, sub 2.2.

[115] KNAU Dopingreglement, Art. 2 – Verbod en verplichting, sub 3. a.

1e (degradation products of) doping or

2e concentrations of (degradation products of) endogenous spheroid hormones or of peptide hormones, analoga and respective 'releasing factors' which, according to current medical opinion, deviate from the levels which are normally found in humans to such an extent that these findings do not correspond to ordinary body production levels, or

3e in the event that endogenous spheroid hormones are found in mutual relations deviating from the levels which, according to current medical opinion, are normally found in humans to such an extent that these findings do not correspond to ordinary body production levels."

And the *Nederlandse Basketball Bond* (NBB)[116] provided that:

"An athlete is considered to have used doping when:
after the doping control the urine of the athlete is found to contain (degradation products of) prohibited designated doping substances [...]."

The definitions of the *Koninklijke Nederlandse Gynmnastiek Bond* (KNGB) and the *Judo Bond Nederland*[117] are rather more like the absolute liability definitions used by various federations in Great Britain:

"Doping has occurred when:
after the doping control the athlete's urine is found to contain (degradation products of) prohibited designated doping susbtances [...]."

This is also the case for the definition in the doping regulations of the *Koninklijke Nederlandse Zwembond* (KNZB):[118]

"Doping is defined as follows:
the presence of a prohibited substance [...] in the body tissue or body fluids of a competitive athlete; [...]."

---

[116] Dopingreglement, Verboden en verplichtingen, Art. 2, sub 3. *Idem:* Koninklijke Nederlandse Algemene Schermbond: Dopingreglement, Titel I – Verboden en verplichtingen, Art. 2, sub 3; Koninlijke Nederlandse Hockey Bond: Dopingreglement, Titel I, Verboden en verplichtingen, Art. 2; Koninklijke Nederlandse Lawn Tennis Bond: Dopingcontrolereglement, Hoofdstuk 1 – Begripsbepalingen, Art. 2 – Verboden en verplichtingen, sub 3; Nederlandse Tafeltennis Bond: Dopingcontrole-Reglement, Art. 7 Verboden en verplichtingen, sub 3; Koninklijke Nederlandse Schutters Associatie KNSA: Dopingreglement, Titel I – Verboden en verplichtingen, Art. 2, sub 3; Nederlandse Handboog Bond: Dopingreglement, Titel I – Verboden en verplichtingen, Art. 2, sub 3; Nederlandse IJshockey Bond: Dopingreglement, Titel I – Verboden en verplichtingen, Art. 2, sub 3; Nederlandse Boksbond, art. 33: Dopingreglement, sub 33.1.3; Koninklijke Nederlandse Baseball en Softball Bond, Reglement van wedstrijden, Doping, 2. Verboden en verplichtingen, sub 3; Nederlands Handbal Verbond: Huishoudelijk reglement NHV, para. 6.3 Doping, Art. 6.3.1.2 Verboden en verplichtingen, sub 3; Nederlandse Ski Vereniging: Dopingreglement, Begripsbepalingen, Verboden en verplichtingen, Art. 2, sub 3.

[117] Koninklijke Nederlandse Gymnastiek Bond: Huishoudelijk Reglement, Hoofdstuk 4 Dopingcontrole, 4.0 Algemene bepalingen, 4.0.02. Verboden, sub 2 a; Judo Bond Nederland: Bonds Vademecum, Hoofdstuk 2 – Regelingen, 2.5 Dopingreglement, Art. 1 – Verboden en verplichtingen, sub 2. a.

[118] KNZB-Reglement Dopingcontrole, Art. P2 Doping, 2.1, sub a.

The Finnish sport federations followed the lead of the legislation on doping of the *Suomen Antidoping-Toimikunte* (SAT) (the Finnish Anti-doping Committee). The *Urheilujärjestöjen Doping-Säännöstö* (UDS) (Doping Regulations for Sport Organisations) provided that:

> "[...] the contents and limits of doping are determined by the rules of the International Olympic Committee and international sport associations, the Council of Europe's Antidoping agreement and the Nordic Antidoping agreement, as well as other international agreements Finland has entered into."

2.1.5. *The description of the offence of the use of doping in the Olympic Movement Anti-Doping Code*

The influence which the IOC Medical Code (MC) had on these descriptions must not be underestimated. Because of its comprehensive character, the IOC Medical Code for many years used to be the focal point in the debate within the international sports community concerning the harmonisation of anti-doping rules and regulations. Not surprisingly (but not widely publicised), one of the first tangible results of the World Conference on Doping in Sport which took place in early 1999 turned out to be a revised Medical Code, now called the Olympic Movement Anti-Doping Code (OMADC).[119]

According to the MC, doping was understood to mean the use of prohibited (classes of) substances and methods capable of enhancing an athlete's performance in sports, or of prohibited (classes of) substances and methods which could have such an effect. Such practices were deemed a violation of medical ethics and were *generally* regarded as doping.[120] Accordingly, the MC defined doping specifically as "the use of any substance and/or method featuring on the list of prohibited classes of substances and prohibited methods contained in Chapter II of the MC." The MC thus essentially provided the same kind of circular definition of doping as provided for in the anti-doping regulations of other international sports-governing bodies. What *exactly* constituted doping we still did not know.[121] In practice, doping was

---

[119] *"Lausanne, 2nd August 1999*
As you know, following the agreement which the Olympic family reached at the meeting on 27th November 1998, the draft Olympic Movement Medical Code was adopted under the title 'Olympic Movement Anti-doping Code' at the World Conference on Doping in Sport in Lausanne on 2nd, 3rd and 4th February 1999. This was a major event, as it means that all the constituents of the Olympic Movement now have a common instrument with which to combat doping in sport. This Code will come into force on 1st January 2000.
In the meantime, I remain,
Yours faithfully, Juan Antonio Samaranch, Marqués de Samaranch." www.nodoping.org/pos-anti-dop_code-e.html.
[120] Second "whereas" of the preamble.
[121] "The biggest problem, Verbruggen said [...] are the untraceable substances. At the moment, it's EPO, which use cannot or only barely be proven. In a while, it will be even newer substances. Cell

regarded as the use of banned (classes of) substances and/or methods which had been identified as such by the IOC.

As the definition of doping contained within the MC was felt to be incomplete, the working group established by the IOC for the purpose of redrafting its MC, was required to re-orientate itself regarding this issue. In the words of Mbaye, the working group had to achieve:

"a definition of doping which would not sacrifice the effectiveness of prevention and punishment nor change current practice, but would include an additional weapon with which to pre-empt offenders, as this is what seemed to be needed in the fight against this scourge."

The results of this reorientation process can be found in a document entitled "The offence of doping and its punishment" which was drafted by Mbaye on 24 December 1998 in Dakar. Unfortunately, the working group did not consider it part of its assignment to formulate a definition of what constitutes doping that did justice to the essence of the phenomenon itself, while, at the same time, retaining a level of abstraction allowing it to be used as a legal concept in its own right. According to Mbaye, doping had to be defined as:

"1. the use of an expedient (substance or method) which is potentially harmful to athletes' health and capable of enhancing their performance.
2. the presence in the athlete's body of a substance or evidence of the use of a method where such substance or method appears on the list annexed to the present Code."

However, this provision (included unaltered in the OMADC as Article 2 of Chapter II) contained not one, but four definitions of doping.[122] Doping was:

"1. the use of an expedient (substance or method) which is potentially harmful to athletes' health;
2. the use[123] of an expedient which is capable of enhancing performance;
3. the presence in the athlete's body of a substance that appears on the IOC list of prohibited classes of substances and prohibited methods; and

---

implants, genetic engineering, the end is nowhere near in sight." Investigating these offences is getting harder and so is punishing them. There are always borderline cases. "And what exactly is doping?," Verbruggen wonders. *NRC* of 3 February 1999.

[122] "Une définition claire et suffisammant large du dopage parait nécessaire. D'une part pour couvrir tous les cas de figure et d'autre part pour une bonne conduite de la procédure menée par une autorité sportive ou judiciaire à l'encontre d'une personne, athlète ou non, poursuivi pour dopage. Une définition imprécise ou incomplète permaittrait à des personnes responsables d'une manquement à la réglementation sur le dopage d'échapper aux sanctions," says La Rochefoucauld in a memo to the working group. Rap Conf Mond fev 99.lwp, p. 10/33.

[123] The OMADC in Art. 1, Ch. I considers use "the application, ingestion, injection, consumption by any means whatsoever of any Prohibited Substance or Prohibited Method. Use includes counselling the use of, permitting the use of or condoning the use of any Prohibited Substance or Prohibited Method."

4.   evidence of the use of a method that appears on the IOC list of prohibited classes
      of substances and prohibited methods."

It could be argued that, by formulating four definitions, the working group's task to
provide one definition of what constituted doping had been sufficiently accom-
plished. This point of view, however, was certainly not shared by Mbaye, who
argued that one legal gap remained: "We have never clearly differentiated between
doping, the mere detection of which is sufficient to result in certain measures and
sanctions (doping as a kind of petty offence), and intentional doping, which should
be punished more severely." A description of the concept of intentional doping was,
however, not included in the December 1998 document. It did, however, feature in
Article 1 of Chapter I of the OMADC:

> "Intentional doping means doping in circumstances where it is established, or may rea-
> sonably be presumed, that any Participant acted knowingly or in circumstances
> amounting to gross negligence."

While arguing the need to differentiate between doping and intentional doping,
Mbaye threw together two distinct legal phenomena: the definition of doping and
the description of the doping offence. The actions described *in abstracto* provided
but one of the constituent elements of the doping offence. An athlete cannot be
punished based on the fact that his actions match those described in the definition
alone. The possibility of punishment also requires that his actions are regarded as
reprehensible and thus punishable. Article 1 of Chapter II of the December 1998
document and the OMADC both stipulated that "doping is prohibited." Only after
linking Article 2 with Article 1, one could arrive at a complete description of the
doping offence. In other words, the additional element required for the description
to become a description of an unlawful act was the interconnection of the two provisions cited. In order to arrive at a better understanding of the four separate definitions of doping in the OMADC – and because Mbaye has already pointed us in that
direction – one should keep in mind that these definitions are only part of the description of the offence. The OMADC also featured the concept of intentional doping. Our first examination of the offence of doping will be of doping as a petty
offence.[124]

The MC used to distinguish between *prima facie* cases of doping and definitive
cases of doping.[125] A *prima facie* case of doping would occur when an athlete tested
positive for ephedrine, pseudo-ephedrine, phenylpropanolamine and cathine, as well
as testosterone and, more recently, nandrolone. While the mere detection of other
banned substances in an athlete's urine sample would automatically constitute a
definitive case of doping irregardless of either the athlete's intentions or the actual

---

[124] As an aside, it could be mentioned that most athletes will not consider an offence punishable by
exclusion for a minimum of two years a "petty offence."

[125] MC, Arts. IV and V, Ch. II.

concentration of the banned substance found, in *prima facie* cases of doping the concentration of the banned substance had to be considered first. This meant that in definitive cases of doping athletes were not given any opportunity to present evidence as to their lack of intent or the actual amount of the substance found, but in *prima facie* cases they could raise a defence.

The introduction of the OMADC also saw the introduction of the concept of intentional doping. It remained unclear, however, how intentional doping actually differed from doping as it was understood at the time. Because of the evidentiary problems that sports-governing bodies had encountered in the past when trying to prove that athletes who had tested positive had intended to use doping to enhance their performance, the anti-doping rules and regulations establishing what constitutes a doping offence gradually shifted away from specified actions to mere factual findings – i.e., was a banned substance found in the athlete's urine sample or not – resulting in the introduction of a strict liability approach. The mere finding of a banned substance rendered the athlete fully liable. This made any discussion of intent or guilt superfluous. With the introduction of the concept of intentional doping, however, this discussion appeared to have regained relevance.

The confusion regarding the difference between these two doping offences was exacerbated by the structure used in the OMADC. The definition of doping offence was included at length in Chapter II entitled "The offence of doping and its punishment." It would therefore have made sense to include the definition of intentional doping in this chapter as well. However, Mbaye drafted Chapter II at some point in December of 1998 and he did not include a definition of intentional doping. As Mbaye's draft Chapter II was included in the final draft of the OMADC practically unaltered, it must be assumed that the definition of intentional doping was not established until some time after and was subsequently introduced in Article 1 of Chapter I. As a result, the definition of intentional doping came to precede the general definition of doping, of which it was actually an aggravated form. This inconsistency might have come to light at an earlier stage, as Article 3 of Chapter II specified the penalties for intentional doping, while Article 4 of Chapter II contained further provisions concerning evidence of intentional doping. The provision that became Article 4 could be found *in statu nascendi* in Mbaye's draft of December 1998: "Evidence of fraudulent intent in cases of doping can be adduced by any means whatsoever, including presumption." In the OMADC this rule read: "Intentional doping can be proved by any means whatsoever, including presumption."[126]

---

[126] A salient editorial difference between the two categories of doping definitions may still be spotted. The doping definitions of Art. 2, Ch. II address "athletes," while the definition of intentional doping in Art. 1 of Ch. I uses the term "participant." It is possible that it was simply omitted to "readdress" the provision of Art. 2. "Participant" in Art. 1 is understood to mean: "any athlete, coach, trainer, official, medical or para-medical personnel working with or treating athletes participating in or preparing for sports competitions of the Olympic Games, those competitions to which the IOC grants its patronage or support and all competitions organized under the authority, whether direct or delegated, of an IF or NOC." If intentional doping is an aggravated form of doping, it is highly relevant that the group of persons addressed by the provisions is the same.

Article 2 of Chapter II of the OMADC contained a provision detailing what constituted doping in a similar fashion to Article IV of the MC and to provisions in the anti-doping rules and regulations of many international sports-governing bodies.[127] The provision was based on CAS case law establishing a two-step system for concluding that doping had occurred. The system followed the strict liability approach. As step one, the sports-governing body had to establish that a doping offence had indeed been committed by showing that a banned substance was present in the athlete's body tissue or fluids.[128] This led many sports administrators to believe that according to the strict liability approach they did not need to prove intent before they could impose sanctions upon the athlete: "[...] the principal offence of doping consists merely of the finding of the presence of a prohibited substance in an athlete's body tissue or fluids. The rule does not provide that an athlete must have taken the substance deliberately. It creates an offence of strict liability in that the athlete's intent is completely irrelevant."[129]

However, the CAS ruled otherwise on the requirements for proving a doping offence.[130] In *Bernhard v. ITU* the Panel argued that if a sports-governing body opted to sanction the consequences of the unlawful act rather than the unlawful act itself, it first had to establish the causal relationship between the unlawful act and the consequences in a manner that was completely clear and incontestable. Generally speaking, if we look at tort law, we also find that the causal link between the unlawful act and its consequences is not automatically assumed, but requires proof. Even in cases of strict liability – where guilt does not need to be proven – the causal relationship between the unlawful act and its consequences remains an element requiring proof by the party invoking liability. This should therefore be even more the case in matters dealt with by disciplinary law, with its quasi-criminal law character. The Panel accordingly considered it unacceptable if the concept of strict liability were to be applied more strictly against an athlete accused of doping offence than it would have been in a case under private law in which the strict liability concept is firmly rooted. This led the Panel to rule that the causal link between the unlawful act and the consequences still required proving. In other words, although the strict liability rule means that sports-governing bodies do not need to prove guilt (i.e. that the athlete was guilty of the fact that a banned substance was present

---

[127] IAAF Rules and Regulations, Rule 55, para. 2; FISA Rules of racing and related By Laws, Rule 80, para. 2; IWF Anti-doping Policy, Art. 5.1; FINA Doping Control, DC 1.2; IBU Anti-doping, Blood Test and Gender Verification Rules; ITF Anti-doping Programme (c)2; ITU Doping Control Rules and Procedural Guidelines, 2.2; FIS Doping Rules – Rules 1 – 3; ATP and WTA Official Rulebook – Players – Tennis' Anti-doping Program – C.1.

[128] See CAS 95/142, 14-2-1996, *Lehtinen v. FINA*, Matthieu Reeb, ed., *Digest of CAS Awards 1986-1998* (Berne, Editions Stämpfli 1998) pp. 225-244.

[129] M. Gay in a speech during the International Symposium on Sport & Law at the beginning of 1991, International Athletic Foundation, International Symposium on Sport & Law, Official Proceedings, Monte Carlo 1991 (Gay 1991), p. 66.

[130] CAS 98/222, 9-8-1999, *Bernhard v. ITU*, Matthieu Reeb, ed., *Digest of CAS Awards II 1998-2000* (The Hague, Kluwer Law International 2002) pp. 330-344.

in his body), the rule still means that sports-governing bodies have to prove that the presence of the substance was the result of use by the athlete.[131]

After establishing that a doping offence had in fact occurred, tribunals had to turn to step two, where the burden of proof shifted from the sports-governing body to the athlete.[132] At this stage, the athlete was given the opportunity to raise a defence, so that the tribunal could decide on the (severity) of the applicable sanction, bearing in mind the principle of proportionality, provided the sports-governing body in question applied a flexible sanctioning system.

Apart from the strict liability definition of doping, in which the issues of guilt and intent are absent, the OMADC featured three other definitions of doping which focused on the unlawfulness of the act of doping and required proof of culpability (either negligence or intent). One definition concerned banned methods, and two concerned the use of banned substances in general.

According to the first sentence of Article 2 of Chapter I of the OMADC, the use of an expedient (either a substance or method) which was potentially harmful to an athlete's health was prohibited. This provision must have been directed at substances and/or methods not listed on the IOC list of prohibited classes of substances and prohibited methods. If not, the situation would already have been fully covered by the provisions of Article 2, Chapter II OMADC. However, having to show that an athlete used a substance or a method which was not listed by the IOC, but was still harmful to the athlete's health and thus constituted doping once again confronted sports-governing bodies with insurmountable obstacles in the shape of the required scientific evidence. The definition in question was perhaps merely intended as a reflection of the first "whereas" in the OMADC preamble, i.e., "[...] the Olympic Movement, [...] takes measures, the goal of which is to prevent endangering the health of athletes," rather than as a serious attempt to provide a new and complementary definition of doping.[133]

---

[131] Critics have not entirely ignored the strict liability rule. Lob, for example, in his article "Dopage, responsabilité objective ('strict liability') et de quelques autres questions" (*SJZ* 95(1999) no. 12, p. 272) considers that: "Il nous paraît qu'une sentence du TAS fondée sur le principe de la responsabilité objective pourrait étre attaquée devant les tribunaux ordinaires. L'art. 36 g du Concordat du 27 août 1969 sur arbitrage permet en effet l'annulation d'une sentence arbitrale lorsque la sentence est arbitraire, parce qu'elle constitue une violation évidente du droit ou de l'équité. Le principe de la responsabilité objective apparaît aussi critiquable s'il est appliqué á la durée de la suspension. Les règles statutaires peuvent certes prévoir des normes, mais il appartient aux fédérations de tenir compte de toutes les circonstances et de prendre en considération en particulier la gravité de la faute de l'athlète concerné."

[132] See CAS 98/208, 22-12-1998, *Wang Lu Na, Cai Hui Jue, Zhgang Yi, Wang Wei v. FINA*, Matthieu Reeb, ed., *Digest of CAS Awards II 1998-2000* (The Hague, Kluwer Law International 2002) pp. 234-254, ground 5.10: "If the presence of a prohibited substance is established to the high degree of satisfaction required by the seriousness of the allegation, then the burden shifts to the competitor to show why, in the case of a diuretic, the maximum sanction should not be imposed. The Panel repeats that under the new FINA rules it is only at the level of *sanction* not of finding of innocence or guilt, that the concept of shifting the burden becomes relevant at all. And it is only at this juncture too that questions of intent become relevant."

[133] "To most sporting participants the side effects of these drugs outweigh the advantages of taking them. However, at the highest level the competitive instincts of many participants may blind them to

The second part of Article 2, Chapter I in conjunction with Article 1, Chapter II OMADC prohibited the use of any expedient – substance or method – which had the potential of enhancing athletic performance. Concerning this provisions Bette and Schimanck considered that it

> "hängt für eine – insbesondere auch rechtliche – Handhabbarkeit dieser Art der Dopingdefinition alles davon ab, inwieweit sich in sachlicher Hinsicht hinreichend präzise und umfassend, in zeitlicher Hinsicht hinreichend dauerhaft und in sozialer Hinsicht hinreichend intersubjektiv einheitlich bestimmen läßt, welche Art von Handeln sich als 'unnatürliche' sportliche Leistungssteigerung begreifen läßt. In dem Maße hingegen, wie genau diese Spezifizierungen nicht gelingen, erweist sich eine Wesensdefinition des Dopings als unbrauchbar."[134]

The 1996 *Bromantan* case provided a perfect example of the caveat voiced by Bette and Schimanck, as it revealed the systematic defect in the rules and regulations on which the fight against doping was based, namely that they allowed athletes using performance-enhancing substances and methods which were not on the IOC list to go free. With the introduction of the provision of Article 2, Chapter II (first sentence, second part) the Working Group attempted to remedy this defect, as neither it, nor Mbaye were blind to the limitations of the elected approach from an evidentiary point of view:

> "while [this provision] will [...] enable the Olympic Movement to guard against such a case [as the Bromantan Case; *JWS*], it should nevertheless be noted that doping will be counteracted essentially on the basis of detection of the presence or use of prohibited substances and methods."

The last definition of doping in the OMADC concerned the use of IOC-listed methods. As the use or application of banned methods remained difficult to prove directly, given that it often depended on indirect proof, such as the of occurrence of subsequent side effects, this offence did not lend itself for application of the strict liability principle.

In conclusion, it may be stated that the OMADC did not offer any innovative approaches to the definition of doping. The MC and many of the anti-doping rules and regulations of international sports-governing bodies already contained similar provisions.

---

the dangers. So how justified are NGBs in taking a paternalist approach and protecting the welfare of sporting participants? Traditional paternalist jurisprudence would argue that this approach is only valid if the effect of the prohibition is to protect those unable to make an informed and rational judgment for themselves or to prevent harm to others. The obvious example of the former would be a ban on the taking of performance-enhancing drugs by children and junior athletes but extending the ban beyond this point is difficult to justify on this basis." Gardiner et al., *Sports Law*, p. 164.

[134] Bette/Schimank 1998 (*supra* nt. 7), p. 359.

The introduction of the concept of intentional doping begged the question of whether the IOC was not raking up old and awkward matters? Old, because the evidentiary problems involved in proving intent had already led to the development of the strict liability approach and awkward, because "establishing proof of such intention will clearly be difficult, and for that reason it is necessary to establish regulations governing it."[135] New regulations, however, did not appear to be necessary. Although the OMADC did not expressly say so,[136] it is quite obvious that intentional doping had to be considered something different from doping as defined in Article 2 of Chapter II. Apparently, intentional doping was an aggravated form of doping. If a sports-governing body was successful in establishing a doping offence resulting in the strict liability of the athlete, it could then proceed to prove intent making it possible to impose severer penalties, such as life-long bans rather than temporary suspensions, or higher fines (the maximum fine in case of proven intent was US$ 1,000,000.–, as compared to US$ 100,000,– if intent could not be proven).[137, 138]

In summary, the OMADC[139] defined doping as follows:

"1. the use of an expedient (substance or method) which is potentially harmful to athletes' health and capable of enhancing their performance.
2. the presence in the athlete's body of a substance or evidence of the use of a method where such substance or method appears on the list annexed to the present Code."

In this provision we find not one, but four definitions of doping,[140] i.e. doping is: 1° the use of an expedient (substance or method) which is potentially harmful to athletes' health;[141] 2° the use of an expedient which is capable of enhancing perfor-

---

[135] Mbaye in his introduction of 30 September 1998.

[136] Nor does it follow from what Mbaye wrote in his introduction. "[...] we have never clearly differentiated between doping [...] and intentional doping."

[137] OMADC Ch. II, Art. 3 (1) and (2).

[138] This elaboration on the subject of "intentional doping" is relevant to the subject at hand, now that various sports federations in the European Community follow the IOC's lead. The Finnish Anti-Doping Committee, for example, laid down in its regulations that "the contents and limits of doping are determined by the rules of the International Olympic Committee." In the Rahmen-Richtlinien des Deutschen Sportbundes zur Bekämpfung des Dopings (Erster Abschnitt – Dopingverbot, para. 2 Begriffsbestimmungen, sub 5) it is stated that "die 'Dopingdefinition der Medizinischen Kommission des IOC' [...] ist Bestandteil dieser Rahmen-Richtlinien. Sie ist von den Spitzenverbänden zum Bestandteil ihrer Wettkampfbestimmungen zu machen."

[139] Chapter II, Art. 2.

[140] "Une définition claire et suffisammant large du dopage parait nécessaire. D'une part pour couvrir tous les cas de figure et d'autre part pour une bonne conduite de la procédure menée par une autorité sportive ou judiciaire à l'encontre d'une personne, athlète ou non, poursuivi pour dopage. Une définition imprécise ou incomplète permaittrait à des personnes responsables d'une manquement à la réglementation sur le dopage d'échapper aux sanctions," says La Rochefoucauld in a memo to the working group. Rap Conf Mond fev 99.lwp, p. 10/33.

[141] By this wording the IOC attempted to drive one more nail in doping's coffin. In the Explanatory Memorandum concerning the application of the OMADC: p. 7 it is stated that Art. 2(1) "refers to new

mance; 3° the presence in the athlete's body of a substance that appears on the IOC list of prohibited substances, and 4° evidence of the use of a method that appears on the IOC list.

2.1.6. *The description of the offence of the use of doping in the World Anti-Doping Code*

The World Conference on Doping in Sport, which took place in Lausanne from 2 to 4 February 1999, led to the adoption of the Lausanne Declaration by representatives of governments, intergovernmental organisations and the international sports organisations, the IOC among them. The establishment of the World Anti-Doping Agency (WADA) was a direct result of this Conference. The WADA was established on 10 November 1999. The reason for establishing a WADA was the assumption that the fight against doping could be fought more effectively if the Olympic Movement (including the athletes) and public authorities would cooperate. It may therefore be considered the first "joint venture" between sports and public authorities. Initially the WADA had its headquarters in Lausanne, but on 21 August 2001 the Foundation Board put the permanent seat to the vote, and as a result the WADA seat was transferred to Montréal.[142] The IOC committed itself to financing the WADA until the end of 2001, by which time the sport movement and the public authorities would jointly take over the funding. "The mission of the Agency shall be to promote and coordinate at international level the fight against doping in sport in all its forms; to this end, the Agency will cooperate with intergovernmental organisations, governments, public authorities and other public and private bodies fighting against doping in sport, inter alia, the International Olympic Committee (IOC), International Sports Federations (IFs), National Olympic Committees (NOCs) and the athletes," according to the Draft Mission Statement.[143]

The WADA is also assigned the task of "[promoting] harmonised rules, disciplinary procedures, sanctions and other means of combating doping in sport, and contribut[ing] to the unification thereof taking into account the rights of athletes."[144] After the establishment of the WADA, the International Intergovernmental Consultative Group on Anti-Doping in Sport (IICGADS) was created "to coordinate the efforts of the public authorities in the WADA."[145] The role which national and regional authorities were supposed to play in the WADA was subsequently clarified during various meetings of the IICGADS.

---

substances that have been discovered but which have not yet been added to the list as specifically identified substances. It is to be noted that Article 2(1) and 2(2) are not linked and that a prohibited substance or method may be qualified as doping without necessarily meeting the criteria provided in Article 2(1)."

[142] http://www.wada-ama.org/asiakas/003/wada_english.nsf/.
[143] Available on the WADA website.
[144] Draft Mission Statement, 4.6.
[145] Balfour, ibidem.

After its establishment the first priority of the WADA was the drafting of universally applicable anti-doping regulations. To this end, a Code Project Team was created. "There had been several stages within an eighteen-month period; the consultation process had involved all categories of stakeholders in addition to independent experts for certain key areas; the comments and suggestions received had been addressed and incorporated into each new version of the document."[146] Immediately after the meetings of the Executive Committee and the Foundation Board between September and November 2001, a start was made on outlining the framework of the WADC. This process involved athletes, the IICGADS, the Council of Europe, various governments, various National Anti-Doping Organisations (NADOs), several IFs, the General Association of International Sports Federations (GAISF), the CAS and all the members of the various WADA working committees. The foundations for the Code were laid between December 2001 and April 2002 and were the product of consultations between all these groups. Approximately 130 individuals and organisations submitted comments. During this stage, about 30 experts in the field of doping were involved as content producers. Meetings were held with athletes, IFs, the European Commission, the Council of Europe, governments, NOCs and NADOs. The WADA participated in the Harmonisation Conference in the Netherlands and in the IICGADS meeting in Kuala Lumpur in 2002. After the first version of the Code had been completed, it was circulated between May and September 2002. Meetings followed involving athletes, the IOC Athletes' Commission, the European Olympic Committees Athletes' Commission, the IOC, the majority of IFs, the GAISF,[147] the ASOIF,[148] the ARISF,[149] the AIOWF,[150] several governments, the Council of Europe, the IICGADS, the European Union Presidency, a number of NOCs and various NADOs. The expertise of several key drafting experts was drawn on. Over 120 comments resulted from this exploration. The second draft of the Code was published on 10 October 2002. Again, meetings were held attended by practically all the parties mentioned above who had also been involved previously. This round of consultations yielded another 90 comments. The third draft dates from 20 February 2003 and was circulated in the final quarter of that month.

The second World Conference on Doping in Sport took place in Copenhagen from 3 to 5 May. The purpose of this conference "[...] was to review, discuss and agree upon the Code content and its use as the basis for the fight against doping in sport. The approach had been to highlight the importance of the athletes, and its basis was the integrity of sport."[151] Taking part in the Conference were representatives of the IOC and of 80 governments, 60 NOCs, 70 IFs, 30 NADOs and 20 athletes, all in all around 1000 persons. The first day was set aside for the discus-

---

[146] World Conference on Doping in Sport, plenary sessions, Summary Notes, p. 12.
[147] General Association of International Sports Federations.
[148] Association of Summer Olympic International Federations.
[149] Association of IOC Recognized International Sports Federations.
[150] Association of International Olympic Winter Sports Federations.
[151] World Conference on Doping in Sport, plenary sessions, Summary Notes, p. 13.

sion of the content of the third draft of the Code. The WADA Foundation Board would adopt the Code on the third day of the Conference. A Conference Resolution would also be drawn up on that day, based on the interventions. With the Resolution "the World Conference accept[ed] the World Anti-Doping Code [...] as the basis for the fight against doping in sport throughout the world."[152] The governments present at the Conference declared among other things that they would "support a timely process leading to a convention or other obligation concerning, among other things, the Code, to be implemented through instruments appropriate to the constitutional and administrative contexts of each government on or before the XX Olympic Winter Games in Turin in 2006."[153] The governments agreed to a joint meeting in Copenhagen in order to discuss intergovernmental aspects and to arrive at a Government Declaration which was to supplement the Conference Resolution.

"There should be no place at the Olympic Games for IFs or NOCs that refused to implement the Code. Likewise, no organisation of the Olympic Games should be awarded to a country whose government had neglected or refused to implement the Code," IOC chairman Rogge warned all concerned in his opening address, and he further urged all IFs and NOCs "to apply the same philosophy."[154]

Core elements of the WADC are *inter alia*:

"1.   The broadened scope of the concept of doping. According to the new concept doping is not only understood to be the act of doping itself, but also attempted doping and the possession of or trafficking in doping products and methods.
2.   Strict liability as the starting point. The athlete is strictly liable for the presence of any prohibited substance in his or her body. Although the WADC includes some exceptions to this rule, every participant in the Olympic Games and world championships is tested for doping and, if found positive, automatically disqualified.
[...]."

Now, in the final version of the WADC, Article 1 defines doping as follows:

"Doping is defined as the occurrence of one or more of the anti-doping rule violations set forth in Article 2.1 through Article 2.8 of the Code."

The descriptions of the doping offence used in the codes preceding the WADC were similar in structure to the description of offences under criminal law. A certain act or situation was considered undesirable and a penalty was attached to it. The drafters of the WADC decided to abandon this approach. Doping is no longer considered a specified condemnable human act or the result of such an act, but rather a violation of the rules describing that act or result. The concept of doping has been com-

---

[152] World Conference on Doping in Sport Resolution, adopted by the World Conference on Doping in Sport, Copenhagen, Denmark, 5 March 2003, sub 1.
[153] World Conference on Doping in Sport Resolution, adopted by the World Conference on Doping in Sport, Copenhagen, Denmark, 5 March 2003, sub 2.
[154] World Conference on Doping in Sport, plenary sessions, Summary Notes, p. 1.

pletely detached, abstracted and instrumentalised. Doping is no longer viewed as an act knowingly performed by an athlete, but rather as an act performed by an athlete in a legal dimension: doping is the violation of an anti-doping rule. As such violations of the anti-doping rule also comprise situations which are not directly considered doping offences in the classical sense of the word.[155] It is understandable that the term doping has had to be defined in two stages, although this is not very elegant, nor very clear. The substantive norm, i.e. the norm that should be complied with and on the basis of which an act or a situation can be tested and punished, has been pushed to the background. Subsequent to the framework rule it is indicated when the anti-doping regulations can be said to have been violated. The substantive norm which was taken as the starting point in the WADC says that no underlying substantive norms may be violated. These rules essentially indicate what the drafters of the Code considered doping to be.

Relevant within the present framework are subsections 1 and 2 of Article 2 WADC.

"Article 2: Anti-doping Rule Violations[156]
The following constitute anti-doping rule violations:
2.1   The presence of a prohibited substance or its metabolites or markers in an athlete's bodily specimen.
2.1.1 It is each athlete's personal duty to ensure that no prohibited substance enters his or her body.[157] Athletes are responsible for any prohibited substance or its metabolites or markers found to be present in their bodily specimens. Accordingly, it is not necessary that intent, fault, negligence or knowing use on the athlete's part be demonstrated in order to establish an anti-doping rule violation under Article 2.1.
2.1.2 Excepting those substances for which a quantitative reporting threshold is specifically identified in the prohibited list, the detected presence of any quantity of a prohibited substance or its metabolites or markers in an athlete's sample shall constitute an anti-doping rule violation.
2.1.3 As an exception to the general rule of Article 2.1, the prohibited list may establish special criteria for the evaluation of prohibited substances that can also be produced endogenously.
2.2   Use or attempted use of a prohibited substance or a prohibited method.
2.2.1 The success or failure of the use of a prohibited substance or prohibited method is not material. It is sufficient that the prohibited substance or prohibited meth-

---

[155] The possession of doping substances by persons in the athlete's entourage is very far removed from an actual act of doping by the athlete.

[156] The comment to Art. 1.2 – Anti-doping rule violations, in the second draft of the WADC in part read as follows: "The purpose of this Article is to specify the circumstances and conduct which constitute violations of anti-doping rules. Hearings in doping cases will proceed based on the assertion that one or more of these specific rules have been violated. Most of the circumstances and conduct on this list of violations can be found in some form in the OMADC or other existing anti-doping rules." This comment was subsequently and rightly omitted from the final version of the WADC.

[157] It is somewhat incongruous that the description of the doping offence should contain a warning to athletes that it is their duty to ensure that no banned substances enter their body. It would have been more obvious to caution athletes of this fact prior to the anti-doping code.

od was used or attempted to be used for an anti-doping rule violation to be committed."

In defence of the strict liability system, the comments to Art. 2.1.1 WADC refer to a ground in the *Quigley* case where it was held that, on the one hand, it might be unfair in a given case to hold an athlete strictly liable when he/she was not to blame, but that on the other hand it would be equally unfair to the other athletes to allow banned substances if they were taken unintentionally. This quotation rightly caused Petri[158] to observe that:

> "diese Begründung [...] indes nicht den Kern der Sache [trifft]. Sie vermischt Disquali-fikation und echte Strafe (Zeitsperre), die sich in ihrem Schutzzweck unterscheiden. Die im WADC genannte Unfairness ist ein Verstoß gegen die Chancengleichheit im Wettbewerb. Sie ist gesichert, solange keine gedopten Sportler am Wettbewerb teilnehmen. Dieses Ziel kann durch Disqualifikationen erreicht werden – sie führen zur Annullierung aller Ergebnisse, die unfair erzielt wurden, un stellen so die Chan-cengleichheit wieder her. Die Disqualifikation erhebt dabei keinen Schuldvorwurf, sondern ist als Maßnahme der Gefahrenabwehr zu betrachten und deshalb ohne Schuldnachweis zulässig. Das unterscheidet sie von der Sperre als einer Strafe, deren Auswirkung über den Schutz des Wettbewerbs hinaus geht und eine persönliche Schuld zwingend voraussetzt. Deshalb is die Strict Liability für Disqualifikationen zulässig, für Sperren aber nicht."

In sum, in the above I have given a description of the evolution of the description of the doping offence. The first descriptions to be used penalised the use of unspeci-fied substances intended to enhance athletic performance. These descriptions proved vulnerable on two points. The sports organisation prosecuting the offence first had to show that the substance used was actually capable of enhancing performance and secondly, if they had been successful in proving this, that the substance had entered the athlete's body through an act of intent or negligence. The next generation of descriptions added a link to lists of prohibited substances. From then on, doping was considered the use of specified substances. This type of description released sports organisations from the duty to demonstrate that any substance found had indeed enhanced the athlete's performance. Legally speaking, the doping offence was no longer directed at the illegal enhancement of athletic performance, but at the use of certain substances. However, this did not alter the fact that the prosecuting sports organisation still had to show guilt or intent on the part of the athlete. This meant that this type of description also failed to satisfy in the long run. The sports organisation were seeking ways to eliminate their evidentiary problems. The solu-tion was found in the reversal of the burden of proving intent or guilt, elements which were implied by the existing descriptions. Accordingly, the next generation of descriptions resulted in *prima facie* guilt of the athlete after the discovery of a banned substance in his/her sample. Athletes could no longer easily ward off accu-

---

[158] Grischka Petri, "Die Sanktionsregeln des Worl Anti-Doping-Codes," (2003) *SpuRt* 6, p. 232.

sations of doping simply by pointing out that they were not to blame. This comfortable position was now reserved for the sports organisations. They only needed to prove that banned substances were present in the athlete's sample. Finally, the WADC gave us the final step in the evolution of the description of the doping offence. The strict liability approach was maintained, although the focus is no longer on the prohibited human act, but on the fact that the athlete violated the rules containing the description of the doping offence. Instead of doping violations, the WADC establishes anti-doping rule violations.

Many national and international federations also explicitly considered various offences as doping that were not actually acts of doping in themselves, but were related to the act of doping. Among these were: failing to report to doping control, refusing to submit to doping control, and admitting to having used a prohibited substance or method.

2.2. The description of the ancillary doping infractions

2.2.1. The failure to report to doping control and the refusal to submit to doping control

The mechanisms contained in the anti-doping regulations could not function unless the refusal to undergo a doping test was threatened with some form of penalty.[159] Various IFs made the failure to report to a doping test – when invited to take one – or the refusal to submit to such a test into constituent elements of the doping offence. In these cases the act or omission was considered a doping offence of its own accord by many international[160] and national[161] federations, and even by some national legislators.[162]

---

[159] The Dutch cyclist Michael Boogaard failed to report to the doping control at the regulated time after the team time-trial, which took place in the framework of Olympia's Tour of the Netherlands. The KNWU suspended Boogaard in conformity with the penalty set for failing to report to doping controls. In interim injunction proceedings, Boogaard requested that the suspension be lifted. Every argument Boogaard adduced in order to justify his non-appearance failed. Boogaard could have known that he had to report for doping control. The district court of Amsterdam in its decision on the application of interim injunctions of 21 June 1991 (KG 91, 230) held that, given the fact that bringing the case before the arbitration commission had to be considered of no avail, the arrangements requested of it should be denied. The Court of Appeal of Amsterdam upheld this judgment on appeal (19 December 1991, *Gids Lichamelijke Opvoeding Sport en Spel*, no. 79).

[160] IAAF: Rules and Regulations, Rule 55, subsection 1: "An athlete who fails or refuses to submit to doping control after having been requested to do so by the responsible official will have committed a doping offence and will be subject to sanctions in accordance with Rule 60"; ICF: Doping Rules, Rule 2, subsection 1: "An athlete participating in an ICF competition who has failed to report to doping control or who has rejected doping control after having been requested to do so by the responsible official will be judged to have committed a doping offence and will be subject to sanctions in accordance with Rule 6."; FIS: Doping Rules – Rule 2 – Ancillary Offences: "A FIS competitor who fails to attend for doping control or who refuses doping control after having being requested to do so by an appointed official will have committed a doping offence and will be subject to sanction in accordance to Rule 6. This fact shall be reported to the FIS by his national member association."

[161] Fédération Royale Belge de Patinage Artistique: Chapitre I – Reglement Sportif Général, Art. 093 – Antidopage, 093.1.: "Le résultat d'un contrôle de dopage d'un membre de la FRBN ou d'un concurrent participant à une compétition sportive organisée sous l'égide la FRBN est considéré comme positif: si l'athlète ou le concurrent refuse de soumettre à un contrôle antidopage regulierement requis par la FRBN, par un organisme reconnu par la FINA, le COIB, le CIO ou par les authorites judiciaires de territoir ou il se trouve [...]"; Deutscher Schwimm-Verband: DSV- Antidopingbestimmungen, para. 3 Dopingverstöße, (1) d) "Als Dopingverstöße gelten: Unterlassen einer Dopingkontrolle oder deren Verweigerung durch einen Schwimmer [...]"; Real Federación Española de Atletismo: D) Reglamento de los Controles de Dopaje de la Real Federación Española de Atletismo: Capitolo I – Disposiciones Generale, Articulo 4, sub 4): "Cualquier acción u omisión tendente a impedir o perturbar la correcta realización de los procedimientos de represión del dopaje"; *Idem:* Real Federación Española de Fútbol: Estatutos. Título VIII Del Régimen Disciplinario y Competicional, Capítulo 3 – De las infracciones y sus sanciones, Sección 4a – De las infracciones especificas en relación con el dopaje. Tipificación de las infracciones, Articulo 143, sub d); Fédération Française de Handball: Lutte contre le dopage, Titre 1, Chapitre 1 – dispositions générales, Art. 2: "Tout participant aux compétitions et manifestations sportives et aux entraînements y préparant, est tenu de se soumettre aux prélèvements et aux examens destinés á déceler la présence de substances [...]"; *Idem:* Fédération Française de Boxe: Règlement Féderal, Lutte contre le Dopage, Titre I – Dispositions Générales, Art. 1; UK Athletics: UK Current Doping Rules and Procedures, Rule 24 Doping, (5) (d) "The offence of doping takes place when: an athlete fails or refuses to submit to doping control and produce a sample after having been requested to do so by an authorised official [...]"; *Idem:* British Bobsleigh Association, Rules for Doping Control, 2. Doping Offences, 2.2 sub (vii), The Lawn Tennis Association, LTA Rules, Appendix 4 – Tennis Anti-Doping Programme, A. General Statement of Policy, 2., sub (iii); Amateur Swimming Federation of Great Britain, ASFGB Doping Control Rules and Protocols, 3. Doping Offences, 3.1, sub 3.1.3; Badminton Association of England, Doping Control Rules for the Badminton Association of England, Appendix A – Doping Offences, 2, sub (vii); English Table Tennis Association: Rules, 32.14 Doping, sub 32.14.4; Football Association, Drug Testing Programme, Memorandum and Procedural Guidelines for the Conduct of Drug Testing, Season 2000/2001, Memorandum, Drug Testing, 1, sub (iii); British Canoe Union: BCU Sports Management Committee, Doping Control Rules, 2. Submission to tests, 2.3 "Any refusal or failure to submit to a doping control test when required to do so shall be treated as *prima facie* evidence of a contravention of rule 1.1 and shall be reported to the BCU Drugs Advisori Committee, who shall institute disciplinary procedures as if the test had been carried out and a positive result found."; The Scottish Football Association: Doping Charter, 4. The SFA Doping Regulations, sub 5: "Any player who refuses to provide a Sample or refuses to permit that Sample to be submitted to the Test, or where appropriate, whose parent or guardian refuses to consent to a request being made to that player to provide a Sample or whose parent or guardian refuses to permit that Sample to be submitted to the Test, shall be deemed to have failed the Test and the Reserve Test and shall be in breach of Regulation 1."; The Football Association of Wales: Memorandum on the use of drugs: "Any player must, if requested bv an official designated by the Governing body for the purpose of doping control, submit to a doping control test. Failure to do so will be taken as if a positive test result had been obtained, and dealt with accordingly."; Irish Canoe Union, Irish Canoe Union Doping Control Regulations, 6.00 Offences, 6.02 sub (a): "An Ancillary Doping Offence may have been committed when: an athlete participati:ong in a competition organised under the auspices of the International Canoe Federation or the Irish Canoe Union fails to report to, and/or fails to cooperate with doping control after being requested to do so by an appropriate official [...]"; Volleyball Association of Ireland: Doping Control Policy of the Volleyball Association of Ireland, 1.2 The Doping Offence. 1.2.2, sub h.:
"Under these Rules doping is illegal and an offence is committed when: a person wilfully obstructs or interferes with the carrying out of anything in these Rules, including failure to co-operate with investigations carried out by the Volleyball Association of Ireland in accordance with Clause 1.2.3. hereof."; Fédération Luxembourgeoise de Football: Kapitel IX: Doping, para. 12, sub III.: Behinderung der zuständigen Instanz und/oder Weigerung des (der) Verantwortlichen zur Mithilfe bei der Durchführung der Doping- Kontrollen; Koninklijke Nederlandse Atletiek Unie: KNAU Dopingreglement, Artikel 2 – Verbod en verplichting, sub 2.: "Athletes are obliged to co-operate fully, timely and correctly with doping controls."; Nederlandse Basketball Bond: Dopingreglement, Verboden en verplichtingen, Artikel 2, sub 2: "Athletes and associations are obliged to co-operate fully, timely and correctly with doping

In addition to this active approach there was also an abstract approach by which the description of the doping offence also included refusal to comply with a request by an authorised drug-testing authority to provide a urine sample.[163] This indirect approach also existed before the acceptance of the WADC when the refusal to submit to doping control was considered to equal a positive doping test result.[164] Two

---

controls. They must follow the instructions of the doping control official."; *Idem:* Koninklijke Nederlands Algemene Schermbond: Dopingreglement, Titel I – Verboden en verplichtingen, Artikel 2, sub 2; Koninklijke Nederlandse Schutters Associatie KNSA: Dopingreglement, Titel I – Verboden en verplichtingen, Artikel 2, sub 2.; Koninklijke Nederlandse Baseball en Softball Bond: Reglement van wedstrijden, Doping, 2. Verboden en verplichtingen, sub 2.; Nederlands Handbal Verbond: Huishoudelijk reglement NHV, para. 6.3 Doping, Artikel 6.3.1.2 Verboden en verplichtingen, sub 2.; Nederlandse Ski Vereniging: Dopingreglement, Begripsbepalingen, Verboden en verplichtingen, Artikel 2, sub 2.; Koninklijke Nederlandse Voetbalbond: Dopingreglement KNVB, Verboden en verplichtingen, Artikel 1, sub 2: "KNVB members are obliged to co-operate with doping controls. They must follow the instructions of the observer and the doping control doctor. Violation of this provision may give rise to the imposition of disciplinary sanctions."; *Idem:* Koninklijke Nederlandse Hockey Bond: Dopingreglement, Titel I – Verboden en verplichtingen, Artikel 2, sub 2.; Koninklijke Nederlandse Lawn Tennis Bond: Dopingcontrolereglement, Hoofdstuk 1 – Begripsbepalingen, Artikel 2 – Verboden en verplichtingen, sub 2.; Nederlandse Handboog Bond: Dopingreglement, Titel I – Verboden en verplichtingen, Artikel 2, sub 2.; Nederlandse IJshockey Bond: Dopingreglement, Titel I – Verboden en verplichtingen, Artikel 2, sub 2.; Koninklijke Nederlandse Zwembond: KNZB-Reglement Dopingcontrole, Artikel P2 Doping, 2.1, sub d.: "Doping is defined as follows: failing to report to or refusing to co-operate with doping controls in a competitive sport."; Federação Portuguesa de Basquetebol: Regulamento Antidopagem da Federação Portuguesa de Basquetebol, Capítulo I – Âmbito de aplicação, Artigo lo, sub 3 b): "É igualmente considerado dopado o atleta: Que, por qualquer forma, recuse, impeça ou defraude a realização do respectivo controlo antidopagem."

[162] Decreet inzake Medisch Verantwoorde Sportbeoefening: Titel IV – Voorwaarden inzake de medisch verantwoorde sportbeoefening, Hoofdstuk III – Regelen ter bestrijding van dopingpraktijken, Art. 21, para. 2, sub 3o: "To the doping practices referred to in para. 1 are equated: refusing, manipulating or obstructing doping controls [...]"; Real Decreto 255/1996, de 16 de febrero, por el que se establece el régimen de infracciones y sanciones para la represión del dopaje: Titulo 1 – Régimen Disciplinario del Dopaje, Articulo 1 – Tipificación de las infracciones, sub 1.: "Se consideran como infracciones muy graves a la discipline deportiva las siguientes: Cualquier acción u omisión tendente a impedir o perturbar la correcta realización de los procedimientos de represión del dopaje."

[163] IWF: Anti-doping Policy – 5. Doping Offence, 5.1: "- For the purpose of this Policy a Doping Offence is: [...] refusal to comply with a request to provide a sample for testing when requested by a properly authorised drug testing authority." FINA: Guidelines for Doping Control: "The offence of doping occurs when: [...] the failure or refusal of the athlete to submit to doping control." DC 4 Ancillary offenses, DC 4.1 "A competitor who fails or refuses to submit to doping control after having been requested to do so by the authorised official will have committed a doping offence and will be subject to sanctions in accordance with DC 9. This fact shall be reported to FINA and the competitor's Member federation"; ITF: 8. Tennis Anti-doping Programme – (c) Doping Offences: 2. "Under this Programme the following shall be regarded as doping offences: [...] A player refuses to comply with any provision of this Programme"; ITU: Doping Control Rules and Procedural Guidelines, 2. Definition of Doping: 2.2 "For the purpose of these Rules, the following are regarded as doping offenses: [...] refusal or failure to submit to doping control."; ATP: Official Rulebook – Players – Tennis Anti-doping Program – C. Doping Offenses, 1. "Under this Program the following shall be regarded as doping offenses: [...] a player fails or refuses to submit to a doping test after having been notified or fails or refuses to comply with any provision of this Program."

[164] IHF: Anti-doping Regulations – 6. Refusal to undergo a doping control: AShould a player refuse to supply a urine sample, he or she will be acquainted with the possible consequences. Refusal to undergo a doping check is tantamount to a positive test result. Should the player still refuse, this fact

IFs threatened athletes refusing to cooperate with doping tests with sanctions. The International Wrestling Federation (FILA)[165] excluded such athletes from further participation in the match, while the International Ice Hockey Federation (IIHF) [166] threatened such athletes with the same sanctions that applied in case of positive test results.

In addition to the provisions expressly declaring that refusing to undergo testing is a doping offence, sports organisations could also rely on the more general elastic provisions in their general disciplinary rules in cases of non-cooperation with doping controls. The disciplinary rules of sports organisations usually contain a provision to the effect that any act which is prejudicial to the interests of the organisation or of the sport which the organisation represents are punishable.[167] Elastic provisions, according to Wassing,[168] "may include any act which is relevant from a disciplinary law perspective."

However, pursuant to Art. 2.3 WADC, refusing, or failing without compelling justification, to submit to sample collection after notification as authorised in applicable anti-doping rules or otherwise evading sample collection is considered a violation of the anti-doping rule.

2.2.2. *No change of address*

At the beginning of the sixties anabolic steroids first appeared on the market. The introduction of these substances and the fact that they were relatively easy to obtain

---

is noted on the form, which is to be signed by the IHF doping official." Anti-doping Regulations – 7. Failure to appear for a doping control: "Should a player fail to appear for a doping control at the previously determined time, the form should state that fact. Failure to appear is tantamount to a positive test result"; IJF: Regulations Concerning Dope Tests, 2: "Any refusal to undergo a check or any attempt to avoid one shall be considered as tantamount to doping."; FILA: Disciplinary Regulations, Art. 13: "In accordance with Article 10 of the Constitution, any wrestier who refuses to submit to the doping test shall be considered as having tested positive and will be banned from the entire competition, as well as being banned from participating in international events for a period of two years"; FITA: Appendix 4 Doping Control Procedures, 1 Doping – Preamble And Principles 1.5 "Any athlete must submit to the doping control if he/she has been selected." Appendix 4 Doping Control Procedures, 1 Doping – Preamble And Principles 1.6 "Any athlete refusing to submit to the doping control will be considered as if the result of this control has been positive."

[165] WCF: Rules of Play – 16. Doping: "(4) A competitor refusing to submit to testing will be banned from further participation in the competition."

[166] IIHF: By Laws – 600 Competition By Laws, 608. Medical Control (Doping): "In the event of a [...] refusal to undergo a test [...] the sanctions specified in the IIHF Bylaws will apply."

[167] See e.g. UCI Part. XII Discipline and Procedures, 12.1.005: "Anyone subject to UCI Regulations shall be suspended for a minimum of one and a maximum of six months, who: [...] 2. behaves in such a way as to blemish the image, the reputation or the interests of cycling or the UCI, or 3. without valid reason, fails to respond when convened or summoned by a UCI authority or disciplinary body," and Rules of the International Badminton Federation, 17.1: "Council, or any Disciplinary Committee it appoints, shall have power on behalf of the Federation to penalise a Member Association, player, competition official, or other person for infringement of the IOC regulations (see Competition Regulation 23), for misconduct during competition, or for actions that bring the game of badminton into disrepute."

[168] A. Wassing, *Het tuchtrecht van het publiekvoetbal*, PhD. 1978 (Rotterdam, Erasmus Universiteit 1978) (Wassing 1978) p. 16.

completely and suddenly changed the entire nature of the doping problem. The use of anabolic steroids, among which the male growth hormone testosterone, enabled athletes to increase muscle volume without having to undergo rigid training.[169] These substances were mainly administered in the out-of-competition season and during periods of training. Initially, showing the use of anabolic steroids from the analysis of the urine samples of the athletes tested was a huge problem. After some time, however, an effective method of analysis was developed. This method was applied for the first time in the analysis of the samples taken during the European athletics championships in Rome in 1974. A new problem revealed itself. As the steroids were used during periods of training and any traces of them in the athletes" bodies during competitions (i.e. a month later) would have virtually disappeared, the analyses often failed to render positive results.[170] As far as anabolic steroids were concerned, doping control at competitions was simply an inadequate tool. An effective anti-doping programme "to deter athletes from using these substance[171] would therefore need to target these controls.[172, 173] At the end of the 1980s, rules

---

[169] "Testosterone and Growth Hormones are used by athletes in many sports. It is thought that one of the advantages of anabolic steroids is that they permit the athlete to train more rigorously and to recover more rapidly than would be possible without. The side effect of increased aggression could be dangerous to opponents in a field sport," according to ISAF Doping Control in Yacht Racing. Why We Test – What We Test for – How We Test, Cheating.

[170] "It is thought that some sailors in the Olympic Classes may have taken Anabolic Steroids to increase their muscle bulk, strength and weight. Clearly sailors in the Finn Dinghy, Star and Tempest Crews, and Soling middle men would find such gains attractive. Winch men in America's Cup, Admiral's Cup and Maxi Racing would derive similar benefit. Detection of such medication is not certain if the steroid is stopped long enough before the test, which is why out of competition testing is undertaken," says ISAF Doping Control in Yacht Racing. Why We Test – What We Test for – How We Test, Cheating.

[171] "Out of Competition doping control is used as a deterrent for the use of anabolic agents and peptide hormones. Application for exemption of drug use during training is, therefore, needed only for these substances," according to ITU Doping Control Rules and Procedural Guidelines, 6. Procedures for Application for Exemption to Use Prohibited Substances, General [...] 6.3. The IAAF rules contain a corresponding provision. Procedural Guidelines for Doping Control, 5. Procedures for Application for Exemption to Use Prohibited Substances, General, 5.3: AOut-Of-Competition doping control is used as a deterrent for the use of anabolic agents and certain listed hormones, including the substances under prohibited techniques. Application for exemption of drug use during training is, therefore, needed only for these substances."

[172] In Art. 116 of Chapter XI Out-of-competition Tests (Part XIV – Antidoping Examination Regulations of the UCI) a definition of out-of-competition tests is given: "By out-of-competition tests is meant all drug tests conducted other than those conducted after an event as provided for in Chapter II above. Out-of-competition tests may, for example, be conducted: [...] – during stage events or World Championships on rest days or before the start of a stage, after an event where the test was not mandatory pursuant to Article 8, during training, especially outside the season for the discipline." The IWF Anti-Doping Policy, 6. Definitions stipulate that "'out-of-competition testing' means any time other than during an event." Cf., IPC: Doping, 8.1 Doping Operating Procedure, 7.0 Procedures for Unannounced Doping Controls, 7.1 Definition, 7.1.1: "Unannounced Doping Control is defined as unscheduled tests which are administered at any time on a 'short' or 'no-notice' basis." UIPM: Anti-doping Controls, 10. Out of Competition Controls, 10.2: "With out of competition controls we mean the antidoping controls in addition to those carried out at the end of competitions."

[173] It is relatively easy to organise doping controls within a competition context; the athletes, the doping control officials and the place where the controls are carried out are all situated closely together.

were included in the doping regulations of a number of international federations making (unannounced)[174] "out-of-competition" doping controls possible.[175] These federations subsequently applied some degree of pressure on their members – the national sports federations – to lay down similar rules in their doping regulations and to establish and carry out national out-of-competition doping control programmes.[176] In order to be able to adequately carry out such programmes, the

---

Organising controls out of competition is a completely different matter. You must know where a particular athlete is and ideally the doping control official should be able to appear at his/her door unannounced, because any prior warning would render the controls meaningless. Finally, controls under these conditions are often quite difficult to carry out.

[174] "The nature of out-of-competition testing makes it desirable that little or no prior warning is given to the player being tested," says ITF: 8. Tennis Anti-doping Programme, (H) Out-Of-Competition Testing, 6; FITA: Appendix 4, Doping Control Procedures, 13 Out-of-competition Doping Controls, 13.1: "Out-of-competition doping controls are administered without warning to the competitor during the training period."; FINA: Doping Control, DC 6 – Unannounced Testing, DC 6.2: "[...] It is also understood that it is preferred that unannounced testing be unannounced to the competitor or his or her federation," and Guidelines for Doping Control, Unannounced out of competition Doping Control, 7. Unannounced Doping Control, 7.8: "The nature of unannounced, out-of-competition, doping control makes it desirable that little or no prior warning is given to the competitor."; IAAF: Procedural Guidelines for Doping Control, 3. Out-of- competition Testing, International Doping Control Officers (IDCOs), Waiver, 3.25: "The nature of Out-Of-Competition doping control makes it inevitable that little or no prior warning is given to the athlete."; ICF: Procedural Guidelines for Doping Controls, 2. Out-of-competition Doping Controls, 9. Waiver: "The nature of out-of-competition doping control makes it inevitable that little or no prior warning is given to the athlete."; UCI: Part XIV – Antidoping Examination Regulations, UCI Cycling Regulations, Chapter XI Out-of-competition Tests, Art. 118: "UCI representatives, the Doctor and the Inspector may appear without prior warning wheresoever they expect to be able to find the rider."; IBU: Anti-doping, Blood Test and Gender Verification Rules, II. Out-of-competition Doping Controls, 9. Waiver: "The nature of out-of-competition doping control makes it inevitable that little or no prior warning is given to the athlete."; ITU: Doping Control Rules and Procedural Guidelines, 4. ITU Out of Competition Testing, International Sampling Officers (ISOs), Waiver, 4.17: "The nature of Out of Competition doping control makes it inevitable that little or no prior warning is given to the athlete."; FIS: Procedural Guidelines for Doping and Hemoglobin Control, B. Out-of-competition Doping Control, 9. Waiver: "The nature of out-of-competition doping control makes it inevitable that little or no prior warning is given to the athlete."

[175] In this context we may point to a rather odd provision (declaration of support) in the Technical Regulations, Chapter XI – Doping Control, regn. 11.1 – General Principles of the FIG. "Doping is prohibited. In this regard, the FIG recognises and gives full support to the requirements of the International Olympic Committee that provision should not only be made for checks at international and national competitions but, also, that spot checks should be carried out during training sessions."

[176] At the moment the regulations of a considerable number of these federations include rules obliging the national sport federations to lay down such rules in their doping regulations.
IAAF: Rules and Regulations, Division III, Control of Drug Abuse, Rule 57 – Out-of-Competition Testing, "1. It is a condition of membership of the IAAF that a Member includes within its constitution: 1. a provision obliging that Member to conduct out-of-competition doping control, a report of which must be submitted to the IAAF annually; and 2. a provision allowing the IAAF to conduct doping control at that Member's National Championships or any similar meeting; and 3. a provision allowing the IAAF to conduct out-of-competition testing on that Member's athletes."
FISA: 4. Obligations of the Federations: 4.1 "Before the 31st January each year, each national federation shall provide to the Executive Director a report on the anti-doping tests which it has conducted during the preceding year, indicating: [...] the distribution of these tests ([...] tests out-of-competition)."
ICF: Procedural Guidelines for Doping Controls, 2. Out-of-competition Doping Controls, 1. General,

federations needed to know at what location, wherever in the world, an athlete underwent his training regime. Some doping regulations even stipulated that an athlete who did not reveal his whereabouts was guilty of doping by this fact alone. Apart from the fact that the national federations had to apply out-of-competition controls to the athletes registered with them, the international federations reserved the right to conduct such tests throughout the world with the co-operation of their members. The national federations were obliged to supply the addresses of the athletes registered with them to the international federations. Parallel to the efforts which the international federations displayed at the end of the 1980s with respect to worldwide, unannounced out-of-competition controls ran the activities in this area of the Council of Europe.[177] Article 4(3)(c) and (d) of the 1989 Anti-Doping Convention, concerning measures to curb the availability of prohibited doping substances and methods, read:

> "Furthermore, the Parties shall:
> 1. encourage and, where appropriate, facilitate the carrying out by their sports organisations of doping controls required by the competent international sports organisations [...] outside competitions; and
> 2. encourage and facilitate the negotiation by sports organisations of agreements permitting their members to be tested by duly authorised doping control teams in other countries."

In December 1991 the IOC Medical Commission established a working group with out-of-competition doping control as its field of study. One of the first findings of this working group was that, although some international federations (the IAAF, the International Rowing Federation (FISA) and the IWF) had proceeded to carry out this type of controls, these isolated attempts were inadequate. "Effective coordination and harmonization between the various authorities responsible for these

---

1.4. "Any National Member Federation which does not co-operate with the conduction of out-of-competition doping controls, or which in any way prevents the test from achieving his purpose, will be subject to sanctions."

IWF: IWF Anti-doping Policy, 2. Object of the Policy, 2.1 "The object of this Policy is to: [...] b. assist in ensuring that National Federations implement their own effective competition and out of competition drug testing programmes."

FINA: Constitution, C 6 Rights and Duties of Members, [...] C 6.2 "All Members are obliged [...] C 6.2.4 to include within its constitution a provision which allows out-of-competition doping control by FINA."

WTF: Regulations for Doping Control, 12. Out-of-Competition and Short Notice Testing, 12.1 "All Member National Federations are encouraged to conduct out-of-competition (doping control) testings."

FIS: FIS Doping Rules, Rule 4 – Out of Competition Testing, "1. It is a condition of membership of the FIS that a National Member Association includes within its constitution: 1.1 a provision obliging that National Member Association to conduct out-of-competition, no-notice doping control, a report of which must be submitted to the FIS annually; and; 1.2 a provision allowing the FIS to conduct out-of-competition, no- notice testing on that member's athletes."

[177] Out-of- competition testing was on the agenda of the European Sports Conference held in Börlange (Sweden) on 30 October 1988. This was also the case at the second "Permanent World Conference on Anti-doping in Sport" of 1989.

activities are indispensable; this should be undertaken by an ad hoc committee under the moral authority and guidance of the IOC." In order to achieve some level of harmonisation in the then current rules that the various international federations had established with respect to out-of-competition testing, this issue was included on the agenda for the meeting in Lausanne on 13 January 1994. The representatives of the IOC, the ASOIF, the AIOWF, the Association of National Olympic Committees (ANOC), and the athletes adopted principles which had to lead to the unification of "their anti-doping rules and procedures for controls they performed out of competition (unannounced tests)."[178, 179] In June 1999 the executive organ of the IOC during a meeting in Seoul decided that doping controls would be carried out during training at the Olympic Games in 2000. After this, it became common practice for the sports organisations to include rules in their anti-doping regulations which made out-of-competition testing possible. Often national federations are obliged under pain of some kind of penalty to cooperate in out-of-competition controls undertaken on the initiative of their international federations and various doping regulations of international federations oblige individual athletes to cooperate in such tests.[180]

Out-of-competition doping control means that athletes have to be visited, usually at an address supplied by the athletes themselves. The international federations must have these addresses at their disposal in order to be able to effectively carry out controls. The national federations have the task of informing the international federations of the whereabouts of the athletes.[181] In case an athlete selected for an

---

[178] See: International Badminton Federation (IBF): Competition Regulations, Appendix 3, Preventing and Fighting Against Doping in Sport.

[179] In the so-called Lausanne Declaration "Preventing and fighting against doping in sport" it was agreed that the first stage in the fight against doping would be for the "voluntary" bodies to reach an agreement to enable them to negotiate with the governmental bodies, with a view to eliminating the existing contradictions between national legislation and the rules of the sports movement."

[180] E.g. FISA: Rules of Racing and Related By Laws, Part VII – Medical Provisions, Rule 82 – Penalties for Doping: "The Executive Committee may also impose [...] penalties against any person, club [...] who does not co-operate in the conduct of any anti-doping test, in particular of such a test conducted outside of competition. In the latter case, it may even impose penalties against the rowers and coxswains of the federation concerned."

[181] IWF: Anti-doping Policy, 9. Drug Testing, Out of Competition Testing, 9.11: "All National Federations are required to provide the IWF Secretariat with the list of their national team members (men, women and junior) when requested. The IWF Out of Competition testing programmes will be based on these lists. The IWF Secretariat must be advised, within reasonable time, of any changes to the composition of these team lists."
Anti-doping Policy, 9. Drug Testing, Out of Competition Testing, 9.12: "The IWF must be kept informed about national training camps and periods of time when these lifters are not in their own country."
FINA: Doping Control, DC 6 Unannounced Testing, DC 6.6: "Member Federations shall have the obligation to submit the names, addresses and telephone numbers of competitors as requested by FINA, to enable FINA to conduct unannounced testing."
Guidelines for Doping Control, Unannounced Out of Competition Doping Control, 7. Unannounced Doping Control, 7.10: "Member Federations shall have the obligation to submit the names, addresses and telephone numbers of competitors as requested by FINA, to enable FINA to conduct unannounced testing (Appendix 2d)."

out-of-competition test cannot be located, the international federation concerned will give the designated authorities of the national federations one final opportunity to find the athlete.[182] If the national federation is unable to find him/her, the international federations will consider this a refusal to submit to doping tests or a positive doping test result.[183] In case an athlete is found at the address supplied, but refuses

---

FIS: Procedural Guidelines for Doping and Hemoglobin Control, B. Out-of-competition Doping Control, 2. Procedure for registration of competitors that may be selected for out-of-competition doping controls, 2.2: "When required to do so, the NMA must be able to provide the following information on all targeted athletes: 1. Date of birth, 2. Passport (or equivalent document) number, 3. Full address and telephone number (home or training site) where, the competitor can be contacted during the period of preparation. 4. Number of years competing for NMA and events attended."
FIBT: Doping Control Regulations, 5. Selection of Athletes for Doping Control, 5.2. Doping control effected outside competitions, 5.2.2.: "Once the draw has been made, the FIBT will inform, by telegraph, the national federations to which the drawn athletes belong. Within 48 hours of receiving this information, the national federations to which the drawn athletes belong shall inform the FIBT, by telegraph, of the addresses at which the athletes can be contacted over the following 72 hours. This information must be provided also for those athletes who might be a long way from their usual place of abode."

[182] E.g. ICF: Procedural Guidelines for Doping Controls, 2. Out-of-competition Doping Controls, 2. Procedure for registration of competitors that can be selected for out-of-competition doping controls, 2.3. "Each National Member Federation shall upon simple request provide the ICF or its mandatory with all the necessary information to contact the athlete. It should be emphasised that in all cases of holiday, training camp or foreign travel the National Member Federation must be able to contact an athlete within 24 hours." UCI: Cycling Regulations, Part XIV – Antidoping Examination Regulations, Chapter XI Out-of-competition Tests, Art. 125. "During stage events and World Championships, the team leader or the team manager shall always be able to indicate the place where riders are to be found so that they may be contacted as rapidly as possible. Team leaders and/or team managers who provide incorrect information, who refuse to provide information at all or who hinder the proper conduct of the drug test in any way shall be liable to the disciplinary measures in Article 93."

[183] IAAF: Procedural Guidelines for Doping Control, 3. Out-of-competition Testing, Contacting the Athlete, 3.8: "The IDCO will wait up to 2 hours beyond the time agreed but thereafter the athlete will be declared absent from testing. An appeal on the grounds that the athlete did not fully understand where to go, or went at the wrong time, will not normally be considered. An athlete who is absent from testing will be deemed to have refused to submit to doping control contrary to Rule 56 and may be subject to sanctions under IAAF Rule 60."
FINA: Doping Control, DC 6 Unannounced Testing, DC 6.7: "If FINA attempts to conduct unannounced testing but is twice unable to locate a competitor at the address or location provided to FINA for such purposes, FINA shall send notice regarding the situation to both the competitor and his or her federation, requesting more detailed information as to the competitor's schedule. If the competitor cannot be located thereafter for a doping control test during a period up to eighteen (18) months from the first date the competitor was unable to be located, the competitor may be considered to have refused to submit to doping control."
Guidelines for Doping Control, Unannounced Out of Competition Doping Control, 7. Unannounced Doping Control, 7.11: "If FINA attempts to conduct unannounced testing but is twice unable to locate a competitor at the address or location provided to FINA for such purposes, FINA shall send notice regarding the situation to both the competitor and his federation, requesting more detailed information as to the competitor's schedule. If the competitor cannot be located thereafter for a doping control test, the competitor may be considered to have refused to submit to doping control."
FIBT: Doping Control Regulations, 5. Selection of Athletes for Doping Control, 5.2. Doping control effected outside competitions, 5.2.3.: "If, for a chosen athlete, the national federation to which this athlete belongs is unable to provide a contact address, the athlete shall provided the FIBT within 30 days, with documentation justifying his absence from his usual place of abode (e.g. airline ticket, hotel

to undergo the test, the doping official must point out to him/her the consequences (sanctions) of his/her refusal.[184] In some cases it was stated rather more specifi-

---

bills, passport bearing exit and entry stamps, etc.). Otherwise, the athlete will be considered as 'positive' and will be subject to the sanctions applied to 'positive' cases."
Doping Control Regulations, 5. Selection of Athletes for Doping Control, 5.2. Doping control effected outside competitions, 5.2.5.: "If the athlete cannot be contacted at the address indicated by the federation to which he belongs, he will be considered 'positive' and subject to the sanctions applied to 'positive' cases."
Doping Control Regulations, 5. Selection of Athletes for Doping Control, 5.2. Doping control effected outside competitions, 5.2.6.: "If the national federation of an athlete drawn for the doping control fails to communicate, within the established 48 hours, the address at which the athlete can be contacted, this athlete will be considered 'positive'."
[184] IAAF: Procedural Guidelines for Doping Control, 3. Out-of-competition Testing, Collecting the Sample, 3.20: "if the athlete refuses to provide a urine sample (or a second sample), the IDCO should explain to the athlete that by refusing to provide a sample, he shall be deemed to have refused to submit to doping control and may be subject to sanctions under IAAF Rule 60. If the athlete still refuses to provide a sample (or a second sample), the IDCO should note this on the Doping Control Form, sign his name and ask the athlete to sign the form. The IDCO should also note any other irregularities in the doping control process."
ICF: Procedural Guidelines for Doping Controls, 2. Out-of-competition Doping Controls, 6. Procedure for out-of-competition doping control, 6.4.: "If the athlete refuses to provide a urine or blood sample, the ISO should explain to the athlete that by refusing to provide a sample, he shall be deemed to have refused to submit to doping control and may be subject to sanctions under the ICF Rule 6.1.4. If the athlete still refuses to provide a sample, the ISO should note this on the Doping Control Form, sign his name to the form and ask the athlete to sign the form. The ISO should also note any other irregularities in the doping control process."
FINA: Guidelines for Doping Control, Unannounced Out of Competition Doping Control, 7. Unannounced Doping Control, 7.7: "If the athlete refuses to provide a urine sample, the, SO shall explain to the athlete that by refusing to provide a sample, he shall be deemed to have refused to submit to doping control and may be subject to sanctions under DC 9. If the athlete still refuses to provide a sample, the test person shall note this on the doping control form, sign his name to the form and ask the athlete to sign the form. The test person shall also note any other irregularities in the doping control process."
IBU: Anti-doping, Blood Test and Gender Verification Rules, II. Out-of- competition Doping Controls, 6. Procedure for Out-of- competition Doping Control, 6.4: "If the athlete refuses to provide a sample, the ISO must explain to the athlete that by refusing to provide a sample, he shall be deemed to have refused to submit to doping control and will be subject to sanctions under Chapter IV of these Rules. If the athlete still refuses to provide a sample, the ISO shall note this on the Doping Control Form, sing his name on the form and ask the athlete to sign the form. The ISO should also note any other irregularities in the doping control process."
ITU: Doping Control Rules and Procedural Guidelines, 4. ITU Out of Competition Testing, Collecting the Sample, 4.14: "If the athlete refuses to provide a urine sample (or second sample), the ISO should explain to the athlete that by refusing to provide a sample, he/she shall be deemed to have refused to submit to doping control and may be subject to sanctions under ITU rules. If the athlete still refuses to provide a sample (or second sample), the ISO should note this on the Doping Control Form, sign his/her name and ask the athlete to sign the form. The ISO should also note any other irregularities in the doping control process."
FIBT: Doping Control Regulations, 5. Selection of Athletes for Doping Control, 5.2. Doping control effected outside competitions, 5.2.7.: "If the athlete refuses to provide a urine sample, -the person entrusted to perform the doping control should explain to the athlete that by refusing to provide a sample, he shall be deemed to have refused to submit to doping control and may be subject to sanctions under the FIBT Rules. If the athlete still refuses to provide a sample, the person entrusted to perform the doping control should note this on the Doping Control Form, sign his name and ask the athlete to

cally that refusal was equated to a doping offence of the gravest category.[185]

In sum, an athlete's failure to pass on his training address at which he may undergo out-of-competition testing is comparable to failure to report to doping control during competition.

Art. 2.4 WADC provides that the "violation of applicable requirements regarding athlete availability for out-of-competition testing including failure to provide required whereabouts information and missed tests which are declared based on reasonable rules" constitutes a violation of the anti-doping rules. Unannounced out-of-competition testing is currently considered a core element of effective doping control. Without current information concerning the exact whereabouts of the athlete when he/she is not competing doping control would be ineffective and often prove impossible. According to the comments to this provision "this Article, which is not typically found in most existing anti-doping rules, requires athletes that have been identified for out-of-competition testing to be responsible for providing and updating information on their whereabouts so that they can be located for no advance notice out-of-competition testing." The "applicable requirements" referred to in the Article must be established by the athlete's international federation and the national anti-doping organisation in order to "allow some flexibility based upon varying circumstances encountered in different sports and countries." An important comment is that "a violation of this article may be based on either intentional or negligent conduct by the athlete."

To sum up, refusal to undergo doping control, failure to report to doping control, and being untraceable in case of an out-of-competition control are all considered doping offences for which there is no need to specifically demonstrate that banned

---

sign the form. The person entrusted to perform the doping control should also note any other irregularities in the doping control process."

FIS: Procedural Guidelines for Doping and Hemoglobin Control, B. Out-of-competition Doping Control, 6. Procedure for out-of-competition doping control, 6.4: "If the athlete refuses to provide an urine sample, the FASC should explain to the athlete that by refusing to provide a sample, he shall be deemed to have refused to submit to doping control and may be subject to sanctions under FIS Rule 6. If the athlete still refuses to provide a sample, the FASC should note this on the Doping Control Form, sign his name to the form and ask the athlete to sign the form. The FASC should also note any other irregularities in the doping control process."

[185] ITF: 8. Tennis Anti-doping Programme, (H) Out-Of-Competition Testing, 5.: "If a player fails or refuses to submit to testing or otherwise fails or refuses to comply with the provisions of this Programme, then the APA shall certify to the ITF Medical Executive Director that such player was absent from or has refused or failed to submit to the provisions of the Programme and that the player is in violation of the Programme. The ITF shall notify the player that he is in violation of the Programme and that he shall be subject to the penalties set out under the provisions of the Programme. A failure or refusal to submit to or comply with the provisions of the Programme shall be treated as a doping offence involving a Class I Prohibited Substance and the player shall, subject to his entitlement to appeal in accordance with Section (L), be subject to the penalties set out in Section (M)1(a) or (M)1(b) as appropriate."

FITA: Appendix 4, Doping Control Procedures, 13 Out-of-competition Doping Controls, 13.5: "Refusal to submit to an authorized out-of-competition doping control has the same disciplinary consequences as a positive test for anabolic steroids."

substances were found in the athlete's blood or urine. In the next section, we will see that proof is also unnecessary in case an athlete at any given time during his career announces that he has used prohibited substances in the past.

2.2.3.   *The admission to having used a prohibited substance or method*

It is possible that an athlete's use of doping substances or methods goes undetected, either because he was not invited to take a doping test or because the test failed to show any irregularities. Various anti-doping regulations provided for the event that an athlete later confessed to the use of doping. The sports organisations that laid down rules for this occurrence responded to this kind of honesty by equating the user with athletes who *were* caught during tests. Some regulations started from the point of view that the confession caused the offence to have been committed,[186] while others considered that the confessing athlete's actions constituted the doping offence.[187]

The doping regulations of the national federations only very rarely included the admission to having used doping in the acts constituting the doping offence. If at

---

[186] IAAF: Rules and Regulations, Rule 55, subsection 2 "The offence of doping takes place when [...] an athlete admits having used or taken advantage of a prohibited substance or a prohibited technique.";
ICF: Doping Rules, Rule 1, subsection 4: "The offence of doping takes place when [...] an athlete uses a banned method, or an athlete admits having used a prohibited drug or a banned method on the IOC list of doping classes and methods." ICF Doping Rules, Rule 1, subsection 5: "An admission may be either orally in a verifiable manner or in writing. For the purpose of these rules, a statement is not to be regarded as an admission where it was made more than six years after the facts to which it relates.";
FINA: Doping Control: DC 1.2 "The offence of doping occurs when: [...] a competitor admits having used or taken advantage of a banned substance or a banned technique." Doping Control: DC 1.3 "An admission may be made either orally in a verifiable manner or in writing. For the purpose of FINA Rules, a statement is not to be regarded as an admission where it was made more than twenty-one years after the fact to which it relates." Guidelines for Doping Control: "The offence of doping occurs when: [...] an athlete admits to having used or taken advantage of a banned substance or a banned technique.";
IBU: IBU Anti-doping, Blood Test and Gender Verification Rules, I. Doping controls, 1. Principle: "The offence of doping takes place when [...] an athlete admits having used a prohibited drug or a banned method on the IOC list of doping classes and methods.";
FIS: Doping Rules – Rule 1 – Doping: A3. The offence of doping takes place when [...] an athlete admits having used a prohibited drug or a banned method on the FIS list of doping classes and methods." FIS Doping Rules – Rule 1 – Doping: "4. An admission may be made either orally in a verifiable manner or in writing."

[187] ITF: 8. Tennis Anti-doping Programme – (c) Doping Offences: 2. "Under this Programme the following shall be regarded as doping offences: [...] In accordance with Section (K) of this Programme, a player admits having used a Prohibited Substance or Doping Method.";
ITU: Doping Control Rules and Procedural Guidelines, 2. Definition of Doping: 2.2 "For the purpose of these Rules, the following are regarded as doping offenses: [...] admitting to having used or taken advantage of a prohibited substance or a prohibited technique."; ATP: Official Rulebook – Players – Tennis" Anti-doping Program – C. Doping Offenses, 1. "Under this Program the following shall be regarded as doping offenses: [...] in accordance with section K of this Program, a player admits having used a Prohibited Substance or Doping Method."

all, regulations concerning the phenomenon were mostly found in the regulations of the British, Irish and Dutch sports organisations.

British Bobsleigh Association (BBA):[188]

> "Under these Rules doping is illegal and an offence is committed when: a person admits using a prohibited substance or a prohibited method [...]."

Amateur Swimming Federation of Great Britain (ASFGB):[189]

> "Doping is strictly forbidden and constitutes a breach of the FINA Doping Control Rules and these Rules. For the purposes of these Rules, the following shall be regarded as doping offences: if a person admits having assisted, encouraged or caused another to use a prohibited substance or prohibited technique or to commit any offence under these Rules [...]
> A person may at any time admit that he has committed a doping offence. An admission for the purposes of these Rules means a statement made in writing or orally, but in a verifiable manner, by the person alleged to have committed a doping offence which acknowledges directly or indirectly a violation of these Rules."

Badminton Association of England (BAE):[190]

> "Under these Rules doping is illegal and an offence is committed when: a person admits using a prohibited substance or a prohibited method [...]
> An admission made more than 5 years after the facts to which it relates shall not constitute an offence under these Rules."

The Scottish Football Association (SFA):[191]

> "Use of prohibited substances and prohibited techniques: Should a player admit to having used or taken advantage of a Prohibited Substance or Prohibited Technique at any time then the General Purposes Committee may impose such penalty as is provided for in this Charter."

The doping regulations of five Irish federations contained a standard clause stating that "a doping offence may have been committed when an athlete admits to having used a prohibited substance or a prohibited method."[192] Two Dutch federations provided for admissions, namely:

---

[188] Rules for Doping Control, 2. Doping Offences, 2.2, sub (iii).

[189] ASFGB Doping Control Rules and Protocols, 3. Doping Offences, 3.1, sub 3.1.6 and 3.2.

[190] Doping Control Rules for the Badminton Association of England, Appendix A – Doping Offences, 2., sub (iii) and 3.

[191] Doping Charter, 4. The SFA Doping Regulations, sub 2.

[192] Irish Canoe Union: Irish Canoe Union Doping Control Regulations, 6.00 Offences, 6.01, sub (c); Equestrian Federation of Ireland: Model Doping Control Policy for National Governing Bodies, 2. Doping Control Policy, 2.2 What is a Doping Offence?, 2.2.2, sub (c); Tennis Ireland: Doping Control Policy, 2. Doping Offences, 2.2, sub (c); Irish Triathlon Association: Doping Control Policy, 2.2 What is a Doping Offence? 2.2.2, sub (c); Volleyball Association of Ireland: Doping Control Policy of the Volleyball Association of Ireland, 1.2 The Doping Offence, 1.2.2, sub c.

Koninklijke Nederlandse Atletiek Unie (KNAU):[193]

> "It is also likely that the athlete has used doping when: he firmly and unreservedly declares that he has used doping or a prohibited technique."

Koninklijke Nederlandse Zwembond (KNZB):[194]

> "Doping is defined as follows: admitting to having benefited from or made use of a prohibited substance or a prohibited technique [...]
> The admission (in the sense of Article P2 subsection 1 sub c) involves a written or oral, but in any case verifiable, declaration by the person chargable with doping that he/she has violated this doping regiment directly or indirectly."

In Germany, only one federation included an express provision with regard to confessions, i.e., the *Deutscher Schwimm-Verband* (DSV).[195] The provision in question is not entirely clear on whether the admission as such already constituted a doping offence. Rather, it could sooner be deduced from the text that an offence would have been committed in case the athlete admited to having gained an advantage through the use of doping.

> "Als Dopingverstöße gelten:
> das Eingeständnis, einen Vorteil nach Anwendung einer verbotenen Substanz oder verbotenen Technik erlangt zu haben [...]."

It is noteworthy that in some of the doping regulations of national and international federations which do contain provisions on admission the focus is on the abstract description of the doping offence, while in others it is on the athlete's actions. The result in both cases is, however, the same, namely that the "loose-lipped" athlete lays himself open to punishment for doping. In cases where confessions are withdrawn at a later stage the question is which should be accorded more weight: the initial confession, or its subsequent withdrawal?

2.2.4. *Masking agents and methods*

The doping regulations of the international federations determine that manipulative acts which hamper the detection of doping substances or mask their presence entirely are also to be counted as doping. "Doping consists of [...] and/or pharmacological, physical or chemical manipulation aimed at making these substances difficult to detect," according to the doping regulations of the International Rowing Federation (FISA).[196]

The concept of doping, according to the regulations of the baseball federation IBA,[197] also covers "pharmacological, classes of agents or methods masking the

---

[193] KNAU Dopingreglement, Art. 2 – Verbod en verplichting, 3. b, 2e.
[194] KNZB-Reglement Dopingcontrole, Art. P2 Doping, 2.1, sub c. and 2.2.
[195] DSV-Antidopingbestimmungen, para. 3 Dopingverstöße, (1) sub c).
[196] FISA: Rules of racing and related By Laws, Rule 80, para. 1.
[197] IBA: Anti Doping Rules, Ch. 1, Art. 1.1.

use of substances or methods having this property [...]." The judo federation IJF[198] and the field International Hockey Rederation (FIH)[199] use similar wording when they consider doping to include the "manipulation of urine, whether pharmacological, chemical or physical." The International Table Tennis Federation (ITTF)[200] also understands doping substances and methods to mean "substances and methods which alter the integrity and validity of urine samples used in doping controls." The International Amateur Swimming Federation (FINA)[201] considers the manipulation of urine samples a prohibited technique, i.e. "the use of substances and methods which alter the integrity and validity of urine or blood samples used in doping control." The analysis of the urine sample of Michelle Smith de Bruin revealed that the urine contained large doses of alcohol. The fact that alcohol is in general not considered a masking agent was of no avail to Smith in her defence that she had not used doping. The FINA and the CAS[202] found her guilty of a doping offence, although there was no hard evidence that her urine contained prohibited substances.

Masking the use of doping need not necessarily take place through administration of a substance to the athlete. Manipulation can also take place during or after the doping test. For example, had it been imbibed, the amount of alcohol found in Smith's sample could have led to her death, making it unlikely that she actually drank it.

The defence may put forward the argument that a sample has been manipulated.[203] The possibility that a sample could be manipulated may in extraordinary cases also prove to be to the suspected athlete's advantage.[204]

---

[198] IJF: Regulations Concerning Dope Tests, Art. 2.

[199] FIH: Doping Policy, Art. 1.

[200] ITTF: Anti-Doping Regulations, Art. 1.1.2.

[201] FINA: Doping Control, Art. DC 3.

[202] CAS 98/211, 7-6-1999, *Smith-De Bruin v. FINA*, Matthieu Reeb, ed., *Digest of CAS Awards II 1998-2000* (The Hague, Kluwer Law International 2002) pp. 255-273, grounds 12-15: "In this context, we draw attention again to the conclusion of the laboratory in respect of the 'A' and the 'B' samples: Unequivocal signs of adulteration have been found in sample [...]. The content of alcohol of the sample (concentration higher than 100 mg/ml) is in no way compatible with human consumption and the sample shows a very strong whisky odour. Its very low specific gravity (0.983 g/mi) is also compatible with physical manipulation. [...] It matters not, for present purposes, that the substance referred to could not be specifically identified [...]. The fact remains that there is unchallenged evidence that what was, even at the date of the testing, a banned substance (because it fell within the general category of substances related to those specifically listed) was found in the Appellant's urine; there is, therefore, actual evidence before the Panel that there was something to conceal. Not only was the manipulating not wholly successful, but there was an obvious motive for it."

[203] In CAS 92/63, 10-9-1992, *G. v. FEI*, Matthieu Reeb, ed., *Digest of CAS Awards 1986-1998* (Berne, Editions Stämpfli 1998) pp. 93-103, ground 6, it was considered that the defence "firstly drew attention to the late sending of the urine samples to the HFL. In fact, the samples were taken on 19th June 1991 and did not reach the HFL until 26th June 1991. Accepting that the sample had probably been sent on 24th June 1991, i.e the day after the event ended, the appellant notes that 5 days elapsed between the taking and sending of the sample, whence the risk that the disputed samples might have been interchanged or manipulated."

[204] In CAS 91/56, 25-6-1992, *S. v. FEI*, Matthieu Reeb, ed., *Digest of CAS Awards 1986-1998* (Berne, Editions Stämpfli 1998) pp. 93-103, it was considered that Athrough the showing of a video brought by the witness Donike, it could be established that the airtightness of the jar was affected if its

In a large number of doping regulations of national sports organisations the practice of doping – as it is called in the Belgian *Decreet inzake Medisch Verantwoorde Sportbeoefening*[205] – is also considered to be "the use of substances or the use of means which aim to mask doping practices."[206]

---

lid was unscrewed, even slightly. It was also demonstrated that the lid could be unscrewed in spite of the metal wire when it was possible to slide the incorrectly sealed seal along the wire. This operation was facilitated when the jar was small, as it was then possible to free and dispose of a greater length of wire. It was then possible to contaminate the contents of the jar by introducing a foreign liquid, and then once more sliding the seal without such manipulation being noticeable. Now, according to the evidence of Prof. Donike, not contested by the respondent, the two jars examined in Newmarket on 12th February 1991 were small in size."

[205] Titel I – Definities, Art. 2, 6°, sub c.

[206] Para. 1: Stk. 2. "The use of banned substances, their presence in urine or blood samples and the use of methods with the purpose of altering the result of an analysis of a urine or blood sample are prohibited." Deutscher Fussball-Bund: Durchführungsbestimmungen – Doping, para. 1 – Dopingbegriff: "Verbotene Methoden (z.B. Blutdoping) oder Manipulation der Dopingproben werden ebenfalls als Doping eingestuft. Diese Bestimmung gilt auch außerhalb des Wettbewerbs." Real Decreto 255/1996, de 16 de febrero, por el que se establece el régimen de infracciones y sanciones para la represión del dopaje: Titulo 1 – Régimen Disciplinario del Dopaje, Articulo 1 – Tipificación de las infracciones, 1.: "Se consideran como infracciones muy graves a la discipline deportiva las siguientes: [...] La utilización de las sustancias y grupos farmacológicos probibidos, asi como de métodos no reglamentarios destinados a aumentar artificialmente las capacidades fisicas de los deportistas o a modificar los resultados de las competiciones." *Idem*: Real Federación Española de Atletismo: D) Reglamento de los Controles de Dopaje de la Real Federación Española de Atletismo, Capitolo I – Disposiciones Generales, Arts. 2 and 4; Federación Española de Baloncesto: Reglamento Contro de Dopaje, Titulo Primero – Disposiciones Generales, Art. 2; Real Federación Española de Balonmano: RFEBM Estatutos y Reglamentos, Reglamento Control de Dopaje, Art. 2; Real Federación Española de Fútbol: Estatutos, Título VIII Del Régimen Disciplinario y Competicional, Capítulo 3 – De las infracciones y sus sanciones, Sección 4a – De las infracciones especificas en relación con el dopaje, Tipificación de las infracciones, Art. 143 a) Loi no. 99-223 du 23 mars 1999 relative à la protection de la santé des sportifs et à la lutte contre le dopage, Titre II B De la prevention et de la Lutte contre le dopage, Section 2 Des Agissements interdits. Art. 17: "Il est interdit à toute personne, au cours des compétitions et manifestations sportives organisées ou agréées par des fédérations sportives ou en vue d'y participer: [...] d'utiliser des substances et procédés de nature à modifier artificiellement les capacités ou à masquer l'emploi de substances ou procédés ayant cette propriété [...]." *Idem*: Décret no. 2002-36 du 11 janvier 2001 relatif aux dispositions que que les fédérations sportives agréées doivent adopter dans leur règlement en matière de contrôles et de santions contre le dopage en application de l'article L.3634-1 du code de la santé publique, Annexe – Règlement Disciplinaire type des Fédérations Sportives agréées relatif à la Lutte contre le dopage, Art. 2; Fédération Française des Sociétés d'Aviron (FFSA), Réglementation Antidopage, Principes, 1.3.; Fédération Française de Boxe, Règlement Féderal de Lutte contre le Dopage, Titre I – Dispositions Générales, Art. 1. Hockey Club Luxembourg: Mesures contre le dopage, Art. 1: "Est considéré comme dopage et donc interdite l'utilisation, par des licenciés actifs, de toute substance ou tout moyen figurant sur la liste établie par l'organisme national de coordination en matière de dopage, ci-après 'l'instance de contrôle', susceptible d'infuencer les capacités et performances sportives ou de masquer l'emploi de telles substances, ci-après 'substances dopantes'." *Idem*: Fédération Luxembourgeoise de Lutte: Statuts, VII – Du Dopage, Art. 23; Federation Luxembourgeoise de Tennis: Chapitre XIV – Mesures contre le dopage, Art. 1; Fédération Luxemburgeoise de Volley-Ball: F.L.V.B. Règlement d'Ordre Intérieur, 4.6. Mesure contre le dopage, 4.6.1; Fédération Luxembourgeoise de Natation et de Sauvetage, Mesures contra le dopage, Art. 38. Federação Equestre Portuguesa: Regulamento de Controlo de Antidopagem de Cavaleiros/condutores, Capitulo 1 – Disposições gerais, Artigo 2o – Definição de dopagem, 2.: "São também consideradas como dopantes as substâncias ou métodos de dopagem que, embora não sendo susceptíveis de alterar o rendimento desportivo do

What non-appearance at a doping control, refusing to be tested and confessing to doping afterwards all have in common is that they do not hinge on the fact that doping substances were found in the athlete's sample. This is also true for the presence of masking agents, which often makes it impossible to verify whether the athlete actually used a banned substance. In all these cases, the athletes in question can be said to be under grave suspicions of doping. After all, if an athlete is "clean," he/she has no need to revert to such measures. Another instance in which a doping offence can be said to have been committed without the need for actual use to occur is when an athlete lays him/herself open to suspicion by having doping substances in his/her possession.

2.2.5. *Possession of a prohibited substance*

Only Belgian law contained a provision with respect to the possession of prohibited substances in the *Decreet inzake Medisch Verantwoorde Sportbeoefening*.[207] The Flemish legislator equated the possession of doping substances to doping practices.[208]

> "Para. 2. To the doping practices referred to in para. 1 are equated:
> the possession during or during the preparations for a sports event of substances and means as referred to in Article 2, 6°."

The drafters of the WADC were also inclined towards the view that possession of doping substances quite naturally leads to a suspicion of actual use. Where the Flemish legislator spoke of doping substances in general, Art. 2.6.1 WADC merely mentions substances that are prohibited in out-of-competition testing:

> "2.6   Possession of prohibited substances and methods:
> 2.6.1   Possession by an athlete at any time or place of a substance that is prohibited in out-of-competition testing or a prohibited method unless the athlete establishes that the possession is pursuant to a therapeutic use exemption granted in accordance with Article 4.4 (Therapeutic Use) or other acceptable justification."

---

praticante, sejam usadas para impedir ou dificultar a detecção de substâncias dopantes." *Idem:* Federação Portuguesa de Andebol, Regulamento Geral da Federação Portuguesa de Andebol e Associações, Titulo 9 – Regulamento de Controlo Antidopagem, Capítulo I – Disposições gerais, Art. 2: Federação Portuguesa de Hoquei, Regulamento Antidopagem, Título 1 – Da Antidopagem, Capítulo 1 – Disposições Gerais, Art. 2o, sub 5; Federação Portuguesa de Remo, Regulamento do Controlo Antidopagem, Capitulo I – Disposições gerais, Art. 3, sub 2; Federação Portuguesa de Halterofilismo, Regulamento Antidopagem, Art. 5, sub 3; Federação Portuguesa de Basquetebol, Regulamento Antidopagem da Federação Portuguesa De Basquetebol, Capítulo I – Âmbito de aplicação, Art. 1o, sub 3. a); Federação Portuguesa de Tiro com Arco, Regulamente do Controlo Antidopagem, Capítulo I – Disposições Gerais, Art. 2, sub 2.

[207] Titel IV – Voorwaarden inzake de medisch verantwoorde sportbeoefening: Hoofdstuk III – Regelen ter bestrijding van dopingpraktijken, Art. 21, 1 and 2, sub 2°.

[208] See also British Bobsleigh Association, *infra* Section 3.3.

2.2.6. *Criminal conviction*

Criminal conviction constituted an ancillary doping infraction that may be termed a rarity. Only in the doping regulations of certain sports federations in Great Britain and Ireland a rule was included providing that persons – athletes or otherwise – who had been criminally convicted of an act involving prohibited substances (e.g. drug trafficking) were considered to have committed a doping offence. Two British[209] and five Irish[210] sports organisations had included this provision which read as follows:

> "Under these Rules doping is illegal and an offence is committed when: [...] a person (athlete or individual) is convicted of a criminal offence involving a prohibited substance."

2.2.7. *Elastic provisions*

To conclude our list of ancillary doping infractions we must not fail to mention infractions described in elastic provisions. It is quite possible that the "ordinary" doping offences also came within the scope of these provisions, but there were a number of extraordinary doping offences which could only be brought under this heading, such as preventing athletes from reporting for doping controls.

Various doping regulations provided for such occurrences by including a formulation that was couched in such open and general terms that many undesirable acts could come under its heading and be declared doping offences. The Amateur Rowing Association,[211] for example, had a rule stipulating that:

> "The mis-use of drugs [...] is prohibited and any person who is involved in the mis-use of drugs will be subject to a penalty which could involve a life time ban from participation in the sport and associated activities."

The British Cycling Federation (BCF)[212] used fraud as the common denominator:

> "The administration to, or use by, a rider of a banned substance or method shall be a breach of the Technical Regulations. This breach takes place when either: [...] a rider commits or attempts to commit a fraud in connection with the provision of a urine sample."

---

[209] British Bobsleigh Association: Rules for Doping Control, Doping Offences, 2, sub (v); Badminton Association of England Ltd.: Doping Control Rules for the Badminton Association of England, Appendix A – Doping Offences, 2., sub (v).

[210] Irish Canoe Union: Irish Canoe Union Doping Control Regulations, 6.00 Offences, 6.02, sub c.; Equestrian Federation of Ireland: Model Doping Control Policy for National Governing Bodies, 2. Doping Control Policy, 2.2 What is a Doping Offence?, 2.2.2, sub (e); Tennis Ireland: Doping Control Policy, 2. Doping Offences, 2.2., (e); Irish Triathlon Association: Doping Control Policy, 2.2 What is a Doping Offence?, 2.2.2, sub (e); Volleyball Association of Ireland: Doping Control Policy of the Volleyball Association of Ireland, 1.2 The Doping Offence, 1.2.2, sub e.

[211] Mis-use of Drugs By Laws, 1. Principles, 1.4.

[212] Anti Doping Regulations, Principles, 1. sub d).

Even more generally worded, a number of British and Irish sports organisations considered it a doping offence when a person failed or refused to abide by the rules laid down in the doping regulations. These included:

British Bobsleigh Association (BBA):[213]

"Under these Rules doping is illegal and an offence is committed when: [...]
a person fails or refuses to comply with any provision of these Rules after having been requested to do so; or
a person wilfully obstructs or interferes with the carrying out of anything in these Rules."

Amateur Swimming Federation of Great Britain (ASFGB):[214]

"Doping is strictly forbidden and constitutes a breach of the FINA Doping Control Rules and these Rules. For the purposes of these Rules, the following shall be regarded as doping offences: [...] a person obstructs or interferes or attempts to obstruct or interfere with the carrying out of any provision of these Rules and Protocols."

The only sports organisation on the EU continent to use a similar elastic provision was the *Fédération Luxembourgeoise de Football* (FLF):[215]

"Behinderung der zuständigen Instanz und/oder Weigerung des (der) Verantwortlichen zur Mithilfe bei der Durchführung der Doping-Kontrollen."

One may concede that evading doping control is rightly considered a doping offence. If this were otherwise, the prosecution of doping offenders would be considerably hampered. An athlete who has nothing to hide should ordinarily have no objection to the fact that his urine or blood is tested for the presence of banned substances. If, however, the athlete fails to cooperate he/she lays him/herself open to suspicion, even if he/she did not test positive. This is also the case if the sample contains excessive amounts of non-prohibited substances that are not normally produced by the human body or if an athlete is in possession of prohibited substances not required for health reasons.

---

[213] Rules for Doping Control, 2. Doping Offences, 2.2, sub (vii) and (viii). *Idem*: Badminton Association of England Ltd.: Doping Control Rules for the Badminton Association of England, Appendix A – Doping Offences, 2., sub (vi) and (viii); Irish Canoe Union: Irish Canoe Union Doping Control Regulations, 6.00 Offences, 6.02, sub (e) and (f); Equestrian Federation of Ireland: Model Doping Control Policy for National Governing Bodies, 2. Doping Control Policy, 2.2 What is a Doping Offence?, 2.2.2, sub (g) and (h); Tennis Ireland: Doping Control Policy, 2. Doping Offences, 2.2., sub (h) and (i); Irish Triathlon Association, Doping Control Policy, 2.2 What is a Doping Offence?, 2.2.2, sub (g) and (h); Volleyball Association of Ireland: Doping Control Policy of the Volleyball Association of Ireland, 1.2 The Doping Offence, 1.2.2. sub g. and h.; The Irish Amateur Wrestling Association: 2 Doping Offences, 2.2 sub (g) and (h).

[214] ASFGB Doping Control Rules and Protocols, 3. Doping Offences, 3.1, sub 3.1.8.

[215] Kapitel IX: Doping, para. 12, III.

However, in the case of admissions and confessions greater caution should be exercised. It is not unusual that under pressure of circumstances people make statements which they later regret.

Finally, the example of a criminal conviction for offences involving banned substances may be considered the least indispensable ancillary doping infractions in terms of the possibility of prosecuting doping offences.

So far, we have examined practices by which the athlete him/herself administered the drugs in some way. We have also discussed situations where it was likely that the athlete had availed him/herself of such practices. However, besides these "stand-alone" infractions, doping offences can also be committed by third parties. One might think of assisting athletes in the administration of doping and doping of horses.

3.   OFFENCES RELATED TO THE USE OF DOPING

3.1.   Third-party assistance in the use of doping

Many doping regulations of international sports organisations considered the intervention of third parties in the doping offence to be a doping offence of its own accord. A third party may be guilty of complicity to, condoning or counselling of the use of doping by an athlete.[216] Federations that equated assistance with doping would likewise apply the sanctions by which the "ordinary" doping offence was punishable to this offence.[217] Other federations included a separate description of the offence of third-party assistance in doping.[218] The International Archery Fed-

---

[216] IPC: Ch. 8.2, 1.1: Doping infractions fall into two broad categories: a. Use of banned substances or practices; and b. infractions other than use – ie. aiding, abetting, condoning, counselling [...].

[217] IAAF: Rules and Regulations, Rule 55, subsection 3: "or prohibited techniques, shall have committed a doping offence and shall be subject to sanctions in accordance with Rule 60. If that person is not an athlete, then the Council may, at its discretion, impose an appropriate sanction."; ICF: Doping Rules, Rule 2, lid 2: "Any person assisting or inciting others, or admitting having incited or assisted others, to use a prohibited substance or prohibited techniques, shall have committed a doping offence and shall be subject to sanctions in accordance with Rule 6."; FIS: Doping Rules – Rule 2 – Ancillary Offences: "2. Any person assisting or inciting others, or admitting having incited or assisted others, to use a prohibited substance, or prohibited techniques, shall have committed a doping offence and shall be subject to sanctions in accordance with Rule 6."

[218] IWF: Anti-doping Policy – 1. Position Statement, 1.2 "No person who is subject to this Policy shall [...] assist, encourage or otherwise be a party to a doping offence." Anti-doping Policy – 5. Doping Offence, 5.1: "For the purpose of this Policy a Doping Offence is: [...] assisting, or being knowingly involved in a Doping Offence as in (i) and (ii) above"; FINA: Guidelines for Doping Control: The offence of doping occurs when: [...] assisting or encouraging others to use a banned substance or banned technique, or having assisted or incited others. IBU: Anti-doping, Blood Test and Gender Verification Rules, I. Doping controls, 1. Principle: The offence of doping takes place when [...] an athlete/medical doctor/coach used a banned method [...] ITU: Doping Control Rules and Procedural Guidelines, 2. Definition of Doping: 2.2 "For the purpose of these Rules, the following are regarded as doping offenses: [...] assisting or inciting others to use a prohibited substance or prohibited technique."

eration (FITA) and the International Skating Union (ISU) merely stated that any person assisting would be punished.[219] The International Luge Federation chose the same approach, but only imposed sanctions when a violation of the anti-doping regulations had actually occurred.[220]

The doping rules of the various EU countries made frequent mention of assistance in the use of prohibited doping substances. Given that the approach taken towards the concept of "assistance" differed per country, the descriptions below will also be given per country.

In the doping regulations of the *Union Royale Belge des Sociétés de Football Association* (URBSFA/KBVB)[221] doping was considered to be: "the fact, however brought about, of facilitating the use of doping." Third-party assistance was implied here, as only third parties could manipulate the athlete's situation in such a way that "facilitating" could be the result.

In the regulations of the German sports organisations the use of prohibited substances was usually described in closer detail. Use, besides ingestion or injection, was also understood to mean distribution (*Verabreichung*). Only a third party could distribute the prohibited substances and thus assist in the use of doping. The distribution of doping substances could also be considered their trade. Only the *Deutscher Schwimm-Verband*[222] was explicit on the subject of third-party assistance:

> "Als Dopingverstöße gelten: die Hilfe bei oder die Anstiftung zur Anwendung einer verbotenen Substanz oder verbotenen Technik oder das Eingeständnis, anderen geholfen oder diese angestiftet zu haben, dies zu tun."

Spanish provisions used terms like "*promoción*" and "*incitación*" when dealing with third-party assistance in the use of prohibited substances. The relevant provision in the Real Decreto of 1996[223] which was repeated by a number of Spanish federations in their regulations[224] stipulated that:

---

[219] FITA: Appendix 4 Doping Control Procedures, 1 Doping – Preamble And Principles 1.7 Any person who aids in doping will be sanctioned. ISU: Communication no. 956 – Doping: "1.1 Doping or Doping Methods are contrary to the spirit of good and fair sportmanship and are forbidden according to ISU Rule 139. [...] any person who has aided the competitor in the use of doping substances or methods is subject to sanctions of this Rule."

[220] FIL: IRO – International Luge Regulations – Artificial Track – Supplement 4 – Medical Code – Chapter I General Provisions, art. IV. "[...], counselling of the use of, permitting the use of or condoning the use of any substance or method outlawed within the FIL Medical Code is prohibited. Sanctions are applicable in the event of any breach of the provisions of the FIL Medical Code."

[221] Art. VII/82 – Daden van doping, 2. Definitie, sub b).

[222] DSV-Antidopingbestimmungen, para. 3 Dopingverstöße, (1), sub e).

[223] Real Decreto 255/1996, de 16 de febrero, por el que se establece el régimen de infracciones y sanciones para la represión del dopaje: Titulo 1 – Régimen Disciplinario del Dopaje, Articulo 1 – Tipificación de las infracciones, 1.

[224] Real Federación Española de Atletismo: D) Reglamento de los Controles de Dopaje de la Real Federación Española de Atletismo, Capitolo I – Disposiciones Generales, Articulo 4 – Tipificación de las infracciones, sub 2); Real Federación Española de Fútbol: Estatutos, Título VIII Del Régimen Disciplinario y Competicional, Capítulo 3 – De las infracciones y sus sanciones, Sección 4a.

"Se consideran como infracciones muy graves a la discipline deportiva las siguientes:
– La promoción o incitación a la utilización de tales sustancias o métodos.
Se considera promoción la dispensa o administración de tales sustancias, asi como la colaboración en la puesta en práctica de los métodos no reglamentarios."

In Great Britain and Ireland provisions concerning third-party assistance were more explicit:

UK Athletics:[225]

"Doping in or out of Competition is strictly prohibited and is an offence. The offence of doping takes place when: a person assists or incites others, or admits having assisted or incited others to use prohibited substances or prohibited techniques [...]"

Amateur Rowing Association:[226]

"The mis-use of drugs, as defined, is prohibited and any person who is involved in the mis-use of drugs will be subject to a penalty which could involve a life time ban from participation in the sport and associated activities."

British Bobsleigh Association (BBA):[227]

"Under these Rules doping is illegal and an offence is committed when: a person assists, procures, induces or causes others or admits having assisted, procured, induced, or caused others to use a prohibited substance or a prohibited method or to commit any other offence under these Rules [...]"

The Lawn Tennis Association (LTA):[228]

"The following matters shall be regarded as 'Doping Offences' for the purpose of Rule 32: Inciting or assisting a player to use a Prohibited Substance or Prohibited Method."

Amateur Swimming Federation of Great Britain (ASFGB):[229]

"Doping is strictly forbidden and constitutes a breach of the FINA Doping Control Rules and these Rules. For the purposes of these Rules, the following shall be regarded as doping offences: if a person assists, induces, encourages or causes another to use a prohibited substance or prohibited technique or to commit any offence under these Rules [...]"

---

[225] UK Current Doping Rules and Procedures, Rule 24 Doping, (1) and (5), sub (e).
[226] Mis-use of Drugs By Laws, 1.Principles, 1.4.
[227] Rules for Doping Control, 2. Doping Offences, 2.2, sub (iv).
[228] LTA Rules, Appendix 4 – Tennis Anti-Doping Programme, A. General Statement of Policy, 2., sub (iv).
[229] ASFGB Doping Control Rules and Protocols, 3. Doping Offences, 3.1, sub 3.1.5.

British Canoe Union (BCU):[230]

"Any person assisting or inciting others in the contravention of any provision of these Rules shall be presumed to have committed an offence against these Rules and may be subject to disciplinary action."

English Table Tennis Association (ETTA):[231]

"A Member or Affiliated Organisation must not assist or incite any Member to contravene Rule 32.14.1."

The Football Association (FA):[232]

"The following matters will be regarded as amounting to 'Misconduct' for the purposes of Rule 26: inciting or assisting a player to use a prohibited substance or technique [...]"

The Football Association of Wales (WFA):[233]

"Any person assisting or inciting others in the contravention of doping regulations shall be considered as having committed an offence against the Rules of The F.A. of Wales and may be subject to disciplinary action [...]"

Welsh Badminton Union (WBU):[234]

"Any person assisting or inciting others in the contravention of doping regulations shall be considered as having committed an offence against these rules and may be penalised."

Irish Canoe Union:[235]

"An Ancillary Doping Offence may have been committed when: an athlete or individual is found to have assisted, incited, or caused others to use a prohibited substance or a prohibited method [...]"

Equestrian Federation of Ireland:[236]

"Under these Rules doping is illegal and an offence is committed when: a person assists, procures, induces or causes others or admits having assisted, procured, induced, or caused others to use a prohibited substance or a prohibited method or to commit any other offence under these Rules [...]"

---

[230] BCU Sports Management Committee, Doping Control Rules, Definitions, 2. Submission to tests, 2.6.

[231] Rules, 32.14. Doping, 32.14.5.

[232] Drug Testing Programme, Memorandum and Procedural Guidelines for the Conduct of Drug Testing, Season 2000/2001, Memorandum, Drug Testing, 1, sub (iv).

[233] Memorandum on the use of drugs.

[234] Positive Dope Test Protocol, Section One – Regulations, 1.7.

[235] Irish Canoe Union Doping Control Regulations, 6.00 Offences, 6.02, sub (b).

[236] Model Doping Control Policy for National Governing Bodies, 2. Doping Control Policy, 2.2 What is a Doping Offence?, 22.2.2, sub (d). *Idem:* Tennis Ireland: Doping Control Policy, 2. Doping

We again encounter the concept of "*Verabreichung*" in the regulations of two Luxembourg federations, although here it was not used to illustrate what is to be understood by "use."

Fédération Luxembourgeoise de Football (FLF):[237]

"Unterstützung oder Aufforderung zur Verabreichung, sowie eigenhandige Verabreichung von Dopingmitteln an Spieler(in)."

Fédération Luxembourgeoise de Tennis de Table (FLTT):[238]

"Jedem Verbands- und jedem Vereinsmitglied ist jedwede Tätigkeit in Bezug auf Doping oder andere vom Staat, der ITTF, der ETTU bzw. der FLTT als gefährlich oder gesundheitsschädigend eingestufte Substanzen strengstens untersagt; dies betrifft sowohl die Verabreichung als auch den Gebrauch entsprechender Mittel."

In three more Luxembourg regulations the prohibition of assisting an athlete in the use of doping was – strangely – only addressed to members of the respective federations.

Fédération Luxembourgeoise de Lutte (FLL):[239]

"Il est interdit à tout membre licencié d'administrer, d'encourager ou d'inciter à administrer une substance dopante à un licencié actif."

Fédération Luxemburgeoise de Volley-Ball (FLVB):[240]

"Il est interdit à tout membre licencié d'administrer, d'aider, d'encourager ou d'inciter à administrer une substance dopante à un licencié actif."

Fédération Luxembourgeoise de Natation et de Sauvetage (FLNS):[241]

"Il est interdit à tout licencié d'administrer, d'aider, d'encourager ou d'inciter à administrer une substance dopante à un compétiteur."

The doping regulations of some 14 Dutch federations[242] all included the following provision with respect to third-party assistance in the use of doping:

Offences, 2.2., sub (d); Irish Triathlon Association: Doping Control Policy, 2.2 What is a Doping Offence?, 2.2.2, sub (d); Volleyball Association of Ireland: Doping Control Policy of the Volleyball Association of Ireland, 11.2 The Doping Offence, 1.2.2, sub (d).

[237] Kapitel IX: Doping, para. 12, II.: Begünstigung.

[238] Statuten, 4.2 Doping / gefährliche und gesundheitsschädigende substanzen, Art. 4.21.

[239] Statuts, VII – Du Dopage, Art. 26.

[240] F.L.V.B. Règlement d'Ordre Intérieur, 4.6. Mesure contre le dopage, 4.6.4.

[241] Mesures contra le dopage, Art. 41.

[242] Nederlandse Basketball Bond, Dopingreglement, Verboden en verplichtingen, Art. 2, sub 5; Koninklijke Nederlands Algemene Schermbond: Dopingreglement, Titel I, Verboden en verplichtingen, Art. 2, sub 5; Koninklijke Nederlandse Voetbalbond: Dopingreglement KNVB, Verboden en verplichtin-

"It is prohibited to incite athletes to use doping or, by whatever means, either through action or omission, to assist in its use or in the failure to meet the obligations referred to in subsection 2."

Five of them added that: "Any violation of this provision may give rise to disciplinary sanctions."[243] The *Judo Bond Nederland*[244] merely stated that "It is prohibited to incite participants to use doping or in any way assist them in the use of doping." Only the *Koninklijke Nederlandse Zwembond*[245] used a provision, which deviated from the standard clause cited above:

"Doping is defined as follows: [...] assisting or encouraging others to use a prohibited substance or a prohibited technique, or admitting to having so assisted or encouraged others."

Finally, the *Swedish Riksidrotts Förbundet* (SRF)[246] provided in its *Dopingregler* that were binding on all Swedish sports federations that any person offering assistance to athletes in the use of doping substances were guilty of doping:

"Idrottsutövare som gör sig skyldig till doping, liksom annan person som är idrottsutövare behjälpig med doping eller som förser idrottsutövare med dopingmedel, kan bestraffas enligt 14 kap RF:s stadgar."[247]

Various regulations of international federations in respect of penalties distinguished between athletes assisting athletes and non-athletes assisting athletes. This distinction – which did not reappear in any of the doping regulations of the national federations – was based on the fact that athletes were in a subordinate position to the

---

gen, Art. 1, sub 3; Koninklijke Nederlandse Gymnastiek Bond: Huishoudelijk Reglement, Hoofdstuk 4 Dopingcontrole, 4.0 Algemene bepalingen, 4.0.02., sub 3: Verboden; Koninklijke Nederlandse Schutters Associatie KNSA: Dopingreglement, Titel I – Verboden en verplichtingen, Art. 2, 5; Nederlandse Boksbond: Artikel 33: Dopingreglement, 33.1. Verboden en Verplichtingen, 33.1.5; Koninklijke Nederlandse Baseball en Softball Bond: Reglement van wedstrijden, Doping, 2. Verboden en verplichtingen, 5; Nederlands Handbal Verbond: Huishoudelijk reglement NHV, para. 6.3 Doping, art. 6.3.1.2 Verboden en verplichtingen, 5; Nederlandse Ski Vereniging: Dopingreglement, Begripsbepalingen, Verboden en verplichtingen, Art. 2, 4.

[243] Koninlijke Nederlandse Hockey Bond: Dopingreglement, Titel I, Verboden en verplichtingen, Art. 2, sub 5; Koninklijke Nederlandse Lawn Tennis Bond: Dopingcontrolereglement, Hoofdstuk 1 – Begripsbepalingen, Art. 2 – Verboden en verplichtingen, 5; Nederlandse Tafeltennis Bond: Dopingcontrole-Reglement, Art. 7 Verboden en verplichtingen, 5; Nederlandse Handboog Bond: Dopingreglement, Titel I – Verboden en verplichtingen, Art. 2, 5; Nederlandse IJshockey Bond: Dopingreglement, Titel I – Verboden en verplichtingen, Art. 2, 5.

[244] Bonds Vademecum, Hoofdstuk 2 – Regelingen, 2.5 Dopingreglement, Art. 1 – Verboden en verplichtingen, 3.

[245] KNZB-Reglement Dopingcontrole, Art. P2 Doping, 2.1, sub e.

[246] Dopingregler, 13 kap, RF:s stadgar, 1 para. Doping.

[247] Any athlete found guilty of doping, as well as any person assisting the athlete in doping or who provides the athlete with doping substances can be punished in accordance with Chapter 14 of the Swedish Sports Confederation Statutes.

federation, while non-athletes usually were not.[248] Although this appears as a rational argument, an emotional argument probably lay behind it. An element of intent is necessarily always present in a doping offence committed by a third party. It can never be just a case of "negligent participation." Given that sports organisations already responded sharply to the offence of "use," it was to be expected that they would respond even more sharply to an offence of "non-use" which was indisputably intentional.

3.2. **The doping of horses**

To the International Equestrian Federation (FEI) and the International Union for Modern Pentathlon (UIPM) the horses are the athletes; without them, horse racing and dressage are simply not possible. The doping of horses can be regarded as an offence of non-use, corresponding to that committed by third parties, as although horses may in some respects be considered athletes, they are not capable of doping themselves. Although the doping of horses is not a rare phenomenon in these sports, the UIPM regulations were extremely brief on the problem. The UIPM merely "also condemned doping for animals, horses included," according to the UIPM Medical Rulebook. The FEI, on the other hand, provided a lengthy regulation of the problem in its General Regulations. Any horse which was discovered to have prohibited substances present in its body was automatically disqualified, together with the competitor, unless the Ground Jury decided otherwise.[249] The Veterinary Commission had to give its approval in writing before any veterinary treatment with the aid of medication was permitted or a prohibited substance was administered to a horse during the entire course of an event. If during that period it was necessary to treat a horse with a prohibited substance, the Commission had to be informed immediately.[250] With respect to any kind of veterinary treatment or medication, a horse

---

[248] IAAF: Rules and Regulations, Rule 55, subsection 3: "[...] If that person is not an athlete, then the Council may, at its discretion, impose an appropriate sanction."; ICF: Doping Rules, Rule 2, subsection 2: AIf that person is not an athlete, then the ICF may, at its discretion, impose an appropriate sanction."; FINA: Guidelines for Doping Control DC 4.3: "Any coach, physician, trainer, administrator, or other individual found to be assisting or inciting others, or admitting to having incited or assisted others, to use a banned substance, or banned technique, shall have committed a doping offence and shall be subject to sanctions in accordance with DC 9."; ISU: Communication no. 956 – Doping: 1.2 Definitions: "1.2.1 Doping – is [...] the administration or supply of these substances to a competitor by another person such as physician, teamleader, physiotherapist, coach, parent or other person and is forbidden."; FIS: Doping Rules – Rule 2 – Ancillary Offences: 2. "[...] If that person is not an athlete, the FIS Council may, at its discretion, impose an appropriate sanction."

[249] FEI: General Regulations – Chapter VII, Art. 146, subsection 2: "Any horse found to have a Prohibited Substance in any of its tissues, body fluids or excreta at an event as the result of a Medication Test, is automatically disqualified, together with the competitor, from all competitions at that event and the classification adjusted accordingly, unless the Ground Jury has authorised the horse to continue in the event in accordance with paragraph 3. below."

[250] FEI: General Regulations – Chapter VII, Art. 146, subsection 3. "The Veterinary Commission/ Delegate must give written approval before any veterinary treatment or medication with a Prohibited Substance is administered to a horse during the entire course of an event. If during this period it is

involved in the usage of prohibited substances had to have the written approval of the Veterinary Commission during the course of the event.[251] Horses were allowed to take part in events while certain substances were present in their bodies, unless the amount of those substances succeeded certain threshold levels.[252] The term "prohibited substances" was understood to mean a substance, the metabolites and the isomers or biological indicators of such a substance, which had been included in the list of prohibited substances.[253] The list of prohibited substances was submitted for approval by the General Assembly on the recommendation of the Bureau.[254] In view of the rapid development of new drugs and pharmacological agents and of the changes in the methods of preparing horses for competition, the regulations governing the use of new products and new techniques would be kept under review and might be changed at any time.[255]

Relevant provisions in doping regulations at the national level establishing that certain acts involving horses were considered doping were the following:

Fédération Royale Belge des Sports Equestres (FRBSE):[256]

"Les chevaux prenant part aux concours doivent être en bonne santé et réaliser leurs performances sur le base exclusive de leur potentiel propre. L'emploi d'un Produit Interdit peut modifier la performance d'un cheval ou cacher un problème de santé sous-jacent et donc falsifier le résultat d'une épreuve. La liste des Produits Interdits a été établie afin d'inclure toutes les catégories d'action pharmacologique."

Deutsche Reiterliche Vereinigung (DRV):

"2. Einen Verstoß begeht insbesondere, wer
   [...]

---

urgently necessary to treat a horse with a Prohibited Substance, the Veterinary Commission/Delegate must be informed at once and the circumstances reported to the President of the Ground Jury. Any treatment so administered must be indicated to the Veterinary Commission/Delegate by written certification. The Ground Jury must, on recommendation of the Veterinary Commission/Delegate, decide whether the horse may further take part in the event."

[251] FEI: Veterinary Regulations – Chapter III, Art. 1006, subsection 7: "In regard to any form of veterinary treatment or medication of a horse involving the use of a Prohibited Substance during an event, written approval from the Veterinary Commission/Delegate must be obtained, using the standard Authorisation Form for Emergency Treatment."

[252] FEI: Veterinary Regulations – Chapter V, Art. 1013, subsection 3: "Horses may compete with the presence of certain substances in their tissues, body fluids or excreta for which these Regulations have established threshold levels/ratios as laid down in Annex IV, provided the concentration of the substance is not greater than the threshold level/ratio indicated in this Annex."

[253] FEI: Veterinary Regulations – Chapter V, Art. 1013, subsection 2: "The term 'Prohibited Substance' means a substance, the metabolite(s) and the isomers or biological indicators of such substance (including any metabolite(s) originating externally) whether or not they are endogenous to the horse and which are contained in the list of Prohibited Substances (Annex IV)."

[254] FEI: Veterinary Regulations – Chapter V, Art. 1013, subsection 5: "The list of Prohibited Substances is submitted for approval by the General Assembly on the recommendation of the Bureau."

[255] FEI: Veterinary Regulations – Chapter V, Art. 1013, subsection 6 (see Art. 1001.2).

[256] Règlement Vétérinaire, Annexe IV – Produits Interdits.

e)   als Teilnehmer, Besitzer oder Pfleger in zeitlichem Zusammenhang mit
     einer PS/PLS
     aa) ein Pferd/Pony
          – bei Vorhandensein einer nach para. 67 a Ziffer 1 verbotenen
             Substanz einsetzt oder
          – bei Vorhandensein einer in para. 67 a Ziffer 1 mit Grenzwert an-
             gegebenen Substanz einsetzt und diese den Grenzwert übersteigt
             oder
          – bei Anwendung einer nach para. 67 a Ziffer 1 verbotenen Methode
             einsetzt (Doping)
     bb) ein Pferd/Pony bei Vorhandensein
          – eines nach para. 67 a Ziffer 2 verbotenen Arzneimittels einsetzt
             oder
          – eines in para. 67a Ziffer 2 mit Grenzwert angegebenen Arztnei-
             mittels einsetzt und dieses den Grenzwert übersteigt (Anwendung
             eines verbotenen Arzneimittels)
     cc) bei einem Pferd/Pony einen verbotenen Eingriff oder eine Manipula-
          tion zur Beeinflussung der Leistung, der Leistungsfähigkeit oder Leis-
          tungsbereitschaft vornimmt (Manipulation).

Einen Verstoß im obigen Sinne begeht auch, wer sich nicht, mit allen ihm zu
Gebote stehenden Mitteln vergewissert oder nicht durch geeignete Maßnahmen
hinsichtlich der Beaufsichtigung des Pferdes/Ponys sicherstellt, dass kein Doping, keine Anwendung eines verbotenen Arzneimittels, kein Einsatz behandelter
Pferde/Ponys und keine Manipulation vorgenommen wurde."

Bundesfachverband für Reiten und Fahren in Österreich (BRF):[257]

"Eines Verstoßes macht sich insbesondere schuldig, wer:
– Mittel anwendet, die geeignet sind, die Leistungsfähigkeit eines Pferdes während
   einer Prüfung vorübergehënd künstlich zu beeinflussen,
– die Anwendung solcher Mittel versucht, dazu anstiftet oder Beihilfe leistet,
– ein Pferd, das unter dem Einfluß solcher Mittel steht, an den Start bringt, oder
– die Teilnahme an einer Verfassungsprüfung oder Dopingkontrolle gemäß para. 56
   verweigert."

British Equestrian Federation (BEF):[258]

"Horses taking part in a competition must be healthy and compete on their inherent
merits. The use of a prohibited substance might influence a horse's performance or
mask an underlying health problem and could falsely affect the outcome of a competition. The list of prohibited substances has been compiled to include all categories of
pharmacological action.
Prohibited substances in horses are those originating externally whether or not they are
endogenous to the horse. [...]"

---

[257] Para. 2302 Doping.
[258] Rulebook, Disciplinary and Doping Control Procedures, Annex E-1 – Prohibited Substances –
Horses.

I have discussed assisting athletes in doping and the doping of horses within the same framework as these offences are largely corresponding. However, one obvious difference is, of course, that the athlete may actively seek the assistance of a third party or consent to it, whereas a horse must simply submit to the procedure. Another important difference is that the penalisation of third-party horse doping touches upon the core of the anti-doping system, whereas the system would not suffer if a third-party assisting an athlete would not be punishable.

So far, I have discussed rules regulating the actual and suspected doping of athletes. Although the next section does not quite fall within the scope of this book, I would still like to say a few words about what could be called a quasi-doping offence, namely trafficking in doping substances and methods.

3.3.   The illegal trade in prohibited doping substances

Sports organisation may punish third parties assisting athletes in using doping when these third parties are within the scope of the organisation's authority. However, dope dealers usually operate outside this scope which means that their punishment will not be for the organisation to decide upon either. Besides, sports organisation will also lack the necessary facilities for investigation. Nevertheless, a number of federations included rules in their regulations which threatened dealers, distributors and sellers with sanctions. The International Paralympic Committee divided doping offences into two categories: one consisted of the "use of banned substances or practices" and the other of "infractions other than use – i.e. [...] distributing banned substances or the material used in banned substances or practices."[259] Only the World Curling Federation stipulated that persons in the athlete's entourage had to subscribe to the provisions of the IOC Medical Code regarding trafficking in doping products.[260] Four other international federations also considered trafficking in doping substances a doping offence and established penalties.[261]

---

[259] IPC: Doping, Ch. 8.2, Art. 1.1.

[260] WCF: By Law No. 8 doping – I General: Art. 1: All competitors, coaches, doctors, physiotherapists or other officials of all WCF Member Nations undertake to accept the rules of the IOC Medical Code concerning [...] trafficking of prohibited substances.

[261] IAAF: Rules and Regulations, Rule 55, subsection 4: "Any person trading, trafficking, distributing or selling any prohibited substance otherwise than in the normal course of a recognised profession or trade shall also have committed a doping offence under these Rules and shall be subject to sanctions in accordance with Rule 60."; IWF: Anti-doping Policy – 5. Doping Offence, 5.1: "For the purpose of this Policy a Doping Offence is: [...] being found guilty of dealing or trafficking in prohibited substances."; FINA: Guidelines for Doping Control: "The offence of doping occurs when: [...] trading, trafficking, distributing or selling any banned substance." DC 4 Ancillary offenses, DC 4.4 "Any person trading, trafficking, distributing or selling any banned substance otherwise than in the normal course of a recognized profession or trade shall have committed a doping offence under these Rules and shall be subject to sanctions in accordance with DC 9."; ITU: Doping Control Rules and Procedural Guidelines, 2. Definition of Doping: 2.2 "For the purpose of these Rules, the following are regarded as doping offenses: [...] trafficking, distributing, or selling any prohibited substances other than in the normal course of a recognised profession or trade."

At the national level, there were but few sports organisations to include relevant provisions. The ones that did were mainly British or Irish. Only two continental federations, one German and one Dutch, also penalised trafficking:

Deutscher Schwimm-Verband (DSV):[262]

"Als Dopingverstöße gelten: [...] Kaufen, Handeln, Verkaufen oder Aushändigen einer verbotenen Substanz."

Koninklijke Nederlandse Zwembond (KNZB):[263]

"Doping is defined as follows: [...] the purchase, sale, trade, distribution or handing out of any kind of prohibited substance."

The British sports organisations dealt with the problem from various different angles. Often they focused on trade in doping substances "proper," at other times they were concerned with the trade in "social drugs." Sometimes only "trafficking" was an issue, and sometimes a whole range of undesirable acts was targeted. One organisation made trafficking punishable, while another limited itself to issuing a postulate.

British Bobsleigh Association (BBA):[264]

"Under these Rules doping is illegal and an offence is committed when: a person supplies or deals in or has been in possession of a prohibited substance or admits supplying, dealing in or possession of a prohibited substance [...]"

The Lawn Tennis Association (LTA):[265]

"The following matters shall be regarded as 'Doping Offences' for the purpose of Rule 32: [...] Trafficking in the substances specified in class I and class II of paragraph G2."

Amateur Swimming Federation of Great Britain:[266]

"Doping is strictly forbidden and constitutes a breach of the FINA Doping Control Rules and these Rules. For the purposes of these Rules, the following shall be regarded as doping offences: [...] if, save in the normal course of a recognised profession or trade, a person is in possession of any prohibited substance or purchases, supplies, deals in, distributes or hands out or offers to purchase, supply or deal in, distribute, or hand out any prohibited substance; or admits to being in possession of any prohibited substance or to purchasing, supplying, dealing in, distributing or handing out or offering to purchase, supply, deal in, distribute or hand out any prohibited substance."

---

[262] DSV- Antidopingbestimmungen, para. 3 Dopingverstöße, (1), sub f).
[263] KNZB-Reglement Dopingcontrole, Art. P2 Doping, 2.1, sub f.
[264] Rules for Doping Control, 2. Doping Offences, 2.2, sub (vi).
[265] LTA Rules, Appendix 4 – Tennis Anti-Doping Programme, A. General Statement of Policy, 2., sub (vii).
[266] ASFGB Doping Control Rules and Protocols, 3. Doping Offences, 3.1, sub 3.1.7.

Badminton Association of England (BAE):[267]

"Under these Rules doping is illegal and an offence is committed when: [...] a person manufactures, extracts, transforms, prepares, stores, expedites, transports, imports, exports, transits, offers subject to payment or free of charge, distributes, sells, exchanges, undertakes the brokerage of, obtains in any form, prescribes, commercialises, makes over, accepts, possesses, holds, buys or acquires in any manner prohibited substances, procures, induces or causes others or admits having assisted, procured, induced or caused others to use a prohibited substance or a prohibited method (an action known as trafficking,) or to commit any offence under these Rules [...]"

English Table Tennis Association (ETTA):[268]

"A Member or Affiliated Organisation must not distribute any banned substance to any player."

The Football Association (FA):[269]

"The following matters will be regarded as amounting to 'Misconduct' for the purposes of Rule 26: [...] possession or trafficking in a prohibited substance or in any of the substances set out in Schedule 1, Section III C (Social Drugs) of the Procedural Guidelines for the Conduct of Drug Testing.
The expression 'trafficking' in paragraph 1 (vii) above shall include the possession of prohibited substances or social drugs in quantities inconsistent with personal consumption, the possession of such substances with the intent to supply, or being concerned in the supply and distribution of such substances."

In Ireland the rules were rather more uniform, although slight differences were to be found here as well.

Irish Canoe Union (ICU):[270]

"An Ancillary Doping Offence may have been committed when: [...] an athlete or individual is found to have supplied, or dealt in, or is, or has been in possession of a prohibited substance or admits supplying, dealing in, or possession of a prohibited substance [...]"

Equestrian Federation of Ireland:[271]

"Under these Rules doping is illegal and an offence is committed when: [...] a person supplies or deals in or has been in possession of a prohibited substance or admits supplying, dealing in or possession of a prohibited substance [...]"

---

[267] Doping Control Rules for the Badminton Association of England, Appendix A – Doping Offences, 2., sub (iv).

[268] Rules, 32.14. Doping, 32.14.6.

[269] Drug Testing Programme, Memorandum and Procedural Guidelines for the Conduct of Drug Testing, Season 2000/2001, Memorandum, Drug Testing, 1, sub (vii) and 5.

[270] Irish Canoe Union Doping Control Regulations, 6.00 Offences, 6.02, sub (d).

[271] Model Doping Control Policy for National Governing Bodies, 2. Doping Control Policy, 2.2 What is a Doping Offence?, 2.2.2, sub (f). *Idem:* Tennis Ireland: Doping Control Policy, 2. Doping

The Irish Amateur Wrestling Association (IAWA):[272]

> "Under these Rules doping is illegal and an offence is committed when [...] a member supplies or deals in or is or has been in possession of a prohibited substance or admits supplying, dealing in or possession of a prohibited substance [...]"

The sports organisations which included the above provisions in their anti-doping regulations went to great lengths to describe the offence as accurately as possible. By contrast, Art. 2.7 WADC simply designates "trafficking in any prohibited substance or prohibited method" a doping offence. If one wishes to eliminate doping from sport, the obvious approach would be to close down on the criminal gangs involved in the trafficking in doping substances and methods. The provision of Art. 27 WADC addresses the governments which have signed the WADC, not the sports organisations. These organisations lack the authority and the means to deal with trafficking.

One criterion from the doping definition in the 1967 Resolution has not yet been discussed above, namely that of "a healthy person." A great many substances of which it was thought that they could enhance athletic performance – and which were subsequently placed on doping lists – were in fact regular medicinal drugs, which could be prescribed to cure regular ailments or be used in surgery. For this reason, it is essential to make a clear distinction between the use or administration of drugs for doping purposes and their use or administration for medical purposes.

The Resolution's definition of doping indicated that there could only be a case of doping if the substances specified had been used by a healthy person. As a result, persons who were able to prove that they were not healthy fell outside its scope. For this reason, the definition was not widely copied. In addition, it could give rise to a difference in treatment. Athletes may fall ill and be in need of medication. In that case, they should be entitled to the same treatment as non-athletes without having to worry about the impact of drugs on doping tests. However, even if the "healthy person" clause has not subsequently returned in definitions, the problem remains in practice, as will be discussed below.

Offences, 2.2., sub (f) and (g); Irish Triathlon Association: Doping Control Policy, 2.2 What is a Doping Offence?, 2.2.2, sub (f); Volleyball Association of Ireland: Doping Control Policy of the Volleyball Association of Ireland, 1.1 Position on Doping, 1.2 The Doping Offence, 1.2.2, sub f.

[272] 2 Doping Offences, 2.2, sub (f).

4. DOPING SUBSTANCES AND METHODS

4.1. Doping substances[273]

4.1.1. *Doping substances which are prohibited unconditionally ("hard doping")*

The greater part of doping definitions are based on the prohibition of pharmacological substances. These substances have been subdivided into classes: 1. stimulants, 2. narcotics, 3. anabolic substances, 4. diuretics and 5. peptide hormones. On the doping lists examples are given per class. Substances belonging to these classes – including the ones not expressly named – may never be used in medical procedures.

Stimulants are drugs which cause a heightened state of awareness and lessen fatigue. These substances can induce a heightened sense of competition and aggression. Narcotics – such as morphine – are used to suppress pain. Anabolics – related to the male hormone testosterone – are substances used to stimulate the development of muscle tissue. These substances give the athlete more strength and energy. Diuretics are used to remove fluids from body tissue, which can reduce weight in the short term. Because they induce the excretion of urine, these substances are also used to reduce the concentration of drugs in urine and thereby reduce the risk that the presence of such drugs is detected. HCG, causing the heightened production of testosterone, the human growth hormone (HGH) and erythropoetine (EPO), improving the flow of oxygen through the bloodstream, are all peptide hormones.

4.1.2. *Doping substances which are prohibited conditionally ("soft doping")*

In addition to substances and methods which are prohibited at all times, practically all doping lists contain a class of substances "subject to restrictions." These substances are prohibited in principle, but may still be used for a plausible medical reason, if the authorities have been informed in advance of such use and the substances have been administered in a certain way. Linck[274] is of the opinion that

---

[273] Compare Tj.B. van Wimersma Greidanus and P.A.G.M. de Smet, "Geneesmiddelen en doping," in P.A.G.M. de Smet, A.C. van Loenen, L. Offerhaus and E. van der Does, eds., *Medicatiebegeleiding* (Houten, Bohn, Stafleu & Van Loghum 1990) pp. 412-419; Tj.B. van Wimersma Greidanus, *Doping in de sport; definities en middelen*, TGO/JDR March (1991) 3, pp. 4-10 and Tj.B. van Wimersma Greidanus, *Doping – feiten en achtergronden*. See also H.T. van Staveren and M.J.G. Das, *Aspecten van strafrecht en geneesmiddelenrecht bij dopinggeduide middelen* (VU Amsterdam 1990).

[274] Joachim Linck, "Doping und staatliches Recht," *NJW*, 1987, p, 2547. See also Klaus Vieweg, "Doping und Verbandsrecht," *NJW* 1991 p. 1511: "[muß] eine Abgrenzung vorgenommen werden zur – zulässigen – Zuführung solcher Substanzen, die medizinisch angezeigt ist. Hierbei handelt es sich zum einen um die sogenannte Substitution von Wirkstoffen wie Vitaminen, Elektrolyten und Spurenelementen sowie von Nährstoffen wie Kohlehydraten und Eiweiß. Zum anderen kann eine therapeutische Zuführung von Substanzen als zulässig bewertet werden, wenn es um die Heilung eines erkrankten oder verletzten Athleten geht."

"die Abgrenzung zwischen medizinisch indizierter Verabreichung von Pharmaka und Doping [...] in konkreten Einzalfall, insbesondere bei der Beweisführung, Probleme [mag] bereiten, im Grundsatz ist die Trennungslinie jedoch eindeutig zu ziehen: setzen sich Sportler extremen Leistungsanforderungen aus, die zu Gesundheitsgefährdungen oder -schädigungen führen, so ist auch die Medizin gefordert, werden hingegegen einem gesunden Sportler Mittel zur Leistungssteigerung verabreicht, wird gedopt; oder m.a.W. mit hilfe von Pharmaka darf ein Verlust an – individuell normaler – Leistung ausgeglichen, ein Zuwachs jedoch nicht gefördert werden."[275]

The substances concerned are, among others, ephedrine, phenylproponolamine and codeine, which can all be found in regular painkillers or cough remedies and which are usually available over the counter. The reason that these drugs appear on doping lists is that they are assumed to also have performance-enhancing qualities. The injection of certain anaesthetics – with the exception of cocaine – is also permitted, subject to certain conditions. Anaesthetics may only be injected locally (intra-articularly, not intra-vascularly). The use of these substances must also be medically accounted for and must be reported to the medical commission shortly after their administration. Usually, the class of conditionally prohibited substances also contains corticosteroids. These substances are medically prescribed as anti-inflammatory drugs and painkillers but have the additional quality of being able to induce euphoria. Corticosteroids may only be administered through inhalation or by means of an intra-articular and local injection.[276] As corticosteroids were used in various branches of sport for non-therapeutic reasons, they were placed on the doping lists. Beta-blocking drugs are also conditionally prohibited. They are therapeutic in cases of hypertensia, angina pectoris and migraine, but also work as sedatives. The UIPM, World Taekwondo Federation (WTF), FIBT, WCF and IIHF all unconditionally prohibited the use of beta-blockers, as opposed to the International Sport Shooting Federation (ISSF) and the FITA, of which one would have expected an unconditional prohibition.

The consumption of alcohol is usually not subject to restrictions, unless it is excessive. Still, the IOC has included alcohol as a conditionally prohibited substance.

---

[275] Linck (*supra* nt. 274) rather lightly sidestepped the various problems of an evidentiary nature in claiming that there is no real need for linking the doping definition to a doping list. "Wenn im folgende von Doping die Rede ist, zo wird darunter jede Zufuhr von Substanzen, insbesondere von medizinisch nicht indizierten Pharmaka zum Zwecke künstlicher Leistungssteigerung, verstanden, sofern mit ihnen – auch z.B. infolge von Neben- oder Folgewirkungen – in die köperliche Integrität von Sportlern eingegriffen wird; ob diese Substanzen in den Dopinglisten der Sportverbände enthalten sind, ist dabei unbeachtlich."

[276] Cf., Doping Regulations of AIBA, Art. III, sub B: "The AIBA Medical Commission has introduced mandatory reporting of athletes requiring corticosteroids by inhalation during competitions. Any team doctor wishing to administer corticosteroids by local or intra-articular injection, or by inhalation, to a competitor must give written notification to the Chairman of the AIBA Medical Commission or to the Chairman of the Medical Jury."

"In agreement with the International Sports Federations and the responsible authorities, tests may be conducted for ethanol. The results may lead to sanctions."

The UIPM permitted the use of alcohol subject to restrictions. The restrictions were not listed in its regulations and it is difficult to imagine a therapeutic reason for the consumption of alcohol which a doctor would support. The regulations did state that there would be tests for alcohol. Should the use of alcohol in the present-day pentathlon be considered a violation of the principles of fair play? Those who have been selected for testing are obliged to co-operate. "If the athlete refuses, he is guilty."[277] The WTF included alcohol in its "classes of drugs with certain restrictions" and further provided that "alcohol is not prohibited" and that "breath or blood-alcohol level may be determined on request." It would be understandable if a sport like crossbow shooting would consider alcohol a means of doping, because of its calming qualities. Still, the FITA did not list alcohol as unconditionally prohibited; "[...] tests may be conducted for ethanol. The results may lead to sanctions." The International Sailing Federation (ISAF) did not test for alcohol. "It is a sedative and will impair judgment, as such it is a danger to sailors when afloat." For the sake of the safety of the athletes the FIBT did conduct alcohol tests, but only "in case of justified suspicion and in accordance with item 7.2. of the Regulations." Item 7.2. provided that the analysis of the urine sample would take place in accordance with internationally recognised methods. For this reason, the FIBT also examined urine samples for traces of alcohol, but it did not perform breath or blood tests. The International Luge Federation (FIL) did not consider alcohol capable of enhancing athletic performance. "The FIL considers the use of such substances a significant personal danger to the competitor within the sport of luge and strongly advises their avoidance at all times." The FIS was the only IF to unconditionally prohibit the use of alcohol.

"Alcohol is prohibited, in all skiing events. Breath and/or blood alcohol levels may be determined at the request of the FIS Medical Committee. The FIS require a 'zero' level of alcohol during competition and positive results may lead to sanctions."

The provision in the IOC Medical Code concerning marijuana and hashish bore a marked resemblance to that concerning alcohol.

"In agreement with the International Sports Federations and the responsible authorities, tests may be conducted for cannabinoids (e.g. Marijuana, Hashish). The results may lead to sanctions."

---

[277] UIPM: Medical Rulebook, Anti-Doping Controls, 8. Alcohol Test, 8.1 and 8.2: "The test for alcohol is performed by a screening test of expired air, from a number of competitors selected at the direction of the UIPM medical and/or UIPM technical delegate during the shooting event. If the screening test is positive (over 0,1g/l), the male (female) competitor has to undergo taking of vein blood. The blood collection is obligatory. If the athlete refuses, he is guilty. If the result is again positive, the respective sanction in accordance with Rule 7.8 will be applied. The analysis of the blood sample will be conducted at a suitable laboratory in the host country in the presence of the doping control supervisor and/or a member of the UIPM Medical Committee and/or the UIPM Technical Delegate."

Some IFs only included marijuana and hashish in the class of substances which were prohibited subject to restrictions,[278] while other IFs merely repeated the IOC Medical Code's rule.[279] The UCI did not generally prohibit the use of marijuana, "except in the discipline "downhill" in MTB, where a sample would be declared positive as from the detection of more than 40 ng/ml." The ISAF allowed the use of marijuana in all its disciplines, but pointed out to the athletes that "in many countries possession is against the law. Sailors are warned that they may bring the regatta and organising authorities into disrepute if arrested by local police during an event." As it did with respect to alcohol, the FIL warned its athletes of the personal risk involved in smoking marijuana. The only IF to include the use of marijuana in its provisions concerning conditionally prohibited substances was the FINA.[280] Four IFs: the (International Gymnastics Federations) FIG, the IWF, the WCF and the FIS, included cannabinoids like marijuana and hashish in the class of unconditionally prohibited substances. The FIS established a threshold level:

> "Marijuana is prohibited in all skiing disciplines. The FIS accept a threshold level of 15 ng/ml for using gc/as, and levels of 15 ng/ml or above will be declared as a positive result. Positive results lead to sanctions."

If consent had been sought and given for the use of conditionally prohibited substances, their detection would not result in negative consequences for the athlete. Only a small number of IFs included a description of the doping offence in their regulations which specifically addressed the use of conditionally prohibited substances. Only athletes who did not report their use of these substances to the authorities on time or at all could be found guilty of a doping offence. A large number of IFs to include conditionally prohibited substances in their doping lists only distinguished between them and unconditionally prohibited substances insofar as the severity of the penalty was concerned. The general description of the doping offence would normally also apply to the conditionally prohibited substances. If we look at the different penalty norms it is notable that of the conditionally prohibited substances alcohol, marijuana and hashish were not typically mentioned.

The use of conditionally prohibited substances had to be reported during doping control by means of a specific form. Lehtinen had failed to mention in his FINA "Declaration of medication taken recently" that he had used Ventolin. Although it was known at the FINA that Lehtinen suffered from asthma and although he had completed the form truthfully at all previous doping controls, the FINA still instituted doping proceedings against him after he had tested positive for salbutamol, a substance present in Ventolin and appearing on the FINA doping list of condition-

[278] IBA and ISF.

[279] FITA and IIHF.

[280] FINA Doping Control, DC 9 Sanctions, DC 9.2, (d): "Sanctions shall include the following: [...] Ephedrine, phenylpropanolamine, caffeine (the level of caffeine must, however, be taken in consideration), cannabinoids (such as marijuana and hashish), and all other banned substances not otherwise set in DC 9.2 (a) through (c): First offence: [...]"

ally prohibited substances. The FINA Executive excluded Lehtinen for a period of two years. He appealed the decision before the CAS.[281] Based on the starting point that "the absence of a declaration does not in itself constitute a doping offence" and after the CAS had established that to Lehtinen the use of Ventolin is a necessity and that he had used the substance through inhalation alone, in the opinion of the CAS the

> "necessary prerequisites of a doping offence under the FINA doping rules have not been fulfilled in the present case. Consequently, no sanction should be imposed. Thus, the two year sanction imposed on L. must be lifted."[282]

One year after the *Lehtinen* case, the CAS was once more petitioned to decide on the unreported use of salbutamol. However, this case involving the New-Zealand water polo player Cullwick[283] is not relevant in the present context as it revolved around false information supplied by the national federation which had told Cullwick that Ventolin could be used without restrictions to relieve asthma.

The possibility of therapeutic use of certain substances is treated at length in Art. 4.4 WADC:

> "WADA shall adopt an International Standard for the process of granting therapeutic use exemptions.
> Each International Federation shall ensure, for international-level athletes or any other athlete who is entered in an international event, that a process is in place whereby athletes with documented medical conditions requiring the use of a prohibited substance or a prohibited method may request a therapeutic use exemption. Each National Anti-Doping Organization shall ensure, for all athletes within its jurisdiction that are not international-level athletes, that a process is in place whereby athletes with documented medical conditions requiring the use of a prohibited substance or a prohibited method may request a therapeutic use exemption. Such requests shall be evaluated in accor-

---

[281] CAS 95/142, 14-2-1996, *Lehtinen v. FINA*, Matthieu Reeb, ed., *Digest of CAS Awards 1986-1998* (Berne, Editions Stämpfli 1998) pp. 225-244.

[282] A first remarkable aspect is that the ground cited (ground 39) ends in the sentence "Under these circumstances there is no need to examine, whether the FINA doping rules themselves comply with the applicable (i.e. Swiss) law." (Cf., M. Beloff, T. Kerr, M. Demetriou: *Sports Law* (Oxford, Hart Publishing 1999) (Beloff 1999), p. 182, no. 7.28). Although the FINA was familiar with Lehtinen's ailment and knew of his use of Ventolin, the FINA instituted proceedings against him after he had forgotten to complete the requisite form only once. Equally remarkable, therefore, is the ground employed by the CAS in the event of his claim for "moral damages" against the FINA, in which it is stated that the FINA "has not committed any unlawful act by initiating a doping procedure when L. failed to declare his taking of Ventolin on the doping test form. Furthermore, the FINA Executive and the FINA Bureau did not act in bad faith or abusively when it decided against L. and imposed the sanction provided in the FINA rules. Therefore, the necessary prerequisites to award damages are not present." If the FINA, according to the CAS, had every right to institute proceedings against Lehtinen, then why did the CAS not rule against Lehtinen in the proceedings on the substance of the case?

[283] CAS 96/149, 13-3-1997, *Cullwick v. FINA*, Matthieu Reeb, ed., *Digest of CAS Awards 1986-1998* (Berne, Editions Stämpfli 1998) pp. 251-263.

dance with the International Standard on therapeutic use. International Federations and National Anti-Doping Organizations shall promptly report to WADA the granting of therapeutic use exemptions to any international-level athlete or national-level athlete that is included in his or her National Anti-Doping Organization's registered testing pool.

WADA, on its own initiative, may review the granting of a therapeutic use exemption to any international-level athlete or national-level athlete that is included in his or her National Anti-Doping Organization's Registered testing pool. Further, upon the request of any such athlete that has been denied a therapeutic use exemption, WADA may review such denial. If WADA determines that such granting or denial of a therapeutic use exemption did not comply with the International Standard for therapeutic use exemptions, WADA may reverse the decision."

The 2005 Prohibited List of the WADA under "Specified Substances" lists all doping substances which are prohibited conditionally.[284] The WADA stipulates that doping lists may designate as specified substances, "substances which are particularly susceptible to unintentional anti-doping rule violations because of their general availability in medicinal products or which are less likely to be successfully abused as doping agents." Pursuant to the WADC penalties for doping offences involving the use of specified substances can be mitigated if "the athlete can establish that the use of such a specified substance was not intended to enhance sport performance."

4.2. Doping methods

Doping lists differentiate between prohibited substances and prohibited methods. Methods are blood doping and all the pharmacological, chemical and physical manipulations already mentioned above. As opposed to the description of the offence involving the use of prohibited substances, the description of the doping offence involving the use of prohibited methods remained unchanged until the adoption of the WADC. Despite the fact that there was no reliable means of testing the IOC and the Olympic federations still included blood doping in their lists of prohibited methods. However, due to the lack of a reliable test, it was not possible to apply the strict liability regime to blood doping. This meant that fault liability was applicable. With the introduction of the WADC the situation changed, however. In Art. 2.2.1 the concept of a prohibited method is first mentioned: "The success or failure of the use of a prohibited method is not material. It is sufficient that the prohibited method was used or attempted to be used for an anti-doping rule violation to be committed." Blood doping is also a prohibited method: "Unless the act can be medically justified, the administration of blood or blood-related products to an athlete will be considered blood doping." In blood doping, an athlete's blood is taken some time before the game and is re-infused shortly before. This method of doping aims to not

---

[284] Ephedrine, L-methylamphetamine, methylephedrine; cannabinoids; all inhaled beta-2 antagonists, except clenbuterol; probenecid; all glucocorticosteroids; all beta-blockers and alcohol.

only increase the athlete's overall blood volume, but also his haemoglobin count, which will both increase the oxygen transporting capacity of his blood and the maximum oxygen intake.[285] The idea behind these manipulations is that the athlete will improve his performance during protracted exertion.[286]

Gene doping is defined by the WADA as "the non-therapeutic use of cells, genes, genetic elements, or of the modulation of gene expression, having the capacity to enhance athletic performance."[287] Gene doping was on the IOC list from the beginning of 2003. The WADA includes gene doping in the doping list as of 2004.[288]

5. Conclusion

The different descriptions of the doping offence can be broken down into descriptions of the offence of the use of doping and descriptions of the offence of doping not involving use. The focus is primarily on the offence of use, i.e. on offences committed by the athletes themselves through their own actions. In addition some forms of ancillary doping offences, i.e. offences other than actual use, but committed by the athletes themselves, such as failing to report to doping control or refusing to undergo testing, confessing to doping, use of masking agents and methods, etc. are dealt with. Finally, there are non-use third-party offences whereby third parties in the doping use of others.

The definitions of doping in the various regulations at the same time contain the main elements of the doping offence. These elements together make up the description of the doping offence which indicates when the transgression of the primary norm is punishable. The descriptions are therefore the relevant formulation under disciplinary law of that primary norm; they are primary norms settled into concrete rules.

"Use" infractions

1. A handful of national or international federations prohibited the use of unspecified doping substances and methods, if such use was primarily intended to enhance athletic performance;

---

[285] The American cyclist Tyler Hamilton was the first athlete to test positive for a blood transfusion after winning the Olympic time trial gold medal on 18 August 2004. The IOC stated that the B sample had been destroyed by having been deep-frozen.

[286] E.g. erythropoietin (EPO) is a substance used in what is commonly known as "blood doping." It works by stimulating the production of red blood cells, which can enhance performance in endurance sports. See CAS CAS 2002/A/370, 29-11-2002, *Lazutina v. IOC*, Matthieu Reeb, ed., *Digest of CAS Awards III 2001-2003* (The Hague, Kluwer Law International 2004) pp. 273-285, ground 6.

[287] The WADC, The 2005 Prohibited List – International Standard.

[288] Prof. Dr. H.J. Haisma, *Genetische doping*. Met bijdragen van O. de Hon, P. Sollie en J. Vorstenbosch, Nederlands Centrum voor Dopingvraagstukken, Februari 2004: "It is unlikely that a method for detecting gene doping will be developed over the next few years. Either these methods would involve invasive action and offer only limited possibilities, or it would only be possible to use them with the full cooperation of many parties involved."

2. A larger number of federations prohibited the use of certain specified substances and methods;
3. Other federations prohibited the use of specified substances and methods if they enhanced performance; and
4. Some federations penalised the presence of specified substances in the athlete's body.

As the stakes in the business of sport increased, both commercially and in terms of prestige, and lawyers began to act as counsel to athletes who were suspected of the use of doping, the definitions mentioned under 1. were no longer sufficient. The vagueness of the concepts used meant that they were no match for the legal profession. The sports organisations needed to come up with a new design for the description in order not to be given the go-by in every doping trial. The new direction in design was found with the drawing up of lists specifically naming the substances and methods that were prohibited in the business of sport. Doping was now understood to mean the use of substances and methods appearing on the doping list.

In practice and over time the "referring" description also proved to be inadequate. Problems of an evidentiary nature were constantly causing trouble for the federation having to prove that the athlete was guilty of the act of doping. It became clear that in order to conclude that the act of doping was punishable it was not enough to show through doping analysis that that act had taken place. An additional shortcoming of the first generation descriptions of the doping offence, namely that the guilt or intent of the athlete had to be proven, remained unaddressed in the referring description of the doping offence. A description needed to be found which would make things easier from an evidentiary point of view for sports organisations that were involved in doping trials. The solution that a number of IFs came up with consisted of moving the gravamen in the description of the doping offence. Where the gravamen of earlier descriptions consisted of the act itself, it now came to consist of the discovery of the prohibited substance. The presence of a prohibited substance in the sample had to demonstrate that the athlete had committed an act of doping of which he was guilty *prima facie*. The description of the doping offence which applied until the acceptance of the WADC, for example, stipulated that "the offence of doping takes place when a prohibited substance is found to be present within an athlete's body tissue or fluids" and that the athlete was presumed guilty of the offence of doping, if the analysis showed a positive result.

The strict liability definition causes the athlete involved to be found guilty *prima facie* of a doping offence whenever a prohibited substance has been shown to be or have been present in his body. However, as it not possible to conclude from the presence or absence of certain prohibited substances that a certain prohibited method or technique was used, this element of the description of the doping offence remained within the regime of fault liability. For this reason, a large number of international federations decided to no longer take the use or administration of certain substances as the starting point in their doping definitions. For these federations, doping was only the presence in an athlete's body of prohibited substances. Only a limited number of national federations and central doping committees proceeded to include a definition of doping in their doping regulations which established strict liability upon testing positive.

Many sports administrators applying the strict liability regime were of the opinion that they were no longer required to show intent before they could impose sanctions upon the athlete. They considered that the principal offence of doping consisted merely of the finding of the presence of a prohibited substance in an athlete's body tissue or fluids. The rule did not provide that an athlete must have taken the substance deliberately and therefore created an offence of strict liability in the sense that the athlete's intent was completely irrelevant. However, the CAS ruled otherwise on the requirements for proving a doping offence. In *Bernhard v. ITU* the Panel argued that if a sports-governing body opted to sanction the consequences of the unlawful act rather than the unlawful act itself, it first had to establish the causal relationship between the unlawful act and the consequences in a manner that was completely clear and incontestable. Generally speaking, if we look at tort law, we also find that the causal link between the unlawful act and its consequences is not automatically assumed, but requires proof. Even in cases of strict liability – where guilt does not need to be proven – the causal relationship between the unlawful act and its consequences remains an element requiring proof by the party invoking liability. This should therefore be even more the case in matters dealt with by disciplinary law, with its quasi-criminal law character. The Panel accordingly considered it unacceptable if the concept of strict liability were to be applied more strictly against an athlete accused of a doping offence than it would have been in a case under private law in which the strict liability concept is firmly rooted. This led the Panel to rule that the causal link between the unlawful act and the consequences still required proving. In other words, although the strict liability rule means that sports-governing bodies do not need to prove guilt (i.e. that the athlete was guilty of the fact that a banned substance was present in his body), the rule still means that sports-governing bodies have to prove that the presence of the substance was the result of use by the athlete.

After establishing that a doping offence had in fact occurred, tribunals had to turn to step two, where the burden of proof shifted from the sports-governing body to the athlete.[289] At this stage, the athlete was given the opportunity to raise a defence, so that the tribunal could decide on the (severity) of the applicable sanction, bearing in mind the principle of proportionality, provided the sports-governing body in question applied a flexible sanctioning system.

---

[289] See CAS 98/208, 22-12-1998, *Wang Lu Na, Cai Hui Jue, Zhgang Yi, Wang Wei v. FINA*, Matthieu Reeb, ed., *Digest of CAS Awards II 1998-2000* (The Hague, Kluwer Law International 2002) pp. 234-254, ground 5.10: "If the presence of a prohibited substance is established to the high degree of satisfaction required by the seriousness of the allegation, then the burden shifts to the competitor to show why, in the case of a diuretic, the maximum sanction should not be imposed. The Panel repeats that under the new FINA rules it is only at the level of *sanction* not of finding of innocence or guilt, that the concept of shifting the burden becomes relevant at all. And it is only at this juncture too that questions of intent become relevant."

Ancillary doping infractions

Many national and international federations also explicitly considered various of-fences as doping that were not actually acts of doping in themselves, but were related to the act of doping. Among these were: failing to report to doping control, refusing to submit to doping control, and admitting to having used a prohibited substance or method.

Intentional doping
The introduction of the OMADC also saw the introduction of the concept of inten-tional doping. It remained unclear, however, how intentional doping actually dif-fered from doping as it was understood at the time. Because of the evidentiary problems that sports-governing bodies had encountered in the past when trying to prove that athletes who had tested positive had intended to use doping to enhance their performance, the anti-doping rules and regulations establishing what consti-tutes a doping offence gradually shifted away from specified actions to mere fac-tual findings – i.e., was a banned substance found in the athlete's urine sample or not – resulting in the introduction of a strict liability approach. The mere finding of a banned substance rendered the athlete fully liable. This made any discussion of intent or guilt superfluous. With the introduction of the concept of intentional dop-ing, however, this discussion appeared to have regained relevance.

It begged the question of whether the IOC was not raking up old and awkward matters? Old, because the evidentiary problems involved in proving intent had al-ready led to the development of the strict liability approach and awkward, because "establishing proof of such intention will clearly be difficult, and for that reason it is necessary to establish regulations governing it."[290] New regulations, however, did not appear to be necessary. Although the OMADC did not expressly say so, it is quite obvious that intentional doping had to be considered something different from doping as defined in Article 2 of Chapter II. Apparently, intentional doping was an aggravated form of doping. In the context of the present research intentional doping is relevant because various sports federations within the EU used to follow the IOC's lead and refer to its regulations concerning doping. The Finnish Anti-doping Committee and the *Deutscher Sportbund*, for example, had both included provi-sions in their regulation to the effect that their concept of doping would be defined by the IOC rules.

"Non-use" infractions

Many doping regulations of international sports organisations considered the inter-vention of third parties in the doping offence to be a doping offence of its own accord. A third party may be guilty of complicity to, condoning or counselling of

---

[290] Mbaye in his introduction of 30 September 1998.

the use of doping by an athlete. Federations that equated assistance with doping would likewise apply the sanctions by which the "ordinary" doping offence was punishable to this offence. Other federations included a separate description of the offence of third-party assistance in doping.

Sports organisation may punish third parties assisting athletes in using doping when these third parties are within the scope of the organisation's authority. However, dope dealers usually operate outside this scope which means that their punishment will not be for the organisation to decide upon either. Besides, sports organisation will also lack the necessary facilities for investigation. Nevertheless, a number of federations included rules in their regulations which threatened dealers, distributors and sellers with sanctions.

At the national level, there were but few sports organisations to include relevant provisions concerning trafficking in doping substances. The ones that did were mainly British or Irish. Only two continental federations, one German and one Dutch, also penalised trafficking

Doping substances and methods

Doping lists differentiate between prohibited substances and prohibited methods. Methods are blood doping and all pharmacological, chemical and physical manipulations involved in doping. As opposed to the description of the offence involving the use of prohibited substances, the description of the doping offence involving the use of prohibited methods remained unchanged until the adoption of the WADC. Despite the fact that there was no reliable means of testing the IOC and the Olympic federations still included blood doping in their lists of prohibited methods. However, due to the lack of a reliable test, it was not possible to apply the strict liability regime to blood doping. This meant that fault liability was applicable.

CHAPTER 3
THE PUNISHABILITY OF THE ACT OF DOPING

1. INTRODUCTION

An act of doping only becomes an offence when it falls within the scope of the description of the doping offence, when it is illegal and when the offender can be held liable for the act. Here, the focus shall be on punishability. According to Enschedé,[291] if one asks "whether a person is acting illegally, then one asks whether this person's behaviour either corresponds to or conflicts with a rule that applies to him, i.e. with a material rule directed at him. Given that by the nature of things it does not make sense to punish behaviour that is not illegal, the punishability of the behaviour is a requirement for the punishability of the offender." Vermunt[292] cites the German philosopher of law Binding, who considers general illegality to consist of "alles einem subjektiven Recht widerstreitende Verhalten oder Geschehen." Remmelink[293] speaks of the non-punishability of an act due to a lack of criminal law injustice. This is what he reserves the term "material illegality" for. The difference between formal and material illegality is made as follows by German legal philosopher Liszt as quoted by Vermunt:[294]

"Formell rechtswidrig ist die Handlung als Übertretung einer staatlichen Norm, eines Gebotes oder Verbotes der Rechtsordnung. Materiell rechtswidrig ist der Angriff auf die durch die Rechtsnormen geschützten Lebensinteressen des einzelnen oder der Gesammtheit, mithin als die Verletzung oder Gefährdung eines Rechtsgutes."

A soldier at war who shoots an enemy soldier cannot be prosecuted under Article 287 of the Dutch Criminal Code, now that this act is not punishable under these circumstances (not illegal), even though all the objective elements of the offence have been fulfilled and the soldier is guilty in respect of his act (Cf., "schuldhafte Normübertretung").[295] This chapter also deals with the absence of material illegal-

---

[291] Enschedé 1974 (supra nt. 33), pp. 132-133.
[292] D.J.P.M. Vermunt, Onrecht en wederrechtelijkheid in de strafrechtsdogmatiek, PhD 1984 (Arnhem, Gouda Quint 1984) p. 201.
[293] J.R. Remmelink, Mr. D. Hazewinkel-Suringa's Inleiding tot de studie van het Nederlandse Strafrecht (Arnhem, Gouda Quint 1994) (Remmelink 1994) p. 247.
[294] Vermunt 1984) (supra nt. 292), p. 203.
[295] Pursuant to Art. 30 of the Statute of the International Criminal Court (Part 3. General Principles of Criminal Law) shall be criminally responsible and liable for punishment "[...] for a crime within the jurisdiction of the Court only if the material elements are committed with intent and knowledge." [emphasis added].

ity based on the interpretation of altered group or scientific norms. The absence of material illegality as a result of the existence of an exceptional situation, such as the abovementioned state of war, does not occur in disciplinary doping law and will therefore not be considered in this chapter.

In disciplinary doping law, illegality is not an element of the offence in the sense that every time that a material rule is breached the sports organisation must prove the illegality of the challenged act. Illegality should rather be regarded as a characteristic, an aspect, of the doping offence. Just as liability is presumed in the case of strict liability (which will be dealt with in the next chapter) the illegality of the act of doping is also presumed as soon as the sports organisation has proven the objective elements of the offence. In the case of the presumption of liability, the defence cannot be directed against the actual liability, but may only concern the severity of the penalty. The defence that there is no illegality may be put forward as soon as an athlete is involved in a doping trial. If the athlete is able to prove that illegality is lacking or that his act was justified, he/she will be acquitted due to the non-punishability of the act.[296]

The issue of punishability may be divided into two parts. The first part concerns "technical" aspects, such as gaps in the chain of custody (Section 2), while the other part concerns "legal" aspects, such as the non-appearance of a substance on the doping list[297] (Section 3).

2.   DEFECTS IN THE "CHAIN OF CUSTODY"

At the doping control station, the athlete's urine sample is split in two and each portion is decanted into a leak-proof bottle. The bottles are each given a unique number and are then sealed. Then they are each placed in a container – the Envopak – which is also sealed and labelled with the unique number. The samples are then transported to a laboratory where they are stored until they are analysed. All these steps have to be documented in order to ensure that the samples that are analysed truly do contain the relevant athlete's urine. If the number on the Envopak corresponds to the number which the laboratory was given and if the number on the bottle corresponds to the number on the form, then it will be virtually impossible for the athlete to contend that the sample does not contain his/her urine. Only if the sports organisation is able to produce a clear paper chain of custody, the positive outcome of the analysis may be accepted. However, not one set of anti-doping regulations establishes that the sports organisation has to prove the technical chain of custody. It is the task of the sports organisation to prove that the sample is that of

---

[296] Remmelink 1994 (*supra* nt. 293), p. 249.
[297] According to the CAS in CAS 99/A/234 & CAS 99/A/235, 29-2-2000, *David Meca-Medina v. FINA & Igor Majcen v. FINA*, such arguments may "provide a defence to the original charge or result in the appellant's entire exculpation."

the athlete in question.[298] In the *Smith-de Bruin* case[299] the term "chain of custody" was understood to comprise several stages, namely the "collecting, transporting and testing" of an athlete's samples. In the Quigley case[300] the CAS spoke of "sampling/custody/testing procedures," whereby the term "chain of custody" is reserved for the documented procedure at the laboratory. Similarly in the Korda case:[301] "sample collection, chain of custody, laboratory analysis." In the *Foschi* case[302] the CAS considered that "the chain of custody documents demonstrate that from the moment Appellant's samples arrived in the UCLA Laboratory they were both kept under control." In the *Meca-Medina* case and in the *Smith-de Bruin* case, several stages were dealt with separately, although in the latter case all under the heading of "chain of custody." In the collection, transport and analysis of the sample many things may of course go wrong, as Morton-Hooper[303] not without a touch of irony describes:

> "We are talking about carrying out tests on one of the body's waste products. These samples are collected often by unqualified people in chaotic circumstances, transported across national boundaries and arriving at the laboratory very often without any kind of proper manifest evidencing what is called the chain of custody, that is the documentary proof of continuity of evidence without which the identification and integrity of the sample cannot be guaranteed. Things can and do go wrong. When you are talking about the mere presence of a banned substance constituting an offence, even prima facie evidence of an offence, how would you know that the risk of contamination has been controlled and minimised with the same degree of skill and care that our mad scientists use in their gleaming temples of high tech."

At every stage of the process starting at the doping control station and ending in the laboratory it is possible that mistakes are made. If these mistakes are such as to invalidate the sample, the sports organisation will no longer be able to use the

---

[298] M. Gay has said (Gay 1991, *supra* nt. 129, p. 68) "The effect of accepting a technical custody doctrine is to introduce an unwarranted and unmeritorious technicality into the area of doping control. For if this approach is accepted, then an athlete is entitled to be exonerated despite the fact that there is no evidence of tampering and no real doubt that the sample is that of the athlete. The effect of this would be simply to bring the sport into disrepute and to send a message to athletes and the public that athletics is not seriously interested in stamping out drugs. Therefore I believe that while it is important that athletes have the safeguard of knowing that the sample tested by the laboratory is really their sample, athletes should not be exonerated merely for alleged technical breaches in the chain of custody."

[299] CAS 98/211, 7-6-1999, *Smith-De Bruin v. FINA*, Matthieu Reeb, ed., *Digest of CAS Awards II 1998-2000* (The Hague, Kluwer Law International 2002) pp. 255-273, ground 10.5.

[300] CAS 94/129, 23-5-1995, *USA Shooting & Quigley v. UIT*, Matthieu Reeb, ed., *Digest of CAS Awards 1986-1998* (Berne, Editions Stämpfli 1998) pp. 187-204, ground 39.

[301] CAS 98/223, 31-8-1999, *Korda v. ITF*, Matthieu Reeb, ed., *Digest of CAS Awards II 1998-2000* (The Hague, Kluwer Law International 2002) pp. 345-360, ground 37.

[302] CAS 96/156, 6-10-1997, *Jessica K. Foschi v. FINA*, ground 6.2.2.

[303] Tony Morton-Hooper: *Have we created a Monster? – a brief look at some striking features of anti-doping rules and procedures*, *Drugs in Sport – A Time for Re-evaluation?* A symposium on Legal and Ethical Issues 23-4-1999 (Morton-Hooper 1999).

sample's final test results as proof that a doping offence was committed. The athlete has every interest in being able to show that at some point between the turning in of the sample and its analysis at the laboratory an incident occurred to frustrate the furnishing of proof by the sports organisation prosecuting the athlete. In principle, major gaps in the chain of custody should lead to a lack of evidence. The punishability of a possible doping offence is thereby also rendered lacking and this should lead to the dismissal of the case.

Below, the various stages between the doping control and the sample analysis will be discussed separately in accordance with relevant judgments of the CAS.

2.1. Mistakes made during the doping control

When a prohibited substance was found in a horse's sample, the FEI, based on its anti-doping regulations, could maintain the rebuttable presumption that the person responsible for the horse was guilty of a doping offence. The presumption could be lifted by proof of the opposite. The person responsible for the horse could also demonstrate that the doping control or analysis "was invalidated in the sense that the FEI Veterinary Regulations, which establish extremely precise rules in this regard, were not respected." The presumption of the liability of the responsible person was only considered lifted if the alleged error was proven and could have influenced the test result. The two bottles containing the B sample had not been sealed in the manner stipulated by the FEI Veterinary Regulations, allowing for the possibility that the bottles were no longer airtight.

> "It is therefore not possible to exclude definitely the possibility of manipulation and thus contamination of the contents of the two jars by an external substance. On this point, doubt exists which must be to the benefit of the appellant.
> Indeed, it follows, from the final paragraph of article 1024 of the Veterinary Regulations that, in the case where a confirmatory analysis is performed, for there to be cause to apply a sanction, the analysis of the 'B' sample must confirm the positive result of the analysis of the 'A' sample, which cannot be the case unless all the provisions of Annex III of the Veterinary Regulations have been scrupulously observed, in such a way as to eliminate any possibility of manipulation. The appeal by the appellant must therefore be upheld and the decision by the FEI Judicial Committee of 3rd June 1991 must be quashed."[304]

In the *Meca-Medina v. FINA* case[305] the athletes listed numerous violations of the rules concerning the selection of doping control participants, the gathering of the samples, the timing of the control, the arrangement of the room used for the control, the conduct of the staff, etc. These alleged breaches were disputed by the official in

---

[304] CAS 91/56, 25-6-1992, *S. v. FEI*, Matthieu Reeb, ed., *Digest of CAS Awards 1986-1998* (Berne, Editions Stämpfli 1998) pp. 93-103, ground 7.

[305] CAS 99/A/234 & CAS 99/A/235, 29-2-2000, *David Meca-Medina v. FINA & Igor Majcen v. FINA*.

charge of the doping controls. According to his report, the doping procedures had been carried out under the usual circumstances.

"It is not necessary for the Panel to comment on all these criticisms, some of which at least were palpably ill-founded,[306] nor to resolve such conflicts of evidence. The Panel is entirely satisfied that (i) the samples collected and subsequently analysed were the Appellants" samples (indeed, the Panel repeat, the Appellants acknowledged as much) (ii) the samples were collected in a manner which guaranteed their integrity.
Moreover, the Appellants in no instance specify to what extent the many defects they detail, (assuming for the purpose of discussion that they would be established), would cast doubt on the results of the test of samples they expressly admit to be theirs. Only defects which are likely to cast a genuine doubt on the results may be a ground not to rely on sample analysis results (see DC 1.6). The Appellants signed the declaration acknowledging that they 'approved the testing procedure' and left the box 'remarks' just below their signatures completely blank. In the Panel's judgment this effectively estops them from raising these complaints. The Panel find unconvincing their explanation that they wished to terminate the procedure as soon as possible. Those competitors who do not make use of opportunities designed to provide protection for them have only themselves to blame for the consequences of such failure."[307]

Not only did the athletes' arguments fail to impress the CAS, they were also too late in bringing them forward. However, even if the complaints had been voiced on time, they would still not have been processed unless they could have elicited doubt concerning the outcome of the analysis which would still have had to be carried out.
In the *Smith-De Bruin v. FINA* case the CAS accepted the evidence provided by the doping controllers (Mr and Mrs Guy) that the samples had been stored securely at all times. Smith had argued that leaving the samples in the fridge for a weekend had been an act of carelessness on the part of the controllers. The CAS failed to see why this was so.

"Who knew of the sample's whereabouts or could have had access to a private fridge other than the custodians themselves? Moreover, although the Guys could not recollect consistently the one with the other precisely on which shelf in the fridge the sample was placed, both assure us that, come Monday morning, it had not been moved from where it had been originally placed. We accept that evidence."[308]

In a CAS case decided in 2004[309] swimmer A. contended that she, while in the process of delivering her urine sample, had briefly left the toilet of the doping sta-

[306] It is claimed, for example, that the Appellants were not asked to identify themselves: one then wonders how their passport numbers came to be recorded on the forms.
[307] CAS 99/A/234 & CAS 99/A/235, 29-2-2000, *David Meca-Medina v. FINA & Igor Majcen v. FINA*, ground 7.3-7.4.
[308] CAS 98/211, 7-6-1999, *Smith-De Bruin v. FINA*, Matthieu Reeb, ed., *Digest of CAS Awards II 1998-2000* (The Hague, Kluwer Law International 2002) pp. 255-273, ground 11.3.
[309] CAS 2003/A/510, 15-1-2004, *A. v. Confederaçào Brasiliera de Desportos Aquàticos (CBDA)* & CAS 2003/A/514, *FINA v. A.*

tion to speak to her coach and drink some water and that her sample had not been sealed. In the second place, she argued that the sample that was analysed did not contain her urine. The CAS Panel concluded that the first defect adduced by A. did not lead to the invalidity of the testing procedure. The sample could have been invalidated if it had been proven that someone had entered the toilet during A.'s brief absence. However, A. had not furnished any evidence to that effect. Under these circumstances the CAS held that the chain of custody had not been breached. A. was furthermore also unable to demonstrate her second claim.

2.2.   Mistakes made during the transport of the sample

In the event that during the transport of the samples from the control post to the laboratory problems occur which affect the samples" integrity so that a correct analysis can no longer be performed, the sports organisation will be unable to succeed in proving that a doping offence has been committed. Meca-Medina and Majcen considered the time which it had taken to transport the samples from Salvador de Bahia via Sao Paulo to the laboratory in Montreal to be excessively long and therefore suspect. The doping control had taken place on 31 January and the samples were taken to Sao Paulo the next day. From there, UPS transported the samples to Canada where they were delivered to the laboratory on 10 February. The CAS held that the transport had been documented correctly. Why the transport took such a long time and whether the samples suffered as a result partly depends on the subjective assessment of the CAS: "Brazil is a very large country: the journey from Bahia to Sao Paulo necessarily takes time. Moreover, apparently, some delay occurred in the customs clearance process upon arrival in Canada." This does not appear to be a very strong argument, as of the ten days it took to transport the samples only two had been needed for transport within Brazil. The CAS found a way out by pointing out that the athletes had failed to indicate in what way the time that had passed could have influenced the validity of the analysis. The athletes had furthermore signed forms indicating their satisfaction with the integrity of the B samples to be analysed.

> "There was, according to Professor Ayotte's oral evidence, no evidence of contamination by bacterial growth in the samples such as would suggest that they had been adversely affected in transit. She said that the admitted absence of gravity/ph records on the doping control forms was not relevant and the Panel neither heard nor read any evidence which undermined that proposition."[310]

Now that nothing could be found wrong with the samples, it was possible to perform a completely valid analysis whose outcome could be used by the FINA in evidence to complete its proof of the offence.

---

[310] CAS 99/A/234 & CAS 99/A/235, 29-2-2000, *David Meca-Medina v. FINA & Igor Majcen v. FINA*, ground 7.8.

Smith-De Bruin pointed out to the CAS that during a previous transport by DHL the samples had gone missing for a fortnight. For her, this was reason to consider the transport of her samples to the laboratory by the same carrier as "suspect and insecure." This was evidently a weak argument and the CAS did not expend many words considering it.

> "DHL is a carrier of international reputation. We see no reason to assume that the sample, which arrived timeously on this occasion, was not in DHL's custody through-out. IDTM has since enquired of DHL whether it could confirm that there was no de-parture from proper practice in relation to this sample; in response, a letter from DHL to this effect was supplied to us."[311]

2.3. Mistakes made during the analysis of the sample

In the event that gaps are discovered in the documentation of the manner of storage or transport of the samples or of any other act performed in relation to these samples, they can no longer be deemed suitable for demonstrating an offence. The IOC Medical Code with respect to the chain of custody determined that:

> "Proper Chain of Custody control shall always be enforced during all testing and specimen handling. Only authorized personnel may handle specimens to be tested and they shall sign chain of custody forms to document when specimens are in their pos-session. Authorized technicians shall sign chain of custody forms and be responsible for each urine specimen to be tested."[312]

In *Foschi v. FINA* the swimmer involved attempted to convince the CAS that mis-takes had been made at the laboratory, simply because mistakes are often made in such institutions.

> "It is the Panel's view that laboratory error has not been established [...] because [...] the general suggestion that laboratory error is always a possibility and more likely than commonly believed is no evidence that a laboratory error was made in this particular case."[313]

Given the provisions contained in most doping regulations concerning the chain of custody it is extremely difficult for the defence to show that gaps have occurred in this chain and that these have affected the sample's integrity. In DC 8.1 of the FINA it is provided with respect to this chain of custody that:

---

[311] CAS 98/211, 7-6-1999, *Smith-De Bruin v. FINA*, Matthieu Reeb, ed., *Digest of CAS Awards II 1998-2000* (The Hague, Kluwer Law International 2002) pp. 255-273, ground 11.5.

[312] IOC Medical Code Appendix D, of which point 1.1(a) establishes that "the laboratory must have written procedures designed to maintain control and accountability from the receipt of urine specimens until testing is completed, results are reported and while specimens are in storage."

[313] CAS 96/156, 6-10-1997, *Jessica K. Foschi v. FINA*, ground 12.3.6.

"Analysis of all samples shall be done in laboratories accredited by the IOC. Such laboratories shall conclusively be deemed to have conducted tests and analysis of samples in accordance with a higher scientific standard and the results of such analysis shall conclusively be deemed to be scientifically correct. Such laboratories shall be presumed to have conducted custodial procedures in accordance with prevailing acceptable standards of care; this presumption can be rebutted by evidence to the contrary, there shall be no burden on the laboratory in the first instance to establish its procedures."

In April 1999 during a symposium on legal and ethical issues it was discussed who is responsible for proving that a doping offence has occurred. During this discussion Morten-Hooper commented that the laboratory report is often taken as proof guaranteeing the identity and integrity of the sample.

"On the face of it an offence has been committed. Now it is over to you. Can you do anything to rebut that evidence? It gets pretty tricky. Buried deep in the IOC Medical Code is this gem:

'Laboratories accredited by the IOC shall conclusively be deemed to have conducted tests and analyses of samples in accordance with the highest scientific standards and the results of such an analysis shall conclusively be deemed to be scientifically correct.'

It gets worse:

'Laboratories accredited by the IOC are presumed to have conducted testing and custodial procedures in accordance with prevailing and acceptable standards of care. The presumption can be rebutted by evidence to the contrary but the IOC accredited laboratory shall have no onus in the first instance to show that it conducted the procedures other than in accordance with its customary practices.'

So you are two nil down and you haven't even touched the ball,"[314]

Morton-Hooper concluded. The CAS[315] admitted that the wording of the above-cited provision of the FINA (when read out of context) gives the impression that an analysis by an accredited laboratory is almost impossible to challenge. However, the CAS suggested that the provision should be read against the background of the appeal provisions of DC 8.7, which clearly allow the athlete to show that the urine was contaminated or that the analysis was performed incorrectly. The CAS then assessed the complaints concerning the accuracy of the analyses performed on the samples of Meca-Medina and Majcen in accordance with the manner in which it considered that the provision had to be read.

"The Panel have noted that all the dealings of the laboratory are documented for both samples (the samples are referred initially by their lab codes and then by the original sample codes, this not to confuse the parties attending the 'B' tests). They detect no

---

[314] Morton-Hooper 1999 (*supra* nt. 203).
[315] CAS 99/A/234 & CAS 99/A/235, 29-2-2000, *David Meca-Medina v. FINA & Igor Majcen v. FINA*, ground 8.2.

inadequacy or unpropriety in that documentation. The chain of custody is therefore complete and satisfactory. DC 1.6 is in any event in play and there has been no sufficient identification by the Appellants of how any alleged departure from the procedures cast 'genuine doubt' on the reliability of any finding."[316]

Upon reading these considerations one cannot but receive the impression that the athlete is put at a disadvantage by the disciplinary tribunal which appears to take a rather different view of the matter: "two nil down" indeed.

In *Korda v. ITF*[317] the CAS considered that most complaints concerning laboratory procedures have to fail unless in a given case there is reason to believe that the procedure has unduly affected the identification of prohibited substances. As an aside, it should be noted here that the defence is only very rarely given access to the full laboratory report. Any attack on the chain of custody at the laboratory will therefore often have the nature of a "fishing expedition."[318]

"Any deviation or deviations from the anti-doping control procedures including, but not limited to, sample collection, chain-of-custody or laboratory analysis, do not invalidate any finding, procedure, decision or positive test result unless that deviation or deviations raises a material doubt as to the reliability of the finding, procedure, decision or positive test result."

Smith-De Bruin put forward an argument concerning the lack of due care on the part of the laboratory. In the briefest of terms laden with condescension the CAS dealt with this argument without entering into the merits.

"At this juncture, the Appellant faced the high hurdle of the presumption of regularity embodied in the FINA Rule DC 6.1. It seems to us that such presumption is not disturbed by the astute tactics, employed by Appellant, of first compelling the laboratory to produce documents which it is not normally obliged to produce, and then suggesting that not all documents evidencing the location of samples on a day-by-day and hour-by-hour basis had been produced, thereby suggesting that there was – or may have been – a break in the chain of custody."[319]

---

[316] *Idem*, ground 8.3.

[317] CAS 98/223, 31-8-1999, *Korda v. ITF*, Matthieu Reeb, ed., *Digest of CAS Awards II 1998-2000* (The Hague, Kluwer Law International 2002) pp. 345-360, ground 37.

[318] In CAS 94/129, 23-5-1995, *USA Shooting & Quigley v. UIT*, Matthieu Reeb, ed., *Digest of CAS Awards 1986-1998* (Berne, Editions Stämpfli 1998) pp. 187-204, ground 39, the CAS wondered: "Does every athlete found by his federation to have tested positive for a banned substance have the absolute right to demand the production of detailed laboratory documentation establishing beyond doubt that every aspect of the sampling/custody/testing procedure has been followed to the letter?" The CAS then evaded the question by observing that "this is not a question on which this Panel is required to rule in order to resolve this case [...] nor will it make such a ruling." In CAS 96/156, 6-10-1997, *Jessica K. Foschi v. FINA*, ground 12.3.6. the CAS considered: "the fact that the [...] laboratory did not produce all of its documents relating to the Appellant's 'B' test does not alter the clear findings stated in the documents actually produced."

[319] CAS 98/211, 7-6-1999, *Smith-De Bruin v. FINA*, Matthieu Reeb, ed., *Digest of CAS Awards II 1998-2000* (The Hague, Kluwer Law International 2002) pp. 255-273, ground 11.6.

Only very rarely is an athlete given the opportunity to rely on a laboratory error invalidating the outcome of the test.

> "A prime example of this was the case of Trine Solberg, a Norwegian athlete who was found positive after a drug test in the European cup. The 'A' sample undoubtedly showed the presence of en anabolic steroid, the 'B' sample seemed also to do this and the case was reported as a positive. In the course of the review of the analytical material on the 'B' sample it became obvious that it was by no means clear that the 'B' sample had confirmed the presence of the substance found in the 'A' sample. As a result of this, unilaterally, and without pressure from the athlete, the IAAF reached a decision that the positive could not be relied upon and lifted the athlete's suspension."[320]

In brief, once a laboratory analysis of the A and B sample has signified that the samples contain prohibited substances, the prosecuting body, the sports organisation or the anti-doping agency in principle has all the evidence it needs to prove that a doping offence has been committed. The athlete is given a chance to prove that in the period between the collection of the sample and its eventual analysis an incident has occurred that affects the sample's integrity to such an extent that the analysis can no longer yield proof of a doping offence. If the athlete is successful in his/her defence the case against him/her must be dismissed. However, it has emerged that so far athletes have never – or only very rarely – been able to undermine the chain of custody.

The chances that the (formal) illegality of an alleged doping offence can be removed by pointing out that the substance found in the sample does not appear on a doping list or that the amount found remains below the threshold level are far greater, as will be discussed next.

3.   ABSENCE OF FORMAL ILLEGALITY

In the practice of disciplinary doping law cases have occurred where sports organisations imposed sanctions on an athlete for a doping offence for which he/she was held liable, while subsequently it emerged before a higher instance that the athlete's actions could not be deemed illegal. Three situations may be distinguished in which an athlete can successfully rely on absence of illegality:

– The athlete made it sufficiently clear beforehand that he was using a conditionally prohibited substance;
– The athlete used a substance that does not appear on the doping list; and
– The athlete's body produced the prohibited substances endogenously.

---

[320] Gay 1991 (*supra* nt. 129), p. 69.

3.1. Use of conditionally prohibited substances

Several substances appear on doping lists that are prohibited in principle, but whose detection in a sample does not automatically lead to a doping offence if certain conditions are fulfilled. The substances in question belong to "classes of drugs subject to certain restrictions." Firstly, these substances must have been prescribed by a doctor and, secondly, the competent authorities must have been informed of their use prior to the competition, while, thirdly, these substances may only be used in a certain way. In the next chapter, we will see that one athlete, Mr Cullwick, was found to have committed a doping offence, because he had failed to inform the medical authorities beforehand of the fact that he used Ventomil inhalers. As Cullwick had been incorrectly informed by his own national federation and therefore found himself in a position of excusable error (technical breach only) the penalty imposed by the FINA was reversed, even though he was held liable for a doping offence.

The starting point in *Lehtinen v. FINA*[321] was almost identical to that in *Cullwick v. FINA*. Lehtinen also suffered from asthma and he also fought the disease under medical supervision by using Ventolin inhalers. The difference with the *Cullwick* case is that Lehtinen forgot to indicate his use of Ventolin on the doping control form. Cullwick had also omitted to inform the authorities of his use of salbutamol, but he had been under the impression that he did not need to inform them. An additional factor to Lehtinen's advantage was that the medical authorities knew that he suffered from asthma and that from the beginning of Lehtinen's sporting career the competent medical authorities had been repeatedly informed of his medication which contained salbutamol. At previous doping controls, Lehtinen had always notified the authorities of his medication and he had never tested positive. Given all this information that was known to the FINA it is remarkable that this sports organisation after having identified traces of salbutamol in Lehtinen's urine sample nevertheless proceeded to prosecute him for the use of doping. After the FINA's Medical Committee had recommended that Lehtinen be sent a "warning letter" the Honorary Secretary of the FINA sent Lehtinen's national federation the following fax:

> "Please be informed that the FINA Executive, in accordance with FINA Rule MED 4.17.4.1, has sanctioned [L.] of the [national] Swimming Association with two years' suspension for the positive result of the banned substance salbutamol found at the occasion of FINA out-of-competition doping control."

Lehtinen's national federation appealed against this decision to the FINA Bureau. The notice of appeal in which the facts and circumstances were once more set out ended with the remark "that Lehtinen cannot be punished according to existing rules and regulations." The Bureau subsequently informed the national federation by fax of the following:

---

[321] CAS 95/142, 14-2-1996, *Lehtinen v. FINA*, Matthieu Reeb, ed., *Digest of CAS Awards 1986-1998* (Berne, Editions Stämpfli 1998) pp. 225-244.

"Please be informed that your appeal against the FINA Executive decision of 23 June 1995 to suspend you for two years starting from 16 March 1995 has been rejected by the FINA Bureau in a mail vote concluded on 27 July."

Lehtinen consequently appealed against both FINA decisions to the CAS. The FINA argued that Lehtinen had not informed the medical authorities as required by the FINA Guidelines of his use of salbutamol and had not indicated the use of this substance on the "Declaration of medication taken recently" form which he had had to complete as part of the doping control.

"According to FINA, these duties of notification and declaration must be strictly followed. Otherwise, the detection of salbutamol is considered a definitive case of doping, since the principle of 'strict liability' excludes any excuses other than prior notification to the relevant medical authority and the 'declaration of medications taken' in the doping control form. Generally, FINA does not accept the defence that a banned substance has either been taken unintentionally or even given without the competitor's awareness."[322]

The FINA took the position that Lehtinen had committed a doping offence whereby intent or guilt were irrelevant as criteria for testing liability. The strict liability standard had to be upheld as an effective tool in the fight against doping. The FINA further pointed out that the CAS Panels "have always supported the application of such a 'strict liability' standard in other doping cases." However, the CAS considered:[323]

"In this case, the question of intent is not at stake: the appellant neither contests having taken salbutamol nor does he assert having taken it unintentionally. He asserts only that the mere identification of salbutamol in his urine sample is in itself not sufficient to constitute a doping offence."

As a fundamental rule, no sanctions are to be imposed if an offence has not been proven. The principle of strict liability did not relieve the FINA of the task of having to show a doping offence; "[...] the only issue is to determine under what conditions the identification of salbutamol may be considered as doping, and whether these conditions were met in L.'s case,"[324] according to the CAS. Salbutamol had a special position on the FINA doping list. The prohibition of its use was not absolute; inhaling was expressly allowed if such use had been notified to the authorities in advance. The CAS took the material rule as a starting point. This rule indicated that the identification of a prohibited substance was not in itself sufficient to establish a doping offence. The CAS phrased the issue of illegality as follows: "the mere presence of salbutamol is not conclusive evidence of a doping offence." It then recalled that inhaling was allowed for medical reasons: "This requirement is not

---

[322] *Idem.*
[323] *Idem*, ground 15.
[324] *Idem*, ground 16.

expressly mentioned in the FINA rules but it is a strict consequence of FINA Guidelines."[325] The use of salbutamol was only allowed – in other words: no doping offence would have been committed – in case the team physician reported this use to the medical authorities through prior notification. The notification contributed to the evidence that there was a medical need to use salbutamol. However, the notification was not conclusive in this respect. The sports organisation had the right to dismiss it in the event of abuse.

> "Thus, since the mere submission of a notification form is in itself not sufficient, the medical necessity alone may constitute an exemption with respect to salbutamol. Furthermore, the Panel agrees with FINA that the admissibility of *a posteriori* notification of the medical necessity of salbutamol would encourage abuse and weaken the fight against doping. The duty of prior notification may serve as a strong deterrent against some forms of possible cheating. Therefore, the Panel agrees with FINA that one should not admit any evidence to prove medical necessity otherwise than through prior notification. The Panel also considers that the prior notification of a banned substance may lead to an exemption only if provided such an exemption is expressly stated in the relevant doping list (as is the case in FINA's doping list)."[326]

The FINA also remained convinced that if an athlete failed to indicate his/her use of salbutamol on the doping form during the doping control a doping offence was established. The mere declaration that salbutamol had been used was not in itself sufficient to change a banned substance into a permitted substance. If a banned substance was found a prior declaration constituted no justification. This was also true for salbutamol. The declaration neither constituted proof that the salbutamol had been used by medical indication, nor did it show that the salbutamol had been ingested through inhalation.

> "The declaration essentially serves the purpose of supporting the laboratory in analysing the test sample. The absence of a declaration does not in itself constitute a doping offence. However, the Panel agrees with FINA that failure to comply with the duty to declare a certain medication in the test form may indeed raise serious doubts about the medical necessity to use that medication and even lead to the assumption that there was a doping offence. However, there may be exceptional limited situations in which such would not be the case, e.g. if a competitor can demonstrate that the use of salbutamol had been well known by the relevant medical authorities and that only exceptional and understandable circumstances led to his omission."[327]

When salbutamol was found in an athlete's sample, this constituted *prima facie* proof of a doping offence. An exception was made, however, if the salbutamol had been used for reasons of medical necessity. The athlete had to show such medical necessity. The FINA did not doubt the fact that Lehtinen suffered from asthma or

---

[325] *Idem*, ground 17.
[326] *Idem*, ground 20.
[327] *Idem*, ground 22.

that he needed the salbutamol for training and being able to compete. The FINA only adduced that Lehtinen had omitted to inform the relevant medical authorities of his use of the substance.

The CAS first examined the matter of the prior notification. It did not emerge from the evidence produced by Lehtinen that he had made such a prior notification. As to the FINA regulations the CAS concluded that these included instructions which were directed at team physicians. The instructions were drafted with competition conditions in mind, not for out-of-competition conditions where there are usually no team physicians present. The duty to report could, according to the CAS, not simply be shifted to the athlete. The CAS further came to the conclusion that the instructions did not require that every use of salbutamol had to be reported. The aim of the notification was in the first place to inform the relevant medical authorities of the fact that salbutamol had been prescribed for medical reasons. "If the permitted use of salbutamol is well known to the relevant medical authority, there is no need to ask for additional notifications." Then the CAS concluded from the instructions that it was not precisely clear who was to be notified of the use of salbutamol. At previous doping controls, salbutamol had also been found in Lehtinen's sample, but he had never been punished as he had always notified his national anti-doping committee beforehand of his use of the substance. It was evident that Lehtinen had asthma, and that as a consequence he had to rely on salbutamol and that in the past the relevant medical authorities had always been notified.

> "Under these circumstances, it can be left open whether the FINA itself was also in possession of a notification of L.'s medical status. However, before and after the test on 16 March 1995, L. was tested at least twice under the direct supervision of FINA. In both cases, L. mentioned Ventolin on the test form and was found negative. Following the argumentation of FINA, the mere indication of Ventolin on the test form would have been insufficient if no prior notification of L.'s medical status had been submitted to FINA."

Perhaps as a face-saving effort on behalf of the FINA which should have had ample reason to dismiss the case the CAS considered that:

> "[...] a competitor must be well aware that such a failure may involve him into a formal doping procedure with all its deplorable side-effects. It is therefore very difficult to understand why L. as a competitor of the highest level failed to comply with one of his most important professional duties and was not able to present any excuses for his negligence other than fatigue and forgetfulness."[328]

Given the circumstances of this specific case and the fact that the CAS had reason to believe that there was a medical necessity for Lehtinen to use salbutamol the Panel considered the evidence "as sufficient to make up for the failure to declare Ventolin on the control form in this particular doping test." This for the main part

---

[328] *Idem*, ground 35.

removed the illegality of the use of Ventolin. The only fact that remained to be established was that the substance had been ingested by inhalation. Based on Section 8 of the Swiss Civil Code, the CAS in this matter also considered that the athlete who relied on an exception to the rule had to bear the onus of proof. Now that Lehtinen did not have the exact test results in his possession there was no direct evidence that he had inhaled the salbutamol. However, if he was able to show that he suffered from asthma, that the medication containing salbutamol was an acknowledged asthma remedy and that the relevant prescription instructed its use by inhalation, then this would justify the assumption that the salbutamol could not have been used by other means than inhalation. Lehtinen was able to demonstrate each of these points.

> "it is established that the use of salbutamol by L. was medically indicated, that the relevant medical authorities were informed about that medication in good time and that there is no reason to believe that L. took Ventolin other than by inhalation. Therefore, these necessary prerequisites of a doping offence under the FINA doping rules have not been fulfilled in the present case. Consequently, no sanction should be imposed. Thus, the two-year sanction imposed on L. must be lifted. Under these circumstances, there is no need to examine, whether the FINA doping rules themselves comply with the applicable (i.e. Swiss) law."[329]

As the illegality of the alleged doping act was lacking in the *Lehtinen* case, the material rule of the FINA became retroactively inapplicable. Interestingly, this had the consequence that "there is no need to examine whether the [association's] doping rules themselves comply with the applicable (i.e. Swiss) law," Beloff[330] commented, or, in other words: when this rule – and with it all the other rules laid down in the FINA anti-doping regulations – did not apply, the rules no longer needed to be tested against the applicable law. Beloff went on, however, and in my opinion, incorrectly, to consider the lack of illegality in the light of liability.[331]

> "So we may conclude that strict liability doping offences are acceptable and indeed regarded as appropriate by the highest international sporting judicial authorities. But those same authorities are loath to allow such rules to operate unfairly so as to punish the innocent in a case where the rules themselves are unclear or their applicability to the facts of the case doubtful."

In the *Lehtinen* case there was no inclination whatsoever to leave aside rules whose application would result in unfairness *vis-à-vis* the athlete. There was no question of punishing the innocent either, and the FINA rules were not unclear. In this case, the facts resulted in the non-fulfilment of one of the objective elements of the offence: there was no illegality.

---

[329] *Idem*, ground 39.
[330] Beloff 1999 (*supra* nt. 282), 7.28.
[331] *Idem*, 7.32.

In sum, certain substances appearing on doping lists could be used provided that certain conditions are fulfilled. When these conditions had been met in practice or when, having due regard to the circumstances of the case, it had to be assumed that they had been met, one could no longer speak of a doping offence.

3.2. Use of substances not appearing on the doping list

The IOC's Medical Commission's definition of doping and that of the IFs was based on the prohibition of pharmacological groups of substances. The substances listed per doping group were examples to illustrate the definition of doping. The term "and related substances" was intended to cover medication which was related to these substances based on their pharmacological effect and/or chemical structure. The IFs pointed to the advantage of the definition that it also included possible new remedies, some of which might have been specifically developed for doping purposes.

Some athletes were convinced that the use of a substance or method when it did not appear on the doping list was perfectly legitimate. On this, Bette[332] has commented as follows:

"If an athlete is found to be cheating he points to the legality of his action and plays down his deviant behaviour. Even substances used for calf-fattening, which are hidden in other medicines such as asthma remedies, but which are proven to have an anabolic effect, are thus seen to be perfectly legitimate. As Katrin Krabbe put it: 'We have checked the list of banned drugs and found out that our medicine was not listed. This list is meant to protect athletes. Doctors are supposed to look at the list in order to see whether they can describe a medicine or not. If a medication is not on the list I cannot be condemned.'

Generally speaking we can say that the social figures of top athletes make use of specific techniques in order to calm down reactions to their breach of rules. They construct justifications which are meant to gloss over their deviant behaviour. This kind of rhetoric offers the pleasant opportunity to the community of deviants to believe in the conformity of their action. It is nothing unusual if the reasons given for the use of performance-enhancing drugs are based on the disapproval of these drugs. It is remarkable that these various neutralisation techniques are overdetermined: a single argument is enough to justify deviance."

The advantage of the way in which the definition of doping was laid down was not felt across the board. There was also an inherent disadvantage, as Summerer[333] pointed out.

---

[332] Karl-Heinrich Bette "Doping: Studies in the Sociology of Deviance" in K.-H. Bette and A. Rütten, eds., *International Sociology of Sport: Contempory Issues, Festschrift in honour of Günther Lüschen* (Stuttgart, Naglschmid 1995) p. 241.

[333] Th. Summerer, Internationales Sportrecht Kongreß. 4./5, November 1999. Vgl. L. Tarasti: *When can an athlete be punished for a doping offence*, World doping conference 1999 (Tarasti 1999): "The list must according to my opinion be so complete as possible. All efforts should be made to ensure that there is no space for such kind of 'related substances,' because without the help of a specialist an athlete cannot know these substances. This is also a juridical problem."

"Unzureichend ist ein *pauschales* Dopingverbot. Dopingregeln müssen explizit aufführen, welche Substanzen verboten sein sollen. Eine nur beispielhafte Aufzählung einiger Wirkstoffe ist im Zeitalter ausgereifter chemischer Analysetechniken nicht ausreichend. Nicht ausreichend ist ferner, wenn bei den verbotenen Verbindungen auf das Kriterium der 'Verwandtschaft' abgestellt wird, weil offen bleibt, ob der chemische Wirkmechanismus oder der anabole Effekt maßgeblich sein soll."

Summerer acted as lawyer for Katrin Krabbe in her protracted legal battle against the *Deutscher Leichtatlethik Verband* (DLV) and IAAF. In July 1992, Katrin Krabbe's urine sample was found to contain clenbuterol. This substance, which is a component of an asthma remedy called Spiropent, did not appear on the doping list. Nevertheless, the DLV imposed a four-year suspension on Krabbe for having committed a doping offence. On appeal, the term of suspension was reduced to one year. The penalty, however, was not imposed for a doping offence, but for unsporting behaviour (*"sportwidriges Verhalten"*).[334] In proceedings before the German courts the sports organisation's discretion to impose a penalty for unsporting behaviour once it became clear that the penalty could not be based on a doping offence was challenged. On appeal, however, the *"Oberlandesgericht"* (OLG) München allowed such discretion.[335] With the substitution of the objective elements of the doping offence for the objective elements of a different offence, the *Krabbe* case ceased to be a doping case.[336] The case no longer concerned the violation of a material doping rule.[337]

During the 1996 Summer Games in Atlanta, the swimmer Korneev and the wrestler Gouliev were disqualified by the IOC after the substance of bromantan had been found in the analysis of their urine samples. The IOC considered bromantan as

---

[334] Tarasti 1999 (*supra* nt. 333): "The Arbitration Panel of the IAAF affirmed that the conduct of these athletes [Krabbe and Breuer; *JWS*] has been likely to bring the sport into disrepute and they have acted in an unsportsmanlike manner."

[335] Under Dutch criminal law, a wrong choice by the Public Prosecutor will usually lead to discharge from further prosecution, because, as Remmelink explains, "the charges, even if proven, are classified under a provision of criminal law that was not intended to cover them. Certain elements will then be found lacking and the facts found will therefore not qualify as an offence."

[336] Gardiner and O'Leary 1998 (*supra* nt. 14), pp. 193-194, nevertheless do consider the Krabbe case to be a real doping case. The German courts upheld the nulla poena sine culpa rule which is enshrined in German law, but Krabbe's suspension was left intact "on the basis only that she had taken the drugs deliberately." Although in principle it is true that Krabbe took the clenbuterol deliberately, her use of the substance could not lead to a penalty on the basis of the description of the doping offence. Another interesting aspect of this case was the question of whether the strict liability statute of the doping offence also applied to the offence based on unsportsmanlike behaviour.

[337] In mid-January 2000, the footballer Quido Lanzaat tested positive for tetrahydrocannabinol (15 ng/ml). Hashish and marijuana contain this substance, and Lanzaat admitted that he had smoked several joints on New Year's Eve in the Netherlands. At that time, he was still under contract with Ajax and according to the KNVB guidelines the use of hashish was not an offence. At that time, Lanzaat did not yet know that he would be playing in Germany shortly afterwards. On 4 January he was negotiating with Borussia Mönchengladbach and on 11 January he signed a contract with this club. Traces of tetrahydrocannabinol may still be found in the body four weeks after it has been used. At the moment of detection the substance no longer affected athletic performance. The Sportgericht des Deutschen Fußball-Bundes (DFB) could not charge Lanzaat with doping, but suspended him for a period of eight weeks for "unsportliches Verhalten." (*Stuttgarter Zeitung*, 22 March 2000).

"a substance prohibited by the Rules of the IOC Medical Commission."[338] The President of the Russian Olympic Committee on behalf of the athletes appealed against the IOC decisions to the CAS Atlanta Ad Hoc Division.[339] The cases were joined as they concerned "substantially similar issues." It was suspected that Russian athletes had already been using bromantan during the 1988 and 1992 Games. However, the IOC had been unable to detect these substances by means of the methods available at the time. Neither the Russian Olympic Committee, nor the Russian athletes had kept silent concerning the existence of the substance. In June 1996, the IOC Medical Committee received a letter from the IAAF, but as the person it was addressed to (De Mérode) was abroad, some time passed before its contents became known. In this letter, the IAAF made it known that:

> "testing of the athletes in 1994 and 1995 had disclosed the presence of an unidentified substance the use of which had not been disclosed by the athletes. The laboratories had been unable to identify either the substance or its properties.
> At the World Figure Skating Championships held in Madrid in March 1996 a Russian athlete had declared using a substance known as bromantan. When tested the results showed identical results to those for the athletes referred to in (the foregoing) paragraph [...]"

A Russian member of the IAAF Medical Committee responded to a request for clarification from the IAAF that: "this medicine is produced not by Pharmacy, but unofficially." This official succeeded in securing 50 tablets. A search was performed for literature concerning the mysterious substance which yielded some results although the information was sketchy and in Russian. The Commission's Subcommission on Doping and Biochemistry of Sport nevertheless convened a meeting to discuss the information and at the end of it proposed to classify bromantan as "a related substance to the forbidden class I.A." During the meeting of the Commission with representatives of the Russian Olympic Committee to discuss the doping cases of Korneev and Gouliev one of the Russian delegates, Mr Semenov, who was the head of the medical centre for sports of the Russian Olympic Committee, declared that the use of bromantan had been detected five years earlier in their laboratory. He had no information about the substance's formula, or its physical and chemical qualities. He did know, however, that the substance was used in the Russian army as an immune booster and that it increased endurance. "He further said that in his view the drug should be banned for young athletes but that the Russian authorities could not do so as it was not on the list of banned substances."[340] The expert appointed by the Panel reported as follows:

---

[338] According to the IOC, bromantan belonged "to class I.A (stimulants) of the Prohibited Classes of Substances."

[339] CAS 96/003-4, 04-8-1996, *Andrei Korneev v. IOC & Zakhar Goukiev v. IOC*.

[340] *Idem*, ground 44.

"Since bromantan is in the same chemical category as amantadine and has been reported to produce effects on neurotransmitters in the central nervous system which are similar to those reported with amantadine and, since it has been categorized in the current literature as a psychostimulant, it must be assumed that bromantan has the capacity to produce the same central nervous system stimulant effects as other drugs in the category which include an enhanced sense of well being, mood elevation, insomnia, loss of appetite and nervousness. These effects are dose dependent and variable depending on the individual."[341]

Amantadine was neither a prohibited, nor a related substance. During questioning the expert was unable to provide any further information concerning bromantan. "He was not able to express any view as to the quantitative effect of bromantan because of the lack of data. The effects of amantadine are the same as amphetamine on neurotransmitters but he was unable to express a view of the dosage required to produce a stimulant effect.[342] "According to Semenov, bromantan had been researched in Russia, but "the materials supporting the studies he had referred to could not be made available to the Court as "the entire month of August everybody is on vacation."[343] Semenov declared that he had not given bromantan to the Russian athletes, but that the substance was for sale in Moscow.

The crucial issue which the Panel had to resolve was whether bromantan was "a stimulant within the meaning of the Medical Code." The substance was not listed in the Code as prohibited.

"Accordingly, in order to justify the disqualification of an athlete for the use of bromantan it must be established that bromantan is a stimulant within the meaning of the Medical Code. The burden of establishing that fact, if disputed, is on the suspending body."

The data gathered by the CAS gave rise to the suspicion that bromantan had all the qualities of a performance-enhancing drug. If the substance was factually performance- enhancing, then it was prohibited under the Medical Code "regardless of whether or not it is specifically listed as an example or not." The expert opinions gave the CAS the impression that scientifically speaking bromantan could be considered a stimulant within the scope of the Medical Code. However, according to the CAS, there was insufficient evidence to warrant this conclusion.

"The surrounding circumstances while suspicious do not form a basis for concluding, in the light of the scientific evidence, that bromantan is a stimulant. The surrounding circumstances, of themselves, are not evidence of the objective fact of the actual chemical composition and qualities of bromantan. They could be evidence of the belief of those using the substance but not of the correctness of that belief.
While it may be that further study may establish that bromantan is a prohibited substance the totality of the materiel before us does not allow us to reach that conclusion."

---

[341] *Idem*, ground 48.
[342] *Idem*, ground 51, sub 6 and 7.
[343] *Idem*, ground 55.

The CAS Ad Hoc Division upheld the appeals of Korneev and Gouliev and an-
nulled the decisions of the IOC to disqualify the athletes.

The FINA doping rules required that "a banned substance (be) clearly identified"[344]
and that the athlete be informed of any "adverse report for a banned substance."[345]
Meca-Medina and Majcen were informed that the prohibited substance found in
their samples had been identified by the laboratory as nandrolon. During the first
hearing before the FINA Panel on 14 June 1999, the FINA amended the charges
with respect to the prohibited substance. During another hearing on 8 August 1999
the Doping Panel established that the positive outcome of the analysis could have
been caused by nandrolon precursors such as norandrostenedion and
norandrostenediol. The swimmers' lawyers pointed out that as opposed to nandrolon
itself, the precursors mentioned did not appear in the doping list of the FINA Guidelines and had not been included in the most recent list which applied during the
swimming competition. On appeal to the CAS the swimmers argued that:

> "[...] in changing the offence which Applicants are alleged to have committed by pos-
> tulating that the positive test results of both Applicants might have come from
> nandrolon precursors, such as norandrostenedione and norandrostenediol, instead of
> from nandrolon as had been suggested, the FINA Doping Panel violates the legal prin-
> ciple of 'nulla poena sine lege', since neither nandrolon precursors in general, nor
> norandrostenedione and norandrostenediol in particular, were listed as banned sub-
> stances at the time the alleged offence was committed by both Appellants. [...] Conse-
> quently, in the absence of any provision in FINA's Doping Rules banning the use of
> nandrolon precursors in general or norandrostenedione and norandrostenediol in par-
> ticular – signified by the expression 'sine lege' -, no offence has been committed by
> the Applicants and thus no sanction – 'nulla poena' – can be issued."[346]

By the time that the CAS reached its decision in this case, the FINA had included
norandrostenedion and norandrostenediol in its doping list. The swimmers could,
however, not rely on the fact that these metabolites were absent from the list when
their samples were found to contain them, because:

> "Before their express inclusion, both the above substances were prohibited as part of
> the 'related substances'. There is a definite chemical relationship – as the IOC amend-
> ments suggest.
> It has never been put into question that the presence of nandrolon metabolites was the
> conclusive proof of the presence of a prohibited substance, be it nandrolon itself or a
> related substance including in particular the two above mentioned precursors."[347]

---

[344] FINA DC 8.6.
[345] FINA DC 8.2.
[346] Applicant's Brief, p. 9, points 3.1 and 3.2.
[347] CAS 99/A/234 & CAS 99/A/235, 29-2-2000, *David Meca-Medina v. FINA & Igor Majcen v.
FINA*, ground 9.3-9.4.

During the 1998 Winter Games at Nagano, the snowboarder Rebagliati won the gold medal in the giant slalom. The next day, the IOC Executive Board informed the athlete that he had to return his medal as his urine had been found to contain marijuana metabolites. Rebagliati appealed against this decision to the CAS where he argued that he had not actively used marijuana himself, but that the metabolites must have ended up in his urine "from exposure to second hand marijuana smoke" during a number of parties. The IOC contended, however, that even if Rebagliati was telling the truth, the penalty had still been correctly imposed given the provisions of Chapter II, Article III, paragraph B of the IOC Medical Code.

> "Marijuana
> In agreement with the International Sports Federations and the responsible authorities, tests may be conducted for cannabinoids (e.g. Marijuana, Hashish). The results may lead to sanctions."

Did the finding of marijuana metabolites establish a doping offence under paragraph B? The CAS examined the relationship between paragraph B and other parts of the IOC Medical Code and came to the conclusion that marijuana was not mentioned anywhere else. Two members of the IOC Medical Commission testified that marijuana was not a prohibited substance in the framework of the Code. Only if the IF in question had declared marijuana to be a prohibited substance could the IOC make use of paragraph B.

> "In summary, the IOC Medical Code standing alone does not provide a basis for treating marijuana as a banned substance justifying the finding of a doping offence and resulting sanctions.
> Since the effect of paragraph B is to require a joint approach by the IOC and FIS to create sanctions for the use of marijuana, the testimony of Mr Hodler, FIS President, was of the first importance."[348]

Mr Hodler pointed out that the FIS had simply copied the doping offences set out in the IOC Medical Code without adding any rules of its own. Where paragraph B was concerned, the FIS had not concluded any further agreements with the IOC. Literally, Mr Hodler's words were:

> "We have never been asked for approval. We would never give approval for a giant slalom [...] There is absolutely no risk. We have safety measures. Even if he goes too fast and misses lots of gates, nothing much happens. I believe some very basic conditions are missing, in this particular case."[349]

Now that an agreement had not been concluded between the FIS and the IOC concerning paragraph B, the CAS held that the IOC Executive Board's decision to

---

[348] CAS AH 98/002, 12-2-1998, *Rebagliati v. IOC*, Matthieu Reeb, ed., *Digest of CAS Awards 1986-1998* (Berne, Editions Stämpfli 1998) pp. 419-434, grounds 16 and 17.
[349] *Idem*, ground 21.

punish Rebagliati for the presence of marijuana metabolites in his urine lacked legal basis. In conclusion of its decision the Panel expressed its concern

> "[...] that Rebagliati should not suffer from any needless embarrassment on account of misunderstandings or distortions of the factual circumstances of this matter. His performance should not be tarnished by any suggestion that he deserved his punishment but is being saved by a technicality. Rebagliati has affirmed that he has not ingested cannabis since April 1997, and that any exposure he has had to it since then was second hand. The Panel emphasises that these facts have not been challenged by either the FIS or the IOC. Rebagliati has not been accused of being a current cannabis user, but of having residual traces in his urine. For the reasons given above, this is not a punishable offence under the applicable rules."[350]

Pursuant to Article 5.5. of Appendix C to the IOC Medical Code the President of the Medical Committee immediately had to warn the *chef de mission* of a delegation of which an athlete tested positive for his/her A sample. In case the B sample also tested positive the President had to convene a meeting of the Medical Committee at which the case should be discussed. A noteworthy aspect of the *Rebagliati* case was that two august members of the Medical Committee, Prince de Mérode and Dr Schamasch, testified that marijuana was not a prohibited substance in the framework of the Code and that only in case the IF had banned marijuana paragraph B of the Code could provide the necessary legal basis for imposing a sanction. One has to assume that the Committee members were aware of the fact that the FIS had not penalised the use of marijuana. This means that the Committee must also have been aware that no offence had been committed in this case. Nevertheless, the Committee must have signalled to the IOC Executive Board that a violation of the Medical Code had occurred. The members of the Executive Board must also be presumed to have known the rules on which they based Rebagliati's penalty, and yet, impose it they did.

To conclude, an act of doping only became an offence when the athlete's sample had been shown to contain a substance – usually in the shape of one of the substance's possible metabolites – that was expressly included in the list of prohibited substances.[351] If use had been made of a substance that might in extremis be performance enhancing, but which did not appear on the list, then the description of the doping offence was not fulfilled. Athletes were not prohibited from using performance-enhancing substances per se; they were only prohibited from using substances appearing on the doping list. The moral pressure to abstain from the use of

---

[350] *Idem*, ground 28.

[351] On <www.sportgericht.de> the following item recently appeared: "Dienstag, der 18. Januar 2005, Kein Dopingfall trotz positiven Befundes. Swetlana Kusnetsowa hat trotz ihres positiven Doping-Befundes in Belgien nichts zu befürchten: Außerhalb der offiziellen WTA-Turniere ist das gefundene Stimulanzmittel Ephedrin nicht verboten. Damit liegt die Damen-Profi-Tour auf einer Linie mit der Welt-Anti-Doping-Agentur (WADA). Dies betonte WTA-Chef Larry Scott und stellte sich ebenfalls vor die Weltranglisten-Fünfte."

doping in general was in essence removed by the introduction of doping offence descriptions coupled with a list of prohibited substances. In three out of the four doping cases dealt with above the respective athletes had been allowed to use a certain substance which was possibly a stimulant. They did not act illegally, as it could not be proven that the substance was related to a substance appearing on the list. One sports organisation, however, managed to bypass the argument of the absence of illegality by replacing the offence with which the athlete had been charged with another in the course of the proceedings.

3.3. Endogenous production of prohibited substances and the "grey area"

When dealing with threshold values, one literally finds oneself on a threshold, namely that between legality and illegality. If the amount of the substance found remains below the threshold value illegality is absent and no doping offence has taken place. If, however, the amount of the substance found has risen above the threshold level, it is assumed that the athlete has used doping. This establishes illegality and thereby a doping offence according to the strict liability rule. A remaining option for the athlete is to demonstrate by means of medical testing that in specific circumstances his/her body, as opposed to that of the average person, is capable of producing prohibited substances above threshold level. If he/she is able to show this fact, this will remove the element of illegality from his/her act. If the athlete's evidence fails, however, the question of guilt comes into play. The question of guilt will be dealt with in Chapter 4 below. For this reason, it will not be further pursued here.

4. CONCLUSION

Technical aspects

The illegality of the doping offence was presumed from the moment that the prosecuting body had demonstrated the objective elements of the offence. The athlete who was suspected of having used doping had to examine whether during the transport of the sample from the doping control station to the laboratory and during the time the sample was stored and processed there any circumstances occurred which rendered the sample unfit for analysis. A positive test result was only acceptable when the sports organisation was able to produce a clear paper chain of custody. If the athlete was able to show that a dubious gap occurred in this chain of custody, this invalidated any evidence of doping which the prosecuting body adduced. Indeed, this would prove absence of illegality and force the disciplinary body to acquit him/her.

However, none of the doping regulations used to provide that the sports organisation had to prove the technical chain of custody. Rather, the task of the organisation was to prove that the sample was truly that of the athlete in question.

Various CAS decisions show that the CAS did not always consider the term chain of custody to mean the same thing. Sometimes the concept was understood to denote the various stages which the sample had to complete, i.e. "collecting, transporting and testing," while at other times the term was reserved for the documented procedure at the laboratory. In this chapter, the various stages between the doping control and the analysis of the sample were treated individually, as mistakes made during any of these stages might lead to acquittal.

Complaints concerning mistakes allegedly made by doping officials during testing were only dealt with by the CAS if they were able to cast doubt on the outcome of the analysis. It was however only rarely that such arguments made any impression on the CAS. The same was true when the athlete attacked the validity of the outcome of his test by pointing to mistakes made during the transport of the samples to the laboratory; here, too, the arguments had to be extremely convincing in order for the CAS to take them seriously. Given the provisions laid down in most doping regulations concerning the chain of custody it was very difficult for the defence to prove that a gap occurred in the chain and that this gap affected the integrity of the samples. Finally, it was harder still to prove that errors had been made at the laboratory. Most anti-doping regulations took as a starting point that laboratory tests and analyses were conducted in accordance with the highest scientific standards. For example, the IOC Medical Code contained a rule which was much copied by the individual IFs that: "Laboratories accredited by the IOC are presumed to have conducted testing and custodial procedures in accordance with prevailing and acceptable standards of care. The presumption can be rebutted by evidence to the contrary, but the IOC accredited laboratory shall have no onus in the first instance to show that it conducted the procedures other than in accordance with its customary practices." It should also be noted here that the defence was only very rarely given access to the full laboratory report. Any attack on the chain of custody at the laboratory must therefore often have had the nature of a "fishing expedition."

Legal aspects

Three situations could be distinguished in which an athlete could successfully rely on absence of illegality:

1. *The athlete made it sufficiently clear beforehand that he was using a conditionally prohibited substance.*
Firstly, these substances must have been prescribed by a doctor; secondly, the competent authorities must have been informed of their use prior to the competition; and, thirdly, these substances might only be used in a certain way.

– *The athlete used a substance that does not appear on the doping list.*
In order to still have a case if an athlete used a substance not appearing on the doping list, the IOC Medical Code provided that such substances also had to be considered prohibited if they could be decisively shown to be performance enhanc-

ing. However, even if in a given case the substance used did not appear on the doping list and could not be shown to be performance enhancing, there was still a possibility for the prosecuting body to secure the athlete's conviction by basing it on unsporting behaviour.

– The athlete's body produced the prohibited substances endogenously.
The once so clear rule that the mere finding of certain substances in athletes' samples established an offence for which the athlete was *prima facie* liable and which demonstrated the illegality of the act and consequently its punishability was made less transparent by new scientific insights concerning these substances. Medical science after some time discovered that various substances of which it was previously thought that they could never be produced by the human body could in fact be endogenous. The grey area between the natural production of certain substances and the level at which it can no longer be disputed that they have been administered artificially gave rise to much scientific debate. If the athlete was able to demonstrate by means of medical testing that in specific circumstances his/her body, as opposed to that of the average person, was capable of producing prohibited substances above threshold level, this would remove the element of illegality from his/her act. If the athlete's evidence failed, however, his act would be considered illegal and the athlete him/herself strictly liable. Threshold levels are further discussed in the context of the question of guilt in Chapter 4 below.

CHAPTER 4
THE LIABILITY OF THE PERPETRATOR FOR THE ACT OF DOPING

1. INTRODUCTION

De Doelder refers to various authors who have argued that guilt could and should never be an element of a disciplinary offence.[352] One of these authors is Verpalen[353] who considered it "one of the especially attractive aspects of disciplinary law that the principle of "no punishment without guilt" does not apply there."[354] Based on a study of the literature De Doelder concludes that the opinions of writers concerning the question of whether disciplinary law requires intention or guilt "is not uniform." De Doelder's own opinion is however clear: "[...] throughout disciplinary law as a whole, as in criminal law, the principle of no punishment without guilt applies."[355]

The disciplinary law dealing with doping offences did not develop until the second half of the 1980s. This disciplinary law – as opposed to that studied by De Doelder until 1981 – certainly does give prominence to the element of guilt. Before being able to proceed to the stage of punishment of an athlete it is thus necessary to examine the issue of whether he/she is in fact guilty of the offence. For the actual punishment of an athlete (or a third party) for the use of doping substances or methods it is not only relevant that his/her actions fall within the limits of the description of the doping offence (the material rule), but also that these actions are illegal and culpable. The inherent objectives of the description of the doping offence are to prohibit and to prevent any acts or behaviour which, if not justifiable or excusable, violate or threaten the general interest of sport. The presence or absence of a ground for justification (the element of illegality) has been discussed in the previous chapter. The other element in the description of the doping offence, namely culpability, is the focus of the present chapter. Criminal law literature distinguishes between guilt (ground for exculpation) as an element of the description of the offence and guilt in the meaning of culpability. In this latter guise guilt – also in the disciplinary

---

[352] H. de Doelder, *Terrein en beginselen van tuchtrecht*, PhD. 1981 (Alphen aan den Rijn, H.D. Tjeenk Willink 1981) (De Doelder 1981) p. 102.

[353] *Handelingen 1971 der Nederlandse Juristen-Vereniging*, deel 2, pp. 110-111.

[354] Another author cited by De Doelder is Kamminga, *Tuchtrecht, preadvies Calvinistische Juristenvereniging*, 1949, p. 6, who argued that intent "[...] is never an element of a disciplinary offence. Even the establishment of guilt is not usually a requirement for disciplinary measures. If a member of the group is unwilling or unable to adapt to the interests of the group he/she will eventually be excluded from the group, also in the case that this adaptibility has been affected by influences for which he/she cannot be blamed." De Doelder 1981 (*supra* nt. 352), p. 102.

[355] De Doelder 1981 (*supra* nt. 352), p. 109.

law on doping – serves as a tacit requirement for punishability. Although the material rule does not mention the element of guilt in so many words (see *supra* Chapter 2) it was from the very beginning considered a requirement in disciplinary doping law which had to be assessed before the imposition of a penalty became possible. Later, a number of IFs included the principle of liability without guilt (strict liability) in their disciplinary doping laws, but that did not automatically imply that guilt as a subjective element disappeared from the description of the doping offence; the element was made objective. Within the sporting community, which applies its own ethical standards of appreciation in the field of doping, culpability is directed at the avoidable deviant behaviour of an athlete caught using doping. The assessment of this behaviour expresses what in the sporting community is considered as a lack of social feeling and as a form of egoism that is unacceptable to that community.

As has been mentioned above, the psychological concepts of guilt and intent are not expressly mentioned – as general requirements – in the descriptions of the doping offence. Under Dutch law, intent is defined as knowingly and wilfully fulfilling the elements of an offence description. Extrapolated to doping law, this results in the knowing and wilful fulfilment of the elements of the doping offence as described, for example "use" or "administration." Most legal systems have a similar approach to the aspect of intent as under Dutch law, i.e. focusing on the directed will and awareness of the circumstances.[356] The gradations of the subjective element, which in international criminal law is termed individual responsibility, range from malice to the most minor degree of guilt. As opposed to intent, which focuses on will and awareness, guilt involves an unwilful and unknowing act (negligence). Viewed from the perspective of Dutch law, guilt in doping law can be understood to mean that the athlete in question failed to make an adequate assessment or did not make such an assessment at all of the fatal consequences – which are repudiated by

---

[356] Cf., for common law systems, Elies van Sliedregt, *The criminal responsibility of individuals for violations of international humanitarian law*, PhD. Tilburg 2003 (The Hague, T.M.C. Asser Press 2003) Van Sliedregt 2003) p. 43. She cites Justice Devlin who considered that "[M]ens rea consists of two elements. It consists first of all of the intent to do an act and secondly of the knowledge of the circumstances that makes that act a criminal offence. For civil law in general Van Sliedregt concludes that: AIntent includes an element of knowledge and volition."
The most authoritative description of intent – as the only international criminal law description which is accepted as such by the international community of states – can be found in Art. 30 – Mental Eelement – of the Statute of the International Criminal Court (Part 3. General Principles of Criminal Law):
"1. Unless otherwise provided, a person shall be criminally responsible and liable for punishment for a crime within the jurisdiction of the Court only if the material elements are committed with intent and knowledge.
2. For the purposes of this article, a person has intent where:
(a) In relation to conduct, that person means to engage in the conduct;
(b) In relation to a consequence, that person means to cause that consequence or is aware that it will occur in the ordinary course of events.
3. For the purposes of this article, knowledge means awareness that a circumstance exists or a consequence will occur in the ordinary course of events. Know and knowingly shall be construed accordingly."

the sporting community – of his actions, even though he/she easily could have.[357] Dutch case law has recognised guilt in the meaning of culpability as an essential requirement for the punishability of the suspect. Van Sliedregt[358] argues that in civil law systems in general it can be said that "[...] the essential aspect of negligence is not what a person's state of mind was, but what is *should* have been. The element dividing *culpa* and *dolus* is will, the volitional element."[359]

Ethical standards were not involved in the descriptions of the psychological criteria given above. The exclusion of such standards also excludes the possibility to allow for the eventuality that the athlete reached his erroneous conclusion in utter good faith. Criminal law in this respect speaks of mistake and absence of guilt. The adage "no punishment without guilt" which does not appear in the Criminal Code has developed in case law as a generally applicable standard in assessing whether a penalty should be imposed. In this chapter it will be examined whether a similar development – whereby guilt as *culpa* has merged with general culpabilility – has taken place in the disciplinary law on doping.

Every top athlete who comes under the scope of the doping regulations of the IOC, the International Paralympic Committee or of the regulations of an Olympic IF is presumed to be aware of the fact that the use of doping substances and methods is not allowed. The material rule does not only serve as a yardstick to measure the athlete's behaviour by in a doping trial, but also as an ethical standard to be applied by the athlete in the exercise of his sport. If he/she has voluntarily used prohibited substances and methods, it is presumed that he/she did so intentionally. Under doping law, intent is deemed to be directed at the impermissibility of the act.

Over the past few years, a consensus has emerged concerning what is to be considered intent in the international context. However, less unanimity exists internationally concerning liability for certain actions that are described as undesirable and punishable (the element of guilt). Although at several times during the reasoning brought forward below opinions which prevail in Dutch law will be taken as a starting point, readers must be aware that slight differences could occur under their own national systems. Van Sliedregt in her doctoral thesis observes the following concerning individual criminal responsibility:[360]

"It seems that in establishing criminal responsibility most national criminal legal systems distinguish the following steps: 1) the conduct (act or omission) satisfies the defi-

---

[357] Vgl. Remmelink 1994 (*supra* nt. 293), pp. 191-192).

[358] Van Sliedregt 2003 (*supra* nt. 356), p. 47.

[359] The Statute of the International Criminal Court (Part 3. General Principles of Criminal Law) does not include a description of individual guilt, i.e. the subjective element that does not start from the volition to commit the offence. In case the Statute does not provide a solution, the Court, where appropriate, should look for general principles in "[...] applicable treaties and the principles and rules of international law [...]" (Art. 21(1)(b)) and, failing that, "general principles of law derived by the Court from national laws of legal systems of the world including, as appropriate, the national laws of States that would normally exercise jurisdiction over the crime [...] (Art. 21(1)(c))."

[360] Van Sliedregt 2003 (*supra* nt. 356), p. 5.

nitional elements of a crime; 2) the conduct is not justified by law; 3) the perpetrator cannot be excused."

She further writes that[361]

"[...] in determining whether a person's conduct can be qualified as criminal under law, one needs to establish that his act or omission can be traced back to a guilty mind and constitutes voluntary conduct, which is blameworthy. Individual criminal responsibility turns on culpability and requires proof of *personal* guilt (i) relating to one's *own* conduct (ii). Another element often mentioned in association with the previous two is that criminal responsibility can only attach to precisely defined conduct. [...] The other two elements [...] constitute the parameter of culpability that underlie the process of attributing and averting criminal responsibility and as such play a vital role in the [...] three-stage process [...]. To qualify as a sophisticated and coherent criminal law system where the concept of criminal responsibility is respected and endorsed, international criminal law should respect the parameters of culpability as well."

In Section 2 of this chapter it will be examined what position liability occupies in disciplinary doping law as a general requirement (subjective element) for punishability. This will also entail an examination of how the concept has influenced the evolution of the material rule. Sections 3 and 4 focus on the strict liability rule and how this rule has been interpreted by the CAS. Section 5 discusses the relationship between guilt and the punishment imposed. Finally, Sections 6 and 7 further examine the position of the subjective element in "ancillary doping infractions" and "non-use" offences (participation).

2.   THE METAMORPHOSIS OF THE MATERIAL RULE

As opposed to the previous chapter, this chapter does not focus on the wording of the material rule, but on the relationship between this rule and general requirements such as guilt and intent (i.e. individual responsibility). In the material rule, in which the essence of doping constitutes the central element, all the elements which together make up the term doping must each be confronted with intent and guilt.

From the survey of the literature carried out by De Doelder[362] it emerged that intent usually remained outside the scope of the discussion; his conclusion was that "[...] it seems undisputed that intent is generally not necessary." He also considered that: "If we look at the standard of "failing to observe the care which a good group member should observe" it is not necessary that one fails in this 'intentionally'. At least not if we understand intentionally to mean what it means under criminal law: wilfully and knowingly. It is even doubtful whether *culpa* is required. However, evidently this does not preclude the possibility that for certain specifically defined

---

[361] *Idem*, p. 6.
[362] De Doelder 1981 (*supra* nt. 352), p. 103.

prohibited acts under disciplinary law intent or *culpa* may in fact be required." The focus of doping law is such a specifically defined prohibited act. The definition of the term doping in the 1967 Council of Europe Resolution (which forms an example of the "essential" definition referred to above) demonstrates the position of intent and guilt in doping law. Doping was understood to mean:

> "[...] the administration to or use by a healthy person, in any manner whatsoever, of agents foreign to the organism, or of physiological substances in excessive quantities or introduced by an abnormal channel, with the sole purpose of affecting artificially and by unfair means the performance of such a person when taking part in a competition."

The athlete who is being prosecuted for use of doping and any third parties who were involved in this use will immediately counter an accusation based on a rule such as this by pointing out that the athlete was not healthy at the time of use and that therefore no blame attaches to him/her or the third party. The rule also leaves room for arguing that the athlete cannot be blamed if he is able to demonstrate that the substances, although foreign to the organism, were not used in excessive quantities or introduced abnormally. A rule worded in this way could never result in punishability of the athlete based on a doping offence. Any alleged liability based on the fact that the substances were used with the sole purpose of artificially and unfairly affecting performance could also easily be parried by arguing that this purpose was not the object of the athlete's or third party's volition. The condition of responsibility based on such a material rule as that drawn up by the Council of Europe could not but frustrate the fight against doping.

The sporting community came to the conclusion that the discussion concerning the performance-enhancing capabilities of certain pharmaceutical and chemical substances had to be cut short. The solution found was to compile lists on which prohibited classes of substances and methods could be placed. The material rule simply referred to the lists. It thus became sufficient to state in the material rule that the use or administration of substances on the list was prohibited and liable to punishment: "Doping is the use or administration of prohibited classes of drugs and of banned methods."

It was thought that all the elements appearing in the first-generation descriptions of the doping offence for which liability had been difficult if not impossible to establish would be set aside by this new and simply worded material rule. As has been touched upon in the previous chapter, not all IFs were convinced that the fight against doping could be successful using such a simple rule, and although these IFs did establish rules referring to their own or the IOC's doping list, they also continued to cling to certain relics of the past.[363] Thus they positioned the element of the rule prohibiting the use and administration of performance-enhancing substances next to the element prohibiting the use and administration of substances appearing

---

[363] See Chapter 2, Section 1.1.3.

on the doping list. From some of the material rules drafted in this way it becomes clear that primacy is accorded to the reference to the list and that the wording relating to the purpose of the use of these substances were merely intended as window dressing. From other material rules such a hierarchy is difficult to conclude and here the requirement of purpose can be read as an added condition next to the use of substances or methods appearing on the list.[364]

Material rules that refer to a doping list, but are also intertwined with added constitutive elements of which the sports organisation has to provide proof every time it asserts the punishability of an athlete's acts, lose much of their clout. By applying such a rule, sports organisations make it virtually impossible for themselves to obtain the conviction of a doping suspect. Moreover, these cumulative elements are not truly necessary.

A number of IFs did consider the material rule prohibiting the use and administration of substances appearing on the doping list sufficient. However, it soon emerged in practice that from an evidentiary perspective this material rule was not conclusive either. Once a sports organisation had been able to show on the basis of the laboratory results that the athlete's conduct corresponded to the actions described in the material rule it still, in case the athlete argued that his/her act had been unintentional, had to prove that the use of doping had been the object of the athlete's will. If the athlete could conclusively demonstrate that he/she had not acted with intent or that he/she had been unaware of the fact that the substance he/she was using was a doping substance, the prosecution would still fail. During the 1991 IAF International Symposium Gay remarked that:[365]

"[...] the athlete did have some basis for arguing that his intent was relevant. It could be argued that as the words refer to the use by an athlete of a prohibited substance, the Rules envisaged that this use must be a knowing use."

Some IFs were looking for a material rule which would rid them of the burden of having to prove the liability of an athlete for the use of doping if the athlete argued that he/she was not liable. A rule had to be found which would render the athlete *prima facie* liable once his urine or blood had been shown to contain a prohibited

---

[364] For the purpose of clarification, we will cite two more examples of material rules containing this element for which liability still had to be demonstrated:
"[...] the use or the administration to athletes of pharmacological classes of doping agents or doping methods banned by the I.O.C. or having either adverse effects on the health of those who take them, or of pharmacological classes of agents or methods masking the use of substances or methods having this property in order to obtain an unfair advantage of the athletes performance during competition, training, or recuperation after competition or training."
"The sport of weightlifting involves physical health and fitness, mental application and dedication to training. The use of banned substances and other doping methods to artificially enhance performance can endanger the health of athletes and is unethical, contrary to the concept of fair play and undermines the values of sport. The International Weightlifting Federation (IWF), condemns the use of banned substances and doping methods."
[365] Gay 1991 (*supra* nt. 129), p. 66.

substance. Doping in the newly established material rule was defined as the presence in the athlete's body of one or more substances appearing on the doping list. By such a rule, the human act which had been the focal point of previous rules was replaced by a factual circumstance. Liability for any human acts preceding this circumstance was thereby subsumed under the finding of prohibited substances. A positive test result thus precluded almost all excuses which an athlete could possibly formulate. An example of such a rule was the rule of the IAAF:[366]

> "The offence of doping takes place when [...] a prohibited substance is found to be present within an athlete's body tissue or fluids [...]."

A large number of IFs proceeded to include similar rules in their anti-doping regulations.[367] These rules were directed at the finding of prohibited substances. However, it proved necessary to establish a separate rule for the use of prohibited methods. The wording of this norm corresponded to the wording that was previously used to prohibit the use of certain substances.[368]

> "The offence of doping takes place when [...] an athlete uses or takes advantage of a prohibited technique."

Complicity, which in the old material rule was expressed by the term "administration," could not by its nature be included in the new rule. The punishability of third parties for involvement in the use of doping by an athlete will be dealt with further on in this chapter.

3. THE *PRIMA FACIE* LIABILITY RULE

Gay,[369] who was closely involved in the drafting of the IAAF anti-doping regulations in which the rules cited above were laid down, was of the opinion that by its unambiguous nature the new material rule constituted an effective instrument in the fight against doping.

> "Intent is irrelevant and so are the athlete's mere protestations of innocence if they are unsupported by other evidence."

---

[366] IAAF Rules and Regulations, Rule 55, Section 2. M. Gay: (Gay 1991 *supra* nt. 129, p. 66) "The new Rules are quite unambiguous. The offence is committed merely by the detection of a prohibited substance in an athlete's urine. Intent is irrelevant and so are the athlete's mere protestations of innocence if they are unsupported by other evidence."

[367] FISA, IWF, FIH, FINA, IBU, ISF, ITF, ITU, ISAF, ISU, FIS, ATP andn WTA. See Chapter 2, Section 1.1.4.

[368] IAAF Rules and Regulations, Rule 55, para. 2.

[369] Gay 1991 (*supra* nt. 129, p. 68), p. 6.

O'Leary[370] agreed with those who found a material rule under which a positive test automatically resulted in punishment an attractive proposition because of its clarity and simplicity. "However," he went on to say,

"[...] this rule denies what many of us would view as the fundamental right of an opportunity to prove a lack of fault, knowledge or intent. In practice this would mean that even if an athlete could prove that the consumption of the drug was accidental or the result of malice on the part of another, the athlete would still be found guilty. This may appear to be a draconian provision. The reason for it is a fear that rules requiring proof of intent would be impossible to implement and it is likely that athletes would find little difficulty in producing a coach or doctor prepared to take responsibility and vouch for the athlete's innocence."

These two quotes reveal in a nutshell that there were two diametrically opposing ambitions here. According to the one, the athlete must be given as little opportunity as possible to frustrate the doping trial by arguing that he/she was not to blame; according to the other, disciplinary law should leave room for the athlete to defend him/herself. The new material rule left no room for compromise, or at least, so the drafters had intended. Under the old rule, the sports organisation was at a disadvantage, as it could not respond adequately to the athlete's defence that for whatever reason he/she was not to blame for doping. The roles were reversed by the new rule which put the athlete at a disadvantage as nearly all of his/her defences were taken from him/her and a finding of prohibited substances in his/her blood or urine would almost automatically lead to conviction for a doping offence. The interests of the collective were thus placed above the just treatment of the individual. The group dilemma found expression in the wording of the material doping rule: uniformity as opposed to diversity.[371]

The rule established by the IAAF was harsh, but clear and simple, although one could perhaps wonder whether the doping offence only occurred at the moment of the discovery of a prohibited substance, or whether it already occurred at the moment of use. What was probably intended was that upon discovery of the substance the doping offence came to light. According to the FISA rule[372] doping was the presence in the athlete's body of one or more prohibited substances "above the permitted concentration."[373] To this rule was added the provision that the presence of such a substance "shall constitute a rebuttable presumption of voluntary use."

---

[370] Gardiner/O'Leary 1998 (*supra* nt. 14), pp. 190-191.

[371] The CAS in CAS 94/129, 23-5-1995, *USA Shooting & Quigley v. UIT*, Matthieu Reeb, ed., *Digest of CAS Awards 1986-1998* (Berne, Editions Stämpfli 1998) pp. 187-204, ground 215, considered that: "[...] it appears to be a laudable policy objective not to repair an accidental unfairness to an individual by creating an intentional unfairness to the whole body of other competitors."

[372] FISA: Rules of Racing and related By Laws, Rule 80, paras. 1 and 2.

[373] The FIH also only made the presence of prohibited substances in the body an offence if the quantities rose above a certain threshold level. Doping Policy, Art. 1: "Doping is defined as the presence in the athlete's body of one or more substances in the prohibited therapeutic categories [...] above the allowed concentration [...]."

These two additional requirements did nothing to improve the clarity and simplicity of the rule. The harshness which characterised the IAAF rule was probably a step too far in the eyes of the FISA. The material rule of the IWF[374] considered as a doping offence "the presence of a prohibited substance or metabolite." Although it was part of the essence of the new rule that a location was expressly indicated it can be concluded from the term "metabolite" that the location in question was the athlete's body. The IHF[375] and FIH[376] rules were very similar to those of the IAAF; however, as opposed to the IAAF approach, these two IFs for clarity's sake added that with the finding of the prohibited substances the athlete's liability was *prima facie* established. If the FISA still left some room for the athlete to defend him/herself by arguments concerning guilt or intent, the IHF and the FIH (like the IAAF and the IWF) virtually reduced this possibility to nil.

The number of IFs which opted in favour of the new approach to the doping problem was considerable.[377] In the new approach doping was thus not considered to be the description of an undesirable act, but rather the description of an undesirable state of affairs, i.e. the finding of a fact. The proven presence of a prohibited substance in a sample led to almost complete liability. In order to reinforce this liability and to dispel any illusions which the athlete might still have had concerning his/her chances to aver a lack of guilt or intent on his/her part the IAAF, the FINA, the FIL and the international tennis organisations included a provision in

---

[374] IWF: Anti-Doping Policy, Art. 5.1.

[375] IHF: Anti-Doping Regulations, Art. 1: "In this context, may we mention that the presence of prohibited substances represents a violation of the regulations regardless of the application method."

[376] FIH: Doping Policy, Art. 1: "The presence of such a substance in an athlete's urine or blood entails the presumption of voluntary use."

[377] FINA: Doping Control: DC 1.2: "The offence of doping occurs when: (a) a banned substance (see DC 2) is found to be present within a competitor's body tissue or fluids."
IBU: Anti-doping, Blood Test and Gender Verification Rules: "The offence of doping takes place when a prohibited drug is found to be present within an athlete's body tissue or fluids [...]."
ISF: Doping Control and Testing as Established by the ISF Medical and Doping Commission: "It should be noted that the presence of the drug in the urine constitutes an offense, irrespective of the route of administration."
ITF: Tennis Anti-doping Programme – (c) 2: "Under this Programme the following shall be regarded as doping offences: A Prohibited Substance is found to be present within a player's body [...]."
ITU: Doping Control Rules and Procedural Guidelines, 2. Definition of Doping: 2.2: "For the purpose of these Rules, the following are regarded as doping offenses: – the finding in an athlete's body tissue or fluids of a prohibited substance [...]."
ISAF: 1998 ISAF Regulations – Medical Code (Old 17): "It should be noted that the presence of the drug in the urine constitutes an offence, irrespective of the route of administration."
ISU: Communication no. 958, Art. 1.2.1.: "Doping is the detection of any substance contained in the current International Olympic Committee's list of doping classes by (sic!) the competitor [...] and is forbidden."
FIS: Doping Rules – Rule 1 – Doping: 3: "The offence of doping takes place when a prohibited drug is found to be present within an athlete's body tissue [...]."
ATP: Official Rulebook – Players – Tennis Anti-doping Program – C. Doping Offenses, 1, and:
WTA: Official Rulebook – Tennis Anti-doping Program – C. Doping Offenses, 1: "Under this Program the following shall be regarded as doping offenses: a. a Prohibited Substance is found to be present within a player's body [...]."

their regulations which made it clear to the athletes that they would be held liable for any prohibited substances found in their samples.

IAAF:[378] "It is an athlete's duty to ensure that no substance enters his body tissues or fluids which is prohibited under these Rules. Athletes are warned that they are responsible for all or any substance detected in samples given by them."

FINA:[379] "It is a competitor's duty to ensure that no banned substance enters his body tissues or fluids. Competitors are responsible for any substance detected in samples given by them."

FIL:[380] "Notwithstanding the obligations of others to comply with the provisions of the FIL Medical Code, it is the personal responsibility of any competitor subject to the provisions of the FIL Medical Code to ensure that he/she does not ingest any prohibited substance or engage in any prohibited method."

ITF:[381] "A player is absolutely responsible for any Prohibited Substance found to be present within his body."

ATP:[382] "A player is absolutely responsible for any Prohibited Substance found."

WTA:[383] "[...] to be present within his body. Accordingly, it is not necessary that intent or fault on the player's part be shown in order for a doping offence to be established under paragraphs 1a, 1b and 1e of this section C; nor is the player's lack of intent or lack of fault a defense to those doping offences."

From the above it has already emerged that a few federations still offered caught athletes an opportunity to give evidence to the contrary. For example, the FISA anti-doping regulations spoke of a "rebuttable presumption of voluntary use." Usually, the possibility to put forward a defence was only reserved for cases involving the use of conditionally prohibited substances. For example, the IOC Medical Code offered this opportunity,[384] but only if there had been no intent, gross negligence or wilful negligence in the use of the challenged substance.

"The person affected shall have the opportunity to rebut the presumption of doping by providing evidence that the substance was present under circumstances which, on a balance of probabilities, including the quantity of substance detected, would support a conclusion that doping was neither intended, nor the result of gross negligence, wilful negligence or imprudence. In all cases, the onus of rebutting the presumption of doping, when the substance has been detected, shall rest with the person affected."

The International Amateur Boxing Association (AIBA)[385] had also included a similar provision in its regulations.

---

[378] IAAF: Procedural Guidelines For Doping Control, 4.

[379] FINA: Doping Control, DC 2.2.

[380] FIL: Medical Code. Chapter I, Art. V.

[381] ITF: Tennis Anti-doping Programme – (c) Doping Offences, 2.

[382] ATP: Official Rulebook – Players – Tennis Anti-doping Program – C. Doping Offenses, 2.

[383] WTA: Official Rulebook – Tennis Anti-doping Program – C. Doping Offenses, 2.

[384] IOC: Medical Code, Chapter II, Art. V.

[385] AIBA: Doping Regulations, Art. IV(2).

"[...] the person affected shall have the opportunity to rebut the presumption of doping by providing evidence that the substance was present under circumstances which, on a balance of probabilities, including the quantity of the substance detected, would support a conclusion that doping was neither intended, nor the result of gross or wilful negligence or imprudence."

The Internatinonal Cycling Union (UCI) also restricted discussions on liability in the case of medical treatment and thereby also any arguments the defence might have raised to the effect that the prohibited substances shown to be present were not intended to enhance performance but had been used for medical reasons. Concerning use for medical purposes the UCI's anti-doping provisions contained a "No, unless..." rule.

"No substance belonging to a forbidden class or doping method may be used for medical treatment unless otherwise specified in the list. In the latter case, the burden of proof of medical treatment and the use of the substance or method for the purposes of that treatment shall lie with the rider."

The FIFA[386] also prohibited the use of listed substances for medical reasons during the athlete's participation in a competition.

"Players are also prohibited from using (taking, injecting or administering) any of the substances listed on appendix B, even for medical purposes, while they are taking part in a competition."

Despite the fact that the International Triathlon Union (ITU)[387] had also adopted the new material rule, its stance on the use of prohibited substances for medical treatment was less rigid. The ITU rules

"[...] make it possible for an athlete, who for a limited or prolonged period of time needs a prohibited substance for medical reasons, to participate in sport. An athlete may request that the Doping Commission grant prior exemption allowing him/her to take a substance normally prohibited under ITU Rules. Such exemption will only be granted in a case of clear and compelling clinical need.
Exemption will not normally be granted in cases of acute disease and never when sporting activity may be hazardous to the athlete."

In sum, therefore, the material rules which resulted in *prima facie* liability after a positive test result still left some room to put forward the defence that the athlete caught using doping was not to blame. In some cases, this defence might consist of the argument that the quantities of the substance found were within the allowed concentration, while in other cases liability could be minimalised if it could be shown that the substance had been used exclusively for medical purposes. In the

---

[386] FIFA: Doping Control Regulations for FIFA Competitions.
[387] ITU: Doping Control Rules and Procedural Guidelines, Arts. 6.1 and 6.2.

majority of cases, however, the presumption of liability could not be overturned and the athlete's only remaining option was to contest the course of events during the analysis in the hope that the test results would be declared invalid.

The events which shocked the cycling world in the summer of 1998, made the IOC decide to organise a World Conference on Doping. For this conference, which was held at Lausanne from 2 to 4 February 1999, all the parties involved in the fight against doping convened. At the end of the conference the Lausanne Declaration on Doping in Sport was drawn up. This document provided for the creation of an independent WADA. This Agency had to become fully operational before the Olympic Games in Sydney. The WADA drafted an anti-doping code, WADC which has now been adopted by the majority of international sports organisations and the Governments of over 160 countries. Article 2 of the Code lays down the strict liability principle. The athlete is strictly liable for the presence in his or her body of any prohibited substance. This principle now also applies to every sports organisation that has signed the Code. The descriptions of the doping offence used in the codes preceding the WADC were similar in structure to the description of an offence under criminal law. A certain act or situation was considered undesirable and a penalty was attached to it. The drafters of the WADC decided to abandon this approach. Doping is no longer considered a defined condemnable human act or the result of such an act, but rather a violation of the rules describing that act or result. The concept of doping has been completely detached, abstracted and instrumentalised. Doping is no longer viewed as an act knowingly performed by an athlete, but rather as an act performed by an athlete in a legal dimension: doping is the violation of an anti-doping rule.[388] As such violations of the anti-doping rule also comprise situations which are not directly considered doping offences in the classical sense of the word,[389] it is clear that the term doping has to be defined in two stages, although this is neither very elegant, nor very clear. The substantive norm, i.e. the norm that should be complied with and on the basis of which an act or a situation can be tested and punished, has been pushed into the background. Subsequent to the framework rule it is indicated when there can be said to have been a violation of the anti-doping regulations. The substantive norm which was taken as the starting point in the WADC says that no underlying substantive norms may be violated. These rules essentially indicate what the drafters of the Code considered doping to be.

"Article 2 Anti-doping rule violations
The following constitute anti-doping rule violations:
2.1 The presence of a *Prohibited Substance* or its *Metabolites* or *Markers* in an *Athlete's* bodily *Specimen*.

---

[388] Art. 1 WADC: "Doping is defined as the occurrence of one or more of the anti-doping rule violations set forth in Article 2.1 through Article 2.8 of the Code."

[389] The possession of doping substances by persons in the athlete's entourage is very far removed from an actual act of doping by the athlete.

2.1.1 It is each Athlete's personal duty to ensure that no *Prohibited Substance* enters his or her body. *Athletes* are responsible for any *Prohibited Substance* or its *Metabolites* or *Markers* found to be present in their bodily *Specimens*. Accordingly, it is not necessary that intent, fault, negligence or knowing *Use* on the *Athlete's* part be demonstrated in order to establish an anti-doping violation under Article 2.1."[390]

4. INTERPRETATION BY THE CAS OF THE *PRIMA FACIE* RULE

Over the past few decades the CAS in numerous doping cases has been required to give an interpretation of the new material rules at issue, metaphorically termed by it "strict liability rules." The CAS did not only make a valuable contribution to the legal reasoning underlying the rule itself, but in its considerations it also examined various additional aspects in the framework of liability for the athlete's actions. Of this one CAS arbitrator, Mr Beloff, has said:[391]

"In a series of cases decided by the CAS the correct interpretation of anti-doping provisions has been debated. The principal issue has been whether particular rules under consideration create a strict liability offence of ingesting a banned substance, or whether knowledge and/or intention to ingest the substance must additionally be proved."

4.1. Between the old and the revised material rule

After the analysis of Quigley's sample produced a positive result, the International Shooting Union (UIT) suspended him for a period of three months. Although the UIT was aware that Quigley had used the substances of which traces were later found in his urine to treat an acute complaint, and not to enhance his athletic performance, it could still ban Quigley as it was accepted among its membership that the finding of a prohibited substance implied *prima facie* liability. Quigley and his national federation appealed against the judgment of the UIT to the CAS.[392] Quigley based his appeal amongst other things on the then material rule in the UIT doping regulations which provided that an athlete could only be penalised if he/she could be blamed for using the medication in question.[393]

---

[390] In order to indicate that the WADC does not signify a break with the anti-doping rules previously in force, Art. 2 starts out by stating that "the purpose of Article 2 is to specify the circumstances and conduct which constitute violations of anti-doping rules. Hearings in doping cases will proceed based on the assertion that one or more of these specific rules have been violated. Most of the circumstances and conduct on this list of violations can be found in some form in the OMADC [Olympic Movement Anti-Doping Code; *JWS*] or other existing anti-doping rules."

[391] Beloff 1999 (*supra* nt. 282), 7.27.

[392] CAS 94/129, 23-5-1995, *USA Shooting & Quigley v. UIT* (Paulsson, Oswald, Argand), Matthieu Reeb, ed., *Digest of CAS Awards 1986-1998* (Berne, Editions Stämpfli 1998) pp. 187-204.

[393] UIT Anti-Doping Regulations, Art. 2.

"Doping means the use of one or more substances mentioned in the official UIT Anti-Doping List with the aim of attaining an increase in performance [...]."

Quigley considered that he had not been at fault because he had not attained any sporting advantage. Even under a strict liability regime, therefore, he could not be punished, or could only be mildly punished at best. The UIT argued that its decision, although based on its anti-doping regulations, was not based on the assumption that Quigley had used a substance which could enhance his performance and that he had used it for that purpose. "In other words, doping is a strict liability offence which is established once the presence of a prohibited substance is established." The UIT in its own opinion could not have reached any other verdict.

Although the Panel admitted its sympathy for the material rule[394] establishing *prima facie* liability,[395] in its opinion such a standard could only be applied if it was clearly defined. "This is where we reach the heart of the problem of this case." The UIT further adduced that its material rule had to be read as a strict liability rule, that its policy was directed towards strict liability and that it had experienced some practical difficulties in the implementation of its anti-doping programme, but all to no avail. The UIT's right to punish Quigly could only derive from the rules in force.

"The Panel has reviewed the UIT's arguments with sympathy for the objectives and practical difficulties of its anti-doping programme. But the fact that the Panel has sympathy for the principle of a strict liability rule obviously does not allow the Panel to create such a rule where it does not exist. Nor would the fact that the UIT is said to be in the process of aligning its rules with an IOC-inspired strict liability principle justify punishment on the basis of rules which do not yet exist, and indeed contradict the rule presently in force."[396]

"The Panel has carefully examined the textual arguments by which the UIT seeks to get around what it today plainly views as an unfortunate definition surviving in its Regulations. As we shall now see, none of those arguments stand up. The fact that article 1 of the UIT Anti-Doping Regulations recites that they are based on the IOC Rules cannot mean that any provisions in any IOC rules which contradict the UIT Regulations will take precedence. The statement in Article 1 may very well be of as-

[394] CAS 94/129, 23-5-1995, *USA Shooting & Quigley v. UIT*, Matthieu Reeb, ed., *Digest of CAS Awards 1986-1998* (Berne, Editions Stämpfli 1998) pp. 187-204, ground 21.
[395] According to A.N. Wise (*Legal Status and Problems of Foreign Athletes in the United States*, Paper presented at the T.M.C. Asser Institute Round Table Session entitled "The Americanization of Sports Law? The American and European Sports Models Compared," Utrecht, The Netherlands, 9 March 2000 (Wise 2000)) the CAS's preference for a material rule which starts from *prima facie* guilt has not always been as marked as it would appear from this judgment. "TAS arbitrators have been extremely inconsistent over the years on these issues. Up until around 1993-1994, TAS arbitrators had, in several cases, rejected strict liability in doping cases. Then, probably due in part to certain pressures, TAS panels began to apply strict liability doping rules." Unfortunately, this claim was not followed up by further elaboration.
[396] CAS 94/129, 23-5-1995, *USA Shooting & Quigley v. UIT*, Matthieu Reeb, ed., *Digest of CAS Awards 1986-1998* (Berne, Editions Stämpfli 1998) pp. 187-204, ground 21.

sistance if there is an issue of interpreting the Regulations. But it is for the UIT, if it so wishes, to ensure that its Regulations do indeed incorporate relevant IOC texts. Persons subjected to the UIT Regulations can only read what is said. They cannot be asked to consider that any or all of the UIT Regulations might in fact be invalid due to the existence or emergence of unspecified IOC rules.

[...]

1)   Article 2 requires a finding of culpable intent,
2)   the Executive Committee explicitly concluded that there was no such intent, and therefore
3)   there could be no punishment under the UIT Anti-Doping Regulations."[397]

The CAS upheld these brief but powerful arguments by Quigley. The defence of the UIT which started from the scope of Article 2 being different from what it would appear to be on first reading as this scope was embedded in the UIT's overall strict liability policy was unsuccessful.[398] The battle was effectively lost. However, at first glance it seems odd from the viewpoint of procedural strategy that the UIT did not simply point to Supplement C of its Anti-Doping Regulations, which read that: "The inadvertent use of forbidden doping substances such as Ephedrine [...] shall be penalized." Such a rule may be considered as a description of the doping offence, and one which is specifically tailored to the case in hand at that, as opposed to the rule contained in Article 2 which only provides a definition of doping. It has to be stressed that this rule did not establish strict liability either as it left room to demonstrate that use took place negligently. The crucial issue was what the status of a rule in a supplement is. The CAS put a different question and asked: does the rule in the supplement set aside the rule in Article 2? The CAS answered in the negative. The Regulations did not contain any provisions stipulating that Supplement C applied. The answer would have been in the affirmative if the Regulations had been worded more adequately. "[...] one cannot encourage a sport federation to adopt a drafting style which overrules in one place what it has ruled in another, thus creating traps for the unwary." Initially, the difference in status based on a hierarchical distinction between the two sets of rules containing the respective provisions did not appear to be at issue, but rather the fact that the rules contained contradictory elements. The definition imposes the requirement that the object of the athlete's will has to be to act illegally, while in the description of the offence any discussion of the question of object is avoided. Next, however, the question of hierarchy was introduced after all, as this might eliminate the contradiction between the provi-

---

[397] *Idem*, ground 23.

[398] The statement of the CAS in ground 34 of *Quigley* has become quite famous. In later judgments, this passage is often referred to: "The fight against doping is arduous, and it may require strict rules. But the rule makers and the rule appliers must begin by being strict with themselves. Regulations that may affect the careers of dedicated athletes must be predictable. They must emanate from duly authorised bodies. They must be adopted in constitutionally proper ways. They should not be the product of an obscure process of accretion. Athletes and officials should not be confronted with a thicket of mutually qualifying or even contradictory rules that can be understood only on the basis of the de facto practice over the course of many years of a small number of insiders."

sions. The Comment to the Supplement that "supplements are issued immediately upon receipt of official changes in information and are an official part of this Annex (sic!)" was considered insufficient by the CAS. Reaching for such a weak argument to confirm the supremacy of Supplement C was considered by the CAS to be tantamount to admitting defeat. The anti-doping regulations of the UIT therefore left no room for the CAS to decide otherwise. The UIT doping rules provided no basis for Quigley's punishment without a prior examination of the question of whether he had been responsible for his actions. For this reason, the CAS reversed the penalties imposed by the UIT.

> "Reading the UIT Regulations (as they currently appear) in the light of these desiderata, the Panel has no alternative but to reach the conclusion that the UIT had no legal basis for the sanctions it pronounced against the appellants. The sanctions must therefore be reversed."[399]

One remarkable aspect of the *Quigley* case has yet to be discussed. At the heart of the arguments was Article 2 of the UIT Anti-Doping Regulations, which gave a definition of the term doping. Doping was the use of UIT-prohibited substances, unless these were not used to enhance performance. Here, mention was only made of certain behaviour. Article 2 did not provide a description of the doping offence whereby this behaviour was declared undesirable and thus prohibited. Penalties could only be imposed on the basis of such a description. The rule included in Supplement C did contain such a description, but had to be left aside for various reasons. On the face of it, the description of the term doping could be taken as the starting point for imposing sanctions, now that within the sport it was *prima facie* assumed that doping was undesirable behaviour, which was prohibited. However, such a biased starting point turns the definition from merely an element of the description into the description itself.

An IF upon finding a prohibited substance could only assume an act of doping for which the athlete was liable if this had been laid down in its doping regulations and was recognisable to all. The athlete should not at some point be confronted with the fact that the sports organisation's policy differed from what was laid down in the regulations. If the regulations did not contain a rule which allowed the sports organisation *prima facie* to assume the liability of the athlete it could be required to demonstrate such liability after all. The predictability of the rules took precedence over what the organisation considered the customary practice, but had omitted to lay down in the rules. If, however, the IF had included a material rule in its regulations which provided that upon the finding of a prohibited substance in the urine or blood of the athlete he/she was automatically presumed to be liable for an act of doping there was nothing to stand in the IF's way to implement this provision. This starting point was repeated by the CAS in subsequent case law:

---

[399] CAS 94/129, 23-5-1995, *USA Shooting & Quigley v. UIT*, Matthieu Reeb, ed., *Digest of CAS Awards 1986-1998* (Berne, Editions Stämpfli 1998) pp. 187-204, ground 35.

"If a federation wants to allow no defences at all (assuming this is legal [...]) in the event that a banned substance is found in an athlete's body it must express this in a manner which is absolutely crystal clear and unambiguous."[400]

"It is important that the fight against doping in sport, national and international, be waged unremittingly. The reasons are well known [...]. It is equally important that athletes in any sport [...] know clearly where they stand. It is unfair if they are to be found guilty of offences in circumstances where they neither knew nor reasonably could have known that what they were doing was wrong (to avoid any doubt we are not to be taken as saying that doping offences should not be offences as a strict liability, but rather that the nature of the offence [as one of strict liability] should be known and understood)."[401]

In *Cullwick v. FINA* the CAS elaborated a test to decide whether the rules were sufficiently clear and unambiguous. The standard for this test was not whether a legally trained person considered the rules crystal clear and unambiguous, but whether an athlete who was subject to these rules but had not had any legal training and had no experience with legal matters considered that the rules fulfilled the criteria mentioned. The problem with a test like this, however, – and this is something which the CAS glossed over – is that arbitrators with experience in legal interpretation have to determine what a person without any legal training should be able to understand.

The CAS case *NWBA v. IPC*[402] corresponds to the *Quigley* case to the extent that in this case too an athlete was held *prima facie* liable for a doping offence while the doping regulations of the sports organisation in question did not expressly provide a material rule to that effect.[403]

"It is true that the ICC rules do not contain a provision that clearly calls the reader's attention to the establishment of the strict liability principle. (Thus: Definition of doping: an athlete in whose body banned substances are detected shall be guilty of doping.) It may well be desirable for such a provision to be articulated."

The athlete was nevertheless considered *prima facie* responsible and the sports organisation was released from the duty to prove intent or guilt. How was this possible? In the Medical Control Guide for the 1992 Barcelona Paralympics the Medical Chairman of the sports organisation concerned (the ICC) in a personal introduction referred to the ICC's "strict plan to deal with doping" and made it clear that "innocent motives such as relieving nervous tension or reducing fatigue are for

---

[400] CAS 96/156, 6-10-1997, *Jessica K. Foschi v. FINA*, ground 13.3 (Martens, Oswald, Campbell).
[401] CAS 96/149, 13-3-1997, *Cullwick v. FINA*, ground 31 (Beloff, Castle, Carrard), Matthieu Reeb, ed., *Digest of CAS Awards 1986-1998* (Berne, Editions Stämpfli 1998) pp. 251-263.
[402] CAS 95/122, 5-3-1996, *National Wheelchair Basketball Association (NWBA) v. IPC*, Matthieu Reeb, ed., *Digest of CAS Awards 1986-1998* (Berne, Editions Stämpfli 1998) pp. 173-185 (Paulsson, Argand, Dixon).
[403] *Idem*, ground 12.

this purpose no different from seeking to increase muscle strength or to improve performance," also stating that "the presence of the drug in the urine constitutes an offence, irrespective of the route of administration." Contrary to what the CAS had considered in Quigley that despite its sympathy for the strict liability rule this could not be applied "when faced with a clearly inconsistent provision" and contrary to the test developed by the CAS to establish whether to a lay person the rules could be considered to be clear and unambiguous, the athlete in the *NBWA* case could apparently be held *prima facie* liable for a doping offence based on some statements in a personal introduction. This is all the more puzzling, now that in one of the grounds[404] the CAS lets it slip that it "[...] has seen ample evidence of the fact that the ICC authorities themselves had an imperfect understanding of their Rules." As in Quigley, the CAS should have taken a more detached view of the matter and curbed its enthusiasm for the strict liability rule, as the application of this rule had no true legal basis in the doping regulations of the sports organisation concerned.

4.2.   The reasons for the CAS's preference for the strict liability rule

In *Quigley* and in the *NWBA* case the CAS had thus expressed sympathy for the material rule starting from the presumed liability of the athlete whose sample contained prohibited substances, despite the fact that the application of this norm put the athlete at a serious disadvantage. The CAS qualified this rule as the "strict liability rule"; a rule which establishes liability without guilt, in fact presumes guilt when the athlete's body was found to contain prohibited substances. In this section it will be examined why the CAS preferred such a rule.

From the earliest doping cases included in the Digest of CAS Awards it can only be concluded that the CAS had no objection to its application. The tribunal simply applied the material rule of the IF in question if this IF had demonstrated that the athlete's act (in those cases the person in charge of a horse) corresponded to the act described in that rule. If the doping offence had been proven based on a positive test result the athlete was held liable without further explanation.

"In accordance with Article 149.2 of the FEI General Regulations, the presence of the prohibited substance results in a pure strict liability which is expressed in the automatic disqualification of the horse and the rider from all competitions at that event which implies loss of all rankings obtained. This consequence is confirmed by Article 177.5.1 of the FEI General Regulations."[405]
"The appellant is the person responsible for the horse in application of Article 145 of the FEI GR. While it is true that, in application of Article 8 of the Swiss Civil Code, the burden of proof of the presence of a prohibited substance lies with the FEI, it

---

[404] CAS 95/122, 5-3-1996, *National Wheelchair Basketball Association (NWBA) v. IPC*, Matthieu Reeb, ed., *Digest of CAS Awards 1986-1998* (Berne, Editions Stämpfli 1998) pp. 173-185, ground 26.
[405] CAS 91/53, 15-1-1992, *G. v. FEI*, Matthieu Reeb, ed., *Digest of CAS Awards 1986-1998* (Berne, Editions Stämpfli 1998) pp. 67-91, ground 14 (Oswald, Sutter, Benigno).

should be noted that, for his part, the person responsible has a strict liability, as has consistently been accepted in this domain."[406]

In *Quigley v. UIT* the CAS explained why it preferred a strict liability regime to a regime where an IF still had to parry the athlete's claim that he/she was not liable. Although in individual cases *prima facie* liability might result in unfairness,

"[...] it appears to be a laudable policy objective not to repair an accidental unfairness to an individual by creating an intentional unfairness to the whole body of other competitors."[407]

On the other hand, one might wonder whether it is a laudable policy objective to allow the unfairness by pointing out, as the CAS did in *Quigley*, that life in general is not fair:[408]

"[...] it is also in some sense unfair for an athlete to get food poisoning on the eve of an important competition. Yet in neither case will the rules of the competition be altered to undo the unfairness. Just as the competition will not be postponed to await the athlete's recovery, so the prohibition of a banned substance will not be lifted in recognition of its accidental absorption. The vicissitudes of competition, like those of life generally, may create many types of unfairness, whether by accident or the negligence of unaccountable persons, which the law cannot repair."

Individual unfairness aside, however, the tribunal considered that it was possible even in the case of intentional use that the perpetrator might escape punishment due to the fact that intent could not be proven. There was also a financial argument in favour of strict liability:

"[...] it is certain that a requirement of intent would invite costly litigation that may well cripple federations – particularly those run on modest budgets – in their fight against doping."

Summing up, the CAS considered that:

"[...] in principle the high objectives and practical necessities of the fight against doping amply justify the application of a strict liability standard."[409]

---

[406] CAS 92/71, 20-10-1992, *SJ. v. FEI*, Matthieu Reeb, ed., *Digest of CAS Awards 1986-1998* (Berne, Editions Stämpfli 1998) pp. 125-143, ground 16 (Rasquin, Klimke, Lévy). The only reported case in which the strict liability rule was applied is CAS 91/53, 15-1-1992, *G. v. FEI*, Matthieu Reeb, ed., *Digest of CAS Awards 1986-1998* (Berne, Editions Stämpfli 1998) pp. 67-91, so that we will just have to take the CAS's word for it that this rule "has consistently been accepted in this domain."

[407] CAS 94/129, 23-5-1995, *USA Shooting & Quigley v. UIT*, Matthieu Reeb, ed., *Digest of CAS Awards 1986-1998* (Berne, Editions Stämpfli 1998) pp. 187-204, ground 15.

[408] *Idem*, ground 14.

[409] *Idem*, ground 16.

The CAS therefore put forward two arguments to base its preference for the strict liability rule on. First, the rule can prevent injustice to the collective (a "high objective")[410] and second, it can prevent that a sports federation has to incur great expense (a "practical necessity"). Arguments to the effect that the strict liability rule could conflict with "natural justice" for depriving athletes accused of doping of the opportunity to prove their moral innocence failed to sway the CAS.

In *Chagnaud v. FINA*[411] the CAS subsumed another element under the "high objectives," namely that of "sporting fairness."

> "The Panel is of the opinion that the system of strict liability of the athlete must prevail when sporting fairness is at stake. This means that, once a banned substance is discovered in the urine or blood of an athlete, he must automatically be disqualified from the competition in question, without any possibility for him to rebut this presumption of guilt (irrebuttable presumption). It would indeed be shocking to include in a ranking an athlete who had not competed using the same means as his opponents, for whatever reasons."

In sum, therefore, presumed liability often resulted in disqualification from competing, whereby the interests of the collective took precedence over the interests of the individual. From the way in which the CAS phrased this consideration it could be assumed that the sports organisation had to assess whether "sporting fairness" was at stake. This presumably means that circumstances could occur where this was not the case and where there would be no reason to disqualify an athlete who had tested positive. Criteria which could be used in deciding whether sporting fairness has been violated are not easily devised and the CAS did not provide any. The suggestion that the CAS intended to leave room for assessment was however belied by its reference to the words of Dallèves:[412] "The result of the event has indeed been objectively vitiated and, consequently, the intention of the author is irrelevant." Any sporting sanctions imposed on an athlete based on presumed liability were without prejudice to the imposition by the sports organisation of disciplinary measures on the same basis.

---

[410] Cf., CAS 95/142, 14-2-1996, *Lehtinen v. FINA*, Matthieu Reeb, ed., *Digest of CAS Awards 1986-1998* (Berne, Editions Stämpfli 1998) pp. 225-244, ground 12: "The FINA Medical Rules (MED) provide for the application of what is generally characterized as a strict liability standard as an effective instrument in the fight against doping. The CAS panels have always supported the application of such a strict liability standard in other doping cases." CAS 98/222, 9-8-1999, *Bernhard v. ITU*, Matthieu Reeb, ed., *Digest of CAS Awards II 1998-2000* (The Hague, Kluwer Law International 2002) pp. 330-344, ground 35: "This Panel shares the opinion expressed in the above-quoted awards that the rule on strict liability is essential and, indeed, indispensable for an efficient fight against doping in sport and for the protection of fairness towards all competitors and of their health and wellbeing."

[411] CAS 95/141, 22-4-1996, *Chagnaud v. FINA*, ground 15 (Rasquin, Karaquillo, Carrard), Matthieu Reeb, ed., *Digest of CAS Awards 1986-1998* (Berne, Editions Stämpfli 1998) pp. 205-224.

[412] L. Dallèves: *Sport and Law Conference, Court of Arbitration for Sport* (Geneva, Ed. Médecine et hygiène 1993) p. 26.

4.3. Punishment without guilt? Strict or *prima facie* liability?

The material rule penalising the use of named prohibited substances gave the athlete an opportunity (even if his use had been intentional) to escape conviction by manoeuvring the sports organisation into a position where it had to prove that the athlete's use had been intentional or had come about through culpable negligence. As the burden of proof of liability lay with the sports organisation, the athlete was at a distinct advantage: it was virtually impossible for the sports organisation to prove guilt or intent on the part of the athlete. Whichever reasons – motivated by high objectives – the CAS may have adduced, the main reason for the sports organisations to abandon the regime of fault liability and embrace that of *prima facie* liability was the desire to rid themselves of their evidentiary problems. It has already been remarked above that the strict liability regime was seldom criticised in the legal literature. O'Leary[413] agreed with those who considered that a rule which automatically resulted in exclusion upon the finding of a banned substance was attractive through its clarity and simplicity. However, he went on to observe that such a rule:

> "[...] denies what many of us would view as the fundamental right of an opportunity to prove a lack of fault, knowledge or intent. In practice this would mean that even if an athlete could prove that the consumption of the drug was accidental or as a result of malice on the part of another, the athlete would still be found guilty. This may appear to be a draconian provision."

Under the new regime, the sports organisations were no less bound to demonstrate that a doping offence had occurred.[414] In this, as the CAS held in *Korneev v. IOC*,[415]

---

[413] Gardiner/O'Leary 1998 (*supra* nt. 14), pp. 190-191. Cf., Beloff 1999 (*supra* nt. 279), 7.27: "In a series of cases decided by the CAS the correct interpretation of anti-doping provisions has been debated. The principal issue has been whether particular rules under consideration create a strict liability offence of ingesting a banned substance, or whether knowledge and/or intention to ingest the substance must additionally be proved. As we have already observed in chapter three, strict liability doping offences are not necessarily invalid as contractual terms on public policy grounds, since performance-enhancing drugs confer an unfair advantage even if taken accidentally or without intent to gain advantage."

[414] The burden for the sports organisation to prove that a doping offence had occurred was normally based on the wording of the material rule and on Section 8 of the Swiss Civil Code. See: CAS 92/71, 20-10-1992, *SJ. v. FEI*, Matthieu Reeb, ed., *Digest of CAS Awards 1986-1998* (Berne, Editions Stämpfli 1998) pp. 125-143, ground 16; CAS 95/142, 14-2-1996, *Lehtinen v. FINA*, Matthieu Reeb, ed., *Digest of CAS Awards 1986-1998* (Berne, Editions Stämpfli 1998) pp. 225-244, ground 25; CAS 98/208, 22-12-1998, *Wang Lu Na, Cai Hui Jue, Zhgang Yi, Wang Wei v. FINA*, Matthieu Reeb, ed., *Digest of CAS Awards II 1998-2000* (The Hague, Kluwer Law International 2002) pp. 234-254, ground 5.5; CAS 98/211, 7-6-1999, *Smith-De Bruin v. FINA*, Matthieu Reeb, ed., *Digest of CAS Awards II 1998-2000* (The Hague, Kluwer Law International 2002) pp. 255-273, ground 10.1.

[415] CAS AH 96/003-4, 4-8-1996, *Andrei Korneev v. IOC & Zakhar Goukiev v. IOC* (Bruce, Shycoff, Rasquin).

"It follows that the more serious the allegation being considered the greater is the degree of evidence which is required to achieve the requisite degree of comfortable satisfaction necessary to establish the commission of the offence."

Once the offence had been sufficiently proven by means of a positive doping test result, the burden of proof was reversed and the athlete who was suspected of having used doping had to show that he could not be blamed for his/her actions. The athlete's position which hitherto had been extremely comfortable underwent a dramatic change as a result of the new material rule. In theory, the athlete still had a chance to prove his/her innocence, but in practice the *prima facie*-ness of the liability had rather turned into definitive liability. In the regime developed by the CAS in its case law, athletes who had been caught were fully liable, or in the words of the CAS: strictly liable.[416] Once full liability had been established, the athlete was still given the opportunity to show that he/she was not to blame, either at all, or only partially, as taking all circumstances into account the use of doping was not entirely his/her own fault. A complete or partial lack of liability was only relevant, however, for the severity of the penalty to be imposed.

The outlines of the system just described were already present in *W. v. FEI*,[417] if not as a system developed by the CAS, but as part of the FEI regulations. The FEI had included a rule in its doping regulations which provided that the finding of a prohibited substance in a horse led to the presumption of intent to influence the horse's performance on the part of the person responsible for the horse. If the responsible person was able to show, that it was not a deliberate attempt to affect the performance of the horse or that the findings were the result of legitimate treatment of the horse or of one or more parts of his body, the penalty would be less severe than in the case where the responsible person was unable to demonstrate this.[418]

---

[416] Tarasti (Tarasti 1999, *supra* nt. 333) addressed the question of: "which kind of content strict liability has in doping cases and if it is possible in these cases to deviate from the general principles of criminal law when determining guilt and the necessary intent or negligence." One would have expected that he would take the provisions of the IOC Medical Code dealing with the definitive case of doping and the *prima facie* case of doping as the starting point. However, this was not the case. Instead, Tarasti took the rule included in Art. 1 of Chapter 1 of the IOC Medical Code as his starting point where it provided that the use of certain substances was prohibited and then concluded that the Code did not contain a uniform explanation of the liability of the athlete. This is surprising, especially in Tarasti's capacity of member of the Sport and Law Commission of the IOC. He then turned to the doping definition which was used by the IAAF: "[...] a prohibited substance is found to be present within an athlete's body tissue or fluids." The wording used by the IAAF, according to Tarasti, "can give good reasons to interpret liability as a strict one," while it was obvious that the words chosen by the IAAF clearly indicated full liability, rather than merely the possibility to interpret them as such. Why Tarasti did not choose Art. IV of Chapter 1 of the IOC Medical Code as his starting point is a mystery. This provision was just as clear as that of the IAAF: "[...] the detected presence of any amount of substances in classes (a), (b), (c) and (e) in respect of a test conducted in connection with a competition shall constitute a definite case of doping. The quantity of the substance detected is not material to a definite case of doping."
[417] CAS 92/86, 9-4-1993, *W. v. FEI*, Matthieu Reeb, ed., *Digest of CAS Awards 1986-1998* (Berne, Editions Stämpfli 1998) pp. 161-171 (Rasquin, Klimke, Sutter).
[418] FEI GR, Arts. 177.5.2 and 177.5.3.

The CAS simply followed the provisions established by the FEI:[419]

> "Such modification therefore clearly states the fact that the finding on analysis of a prohibited substance presumes a deliberate attempt by the person responsible to affect the performance of the horse. In other words, the strict liability of the person responsible being established in the case of prohibited substances being discovered, the burden of proof is reversed. It consequently rests with the person responsible to prove either that there was not a deliberate attempt to affect the performance of the horse, or that the horse has undergone legitimate treatment."

Chagnaud could not reconcile herself with a system under which liability was presumed. In her defence, she quoted Dalleves:[420] "one may wonder to what extent sanctions of a penal nature may be imposed without it having been established that the author acted intentionally, or at least displayed culpable negligence, [Principle: *Nulla poena sine culpa*]." The CAS[421] was of the opinion that it would affect the effectiveness of the measures against the use of doping if this principle was understood too literally. On the one hand, it would practically cripple the efforts against doping if in each individual case the athlete's liability had to be established, but on the other hand the CAS considered that a system of definitive liability (irrebuttable presumption) would also lead to unacceptable results.

> "In conjunction with such a sporting sanction, a disciplinary sanction may also be involved in doping cases. In the majority of cases, this is suspension of the athlete who tested positive. On this precise aspect of the issue, the Panel believes that the different sports rules on sanctions in doping cases should make allowance for an appreciation of the subjective elements in each case. For it is indeed the task of the sports authorities to establish the guilt of an athlete in order to fix a just and equitable sanction."[422]
> "[...] the Panel considers that, generally speaking, the principle of presumption of the athlete's guilt may remain but that, by way of compensation, the athlete must have the possibility of shifting the burden of proof by providing exculpatory evidence. The athlete will thus be allowed to demonstrate that he did not commit any fault intentionally or negligently."[423]

The system advocated by the CAS in which the athlete's liability after a positive test result is absolute but the degree of guilt is weighed for the purpose of determining the nature and severity of the sanction to be imposed depended on the way in

---

[419] CAS 92/86, 9-4-1993, *W. v. FEI*, Matthieu Reeb, ed., *Digest of CAS Awards 1986-1998* (Berne, Editions Stämpfli 1998) pp. 161-171, ground 6.

[420] L. Dalleves: *Chapitres choisis du droit du sport*, GISS, 1993, p. 120.

[421] CAS 95/141, 22-4-1996, *Chagnaud v. FINA*, Matthieu Reeb, ed., *Digest of CAS Awards 1986-1998* (Berne, Editions Stämpfli 1998) pp. 205-224, ground 13.

[422] *Idem*, ground 16.

[423] *Idem*, ground 17. In ground 18 the CAS referred to its reasoning in previous cases: "The CAS has already had occasion to recall the above-mentioned principles when the application of the General Regulations (GR) of the International Equestrian Federation were at issue (see cases CAS 92/63 and CAS 92/86)."

which the sports organisations had phrased the sanctions in their doping regulations. It can already be concluded that almost all of the Olympic IFs used fixed sanctions. The severity of such sanctions was not related to the severity of the offence, but to the kind of doping substances used and to the fact whether the athlete was a first offender or a repeat offender. The CAS therefore addressed a practice which it found to exist with the FEI, but which was not shared by the other IFs. By considering "that a fixed-rate system governing sanctions in doping cases is not desirable and that a more flexible system, which provides a sliding scale of suspension periods depending on the degree of fault of the athlete, is preferable" the CAS had so far not managed to convince many sports organisations. The observation by the CAS that the desired development was only possible if the applicable rules permitted it did not undermine the CAS's belief in its own system, despite the fact that most sports organisations continued to use fixed penalties.

The system as advocated by the CAS only nominally removed the unfairness towards athletes who had been caught. Where the establishment of liability was concerned, the athletes were not given any opportunity to defend themselves. They were however offered this opportunity at the second stage of the doping trial where the severity of the sanction to be imposed was at issue. During this stage athletes could put forward arguments to show that – given that no, or only very little, blame attached to them – no penalty or only a very minor penalty could be imposed. Once the defence rested, most IFs were, however, still forced by their doping regulations to impose the maximum penalty. In the Chagnaud case, for example, the FINA could in principle have done very little else now that Article 4.17.4.1. MED provided that: "Sanctions are as follows: Anabolic steroids, amphetamine [...]" (etc., among which the substance found in the swimmer's sample): "2 years for the first offence [...]." The CAS concluded that "in the present case, Article 4.17.4.1. MED provides for a rigid system of suspensions where the athlete's guilt is presumed irrebuttably." If this case had involved any other federation this would have resulted in the immediate bankruptcy of the system. However, the case in question involved the FINA, and its inconsistent sanctioning policy in the past must have seemed heaven sent to the CAS. A few months after the FINA Executive had suspended Chagnaud for two years it was called upon to decide on the use of doping by another swimmer, Ms Riley. In this case, which was "somewhat similar to the present case," the FINA Executive had let Riley off with a warning, which was in direct violation of the fixed penalty system laid down in the FINA anti-doping rules. This gave the CAS a golden opportunity to reduce the penalty of two years' suspension imposed on Chagnaud by the FINA to a period which it deemed proportional due to the swimmer's excellent morality and exemplary conduct.[424] Yet the CAS should have realised that the system divided into liability and punishability could not solely

---

[424] Beloff 1999 (*supra* nt. 282), 7.30 described the CAS's reasoning as follows: "The CAS approved the use of strict liability rules irrespective of any question of guilty intent. Despite this the CAS construed the ruling in favour of the swimmer, relying on previous flexibility by FINA in applying them."

rely on the inconsistency of the sanctioning policy of the IF in question. In most cases the CAS by using the system would only raise the athlete's hopes unnecessarily.

Still, the CAS insisted on the system of full liability. In *Lehtinen v. FINA*[425] it again pointed out that the finding of a prohibited substance in the athlete's blood or urine should not automatically result in the athlete's conviction for doping.

> "There is no tie between sanction and intent. The sanction is an inevitable consequence, if a doping offence has been established. Whether a severe sanction such as a two-year ban may be imposed on an athlete without examining the issue of guilt and intent is not undisputed, particularly in view of Art. 28 of the Swiss Civil Code (Personality rights) and Art. 18 of the Swiss Penal Code (requirement of intent) (see, e.g., Baddeley, L'association sportive face au droit, Basel and Frankfurt, 1994, 240-244; Vieweg, Doping und Verbandsrecht, in: NJW 1991, 1515; and ibid., Questions juridiques relatives au dopage, in Chapitres choisis du droit du sport, Geneva 1993, 119 ff.)."

In this case, the question of whether Lehtinen could be held liable for the use of a prohibited substance (namely salbutamol) was not at issue. Lehtinen had neither denied taking the substance, nor had he argued that he had used the substance unintentionally. What he did argue was that the mere finding of salbutamol in his urine was insufficient to establish a doping offence. This case has been discussed in the previous chapter.

The FINA had suspended swimmer Jessica Foschi for doping for a period of two years. The Appeal Brief drawn up by Foschi's lawyer was a frontal attack on the strict liability system.[426] It stated that absolute liability rules (strict liability with no defences) violated United States law and Swiss law and basic principles of due process, natural justice, and fundamental fairness. Paulsson[427] in 1993 argued that to accept that the mere presence of prohibited substances reverses the burden of proof and establishes a presumption of doping went against Swiss public order.

> "Whether or not the FEI's rules were overly severe in prohibiting substances which in fact do not enhance performance, and whether or not the TAS arbitrators had reversed the burden of proof, the Federal Tribunal held that these were simple issues of evidentiary weight arising in a private law context; it therefore denied the argument to the effect that there had been a violation of the principle of the presumption of innocence (which the petitioner had gone so far as to raise by reference to the European Convention of Human Rights). Such a complaint belongs to the realm of criminal law. In a particularly important passage, the Federal Tribunal declared that whether they are ap-

---

[425] CAS 95/142, 14-2-1996, *Lehtinen v. FINA*, Matthieu Reeb, ed., *Digest of CAS Awards 1986-1998* (Berne, Editions Stämpfli 1998) pp. 225-244, ground 14 (Netzle, Seim-Haugen, Carrard).

[426] CAS 96/156, 6-10-1997, *Jessica K. Foschi v. FINA*, grounds 5.6, 5.7 and 5.8 (Martens, Oswald, Campbell).

[427] Jan Paulsson, *Arbitration of International Sport Disputes*, Arbitration International, Vol. 9, No. 4 [1993] (Paulsson 1993), p. 366.

propriate or not, indeed whether they may or may not be said to be arbitrary, [the FEI doping rules] do not concern fundamental principles of the Swiss legal order in the domain of international relations."

If it was found, however, that the FINA's material rule did not violate every applicable law, the FINA could not impose or enforce such a rule unless and until it was adopted properly, all contradictory rules or guidelines were eliminated, and the new rule was communicated to the community of persons subject to the FINA Rules. The third line of attack was much more moderate, namely "even if the FINA Rules did not require dismissal of the case against the Appellant, she could not be given any more than a strong warning because her fault was much less than Samantha Riley's."

The CAS took the material rule in the FINA anti-doping regulations as its starting point.

"MED 4.3 The identification of a banned substance and/or any of its metabolites in a competitor's urine or blood sample will constitute an offence, and the offender shall be sanctioned. [...]"

According to this rule, a doping offence was deemed to have been committed the moment it had been established that there were prohibited substances present in the athlete's urine. This points to a legal presumption that the athlete is responsible for the presence of the banned substances in his/her body and that he/she may thus be held liable. The FINA did not need to prove the swimmer's intent or guilt; it sufficed that it established that the prohibited substances were correctly identified. In the case concerning *Foschi* the CAS was of the opinion that the FINA had performed its duties properly and considered the swimmer liable for doping. Entirely in keeping with the strict liability system which had been elaborated in previous cases Foschi was subsequently given the opportunity to prove a lack of liability. The old routine was thus followed, although next the CAS suddenly felt the need to defend the reversal of the burden of proof[428] by the following arguments:[429]

"The Panel believes that this legal presumption and the system of a shifting of the burden of proof is legally proper despite the fact that disciplinary sanctions in doping cases are similar to penalties in criminal proceedings where the prosecutor normally has the burden of proving not only the factual elements of an offence but also a degree of guilt on the part of the accused. The panel in the CAS case of Chagnaud vs. FINA (CAS 95/141) also ruled that, the system of strict liability of the athlete must prevail when sporting fairness is at stake and that [...] the principle of presumption of the athlete's guilt may remain but that, by way of compensation, the athlete must have the possibility of shifting the burden of proof by providing exculpatory evidence."

---

[428] Reversal of the burden of proof here means that irrespective of the outcome of the proceedings the burden of proof is placed upon the party other than that which would normally carry the burden of proof.

[429] CAS 96/156, 6-10-1997, *Jessica K. Foschi v. FINA*, ground 12.2.

According to the CAS, therefore, the reversal of the burden of proof was legally sound.[430] This already indicates the outcome of the reasoning following this statement. The first unexpected turn in this line of reasoning is the shift of focus to the result of any trial: the penalty. Disciplinary sanctions in doping trials are similar to penalties in criminal proceedings, the CAS observed. This may be so, but this observation adds nothing to the line of reasoning. Then the CAS addressed the way in which in criminal proceedings the public prosecutor not only has to prove all the elements of the offence, but also that the accused is guilty of the offence. This is also undoubtedly true. Then, however, with no apparent link to the above, the CAS referred to its reasoning in *Chagnaud* ostensibly to show that the prosecuting body in a doping trial does not need to demonstrate the accused athlete's guilt for various reasons. It is difficult to gain any other impression from the way in which the CAS built up its reasoning that it considered it necessary in doping trials, as opposed to in criminal proceedings, to reverse the burden of proof. "[...] The system of strict liability of the athlete must prevail when sporting fairness is at stake," however, it could be argued just as convincingly that there are also numerous reasons to presume the liability of the accused in criminal proceedings.[431] It is just as true for criminal proceedings that the interests of third parties may be harmed if it is necessary first to prove the liability of the accused. The only valid argument for reversing the burden of proof is that doping cases would be so much harder to conduct for sports organisations if the burden was not shifted. Indeed, this is an argument which the CAS put forward further on in the *Foschi* case.

> "In doping cases it would be practically impossible for a sports federation to prove how a banned substance arrived in an athlete's body or that the athlete had knowingly ingested the banned substance. Any such requirement would be the end of any meaningful fight against doping. This approach may seem harsh on a morally innocent athlete found to have a banned substance in his/her body but in order to ensure fairness towards all competitors and to protect their health and well-being, sports federations must have strict and workable doping regulations. Otherwise, as was stated in the case of Chagnaud vs. FINA (CAS 95/141) '[...] if for each case the sports federations had to prove the intentional nature of the act (desire to dope to improve one's performance) in order to be able to give it the force of an offence, the fight against doping would become practically impossible. The floodgates would be opened and the fight against drug-taking in sport would become futile.'"

This reasoning which was based on experiences with doping and gave voice to the frustration of the sports organisations over all those doping cases in which the user

---

[430] It is possible that the CAS was aware that the judgment in *Gasser v. Stinson* (15 June 1988, Scott J.) as cited by Beloff (Beloff 1999, *supra* nt. 282, 3.45) supports this view: "In *Gasser v. Stinson* it was held that an automatic disqualification rule of the International Amateur Athletic Federation (IAAF) applicable to any athlete, regardless of guilty intent, whose urine should contain a banned substance, was justified by the need for certainty and avoidance of evidential difficulties even though the morally innocent may have to suffer in order to ensure that the guilty do not escape."

[431] Compare ECHR 8-2-1996 *John Murray v. United Kingdom*, 41/1994/488/570, 22 EHRR 29, see later in this paragraph.

got off scot-free because his/her liability could not be proven was much more honest than the previous line of argument which pretended to be based on legal considerations.[432]

From the words used by the CAS that the athlete was presumed to have committed a doping offence it could be derived that the athlete still had an opportunity to overturn this presumption through proof of his/her innocence. Logically, the reversal of the burden of proof is expected to concern the question of liability, but in the strict liability system of the CAS this was not the case. The literature also at times suggested the opposite. Netzle,[433] for example, on the strict liability system of the CAS wrote that:

> "Das Schiedsgericht räumte aber ein, daß es zu unakzeptabele Resultaten führen könne, wenn dem Athleten jede Exkulpationsmöglichkeit verwehrt werde. Der Ausweg wurde mit hilfe der Konstruktion einer widerlegbaren Rechtsvermutung gesucht: Liege eine positive Dopingprobe vor, so werde ein Dopingvergehen vermutet. Dem Athleten müsse aber die Möglichkeit gewährt werden, die Vermutung zu entkräften, wenn er nachweisen könne, daß das Testergebnis nicht korrekt oder die verbotene Substanz ohne Wissen und Willen in seinen Urin gelangt sei."

Beloff,[434] a regular CAS arbitrator in doping cases, indicated that: "with this principle [strict liability principle; *JWS*], the subjective elements of the case are not examined: the guilt of the athlete is presumed and she or he does not have the right to supply exculpatory evidence save in relation to mitigation." In other words: if the sports organisation had conclusively shown that banned substances were present in the athlete's samples this also proved that the athlete had committed a doping offence. The penalty to be imposed for this offence as far as its severity was concerned had to be in relation to the degree of liability (culpability) of the athlete. The presumption of full liability concerned the penalty and it was at this point during the doping trial that the reversal of the burden of proof took place by which the athlete was given the opportunity to demonstrate that the liability which he was charged with was less than presumed.[435] After an analysis of relevant CAS case

---

[432] Gay (1991 (*supra* nt. 129, p. 66): "The I am not guilty defence is usually the athlete's first port of call when a positive result has been declared. An athlete will state, often quite convincingly, that he has never taken drugs in his life and would never do so, and that if there was a prohibited substance present in his sample, this was there without his knowledge and against his will. On the old definition of doping, which regarded doping as the use by or distribution to an athlete of a substance which could have the effect of artificially improving that athlete's physical condition and therefore augmenting his performance, the athlete did have some basis for arguing that his intent was relevant. It could be argued that as the words refer to the use by an athlete of a prohibited substance, the Rules envisaged that this use must be a knowing use."

[433] Stephan Netzle: "Wie hält es das Internationale Sportgericht mit dem Doping?," *Doping, Realität und Recht* (1998) (ed. K. Vieweg) (Netzle 1998), p. 208.

[434] Beloff 1999 (*supra* nt. 282), 7.125.

[435] See also: CAS 98/208, 22-12-1998, *Wang Lu Na, Cai Hui Jue, Zhgang Yi, Wang Wei v. FINA*, Matthieu Reeb, ed., *Digest of CAS Awards II 1998-2000* (The Hague, Kluwer Law International 2002) pp. 234-254, *inter alia* ground 5.9, CAS 98/222, 9-8-1999, *Bernhard v. ITU*, Matthieu Reeb, ed., *Di-*

law, Netzle[436] concluded that these cases did not concern the results of evidence to the contrary, but mostly the results of a re-assessment of the penalties in accordance with the question of guilt and any further concrete circumstances of the case.

In *UCI v. Möller*[437] the CAS, after referring to the cases in which the parameters and justification of the strict liability principle were laid down, stated in the principle's defence that:

"The result of the doping test performed on the Respondent established the presence of a prohibited substance. The presence of this substance in the Respondent's body, even if one were to assume the absence of guilt or intent, would quite likely have impacted upon his performance in competition. His competitors, whose bodies were free of performance-enhancing substances, would have been placed at an unfair disadvantage. There can be no doubt that a suspension imposed on the basis of the strict, liability principle can and will lead in individual cases to unfairness and injustice, for example, to an athlete who unwittingly takes a wrong pill or who is intentionally the victim of another's malevolence. The Panel is also not blind to the recent scholarly debate and public hearings before governmental agencies and committees regarding the continued practice of the strict liability principle in sport. But, as the CAS held in *USA Shooting v. UIT*, the continued application of the strict liability principle, however unfair it may appear to be in a given situation, appears to be a laudable policy objective. A set of rules based on proving the athlete's subjective guilt or intent in the taking of a performance-enhancing substance may indeed prevent the occurrence of accidental unfairness to an unwitting athlete. His return to competition would, however, impose intentional unfairness on all those athletes who have played by the rules. The Panel believes that the reasoning which justifies the application of the UCI's strict liability rule, when evaluated in light of the UCI sanctions, their duration and amounts, which can be imposed on the basis of Article 91 AER will indeed withstand the future scrutiny of the civil and constitutional courts both on a national and international level."

The UCI was one of few IFs to include penalties with an upper and a lower limit in its doping regulations. The disciplinary committee in accordance with Article 91 AER was able within these limits to relate the severity of the penalty to the severity of the doping offence. The conclusion of the argument therefore painted too rosy a picture of the future of the strict liability system; a system that could only be justified where penalties could be imposed discretionarily.[438]

---

gest of CAS Awards II 1998-2000 (The Hague, Kluwer Law International 2002) pp. 330-344, *inter alia* ground 34 and CAS 99/A/239, 14-4-2000, *UCI v. Möller, Danmarks Idraets-Vorbund and Danmarks Cykle Union*, grounds 6 and 10-12.

[436] Netzle 1998 (*supra* nt. 429), p. 210.

[437] CAS 99/A/239, 14-4-2000, *UCI v. Möller, Danmarks Idraets-Vorbund and Danmarks Cykle Union*, ground 10.

[438] As opposed to what was the case with IFs which had included fixed penalties in their regulations, the CAS was here permitted (or at least reserved the right to) deviate from the maximum penalty and proportion it to the severity of the offence. The CAS also reserved this right if the IF had not established any precedent, like in Riley. In CAS 96/149, 13-3-1997, *Cullwick v. FINA*, Matthieu Reeb, ed., *Digest of CAS Awards 1986-1998* (Berne, Editions Stämpfli 1998) pp. 251-263, ground 29), for example, the CAS considered that: "We do not believe FINA either would or should have imposed the

Steiner[439] was of the opinion that German law did not object to the way in which the burden of proof was distributed in the strict liability system, at least in the system as he imagined it. Steiner failed to recognise the aspect of the irrebuttable presumption of the strict liability system and assumed that with the reversal of the burden of proof the athlete could advance arguments to lift his/her presumed liability. However, as we have seen above, the reversal of the burden of proof merely concerned the penalties.

> "Ein sportgerichtliches Verfahrensrecht, das dem Athleten in dieser Situation grund-
> sätzlich die Last der Selbstentlastung auferlegt, stellt sich keineswegs außerhalb des
> allgemeinen zivilverfahrensrechtlichen Beweisrechts."

If one were to consider that such a distribution of the burden of proof of an element like liability resulted in too great a risk, Steiner argued that the *Anscheinsbeweis* (*prima facie* evidence) could be invoked. The *Anscheinsbeweis* is not regulated by law in Germany.[440] It is rather a suspicion based on the facts or practical experience. The *Anscheinsbeweis* means that the question of guilt is decided in accordance with the typical course of events. An established cause may be argued to result in a certain effect (or an established effect may be argued to have a certain cause) and this argument may be considered proven. These aspects form part of the weighing of the evidence. They do not concern a reversal of the burden of proof,[441] but an easing thereof. The best known example is the tail-end collision ("Wer auffährt

---

sanction of two years' suspension, if they had enjoyed the freedom as to penalty which we now enjoy, on the facts found by us."

[439] U. Steiner: *Doping aus verfassungsrechtlicher Sicht*, Presentation at the Doping Forum in Cologne, 29 February 2000, organised by the German Association for Sport and Law, the Konstanzer Arbeitskreis, in The International Sports Law Journal, 2000 (Steiner 2000), 1, p. 15.

[440] Dutch law to a certain extent also has the *Anscheinsbeweis*. Art. 339 (2) of the Code of Criminal Procedure provides that: "Facts and circumstances that are generally known do not need to be demonstrated." "Such facts are facts with which every person of average intelligence may be deemed to be acquainted without the need for further research or with which they could become acquainted without any special effort by inspecting generally accessible sources," according to Corstens (*Het Nederlandse strafprocesrecht* (1993), p. 596). The Advocate General of the Dutch Supreme Court in his opinion to the Court's judgment of 13 April 2001 (ELRO no. AB 1065, case no. C99/215HR) in para. 3.8.2. remarked that "it should be mentioned [...] that there is a clear trend towards placing the onus upon the driver of the following vehicle. [...]. The arguments leading to this trend boil down to the following: one has to keep a sufficient distance. If a collission occurs in which the following vehicle collides with the vehicle in front this gives rise to the suspicion that insufficient distance was maintained. However, the driver of the following vehicle may still demonstrate that the vehicle in front braked unexpectedly and needlessly [...]."

[441] Cf., Grischka Petri, "Die Sanktionsregeln des World Anti-Doping-Codes," (2003) *SpuRt*, p. 233, fn. 50: "Der Anscheinsbeweis bedeutet keine Beweislastumkehr." Differently, however: Bernhard Pfister, *Die Doping-Rechtsprechcung des TAS*, (2000) *SpuRt*, pp. 133-137. The OLG Frankfurt in its judgment of 18 May 2000 (13W29/00, (2000) *NJW-RR*, p. 1117) considered that: "In der Rechtslehre ist umstritten, ob bezüglich des Verschuldenstatbestandsmerkmales eine Beweislastumkehr, von der der Beklagte zumindestens bis zu seinem Beschluß vom 15.05.2000 ausging, statthaft ist (verneint z.B. von Summerer, a.a.O. Tz 2/264f, zumindestens bei Unterwerfung unter die Verbandsstrafgewalt durch Satzung)."

hat Schuld"). The *Anscheinsbeweis* may be *"erschüttert"* if it can be proven from the facts that the course of events was different this time. ("Der Vorausfahrende bremste plötzlich grundlos stark ab.")

"Bei positiver A- und B-Probe ist die Verantwortlichkeit des Athleten der 'typische Geschehensablauf'. Dies eröffnet ihm die Chance, konkrete Tatsachen für die Annahme eines atypischen Geschehensablaufs vorzutragen und zu beweisen. Es gilt die Erkenntnis aus dem Beweisrecht, dass in Fällen, in denen die Aufklärung schwierig oder sogar unmöglich ist, schon aus den materiellen Tatbestandsmerkmalen, die ja prozessual handbar bleiben müssen, eine Legitimation dafür hergeleitet werden kann, in Gestalt des Anscheinsbeweises die Anforderungen an die Aufklärungsgenauigkeit zu reduzieren [...]. Die näheren Voraussetzungen zu entwickeln, unter denen der Anscheinsbeweis erschüttert werden kann, ist die Aufgabe der problem- und milieu-erfahrenen Sportrichter."[442]

In the CAS system, the burden of proof was placed upon the athlete as soon as the sports organisation had fulfilled its duty of proving the objective elements of the material rule. However, this by no means entailed a functional – from the viewpoint of judicial efficiency – reversal of the burden of proof and even less *prima facie* evidence. With the proof of the objective elements the CAS also considered the subjective element (liability/culpability) proven. The finding of doping substances in the athlete's sample established irrefutable proof (an irrebuttable presumption) that the athlete was guilty of violating a doping rule.[443] It was not with a view to liability for a doping offence that the athlete was required to counter this proof, but with a view to the degree of the punishment. The OLG Frankfurt in its judgment of 18 May 2000[444] rejected the strict liability rule as unlawful.[445] It reasoned that in disciplinary proceedings concerning a doping offence which might result in a long-term suspension the question of guilt could not be ignored.

"Zumindestens im Geltungsbereich des Grundgesetzes kann para. 84 Abs. 4 RVO i.V.m. der IAAF-Regel 55 Ziff. 2a und weiterer Verbindung mit Ziff. 4, wonach es Pflicht jedes Athleten ist, sicherzustellen, daß kein nach diesen Regeln verbotene Substanz in sein Körpergewebe oder seine Körperflüssigkeit gelangt, nicht so verstanden

---

[442] E. Götze: *Rechtslexikon*: "Anscheinsbeweis: Von einem prima facie Beweis (Beweis des ersten Anscheins) spricht man dann, wenn ein Sachverhalt nach der Lebenserfahrung auf einen bestimmten (also typischen) Verlauf hinweist. Danach kann also von einem bestimmten Erfolg auf eine bestimmte Ursache und umgekehrt geschlossen werden. Der Anscheinsbeweis ist im Rahmen der Beweiswürdigung von Bedeutung. Tatsachen, für die der Beweis des ersten Anscheins spricht, bedürfen keines Beweises. [...] Allerdings kann der Anscheinsbeweis erschüttert werden, indem besondere Umstände für einen abweichenden Geschehensablauf vorgetragen und bewiesen werden."

[443] OLG Frankfurt 18 May 2000: "Der Grundsatz der 'strict liability,' der den IAAF-Regeln zugrundeliegt, und worunter im staatlichen Recht verstanden wird, daß weder Vorsatz noch Fahrlässigkeit erforderlich ist, um eine Haftung zu begründen, ist im übrigen auch international sehr umstritten."

[444] 13W29/00, *NJW-RR* 2000, p. 1117.

[445] See also OLG Frankfurt, 18 April 2001, (2001) *SpuRt*, p. 159 and LG Stuttgart, 2 April 2002, (2002) *SpuRt*, p. 254.

werden, daß auch ohne Verschulden des Athleten gegen diesen eine Disziplinarstrafe verhängt werden darf. Nach deutschem Rechtsverständnis setzt eine Vereinsstrafe, zumindestens wenn es sich um eine folgenschwere oder mit einem Unwerturteil verbundene Aktion handelt, Verschulden voraus.[446] Auch das Schiedsgericht des Deutschen Schwimmverbandes hat im Beschluß vom 23.08.1994,[447] einen Dopingfall betreffend, mit der Begründung im Bereich der Vereinsstrafe müsse die Frage der Strafbarkeit nach allgemein strafrechtlichen Kriterien beurteilt werden, das Verschulden zur Voraussetzung einer Bestrafung erhoben. Für diese Betrachtungsweise spricht auch der Grundsatz der Unschuldsvermutung des Art.6 Abs. 2 EMRK."

An important element in the judgment of the OLG was the consideration that the peculiarities of the disciplinary procedure of the sports organisations on the one hand and the justified desire of those organisations to be able to fight doping effectively on the other hand required that the presumption of innocence which applied in criminal law could not simply and without exception be supplanted to the field of the fight against doping.[448] Further following the OLG's reasoning it was required,

"[...] aber auch ausreichend, davon auszugehen, dass eine positive A-Probe den Anscheinsbeweis für einen schuldhaften Dopingregelverstoß begründet. Es liegt dann an dem Sportler, diesen Anscheinsbeweis nachhaltig zu erschüttern. Gelingt ihm dies, muß der Verband das Verschulden des Sportlers nachweisen. Eine Sanktion ohne individuelles Verschulden [...] ist nicht rechtmäßig und kann, wenn sie denn von einem Verbandsgericht unter solchen Umständen verhängt werden sollte, keinen Bestand haben."[449]

Here an elegant solution was proposed whereby both the conditions established by Article 6(2) ECHR and the evidentiary needs of the prosecuting sports organisation would be met. A positive doping sample could only establish an *Anscheinsbeweis*. It was the athlete's task to shake the evidence.[450] The *Anscheinsbewijs* is also ac-

---

[446] Cf., Reuter-Münchener Kommentar, a.a.O., RN 30 sowie Palandt-Heinrichs, BGB, 59. Aufl. 2000, RN 14 jeweils zu para. 25; Summerer a.a.O., Tz 2/262; a. A. für geringfügige Strafurteile des 2. ZS des BGH vom 26 February 1959 in *BGHZ* 29, S. 352 sowie Soergel-Hadding a.a.O., RN 50 zu para. 25.

[447] (1994) *SpuRt*, p. 210.

[448] "Die Besonderheiten des verbandsgerichtlichen Verfahrens einerseits und das berechtigte Anliegen der Sportverbände, effektiv Doping bekämpfen zu können, bedingt jedoch, daß nicht ohne weiteres ausnahmslos die im Strafrecht geltende Unschuldsvermutung im Dopingbekämpfungsbereich Platz greift."

[449] See also OLG Frankfurt, 18 April 2001, 13U66/01, 2O76/01. The Swiss Tribunal Fédéral held a similar view. In the Aanes judgment (CAS 2000/A/317, 9-7-2001, *F. Aanes v. FILA*) the CAS remarks on this as follows: "It is noteworthy, that the Swiss Federal Tribunal has accepted an interpretation of doping rules to the effect that it is admissible to presume an athlete's guilt if he/she has been tested positive for a prohibited substance. The athlete is then accorded the opportunity to rebut the presumption (Swiss Federal Tribunal, CAS Digest, p. 561, 575 [*G v. FEI*]; Swiss Federal Tribunal, 5P. 83, 1999 [*WCZW v. FINA*], unreported, p. 12)."

[450] See also OLG Dresden, 18 December 2003, (2004) *SpuRT*, pp.74-79. "Die Frage, inwieweit bei der Vorlage eines positiven Dopingtestes gegen den betreffenden Sportler nach den im internationale

cepted by the European Court of Human Rights in *John Murray v. United Kingdom*[451] in case "[...] the evidence presented against the applicant by the prosecution [is] considered [...] to constitute a 'formidable' case against him."

> "It is only if the evidence against the accused 'calls' for an explanation which the accused ought to be in a position to give that failure to give any explanation 'may as a matter of commonsense allow the drawing of an inference that there is no explanation and that the accused is guilty'."

The system of the *Anscheinsbeweis*, also known as the doctrine of *res ipsa loquitur*, has the advantage of allowing greater freedom to weigh the evidence to the contrary than the system of the reversal of the burden of proof does in which evidence to the contrary has to comply with strict requirements. The *Anscheinsbeweis* does more justice to the procedural position of the accused athlete than the strict liability system.

To reiterate, a positive doping test result established a rebuttable presumption of an intentional act of doping. If the athlete was able to demonstrate that there was no intent he/she might still be punished for culpable behaviour. This too could be countered by evidence to the contrary. If the athlete was again successful in his/her proof, he/she would have had to be acquitted. With the introduction of the *res ipsa loquitur* the sports organisations did not need to fear that they would be plunged back into the time when they faced the almost impossible task of proving the athlete's guilt or intent, or that athletes would escape their just punishment. The main advantage of a system allowing room for the *Anscheinsbeweis* was that athletes who were able to show that they were completely innocent of a doping act could be acquitted as opposed to the lack of this possibility in the strict liability system. It moreover made a great deal of sense to turn the element of culpability back into an undivided concept after the ambiguity which had crept into the CAS system under which culpability in respect of liability was an objective aspect and in respect of punishability a subjective aspect. The most important element of the argument against the strict liability system was that general principles of international law, more specifically, the human rights of athletes as laid down in the ECHR and more in particular where doping was concerned in the Anti-Doping Convention of the Council of

---

Sportrecht zumindest terminologisch verbreiteten Grundsätzen der 'strict liability' verschuldensunabhängig eine Sanktion verhängt werden kann bzw. ob dem Sportler nach den Grundsätzen der Sphärentheorie von vornherein die Beweislast für sein fehlendes Verschulden trifft, kan dahinstehen." In between the two extremes the OLG considered that: "Es ist jedenfalls sachlich gerechtfertigt, dem beweisbelasteten Sportverband zumindest die Beweiserleichterungen des Anscheinsbeweises zu Gute kommen zu lassen, wenn bei einem Sportler die Überschreitung eines Grenzwertes festgestellt wird, der nach den aktuellen wissenschaftlichen Erkenntnissen auf die Einnahme anzulässiger leistungssteigernder Mittel schließen und eine Herbeiführung durch unbewusste Nahrungsaufnahme oder körpereigene physiologische Vorgänge als äußerst unwahrscheinlich, wenn nicht sogar ausgeschlossen erscheinen läßt."

[451] ECHR 8-2-1996, 41/1994/488/570, 22 EHRR 29.

Europe imposed restrictions upon the system pursuant to the principle of *nulla poena sine lege*.[452]

The strict liability system was rarely criticised in the legal literature. The main critic of the system was in fact the CAS itself. In *Fritz Aanes v. Fédération Internationale de Luttes Associées (FILA)*[453] the tribunal considered that:

> "[...] the Panel is of the opinion that as a matter of principle [...] an athlete cannot be banned from competition for having committed a doping offence unless he is guilty, i.e. he has acted with intent or negligence. Even if the rules and regulations of a sports federation do not expressly provide that the guilt of the athlete has to be taken into account the foregoing principle will have to be read into these rules to make them legally acceptable."

In the view of the Panel in question an athlete could not be lawfully suspended under Swiss law[454] if no blame attached to him/her.[455] This shows a clear break with the views of previous Panels on this point. From the words "an interpretation to the contrary would lead to the rules being void which would frustrate the objective of the fight against doping pursued by the entire sporting world" it may be derived that this Panel – which was composed of three civil law lawyers – based its reasoning on different starting points from Panels mainly composed of common law lawyers.

> "It is obvious that it would be an important weapon in the fight against doping if the federations were able to impose sanctions on athletes who have tested positive, without having to establish any element of guilt on the part of the athlete. However, this argument, which is one of prevention and deterrence, loses sight of the general objective of doping sanctions, namely the punishment of the athlete for having violated the rules (Baddeley, L'association sportive face au droit (1994), p. 219).
> On the other hand, it has to be recognised that in professional sport doping sanctions have the effect of restraining the athlete from carrying out his chosen trade and thus from earning a living for a certain period of time. In addition, doping sanctions clearly affect the honour and social standing of the athlete concerned and are a stigma on his future.
> When weighing up the interests of both sides the Panel is of the view that the interests of the athlete take precedence over those of the federation to enforce a rule of 'strict liability'. The contrary view would only be acceptable if a strict liability rule were the only meaningful weapon in the fight against doping (see Baddeley in: Fritzweiler (ed.) Doping Sanktionen, Beweise, Ansprüche (2000), p. 9, 22; Scherrer in: Fritzweiler (ed),

---

[452] This will be discussed extensively in a chapter to come.

[453] CAS 2000/A/317, 9-7-2001, *F. Aanes v. FILA*.

[454] According to Rule 45 of the Procedural Rules of the CAS "the Panel shall decide the dispute according to the rules of law chosen by the parties or, in the absence of such a choice, according to Swiss law."

[455] Tribunal Fédéral, 15 May 1993, BGE 119 II 271.

id. at p. 119, 127; see also CAS 95, 142, *L. v. FINA*, CAS Digest, p. 225, 231). [...].
[...]
The so-called strict liability-rule, i.e. a rule as advocated by the Respondent according to which the mere presence of a prohibited substance in an athlete's body justifies his suspension, does not, in the Panel's opinion, sufficiently respect the athlete's right of personality (Persönlichkeitsrecht) as established in Articles 20 and 27 et seq. of the Swiss Civil Code which CAS panels are required to apply (Art. 58 of the Code of Sports-related Arbitration).
[...]
The Panel further notes that in a recent decision the Court of Appeals of Frankfurt/ Main, Germany also held that liability without fault was incompatible with the rights of the athlete and German law (OLG Frankfurt/Main, judgement of May 18, 2000, l3W29/00 [*B. v. DLV*] p. 15)."[456]

The CAS Panel was aware of the fact that the strict liability paradigm as it had been developed by previous Panels was contrary to the prevailing legal opinion in Europe and especially in Germany and Switzerland. The *lex sportiva*[457] of which the CAS has been one of the most important authors could only find universal recognition if its main aspects did not meet with insurmountable resistance in the respective legal systems. The OLG Frankfurt had rejected the CAS's strict liability system and the Panel in the *Aanes* case used the judgment of the OLG as a whetting stone to reshape the position of the athlete in disciplinary doping proceedings in such a way as would be acceptable to the legal community – at least that in Europe.

The Panel held that suspension of an athlete for a doping offence required the athlete's guilt, but not in the way "as is necessary in respect of a criminal act for which a presumption of innocence operates in favour of the accused."[458] However, the sports organisation was not left in any doubt that it did have to prove the objective elements of the offence. As opposed in the case of presumed innocence, the Panel was of the opinion that with respect to the objective elements "this follows

---

[456] CAS 2000/A/317, 9-7-2001, *F. Aanes v. FILA*, ground V.2.3.

[457] James A.R. Nafziger, *Lex Sportiva*, in *ISLJ* 2004/1-2, p. 3 et seq. (Nafziger 2004): "The concept of a *lex sportiva*, as a coherent and influential corpus of practice, has been identified with the *lex mercatoria* or law merchant, a venerable source of law that is said to form the foundation of international commercial practice and commercial arbitration. [...] In practice [...] the awards and opinions of the CAS provide guidance in later cases, strongly influence later awards, and often function as precedent. Also, by reinforcing and helping elaborate established rules and principles of international sports law, the accretion of CAS awards and opinions is gradually forming a source of that body of law. This source has been called the *lex sportiva*."

[458] In the judgment of the DLV-Rechtsausschuß of 13-72000 (RA 1/00) in the *Baumann* case (see also CAS OG 00/006, 22-9-2000, *Dieter Baumann v. IOC, National Olympic Committee of Germany and IAAF*) it is considered that "[...] auf die Unschuldsvermutung gemäß strafrechtlicher Grundsätze [...] sich ein betroffener Athlet nicht berufen [kann]. Das Rechtsverhältnis zwischen Verband/Athlet ist auf vertragliche Basis gestützt. Im Vertragsrecht verteilt jedoch die Rechtsprechung aus praktischen Gründen der Billigkeit und eines gerechten Interessenausgleiches zunehmend die Beweislast nach Risikobereichen." It is correct that the legal relationship between the athlete and the sports organisation is of a private law character. It is, however, not correct that private law-orientated concepts are reflected in the disciplinary procedure which is subject to the penal law of the sports organisation. This mixing of concepts will be discussed further below.

from the general rule that a person who alleges a fact has the burden of proof."
Although this appears contradictory, it is still reasonable as "[...] it would put a
definite end to any meaningful fight against doping if the federations were required
to prove the necessary subjective elements of the offence, i.e. intent or negligence
on the part of the athlete." In weighing up the interests of the sports organisation in
the fight against doping on the one hand and the interest of the athlete not to be
punished when he/she is innocent, the scales in the Panel's view tipped in favour of
the interests of the sports organisation. In principle the athlete was fully responsible
for anything entering his body. "In these circumstances it is appropriate to presume
that the athlete has knowingly or at least negligently consumed the substance which
has led to the positive doping test." If the sports organisation has demonstrated the
objective elements of the doping offence guilt on the part of the athlete must be
presumed. The Panel followed this by an argument along the same lines as that of
the OLG Frankfurt with respect to the *Anscheinsbeweis*.

> "The principle of presumed fault on the part of the athlete does not, however, leave
> him without protection because he/she has the right to rebut the presumption, i.e. to
> establish that the presence of the prohibited substance in his/her body was not due to
> any intent or negligence on his/her part [...] The athlete may for example provide evi-
> dence that the presence of the forbidden substance is the result of an act of malicious
> intent by a third party.
> [...]
> [...] the Panel is conscious of the fact that there have been CAS decisions where the
> Panel was prepared to apply a strict liability standard with respect to suspensions and
> was not willing to take into account the subjective elements of the case in question
> [...]. However, it should be noted that all these decisions took account of the level of
> 'guilt' on the part of the athlete when establishing the duration of the suspension. It
> can also be taken from these awards that their reasoning was often based on arguments
> invoked to justify a simple disqualification. They did not consider the very purpose of
> suspensions as opposed to a mere disqualification and the differences between them.
> For these reasons the Panel is not prepared to follow these decisions.
> The Panel recognises that the opinions of the courts and legal authorities differ as to
> whether the reversal of the burden of proof puts too much burden on the athlete. As an
> example the OLG Frankfurt in its decision of 18 May 2000 [...] is in favour of a rule
> pursuant to which the presence of a prohibited substance in an athlete's body provides
> prima facie evidence of guilt on the part of the athlete; this leaves the athlete with the
> burden of proving that, in his/her particular case, the facts were different from the nor-
> mal sequence of events. In many cases the practical results of both scenarios – a rever-
> sal of the burden of proof or the rebuttal of prima facie evidence – will be the same,
> but the Panel does recognise that the burden on the athlete is slightly less in the latter
> case. The Panel does, however, believe that, as a matter of principle, the reversal of the
> burden of proof and thus the burden being on the athlete to provide full proof of the
> absence of intent or negligence, is adequate and appropriate when weighing the inter-
> ests of both sides.
> In the case in hand, in which none of the objective elements of the offence is in dis-
> pute, the Appellant is thus presumed do have intentionally or negligently committed
> the offence."

Did this mean that the CAS had just executed an about turn where the strict liability rule was concerned or was this merely evidence of a difference of opinion within the CAS between common law and civil law lawyers? As opposed to previous Panels, this Panel was entirely composed of civil law lawyers.[459] Should the *Aanes* judgment be considered a rarity? Indeed: "Other CAS panels were not willing to follow this theory and Aanes remained unique in the history of the court," as Martens,[460] who presided over the Panel in *Aanes*, later observed.[461]

4.4. Absence of guilt

In Dutch case law, absence of guilt – in addition to the general grounds for exemption from criminal liability laid down in Articles 37(1) and 40 to 43 of the Dutch Criminal Code – has also been accepted as an unwritten ground for such exemption.[462] There are two situations in which liability will have to be judged absent.

---

[459] CAS 96/149, 13-3-1997, *Cullwick v. FINA*, *Beloff* (United Kingdom), *Castle* (New Zealand), Carrard (Switzerland), Matthieu Reeb, ed., *Digest of CAS Awards 1986-1998* (Berne, Editions Stämpfli 1998) pp. 251-263.
CAS 98/184, 25-9-1998, *Phoebe Hearst Cooke v. FEI*, *Beloff* (United Kingdom), *Young* (USA), Natter (Switzerland), Matthieu Reeb, ed., *Digest of CAS Awards II 1998-2000* (The Hague, Kluwer Law International 2002) pp. 197-204.
CAS 98/211, 7-6-1999, *Smith-De Bruin v. FINA*, *Fortier* (Canada), *Beloff* (United Kingdom), Oswald (Switzerland), Matthieu Reeb, ed., *Digest of CAS Awards II 1998-2000* (The Hague, Kluwer Law International 2002) pp. 255-273.
CAS 99/A/234 & CAS 99/A/235, 29-2-2000, *David Meca-Medina v. FINA & Igor Majcen v. FINA*, *Beloff* (United Kingdom), *McLaren* (Canada), Oswald (Switzerland).
CAS OG 00/011, 28-9-2000, *Andreea Raducan v. IOC*, Matthieu Reeb, ed., *Digest of CAS Awards II 1998-2000* (The Hague, Kluwer Law International 2002) pp. 665-673, *Kavanagh* (Australia), Netzle (Switzerland), *Oliveau* (USA), Matthieu Reeb, ed., *Digest of CAS Awards II 1998-2000* (The Hague, Kluwer Law International 2002) pp. 665-673.
CAS OG 00/015, 29-9-2000, *Mihaela Melinte v. IAAF*, *Young* (USA), Lee (Malaysia), *McLaren* (Canada), Matthieu Reeb, ed., *Digest of CAS Awards II 1998-2000* (The Hague, Kluwer Law International 2002) pp. 691-695.
CAS 2000/A/270, 23-5-2001, *David Meca-Medina v. FINA & Igor Majcen v. FINA*, *Beloff* (United Kingdom), *McLaren* (Canada), Oswald (Switzerland)
CAS 2000/A/274, 19-10-2000, *Susin v. FINA*, Matthieu Reeb, ed., *Digest of CAS Awards II 1998-2000* (The Hague, Kluwer Law International 2002) pp. 389-409, *Fortier* (Canada), Coccia (Italy), Oswald (Switzerland)
CAS 2000/A/317, 9-7-2001, *F. Aanes v. FILA*, Martens (Germany), Seim-Haugen (Norway), Rochat (Switzerland)
The names in italics belong to common law panel members. In nine out ten cases a common law lawyer presided over the Panel.
[460] Dirk-Reiner Martens, "Landmark decisions," in: *The Court of Arbitration for Sport 1984-2004* (Blackshaw, Siekmann, Soek, eds.), The Hague, T.M.C. Asser Press, 2005, p. 235 et seq.
[461] "Despite a prevailing rule among IFs of strict liability for doping, CAS awards generally disclose an inclination to avoid unnecessarily harsh results," according to Nafziger (James A.R. Nafziger, "Lex Sportiva," in *ISLJ* 2004/1-2, p. 3 et seq.). In a footnote to this statement he referred to the Aanes case to confirm this inclination; however, this is actually the sole exception in a series of CAS judgments on the issue of the strict liability rule.
[462] Cf., R. De Waard, "Schuld en wederrechtelijkheid als elementen van het delict," in J.P. Balkema et al., eds., *Liber Amicorum Th.W. van Veen – Opstellen aangeboden aan Th.W. van Veen ter gelegenheid van zijn vijfenzestigste verjaardag* (1985) p. 381 et seq. (Arnhem, Gouda Quint 1985).

One is if a person makes an excusable mistake of fact, and the other is if he/she makes an excusable mistake of law, i.e. if he/she can show to have been mistaken concerning the illegality of his/her act.

4.4.1. *Mistake of law*

In sport athletes may also make a mistake concerning the rules to which he/she is subject. After a match during the World Junior Championships in Dunkirk, water polo player Cullwick had to undergo doping control. His urine was found to contain salbutamol and the FINA suspended him for a period of two years. On appeal, the FINA Bureau upheld this decision. Cullwick appealed against the decision of the FINA to the CAS. It emerges from the judgment of the CAS[463] that Cullwick had used Ventolin inhalers during the Championships as a remedy against asthma and that he had been using such inhalers prescribed to him by his doctor from the age of ten. Four years before the Dunkirk Championships during a similar event in California Cullwick's national federation had given him a laminated card which read: "Treatment guidelines. Examples of permitted and banned substances (based on IOC doping classes). Asthma: allowed [...] Ventolin, [...] by inhaler only." The athlete had not received any information from his federation since to contradict the information on the card. This case hinged upon two aspects. Cullwick had failed to inform the medical authorities of his use of salbutamol prior to the match and had failed to indicate it on the doping form. With respect to the indication on the form the FINA did not argue that Cullwick's omission resulted in a doping offence, whereby it followed the reasoning of the CAS in *Lehtinen*[464] that the absence of a declaration does not in itself constitute a doping offence. Cullwick argued that his specific use of salbutamol was allowed under the FINA rules given the circumstances of the case and that his behaviour did not fall within the scope of the description of the doping offence. The FINA countered that the use of salbutamol should nevertheless have been reported to the medical authorities. The athlete was of the opinion, however, that the way in which the salbutamol was taken (through

---

In 1930, based on various Dutch judgments, "Vrij in his preliminary report for the Dutch Lawyers Association" (*Handelingen der NJV*, Vol. 60, 1930, 12th piece, and the book "Professor Mr. M.P. Vrij, verzameling uit zijn geschriften op het gebied van strafrecht en criminologie," Zwolle 1956) proposed that two kinds of absence of guilt be included in the Criminal Code as written grounds for exemption from criminal liability.

a: "Not liable to punishment are persons who commit an offence without being in any way at fault in respect of any act or consequence or factual circumstance connected with such act or consequence which is required for the behaviour to become an offence";

b: "Not liable to punishment are persons who commit an offence while they did not know or should have known or should have taken account of the possibility that their actions were illegal."

[463] CAS 96/149, 13-3-1997, *Cullwick v. FINA* (Beloff, Castle, Carrard), Matthieu Reeb, ed., *Digest of CAS Awards 1986-1998* (Berne, Editions Stämpfli 1998) pp. 251-263. Cf., CAS 2003/A/522, 5-3-2004, *C. v. Royale Ligue Vélocipédique Belge (RLVB)*, ISLJ 2004/3-4, pp. 87-88.

[464] CAS 95/142, 14-2-1996, *Lehtinen v. FINA* (Netzle, Seim-Haugen, Carrard), Matthieu Reeb, ed., *Digest of CAS Awards 1986-1998* (Berne, Editions Stämpfli 1998) pp. 225-244.

inhalation) made the substance into a permitted substance and that this conversion did not occur by reporting the use.

"It is, in other words, completely independent of the elements which go to make salbutamol in certain circumstances a permitted substance, and is, moreover, an obligation whose breach is without sanction. Not without hesitation we found ourselves unable to agree."[465]

The CAS's hesitation was caused by a certain distrust of athletes in general: the duty of prior notification may serve as a strong deterrent against some forms of possible cheating. The CAS concluded that a prior notification is not a matter of evidence only going to establish a medical necessity, but a sine qua non of the proof of such necessity. Despite the fact that the disciplinary doping law of the FINA was contained in several volumes which made it difficult for athletes to grasp the precise connection between the rules the CAS considered that:[466]

"In particular we consider that, in this context, we are permitted to have regard to the provisions of the red book, which seem to us to be clarificatory rather than emendatory of the predecessor provisions in the blue book. In this instance, at p. 35, salbutamol is identified as permitted by inhaler only and must be declared to the relevant authority. No competitor, whose case was governed by the Doping Control Guidelines in the red book [...], would be able to advance with any efficacy the argument advanced before us by the appellant."

The CAS rejected the appeal as to liability.[467]

"[...] the appeal as to liability must fail; [...] a doping offence has been proved. [...] we consider the appellant's offence to be of the nature of a technical breach only."

His national federation had led Cullwick to believe that he did not need to notify the medical authorities of his use of salbutamol prior to the match. He believed that in his case the use of his Ventolin inhaler was completely legitimate. His use of salbutamol was for medical reasons and not to enhance his athletic performance. If Cullwick had made a prior notification of his use of salbutamol no doping offence would have been committed. It was non-compliance with procedures rather than abuse of substance, which was the foundation of the charge against him [...].[468] Under Dutch criminal law the circumstances of *Cullwick's* case would be qualified as mistake of law, or in the present case: mistake as to the relevant doping rules. Under Dutch law, a mistake such as this is not a ground for justification – now that, objectively speaking, the behaviour cannot be justified – but as a ground for ex-

[465] CAS 96/149, 13-3-1997, *Cullwick v. FINA*, Matthieu Reeb, ed., *Digest of CAS Awards 1986-1998* (Berne, Editions Stämpfli 1998) pp. 251-263, ground 17.
[466] *Idem*, ground 23.
[467] *Idem*, ground 24.
[468] *Idem*, ground 29, under d).

emption from criminal liability.[469] In 1960, the Dutch Supreme Court[470] as a general guideline for such a ground for exemption indicated that the advice must have been given by a person or institution which may be considered authoritative to the extent that the accused could be said to have reasonably relied on their advice. Where culpable avoidability is absent, according to Remmelink,[471, 472] there is also an absence of guilt, which means that the accused must be acquitted. In a system where an athlete can be liable without guilt – strict liability – there is no room for acquittal based on a ground for exculpation. Absence of guilt cannot be considered until the moment of determining the penalty. The CAS held that the FINA rules had to be clear and precise to the extent "[...] that all athletes could understand them more easily and disputes over the meaning, if possible, avoided." As the FINA rules were unable to pass this test, the CAS in the operative part of its judgment reversed the penalty which had been imposed upon Culwick by the FINA, however, not before repeating the moral of the story.

> "The experience of this appeal allows us to stress the following matters:
> It is important that the fight against doping in sport, national and international, be waged unremittingly. The reasons are well known, and are set out in the introductory notes to the FINA Guidelines.
> It is equally important that athletes in any sport (including Waterpolo) know clearly where they stand. It is unfair if they are to be found guilty of offences in circumstances where they neither knew nor reasonably could have known that what they were doing was wrong (to avoid any doubt we are not to be taken as saying that doping offences should not be offences as a strict liability, but rather that the nature of the offence [as one of strict liability] should be known and understood)."[473]

In short, before the introduction of the WADC and the implementation of this Code by the sports organisations, the doping rules of these organisations could be so complex, opaque and confusing that individual athletes could no longer see the woods for the trees. This situation in which athletes could not be expected to fully grasp these rules could in exceptional cases result in the non-imposition of a penalty.

---

[469] Cf., Remmelink 1994 (*supra* nt. 293), pp. 378 et seq. Under American law this would result in a ground for justification because the accused can reasonably suppose that the requirements for a ground of justification have been fulfilled. Cf., J.A.W. Lensing, *Amerikaans Strafrecht* (Arnhem, Gouda Quint 1996) (Lensing 1996) p. 223.

[470] HR 13 December 1960, *NJ* 61, 416.

[471] Remmelink 1994 (*supra* nt. 293), p. 374.

[472] Under English common law the term is ignorance of the law. When relying on ignorance of the law, the defence has to show that the *mens rea* was lacking when the crime was committed. Art. 32(2) of the Statute of the International Criminal Court provides that "A mistake of law may [...] be a ground for excluding criminal responsibility if it negates the mental element required by [...] a crime [...]."

[473] CAS 96/149, 13-3-1997, *Cullwick v. FINA*, Matthieu Reeb, ed., *Digest of CAS Awards 1986-1998* (Berne, Editions Stämpfli 1998) pp. 251-263, ground 31.

4.4.2. *Mistake of fact*

The second possibility within the framework of absence of guilt as an unwritten ground for exemption from criminal liability is if the accused is able to show that he/she made an excusable mistake of fact.

In the next section it will be explained that sports organisations had to consider the possibility that prohibited substances may have been present in the athlete's food. If the quantities found remained below a fixed threshold no doping offence was considered to have been committed. It is quite common for various hormones to be mixed up with fodder – legally or otherwise – in order to increase meat production. Athletes have to be more than usually cautious in what they eat. Carelessness can be fatal. However, it is also possible that the athlete could not but trust that the food he/she was served fulfilled all the requirements. Yet, in the sporting world and especially in the field of doping, trust had become a rare commodity, as will become clear from the discussion of the CAS case involving the swimmers Meca-Medina and Majcen.

The urine samples of marathon swimmers Meca-Medina from Spain and Majcen from Slovenia were found, both upon the first analysis and the countercheck, to contain the metabolites of the prohibited substance nandrolone. The swimmers among other things argued that "[...] the presence of any banned substance was the result of the innocent ingestion of pork offal." Meca-Medina and Majcen gave as the reason for the positive test result that the substance had been contained in the food which they had consumed at the hotel where they had been accommodated during the competition. They both declared that on five consecutive days prior to the match they had partaken of a local dish called sarapatell.[474] Sarapatell contains pork, liver, kidneys and chitlings. The athletes contended among other things that the meat had been contaminated by nandrolone injections. The suppliers of the meat to the hotel could no longer be traced. An expert witness declared that the use by meat producing companies of growth hormones was legal in Brazil. The Panel was prepared to accept that the sarapatell had been made from meat from uncastrated boars and that the body of an uncastrated pig could contain endogenous nandrolone.[475] An expert declared that "to consume 10 micrograms of Nandrolone, a person has only to eat 50 grams of all products with a Nandrolone content of 200 micrograms per kilogram." From tests on volunteers it had emerged that the consumption of a mere

---

[474] See Appeal brief, p. 33. "Small amounts of Nandrolone metabolites were detectable in the urine after consumption of meat generated from Nandrolone-treated animals." See articles by G. Debruyckere as to influence of the consumption of meat contaminated with anabolic steroids on doping tests in *Analytica Chimica Acta* 275 (1993) pp. 49 to 56. Expert witness Dr Stephany declared that "the use of injected meat is a theoretical possibility and extremely low."

[475] Nandrolone is indeed naturally present in meat, however, only in pork from uncastrated boars. It has never been shown to be present in other types of meat. However, there is thus a possibility that humans ingest the substance naturally, although it should be noted that boar pork is not consumed in Western Europe. Its taste and the smell during preparation is unpleasant to us, according to the NeCeDo, http/www.necedo.nl/nandrolon.htm.

10 to 20 microgrammes of nandrolone could result in the presence in the urine of a quantity of 30 ng/ml.

> "However, the Panel have been provided with no evidence as to why they should read across from results obtained from oral intake of nandrolone or results obtained by eating meat injected with nandrolone to results which would be obtained by eating meat of an uncastrated boar (which has endogenous nandrolone). There has been no experiment, controlled or otherwise, as Dr. Stephany confirmed, to establish results for nandrolone metabolites above the relevant level of 2ngl/ml in the quantities or ratios here in issue (or at all) based on ingestion of meat pork naturally containing nandrolone. [...]."[476]

The only thing that could be established with any certainty was that levels of nandrolone were naturally present in pork and that athletes who ingest nandrolone produce nandrolone metabolites. The Panel considered that no explanation had been provided of the fact that eating pork produced nandrolone metabolites in such quantities as had been found in the two athletes in question. As regards the ratio of NA/NE in Meca-Medina's urine, the expert considered it no more than "theoretically a possibility" that this was the result of the consumption of sarapatell. The Panel was further of the opinion that the athletes could not overcome a fourth obstacle.

> "The raising of an unverified hypothesis is not the same as clearly establishing facts: DC 9.10 requires the latter. The inadequacy of such isolated hypothesis as a means of disproving the culpable use of a prohibited substance is well recognised in the CAS's judgments."[477]

The Panel indicated that the athletes could at any time have had an experiment carried out which could have supported their arguments. However, they had not done so, which caused the Panel sarcastically to remark: "Their resources were apparently expended on other matters."

The swimmers further argued that many positive nandrolone cases had occurred in Brazil in the FINA framework. However, the Panel did not consider the numbers provided to be statistically significant. The Panel also pointed to the tests of the Brazilian swimming federation's own athletes in 1989 and again 1999 at which none of the athletes had tested positive. The out-of-competition controls carried out by the FINA which Brazilian swimmers had undergone during the same period also all came up negative. The CAS Panel therefore failed to be convinced.

The entire case therefore hinged upon an experiment that could prove that the athletes were in the right.

---

[476] CAS 99/A/234 & CAS 99/A/235, 29-2-2000, *David Meca-Medina v. FINA & Igor Majcen v. FINA*, ground 10.10.
[477] CAS 99/A/234 & CAS 99/A/235, 29-2-2000, *David Meca-Medina v. FINA & Igor Majcen v. FINA*, ground 10.12.

The swimmers" urine was found to contain metabolites of nandrolone, i.e. of a prohibited substance. The outcome of the analysis was consistent with the expected outcome after the use of nandrolone precursors. The hypotheses put forward by the swimmers to explain their positive test results were considered to be inadequate by the CAS now that an international federation like the FINA can only base itself on recognised scientific standards and cannot consider unverified and unproven scientific theories,[478] not least because of its responsibility *vis-à-vis* all participants and sport in general. The CAS upheld the penalty imposed by the FINA consisting of suspension for a period of four years.

This, however, was not the end of the *Meca-Medina/Majcen* case. In its judgment, the CAS had considered "that it was at all times open to the swimmers to produce a controlled experiment verifying [...] [the expert's] theory." Such an experiment had in fact been carried out and confirmed the swimmers' sarapatell theory. The result of the controlled experiment only became known after the case was closed and CAS procedure does not include the possibility of review. The swimmers agreed with the FINA to resubmit the case to the CAS upon which the case was reopened.

"Given the considerations of the Panel in its decision of February 29, 2000, the key question in the matter at hand is whether or not Appellants, in submitting (the results of) the study conducted on their behalf, managed to establish, to the comfortable satisfaction of the Panel, that the consumption of flesh/offal of uncastrated boars could have been the source of the presence of metabolites up to the level found, i.e. one exceeding the level of 2 ng/ml."[479]

However, the outcome of the experiment still did not move the CAS[480] to alter its previous judgment.[481]

In the *FINA* case against the swimmers Wang Wei and Xiong Guoming a pig was also allegedly the culprit. In this case the existence of a grey area was not even

---

[478] U. Mareck-Engelke, H. Geyer, W. Schänzer: *19-Norandrosterone – Criteria for the Decision Making Process*, Institut für Biochemie, Deutsche Sporthochschule Köln, Germany (Mareck-Engelke) write that at this time no differentiation between consumption of meat from nandrolone-treated animals and misuse of nandrolone preparations is possible. The main intention for judging criteria should be the prevention of false positive results and protection of the athlete. Norandrosterone generated from endogenous production or consumption of contaminated meat should be excluded even with the ambiguity of positive samples regarded probably negative. One salient aspect of this statement is that it was co-authored by the head of an IOC-accredited laboratory, Prof. Schänzer.

[479] Defence notice in CAS 2000/A/270, 23-5-2001, *David Meca-Medina v. FINA & Igor Majcen v. FINA*, under 2.

[480] CAS 2000/A/270, 23-5-2001, *David Meca-Medina v. FINA & Igor Majcen v. FINA*.

[481] The press release (Lausanne, 23 May 2001) issued as a result of the reopened case declared that: "the new scientific evidence submitted to the CAS was not sufficient to establish satisfactorily that the source of the nandrolone metabolites in the urine of the two swimmers has been consumption of meat from uncastrated pigs. Furthermore, the Panel considered that the swimmers failed to establish that Sarapatel was made from the flesh of uncastrated boars or, even if it is, that Sarapatel of this type was served to the two swimmers."

considered. The urine of the swimmers – who had been caught using doping before – had been found to contain clenbuterol. The cause of the clenbuterol was argued to be pork liver which allegedly contained this substance. The swimmers usually had their meals in the dining hall of the Shanghai Technical Sports Institute for swimmers. Following the advice of the doctor responsible for their care they ate more than a usual amount of pork liver as the doctor had found that their haemachrome levels were depleted. It was assumed that the meat had been contaminated with clenbuterol. Although the Ministry of Agriculture of the People's Republic had prohibited the use of clenbuterol there were still farmers who added the substance to the fodder in order to produce lean meat and increase the revenue from the meat. The dining hall staff who had the task of buying the meat took samples from meat at the market stall where they had bought meat previously. The samples were sent to the Shanghai Supervision Institute of Veterinary Drugs & Foodstuffs for testing. The FINA Doping Panel considered that:[482]

> "There is some likelihood that the swimmers did not ingest the prohibited substance, detected in their urine, on purpose. In some pig liver, purchased by the staff of the dining room for swimmers from a market stand, from which the purchased pig liver was also purchased in the days before the urine collection, clenbuterol was found. However, this likelihood is very low. Only in eleven (11) samples out of sixty (60) was clenbuterol detected. And there is no evidence that the pig liver, purchased from the market stand after the collection of the urine and the pig liver purchased from the same market stand before the day of the collection of the urine came from the same farm.
> And even if the clenbuterol detected in the urine of the swimmers did come from the pig liver eaten, the swimmers are to be sanctioned, as it is their duty always to ensure that no prohibited substance enters their body tissues or fluids (FINA Rule DC 2.2). Both the swimmers have been sanctioned already for having taken a prohibited substance. More than others they had reason to make sure that no prohibited substance would get into their body tissues or fluids."

If a beta-2 agonist was found in the swimmers' urine FINA Rule DC 9.2(b) enabled the imposition of a minimum of two years' suspension to a maximum of suspension for life for a second doping offence. The Doping Panel must have had some doubts concerning culpability as it only suspended the swimmers for a period of three years. In conclusion, however, it can be said that even when an athlete was unaware of ingesting a prohibited substance through his/her food, he/she was still guilty due to a duty of care.

Tennis player Peter Korda, whose urine was found to contain nandrolone metabolites after a match at Wimbledon in 1998, also attributed this in the first place to the consumption of contaminated meat and, in the second place, to the use of a non-prohibited substance. If his arguments were upheld this would result in a consider-

---

[482] FINA Doping Panel 6/99, 9 August 1999.

able reduction of the penalty to be imposed. Section (E)4(c) of the ITF Anti-Doping Programme 1998 contained the following provision:

"The Appeals Committee may reduce the penalties as set out in Section (M) and Sections (N)4 and (N)5 of the Programme (but not overturn the violation of the Programme) only if the player establishes on the balance of probabilities that Exceptional Circumstances exist and that as a result of those Exceptional Circumstances the penalties as set out in Section (M) and Sections (N)4 en (N)5 in the Programme should be reduced. For the purposes of this paragraph, Exceptional Circumstances shall mean circumstances where the player did not know that he had taken, or been administered the relevant substance provided that he had acted reasonably in all relevant circumstances."

Did Korda's actions fall within the scope of the definition of exceptional circumstances? According to the CAS[483] this definition could be interpreted in two ways. In the first place, it could be read to mean that exceptional circumstances had to be assumed if the athlete could demonstrate that he had been unaware of the fact that he was using a prohibited substance. The second interpretation was that the term exceptional circumstances was intended to mean circumstances in which this lack of awareness had occurred. According to the first interpretation, a lack of awareness is necessary, but not sufficient. The CAS however opted for the second interpretation for the following reasons:

"(i) it is the more natural meaning of all the words in the definition;
(ii) it seems to us improbable in the extreme that the player should be able to rely on this mitigation where he offers a denial of a doping offence and no other evidence about the circumstances in which the prohibited substance was found in his body;
(iii) it would also be odd indeed if a player could be absolutely responsible for the prohibited substance found to be present within his body (C2), so that a doping offence was committed ipso facto without knowledge, intent or fault, but that he could mitigate the penalty solely by absence of knowledge. The provisions as to penalty (if so interpreted) would, in our view, fatally contradict the language and undermine the policy of the provisions as to liability;
(iv) the Rule (E4(c)) provides that the player must establish all the relevant circumstances in order (thereafter) to establish the reasonableness of his actions. Relevant circumstances suggests a sifting out from circumstances, as previously defined, between what is relevant and what is irrelevant. This cannot be achieved if the player is ignorant of the circumstances or offers no evidence of or about them."[484]

The evidence submitted by expert witness Dr Sample excluded all possibility of the positive analysis outcome being the result of the consumption of meat or of endog-

---

[483] CAS 98/223, 31-8-1999, *Korda v. ITF*, Matthieu Reeb, ed., *Digest of CAS Awards II 1998-2000* (The Hague, Kluwer Law International 2002) pp. 345-360, ground 48 (Nater, McLaren, Beloff).
[484] CAS 98/223, 31-8-1999, *Korda v. ITF*, Matthieu Reeb, ed., *Digest of CAS Awards II 1998-2000* (The Hague, Kluwer Law International 2002) pp. 345-360, ground 49.

enous production because in those circumstances levels of concentration would not be between 50 and 100 ng/ml as had been found in Korda's urine samples. The case then took a different turn when Korda based his lack of knowledge on the use of Carnitargin. The statements made by Korda as to how he had obtained the substance were contradictory. Dr Sample testified that the examination carried out by him pointed to nandrolone use as the only possible scientific explanation for the levels of nandrolone metabolites found. Korda could not sufficiently explain the presence of nandrolone in his urine. "In short he denies any knowledge whatsoever of how the Prohibited Substance was in his urine sample. He provides a bald denial and nothing more."[485] The Appeal Committee (AC) had still considered that exceptional circumstances were present in the *Korda* case.

> "(1) We heard evidence from the Appellant. Each of us found him to be an honest, open and reliable witness. His evidence was supported by the absence of any prior or subsequent positive result, by the absence of any medical evidence of chronic steroid abuse, and by the character evidence from Mr Boris Becker and from Mr John Pickard. We accept the Appellant's evidence that he did not knowingly take (or have administered to him) a prohibited substance.
> (2) In our judgment, the Appellant has established that he acted reasonably (as well as innocently) in all the relevant circumstances. Whatever the cause of the positive results, we are satisfied that the Appellant could not be faulted in any relevant respect. We reject Mr Stoner's criticism by reference to the Appellant's willingness to take various other preparations (such as minerals and vitamins). There is no evidence to suggest that any of those other preparations contained Prohibited Substances."

The Appeal Committee imposed a relatively mild penalty upon Korda: he would lose all the computer ranking points he had won during Wimbledon and had to return his Wimbledon prize money to the ITF. The ITF appealed against this decision to the CAS.

The CAS's judgment concerning the ITF Appeal Committee's considerations as cited above was not exactly mild.

> "We consider that the AC correctly recognised that there were two elements in the Exceptional Circumstances plea. We cannot fully accept this first finding. We find that the evidence compels us to our conclusion that Mr Peter Korda had motive to take a prohibited substance and that the scientific evidence suggests that on a single occasion he did so by oral ingestion. We reluctantly conclude that he knew what he was doing. We cannot in any event accept their second finding whose very brevity betrays its poverty of analysis. The AC seems to us to regard (wrongly) the first finding as dictating the second. While it is true that it may be reasonable to differentiate between annulment of a competitive result and a consequential sanction (see CAS 95/141 Chagnaud v/FINA in CAS Digest, op. cit., p. 215 ff para 15-17), even in that case at para. 28 the Panel said it is vital that such athlete provide counter-evidence which allows it to be

---

[485] *Idem*, ground 56.

established with near certainty that he has not committed a fault. Mr Peter Korda did not come within measurable distance of satisfying such a test. Even if contrary to our conclusion, he unconsciously broke the anti-doping rules, he fell short of these standards of vigilance in relation to what he took, which is demanded of a player who wishes to establish exceptional circumstances pursuant to ITF Rules. In any event, the Panel in Chagnaud stated expressly 'The Panel observes that such a development is possible only if the applicable rules allow it (para. 19)'. The ITF rules do not."[486]

In the opinion of the CAS Korda had had motive to use performance-enhancing drugs (before saying goodbye to tennis he wanted to achieve a high ranking in a grand slam tournament for the last time), there was scientific evidence that he had used nandrolone and he knew what he was doing. The CAS considered that Korda's actions could not fall within the limits imposed by the CAS on the definition in Section (E)4(c). The CAS amended the Appeal Committee's judgment and imposed the penalty which according to the ITF Programme it was obliged to impose, namely suspension for one year.

In sum, in order to obtain a reduced penalty athletes have often claimed that the prohibited substance entered their body completely without their knowledge. The prohibited substance would have been present in their food or in an innocuous home remedy.

Korda attempted to escape punishment by claiming that he had only used an over-the-counter remedy. His attempt failed, now that the concentrations of the prohibited substance found in his urine told a different story. In the case discussed next, swimmers Wang Lu Na et al. pointed to the innocuous Actovegin as the cause of the finding of triamterene in their urine.[487]

The Sydney Doping Laboratory found that the samples of four Chinese swimmers contained (very low concentrations of) the FINA-prohibited substance triamterene. The FINA subsequently banned the swimmers from participating in the World Championships in Perth. The analysis of the B samples also indicated the presence of triamterene. Again "[...] the observed level of Triamterene and metabolites was very low in these samples." The president of the Shanghai Swimming Association of which the swimmers in question were members in a letter to the FINA president pointed out that the swimmers' consumption of the health food Actovegin could be the cause of the triamterene result. He also cautioned that "[...] further analysis needs to be conducted to clarify the issue." In an analysis report drawn up some time later the Shanghai Institute for Drug Control announced that tests on the Actovegin tablets which the swimmers had used had shown a suspicious peak with the same retention time of Triamterene. During the hearing which was held as a

---

[486] *Idem*, ground 58.

[487] CAS 98/208, 22-12-1998, *Wang Lu Na, Cai Hui Jue, Zhgang Yi, Wang Wei v. FINA* (Beloff, Mingzhong Su, Oswald), Matthieu Reeb, ed., *Digest of CAS Awards II 1998-2000* (The Hague, Kluwer Law International 2002) pp. 234-254.

result of the finding of doping the swimmers denied having committed a doping offence. They stated that they had used the food supplement Actovegin which is a protein-free extract of veal blood. The company producing Actovegin had declared that its product did not contain triamterene and the China Dope Testing Centre had released the product stating that it did not contain any substances appearing on the IOC doping list. A laboratory in Lausanne which had examined the Actovegin at the request of the FINA reported that: "The initial results confirmed the presence of an unidentified substance that appeared as Triamterene in approximately 1/3 of the samples tested." Based on the concentrations of triamterene found in the B samples an Australian laboratory came to the conclusion that you would need to take some 100,000 tablets to arrive at such levels. Based on these findings the FINA Panel held that the swimmers were guilty of a doping offence under FINA Rule DC 9.2. The Panel concluded that the swimmers had used triamterene in order to mask their use of another prohibited substance and suspended them for two years.

The swimmers appealed against the decision of the FINA to the CAS. Before entering into the merits of the case, the CAS made the following statement. It acknowledged:

"that there exists a predisposition in some quarters to assume that Chinese swimmers are guilty of systematic drug taking. FINA's constitution states at C2 that FINA shall not allow any discrimination against [...] individuals [...] on grounds of race [...] or political affiliations. It may be unnecessary to say that, even without reference to that provision, the Panel would, as an international arbitral tribunal, not only be, but trust that it appears to be, free from any taint of such predisposition or discrimination. The Panel considers only the evidence before it: it pays no heed to media hyperbole."[488]

After this unsolicited statement concerning its own impartiality in this case the CAS declared it not proven that taking six tablets of Actovegin daily could produce the result which had emerged from the doping analysis. Before concluding that a doping offence had been committed and that the swimmers had been unable to discharge the burden of proof resting upon them in order to reduce the penalty the CAS recalled that they had denied before the Panel ever having used triamterene. The Panel considered this statement as testimony given under oath. "However, it is regrettable that the currency of such denial is devalued by the fact that it is the common coin of the guilty as well as of the innocent." It did not emerge why the swimmers had used Actovegin, but it was suspected that it had been to mask another substance.

"The Panel was vigorously pressed too with the argument that there was no evidence as to what purpose ingestion of Triamterene might serve for the swimmers at that particular time. The FINA DC Rule, however do not require investigation of purpose. The presence of a prohibited substance – including a diuretic – is sufficient (DC9.2). Given, however, the known propensity of a diuretic to assist in flushing out what

---

[488] *Idem*, ground 5.1.

might be other prohibited substances, it is not impossible for the Panel to construct hypotheses as to why Triamterene might have been ingested. The Panel stresses that it does not rely upon such hypotheses, however, to sustain its conclusion – merely to test whether the clean and sufficient scientific evidence is somehow undermined. The FINA regulatory provisions require the Panel to consider what was in the competitor's fluids, and not why."[489]

If the Panel had been able to define Actovegin as the cause of the analysis results, it would have given serious consideration to whether or not the maximum penalty had to be imposed and possibly to whether this finding could have opened up the possibility that the swimmers had to be fully exonerated. There was insufficient evidence that the Actovegin had been used in the knowledge that it contained triamterene. The CAS aired several more considerations along these lines.

"The Panel readily accepts the submission of the Appellants that prima facie, (although always depending upon the particular circumstances of the case), lack of intent should be a powerful mitigating feature. Such is a consistent theme of all the CAS jurisprudence (CAS 95/141 *C. v. FINA* in Digest, p. 221-222, n. 21-24; CAS 96/149 *A.C. v. FINA* in Digest, p 260-261, n. 29-30 a); CAS 95/150 *V. v. FINA* in Digest, p. 273, n. 20; *Foschi v. FINA* TAS 96/156, para. 15).
In so saying, the Panel is not oblivious to the submission made on behalf of FINA that DC2.2 states that it is it is a competitor's duty to ensure that no banned substances enter his body [...] fluids. Competitors are responsible for any substance detected in samples given by them. Nonetheless if the persons responsible for team management have analysed a particular food product and cleared it of containing prohibited substances, it is not easy to see how much more could reasonably be required of competitors."[490]

Despite this display of sympathy the Panel rejected the swimmers' appeal and upheld the decision of the FINA Doping Panel to suspend them for two years.

Summarising, it has been more or less proven scientifically that the consumption of meat and animal products may cause traces of substances which have been mixed into these animals' food in order to either speed up their growth or increase meat production to end up in the metabolism of the consumer. The sports organisations established threshold values to prevent microscopic quantities of doping-listed substances to result in accusations of doping. However, if the levels found in the sample were above what they might be assumed to be after the consumption of contaminated food it would be concluded that the athlete in question had intentionally used a prohibited substance. The rule was that the athlete is responsible for everything he/she ingests. Even if the athlete argued that the food was consumed in circumstances in which it could be assumed that it met with all the relevant requirements, he/she was still responsible for any concentrations of prohibited substances in his/

---

[489] *Idem*, ground 5.34.
[490] *Idem*, ground 5.35-5.36.

her body that exceeded the threshold value. Such circumstances would at best only be taken into account in determining the penalty to be ultimately imposed.

In addition to mistake of law (i.e. as to the applicable doping rules) and mistake of fact there were other situations in which it can be questioned whether the athlete could be considered guilty of the presence of a prohibited substance in his/her body. In the next section, the circumstance will be discussed that it is not only the athlete's food, but also and especially the biochemical response of his/her own body that causes problems.

4.4.3. *Endogenous production of prohibited substances and the "grey area"*

The presence of a prohibited substance in a doping sample under the strict liability regime developed in CAS case law in principle always resulted in liability without any discussion of the question of guilt. In other words, the sports organisation did not need to show intent or guilt. After some time, however, it became clear from scientific research that various food supplements as well as pork contained substances which appeared on different doping lists.[491] It furthermore emerged from scientific research that certain concentrations of some of the substances appearing on doping lists may be produced by the human body itself. It is argued that these concentrations are above average in athletes who engage in strenuous physical ex-

---

[491] A working group established by UK Atlethics (see: www. ukathletics.org/ukadata/gettitem.idc?/uniqueID313.) concluded:
"– that dietary supplements are a possible cause of some of the positive findings. The athletes recording positive tests have subsequently been negative on a second test carried out within a few weeks, this suggests that injection of nandrolone is unlikely. [...] Three athletes who had previously recorded positive findings supplied urine samples collected over a seven-day period during which they trained but did not take dietary supplements. All values were negative or at the low end of the normal range.
– Two of those three athletes then supplied a further series of samples over a seven-day period during which they continued to train but took the same supplements as they had taken prior to their initial positive test. One set of samples was negative, but the other series all contained 19-norandrosterone, in some cases at levels in excess of 10 ng/ml.
– Three healthy volunteers were then recruited. All provided a morning urine sample, then took the same supplements as taken by the athlete who had registered positive findings before providing a further sample the following morning. All samples from day one were negative, but one of the three recorded a 19-norandrosterone level in excess of 10 ng/ml on the second morning. This was the only subject who trained.
– From these preliminary results, we conclude that a combination of exercise and dietary supplements, none of which appears to contain a prohibited substance, can result in a positive nandrolone finding.
– There is therefore clearly an urgent need for a full investigation of the factors that can give rise to positive nandrolone tests in athletes."
The NeCeDo (op. cit.) also considered it possible that the cause of the increase in nandrolone positive findings has to do with the use of dietary supplements. Some years ago dietary supplements began to appear on the market containing nortestosterone-related substances, mainly in the form of precursors (chemical predecessors) of testosterone, such as 19-norandrosterone and 19-noretiocholanolone. In the Netherlands, these substances are considered medical drugs and are only available on prescription. However, in other countries, such as the United States, they are considered as dietary supplements and are available over the counter.

ercise.[492, 493] In drawing up their lists of prohibited substances, the sports organisations took this into account by establishing threshold values for certain substances.[494] If the concentrations of a certain substance found remained below this value the athlete in question would not be prosecuted; it was then assumed that nothing illegal had taken place and that therefore no doping offence had been committed. A threshold value always gives rise to an area of uncertainty beyond that value connected with the individual physical circumstances of the athlete concerned. Just above the threshold value there is a grey area which also results in a legal grey area. If the athlete was able to show conclusively that his/her body produced a certain substance above the established threshold value he/she could not be considered to have acted illegally.[495] However, if the athlete could not demonstrate the more than aver-

---

[492] In CAS 98/222, 9-8-1999, *Bernhard v. ITU*, Matthieu Reeb, ed., *Digest of CAS Awards II 1998-2000* (The Hague, Kluwer Law International 2002) pp. 330-344, the arbitrators considered: AWhile in earlier days it was possible to maintain that the mere existence of metabolites is conclusive of the presence (application) of nandrolone, the new technique of mass spectrometry (MS/MS), introduced in doping analysis after 1996 enabled the detection of the metabolites already at significantly lower concentrations. The reaction of science was to warn the interested persons that such low concentrations no longer permit a reliable conclusion as to the presence of nandrolone. In other words, it appears to be beyond scientific doubt that such lower concentrations falling within what is now often referred to as Athe grey zone," can as well be the result of endogenous production of the human body (see CAS 98/212, 21-1-1999, *UCI v. Mason* and CAS 98/214, 8-1-1999, *Bouras v. FIJ*)."

[493] B. Le Bizec, F. Monteau, I. Gaudin, F. André: "Evidence for the presence of endogenous 19-norandrosterone in human urine", in: *Journal of Chromatography B*. 723 (1999), pp. 157 et seq. "In 1997, in the scope of antidoping control in sport, a not inconsiderable number of urine analysed by official laboratories revealed the presence of 19-nortestosterone [...] metabolites: 19-norandrosterone [...] and 19-noretiocholanolone [...] These repeated results in a short period of time generated some investigations and especially the verification of the possible production of these metabolites by an unknown endogenous route in adult entire male. Some experiments were conducted on different persons known to be non-treated with steroids and more precisely with nandrolone. Extractive methods were developed focusing on their selectivity, i.e. searching to eliminate at best matrix interferences from the target analytes. Gas chromatography coupled to mass spectrometry (quadrupole and rnagnetic instruments) was used to detect, identify and quantify the suspected signals. Two types of derivatization (TMS and TBDMS), a semi-preparative HPLC as well as co-chromatography proved unambiguously the presence, in more than 50% of the analysed urine (n "40), of 19-NA at concentrations between 0,05 and 0,60 ng/ml. 19-NE was not detected with the developed methods (LOD<0,02 ng/ml). Experiments conducted on athletes showed that after a prolonged intense effort, the 19-NA concentration can be increased by a factor varying between 2 and 4. Even if some complementary research has to be done in order to determine the maximal physiological level of 19-NA and 19-NE, these results should considerably change the strategy of antidoping laboratories." R. Bergés, J. Segura, X. de la Torre, R. Verntura: "Analytical methodology for enantiomers of salbutamol in human urine for application in doping control", in: *Journal of Chromatography B*. 723 (1999), pp. 173 et seq. These authors propose a method which is Arapid, selective and sensitive and seems to be useful to differentiate between an authorized and a prohibited use of the drug in doping control."

[494] In Art. 2.1.2. of the WADC it is provided that: "Excepting those substances for which a quantitative reporting threshold is specifically identified in the prohibited list, the detected presence of any quantity of a prohibited substance or its metabolites or markers in an athlete's sample shall constitute an anti-doping rule violation." Art. 2.1.3. further provides that: "As an exception to the general rule of Article 2.1, the prohibited list may establish special criteria for the evaluation of prohibited substances that can also be produced endogenously."

[495] *Supra* Chapter 4, Section 3.3.

age endogenous production by his/her body of a substance appearing on the doping list, he had to be considered strictly liable. The grey area had an upper limit. Concentrations found above this limit left no more room for doubt and were always an indication of the external administration of the prohibited substance.

When a concentration was found in an athlete's urine which fell within grey area levels this might be an indication that the athlete had either produced the substance him/herself or that he/she had consumed a food supplement or meat that was contaminated with the prohibited substance. The grey area gave rise to much debate among both lawyers and scientists.[496] "At this time, it is not possible to discern clearly between endogenous production, consumption of contaminated meat or misuse," according to some scientists.[497] The IOC was not sympathetic towards the existence of a grey area. The CAS on the other hand used this transitional area in various judgments, although in others it indicated under pressure from the IOC that it declined making such a grey area part of its considerations.

Already in 1983, Joop Zoetemelk appealed to the *Cour d'Appel de Paris*[498] against a penalty which had been imposed on him based on the identification of nandrolone metabolites in his urine.

"Il soutient que de l'avis de plusieurs professeurs, dont le professeur Van Rossum, 'il est possible qu'une autre substance que le nandrolone soit transformé dans le corps en formant cette métabolite, que la présence de nandrolone lui même n'est pas sûr'.
Il précise que plusieurs hormones peuvent avoir le même aboutissement final à la suite de leur passage dans le corps.
Il déclare qu'il y aurait lieu de comparer les métabolites du nandrolone avec les métabolites d'androgènes naturels ou des corticoïdes ou de quelques autres substances qui pourraient éventuellement donner à l'analyse le même résultat.
Il indique qu'il y a de grandes chances pour que l'on retrouve les mêmes métabolites de nandrolone si de nouveaux prélèvements sont effectués hors des courses importantes auxquelles il est inscrit, qu'il sera à nouveau sanctionné et interdit de courses."

As there was a possibility that the nandrolone had been produced by Zoetemelk's own body the Court considered it necessary that evidence was first submitted on this point before being able to pass a verdict.

After a leg in the 1998 Settimana Bergamasca the cyclist Mason had to undergo doping control. The analysis of the A sample revealed the presence of norandrosterone (a nandrolone metabolite) in a concentration of approximately 6ng/ml. Mason requested a countercheck. The second analysis also indicated the presence of this substance, this time in a concentration of 5 ng/ml. The UCI Anti-doping Commis-

---

[496] See also: G. Debruyckere, R. de Sagher, A. de Leenheer, C. van Peteghem: "The impact of nandrolone metabolites, occurring normally in male urines, on the cut-off level stipulated for nandrolon doping," in Advances in steroid analysis 90, *Proceedings of the Symposium on the Analysis of Steroids* (ed. S. Görög) (1991), Pécs, Hungary, 24-26 April 1990.

[497] U. Mareck-Engelke (*supra* nt. 478).

[498] Rép. Gén.: K 15472, 26 October 1993.

sion asked the Italian cycling federation to deal with the matter further. Both the *Commissione Disciplinare of the Lega Ciclismo Professionistico* and on appeal the *Commissione d'Appello Federale della Federazione Ciclistica Italiana* imposed a penalty on Mason of 6 months' suspension and a fine of CHF 2000. The UCI considered the judgment inadequate and appealed to the CAS against the decision on appeal of the Italian cycling federation.[499] The UCI argued among other things that the presence of norandrosterone in an athlete's urine in any concentration above 2 ng/ml established a doping offence.[500] Mason argued to the contrary that experts still differed concerning the question of which maximum concentration of nandrolone the human body was able to produce naturally. From this Mason concluded that a doping offence had not been shown. The CAS considered it essential and necessary that an expert be requested to make a statement concerning the minimum concentration of nandrolone metabolites which could offer sufficient proof to assume a doping offence. Dr Rivier was consequently asked by the CAS to give an expert opinion. According to this, two categories had to be distinguished in the identification of nandrolone in urine:

"Quantities up to 2 ng/ml are not considered to constitute a doping offence. The laboratories do normally not report concentrations below 2 ng/ml to the Federation. The threshold of 2 ng/ml was introduced by an IOC Medical Commission guideline (guideline on 'Analytical criteria for reporting low concentrations of anabolic steroids'). The guideline does not state any reason for the threshold.
Quantities between 2 and 5 ng/ml, however, need to be interpreted cautiously. Findings between 2 and 5 ng/ml do fall in a so-called 'grey zone'. In fact, there is uncertainty among experts as to the maximum concentration of Nandrolone produced by a human body. Consequently, there is high scepticism among scientists whether the mere finding of Nandrolone in a concentration between 2 and 5 ng/ml may be sufficient evidence to assume a doping offence. In other words, the finding may constitute a doping offence, but requires further investigations in order to confirm the result of the analysis. However, within the 'grey zone' the likelihood that Nandrolone is produced endogenously is decreasing exponentially.
The probability of an endogenous production of Nandrolone in quantities beyond 5 ng/ml was held to be very unlikely. Therefore quantities beyond 5 ng/ml are very likely to be confirmed by further investigations and may be regarded as sufficient evidence to constitute a doping offence."[501]

The expert explained the difference in the concentrations measured during the two analyses from the fact that the second analysis took place over a month after the first analysis. He claimed it was perfectly normal for lower concentrations to occur

---

[499] CAS 98/212, 21-1-1999, *UCI v. Mason*, Matthieu Reeb, ed., *Digest of CAS Awards II 1998-2000* (The Hague, Kluwer Law International 2002) pp. 274-282.
[500] IOC Medical Commission's guideline on "Analytical criteria for reporting low concentrations of anabolic steroids."
[501] CAS 98/212, 21-1-1999, *UCI v. Mason*, Matthieu Reeb, ed., *Digest of CAS Awards II 1998-2000* (The Hague, Kluwer Law International 2002) pp. 274-282, ground 4.4.

due to evaporation. Dr Rivier further advised the CAS that there would be no risk in using the first analysis result to base the case on. The CAS subsequently concluded that:

> "[...] Mr. Mason was not able to give any reasonable explanation for the origin of the prohibited substances. He further failed to submit any evidence in order to support the motion that in this particular case the endogenous production of Nandrolone could reach or even exceed the threshold of 5 ng/ml. The Panel therefore held that the analysis of the A-sample, confirmed by the analysis of the B-sample, revealed the presence of prohibited substances in a concentration not only higher than 2 ng/ml but also beyond the unofficial 'grey zone' and as such established an infringement of the AER [de Anti-doping Examination Regulations of the UCI; *JWS*]."[502]

In June 1998, the Swiss tri-athlete Bernhard participated in the Powerman Long Distance World Championships 1998 at Zofingen and claimed the title of World Champion. Immediately after the competition he had to undergo doping control. The subsequent analysis of his sample revealed the presence in his urine of norandrosterone (3 ng/ml) and noretiocholanone (3 ng/ml). Bernhard requested a countercheck and at the same time explained the presence of the metabolites as a possible result of his consumption of meat from animals that had been treated with nandrolone. The analysis of the B sample also produced a positive result. The laboratory did not include the concentrations in its report. The Swiss triathlon federation suspended Bernhard for a year and disqualified him from the Zofingen competition. Bernhard requested a review of this decision by the ITU's Doping and Appeals Board. The Board after a teleconference rejected the appeal. Bernhard subsequently appealed against this decision of the ITU to the CAS.[503] It was argued on his behalf that:[504]

> "the Appellant has never applied nandrolone or any other prohibited substance and, in general, he takes great care of his nutrition;
> – 3 ng/ml of norandrosterone or noretiocholanone are not conclusive evidence for the existence of nandrolone; the sanctioning body has failed to prove the existence of a forbidden substance beyond reasonable doubt;
> – the recently introduced more sensitive techniques of analysis have caused that the prior assumption that any finding of norandrosterone and noretiocholanone was sufficient evidence of the existence of nandrolone, could no longer be upheld; this was recognised also by the IOC Subcommission Doping and Biochemistry of Sport and expressed in a letter by its Secretary Dr. Segura of August 22, 1996;
> – different experts have reported that the results of their research confirmed that, in particular circumstances, these substances can be produced by the human body

---

[502] *Idem*, ground 4.5.

[503] CAS 98/222, 9-8-1999, *Bernhard v. ITU*, Matthieu Reeb, ed., *Digest of CAS Awards II 1998-2000* (The Hague, Kluwer Law International 2002) pp. 330-344.

[504] *Idem*, ground 16.

and recommended caution in sanctioning athletes in cases of concentrations between 1 and 5 ng/ml of NA or NE;
the Appellant has undergone – voluntarily and at his own expense – extended tests with Dr. Dehennin at the Laboratory of Châtenay-Malabry, France (L.A.B.-F.N.C.F.); these tests showed the presence of NA and NE in significant concentrations (0.07 – 2.1 ng/ml for NA and 0.12 – 3.0 ng/ml for NE) and led Dr. Dehennin to conclude that '*the urinary excretions of NA and NE by O. Bernhard are very unusual and require further investigation*'."

The ITU was of the opinion that 3.0 ng/ml of NA or NE in a sample is conclusive evidence of the use of doping. It pointed out that the IOC Medical Committee had repeatedly held that such levels constituted "absolute evidence of doping." The CAS had to answer the question of whether the current state of science still permitted the conclusion or at least the assumption that the presence of nandrolone in the urine was the result of the external administration of this substance. Various experts had demonstrated over the past few years – as was confirmed during the hearing by expert witness Dr Saugy – that recent developments had led to new findings, partly because of new techniques and partly because of improved equipment. Now that significantly lower concentrations could be detected than before science warned that these lower concentrations no longer warranted reliable conclusions with respect to nandrolone.

"In other words, it appears to be beyond scientific doubt that such lower concentrations falling within what is now often referred to as 'the grey zone', can as well be the result of endogenous production of the human body (see CAS 98/212 *UCI v. Mason and FCI* and CAS 98/214 *Bouras v. FIJ*)."[505]

In the Analytical criteria for reporting low concentrations of anabolic steroids, a document which the IOC Medical Committee sent to the IOC laboratories in August 1998, 2.0 ng/ml was indicated as the threshold value for norandrosterone. The CAS held that this document did not contain any legal rules and that the Committee by this document did not intend to establish that concentrations above 2.0 ng/ml should automatically lead to sanctions. The relevant part of the document only stated that "[...] identification of only 19-norandrosterone is sufficient to report for possible sanctions." Dr Rivier, the director of the Laboratoire Suisse d'Analyse du Dopage, further elaborated the statements in the document in a scientific report for the purpose of a CAS seminar in December 1998. Rivier made a number of recommendations for cases in which nandrolone metabolites were at stake.

"– no report on metabolite findings in case of concentrations below 1.0 ng/ml,
– report recommending sanctions in case of concentrations above 5.0 ng/ml,
– report findings between 1.0 and 5.0 for information purposes only and recommend additional target testing of the athlete concerned."[506]

---

[505] *Idem*, ground 29.
[506] *Idem*, ground 31.

During the hearing, Dr Saugy proposed a similar approach. He also confirmed that within the grey area (concentrations between 1.0 en 5.0 ng/ml) the possibility that nandrolone is endogenously produced decreases exponentially. Based on these findings, the CAS considered it necessary to determine what the "legal impact of the emergence of such a "grey zone" had to be.

Having arrived at this point of their judgment, the arbitrators did not directly proceed to the question of whether the concentrations found in Bernhard's urine should lead to the conclusion that the athlete had acted illegally. They first gave an overview of the strict liability system developed by the CAS in previous judgments: "[...] it seems [...] appropriate to examine the exact scope of the 'strict liability' ('responsabilité objective') rule applicable in doping cases in general and in this case in particular." In other words, for the moment the arbitrators presumed the illegality of Bernhard's actions and attempted to arrive at a decision concerning the degree of his liability with a view to the severity of a possible sanction. For a proper understanding of the remainder of the judgment it is useful to follow this liability detour as taken by the arbitrators.

The arbitrators considered the system indispensable for fighting doping in sport effectively. In their view, where proof of liability was concerned, the strict liability rule had to be interpreted in such a way as to extend beyond the mere presumption of the athlete's liability. The term established stricter requirements: "by making the subject liable regardless of his guilt, it renders the question of guilt irrelevant and allows for exoneration only in very limited and usually exhaustively listed cases, such as "force majeure" or wrongful act of a third person (see also the discussion of the term "strict liability" in the context in CAS 142/95 *L. v. FINA*, in *Digest of CAS Awards*, op. cit. p. 230, no. 13)." The case referred to, however, happened to be one in which the CAS did not get around to considering liability as Lehtinen's actions could not be deemed illegal.

The CAS once more pointed out that the sports organisation does not carry the burden of proof of the culpability of the athlete's actions. One of the reasons for accompanying the arbitrators on their liability detour is that here their private law approach is revealed and their tendency to regard the strict liability concept as deriving from notions that were developed in private law, even though in a penalty system such as the criminal law-orientated disciplinary law of doping such a concept apart from when it is used as a metaphor bears no relation to its surroundings.

"This is, on one hand, a faithful transposition of the civil (tort) law concept of 'strict liability' (as distinguished from a 'presumed guilt'), and, on the other hand, also the only interpretation capable to ensure the efficient fight against doping."

After the arbitrators had painted a picture of strict liability and declared that they supported the previous CAS case law on this point the judgment took another turn.

"The situation in the present case is, however, different from those dealt with above. The issue is not whether the Appellant has absorbed the forbidden substance intentionally or negligently, but rather whether he has absorbed it at all."[507]

It appears as though the arbitrators suddenly became aware that their detour into liability had been premature now that they had not yet examined whether Bernhard's actions had been illegal, i.e. whether Bernhard had in fact committed a doping offence at all. How did they approach this matter? Although the question of liability could only be dealt with after the question of illegality had been answered in the affirmative, the arbitrators in the face of logic positioned themselves in the field of liability to answer the question of illegality. After all, within the strict liability system absence of guilt did not lead to absence of illegality.

"The principle of strict liability rule does not exempt the sports federations to prove the existence of a doping offence. As it has been discussed above in the context of law in general the effect of any rule of law imposing strict liability is merely to render obsolete *the proof of guilt* on the part of the person subjected to the regime of strict liability, where on the other hand such rule does not eliminate the need to establish the *wrongful act itself* and the causal link between the wrongful act and its consequences."[508]

On the one hand, the sports organisations had the task of proving the existence of a doping offence and on the other hand they also had to demonstrate the "wrongful act itself." This appears to be the same thing, and perhaps it is. Be that as it may, the sports organisation in any case also had to demonstrate the causal link between the offence and its consequences. What did this involve, however? In the case at hand, the ITU had reasoned that the objective elements of the offence had been fulfilled now that the doping analysis had revealed the presence of a concentration of 3.0 ng/ml. It was the task of the arbitrators to assess whether this value was sufficient to presume the illegality of Bernhard's behaviour. If the arbitrators would find that such concentrations pointed to the use of nandrolone and that illegality was therefore established, Bernhard would be fully and strictly liable for his act. If the arbitrators would however hold that the concentrations found were insufficient to establish illegality, they would have to acquit Bernhard. There is reason to believe that the arbitrators were at a loss as to how to approach the concept of material illegality. They avoided admitting the concept to their considerations and attempted to bring the case to a proper end by starting from private law concepts instead.

Although Bernhard was awaiting an answer to the question of whether the concentrations found in his urine constituted a doping offence, the arbitrators in fact analysed the ITU's material rule and concluded that by this and similar rules of other federations the "emphasis (and, indeed, the critical element of the anti-doping procedures) has been shifted from the wrongful act itself to its consequences."[509]

---

[507] *Idem*, ground 38.
[508] *Idem*, ground 39.
[509] *Idem*, ground 41.

Although according to the CAS this shift was understandable from the point of view of the sports organisations,

> "[...] it is equally true that this shift from the wrongful act to its consequences is capable to have significant impact on the legal situation of the accused athlete and on his right of defence. It is therefore appropriate to scrutinize such regulatory practices and its implementation in practice also from the aspect of general principles of law and the requirements of fair trial."

From this point of view a rule which penalises a prohibited consequence instead of a wrongful act can only be justified from the perspective of general principles of law if there is no doubt whatsoever that the incriminated consequence only occurred as a result of the wrongful act intended by the rule. If a sports organisation opted to penalise the consequence (the presence of a prohibited substance) rather than the wrongful act itself (the use of prohibited substances), the causal link between the consequence and the act had to be completely clear and indisputable. Completely unaware of the fact that a criminal law approach in this case would have resulted in far less complex reasoning and in a more elegant solution, the CAS pulled into the next private law station. Only there did it become clear that the comparison of the doping act with a wrongful act establishing strict liability was not a metaphor.[510]

> "In civil (tort) law, there is no general presumption of causal link between the wrongful act and its consequences. Even in cases of strict liability, where no proof of guilt is required, the causal link between the latter and the former still remains an issue to be proved by the party invoking such liability. Having in mind the specific disciplinary ('quasi-penal') character of the anti-doping investigations and sanctions, it seems to be hardly acceptable to interpret the rule on strict liability against the person submitted to such liability even more severely than in civil law in which this concept has its roots. The existence of a causal link between a wrongful act and its consequence therefore remains to be an item to be proven by the party whose arguments are based on such consequence."[511]

This consideration is a bundle of contradictions. First it is claimed that the strict liability originates from tort law and that the causal link between an act and its consequence in the doctrine of tort has to be proven by the party invoking the liability. At the same time it is stated that anti-doping investigations have a specific disciplinary quasi-penal character and that it is difficult to reconcile with this particular character that the rule on strict liability be interpreted more severely against those submitted to such liability than in civil law in which this concept has its roots. The most intriguing aspect of this line of reasoning by the CAS has to be, however,

---

[510] The last section of this chapter further discusses metaphor or equivalent.

[511] CAS 98/222, 9-8-1999, *Bernhard v. ITU*, Matthieu Reeb, ed., *Digest of CAS Awards II 1998-2000* (The Hague, Kluwer Law International 2002) pp. 330-344, ground 45.

that it was assumed that a doping offence had been committed while it had still not been established whether concentrations of 0.3 ng/ml were capable of producing an illegal act, or in the words of the CAS, a wrongful act. The CAS penetrated deep into liability territory even though according to its own method of structuring a judgment it should not yet have ventured there at all. The consecutive considerations of the CAS in this judgment call to mind the predicament of the traveller who upon discovering that he has pulled into the wrong station has to conclude that all the next stations will be wrong too.

Societal views and/or new scientific insights may (under Dutch criminal law) remove the illegality of an act. Under Dutch law this approach has been laid down as the general ground for justification termed absence of material illegality. In the judgment at hand the CAS attempted to include this approach within the scope of tort law, more particularly within the doctrine of causal link.

> "Although the question of causal link is principally a legal issue, law may (and must) sometimes rely on other rules of science in order to determine the relationship between an event and its consequences. If, for example, the medical science tells us that a particular consequence (disease) can occur only as a result of external infection, than a successful proof of such disease requires no further proof of causal link. If, on the contrary, such disease can arise from a number of different causes, than the proof of actual disease would not be considered sufficient in law and the claiming party will be requested to prove that the disease has actually occurred as a consequence of external infection. It appears, therefore, that in certain circumstances the scientific rules eliminate the need of proof of causality by creating a 'scientific' (as opposed to 'legal') presumption concerning a certain course of events.
>
> As has already been observed, such 'scientific presumption' may justify a legal rule sanctioning a consequence of a wrongful act and not the act itself only in case where the science leaves no doubt that the consequence can occur only in one single manner, i.e. by the wrongful act.
>
> If this might have been the case of anti-doping rules and procedures in their early years, it has been demonstrated recently that in particular circumstances, such as low concentrations of certain anabolic agents, this scientific presumption can no longer be considered as absolute and irrebuttable [...]. In this way, the rule sanctioning the presence of a substance and allowing no discussion of the real cause of such presence, would – according to this Panel – no longer be justified."[512]

According to the reasoning of the CAS the liability of the athlete based on the description of the doping offence might be absent as a result of scientific developments. In this line of argument the presumption of liability is lifted. However, in the system of the CAS this presumption theoretically was not up for discussion as far as liability was concerned. The degree of liability or, like in the case at hand: the lack thereof due to new scientific insights, was only a point for discussion in the CAS system where the severity of the penalty was at stake. The line of thought unfurling in this case meant therefore that if a doping analysis revealed concentra-

---

[512] *Idem*, grounds 46-47.

tions of above 1.0 ng/ml and below 5.0 ng/ml a doping offence had to be assumed, unless the causal link between this finding and certain preceding culpable behaviour could not be demonstrated.

As the sports organisation had to show that a doping offence had been committed it would be logical to assume that the organisation had to be the one to show the causal link. However, because the CAS did not make a sharp distinction between the illegality of an act and liability for this act the assumption fails.

> "According to this Panel, it is a general rule of law that each party should bear the 'onus probandi' with respect to all facts on which it relies in its conclusions, except where such burden has been shifted by a legal presumption, which is not the case in this discussion."[513]

In this case where a grey area had emerged as a result of the uncertainties voiced by science an absolute presumption that the presence of metabolites was the result of external administration could no longer be assumed. Lacking this presumption, the burden of proof had to be divided justly and fairly.

> "It seems therefore proper to distinguish this type of cases related to substances produced endogenously from the cases where the presumption of guilt is the main issue and where it is clearly left to the accused athlete to discharge him(her)self by exoneration, i.e. by providing conclusive evidence rebutting the presumption laid down by the rule of law applicable in the circumstances."[514]

In order to prevent that placing the burden of proof upon Bernhard would manoeuvre him into an impossible situation where he would lose the case beforehand, the CAS came to the rescue.

> "As it is well known in other fields of law, the particular problem of proof in the field of causality lies in the *possible parallel impact* of several causes potentially leading to the same consequence. As soon as science admits that more than one cause can lead to the same result, the legal issue arises who has to prove the exact cause of a given consequence. However, in the majority of cases in real life, it will be impossible for any of the parties to prove that the result has occurred exactly *due to a specific* cause (*'probagio diabolica'*). To charge one of the parties with such a heavy burden would, in fact, amount to a presumption, rebuttable on the face of it, but irrebuttable in reality. Therefore, alternative ways of proving the causal link must exist, such as, e.g., elimination of other causes: a party requested to prove the causal link and unable to demonstrate that a particular cause has led to the consequence, can nevertheless be deemed successful, if it can provide proof *excluding all other possible causes*."[515]

Bernhard was therefore not required to prove that it had not been use of nandrolone which had caused metabolites to be present in his body. The athlete had already

---

[513] *Idem*, ground 53.
[514] *Idem*, ground 55.
[515] *Idem*, ground 56.

submitted scientific evidence. The CAS did not consider it unrealistic to request the sports organisation to prove that other possible scientific causes could not lead to the prohibited consequence in this case. If the sports organisation would test the athlete again out of competition and there were no metabolites present this would be valid proof. Bernhard submitted to the test voluntarily.

The CAS provided another argument as to why a lower degree of proof on the part of the athlete could be considered sufficient in cases falling within the grey area:

> "Namely, account should be taken of the differences between civil (tort) law on the one hand and quasi-penal and disciplinary proceedings on the other hand.[516]
>
> In civil (tort) law, the burden of proof is clear-cut and its sharp edge has the effect to reverse the case against the party which has failed to provide the required proof. This is true both in cases where the burden of proof is 'balanced', i.e. shared between the parties, and in cases where such burden is re-distributed through a legal presumption releasing one party of a particular proof and shifting it to the other party.
>
> The situation in 'quasi-penal' procedures, such as doping in sport, should, on the other hand, be looked at differently, among other reasons also due to *the principle 'in dubio pro reo'*, i.e. the benefit of doubt, which itself is an emanation of one of the most important legal presumptions, the presumption of innocence, deeply enshrined in the general principles of law and justice. This principle has the effect that in criminal and similar proceedings, the two parties do not bear an equal burden of proof; while the accusing party must prove the alleged facts with *certainty*, it is sufficient for the accused to establish reasons for doubt."[517]

In the first place, one may wonder why the CAS did not use a criminal law model as its basis from the beginning of this case; in the second place, the question is why the CAS when it omitted to opt for this model suddenly on the question of evidence did point to the criminal law of evidence as an alternative.

Despite the pressing requirements of the fight against doping these could not set aside the accused's fundamental right provided by the *in dubio pro reo* rule. The CAS declared that the principle laid down in this rule did not go against the spirit of the documents of the IOC Medical Commission which addressed the persons applying the Medical Code. After this intermezzo which the CAS could just as easily have made the starting point of its reasoning the tribunal finally got around to weighing the evidence submitted by the parties.

The urine was found to contain metabolites of nandrolone, namely norandrosterone and noretiocholanone, both in concentrations of 3 ng/ml. The concentrations were considerably lower than those found in the urine of Mason (3.0 / 5 – 6 ng/ml) and Bouras (10.8 / 15 ng/ml). Mason was unable to provide a reasonable explanation for the prohibited substances' origin and had failed in his evidence that his

---

[516] *Idem*, ground 60.
[517] *Idem*, grounds 61-62.

body produced nandrolone in such quantities as to exceed the threshold value of 5 ng/ml. The French judoka Bouras also failed to prove his case conclusively.[518]

> "In the circumstances of this case, it was, however, the Appellant who offered evidence – supported by expert opinion – that the presence of metabolites could have as well been a consequence of endogenous production of his body. The 'Conclusions and Comments' submitted by Dr. L. Dehennin of L.A.B. (Laboratoire de la Federation Nationale des Courses Françaises of Chatenay – Malabry, France) on March 30, 1999 confirm that the Appellant displayed – during the out-of-competition testing between October 1998 and February 1999 – an abnormal urinary excretion profile of nandrolone metabolites, which occasionally exceeded 2 ng/ml. The report of Dr. Dehennin also underlined the correlation between the fat-rich diet to which the Appellant was submitted and the high levels of endogenous creation of norandrosterone and noretiocholanone.'[519]
> '[...] the conclusions of the report of Dr. Dehennin – quoted above -, support the possibility that the presence of nandrolone metabolite in the urine following the competition on June 7, 1999 was not of exogenous origin, or that this becomes at least probable'."[520]

The CAS was of the opinion that Bernhard had demonstrated at least a probability that the concentrations of nandrolone metabolites in his urine were the result of endogenous production by his own body.

> "Although it is clear that the Appellant was unable to prove with *certainty* such endogenous production, the evidence provided can be deemed sufficient to create reasonable doubt concerning external application. In line with the legal reasoning concerning the legal impact of the 'grey zone' cases, developed earlier in this award, the evidence leading to reasonable doubt should – in absence of other evidence – be sufficient to grant the Appellant the benefit of the doubt."[521]

The awareness of the Panel that the possibility that nandrolone[522] is produced endogenously decreased exponentially within the limits of the grey area made it easier to assume this probability in the case of Bernhard, as the concentrations found in his sample corresponded almost exactly to the lower limit of the grey area. Even if Mason and Bouras had been able to provide sufficient evidence to support endogenous production the CAS would not have accepted this as easily, as the concentrations found in their bodies were much higher than those found in Bernhard's body.

---

[518] CAS 98/214, 8-1-1999, *Bouras v. FIJ*, Matthieu Reeb, ed., *Digest of CAS Awards II 1998-2000* (The Hague, Kluwer Law International 2002) pp. 291-324.

[519] CAS 98/222, 9-8-1999, *Bernhard v. ITU*, Matthieu Reeb, ed., *Digest of CAS Awards II 1998-2000* (The Hague, Kluwer Law International 2002) pp. 330-344, ground 68.

[520] *Idem*, ground 69.

[521] *Idem*, ground 71.

[522] *The Examiner*, 6 August 1999: "Among anabolic steroids, nandrolone is virtually prehistoric. A chemical version of the naturally occurring hormone, testosterone, it helps the body to increase muscle mass. Originally, nandrolone was used in an oil-based, injectible form. Sold as Deca Durabolin, nandrolone is still in widespread use in gymnasiums around the world, and is openly sold on the internet."

Although the IOC and the CAS gave the impression that scientific research had clarified the endogenous production of steroids and that this made it possible to apply "hard and fast rules," that same science indicated that clarity was still elusive as regards the production by the human body of steroids in specific circumstances and in relation to the body's chemistry as a whole.

In the *Meca-Medina/Majcen* case the CAS pointed out that the threshold value accepted by the IOC for endogenous NA in urine samples of male athletes was 2 ng/ml.[523]

> "The average value for endogenous production found in all published studies was less than twenty times lower than this level and the highest value found less than one third lower.[524] At a conference of the heads of all the 27 IOC laboratories in October 1999 the validity of the 2ng/ml limit was reaffirmed."

The samples of both athletes revealed the presence of norandosterone (NA) in quantities above the recognised limit. The result of the analyses was indicative of the fact that the origin of the nandrolone metabolites could be nandrolone precursors, such as norandrostenedione, rather than the classical nandrolone itself. A precursor is a substance that has the capacity to change into another substance.

> "Because such precursors, as part of nutritional supplements, have been the source for an increase in positive tests in connection with nandrolone metabolites such as NA and NE over the last years, norandrostenedione and norandrostenediol have now been expressly included in the newer lists of anabolic androgenic steroids.
> Before their express inclusion, both the above substances were prohibited as part of the so-called 'related substances'. There is a definite chemical relationship – as the IOC amendments suggest.
> It has never been put into question that the presence of nandrolone metabolites was the conclusive proof of the presence of a prohibited substance, be it nandrolone itself or a related substance including in particular the two above mentioned precursors."[525]

As opposed to in the *Bernhard* case, the CAS in this case rejected the existence of a grey area.

> "With the confirmation of the limit of 2ng/ml [...], any discussion of possible endogenous production above that level (which includes a safety margin and was never reached in any controlled experiment) has become moot. In particular, there is no grey area between 2 and 5 ng/ml (which would avail Appellant 2 only) and reference to ear-

---

[523] CAS 99/A/234 & CAS 99/A/235, 29-2-2000, *David Meca-Medina v. FINA & Igor Majcen v. FINA*, ground 2.11.

[524] Undated Statement on Nandrolone for Governing Bodies of Sport.

[525] CAS 99/A/234 & CAS 99/A/235, 29-2-2000, *David Meca-Medina v. FINA & Igor Majcen v. FINA*, ground 9.2-9.4.

lier decisions or statements which made reference thereto have become irrelevant.[526] In any event, the Appellants have produced no evidence that they were naturally high producers of endogenous nandrolone."[527]

Not only does a grey area not exist, according to the CAS, but the IOC standard of 2 ng/ml, which in *Bernhard* was still considered a guideline, in *Meca-Medina* was turned into an objective rule. Although the IOC was convinced that the standard was correct, it was still not clear how and based on what scientific grounds the IOC arrived at this conclusion. There was no consensus in medicine or sport concerning the reference value that was to be used for nandrolone. In *KNAU v. Douglas* the question was raised whether according to current medical opinion a reference value of 2 ng/ml or any reference value for that matter could be considered acceptable. The witness Professor J.H.H. Thijssen declared that the reference value of 2 ng/ml as identified and used by Professor Dr. Schänzer was based on two studies of limited scope in Canada. In his opinion there was no consensus in the medical world concerning this reference value as too little research had yet been published. He did consider that there was consensus, however, concerning the fact that it was not precisely known how nandrolone was produced.

"This is all the more troubling, as this involves a substance naturally produced by the body. Both Professor J.H.H. Thijssen and Professor J.M. van Rossum compare this with the developments that have taken place with respect to the testosterone/epitestosterone ratio, which was initially set at 2:1, then 6:1 and some time after at 10:1. They consider that at present the threshold value for nandrolone as it is normally found in the human body according to current medical opinion is as yet insufficiently clear.
In this context, they also refer to the scientific publications of Professor B. Ie Bizec, 'Evidence for the Presence of Endogenous 19-norandrosterone in Human Urine' and of Mr de Backer et al., 'Urinary Metabolites of endogenous nandrolone in Women, a case study', as well as of Professor W. Schänzer et al. himself, '19-Norandrosterone-criteria for the Decision Making Process'."[528]

In a study into nandrolone by the Swiss biochemist Saugy concentrations were measured in 148 footballers. From this research it emerged that strenuous physical exercise could lead to heightened levels of endogenous nandrolone. Saugy's research had been carried out at the request of Professor Toni Graf-Baumann, a member of the FIFA Medical Commission. A FIFA spokesman, Andreas Herren, was

---

[526] The Appellants relied on the case CAS 98/222, 9-8-1999, *Bernhard v. ITU*, Matthieu Reeb, ed., *Digest of CAS Awards II 1998-2000* (The Hague, Kluwer Law International 2002) pp. 330-344, in which Bernhard was acquitted on appeal from a finding of the International Triathlon Union in a concentration of 3 ng/ml. However, this ruling pre-dated the latest IOC promulgation and the Panel accordingly distinguished it from the case at hand.
[527] CAS 99/A/234 & CAS 99/A/235, 29-2-2000, *David Meca-Medina v. FINA & Igor Majcen v. FINA*, ground 10.1.
[528] Disciplinary committee of the Royal Dutch Athletics Union, 8 March 2000, *KNAU v. Douglas*, grounds 13-15.

alleged to have declared at the beginning of March 2000 that the FIFA would no longer impose sanctions following the discovery of nandrolone metabolites in a footballer's urine.[529] This was denied by the FIFA in an official statement the next day: "Contrary to reports issued last weekend, FIFA has not decided to strike nandrolone off the list of prohibited substances. Football's world-governing body categorically denies the contents of such reports."[530]

It is presently the custom with this substance to measure the number of nanogrammes per millilitre, but his method of measurement has also been subject to debate. The IAAF stipulated that the presence of more than 2 nanogrammes per millilitre was an indication of the exogenous use of nandrolone; the triathlon federation set the threshold value at 5 nanogrammes. Despite little scientific knowledge about nandrolone, various experts considered that the best approach was to relate the amount of androlone to other substances naturally present in the body. A comparison was made with the hormone testosterone which occurs naturally. This substance is related to the presence of epitestosterone in the body in ratios on which there is scientific agreement. During a forum on doping which was held on 29 February 2000 in Cologne,[531] Mr Schänzer, who was the head of the doping laboratory at Cologne, which is an IOC-accredited laboratory, was of the opinion that the reference value for nandrolone had to be set at 10 ng/ml; only when this value was exceeded could it be assumed with certainty that a doping offence had been committed.[532] Where exactly Schänzer stands in the nandrolone debate is difficult to say. In an interview with him in August 1999 it is still reported: "Dass der Nandrolon-Grenzwert durch körpereigene Steroidproduktion überschritten werden kann, bestreitet Schänzer energisch: 'Alle wissenschaftlichen Studien sprechen dagegen'."[533] Suddenly, nandrolone metabolites were discovered in the urine of a large number of international top athletes. Among these was Merlene Ottey (along with Christie, Walker, Richardson, Smith, Baumann, Douglas, etc.)[534] After a competition in Luzern on 5 July 1999, Ottey's urine was found to contain 9-norandosterone (NA) in a concentration of 15 ng/ml and 19-noretiocholanolone (NE) in a concentration of 10 ng/ml. (The countercheck revealed concentrations of 14 ng/ml 19-NA and 11 ng/ml 19-NE). The disciplinary committee of the Jamaican athletics federation (JAAA) in its decision of 7 December 1999 acquitted Ottey for the following reasons:

---

[529] *Berliner Zeitung*, 4 March 2000.

[530] Media information – FIFA Executive Committee to debate on the topic of nandrolone, Zürich, 6 March 2000.

[531] *Sportzaken* 2000, p. 63

[532] In an interview held by CNN (100 times the legal level, 8 August 1999) Schänzer stated that: "for me to be absolutely clear, the minimum is 10. Here I am absolutely clear." This statement was also included in *KNAU v. Douglas*, ground 16.

[533] *Berliner Morgenpost*, 20 August 1999.

[534] IAAF press release, 15 February 2000: "The facts do not back up the notion of a sudden increase in nandrolone cases in sport. Furthermore, the frequency of such cases in athletics is lower than the average in all sports together. Nevertheless, on the initiative of UK Athletics and several athletes who are seeking to explain apparent anomalies in nandrolone findings, the IAAF Council has agreed to participate in international research."

"inter alia that of the material adduced before it, the scientific evidence does not support an exogenous source of the metabolites detected in the urine samples; accordingly the JAAA's tribunal was not sure that the substance reported was ingested by her and not produced endogenously."

On 12 February 2000, however, the IAAF Council suspended Ottey after all, based on its recently amended Rule 59.2 "Disciplinary Procedures for Doping Offences."[535] The case was heard anew and in its judgment of 3 July 2000 the IAAF Arbitration Panel first made it clear that IAAF had to prove beyond reasonable doubt that a doping offence had occurred.

"Hence, the Rules do not require that IAAF (or in the case under consideration the JAAA before its relevant tribunal) has to prove that the prohibited substance was exogenously administered. The decision of JAAA's Tribunal is based on a wrongful construction of the pertinent rules."

Ottey denied having committed a doping offence and argued that the level of 19-NA found in the samples had been produced endogenously. It emerged from a growing number of scientific studies that 19-NA was naturally present in low, but clearly recognisable concentrations in the urine of both women and men. The concentration in women appears to be higher particularly in case of pregnancy and at certain times during their monthly cycle.[536] "It is undisputed that Ms Ottey was mid-cycle at the time of the Lucerne Meeting. This time is the most fertile in terms of hormone production."

"[...] the panel considered the impact of naturally produced nandrolone and its metabolites and found that a *lacuna* exists in Schedule 1 Part I(a) of the Procedural Guidelines for Doping Control as read with Rule 55.2(1). It is because the rules as read with the Procedural Guidelines for Doping Control provide, in the case of the endogenous production of testosterone beyond normally acceptable limits, a procedure designed to avoid prejudicing the athlete. By analogy and in fairness to the athlete the Arbitration Panel invokes and applies the underlying principle applicable to testosterone to the issue of nandrolone."[537]

The Panel was of the opinion that it was up to the IAAF to prove that the objective elements of the offence had been fulfilled. Part of this was proving that the amount of 19-NA which was found in Ottey's samples exceeded the values normally found

---

[535] IAAF press release, 12 February 2000 – "Monte Carlo – Monaco – The IAAF Council, during an Extraordinary Meeting in Monte Carlo, has decided to amend IAAF Rule 59.2 (Disciplinary Procedures for Doping Offences). As of midnight on February 13, any athlete who has been cleared by his or her national federation of a doping offence, but whose case has been sent to Arbitration by the IAAF, will now be suspended from competition until the conclusion of that Arbitration."

[536] See: P. van Eenoo, F.T. Delbeke, F.H. de Jong, P. de Backer: *Urinary metabolites of endogenous nandrolone in women: a case study*.

[537] IAAF Arbitration Panel, 3 July 2000, no. 7216, *Ottey v. IAAF*, ground 15.

in humans in the case of endogenous production. If the IAAF had been able to furnish such proof it would have been the task of the athlete to demonstrate "by clear and convincing evidence that the quantity of 19-NA found is attributable to a pathological or physiological condition."

"It was the IAAF's contention that the 'A' sample showing 15 ng/ml of 19-NA exceeds normal endogenous production. Also noted was the Nagano study carried out at the Nagano Olympic Games on 251 women athletes following competition, none of whom produced a 19-NA sample in excess of 5 ng/ml. This and other evidence suggest an upper limit for endogenous production of 19-NA by non-pregnant women of 5 ng/ml."[538]

The Panel also referred to the guidelines which the IOC had established for accredited laboratories, the Analytical Criteria for Reporting Low Concentrations of Anabolic Steroids (August 1998).[539] The document recommended that proceedings should not be instituted against pregnant women if the NA value found was below 5 ng/ml. The documents also mentioned a correction in case the specific gravity of the urine sample exceeded the value of 1.020.

"This is recommended as the IOC recognises that among other factors, during intense physical activity a degree of dehydration may occur, causing urine to become concentrated. This may increase the measured concentration of excreted substances, possibly up to fourfold. The James Report, a report to the UK Sports Council from the Expert Committee, dated 18 January, 2000 [...] approves of this IOC-recommended procedure as the most appropriate method of correction when necessary."[540]

On a day when temperatures ranged between 25.5 and 28 Celsius, Ottey competed in both the 100 metres and the 200 metres within a period of 90 minutes between one o'clock and seven o'clock in the afternoon. Due to dehydration, the specific gravity of the urine had risen to 1.025. The Panel in its considerations took this into

---

[538] IAAF Arbitration Panel, 3 July 2000, no. 7216, *Ottey v. IAAF*, ground 17.

[539] "19-norandrosterone in male urine

In the case of the detection of 19-norandrosterone in the urine of a male the following two aspects should be assessed:

1. Whether the relative signal(s) in the mass spectometry screening analysis for 19-norandrosterone is less than that obtained from the positive control urine (nominal concentration 2 ng/ml) described above.

2. If the urine specific gravity is greater than 1.020, multiply the relative signal from the positive control urine by $I(sg - 1)/0.002$ and determine whether the relative signal obtained from the sample is less.

If either condition is met, do not produce an adverse report for possible sanction. Before issuing an adverse report, repeat the measurements on a further two aliquots of the sample. More than one metabolite may be detected, but the identification of only 19-norandrosterone is sufficient to report for possible sanction.

To summarise, according to this document, the laboratory must verify with a single point of comparison of 2 ng/ml that the signal of norandrosterone in the suspicious sample is higher. The measurements must be repeated with two aliquots."

[540] IAAF Arbitration Panel, no. 7216, 3 July 2000, *Ottey v. IAAF*, ground 18.

account. By applying the correction proposed by the IOC the Panel arrived at a concentration equalling 4.53 ng/ml. This remained within the 5 ng/ml value which the IOC had indicated for non-pregnant women. Ottey's urine therefore did not show any of the characteristics of the urine of athletes to whom nandrolone or nandrolone metabolites had been applied externally. The Panel considered that the IAAF had failed to prove that the concentration in Ottey's urine exceeded the concentration normally produced.

> "According to the evidence and the literature placed before the Arbitration Panel, it is generally accepted that a finding of higher than 5ng/ml is not attributable to normal endogenous production. Nevertheless, the same scientific literature, including the IOC recommendation accepted by the parties, provided the correction formula mentioned in paragraphs 18 and 20. The parties also accepted that the specific gravity dipstick reading (as converted) would fall below 5 ng/ml, if it were to be corrected.
> Under these circumstances, the issue the Arbitration Panel had to determine was which specific gravity reading to rely upon, either the reading taken at the time of the voiding of the sample (1.025), or the later readings at the time of laboratory testing (1.019) for the purpose of triggering the correcting formula. The Arbitration Panel found that the correct specific gravity reading to accept would be that taken at the time of voiding, which would thus trigger the application of the correction formula. As a consequence, the Arbitration Panel accepts that the adjusted 19-NA reading falls below 5 ng/ml and therefore would not require the reporting of the finding of a prohibited substance. In any event, the IAAF failed to discharge its burden of proving, beyond reasonable doubt, that for the 19-NA reading to be at 15 ng/ml, the time for the determination of the specific gravity had to be the time of the laboratory testing and not the time of voiding. Therefore the IAAF has failed to discharge its burden of proof that a doping offence has occurred beyond reasonable doubt."[541]

Nafziger[542] has commented that "all too often, IF decisions appear to be based on political expediency." He not only pointed to the Ottey case, but to that of Javier Sotomayor[543] as well. In his opinion "in both instances clear scientific evidence to support their suspensions seems to have been compromised by either faulty review of the evidence (Ottey) or extrinsic factors such as empathy by the IF administrative council with the particular athlete (Sotomayor) that called into question both the independence and the binding force of the arbitration."

Pursuant to Article 2.1 in conjunction with Article 2.1.1 of the WADC athletes are strictly liable for any prohibited substance or its metabolites or markers found to be present in their bodily specimens. However, in Article 2.1.2 the WADC makes an exception for "those substances for which a quantitative reporting threshold is specifically identified in the prohibited list," but immediately follows this by the provision that "the detected presence of any quantity of a prohibited substance or its

---

[541] IAAF Arbitration Panel, no. 7216, 3 July 2000, *Ottey v. IAAF*, grounds 21-22.
[542] Nafziger 2004 (*supra* nt. 457).
[543] *Sotomayor v. IAAF*, IAAF Decision, 24 July 2000 (unpublished).

metabolites or markers in an athlete's sample shall constitute an anti-doping rule violation." Article 2.1.3 provides another exception to the general rule of Article 2.1, namely that "the prohibited list may establish special criteria for the evaluation of prohibited substances that can also be produced endogenously."

To summarise, the finding of even a small quantity of most substances on the doping list in an athlete's urine in most cases would point to a doping offence. However, the lists also contained substances that are naturally produced by the human body. For these threshold values were established. The finding of a small amount of such a substance in a doping sample did not automatically mean that an illegal act of doping had been committed. Establishing threshold values always gives rise to debate. This was especially the case where one sports organisation established higher values than the other. When something is either allowed or not allowed, this is always easier than if it is slightly allowed. Is it allowed if the amount of prohibited slightly exceeds the threshold level? Is there such a thing as a grey area just above the threshold value? Opinion differed concerning these questions, including the views of the various CAS Panels. The WADC does not mention a grey area, but it does recognise that for certain substances there must be a threshold value and that substances which may be produced endogenously are liable to exceptions.

4.5. Exceptional circumstances according to the WADC

The OMADC did not contain an outright rule for exceptional circumstances. After Article 3(1)(b) penalised the doping offence by a sanction of two years at least, it was further provided that "[...] based on specific, exceptional circumstances to be evaluated in the first instance by the competent IF bodies, there *may* be a provision for a possible modification of the two-year sanction." During the World Conference on Doping the FIFA and UCI chairmen did not attend because their federations could not reconcile themselves with the fixed two-year sanction for the first doping offence.[544] The situation was all the more curious as the first version of the WADC already contained an exceptional circumstances clause which allowed for the flexible application of the prescribed fixed sanction of two years. This clause read as follows:

"8.8.3.2 Exceptional circumstances.
The minimum periods of disqualification provided above may be lessened in proportion to the exceptional circumstances of a particular case, but only if the athlete can

---

[544] "Unter den rund 1000 Delegierten und Beobachtern aus 100 Ländern fehlten ausgerechnet die beiden Weltverbandspräsidenten Sepp Blatter (Fußball) und Hein Verbrüggen (Radsport), die zu den schärfsten Kritikern des Codes zählen. Ihre Abwesenheit wurde von vielen Teilnehmern als Brüskierung angesehen. Sowohl die Fußballspieler als auch die Radsportler wenden sich gegen die vorgesehene Mindeststrafe von zwei Jahren auch für Doping-Ersttäter." *Frankfurter Allgemeine Zeitung*, 4 March 2003, no. 53, p. 31.

clearly establish that the anti-doping rule violation was not the result of his or her fault or negligence."

This clause was worded more broadly than its counterpart in the OMADC, as it did not merely apply in connection with the sanction for a first offence. According to this provision it would in theory be possible to commute the sentence of exclusion for life to a much milder penalty.

The second version saw the clause return in a much-edited version. It had been supplemented to cover cases where an athlete's low age and lack of experience would be relevant in deciding the culpability of his actions.

> "1.9.2.3.3 Exceptional circumstances.
> The periods of ineligibility provided above may be lessened or eliminated in proportion to the exceptional circumstances of a particular case, but only if the athlete can clearly establish that the anti-doping rule violation was not the result of his or her fault or negligence. The athlete's age and competitive experience may be considered in determining whether the anti-doping rule violation was the result of the athlete's fault or negligence."

Why include an exceptional circumstances clause in the WADC? "This approach is consistent with basic principles of human rights and provides a balance between those Anti-Doping Organizations that argue for a much narrower exception, or none at all, and those that would reduce a two-year suspension based on a range of other factors even when the athlete was admittedly at fault."[545] Perhaps partly as a result of pressure from the FIFA and the UCI, the exceptional circumstances clause was expanded considerably.

Where the first version still spoke of a proportional reduction of the period of exclusion, the second mentioned reduction and elimination, and the third now exclusively mentions elimination in cases where there has been no fault or negligence. It must be noted however that the clause may currently only be invoked in case of the violation of the anti-doping rules referred to in Articles 2.1. and 2.2.

> "10.5 Elimination or reduction of period of ineligibility based on exceptional circumstances
> 10.5.1 No fault or negligence
> If the Athlete establishes in an individual case involving an anti-doping rule violation under Article 2.1 [...] or use of a prohibited substance or prohibited method under Article 2.2 that he or she bears no fault or negligence for the violation, the otherwise applicable period of ineligibility shall be eliminated."[546]

---

[545] Comment to Art. 10.5.2 WADC (final version).

[546] The comment to Art. 10.5.1 states that this provision "[...] applies only to violations under Articles 2.1 and 2.2 [...] because fault or negligence is already required to establish an anti-doping rule violation under other anti-doping rules." This gives rise to some confusion as under the strict liability doctrine in the WADC any discussion of culpability is ruled out where the violation of an anti-doping rule is concerned. Such discussion can only take place in the framework of determining punishment.

A rule which has been laid down in the final version of the WADC and which was not found in earlier versions is Article 10.5.2. The Code Project Team considered it appropriate to include another exceptional circumstances clause for cases where there is no significant fault or negligence. This clause may also be invoked by athletes who are suspected of having violated the anti-doping rules laid down in Articles 2.3 and 2.8.

> "10.5.2 No significant fault or negligence
> This Article 10.5.2 applies only to anti-doping rule violations involving Article 2.1 [...], Article 2.2, [...] Article 2.3, or [...] Article 2.8. If an athlete establishes in an individual case involving such violations that he or she bears no significant fault or negligence, then the period of ineligibility may be reduced, but the reduced period of ineligibility may not be less than one-half of the minimum period of Ineligibility otherwise applicable. If the otherwise applicable period of ineligibility is a lifetime, the reduced period under this section may be no less than 8 years."

An additional requirement which was already part of all of the earlier versions of the WADC is that "[...] the athlete must also be able to demonstrate how the prohibited substance entered his or her system."[547]

One could argue that it is hardly proportional that the penalty for a second violation is eliminated when no fault or negligence is at stake, but is upheld for a minimum of eight years if there is no significant fault or negligence.

The Dutch delegate to the World Conference on Doping in Copenhagen criticised the limited role in the doping procedure of the question of the culpability of the athlete in doping violations. The delegate remarked that: "Where exceptional circumstances were concerned, the proposed system for taking into account exceptional circumstances seemed to be limited, therefore limiting the fairness of the anti-doping policy. An athlete should not be restricted in proving exceptional circumstances when accused of an anti-doping rule violation. The Code should explicitly provide that exceptional circumstances will be taken into consideration for each and every anti-doping rule violation. This would promote the credibility of the anti-doping policy by providing greater fairness."[548] This is plausible, but the drafters of the WADC had already opted for a system in which culpability could no longer be discussed for the purpose of determining whether a doping violation had taken place. This system, which had already been laid down in the OMADC, was adopted worldwide after its inclusion in the WADC.

Given the comment to Art. 10.5.2 the Code Project Team was quite aware of this: "These Articles [10.5.1 and 10.5.2] apply only to the imposition of sanctions; they are not applicable to the determination of whether an anti-doping rule violation has occurred."

[547] In the WADC's final version the condition under Art. 10.5.1 is supplemented as follows: "In the event this Article is applied and the period of ineligibility otherwise applicable is eliminated, the anti-doping rule violation shall not be considered a violation for the limited purpose of determining the period of Ineligibility for multiple violations under Articles 10.2, 10.3 and 10.6."

[548] World Conference on Doping in Sport, plenary sessions, Summary Notes, p. 32.

As the OMADC clause did not expressly provide for exceptional circumstances, the IFs were free to apply clauses of their own.[549] The WADC "[...] stated that an athlete needed to exercise the utmost caution. What if an athlete could not meet the test of absolutely no fault? How could proportionality be dealt with? If the athlete could not prove absolutely no fault, then the athlete would have the burden to prove no significant fault or negligence, following which the two years could be reduced to a floor of one year. The opinion of the independent experts was that there had to be a rule that addressed proportionality, and this rule (Art. 10.5) satisfied the requirement," said Richard Young.[550]

Questions still remain however concerning the particular circumstances which according to the drafters of the WADC had to be considered exceptional. These had to be adequately described, as "there is plenty of devil in the detail."[551] The comment to the WADC's Article 10.5 mentions the following concerning the definition of the clause's scope:

"Article 10.5 is meant to have an impact only in cases where the circumstances are truly exceptional and not in the vast majority of cases.
To illustrate the operation of Article 10.5, an example where no fault or negligence would result in the total elimination of a sanction is where an athlete could prove that, despite all due care, he or she was sabotaged by a competitor. Conversely, a sanction could not be completely eliminated on the basis of no fault or negligence in the following circumstances: (a) a positive test resulting from a mislabeled or contaminated vitamin or nutritional supplement (Athletes are responsible for what they ingest (Article 2.1.1) and have been warned against the possibility of supplement contamination); (b) the administration of a prohibited substance by the athlete's personal physician or trainer without disclosure to the athlete (Athletes are responsible for their choice of medical personnel and for advising medical personnel that they cannot be given any prohibited substance); and (c) sabotage of the athlete's food or drink by a spouse, coach or other person within the athlete's circle of associates (Athletes are responsible

---

[549] "[...] as a result, different sporting bodies had set their own, different, criteria. Two examples from two federations could be cited. The FINA rule was based on lack of fault. Since the adoption of the rule, there had been fourteen nandrolone cases, in ten of which it had imposed a four-year sanction, and in four of which it had applied the exceptional circumstances rule to some extent, but in only one of those it had applied the penalty of less than two years (in this case, one year). The FINA had a tight exceptional circumstances rule. The UCI had a very different exceptional circumstances rule, which was much broader, and allowed for consideration of the impact on the athlete, and the impact on his or her standing in the community. The UCI had had four cases since January 2001, when the two-year rule had been adopted. In one of these cases, the athlete had been sanctioned for two years, and in the other three cases athletes had received six months," commented Richard Young, World Conference on Doping in Sport, plenary sessions, Summary Notes, p. 13.

[550] Richard Young, World Conference on Doping in Sport, plenary sessions, Summary Notes, p. 14.

[551] "This has been modified to allow individual sports bodies to reduce the ban in 'exceptional circumstances'." Prof. Jiri Dvorak, the head of FIFA's medical committee, said football had no major disagreements with the code. He said: "We can live with the general estimation of a two-year ban for a first offence but we want the right to increase the bans as well as reduce them – maybe to three or maybe four years." BBC Sport, "Tough new sanctions for drug cheats," 5 March 2003.

for what they ingest and for the conduct of those persons to whom they entrust access to their food and drink). However, depending on the unique facts of a particular case, any of the referenced illustrations could result in a reduced sanction based on no significant fault or negligence. (For example, reduction may well be appropriate in illustration (a) if the athlete clearly establishes that the cause of the positive test was contamination in a common multiple vitamin purchased from a source with no connection to prohibited substances and the athlete exercised care in not taking other nutritional supplements.)

Article 10.5.2 applies only to the identified anti-doping rule violations because these violations may be based on conduct that is not intentional or purposeful. Violations under Article 2.4 (whereabouts information and missed tests) are not included, even though intentional conduct is not required to establish these violations, because the sanction for violations of Article 2.4 (from three months to two years) already builds in sufficient discretion to allow consideration of the athlete's degree of fault."

Despite this explanation, a very real chance remains that the disciplinary bodies of the different IFs will each use their own interpretation of exceptional circumstances. If this interpretation conflicts with the WADA's point of view, the WADA does not need to stand idly by. Under Article 13.2.1 the final decision of an IF disciplinary tribunal may be appealed exclusively (without recourse to the courts) to the CAS when a case is involved arising from competition in an international event or in cases involving international-level athletes. Article 13.2.3 lists the "Persons entitled to appeal." Under (e) the WADA is included in this circle. In the future, CAS case law will further define the term "exceptional circumstances." Given Articles 21.1 and 21.1.3. it will not be easy to demonstrate exceptional circumstances. These Articles provide among other things that the "roles and responsibilities of athletes [are] to be knowledgeable of and comply with all applicable anti-doping policies and rules adopted pursuant to the Code [and] to take responsibility, in the context of anti-doping, for what they ingest and use."

What are the views of the CAS concerning the interpretation of the concept of "exceptional circumstances" under the regulations based on the WADC? It does not consider that the young age of an athlete falls within its scope.[552] The CAS Ad hoc Division – Games of the XXVIII Olympiad – Athens was called upon to give an opinion on this question in the Edwards case.[553] After the finding of salbutamol and nikethamide in her urine, Torri Edwards, a 27-year old athlete and member of the United States Olympic Team, had admitted before an AAA Panel that she had committed a doping offence, but pleaded the existence of exceptional circumstances pursuant to IAAF Rule 38.12 et seq. which would have to result in a reduction or elimination of her sanction by two years which was the period for which the United States Anti-Doping Agency had suspended her. The AAA Panel considered that there was a possibility of exceptional circumstances, but under the IAAF Rules the

[552] CAS 2003/A/447, 20-1-2004, *S. v. FINA*. "The Panel has also considered the age of the Appellant, but has determined that age does not fall within the category of 'Exceptional Circumstances' which warrant consideration in reducing the term of ineligibility."

[553] CAS OG 04/003, 17-8-2004, *Torri Edwards v. IAAF and USA Track and Field (USATF)*.

Panel was not entitled to decide this matter. If there is a possibility of exceptional circumstances, the AAA Panel under Rule 38.16 has to adjourn the hearing and refer the case to the Doping Review Board via the General Secretary. In this case the Doping Review Board decided that there were no exceptional circumstances and the AAA Panel had to abide by this decision. Contrary to Edwards's contention that she had been unaware that the tablets she had taken contained a prohibited substance, the CAS Panel confirmed the findings of the Doping Review Board "that it would have been 'clear to any person reviewing the tablets that there was more than one ingredient in the tablets' and that there was negligence in not ascertaining that no prohibited substance was present within the tablets before they were ingested. In the circumstances of purchasing a product in a foreign country in this packaging, more steps could and, in fact, should have been taken. There is an obligation and a duty on an elite athlete to ensure that no prohibited substance enters his/her body, tissues or fluid. On balance, the Panel finds that there was negligence in failing to inquire or ascertain whether the product contained a prohibited substance."[554] The CAS rejected the defence of exceptional circumstances and the penalty which had been imposed on Edwards earlier remained intact. The CAS's interpretation of the term "exceptional circumstances" had not changed with the introduction of the WADC-related rules of the IAAF. By way of an aside it should be noted however that a change *had* occurred in the attitude towards doping perpetrators: "The Panel is of the view that this case provides an example of the harshness of the operation of the IAAF Rules relating to the imposition of a mandatory two-year sanction. If the breach had occurred at an IAAF Meet some two months earlier, the Panel was informed that it would have resulted in only a public warning under the IAAF Rules then in force. But it will now, as a result of the IAAF Rule which entered into force on 1 March 2004, result in a two-year period of ineligibility."[555]

As we have seen above, the system that provided for strict liability for athletes who tested positive could result in the punishment of more or less innocent people. This could then be mitigated by the reversal of the burden of proof: the athlete was presumed guilty but was at least given the opportunity to prove his/her innocence in order to reduce the sanction. The possibility included in the WADC for an athlete who has been found guilty to claim exceptional circumstances may offer an escape to the athlete who is free of blame or whose guilt is not serious enough to make him pay to the full. The basis for relying on such circumstances is, however, very narrow and the plea does not alter the fact that the athlete remains guilty of the offence; its effect is felt only in the determination of the penalty.

The Comment to Article 10.5 illustrates the effect of the provision by stating that "no fault or negligence" may result in the penalty being lifted if an athlete can prove

---

[554] *Idem*, ground 5.11.
[555] *Idem*, ground 5.13.

that despite all due care he or she was sabotaged by another competitor. Conversely a penalty cannot be completely lifted on the basis of no fault or negligence in the event that the athlete's food or drink is sabotaged by his/her spouse, coach or any other person forming part of his/her entourage. In the next section, it will be examined to what extent sabotage by a third party has contributed to the establishment of exceptional circumstances based on which the athlete, although having tested positive, is not punished as severely or at all.

4.6. Manipulation by the athlete

This section does not deal with the manipulation of samples by taking masking agents or with the manipulation of samples by third parties ("spiking" or "tampering"), but with the manipulation of his/her sample by the athlete him/herself in order to cover up any possibly incriminating components.[556] The analysis of the urine sample of Michelle Smith de Bruin which was supplied at an out-of-competition doping control revealed a high concentration of alcohol. The IOC-accredited laboratory in Barcelona which had been assigned by the FINA to analyse the sample reported to the FINA that in this case there were clear indications of falsification of the samples.[557] The analysis did not conclusively show the presence of any prohibited substance, but the laboratory did report that:

> "Additional laboratory results obtained with the sample (especially steroid profile and isotope ration mass spectrometry measurements) suggest the administration of some metabolic precursor of testosterone. Longitudinal follow-up is recommended."

The FINA doping Panel came to the conclusion that the urine had been tampered with by the swimmer herself, although it could not be established how this had been done. In any case, the manipulation had not taken place at the laboratory or during the sample's transport. The Panel also concluded that the doping controllers had not had any hand in the manipulation. Based on the provisions of Article DC 1.2(b)[558] in conjunction with Article DC 3.1(b)[559] Michelle Smith de Bruin had committed a

---

[556] Including handing in another person's urine, although this possibility is almost completely ruled out. However, in 2004 a case like this still occurred. Süreyya Ayhan, the 2002 European champion on the 1500 metres, handed in a sample to the WADA which did not contain her own urine. The disciplinary committee of the Turkish federation suspended her for two years, <www.sportgericht.de/ Doping>. CAS 2004/A/607, 6-12-2004, *Galabin Boevski v. IWF* (Boevski's urine was identical to that of two other athletes).

[557] "Unequivocal signs of adulteration have been found in the sample coded A 074396. The content of alcohol of the sample (concentration higher than 100 mg/ml) is in no way compatible with human consumption and the sample shows a very strong whiskey odour. Its low specific gravity (0.983 9/ml) is also compatible with a physical manipulation." (B. Bertels: "Geknoei met monsters tijdens onaangekondigde dopingcontrole vastgesteld," *Sportzaken* 1999/1 (no. 9) B 3).

[558] DC 1.2 "The offence of doping occurs when: [...] (b) a competitor uses or takes advantage of a banned procedure (see DC 3)."

[559] DC 3.1 "Banned techniques include: [...] (b) use of substances and methods which alter the integrity and validity of urine or blood samples used in doping control."

doping offence. The Panel suspended her for four years. On appeal to the CAS[560] Smith argued that the proof of the alleged doping offence by the FINA did not comply with the requirements applicable to such proof. Although the CAS admitted that the FINA's standard of proof remained below that required under criminal law, it nevertheless considered that this standard exceeded that normally applied under private law. Adopting a criminal law standard ("at any rate, where the disciplinary charge is not a criminal offence") would furthermore be to confuse the public law of the state with the private law of an organisation, according to the CAS. The tribunal considered the test developed in *Korneev and Ghouliev v. IOC*[561] to be sufficient: "ingredients must be established to the comfortable satisfaction of the Court having in mind the seriousness of the allegation which is made." Given that a charge of manipulation includes an element of mens rea and accuses the athlete of dishonesty ("whereas other doping offences may be ones of strict liability") such a charge has to be of "an extremely high degree of seriousness." However, according to the CAS, the answers to the questions of the burden and standard of proof did not automatically lead to the answer to the question of what precisely had to be proven. This led the CAS to deal with the two arguments of a factual nature which Smith had brought forward to undermine the proof established by the FINA. The first argument was that there were gaps in the chain of custody of the swimmer's samples. If, however, according to the second argument, it were to be established that the samples were her own, the only possible explanation was that they had been manipulated by a third party. However, the CAS considered the statement by the head of the laboratory to the effect that the samples had been stored in the normal fashion convincing. "The Appellant's first line of argument accordingly failed. We are convinced that the sample which was tested was in fact that of the Appellant." The CAS also soon became convinced that there could have been no person other than the swimmer herself who would at any moment have had the motive, opportunity or necessary technical skill to manipulate the urine in such a way as to remain undetected. After the arguments raised by Smith failed to have the desired effect the Panel came to its conclusion. The arbitrators did not consider it relevant that the substance (a testosterone metabolite) revealed by the laboratory could not be identified, nor did it consider it relevant that the substance found (ethanol) did not appear on the FINA doping lists.

> "The fact remains that there is unchallenged evidence that what was, even at the date of the testing, a banned substance (because it fell within the general category of substances related to those specifically listed) was found in the Appellant's urine; there is, therefore, actual evidence before the Panel that there was something to conceal. Not only was the manipulation not wholly successful, but there was an obvious motive for it. [...] the absence of direct evidence of manipulation [...] was in no way fatal to Respondent's case. The substantial circumstantial evidence clearly suffices."

---

[560] CAS 98/211, 7-6-1999, *Smith-De Bruin v. FINA* (Fortier, Beloff, Oswald), Matthieu Reeb, ed., *Digest of CAS Awards II 1998-2000* (The Hague, Kluwer Law International 2002) pp. 255-273.
[561] CAS 96/003-4, 4-8-1996, *Andrei Korneev v. IOC & Zakhar Goukiev v. IOC*.

Using or reaping the benefits of a prohibited procedure according to Article DC 2.1, opening words and under (b), constitutes a doping offence. For the further definition of the term prohibited procedure this provision referred to Article DC 3. Article DC 3.1(b) defined a prohibited technique as the use of substances and methods which affect the integrity and validity of a urine sample. From the wording of Article DC 2.1(b) it can be concluded that its drafters intended to describe a method that affects the organism's functioning. If Article DC 3.1(b) follows on from Article DC 2.1(b) and further defines it, it would seem ineluctable that the substances and methods of Article DC 3.1(b) must have a similar impact on the organism. The verb to use might conceivably be understood to mean any of its equivalents of "application, injection, consumption by any means whatsoever."[562] If this is the case, pouring a slug of whisky into the urine receptacle[563] cannot be considered as "use" pursuant to Article DC 3.1(b), even though such an act significantly affects the integrity and validity of the urine sample. The FINA regulations did not include a general rule prohibiting the manipulation of samples. Following this line of reasoning further, the act with which Smith was charged could not be qualified as a doping offence. However, if this line of argument were brought before a panel in doping proceedings it would probably be dismissed as "astute tactics."

The *Smith* case concerned the type of liability where the subjective element was considered relevant: "[...] an allegation of manipulation includes an element of mens rea and attributes dishonesty to an athlete (whereas other doping offences may be ones of strict liability) [...]."[564] After the sports organisation had proven that the offence was committed, it also still needed to prove that the object of the athlete's volition had in fact been the undesirable behaviour. Despite the consideration quoted above, the Panel in its conclusion changed tack, thereby preventing the consequences of liability based on a subjective element. "The fact remains that there is unchallenged evidence that what was, even at the date of the testing, a banned substance [...] was found in the Appellant's urine [...]" This seems to be based on the laboratory report where it states: "additional laboratory results obtained with the sample [...] suggest the administration of some metabolic precursor of testosterone." Neither the Panel's final consideration, nor the laboratory report statement was transparent. The mainstay of the argument was the debate concerning the manipulation of the sample. At another level, ideas were put forward concerning the possible use by Smith of prohibited substances. These ideas could not be fully developed because the laboratory was unable to make the charges against Smith stick. The Panel retraced its steps:

---

[562] These are the meanings given by Art. 1 of Chapter I of the OMACD which entered into force on 1 January 2000 and replaced the IOC Medical Code.

[563] It emerged from the analysis report that the alcohol had not passed through Smith's body before ending up in her urine, given that: "the content of alcohol of the sample [...] is in no way compatible with human consumption."

[564] CAS 98/211, 7-6-1999, *Smith-De Bruin v. FINA*, Matthieu Reeb, ed., *Digest of CAS Awards II 1998-2000* (The Hague, Kluwer Law International 2002) pp. 255-273, ground 10.3.

"[...] we note that evidence was adduced before us which suggested that previous samples taken from the Appellant (subsequently analysed with the aid of new technology) contained traces of prohibited substances; but since this evidence was and could not be (within the confine of the Appeal) subject to detailed scrutiny or analysis, we declined to weigh it in balance. It is sufficient to note that the Appellant could well have been aware of the growing sophistication of analytical techniques, which might have augmented a desire to manipulate the sample taken [...]"

It cannot exactly be considered elegant or in the spirit of fairness to lay down a line of reasoning in a judgment to the detriment of one of the parties, then explain that this reasoning cannot be followed here and is thus unable to influence the further course of the case, yet ultimately consider it anew in the final assessment. In this way, the Panel clearly established other evidentiary conditions for itself than it did for Michelle Smith de Bruin.

In essence, though, to conclude this section, it has to be shown that it was the athlete him/herself who tampered with the sample instead of other parties. Sabotage by third parties will be dealt with in the next section.

4.7. Manipulation by third parties

Already in 1992 the CAS in a case concerning a race horse which had tested positive considered that: "[...] the Person Responsible has the right to discharge himself through counter-evidence (evidence that the presence of a Prohibited Substance is the result of an act of malicious intent by a third party [...])."

In a case arising five years later the swimmer Foschi argued that there was a possibility that a third party had without her knowledge spiked her food or drink with the mesterolone for which she had tested positive. A journalist had contended that sabotage was a possibility, referring to the animosity that existed between Foschi's swimming club and a rival club. The journalist further contended that the intention had been to entangle a more prominent swimmer but that a mistake had been made due to the fact that Foschi's bag had been standing next to the other swimmer's bag which was almost identical. The CAS did not wish to discuss such speculations.

"The Appellant has put forward the suggestion that the positive test may have been due to an act of sabotage [...] However, this suggestion is, in the opinion of the Panel, pure speculation and no evidence of sabotage has been adduced. The private investigator hired by Ms Foschi [...] produced no conclusive results and unfounded suggestions are not sufficient to rebut the presumption."[565]

In the strict liability era, the *Smith-De Bruin* case provided a more serious story of sabotage. One day after the judgment of the FINA Panel (8 August 1998) the Dutch newspaper *NRC* reported: "According to Smith, there are indications that the FINA

---

[565] CAS 96/156, 6-10-1997, *Jessica K. Foschi v. FINA*, ground 14.17.

intentionally tried to keep her away from the 2000 Sydney Olympics. Especially in Australia, her success has given rise to quite a number of allegations. Smith is planning to submit her findings to the international sports tribunal at Lausanne. Her lawyer Peter Lennon expects the case to be heard at Lausanne within the next six weeks." In an article on the judgment suspending Smith another Dutch newspaper, *Trouw*, reported on that same day: "In Australia, where in 2000 the Olympic Games are due to take place, both the president of the national swimming federation Terry Gathercole and the head coach of the national swimming team Don Talbot appeared elated by the suspension." No lack of enemies, therefore. Still, the CAS[566] immediately took as its starting point that there could have been no person other than the swimmer herself who would at any moment have had motive, opportunity or the necessary technical skill to manipulate the urine in such a way as to remain undetected. Smith's lawyer refused the Panel's invitation to formulate a hypothesis which would point to some other person who could have manipulated the sample. In the Panel's opinion this was because the lawyer was simply unable to. The doping controllers' integrity according to the CAS was beyond any doubt, even though one of them had in the past committed an irregularity in the exercise of his function. The Panel also refused to believe that the FINA could benefit from discrediting the swimmer. The Panel concluded the topic of possible manipulators by remarking that "the fact that Appellant's counsel was constraint (on instructions) to fire off these volleys in all directions, of itself suggests that he had no single legitimate target for his accusations and implications."[567]

Reports had appeared in the press that the Versapak containers in which urine is decanted could be illegally opened and closed without being detected. The Panel dismissed these reports as rumours. There was no "primary evidence that this rumour [...] had any factual substance."[568] Such a rumour could not serve as the basis for a reasonable chance that the Versapaks could be opened and closed without detection. Even if the evidence on this point would be contradictory this would have formed a necessary but far from sufficient basis to support the hypothesis that a third party had manipulated the samples. Such a hypothesis would only be worthy of belief if a remarkable concurrence of circumstances had taken place, for which the Panel had found no proof.

To sum up the case of manipulation or sabotage by third parties, although athletes may attempt to prove their innocence of a doping offence by demonstrating third-party sabotage, practice has shown that it is almost impossible to provide conclusive evidence of malicious acts by third parties.

"Spiking" and "tampering" are also considered third-party manipulation. The relevant description in the Concise Oxford Dictionary of the verb to spike is "make

---

[566] CAS 98/211, 7-6-1999, *Smith-De Bruin v. FINA*, Matthieu Reeb, ed., *Digest of CAS Awards II 1998-2000* (The Hague, Kluwer Law International 2002) pp. 255-273.

[567] *Idem*, ground 12.6.

[568] *Idem*, ground 12.8.

useless," while to tamper is defined as "make unauthorized changes in [...], exert secret or corrupt influence upon [...]."

In *Wang Lu Na et al. v. FINA* and in *Meca-Medina v. FINA* the CAS considered that the presence of a prohibited substance in an athlete's body established a doping offence under the FINA doping regulations, independently of whether the athlete had ingested this substance intentionally or not. In both cases, the CAS added the literally identical footnote that:

> "Whether the FINA DC would be held compatible with general principles of law in so far as they purport to prevent a competitor from establishing his innocence by showing conclusively that the presence of a prohibited substance in his bodily fluid was the product of an ingestion which was neither intentional nor negligent, (e.g. where his drink is spiked with a drug by a rival competitor) is not an issue which falls for decision in this case)."[569]

In *Meca-Medina v. FINA* it was further added to this footnote that in any case new rule DC 9.10 mitigated the penalty. In *Foschi v. FINA* the swimmer argued that a third party had spiked her sample with a prohibited substance. The CAS was quite brief on the matter:

> "[...] there is no evidence to suggest that the UCLA Laboratory aborted its first attempt to test Appellant's B sample in order to spike it with mesterolone metabolite, so the Panel cannot accept this suggestion put forward by Appellant."[570]

It is customary that at the countercheck the athlete fills in a form on which he/she indicates that "there is no evidence of tampering."[571] Foschi argued that the samples had been corrupted at the laboratory. The FINA stated that: "apart from unsubstantiated suggestions by Appellant that the results of her tests may have been wrong or even tampered with by the UCLA Laboratory to hide a laboratory error and even less substantiated suggestions that Appellant's food and/or drink may have been sabotaged, there is no concrete evidence documenting either a lab error or sabotage. Respondent thus alleges that it is established beyond any doubt that Appellant tested positive and that the Laboratory results and procedures were correct." The CAS also held that no evidence resulted from the submitted documents to support that

---

[569] CAS 98/208, 22-12-1998, *Wang Lu Na, Cai Hui Jue, Zhgang Yi, Wang Wei v. FINA*, Matthieu Reeb, ed., *Digest of CAS Awards II 1998-2000* (The Hague, Kluwer Law International 2002) pp. 234-254, ground 5.8, nt. 5 and CAS 99/A/234 & CAS 99/A/235, 29-2-2000, *David Meca-Medina v. FINA & Igor Majcen v. FINA*, ground 4.5, nt. 18.

[570] CAS 96/156, 6-10-1997, *Jessica K. Foschi v. FINA*, ground 12.3.2.6.

[571] Cf., CAS 99/A/234 & CAS 99/A/235, 29-2-2000, *David Meca-Medina v. FINA & Igor Majcen v. FINA*, ground 2.14. In CAS 98/223, 31-8-1999, *Korda v. ITF*, Matthieu Reeb, ed., *Digest of CAS Awards II 1998-2000* (The Hague, Kluwer Law International 2002) pp. 345-360, ground 36(3) it was considered that: "The collection bottle was not subjected to any tampering during the period 18.00-19.20. Mr Your confirmed (and we accept his evidence) that the tamper evident tape was undisturbed. We heard no evidence suggesting any reason for concern that tampering may have occurred."

either the container, the safety tape or the bottles had been tampered with and concluded that:

> "[...] since there is no evidence that the sample bottles were tampered with, it is safe to assume that the urine contained in the sample bottles was the same as the urine voided into the original beaker by Appellant, i.e. Appellant's urine."[572]

Pursuant to Article 2.5 WADC "tampering, or attempting to tamper, with any part of Doping Control" must be considered an anti-doping rule violation. Spiking is not mentioned as such. The Dutch official translation of the WADC uses the term *"fraude."*[573]

In sum, given that in none of the cases that were submitted to the CAS proof of spiking or tampering was found the athletes in question remained strictly liable for the doping offence with which they had been charged. Here again proof of such acts by third parties proved difficult to establish.

As opposed to in the case of third-party sabotage of an athlete's food or drink, the question arises in the case of tampering with a sample whether this, if conclusively demonstrated, would eliminate the illegality from the act, as this would render the sample useless as proof of a doping offence.

The conclusion must be, however, that in practice, also in the case of spiking and tampering, it is nearly impossible to prove malicious acts by third parties.

From the above it has emerged that under the strict liability regime, as opposed to under its predecessor the fault system, it was almost impossible for an athlete who was accused of doping to prove that he/she was not to blame. In the disciplinary proceedings following positive testing in the laboratory the athlete's guilt was presumed. The burden of proof was not reversed and the athlete was not given any opportunity to prove his/her innocence and thus end the proceedings. The question of fault was primarily not an issue in doping proceedings. Only in the determination of the penalty could the degree of or total absence of guilt be discussed. The disciplinary sanction in the strict liability system shifted to a sanction that could be imposed on the playing field. If prohibited substances were found in the athlete's sample he/she must leave the field; this is called disqualification. No discussion of guilt takes place on the field. The presence of prohibited substances falsifies competition results, regardless of whether the athlete was actually aware that his/her body contained these substances or not. On the field, the focus must be on the responsibility of the athlete towards his/her fellow players (sporting fairness); in the disciplinary procedure it is on the responsibility of the athlete towards his/her sport as a whole. Only in a limited number of cases could the athlete conclusively

---

[572] CAS 96/156, 6-10-1997, *Jessica K. Foschi v. FINA*, ground 12.3.2.2.
[573] Dutch translation of the WADC Versie 3.0, © Nederlands Centrum voor Dopingvraagstukken (NeCeDo), Stichting Wetenschappelijk Onderzoek voor de Vereniging voor Sport en Recht.

show in disciplinary proceedings that the minor degree or total absence of his/her guilt had to lead to a reduction of the disciplinary sanction or to its non-imposition. Whichever way the disciplinary sanction turned out, however, the sporting sanction remained unchanged.

So far, circumstances have been discussed where a laboratory found prohibited substances in a sample. Below, doping infractions will be dealt with where no abuse of doping substances needed to be established.

5.   LIABILITY IN CASE OF ANCILLARY DOPING INFRACTIONS

Apart from doping themselves or participating in the doping of an athlete, there were also a number of other acts as has been set out in Chapter 3, Section 3.2.2. entitled "Ancillary doping infractions," which constituted a doping offence. When an athlete failed to report for doping control or if he refused to undergo such a control he/she would commit a doping offence under many of the doping regulations. These offences can be considered the counterpart of the criminal law crime of omission. The athlete would also commit a crime of omission if he/she only later admitted to having used a prohibited substance or method. The illegal trade in prohibited doping substances is not considered as a doping offence here, as these practices fall without the scope of competence of the sports organisations and are more a matter for the justice authorities.

5.1.   Refusing or failing to undergo doping control

The descriptions of the doping offence mainly focused on active behaviour, but it was also possible to commit a doping offence by taking a passive stance towards the mandatory stipulations in the doping regulations, e.g.:

> "An athlete who fails or refuses to submit to doping control after having been requested to do so by the responsible official will have committed a doping offence and will be subject to sanctions [...]"[574]

Such a material rule as this one (which was provided by the IAAF) was to be found in numerous doping regulations.[575] The entire doping policy of the sports organisations would have been completely worthless if such a rule was not included. But what was the refusing athlete actually guilty of? Not of having used a prohibited substance, although quite often this would have lain at the root of the athlete's refusal, namely to prevent that these substances were found. Refusing to undergo

---

[574] IAAF: Rules and Regulations, Division III – Control Of Drug Abuse, Rule 56 – Ancillary Offences.
[575] Pursuant to Art. 2.3. WADC the following is considered a doping offence: "Refusing, or failing without compelling justification, to submit to sample collection after notification as authorized in applicable anti-doping rules or otherwise evading sample collection."

testing would at least have given rise to a suspicion of use. For this reason, it would have made sense if the omission would have rendered the athlete fully liable, but this was not the case, at least, it was not immediately obvious from the provision in question. It is remarked in the Comment to Article 2.3. of the WADC that: "A violation of 'refusing or failing to submit to sample collection' may be based on either intentional or negligent conduct of the athlete, while "evading" sample collection contemplates intentional conduct by the Athlete." Below we will see that the IAAF did in fact consider the omission provision as a strict liability provision. Remmelink[576] has observed that "for an omission the elementary will that is essential for a positive act is not necessary." This is true where the objective element is concerned which is expressed by the term "fail," but in case of a refusal the omission is deliberate. Liability is established once it has been proven that the athlete refused knowingly. Under Dutch criminal law, as Remmelink sees it, "the elements of the description of the offence would have been fulfilled if for example a failure to appear was the result of being locked or tied up, albeit that in such a case as a result of circumstances beyond one's control the accused would have to be acquitted."[577] This of course is an extreme example; another possible scenario is that the athlete agreed to do an on-the-spot interview and for this reason was late for doping control. This would not result in an acquittal as this would involve negligence. However, does it constitute a doping offence? The sports organisation would be hard put to prove that the athlete's intention in agreeing to the interview was to evade the doping control so as to prevent prohibited substances from being found in his/her urine.

In 1994, the Kenyan athlete John Ngugi refused to undergo an out-of-competition control. The IAAF disciplinary tribunal held that the provisions of Rule 56(1) cited above had to result in strict liability.[578] After the consequences of his behaviour had been pointed out to him, Ngugi nevertheless persisted in his refusal. The IAAF had proven beyond reasonable doubt that a doping offence had been committed. Not only was an athlete who refused to cooperate in doping control fully liable for his/her refusal, but this was also presumed to include full liability for a doping offence.

The FINA suspended the 14-year old Dutch swimmer Linda van Herk for a period of two years for failing to cooperate in the doping control. Van Herk was unable to urinate during the control and was urged by her father of whom it was known beforehand that he had to go to an important business meeting to break off the procedure and come home with him. She appealed against the judgment to the CAS. The CAS[579] found Van Herk guilty of a doping offence, but applied the gen-

---

[576] Remmelink 1994 (*supra* nt. 293), p. 163.

[577] It is possible that an athlete after competing and before reporting to doping control becomes involved in an accident and ends up in hospital.

[578] *John Ngugi v. the Kenyan Amateur Athletic Association (KAAA) and the IAAF*, 5 November 1994, L. Tarasti, *Legal Solutions in international Doping Cases* (Milano, SEP Editrice 2000) p. 133-134: "We accept the contention of the IAAF here that Rule 56 paragraph 1 creates a rule of strict liability."

[579] CAS 2003/A/459, 20-10-2003, *VH v. FINA*.

eral principle of sports law according to which the severity of a penalty must be in proportion to the seriousness of the infringement.[580] The tribunal considered that: "taking into account that the athlete concerned is not a mature international athlete apparently attempting to conceal her cheating and retain a major medal, but a young athlete, who through no fault of her own was placed in an unenviable problem and confronted with an unenviable dilemma, the Panel find that the infringement is at the lowest end of the scale and substitute the minimum one-year suspension now contemplated by the FINA Rules."

In short, although the Comment to Article 2.3 WADC would seem to suggest otherwise, a refusal or failure to undergo doping control constitutes a doping offence for which the athlete in question is strictly liable. Refusal will rarely be a reason for reducing the penalty; failure to undergo the control or to undergo it properly may be the result of circumstances which have to be taken into account in the determination of the penalty.

5.2. Confession

The confession is also positioned within the framework of the ancillary doping infractions. A doping offence without actual traces of prohibited substances being found in the athlete's body may occur if an athlete confesses to the use of doping afterwards.[581] Of course, athletes are free to admit to having used a prohibited substance, but they have to be aware of the fact that by doing so they may manoeuvre themselves into the same position as an athlete who has tested positive. After the eleventh leg of the 1999 Tour de France which he had won, Ludo Dierckxens had to undergo a doping test which came out negative. On the form which he had to fill in at the doping control he declared that after a fall in the Tour of Germany in June he had used synacts as prescribed by his doctor to counteract tendinitis. The synacts contained corticoids. This confession could make him liable to six months' to one year suspension. His team decided to expel Dierckxen beforehand. In an official statement the UCI declared that: "even though the effects of this product – the presence of which in the body does not exceed a few days – have probably had no influence on the results of the rider in the Tour, he is liable to disciplinary action."[582] A little under a month after the incident the prosecutor of the Belgian cycling federation demanded six months' suspension, a 2500 guilder fine and disqualification from the leg which he had won.[583] For sports organisations, this has to be the easiest doping offence to establish; after all, the confession turns liability into a fact. But is this truly the case? Under Dutch criminal law, the courts will use a confession if they consider it credible. "In the face of a confession, the courts normally

---

[580] Cf., CAS 2002/A/399, 31-1-2003, *Poll v. FINA*, Matthieu Reeb, ed., *Digest of CAS Awards III 2001-2003* (The Hague, Kluwer Law International 2004) pp. 382-395.

[581] See the material rules in Chapter 2, Section 1.3.2.

[582] Cycling News and Analysis, News for July 20, 1999.

[583] Dutch newspaper *Telegraaf,* 13 August 1999.

tend not to bother too much about proof," according to Corstens.[584] Although Dierckxsens's declaration was probably true, there may be cases where athletes incriminate themselves because they have been pressured or threatened into it. Disciplinary tribunals must realise that athletes on occasion confess offence which they did not commit. And what about liability for Dierckxens's act? His confession was accepted readily, but it was as readily assumed that the cyclist ought to have known that a prohibited substance was involved. However, it was no longer possible to establish this. And how should a disciplinary tribunal respond if an athlete later withdraws his/her confession? Going back on an earlier confession does not render it useless. Corstens[585] as regards Dutch criminal procedural law writes that: "the court [...] will have to ask itself whether, and if so, why, it considers the confession to be more credible than its withdrawal. That is its task. The court must attempt to find out what motives the accused may have had to make the confession at the time and what his/her motives might be in withdrawing it. It is not an easy task. It would be welcome if the court in such a case give an express account of why it accepts the one statement but not the other. In the case law of the *Hoge Raad* [Dutch Supreme Court] this is not a requirement [...]."

In the end, Dierckxsens was suspended for a period of six months and fined BF 50,000. He was not disqualified from the leg in question.[586]

6. GUILT IN CASE OF "NON-USE" OFFENCES

In the material rules prohibiting the use of doping the offence of doping was extended to cover persons who were somehow involved in the offence (Cf. Chapter 3, Section 3.3.: Offences other than the use of doping). This third-party involvement known in criminal law terms as participation was expressed in the material rule by the words "administration to."[587] As opposed to for example in the Dutch Criminal Code where Articles 47 and 48 regulate participation in general and declare it an extension of the separate descriptions of the offences, participation in the anti-doping regulations was directly included in the description of the doping offence itself. Participation in a doping offence can be roughly divided into provocation or incitement on the one hand and, as the IPC put it, "aiding, abetting, condoning, counselling" on the other. The doping regulations of the IAAF, the ICF and the FIS used to speak of "any person assisting or inciting others [...]," while the IWF also added "encourage." Article 2.8. WADC speaks of: "Administration or attempted administration of a prohibited substance or prohibited method to any athlete, or assisting, encouraging, aiding, abetting, covering up or any other type of complicity involving an anti-doping rule violation or any attempted violation."

---

[584] G.J.M. Corstens, *Het Nederlandse strafprocesrecht* (Arnhem, Gouda Quint 1993) (Corstens 1993), p. 600.
[585] Corstens 1993 (*supra* nt. 584), p. 603.
[586] Cycling News and Analysis, News for August 18, 1999.
[587] See *supra* Ch. 2, Section 2.1.

Swimmer Samantha Riley's coach, Scott Volkers, admitted that on the eve of a competition in December 1995 he had given Riley a pain killer which caused her urine sample to test positive for a propoxyphene metabolite. The national federation's disciplinary committee held that: "the breach of the doping Code was caused by the actions of Volkers and whereas he had not acted deliberately, that he had been reckless." In the first instance, the FINA suspended the coach for two years; on appeal, the suspension was reduced to one year. In a concise rendition of the judgments in "FINA News" the following was said of Volkers's involvement:

> "[...] it was ascertained that the fault was the responsibility of the coach, who admitted having given her the tablet in question without taking care beforehand to consult the doctor of the (National) delegation who was accommodated on the same premises.
> For this reason, the Executive decided to suspend the coach for two years. However, on appeal by Volkers, the FINA Bureau changed the suspension to one year in a mail vote [...]."

Volkers appealed against the judgment of the FINA to the CAS.[588] In his first contention he requested that: "the finding of guilt be set aside (as being contrary to law)." Volkers's lawyer subsequently argued that his client:

> "[...] must have mens rea that is to say a 'guilty mind' in order to contravene the relevant FINA Rules. The appellant was a non-competitor within the meaning of FINA Rule MED 4.17.6. The appellant argues that on a plain reading of the FINA Rules, Rule MED 4.17.6 must be read in isolation from the other rules, that is, disjunctively. The appellant's contention that in order to violate this rule a 'guilty mind' is necessary rests upon a disjunctive reading. The respondent on the other hand contends that Rule MED 4.1; 4.3; and 4.17.6 must be read in conjunction with each other and that a coach who distributes a banned substance to a competitor is guilty of a doping offence."

The CAS preferred the FINA's point of view. Volkers then argued that his actions did not fall within the scope of the term "distribute" and that if the FINA rules "could prima facie dispense with the requirement of a guilty mind, it must be done in a clear and unambiguous way, in any event particularly where the consequences of a strict liability finding are severe. It is argued that the appellant was an accomplice with mere ancillary liability." The CAS found that Volkers's actions constituted a "material and operative" cause of the doping offence. In the Panel's opinion his actions fell within the framework of Rule 4.1, even given that the subjective element of intent was lacking. The gravamen of the description of the doping offence was contained in Rule 4.3 and was the identification of a prohibited substance. This case hinged upon the assessment of the connection between the provisions. The method used here by the CAS was to change the subjective element of intent of the non-use offence into the objective element of intent of the use of-

---

[588] CAS 95/150, 28-6-1996, *Volker v. FINA* (Sharad Rao, Faylor, Carrard), Matthieu Reeb, ed., *Digest of CAS Awards 1986-1998* (Berne, Editions Stämpfli 1998) pp. 265-274.

fence using the incantation that otherwise the fight against doping could not be effectively fought.[589]

> "Rule MED 4.3 clearly eliminates the requirement of showing a 'guilty mind' with regard to a competitor. The mischief the rule is designed to combat must be extended in such a way that it can effectively be combated. Rule MED 4.17.6 is such an extension. The appellant advised R. to take the tablet which he had procured to treat her headache. That the appellant could not have known he was advising R. to take a banned substance has no bearing on the quality of the advice given. Self evidently Rule MED 4.17.6 can be read in a number of ways, and in the Panel's view each of which fail within the ambit of the strict liability principle in Rule MED 4.3."

This conciliatory approach by the CAS towards the FINA was rather unexpected given the way in which the tribunal approached the drafters of the UIT regulations in *Quigley*:[590]

> "The fight against doping is arduous, and it may require strict rules. But the rule makers and the rule appliers must begin by being strict with themselves. Regulations that affect the careers of dedicated athletes must be predictable. They must emanate from duly authorized bodies. They must be adopted in constitutionally proper ways. They should not be the product of an obscure process of accretion. Athletes and officials should not be confronted with a thicket of mutually qualifying or even contradictory rules that can be understood only on the basis of the de facto practice over the course of many years of a small group of insiders."

Later, in *Cullwick v. FINA*,[591] the CAS developed a test to decide whether the rules were sufficiently clear and unambiguous. Based on that test, the FINA rules in question would have been interpreted to Volkers's advantage.

In two provisions, the FINA extended the liability to persons who cooperated in the commission of the offence. Where it could normally be assumed that the guilt of the participating party still had to be established, the CAS linked the fate of the participant to that of the offender and considered him/her fully liable as well. In the opinion of the CAS an IF's approach to a participant was dependent upon the IF's approach to the offender. The FINA had indeed adopted the same approach where liability was concerned, but not in respect of punishability. Riley was let off with a warning as the quantity of the prohibited substance found had been so small as to be unable to influence athletic performance. Volkers, however, was initially suspended for two years (which was later for no apparent reason reduced to one year on appeal). Is it possible in disciplinary doping law that the participant is convicted of a more serious offence than the offender? Due to the difference in penalties, one

---

[589] *Idem*, ground 13.

[590] CAS 94/129, 23-5-1995, *USA Shooting & Quigley v. UIT*, Matthieu Reeb, ed., *Digest of CAS Awards 1986-1998* (Berne, Editions Stämpfli 1998) pp. 187-204, ground 21.

[591] CAS 96/149, 13-3-1997, *Cullwick v. FINA*, Matthieu Reeb, ed., *Digest of CAS Awards 1986-1998* (Berne, Editions Stämpfli 1998) pp. 251-263.

might be left under the impression that participation in a doping offence was a separate offence, but the connection which the CAS found between the (irrelevance of the) fault elements of these apparently separate offences dispels the illusion. Under Dutch criminal law persons who participate must be aware of the necessity of every element of an offence. If it is assumed that the same strict liability regime applies to participants, then this awareness is *prima facie* presumed and the question of what the object of the participant's intent was becomes irrelevant. In disciplinary doping law the confession of the coach after prohibited substances were found in the athlete's body resulted in the coach's liability for a doping offence. All differentiations as to the nature of the participation (e.g. complicity, incitement, encouragement, etc.) which in civil law systems like Dutch law make a difference in respect of punishability, become irrelevant when the participant is fully liable.

Under the WADC regime, the administration of a prohibited substance or a prohibited method to an athlete or assisting, encouraging, aiding, abetting, covering up or any other form of complicity in a violation of the anti-doping rules is an independent offence punishable under Article 10.4.2 by a minimum period of four years up to a maximum of lifetime ineligibility. The comment to this provision states that those who are involved in doping athletes or covering up doping should be subject to sanctions which are more severe than the athletes who test positive. As opposed to what the CAS had in mind in respect of complicity this activity (now described in Article 2.8 WADC) does not fall within the strict liability regime.[592] The comment to Article 2.2.1 reads that "For purposes of anti-doping violations involving the presence of a prohibited substance (or its metabolites or markers), the Code adopts the rule of strict liability [...]." The doping offence of Article 2.8 does not focus on the finding of doping, but envisages inter alia the act of administering or the attempt to administer a prohibited substance and in the framework of Article 2 must be considered a separate and independent doping offence.

The drafters of the Code further considered that since the authority of sports organisations is generally limited to ineligibility for credentials, membership and other sport benefits, reporting athlete support personnel to competent authorities is an important step in the deterrence of doping. One of the problems faced by the IOC Medical Code (MC) and the OMADC was the elusiveness of the members of the athlete's supporting staff. These persons where not contractually bound to the sports organisation and therefore remained out of its reach. In this respect the WADC has made a radical change now that it defines the term "participant" as: "Any athlete or athlete support personnel"[593] and "athlete support personnel" as: "Any coach, trainer, manager, agent, team staff, official, medical or para-medical personnel working with or treating Athletes participating in or preparing for sports competition." "By their participation in sport, [...] athlete support personnel should be bound by

---

[592] See the comment to Art. 10.5.1 WADC: "Article 10.5.1 applies only to violations under Articles 2.1 and 2.2 (presence and Use of Prohibited Substances) *because fault or negligence is already required to establish an anti-doping rule violation under other anti-doping rules.*"

[593] Appendix 1 – Definitions – WADC.

anti-doping rules based on Article 2 of the Code by virtue of their agreements for membership, accreditation, or participation in sports organizations or sports events subject to the Code." This puzzling comment on how athlete support personnel is bound by anti-doping rules may be found in the Introduction to Part I of the Code. First it is stated that by their participation in sport, athletes are bound by the competitive rules of their sport. If this obligation did not exist then sport as we know it would not exist either. To this rather gratuitous remark the comment cited above is then added, i.e. that athlete support personnel should be bound by anti-doping rules based on Article 2 of the Code in the same manner as athletes. Each signatory to the Code must take the necessary steps to ensure that all athlete support personnel are brought within the scope of its authority by means of agreements or accreditations.[594] Article 21.2 WADC describes the function and responsibilities of the athlete support personnel:[595]

"21.2.1 To be knowledgeable of and comply with all anti-doping policies and rules adopted pursuant to the Code and which are applicable to them or the athletes whom they support.
21.2.2 To cooperate with the Athlete Testing program.
21.2.3 To use their influence on athlete values and behaviour to foster anti-doping attitudes."

Athlete support personnel may also commit doping offences under the WADC. Article 2.6.2 WADC speaks of:

"Possession of a substance that is prohibited in out-of-competition testing or a prohibited method by athlete support personnel in connection with an athlete, competition or training [...]."

The penalties awaiting members of the athlete's entourage when they commit doping offences are not to be taken lightly. Article 10.4.2 WADC to this end provides that:

"For violations of Articles 2.7 (Trafficking) or 2.8 (administration of Prohibited Substance or Prohibited Method), the period of Ineligibility imposed shall be a minimum of four (4) years up to lifetime ineligibility. An anti-doping rule violation involving a Minor shall be considered a particularly serious violation, and, if committed by Athlete Support Personnel for violations [...] shall result in lifetime ineligibility for such Athlete Support Personnel."

---

[594] There has been some discussion in the past as to whether the athlete's doctor or the team physician fell within the scope of authority of the sports federation. The WADC has made this discussion redundant. See also CAS 2002/A/464, 7-10-2003, *UCI v. L., R., Federação Portuguesa de Ciclismo (FPC)*.

[595] Article 18.2 WADC further extends the scope of the functions of athlete support personnel: "Athlete support personnel should educate and counsel athletes regarding anti-doping policies and rules adopted pursuant to the code."

However, Article 2.8 speaks of complicity in doping offences in general, obviously including athlete support personnel, but also persons who have no formal relations with the athlete or the sports organisation and over whom the sports organisation has no authority whatsoever, including the authority to start disciplinary proceedings against them. And yet, Article 2.8 has the pretension of also covering this kind of complicity. The only recourse open to sports organisations in this case is to inform the competent state authorities of the actions of the person(s) in question and request that they be prosecuted.

To sum up, under Dutch criminal law participants must be aware of all the elements of the offence. The CAS took the position that participants fell within the same strict liability regime as perpetrators by *prima facie* presuming such awareness making the question of the object of the participant's intent irrelevant. In fact, any differentiation as to the nature of the participation (accession, encouragement, incitement, etc.) which under criminal law makes a difference for the punishability of the offence becomes irrelevant when the participant is held strictly liable. Under the system of the WADC the participant has been excluded from the strict liability regime and his/her guilt or intent has to be established every single time.

7. METAPHOR OR EQUIVALENT? COMMENTS ON THE STRICT LIABILITY SYSTEM

The disciplinary law of doping may be considered as a quasi-criminal law sanctioning system. The system is not primarily directed towards remedying material damage but towards enforcing the standards that determine the essence of the organisation per se as well as the special purpose for which it was created. The criminal law-orientated disciplinary law of doping covers an area that is entirely surrounded by a system of norms of a private law character (the law of associations and obligations). The concepts that operate within the two different fields are different both as to their nature and as to their rationale. These concepts, however similar they may seem, must not be made interchangeable, so as to prevent a confusing state of contamination and syncretism. The structure of disciplinary law and disciplinary law interpretation should not be approached in a private law manner. Lehtinen[596] for example considered that the FINA had breached its contractual obligations towards him by the penalty it had imposed upon him. However, for the topic at hand the decision on a private law claim is irrelevant.[597] The invasion of private law con-

---

[596] CAS 95/142, 14-2-1996, *Lehtinen v. FINA* (Netzle, Seim-Haugen, Carrard), Matthieu Reeb, ed., *Digest of CAS Awards 1986-1998* (Berne, Editions Stämpfli 1998) pp. 225-244.

[597] Although not uninteresting. Under (applicable) Swiss law the relationship between a federation and its memebers is not considered a contract. If no special agreement has been concluded between the federation and a (direct or indirect) member, the Swiss courts over time have consistently held that the rules of contractual liability do not apply in case a member claims damages from the federation. To such claims only the rules concerning wrongful act apply (Art. 41 of the Swiss Civil Code).

cepts into the realm of disciplinary doping law may give rise to misapprehension even if these concepts are only used metaphorically.

The CAS termed the material rule under which doping is understood to mean the presence of a prohibited substance in the athlete's body a strict liability rule. In the CAS's opinion, guilt or intent in the commission of the doping offence was established as soon as the doping analysis produced a positive result. In such cases, there was liability without having to consider any subjective elements. It would have made the most sense if in disciplinary doping law the concept of liability would have featured in its criminal law meaning rather than in its private law meaning. In various cases however the CAS used the term in its private law connotation. In *Bernhard v. ITU*[598] the CAS not only held that the strict liability rule had to considered in its private law guise, but also that in respect of the establishment of guilt it had to be interpreted as going beyond the mere establishment of a presumption of the athlete's guilt:

> "The concept of responsabilité objective in civil law (where this rule stems from) is stricter than that: by making the subject liable regardless of his guilt, it renders the question of guilt irrelevant and allows for exoneration only in very limited and usually exhaustively listed cases, such as force majeure or wrongful act of a third person."

Applied to doping cases this strict liability concept not only means that the punishing authority is relieved of the burden to prove that the athlete was guilty or had the intention to allow doping substances to enter his body, but also that even if the athlete is able to prove conclusively that he has not been at fault (no guilt, negligence or intent) this does not release him/her from liability.

> "This is, [...] a faithful transposition of the civil (tort) law concept of strict liability (as distinguished from a presumed guilt) [...]"

The CAS had already given voice to such considerations in *Lehtinen v. FINA*[599] where it not only found the basis for the concept in tort law, but more specifically in product liability law:

> "The use of the term strict liability in the context of doping could be that under the term strict liability one should understand a concept of liability similar to that of civil liability, without fault in tort, or comparable to product liability cases (see, e.g., Honsell, Schweizerisches Haftpflichtrecht, Zürich 1995, 2 L). It does not raise the issue of guilt (or the presumption of guilt) with respect to the applicability of disciplinary sanctions."

---

[598] CAS 98/222, 9-8-1999, *Bernhard v. ITU*, Matthieu Reeb, ed., *Digest of CAS Awards II 1998-2000* (The Hague, Kluwer Law International 2002) pp. 330-344, grounds 35 and 36.
[599] CAS 95/142, 14-2-1996, *Lehtinen v. FINA*, Matthieu Reeb, ed., *Digest of CAS Awards 1986-1998* (Berne, Editions Stämpfli 1998) pp. 225-244, ground 13.

Why in this context did the CAS opt for the private law path? Perhaps the CAS considered that since under the criminal law of most civil law countries liability without guilt[600] is normally applied only very reluctantly it would be more acceptable to these countries to use a private law approach, in the way that, for example, strict liability in the case of faulty products is widely accepted.

As opposed to under the criminal law of most countries on the Western European continent, strict liability is a familiar concept under the criminal law of the United States[601] as laid down in the 1962 Model Penal Code (MPC).[602, 603] In the case of a number of offences the absence of guilt (either completely or only with respect to one or more objective elements) does not lead to impunity (in respect of that element).[604] Liability without the question of guilt coming into play is the ex-

---

[600] The Dutch Supreme Court has several times held that under Dutch criminal law there can be no offence unless guilt or intent is established. HR 1 March 1955, *NJ* 56, 2; HR 6 June 1955, *NJ* 55, 653; HR 10 June 1986, *NJ* 87, 85.

[601] The concept of strict liability under American criminal law is closely linked to the concept under private law, as becomes clear from the description in Rupps Insurance & Risk Management Glossary (1999): "[Strict liability is] liability for injury to others without regard to fault or negligence, arising from inherently dangerous activities (which may have economic or social value). It also may apply to defective or unreasonably dangerous products, provided the product reaches or affects the injured person without having been altered by another. Some states also impose strict liability for some violations of criminal law or public policy. Examples: Strict liability may attach to harm done by a person's pet poisonous snake or by a demolition contractor's use of explosives."

[602] J.A.W. Lensing (Lensing 1996, p. 128) has commented that the drafters of the MPC were generally disapproving of liability without guilt. Model Penal Code and Commentaries, Commentary on 702-212: "The Code takes the general position that absolute or strict liability in the penal law is indefensible in principle if conviction results in the possibility of imprisonment and condemnation. Therefore, within the immediate context of the Penal Code, criminal liability must be based on culpability."

[603] As under US criminal law, under English criminal law one of the most important aspects of guilt is the mental state of the suspect/accused at the time of committing the offence. This mental state, the *mens rea*, must be proven for nearly all crimes. The legislation does not mention the term as such but uses terms like intent or recklessness. However, such terms are lacking in the descriptions of some offences which may therefore be considered as strict liability offences. Kevin's English law glossary (http://kevinboone.com/) gives the following description of strict liability offences: "Offences of strict liability are those where liability is conferred simply by carrying out a particular action, or being in a particular place; the prosecution does not have to show an intention to act, or any blameworthy conduct. Most such offences are statutory, rather than in the common law, and aimed at regulation of activities deemed not to be in the public interest. They include offences related to pollution, driving, food hygene, and safety at work.
Justifications for the existence of strict liability offences may include:
1. they are easier to prosecute, as no mental element need be proved. This is particularly important when the defendant is a corporation;
2. they signal a strong and very clear disapproval of certain acts; this is particularly obvious for offences related, for example, to controlled drugs.
However, courts are reluctant to impose criminal sanctions on people who are easily seen to be morally without blame. Thus there is a strong presumption *against* a statutory offence being treated as one of strict liability."

[604] In CAS 96/156, 6-10-1997, *Jessica K. Foschi v. FINA*, ground 12.2, it was observed that "it is also worth noting that many countries have criminal offences where the burden of proof is shifted to the accused. One example is the offence of the possession of drugs where the burden is shifted to the

ception under American criminal law where it generally has to be established that someone acted "purposely, knowingly, recklessly and negligently." These subjective elements originate in the common law adage *actus non reus nisi mens sit rea*, which means that only persons with a guilty mind (mens rea) can be punished.[605] There is a great similarity between the material rule which lacks the element of guilt so that the accused cannot prove his/her innocence by arguing absence of guilt and the strict liability offences described in the MPC. This similarity makes it likely that despite all the references to private law the strict liability system of the CAS was inspired by concepts in the MPC or at least by the ideas surrounding the concept in US legal doctrine. The resemblance is all the more striking due to the fact that, as Lensing has put it:[606]

> "[...] the liability [...] is generally not defined so narrowly as to completely bar the accused from invoking grounds for exemption from liability. For example, while it is true that the MPC excludes the application of the provisions concerning the voluntary nature of the act and concerning the element of guilt [...], it does not exclude the application of the provisions concerning grounds for exemption from liability."

Under the strict liability system devised by the CAS the question of *culpa* was also excluded in the stage of the doping trial concerned with liability, but it was again included in the stage of the determination of the penalty.

When an element of guilt is not expressly included there are various criteria for determining whether it has been the legislator's intention nevertheless to include such an element. One of these is the seriousness of the consequences of the offence for society: "the more serious the consequences, the more reason for liability without guilt."[607] Within the sports community a doping offence is considered a very serious transgression which if scaled up to the level of society as a whole would be considered a true crime. The sanctions by which a doping offence can be punished are of such a nature as to confirm this view. The consequences of a doping offence are viewed as undermining sports and thus as extremely serious. From this perspective, it seems logical that doping offences can be punished without the need to take the element of guilt into consideration. In the retaliatory criminal law laid down in the MPC the starting point is that guilt is included in the description of true crimes.[608] However, the disciplinary law of doping should rather be viewed as preventive

---

accused to provide (and prove) a sensible explanation as to how the drugs came into his/her possession. Another example is the (irrebuttable) presumption that a person is unfit to drive as soon as the level of alcohol found in his/her blood exceeds a certain limit."

[605] Lensing 1996 (*supra* nt. 602), p. 111. In CAS 95/150, 28-6-1996, *Volker v. FINA*, Matthieu Reeb, ed., *Digest of CAS Awards 1986-1998* (Berne, Editions Stämpfli 1998) pp. 265-274 and CAS 98/211, 7-6-1999, *Smith-De Bruin v. FINA*, Matthieu Reeb, ed., *Digest of CAS Awards II 1998-2000* (The Hague, Kluwer Law International 2002) pp. 255-273, the mens rea element was an important aspect of the CAS's considerations.

[606] Lensing 1996 (*supra* nt. 602), p. 127.

[607] *Idem*, pp. 131-132.

[608] *Idem*, p. 126.

criminal law where it is not necessary to stress the element of guilt to such an extent in the description of the offence. Another criterion by which to judge whether an element of guilt should be considered to be included is the "difficulty for the Prosecutor to prove an element of guilt."[609] Precisely this difficulty led the sports organisations to remove the element of guilt from their material rules. Still, one has to be careful when assessing arguments advocating strict liability. Lensing[610] points to one argument in favour of strict liability which claims that "persons who operate in a field of activity of the kind for which there is liability without guilt have accepted the risk of committing an offence." This has also been contended by advocates of strict liability in disciplinary doping law. A counterargument would be that such acceptance should not imply "that such persons could in fact be punished when they are completely innocent. This touches upon the most fundamental objection against liability without guilt, namely that punishability should be based on culpability." The explanatory memorandum to the MPC provides on this point that:

> "Crime does and should mean condemnation and no court should have to pass that judgment unless it can declare that the defendant's act was culpable. This is too fundamental to be compromised."

At the same time that the drafters of the MPC formulated their arguments against the extensive use under American criminal law of the strict liability principle, the drafters of a great number of doping regulations actually proceeded to include the principle in their rules. Meanwhile, Dutch criminal law also has its share of offence descriptions lacking an element of guilt. For example, in the Netherlands driving a car under the influence of alcohol if this is present in certain quantities in the blood is a liability without guilt offence under Article 8(2) read together with Article 163 of the 1994 Road Traffic Act.

In short, in the judgments discussed above the CAS mentioned the private law origin of the strict liability rule. Perhaps this was intended as a metaphor, but the effect of this can be to confuse different concepts. In fact, the CAS need not have involved private law at all as equivalents under criminal law do exist, not only in the United States, but also in for example the road traffic laws of many other countries.

Pursuant to Article 6(2) ECHR persons who are accused of an offence must be presumed innocent until their guilt has been proven in accordance with the law. In 1988, the ECtHR held that once the objective elements of the offence have been established the burden of proof is allowed to shift. The Court however added that the presumption of guilt created by the legislator has to be rebuttable.[611] Does this mean that in the case of absence of guilt the court has to discharge the accused from

---

[609] *Idem*, p. 132.

[610] *Idem*, pp. 134-135.

[611] EHRM 7 October 1988, A141, *NJB* 1988, pp. 1521-1522 (Salabiaku).

further prosecution? Where guilt is a subjective element of the offence description this is indeed the court's duty, but not where culpability is an objective element.

This concludes the discussion of liability for the doping offence which has led to the following finding: If illegality was established and the athlete was found guilty of a doping offence the disciplinary doping body was free to impose a penalty on the athlete. This leaves the question of what penalties the sports organisations could apply and to what extent the severity of the offence played a role in this. These and other questions relating to penalties will be discussed in the next chapter.

8. CONCLUSION

Under the first descriptions of the doping offence, athletes were not permitted to use substances which enhanced their performance and unfairly affected competition. This type of description made it virtually impossible for the sports organisations to obtain convictions of athletes accused of doping. How could they prove that a substance found in an athlete's sample was performance enhancing and, if they managed that, how could they prove that the athlete's actions were intended unfairly to influence the competition? The sports organisations tried to break through this deadlock by drawing up lists of prohibited substances and methods. The material rules now referred to the lists. However, this only solved part of the problem. It was still almost impossible for a prosecuting body to convict an athlete if the athlete claimed that his will had not been directed at the use of doping. If the athlete was able to offer convincing proof that he had not acted with intent or that he had not known at the time of use that the substance in question was doping, the prosecution would fail time and again. Some IFs went in search of a material rule which could free them from the burden of having to prove the athlete's liability for doping. A rule was drawn up declaring the athlete *prima facie* liable from the moment a prohibited substance was shown to be present in his blood or urine. Doping under the newly established rule was defined as the presence in an athlete's body of one or more substances appearing on the doping list. By such a rule, the human act which had been the focal point of previous rules, was replaced by a factual circumstance. Liability for any human acts preceding this circumstance was thereby subsumed under the finding of prohibited substances. A positive test result thus precluded almost all excuses which an athlete could possibly formulate. The comfortable position in which the athlete previously found him/herself while waiting for the sports organisation to respond to his/her defence of lack of guilt or intent was now reserved for the prosecuting body. With this new material rule the sports organisation could at last be confident about the outcome of the doping proceedings. Liability was assumed when the objective elements had been proven. The interests of the collective were thus placed above the just treatment of the individual.[612] The group

---

[612] The CAS in ground 215 of CAS 94/129, 23-5-1995, *USA Shooting & Quigley v. UIT*, Matthieu Reeb, ed., *Digest of CAS Awards 1986-1998* (Berne, Editions Stämpfli 1998) pp. 187-204, considered

dilemma found expression in the wording of the material doping rule: uniformity as opposed to diversity. In such cases the question of guilt ceased to be relevant for the establishment of disciplinary liability, although it was still relevant in determining the sanction. A system which for pragmatic reasons and reasons of procedural economics starts from a presumption of liability is not necessarily unfair as long as the accused is given the opportunity to submit evidence by which he/she can show that he/she cannot be held liable. The system of strict liability took this one step further because the athlete was not given any opportunity to exonerate him/herself so as to secure his/her acquittal.

The interpretation of the strict liability rule was the focus of various judgments of the CAS. The CAS took as its starting point that the sports organisation might only *prima facie* assume the liability of the athlete if this was expressly laid down in a rule contained in the doping regulations. If such a rule was lacking, the sports organisation was obliged to show liability after all. The predictability of the rules, according to the CAS, took precedence over what the organisation considered the customary practice, but failed to lay down in its rules. The CAS developed a test to decide whether the rules were sufficiently clear and unambiguous. The standard for this test was not whether a legally trained person considered the rules crystal clear and unambiguous, but whether an athlete who was subject to these rules but who had not had any legal training or experience with legal matters considered that the rules fulfilled the mentioned criteria.

Ideally speaking, an athlete should not be punished if he can show that he has no fault in the matter whatsoever. In practice, however, this was not the case due to the fact that many sports federations that used the strict liability system could only impose fixed sanctions. Any discussion of liability in connection with punishability becomes fruitless in such cases. This was one of the weak spots of the strict liability system: its effect in practice made it unfair towards the athlete who "ohne sein Wissen und seinen Willen" had ingested prohibited substances.

Under Dutch law, if culpable avoidability is absent, this is interpreted as absence of guilt. However, in a system where an athlete can be liable without guilt – strict liability – there is no room for acquittal based a ground for exculpation.

The strict liability system was rarely criticized in the legal literature. The main point of criticism was that the system denied the athlete the fundamental right to prove that he could not be held liable for the alleged doping offence. In the CAS judgment in *Fritz Aanes v. Fédération Internationale de Luttes Associées (FILA)* the Panel considered that: "as a matter of principle [...] an athlete cannot be banned from competition for having committed a doping offence unless he is guilty, i.e. he has acted with intent or negligence. Even if the rules and regulations of a sports federation do not expressly provide that the guilt of the athlete has to be taken into account the foregoing principle will have to be read into these rules to make them

that "[...] it appears to be a laudable policy objective not to repair an accidental unfairness to an individual by creating an intentional unfairness to the whole body of other competitors."

legally acceptable." In the view of the Panel in question an athlete could not be lawfully suspended under Swiss law[613] if no blame attached to him/her. This shows a clear break with the views of previous Panels on this point. From the words "an interpretation to the contrary would lead to the rules being void which would frustrate the objective of the fight against doping pursued by the entire sporting world" it may be derived that this Panel – which was composed of three civil law lawyers – based its reasoning on different starting points from Panels mainly composed of common law lawyers.

In order to be able to determine the legal effect of a certain body of disciplinary law and the extent to which certain legal principles should find expression in a given disciplinary law system De Doelder applied the organising criterion of voluntary presence in the group.[614] By contrast, the submission of the athlete to disciplinary doping law shows a high degree of involuntariness. Athletes who play their sport professionally are involuntarily caught up in a web of doping rules. Just like citizens cannot escape from the reach of criminal law, athletes cannot avoid the application of the universally applicable doping rules for their sport and the accompanying disciplinary law. This is one reason why disciplinary doping law has to be considered as being closely related to criminal law. Disciplinary doping law must be considered as quasi-criminal law and should rather be termed doping chastisement law. Although the field of disciplinary doping law is surrounded by private law, within it contract law influences should not be felt and criminal law principles should have the upper hand. It would have made the most sense if in disciplinary doping law the concepts of liability and intent or guilt would have featured in their criminal law meaning rather than in their private law meaning. In various cases however the CAS used these terms in their private law connotation. The strict liability system was introduced for purely pragmatic reasons. If one can admit that, it will no longer be necessary to search for equivalents under private law. Such a comparison will always fall wide off the mark. Imposing a penalty based on the liability which is subsumed in an offence is a completely different thing from the full liability of the producer for the explosion of a lemonade bottle.

Liability in a penalty system is certainly no invention of the sports community. Strict liability was already known under American and English criminal law, but Dutch law also offers a few examples, such as under road traffic laws and social security laws. However, in the case of the strict liability offences in various countries' legislation, the possibility for the accused to exonerate him/herself is never excluded.[615]

Given the fact that some of the substances appearing on doping lists may be produced by the human body itself, threshold values have been established. If the con-

---

[613] According to Rule 45 of CAS's Procedural Rules.

[614] De Doelder 1981 (*supra* nt. 352), p. 41.

[615] Compare ECHR 8-2-1996, 41/1994/488/570, 22 EHRR 29 *John Murray v. United Kingdom*, *supra* paragraph 4.3.

centration found remains below this value the athlete in question will not be prosecuted as he cannot be held liable for a doping offence. Threshold values always leave an area of doubt – the grey area – just beyond it which is connected with the personal physiology of the athlete. This grey area has an upper limit. Concentrations found above this limit are always an indication of external administration and always result in the maximum penalty. Values within the grey area always have to be weighed considering the circumstances of the case. If a concentration is found in the urine of an athlete that falls within the grey area this gives rise to the suspicion that the athlete has consumed a certain food or meat that was contaminated with the prohibited substance. Several times athletes whose values fell within the grey area have tried to demonstrate that they were not guilty of a prohibited act. They regarded the grey area as a final possibility to still raise the question of their liability within the strict liability system. The grey area has given rise to much debate among both lawyers and scientists. The IOC was not sympathetic towards the existence of a grey area. The CAS on the other hand used it in various judgments, although at times it would also indicate under pressure from the IOC that it was disinclined to consider the grey area in a given case.

Finally, although the strict liability system was developed to exclude any claim of absence of liability, several cases are known in which athletes who had tested positive nevertheless appealed on this ground because they believed that they had been sabotaged, in other words, that their samples had been manipulated or their food or drink spiked or tampered with. However, before the CAS all these claims were dismissed.

Apart from using doping or participating in the doping use of others, a number of other acts may also constitute a doping offence (ancillary doping infractions). Under many of the doping regulations, an athlete would commit a doping offence when he/she failed to report for doping control or refused to undergo such a control. Not only was the athlete who refused to cooperate in doping control fully liable for this refusal, it was also assumed that this included full liability for the doping offence itself.

A doping offence may also consist of the fact that an athlete admits to having used doping. Of course, athletes are free to admit to having used a prohibited substance, but they have to be aware of the fact that by doing so they may manoeuvre themselves into the same position as an athlete who has tested positive.

As to the issue of participation, under Dutch criminal law participants must be aware of all the elements of the offence. The CAS took the position that participants fell within the same strict liability regime as perpetrators by *prima facie* presuming such awareness, making the question of the object of the participant's intent irrelevant. In fact, any differentiation as to the nature of the participation (accession, encouragement, incitement, etc.) which under criminal law makes a difference for the punishability of the offence becomes irrelevant when the participant is held strictly liable. The doping offence defined under Article 2.8 of the WADC, however, is not covered by the strict liability regime.

CHAPTER 5
SYSTEM OF SANCTIONS

1. INTRODUCTION

During the first World Doping Conference in 1999, various politicians drew attention to the harmonisation of sanctions. Many of them argued in favour of harmonisation of governmental and non-governmental sanctions.[616] Other speakers who followed[617] were mostly of the same opinion.[618]

There was widespread consensus concerning the severity of the sanctions: penalties for athletes had to be substantial.[619] The Dutch State Secretary for Sport, Mrs Margo Vliegenthart, indicated that sport itself had to come up with solutions. In the imposition of sanctions various politicians were of the opinion that the athlete's environment warranted further attention.[620]

Representatives of the sporting world also concerned themselves with sanctions. Johann Olaf Koss of the Athletes' Commission on behalf of the athletes supported

---

[616] Dr Peter Wittmann, Austria's State Secretary for sport, was of the opinion that this was to occupy an important position in the framework of European co-operation concerning sports policy. Mr Wu Shaozu, President of the Commission for Physical Education and Sport of China also advocated the harmonisation of sanctions, as did Mrs Elsebeth Gerner Nielsen, Denmark's Minister of Culture. She did not, however, want harmonisation to lead to a mitigation of the results.

[617] France's Minister of Juvenile Affairs and Sport, Marie- George Buffet, New Zealand's Sport Minister Mr Tay Wilson, Portugal's State Secretary for Sport, Dr Julio Miranda Calha, and Mr Niels Thogersen, Director General DG X of the European Union.

[618] Tougher sanctions urged Live at the Conference – Wednesday, p. 3, (http://www.nodoping.org/confmond_day2_e.html): "Italian IOC member Mario Pescante cited Aconfusion at government level, contradictory sanctions being applied by different sports federations, delays in scientific research and an absence of 'serious initiatives' in many parts of the world." Mr Pescante warned the Conference: "Public opinion is tired of waiting."

"A report by a special IOC Working Group – set up after last year's Tour de France cycle race – calls for closer cooperation between the Olympic movement and governments in the prevention and punishment of doping. This would include an enhanced international harmonization of legislation and a greater exchange of information."

[619] Dr Andreas Fouras, Under-Secretary of State in charge of sports (Greece): "[...] impose severe penalties." Mrs Giovanna Melandri, Minister for Culture responsible for Sport (Italy): "[...] harmonize sports sanctions internationally, with a minimum 2-year suspension." Tougher sanctions urged Live at the Conference – Wednesday, p. 3, (http://www.nodoping.org/confmond_ day2_e.html): "The report also calls for stricter sanctions against athletes found guilty of doping. These include fines of up to US$ 1 million and a life ban on participation in any sports event, depending on the severity of the doping offence."

[620] Great Britain: The Right Honourable Tony Banks, MP, Minister for Sport (Great-Britain): "Life ban on all coaches guilty of doping practices"; Dr Heinz Keller, Director of the Federal Office of Sports (Switzerland): "[...] impose sanctions on the environment of the athlete who is blamed."

a proposal to suspend convicted athletes for up to 2 years. "Athletes want to compete on a level playing field." John Coates, President of the Australian Olympic Committee, commented that the assistance of national governments was needed as they could adopt specific legislation. In the open discussions in the working group "Prevention: ethics, education and communication," Mr Ulak of the Czech NOC remarked that the administration of doping substances by doctors had to be considered a "major offence," which had best be made subject to severe penalties under (national) law. As far as sanctions were concerned, the outcome of the discussions in the framework of the working group "The Legal and Political Aspects of Doping" was by far the most interesting. The Chairman of this working group, Mr Mbaye, President of the International Council of Arbitration for Sport (ICAS), made a number of statements beforehand, which included the following elements:

- Modulated sanctions, depending on the substances (i.e. establish a scale of sanctions), with a minimum sanction of 2 years, which can be reduced in cases where grounds within existing legislation so provide.
- Intentional offences must be subject to more severe sanctions that unintentional offences.
- Sanctions for trafficking should also be more severe.

Mr Feriencik of the Slovenian NOC found that the distinction between sport sanctions and government sanctions had to be abolished. Mr Brodesser of the German NOC made two points – "the IOC should control general compliance and unify the sanctions" and – "sanctions should be imposed for any offence, warnings only as an additional sanction." Ruben Acosta, the President of the International Volleyball Federation (FIVB), identified an important function to be fulfilled by the respective national authorities – they would have to: 1° adopt a unified medical code and comply with IFs; 2° guarantee that these rules applied in each country; 3° ensure that sanctions imposed by IFs and the IOC cannot be questioned. Although he was of the opinion that sanctions had to be imposed, Pavel Jurak of the Czech NOC did not feel that they should be of a financial nature. According to Lauri Tarasti, a member of the IOC Sport and Law Commission Sport, sanctions must be acceptable according to normal everyday standards and must be applied by the courts. When sanctions last for over a year (a season), according to Hein Verbruggen, the President of the International Cycling Federation (UCI), this could lead to an increase in the number of cases brought before the civil courts. The IFs claimed that they would not be able to bear the resulting financial burden. It is important that we are able to resort to severe penalties, agreed Sepp Blatter, the President of the International Football Federation (FIFA) and Michel D'Hooghe, the Chairman of the FIFA Medical Commission, but the responsibility for these penalties should remain that of the IFs. They further argued that sanctions had to be proportional.[621] They

---

[621] Tougher sanctions urged Live at the Conference – Wednesday, p. 3, (http://www.nodoping.org/ confmond_day2_ e.html): "But Mr Blatter, President of the FIFA, called upon the understanding of the

favoured a sliding scale of sanctions; fixed sanctions were unacceptable. In conclusion, they asked that it be appreciated that some IFs are not in a position to impose a 2-year penalty. Cameron, the Executive Director of the International Badminton Federation (IBF), felt however that there was a "need for a 2-year minimum sanction, without any exception" and Primo Nebiolo, President of the Association of Summer Olympic International Federations (ASOIF) also thought the "minimum required sanction should be 2 years for a first offence." The FIFA officials found support in the statements of Jean-Claude Rochat, Secretary General of the CAS: "Fixed sanctions are conceivable but will not stand up in normal courts, as the principle of individualization of offences is unavoidable in modern legal systems." Baron Pittenger of the United States Olympic Committee (USOC) also supported the concept of flexible sanctions, as did Dennis Oswald, President of the International Rowing Federation (FISA) – "We need flexibility and modulation: sanctions must be proportionate and acceptable to normal courts and in conformity with fundamental principles of law if the Olympic Movement is to be credible. [...] It is important to allow the possibility of interpretation by a court. [...] The problem of the severity of sanctions is different per sport. [...] We should ask for a minimum sanction under 2 years, which would stand up in civil courts and be truly enforceable."

Opinion was thus divided as regards the severity of the sanction: a maximum of one year as opposed to a minimum of two years and, as far as the modality of the sanction was concerned, fixed as opposed to flexible.

In the IOC's report, under the heading "Reply and conclusion," "Judge" Mbaye summarised the outcome of the debate as follows:

"1. Souci de la spécificité du sport dans le domaine de la sanction.
2. Pas de grandes différences entre les sanctions et le code.
3. On peut éduquer, mais il y aura toujours des infractions. Aujourd'hui, il y a sanction, puis rééducation. ONU peut être un cadre pour organiser cette harmonisation."

From the word "debate" it could be deduced that at least some of the time the arguments for and against were heard and responded to. However, the report conveys the impression that although it is true that the numerous opinions concerning sanctions in sport could indeed be aired, that was about all. A proper discussion, of which this topic is in such dire need, never took place. This is why the present chapter will attempt such a discussion.

In the Lausanne Declaration on Doping in Sport[622] which was adopted by the Word Doping Conference on 4 February 1999 it is stated that in accordance with the wishes of the athletes, the NOCs and a large majority of the IFs, the minimum

---

Olympic movement to adopt a more flexible system of sanctions. He argued that professional athletes would be unduly penalized by such strict and extended sanctions."

[622] http://www.nodoping.org/Declaration_e.html.

sanction for the use of prohibited substances shall be a two-year ban for a first offence.

"However, based on specific, exceptional circumstances to be evaluated in the first instance by the competent IF bodies, there may be a provision for a possible modification of the two-year sanction. Additional sanctions or measures may be applied."

Below, much of the focus will be on the situation as it existed prior to the entry into force of the WADC. From this, it will emerge that the cry for harmonisation as it could be heard at the 1999 doping conference was this loud for a reason.

In sports there are two categories of doping substances for which different sanctioning policies are in place, known as "hard doping" and "soft doping" respectively.[623] Hard doping is understood to mean "prohibited classes of substances" and "prohibited methods," i.e. substances and methods prohibited at all times (both in- and out-of-competition); soft doping is understood to mean "classes of drugs subject to certain restrictions," i.e. according to the WADC: "specified substances." The first category of doping substances and methods may never be used by an athlete; the second category of substances and methods may be used, albeit on the condition that the competent authorities are informed of and have consented to this use.[624] Section 2 of this chapter will deal with sanctions imposed on individual athletes for hard doping, and Section 3 deals with soft doping in this respect. Section 4 describes team sanctions and Section 5 discusses sanctions at the national level. The proportionality of sanctions and restraint of trade (right to labour) are dealt with in Section 6. Finally, "sport sanctions" (disqualification, etc.) are discussed separately in Section 7.

2.   SANCTIONS FOR INDIVIDUAL ATHLETES IN CASES OF "HARD DOPING"

Prior to the adoption of the WADC, the sanctions which the various sports organisations used to impose for the use of "hard" doping substances differed widely. Below, it is attempted to introduce some order into this variety of penalties by categorising them. The categories comprise the corresponding sanctions for first and second offences.

---

[623] In CAS 2003/A/522, 5-3-2004, *C. v. Royale Ligue Vélocipédique Belge (RLVB)* the CAS implicitly adopted the distinction between hard and soft substances, judging by its use of the phrase "high doses of ephedrine, which was considered a 'soft' substance."

[624] "Typically, governing body rules will draw distinctions between the various classes of substances contained within the IOC/IF list. Further, as a rule of thumb, those substances which are considered to have the greatest performance-enhancing effect/most damaging effect upon an athlete's health will be subject to the most stringent sanctions. The most severe sanctions are reserved for the use of anabolic steroids and prohibited techniques such as blood doping and the use of EPO." O'Leary, "The State of Play," in J. O'Leary, ed., *Drugs and Doping in Sport* (London, Cavendish 2001) p. 25.

2.1.　The various types of sanctions

2.1.1.　*First offence: 2 years' suspension; second offence: life-long ban*

Pursuant to Article III of the IOC Medical Code, in conjunction with Article II, the sanction for a first doping offence was disqualification if the offence took place during a competition. Apart from this, pursuant to Article II, subsection 1, an athlete who was caught would be punished – both for offences during competitions and those outside a competition context – by a two-year ban on participation in any competition. The period of exclusion started on the day after the use of doping had been established and on the day on which a final decision was rendered on appeal. Article IV stated that the penalty to be imposed on an athlete for a second doping offence would be disqualification from the competition during which the offence was committed coupled with a life-long ban. The same applied when the offence came to light during out-of-competition testing. Besides exclusion from participation in competitions, the athlete in question would also be excluded from any kind of accreditation at the Olympic Games.

For the purpose of determining the penalty, an out-of-competition doping offence was likened to an offence committed during competition.

Corresponding sanctions had to be imposed by the international federations and continental organisations of NOCs if the offence was committed during a competition under their jurisdiction.

Four international federations, the International Badminton Federation (IBF),[625] the International Union for Modern Pentathlon (UIPM),[626] the International Sailing Federation (ISAF)[627] and the International Sport Shooting Federation (ISSF) integrated the IOC Medical Code into their regulations. The ISSF, although using the IOC Medical Code, differed from the IOC in making the severity of the penalty dependent on the seriousness of the offence[628]

---

[625] Art. 16.2 of the Rules of the International Badminton Federation: "In particular, Member Associations must adhere to the IOC requirements on doping, and must co-operate fully with the Federation in measures taken to detect or penalise infringements of those requirements."

[626] UIPM Medical Rulebook, Anti-doping Controls, 7.8 Sanctions: "Sanctions shall be these established by the IOC Rules and adopted by the UIPM Executive Board."

[627] 1998 ISAF Regulations, Art. 3.9: "Sailors in Olympic Classes, when found without doubt to have tested positive for the presence of banned drugs on the ISAF/IOC list, will be subject to the scale of penalties agreed between the IOC and the International Governing Bodies of sport.
Sailors in ISAF World Youth Championships and ISAF World Championship Regattas, when found without doubt to have tested positive for the presence of banned drugs on the ISAF/IOC list, will be subject to the scale of penalties agreed between the IOC and the International Governing Bodies of sport.
Sailors in all other events sailed under RRS'S, when found without doubt to have tested positive for the presence of banned drugs on the ISAF/IOC list, will be subject to a penalty to be determined by the ISAF Executive Committee."

[628] Art. 8.3.1. "The Shooter: the penalty will be determined, taking into account the seriousness of the offense by applying the IOC Medical Code."

Fourteen international federations provided for two-years' suspension for first doping offences and a life-long ban for second offences. These periods of exclusion were in line with the IOC rules, although the regulations in question did not expressly refer to the Medical Code.

International Rowing Federation – FISA

"The penalty for a first infraction by a player shall be disqualification if the infraction occurred during the competition. For the first offence against the regulation if a player is positive for pharmacological classes of doping agents or doping methods banned by the I.O.C. a suspension of two years from all I.B.A.'s international or national competitions.[629]

In case of a second offence the sanction will be a life ban for all I.B.A. international or national games."[630]

As far as sanctions were concerned, the IBA rules did not distinguish between controls during and out of competition.

International Canoe Federation – ICF

"If an athlete commits a doping offence, he will be ineligible for the following periods:

for an offence under Rule 6 above involving substances and methods such as anabolic steroids, peptide hormones and analogues, amphetamine-related and other stimulants, caffeine, diuretics, beta-blockers, narcotic analgesics, designer drugs, blood doping, and manipulations of samples through pharmacological, chemical or physical methods or, for any of the other offences listed in Rule 6.1.:

1.1. first offence: for two years from the date of the provision of the sanctionable action;

1.2. second offence: for life."[631]

The ICF used the IOC list of prohibited substances and methods.[632] When an athlete had tested positive and this had been confirmed after a hearing, he would be excluded. If the control took place during a competition the athlete and his crew would be disqualified. The exclusion period started on the day the sample was taken. It did not appear from the ICF rules dealing with out-of-competition controls whether the same sanctions applied for offence found during out-of-competition testing.[633] If an already banned athlete was again caught in the act of doping this would be considered a separate doping offence "and the athlete [would] be subject to a further sanction as appropriate."[634]

---

[629] Anti-Doping Rules, Chapter 13, Disciplinary Sanctions, Art. 13.1.

[630] Anti-Doping Rules, Chapter 13, Disciplinary Sanctions, Art. 13.2.

[631] ICF Doping Rules, Rule 6 – Sanctions, Rule 6, subsection 2.

[632] ICF Doping Rules, Rule 6 – Sanctions, Rule 1, subsection 3.

[633] Procedural Guidelines for Doping Controls, 2. Out-of-competition Doping Controls.

[634] ICF Doping Rules, Rule 6 – Sanctions, Rule 6, subsection 6.

International Fencing Federation – FIE

"Sanctions
Les sanctions sont obligatoirement les suivantes:
Agents anabolisants, stimulants, analgésiques narcotiques, diurétiques et hormones peptidiques.
1.1. 2 ans pour un premier délit,
1.2. suspension à vie pour un second délit."[635]

The FIE used the IOC list of prohibited substances and methods.[636] As far as sanctions were concerned, the FIE rules did not distinguish between controls during and out of competition. Other national federations were also obliged to enforce sanctions imposed by member federations.

International Weightlifting Federation – IWF

"Subject to other provisions in this section, sanctions will apply for the following periods:
a two (2) years suspension for a first offence involving anabolic agents, peptide hormones, masking agents, diuretics and/or pharmacological, chemical and physical manipulation of urine. For a second offence, the sanction is a life suspension."[637]

The sanctions applied both for during and out-of-competition doping offences. They started on the day of the infraction; in other cases on the day of the ruling.[638] For every infraction the IWF charged the national federation of the athlete concerned a fine of US$ 1,000 and repayment of the costs of the analysis. Any national federation showing 3 cases of doping in a given calendar year would be charged a fine of US$ 50,000.[639]

When the sanction imposed by the NF differed from that of the IWF, the IWF could only accept the minimum sanction of 2 years.[640]

When a doping offence by a foreign athlete was found by a national federation, this federation would impose a sanction. The national federation of the athlete was informed through the IWF. The athlete's federation was then obliged to impose a sanction as well. The athlete had to be banned from participation in international competitions.

The IWF recognised and enforced sanctions imposed by other international federations provided that the control had been carried out according to IOC Medical Code standards.[641]

---

[635] Reglement Technique, Titre Cinquieme – Code Disciplinaire des Epreuves, Chapitre 6 – Dopage, para. 1. Regles Generales, t. 129.

[636] Reglement Technique, Titre Cinquieme – Code Disciplinaire des Epreuves, Chapitre 6 – Dopage, para. 1. Regles Generales, t. 132.

[637] IWF Anti-Doping Policy, 14. Sanctions, Art. 14.2 sub a.

[638] IWF Anti-Doping Policy, 14. Sanctions, Art. 14.3.

[639] IWF Anti-Doping Policy, 14. Sanctions, Art. 14.6.

[640] IWF Anti-Doping Policy, 14. Sanctions, Art. 7.

[641] IWF Anti-Doping Policy, 14. Sanctions, Art. 14.4.

International Judo Federation – IJF

"For a first infraction the incriminated competitor is disqualified from the competition in question. He is removed from the standings. He must return his medal and any other prize received at the prize ceremony, plus
1.   he is suspended by the IJF for 24 months starting with the date of doping notification. He may not take part in a world championship, in a continental championship, in the Olympic Games or in any international tournament held under IJF auspices.[642]
If a competitor repeats the doping offense, he is disqualified from the competition, plus, in cases referred to in paragraph 1 of article 16, he is banned for life.
He is not entitled to take part in any international competition, world championships, the Olympic Games, continental championships or tournaments carried out under IJF auspices.
He is not eligible to be elected to the IJF Executive Committee or the Executive Committee of a continental union, or to vote."[643]

The IJF used disqualification as an equivalent of exclusion. The exclusion started on the day on which the sample was taken. If the athlete took part in a contest after the day the sample was taken, the period of exclusion would be extended by the period between sampling and the contest in question. The IJF recognised the 1994 agreement, which, among other things, provided for the recognition of sanctions of other international federations.

International Amateur Wrestling Federation – FILA

"In accordance with Article 10 of the Constitution, any wrestler who refuses to submit to the doping test shall be considered as having tested positive and will be banned from the entire competition, as well as being banned from participating in international events for a period of two years.
Moreover, if the examinations or tests carried out under the conditions laid down in the FILA Medical Regulations produce a positive result, the wrestler in question shall be disqualified for the entire competition, and shall have his results cancelled, without prejudice to any penalty banning him from international contests for a period of two years. If he offends again, the wrestler at fault shall be banned for life."[644]

The FILA used the IOC list.[645] When a wrestler tested positive he had to be disqualified for the entire competition.[646]

International Biathlon Union – IBU

"A two-year ban will be imposed on competitors who, under the application of the IBU Anti-doping, Blood Test and Gender Verification Rules, are found guilty during

---

[642] Regulations and Procedure concerning Drug Tests, Art. 16, subsection 2.
[643] Regulations and Procedure concerning Drug Tests, Art. 18.
[644] Disciplinary Regulations, Art. 13 – Doping Test.
[645] Constitution, Art. 10.
[646] FILA International Rules, Principe, B), subsection 7.

or out of competition of having used any other forbidden substance. Competitors who are found guilty a second time or more of having been doped in such a way shall be banned for a lifetime from IBU competitions."[647]

Athletes were thus disqualified if they competed while under the influence of doping.[648] The IBU used the IOC list. When the maximum hematocrite level was exceeded an athlete might be suspended for health reasons until the level had dropped to normal (52%).[649] Athletes who refused a blood test were considered to have tested positive.[650] The temporary exclusion started on the day the sample was taken. The life-long ban started on the day the offence was committed.[651] Athletes who tested positive at out-of-competition controls were suspended for two years. Repeat offenders were banned for life.

International Table Tennis Federation – ITTF

"If the use of a banned substance such as anabolic steroids, amphetamine-related and other stimulants, caffeine, diuretics, beta-blockers, narcotic analgesics and designer drugs is established, or if the player refuses to submit to doping control, he/she shall be banned from entering any competitions organized under the auspices of the ITTF and/ or the IOC for a period of two (2) years for the first offence from the date of the provision of the sample or of the sanctionable action. He/she shall be ineligible for life for the second offence."[652]

The ITTF referred to the IOC list of prohibited substances and methods.[653] When a player committed a doping offence he was disqualified immediately.[654] The doping offence caused the athlete to be excluded from competitions under the auspices of the ITTF and the IOC.

International Archery Federation – FITA

"Doping classes and methods prohibited by the IOC and FITA with the exception of substances mentioned in art. 12.2.2
2 years for the first offense;
Life ban for the second offense."[655]

Athletes were disqualified following a positive doping test result.[656] Participants were not allowed to use substances or methods which were prohibited according to

---

[647] IBU Disciplinary Rules, Art. 5.7.2.
[648] IBU Disciplinary Rules, Art. 5.5, sub c.
[649] IBU Disciplinary Rules, Art. 5.6.
[650] IBU Anti-Doping, Blood Test and Gender Verification Rules, I. Doping Controls, Art. 1.
[651] IBU Disciplinary Rules, Art. 5.7.3.
[652] Anti-Doping Regulations, Art. 7.1.2.
[653] Anti-Doping Regulations, Art. 1.1.2.
[654] Anti-Doping Regulations, Art. 7.1.4.
[655] Appendix 4 – Doping Control Procedures, Art. 12.2.1.
[656] Constitution and Administrative Rules, Chapter 10, Art. 10.7.4.

FITA and IOC rules; they had to comply with the FITA and the IOC Medical Code and behave accordingly in all respects.[657]

International Volleyball Federation – FIVB

"A player found positive for anabolic steroids, amphetamine-related and other drugs, is sanctioned:
2-year suspension for the first offence
life ban for the second offence."[658]

Both for the indoor and the beach competition the FIVB used its own list of prohibited substances and methods. An athlete found to have used doping was disqualified and forfeited his/her right to continued participation in the competition.[659]

International Bobsleigh and Tobogganing Federation – FIBT

"The F.I.B.T. Executive Committee shall impose the following penalties in case of a positive result according to items 1 and 3 of the F.I.B.T. Doping Control Regulations.
Two year period of ineligibility in the case of a first-time contravention of the rules
lifelong ineligibility in the case of a repeated contravention of the rules."[660]

The FIBT used the IOC list of prohibited substances and methods, with the addition of beta-blockers.[661]

World Curling Federation – WCF

"The penalty for a first infraction by a competitor shall be disqualification for the duration of the WCF Championship, plus:
except in the cases covered by paragraph (2) of this Article a suspension from all competition for a period of two years from the later date of the positive result and the date on which any appeal from a decision thereon shall be finally determined.[662]
The penalty for a second infraction by a competitor pursuant to the IOC Medical Code and the present by-Law shall be disqualification, if the infraction occurred during a competition, plus, in cases referred to in paragraph (1) of this Article, a lifetime suspension from all WCF competitions and WCF accreditations, in any capacity [...]"[663]

An offence was committed when a provision of the IOC Medical Code was violated. Disqualification took effect starting on the day following the detection of the use of doping or the day on which the decision on appeal became final. The sanction imposed in relation to a particular sport or capacity had to be carried out in full

---

[657] Constitution and Administrative Rules, Chapter 2, Art. 2.2.2.
[658] Medical Regulations, 2. Antidoping Control Regulations, Art. 2.6.2.
[659] Medical Regulations, 2. Antidoping Control Regulations, Art. 2.6.1.
[660] Doping Control Regulations, Art. 9.1.
[661] Doping Control Regulations, Arts. 3.1 en 3.2.
[662] By Law no. 8 Doping, VI Sanctions and Penalties, Art. 13, sub B), a), subsection 1.
[663] By Law no. 8 Doping, VI Sanctions and Penalties, Art. 13, sub B), b).

in relation to other sports or capacities. The sanctions had to be respected throughout their duration by the authorities of other sports.[664]

International Ice Hockey Federation – IIHF

"If the IIHF Directorate or the IIHF Council finds a player tested positive of doping or in the case of refusal of a player to submit to the doping tests, the following sanctions shall apply:

A player with a positive doping test must be sanctioned. Sanctions for the various substances will be as follows and apply to:

Anabolic steroids, amphetamine related or other stimulants, diuretics, narcotics and 'designer drugs':

At the first infraction of the doping regulations – a two-year suspension from participating in any competition of a member national association or of the IIHF starting from the day of detection of the positive doping test;

At the second infraction of the doping regulations – a life-time ban from all games."[665]

Athletes whose A sample had tested positive would be suspended immediately. Suspension did not automatically mean that the athlete was guilty. The suspension started from the day doping was found. If the suspension embraced two separate seasons the athlete would also be suspended for the period in between. If the A sample tested positive, the team leader had to decide whether the player involved had to be allowed to continue to play until the results of the B sample became known. If the B sample also tested positive, the team would be punished for every game it had played in which the doped player had participated.[666]

International Luge Federation – FIL

"The penalty for a first infraction by a competitor shall be disqualification, if the infraction occurred during a competition, plus:

1.3. except in the cases covered by paragraph (2) of this Article, a suspension from all competition for a period of two years from the later of the date of the positive result and the date on which any appeal from a decision thereon shall be finally determined [...][667]

The penalty for a second infraction by a competitor pursuant to the FIL Medical Code shall be disqualification, if the infraction occurred during a competition, plus, in cases referred to in paragraph (1) of Article III, a lifetime suspension from all competition and accreditation, in any capacity, at FIL competitions [...]

The penalty for a second infraction by a competitor in an out-of-competition test shall be a lifetime suspension in cases referred to in paragraph (1) of Article III [...] A previous out-of-competition infraction by a competitor shall be considered as being committed during competition with regard to its effects on the applicable penalty."[668]

---

[664] By Law no. 8 Doping, VI Sanctions and Penalties, Art. 13, sub E).

[665] By laws 1400 Medical Controls (Doping), A. Players, 2).

[666] Doping Regulations, I. IIHF Doping Controls, D, sub e).

[667] IRO – International Luge Regulations, Supplement 4 – Medical Code, Chapter VIII, Art. III, subsection 1.

[668] IRO – International Luge Regulations, Supplement 4 – Medical Code, Chapter VIII, Art. IV.

The suspension started from the date the offence was found or from the date on which a final decision was given on appeal.[669] The sanctions imposed in relation to a particular capacity or sport had to be carried out in full in relation to other capacities and sports. The sanctions had to be respected by the authorities of other sports for their entire duration.[670]

Eighteen international federations imposed the same sanctions for a doping offence as the IOC did: two years for a first doping offence and a life-long ban for a second doping offence. These sanctions were fixed; no consideration was thus given to the seriousness of the offence. There was only one federation which made an exception and also took the seriousness of the offence into account in the imposition of sanctions. In the remainder of cases the determination of punishment was identical, albeit with some minor additions here and there. One federation, for example, did not use the IOC list, whereas all others did. Another also applied the sanctions for "hard" doping for the use of beta-blockers.

2.1.2.   First offence: one-year suspension; second offence: life-long ban

The three international tennis federations, the ITF, the ATP and the WTA applied a sanction of one-year suspension for a first doping offence. As the sanction rules of these federations were identical, only those of the ITF are cited here.

International Tennis Federation – ITF, Association of Tennis Professionals – ATP, Women's Tennis Association – WTA

> "– First Positive/Violation
> A player who is found through the procedures set forth in this Programme to test positive for any Class 1 Prohibited Substance or Method shall be suspended from participation in any and all ITF sanctioned or recognised tournaments or events for a one (1) year period.
> – Second Positive/Violation
> A player who commits a second offence under the Programme involving a Class 1 Prohibited Substance or Method shall be permanently disqualified from participation in or association with any ITF-sanctioned or recognised tournaments or events."[671]

The Appeals Committee was competent to reduce sanctions ("but not overturn the violation of the Programme") in the event that the athlete could show the possible existence of exceptional circumstances and the need for a mitigation of sanctions due to these circumstances. Exceptional circumstances were understood to include circumstances in which the athlete had been unaware that he was using prohibited substances or where they had been administered to him without his knowledge. It

---

[669] IRO – International Luge Regulations, Supplement 4 – Medical Code, Chapter VIII, Art. XI.
[670] IRO – International Luge Regulations, Supplement 4 – Medical Code, Chapter VIII, Art. V.
[671] By Laws of ITF Limited, 8. Tennis Anti-Doping Programme, (M), subsection 1.

was, however, required that the athlete had acted reasonably in the circumstances concerned.[672]

The period of suspension started running either on the day following the expiry of the time-limit for appeal, or on the day after the player had admitted the use of doping, or on the day after the final decision on appeal.[673]

If an athlete had violated the anti-doping rules of an organisation other than the ITF and these rules corresponded to those of the ITF, this violation would be considered a violation of the corresponding ITF rules. In such cases, the ITF would sanction the athlete accordingly.[674]

2.1.3. *First offence: two-year suspension; second offence: minimum suspension of 3 years*

International Skating Union – ISU

"The Council imposes the sanctions for doping.
All IOC-prohibited/restricted classes of substances and methods NOT listed under 9 b) are subject to the following sanctions:
1.1. 2 years for the first offence,
1.2. at least 3 years for the second offence beginning at the day of the sample taking."[675]

In principle, the ISU would adopt sanctions imposed by other international federations, but the ISU Council could alter these on the recommendation of a national member federation.[676] The national federations were not allowed to impose sanctions which were less severe than the minimum penalties established by the ISU.[677]

2.1.4. *First offence: maximum suspension of 2 years; second offence: life-long ban*

Three international federations took the two-year suspension for a first doping offence as an upper limit: the AIBA, the FIG and, partly, the FINA. The sanction for a second doping offence was not fixed either.

International Amateur Boxing Association – AIBA

"A boxer who has been found guilty of doping may be punished by suspension from any competition for a period of up to two years and, in case of recurrence, disqualification for lifetime."[678]

---

[672] By Laws of ITF Limited, 8. Tennis Anti-Doping Programme, (E), sub (c).
[673] By Laws of ITF Limited, 8. Tennis Anti-Doping Programme, (N), subsection 1.
[674] By Laws of ITF Limited, 8. Tennis Anti-Doping Programme, (B), subsection 3.
[675] General Regulations, I. Doping, Rule 139, subsection 9 sub a).
[676] General Regulations, I. Doping, Rule 139, subsection 10.
[677] General Regulations, I. Doping, Rule 139, subsection 11.
[678] Articles of Association and Rules for International Competitions and Tournaments, Art. XXVIII: Disciplinary Action, C. Doping, subsection 2.

It is not entirely clear whether "may be punished" was intended to mean that a doping case might be dismissed or that the sanction might be applied flexibly. Dismissal did not seem to be an option because of the provision that when a boxer was found guilty "he shall be suspended from any competition pending disciplinary action."[679] Elsewhere in the anti-doping rules of the AIBA it was stated that "any boxer [...] infringing this prohibition shall be liable to disqualification or suspension by the A.I.B.A."[680]

International Gymnastics Federation – FIG

"A suspended sanction may be granted in case of the 1st infraction. The sanction may be total or partial.
If the substance found is an: Anabolic Steroid, Diuretic, Narcotic Analgesics, Stimulant, or similar substance:
1st violation: maximum suspension of 2 years
2nd violation: possibility of complete exclusion."[681]

What may be deduced from this? Firstly that the FIG reserved the right to impose a sanction for a first doping offence; secondly that this sanction could be total or partial and thirdly that in the most serious of cases a two-year suspension might be imposed. In the case of repeat offences an athlete could ultimately be banned for life.

The fact that the FIG had imposed a sanction did not stand in the way of the imposition of further sanctions by the IOC, the NOCs or the national federations.[682] This rule might have been the reason that the provision on sanctions offered so much scope for not imposing the maximum penalty. If the FIG imposed a sanction the national federations had to enforce it during national and international competitions.[683]

International Amateur Swimming Association – FINA

"For a doping offence involving stimulants other than those set forth at DC 9.1.4, beta-blockers, beta-2 agonists and related substances:
First offence: – up to two (2) years' suspension.
Second offence: – a minimum of two (2) years' suspension up to a lifetime expulsion."[684]

---

[679] Articles of Association and Rules for International Competitions and Tournaments, Art. XXVIII: Disciplinary Action, C. Doping, subsection 1.
[680] Articles of Association and Rules for International Competitions and Tournaments, Rule XXII: Administration of drugs, etc., sub B.
[681] Medical Regulations, Doping Control Regulations, 3.1. FIG Sanctions, sub A.
[682] Medical Regulations, Doping Control Regulations, 1.4.
[683] Medical Regulations, Doping Control Regulations, 3.2.
[684] FINA Doping Control Rules, DC 9 Sanctions, Art. DC 9.1.2.

The FINA made an exception for the use of beta-blockers, beta-2 agonists and related substances. The principal rule of the FINA will be dealt with later.

The FINA Executive was competent to provisionally exclude an athlete for the duration of the deliberations within the Doping Panel. Exclusions could start either before or after the B sample had been analysed and could be imposed when the Executive considered that there was a well-founded suspicion of guilt. The period of the provisional exclusion had to be deducted from the period of any final exclusion which the Doping Panel might decide to impose.[685]

International Triathlon Union – ITU

> "The ITU Penalties for Doping infractions are:
> For anabolic steroids, amphetamine-related and other stimulants, diuretics, beta-blockers, narcotic analgesics, designer drugs and any other boosting violations not specifically included in paragraph b):
> 1.1. First Offense: up to a maximum of two year suspension.
> 1.2. Second Offense: lifetime ban."[686]

This provision does not belong in the present category where the sanction for a second doping offence is concerned, as this was not a maximum, but a minimum penalty, as becomes clear from the wording that: "A competitor will be expelled for life (but not be limited to): [...] for a second drug offense as outlined in the ITU Doping Control Rules and Procedural Guidelines."[687]

In the event of out-of-competition controls sanctions might be reduced to a warning or other punishment, on condition that the athlete, prior to the control, had indicated his use of the substances tested for, and the substance had been legitimately prescribed by a doctor or was available over the counter and it had been established by the ITU Doping Commission that the substance was not found in such quantities as to constitute doping.[688]

Athletes who had been excluded for doping were not allowed to compete in a different sport whose federation had been recognised by the IOC or the General Association of International Sports Federations (GAISF) either.[689]

The sanctions in this category closely resembled those of the first category. In both categories, the federations took two-year or life-time suspension as their starting point.

The main difference between the respective categories as expressed in the federations' rules was that provisions falling within the second category allowed for a margin of appreciation where the seriousness of the doping offence could be linked to the severity of the sanction.

[685] FINA Doping Control Rules, DC 9 Sanctions, Art. DC 9.6.
[686] ITU Doping Control Rules and Procedural Guidelines, 7. Penalties, Art. 7.2 sub 1.
[687] ITU Competition Rules, III Discipline of Competitors, Art. 5, sub a)(i).
[688] ITU Doping Control Rules and Procedural Guidelines, 7. Penalties, Art. 7.3.
[689] ITU Competition Rules, III Discipline of Competitors, Art. 6, sub b).

2.1.5. *First offence: maximum suspension of 2 years; second offence:*
suspension of 4 years

International Handball Federation – IHF

"In case of a proven doping offence, the players concerned are disqualified from all further tournament matches. The players are also banned from national and international matches for a period of up to two years.
Should a player be in violation of the Anti-Doping Regulations for the second time, the player is banned from national and international matches for a period of four years."[690]

2.1.6. *First offence: minimum suspension of 2 years; second offence: life-long*
ban

This category also started from two-year and life-long bans as sanctions. Here, however, the two years' suspension for a first doping offence was the minimum penalty.

International Amateur Athletic Federation – IAAF

"If an athlete commits a doping offence, he will be ineligible for the following periods:–
For an offence under rule 60.1(i) or 60.1(iii) above involving the substances listed in Part 1 of Schedule 1 of the 'Procedural Guidelines for Doping Control' or, for any of the other offences listed in rule 60.1:–
a.   first offence – for a minimum of two years from the date of the provision of the sample or of the sanctionable offence and any additional period necessary to include a subsequent equivalent competition to that in which the athlete was disqualified;
b.   second offence – for life."[691]

The athlete would be suspended from the moment that the IAAF had informed the national federation that there was proof of a doping offence. If, in the opinion of the IAAF, a national federation had failed without justification to impose a penalty, the IAAF could suspend the athlete in its place.[692]

If an athlete or his/her national federation could not provide a satisfactory explanation for a finding of prohibited substances within a certain time-limit set by the IAAF, the athlete would be considered to have tested positive. If the IAAF was responsible for the control in question it would suspend the athlete with immediate effect as a provisional measure which would remain in force until a decision had been rendered.

---

[690] Anti-Doping Regulations, Art. 11.
[691] Rules and Regulations, Division III – Control of Drug Abuse, Rule 60, subsection 2 sub a.
[692] Rules and Regulations, Division III – Control of Drug Abuse, Rule 59, subsection 2.

If a suspended athlete tested positive, this would be considered a separate doping offence.[693]

International Basketball Federation – FIBA

"Any player whose doping control test proves positive (samples A and B) is subject to:
1.1. Suspension for a minimum of two years for the first infraction,
1.2. Lifelong ban after the second infraction.
This applies to any infraction arising from the use of doping substances and/or methods of doping, as defined by the IOC's List of Doping Classes and Methods."[694]

Athletes would be suspended immediately upon a positive finding in their A sample. The FIBA did not test for beta-blockers. The FIBA could adopt any sanctions imposed by national federations, provided that during the controls the provisions of the FIBA had been closely observed and the samples had been analysed by an IOC-accredited laboratory. Sanctions of the national federation were enforced unchanged, even if they stayed below the minimum corresponding FIBA sanction.[695] In such cases the other national federations also had to enforce the sanction. The sanctions imposed by the FIBA had to be implemented by the national federations in national competitions. With respect to sanctions imposed by organisations outside the FIBA (such as government authorities, the IOC or other international federations), the FIBA had to examine the possibility of also enforcing these sanctions in FIBA games.[696]

World Taekwondo Federation – WTF

"The minimum penalties for doping infractions to be decided by the Executive Council or the Sanction Committee shall be:
A   Doping Class And Methods:
–   Two years for the first offense
–   Life ban for the second offense."[697]

The life-long ban had to be considered a fixed sanction, although from the wording of the provision it could also be concluded that it was a "minimum penalty." Sanctions imposed by the WTF had to be applied by the national and regional Taekwondo organisations.[698]

The sanction for a first doping offence in this category was a minimum of two years. The provisions concerned allowed for the seriousness of the infraction to be taken into consideration in the determination of the sanction's duration. The provi-

---

[693] Rules and Regulations, Division III – Control of Drug Abuse, Rule 60, subsection 7.
[694] Regulations Governing Doping Control, 6.6. Sanctions, Art. 6.6.2.
[695] Regulations Governing Doping Control, 6.6. Sanctions, Art. 6.3.3, subsection 2.
[696] Regulations Governing Doping Control, 6.6. Sanctions, Art. 6.3.3, subsection 5.
[697] Regulations For Doping Control, 1. Disciplinary Procedures and Sanctions, Art. 11.2.
[698] Regulations For Doping Control, 1. Disciplinary Procedures and Sanctions, Art. 11.4.

sions did not give a maximum or contain any restrictions relating to reasonableness or fairness.

2.1.7. First offence: minimum suspension of 4 years; second offence: life-long ban

The penalty provisions under this category corresponded to those under the previous category in the sense that they stipulated a minimum suspension for first offences and a life-long ban for second offences. However, in this category the sanction for a first offence was not two, but four years. Provisions in this category were applied by one umbrella organisation, the IPC, and one international federation, the FINA.

International Paralympic Committee – IPC

> "An athlete who has committed a first major doping infraction will be ineligible to participate in any competition or activity organized, convened, or held or sanctioned by IPC, an International Federation, or a member thereof for a minimum period of four years from the date of the infraction.
> In cases where the infraction occurs at a major sports event (ie. Paralympic Games, World Championships, or Regional Championships) the athlete shall be deemed ineligible for a full four-year period, and will be ineligible for the same Games or Championships at which the original infraction occurred which take place at the approximate end of the four year cycle following the infraction even if the date of those games or championships is beyond the four year time period.[699]
> An athlete who has committed a second major doping infraction will be ineligible for life to participate in activities organized, convened, held or sanctioned by IPC, an International Federation, or member thereof."[700]

Athletes would be disqualified from the competition for which purpose they had used the prohibited substance. Penalties ran from the day on which the offence had been committed. If the doping offence had taken place during one of the main sports events (Paralympics, world championships or regional championships) the suspension would be in force for the full intermediate period of four years and included the next edition of the games or championships during which the initial offence had taken place, "even if the date of those games or championships [was] beyond the four year time period."

The IPC sanctions were minimum penalties. If the athlete was subject to the anti-doping rules of a "world able-bodied" sports organisation which imposed stricter penalties, the athlete would be subject to those instead.[701]

Persons outside the scope of jurisdiction of the IPC or of an international federation might still become subject to their anti-doping provisions if he/she wished to

---

[699] Doping, 8.2 Penalties for doping infractions, Art. 2.1 sub a.

[700] Doping, 8.2 Penalties for doping infractions, Art. 2.1 sub b.

[701] Doping, 8.2 Penalties for doping infractions, Art. 2.3.

participate in any of their activities. Penalties imposed in any sport, any capacity or at any level had to be respected by the authorities functioning on different levels within the same sport and in other sports.[702]

International Amateur Swimming Federation – FINA

"The sanctions for doping offences involving prohibited substances shall be:
For a doping offence involving anabolic agents, diuretics, masking agents, peptide hormones, mimetics and analogues, and chemically or pharmacologically related substances:
First offence:
1.1. a minimum of four (4) years' suspension ; plus
1.2. a retroactive sanction involving cancellation of all results achieved in competitions during the period prior to the date the suspension takes effect and extending back to six (6) months before the collection of the positive sample shall be imposed.
Second offence:
1.3. lifetime expulsion; plus
1.4. a retroactive sanction involving cancellation of all results achieved in competitions during the competitors' career shall be imposed."[703]

The minimum sanction could be reduced if the athlete was able to show conclusively how the prohibited substance had come to be present in his/her body and that this had not been the result of his/her own negligence.[704]

Suspension meant that the punished athlete could not take part in any activity of the FINA or its members in whichever branch of sport and whatever capacity. The suspension started from the date indicated by the competent body.[705]

The next category of penalty provisions differs considerably from the one described above. In this category fall the provisions of the UCI, FEI, FIFA, FIH, the International Softball Federation (ISF) and FIS and the revised IOC provisions.

Although the provisions in this category vary greatly, they have one thing in common: contrary to the provisions of other federations, in addition to penalties for first and second offences, they also provide penalties for third offences.

2.1.8.1. First offence: flexible ban; second offence: flexible ban; third offence: life-long ban

International Cycling Union – UCI

"A rider declared or considered to be positive shall be disciplined as follows:
1)   Elite
MEN

---

[702] Doping, 8.2 Penalties for doping infractions, Art. 1.4.
[703] FINA Doping Control Rules, Art. DC 9.1.1.
[704] FINA Doping Control Rules, Art. DC 9.10.
[705] FINA Doping Control Rules, Art. DC 9.11.

1st offence:
–   disqualification + suspension for six months minimum to one year maximum,
–   fine of SFr. 2,000.- minimum to SFr. 4,000.- maximum.
2nd offence:
–   disqualification + suspension for one year minimum to two years maximum,
–   fine of SFr. 4,000.- minimum to SFr. 6,000.- maximum.
3rd offence:
–   disqualification + permanent debarment,
–   a fine of SFr. 8,000.-.
WOMEN
1st offence:
–   disqualification + suspension for six months minimum to one year maximum,
–   fine of SFr. 1,000.- minimum to SFr. 2,000.- maximum.
2nd offence:
–   disqualification + suspension for one year minimum to two years maximum,
–   fine of SFr. 3,000.- minimum to SFr. 5,000.- maximum.
3rd offence:
–   disqualification + permanent debarment,
–   a fine of SFr. 8,000.
2)   Under 23
1st offence:
–   disqualification + suspension for six months minimum to one year maximum,
–   fine of SFr. 500.- minimum to SFr. 1,000.- maximum.
2nd offence:
–   disqualification + suspension for one year minimum to two years maximum,
–   fine of SFr. 1,500.- minimum to SFr. 3,000.- maximum.
3rd offence:
–   disqualification + permanent debarment,
–   a fine of SFr. 8,000.-.
3)   Other riders
1st offence:
–   disqualification + suspension for six months minimum to one year maximum,
2nd offence:
–   disqualification + suspension for one year minimum to two years maximum,
3rd offence:
–   disqualification + permanent debarment."[706]

These sanctions depended on the category to which the athlete in question belonged: elite, under 23 years of age and other riders. In the elite category the sanction depended on the rider's gender. All sanctions consisted of disqualification, suspension and fines. The periods of suspension for women, the elite under 23's and other elite riders were the same as those for elite men, except that the fines for first and second offences were lower.

Every decision imposing a suspension would give the time of commencement and termination. The suspension would have effect in all sports matters. It had to be

---

[706] 82 Part XIV – Antidoping Examination Regulations, Chapter VI I I, Art. 90, para. 1.

served during the normal active period of the person concerned. For this reason, the suspension might cover various periods of the year.

When the national rules were applied in a national tournament or during an out-of-competition test carried out at the national level, any ban against a rider licensed to another national federation would without exception become applicable in the country in which the tournament or test took place. When the Anti-doping Commission confirmed that the same facts would have led to the same ban as pursuant to the UCI rules, the ban would have worldwide effect. A rider who was caught using doping was excluded from selection for the world championships, Olympic Games and continental championships.

Controls carried out in accordance with different rules than those provided by the Regulations could not lead to the sanctions envisaged in the Regulations. If an offence under the Regulations resulted in a suspension based on the rules of another authority (i.e., not the UCI), the sanction would be reduced by the suspension period. The excessive exclusion period would only apply in the country where the decision was rendered.

International Softball Federation – ISF

"Penalties for testing positive:
1. A minimum of two years disqualification from all ISF competition for the first offense. [...]
2. A minimum of three years for second offense.
3. Life ban for third offense."[707]

Testing positive would result in disqualification. The provision in question had been laid down in two different places in the ISF regulations: first in the ISF Code and again in the Doping Control and Testing Regulations established by the ISF Medical and Doping Commission.

2.1.8.2. First offence: flexible ban; second offence: flexible ban; third offence: flexible ban

International Hockey Federation – FIH

"1st Violation
If any other banned substance or manipulation is discovered, the FIH Disciplinary Committee shall pronounce a suspension from all events for a maximum of two years from the starting date of the provisional suspension;
any interruption of this suspension shall be deducted from the total. In either case, the FIH Disciplinary Committee may pronounce a suspension for a longer period, but which applies only to certain events to be specified.

---

[707] ISF Code, Art. 15.11.

2nd Violation

If any other banned substance or manipulation is discovered, the FIH Disciplinary Committee shall pronounce a suspension from all events for a maximum of two years from the starting date of the provisional suspension;

any interruption of this suspension shall be deducted from the total. In either case, the FIH Disciplinary Committee may pronounce a suspension for a longer period, but which applies only to certain events to be specified.

Further Violations

Upon a third violation, no matter what the substance in question, the FIH Disciplinary Committee shall pronounce a suspension for a minimum of five years, with the option of suspension for life."[708]

Even though the FIH Doping Policy stipulated that the FIH had adopted the IOC Medical Code and that it acted in accordance with it, the sanction provisions of the FIH told a different story.[709]

When imposing a sanction the FIH Disciplinary Committee had to form an opinion concerning the seriousness of the offence (nature of the substance, malice, negligence, etc.), the circumstances under which the offence had been committed (e.g. after encouragement) and the athlete's personal circumstances (age and experience and whether he/she was an amateur or a professional).[710]

When a national federation carried out a doping control, the FIH Disciplinary Committee would review the procedure followed and the decision delivered. When the control was carried out in accordance with the provisions of the FIH Doping Policy or the IOC Medical Code, the FIH Disciplinary Committee could establish a violation of the FIH rules and impose sanctions independently of those imposed by the national federation. The sanctions could be scaled up to the international level or even extended.[711]

The next category comprises penalty provisions which stipulated neither a minimum, nor a maximum suspension period. The competent body was free to determine the length of the sanction. The provisions did not exclude the possibility that a doping panel would try several consecutive doping offences committed by one athlete. Although only the doping provisions of the FISA stated in so many words that a first doping offence could cause an athlete to be banned for life, this was also a possibility under the penalty provisions of the other federations in this category.

---

[708] FIH Doping Policy, Art. 12.3.

[709] FIH Doping Policy, Art. 3: "The I.O.C. has published a detailed Medical Code against Doping in Sport setting out testing procedures, dope classes, a national anti-doping programme, sample analysis, out-of-competition testing, rights and responsibilities of sport organisations and guidelines for sanctions and penalties for breaches thereof.

The FIH has adopted this Medical Code and will act in accordance with its directives and recommendations. Amendments, up-dates, additions and medical control guides relating to the Medical Code and confirmed by the I.O.C. will be similarly adopted."

[710] FIH Doping Policy, Art. 10.

[711] FIH Doping Policy, Art. 13.

In principle, therefore, doping panels of federations falling within this category were free to impose sanctions ranging from a warning to a life-time ban.

2.1.9. *First offence: maximum life-time ban*

International Rowing Federation – FISA

"The penalty will be determined taking into account the seriousness of the offence according to an established scale as follows:
Use of anabolic agents and related substances, diuretics and related substances, peptide hormones and analogues, and all the respective releasing factors of these substances, cocaine and/or pharmacological, physical or chemical manipulation of any biological substance (blood and/or urine) whatever the circumstances of the testing:
Life ban for the first offence."[712]

A rower or coxswain who violated the anti-doping rules of the FISA would be disqualified. The FISA could suspend an athlete temporarily or permanently from the analysis of the B sample until the commencement of the disciplinary Procedure. Moreover, the FISA Executive Committee could impose an additional penalty, which could result in a de facto life-long ban. The Committee could also impose this sanction for a finding of doping at an out-of-competition control.[713] The athlete had the right to be heard. Penalties were determined taking into account the circumstances and the seriousness of the offence.

International Association Football Federation – FIFA

"If specimen 'B' proves positive, the case shall be submitted to the relevant FIFA organising committee. This committee shall investigate the case if necessary with the help of specialists and shall determine the degree of responsibility of the player and/or persons belonging to the national association. The results of their investigation shall be the basis for determining appropriate sanctions."[714]

International Ski Federation – FIS

"When a doping offence is proved (after the mandatory hearing), the FIS Council will be informed and will decide the appropriate sanction(s)."[715]

The national federations would inform the FIS of all positive test results and sanctions. The sanctions were assessed during the next meeting of the FIS Council, which decided whether to accept the sanctions or amend them. Sanctions amended by the Council were final and binding on all national federations.[716]

---

[712] Rules of Racing and Related By Laws, Part VII – Medical Provisions, By Law to rules 80 to 83 – Doping, Art. 9.3.1 sub a).

[713] Rules of Racing and Related By Laws, Part VII – Medical Provisions, Rule 82.

[714] Doping Control Regulations for FIFA, Competitions (Except For FIFA World Cup), II. Doping Control Organisation, 8. Procedure If Specimen "B" Proves Positive, Art. 39.

[715] Medical Guide, FIS Doping Rules, Rule 6.

[716] Medical Guide, FIS Doping Rules, Rule 7, subsection 1.

2.1.10. *No malice: suspension of 1 to 3 months and a fine; malice: suspension of 3 months to 2 years and a fine*

International Equestrian Federation – FEI

"The finding on analysis of a Prohibited Substance as defined in Art. 146.2 is presumed to be a deliberate attempt of the Person Responsible to affect the performance of the horse and will entail the suspension of the Person Responsible from 3 to 24 months. A fine of CHF 1,000.- to 15,000.- can also be imposed.

If the Person Responsible can prove that it was not a deliberate attempt to affect the performance of the horse or that the findings are the results of legitimate treatment of the horse or of one or several parts of his body, the sanction may entail a fine up to CHF 15,000.-, but a suspension from 1 to 3 months may also be imposed.

In the case of repeated violations of Art. 146.2, paragraph 5.2 will always be applied."[717]

The discovery of a prohibited substance always led to the automatic disqualification of both the horse and the rider[718] unless the Ground Jury decided otherwise.[719]

2.1.11. *First offence: ban on participation in one or several competitions, fine of up to US$ 100,000 and suspension from all competition for at least two years; second offence: ban on participation in any competition, fine of up to US$ 1,000,000 and suspension from all competitions for 4 years to life*

International Olympic Committee – IOC

"In a case of doping, the penalties for a first offence are as follows:
if the Prohibited Substance used is one other than those referred to in paragraph a) above:
1. a ban on participation in one or several sports competitions in any capacity whatsoever;
2. a fine of up to US$ 1,00,000;
3. suspension from any competition for a minimum period of two years. However, based on specific, exceptional circumstances to be evaluated in the first instance by the competent IF bodies, there may be a provision for a possible modification of the two-year sanction.[720]
If the Prohibited Substance used is one other than those referred to in paragraph a) above or if it is a repeat offence (a repeat offence being constituted by a further case of doping perpetrated within a period of ten years after the preceding sanction, whatever form it took and whatever the reason for it, became final):
i) a life ban on participation in any sports event in any capacity whatsoever;

[717] General Regulations, Chapter IX, Art. 174 sub 5.2 en 5.3.
[718] General Regulations, Chapter IX, Art. 174 sub 5.1.
[719] General Regulations, Chapter VII, Art. 146, subsection 2.
[720] OMADC, Chapter II, Art. 3, subsection 1 sub b).

ii)   a fine of up to US$ 1,000,000;

iii) suspension (between four years and life) from all sports competition."[721]

The OMADC distinguished between "doping" and "intentional doping."[722] In the event of intentional doping the sanctions would apply which normally applied for a second doping offence.

2.2.   Table of "hard"-doping sactions

Internat. federations	Sanctions		
	1st offence	2nd offence	3rd offence
IOC (MC), IBF, UIPM, ISAF, ISSF, IBA, ICF, FIE, IWF, IJF, FILA, IBU, ITTF, FITA, FIVB, FIBT, WCF, IIHF, FIL	suspension of 2 years	life-long ban	
ITF, ATP, WTA	suspension of 1 year	life-long ban	
ISU	suspension of 2 years	minimum suspension of 3 years	
AIBA, FIG, FINA, ITU	maximum suspension of 2 years	maximum life-long ban	
IHF	maximum suspension of 2 years	suspension of 4 years	
IAAF, FIBA, WTF	minimum suspension of 2 years	life-long ban	
IPC, FINA	minimum suspension of 4 years	life-long ban	
UCI, ISF	flexible ban	flexible ban	life-long ban
FIH	flexible ban	flexible ban	flexible ban
FISA, FIFA, FIS	maximum life-long ban		
FEI	No malice: suspension of 1 to 3 months + fine Malice: suspension of 3 months to 2 years + fine		
IOC (OMADC)	ban + fine + suspension of minimum 2 years	ban + fine + suspension of 4 years to life	

The penalties which the different sports organisations could impose for doping offences involving unconditionally prohibited substances varied widely. Athletes in one sport could be punished by a different penalty for the same offence than athletes in another sport.[723] Footballer Frank de Boer, for example, after having tested

---

[721] OMADC, Chapter II, Art. 3, subsection 2 sub b).

[722] OMADC, Chapter I, Art. 1: "Intentional doping means doping in circumstances where it is established, or may reasonably be presumed, that any Participant acted knowingly or in circumstances amounting to gross negligence."

[723] Another argument put forward in favour of harmonisation was that it was simply not right that two athletes from the same country who had both tested positive for the same prohibited substance under similar circumstances should be punished differently only because they participated in different

positive for nandrolone was suspended for three months, while for the same offence the athlete Troy Douglas was suspended for two years and the Costa Rican
swimmer Claudia Poll for four years even. These differences in punishment had
been the object of protest for years. If anything in particular needed harmonising in
doping law, it was the issue of sanctions. The WADA was given the task of
harmonising the relevant rules and it took this organisation considerable effort to
fulfil it. The discussions between the WADA and the sports organisations concerning the amount of the punishment were exceptionally heated, especially because
opinions were rigid.

The majority of sports organisations were in favour of a two-year suspension for a
first offence and a life-time ban for repeat offenders. These proposals however proved
unacceptable to federations with a professional athlete membership, such as the
football, tennis and cycling federations. The FIFA and the UCI continued to oppose
the proposed penalties. They considered them disproportionate and argued that the
minimum suspension of two years could be regarded as contrary to rules of employment law. The FIFA and the UCI feared that the courts would annul two-year
suspensions leaving them to face huge claims for damages. Based on these arguments, these federations were only prepared to sign the Anti-Doping Code if the
sanctions would be made less severe.

2.3.   Sanctions according to WADC

The WADC[724] includes sanctions for individual athletes (Art. 10), for teams (Art.
11) and for sports organisations (Art. 12). The WADC sanctions for a violation of
the rules in Articles 2.1 – 2.3 and 2.5 – 2.6 – except when the specified substances
referred to in Article 10.3 are found in a sample – are two years' exclusion for a first
offence[725] and life-long exclusion for a second offence.[726, 727] During the 1999 World

---

sports. However, it can also be argued that it makes no difference whether the athletes are from the
same country or not. If this were the only objectionable aspect of the differentiated sanctioning regime,
the argument described above could actually be interpreted to defend differentiated sanctioning per
sport in case the athletes involved were not from the same country.

[724] The WADC is now recognised by a large number of sports organisations and federations, namely
by 28 ASOIF members, 7 AIOWF members, 29 IOC-recognised IFs, 15 (out of 18) non-recognised
GAISF members, 5 international sports federations for disabled athletes, 13 sports for which IPC is the
international federation, 3 other IFs, 9 major games organisations, 41 national anti-doping organisations,
202 NOCs, 158 national Paralympic Committees and 9 others. As of 7 Febuary 2005, 163 governments
have signed the declaration.

[725] *Die Welt* of 3 March 2003 ("Die Radprofis stehen isoliert da"(2)) contained an interview with
WADA president Richard Pound. To *Die Welt*'s question: "Können Sie den Verbänden zusichern, dass
Zwei-Jahres-Sperren juristisch so abgesichert sind, dass ihnen anschließend keine riesigen
Schadensersatzforderungen von gesperrten Athleten drohen?" Pound replied: "Renommierte Sport-
und Menschenrechtsexperten haben uns die Unbedenklichkeit der Vorschriften in Gutachten bescheinigt."

[726] Art. 10.2 WADC.

[727] Pursuant to Art. 10.3 the sanctions for testing positive for certain "specified substances" are:
First violation: at a minimum, a warning and reprimand and no period of ineligibility from future

Conference on Doping it was agreed to introduce flexible sanctions with a minimum of two years following a first offence. The idea of imposing a certain minimum at least has been abandoned in the WADC. The reason could be that various disciplinary tribunals have the discretionary power to respond differently to equal cases, which causes a lack of uniformity. The comment to Article 10.2 explains this as follows: "flexibility in sanctioning has often been viewed as an unacceptable opportunity for some sporting bodies to be more lenient with dopers." The same comment insists that the two-year ban is essential with a view to harmonisation. However, it would be truer to speak of unification, which may actually stand in the way of harmonisation. A two-year ban will have a different impact depending on whether you are a short distance runner or an archer. Harmonisation can only be truly achieved when the sanction is related to the length of the period during the athlete's life when he/she is actually able to participate in his/her sport professionally.

The comment to Article 2.9.1.3. in the second version of the WADC, which is now Article 10.2, was rightly dropped in the third version. This comment defended the instrument of the two-year or life-long ban. It claimed that

> "these disqualification periods are not unduly harsh when compared to the discipline that is applied to other types of professional misconduct. A lawyer who misuses his client's funds, a psychiatrist who has sex with a patient, and an airline pilot who arrives drunk for a flight will, in most countries, be permanently banned from their professions. An athlete who dopes commits a comparable breach of trust in his profession or vocation."

During the Conference another heated discussion took place concerning the question of whether the periods of exclusion (two years and life) were in conformity with human rights, principles of natural justice, general principles of law and fundamental fairness. Richard Young, Team Leader of the WADA Code Project Team,[728] remarked that independent experts had been consulted on this question.

> "Two Geneva law professors, experts in international law and human rights, had been hired, and they had agreed that two years and a lifetime were acceptable and consistent with human rights and natural justice, as long as there were clauses in the rules which said that, if the athlete had absolutely no fault, he or she could not be punished with a suspension or period of ineligibility. They had added that something would need to be built into the rules to deal with the concept of proportionality, so that if the athlete was just slightly at fault, the ineligibility period would have to be less than two years. With regard to the concept of exceptional circumstances, this was a crack in the two-year door."

---

events, and at a maximum, one (1) year's ineligibility. Second violation: two (2) years' ineligibility. Third violation: lifetime ineligibility. Violations of the whereabouts rule may be punished by a minimum of 3 months and a maximum of 2 years (Art. 10.4.3) and trafficking or administration violations by a minimum of four years up to lifetime ineligibility (Art. 10.4.2).

[728] World Conference on Doping in Sport, plenary sessions, Summary Notes, p. 13.

Article 10.4.2 provides that violations of the anti-doping rules referred to in Articles 2.7 and 2.8, i.e. including a failed attempt to administer doping to an athlete, will be punished by a minimum of four years' suspension to life-long exclusion at the most. The same article further provides that any violation of an anti-doping rule involving a minor will be considered an exceptionally severe offence. If a member of the athlete's entourage is involved in the offence, he/she will be banned for life.

This concludes out overview of sanctions provided under the WADC for the use of substances and methods prohibited at all times (both in and out of competition), substances and methods prohibited in competition, and substances prohibited in particular sports.[729] In the next section, sanctions will be discussed which may be imposed for the use of conditionally prohibited substances and "soft" doping substances or, "specified substances" as they are called in the Prohibited List 2005. First, the situation as it existed prior to the adoption of the WADC will be discussed, to be followed by an explanation of how the WADC provides for sanctions in these cases.

3.   SANCTIONS FOR INDIVIDUAL ATHLETES IN CASES OF "SOFT DOPING"

As has done above for penalties imposed for "hard" doping, below the various types of sanctions for "soft" doping will be categorised. Not only was there a great variety of sanctions, but the substances which were considered to result in minor infractions also varied greatly.

3.1.   The various types of sanctions

3.1.1.   *First offence: advice; second offence: suspension of 3 months; third offence: suspension of 1 year*

International Tennis Federation – ITF

"Class III Prohibited Substances
(a) First Positive/Violation
     A player who is found through the procedures set forth in this Programme to test positive for any Class III Prohibited Substance, subject to minimum levels set by the Programme, should be advised by the ML of the medical effects and risks of such usage.
(b) Second Positive/Violation
     A player who commits a second offence under the Programme involving any Class III Prohibited Substance shall be suspended from participation in any and all ITF sanctioned or recognised tournaments or events for a three (3) month period.

---

[729] This distinction is made in the Prohibited List 2005 of the WADA of 23 September 2004.

(c) Third and Subsequent Positive/Violation
     A player who commits a third or subsequent offence under the Programme in-
     volving any Class III Prohibited Substance shall be suspended from participation
     in any and all ITF sanctioned or recognised tournaments or events for a one (1)
     year period."[730]

This offence was understood to include the use of caffeine, corticosteroids and
local anaesthetics. The use of ephedrine, phenyl-propanolamine, pseudo-ephedrine,
cathine (norpseudo-ephedrine), methyl-ephedrine, propyl-hexedrine, 1-methamphet-
amine and methoxyphenamine was allowed.

3.1.2. *First offence: public warning; second offence: minimum suspension of 2 years; third offence: life-long ban*

International Amateur Athletic Federation – IAAF

"If an athlete commits a doping offence, he will be ineligible for the following periods:
[...]
–   for an offence under Rule 60.1(i) or 60.1(iii) above, involving the substances in
     Part II of Schedule 1 of the 'Procedural Guidelines for Doping Control':-
     a.   first offence – shall be given a public warning and be disqualified from the
          competition at which the sample was collected;
     b.   second offence – for two years from the date of the provision of the sample;
     c.   third offence – for life."[731]

When the substances found in the athlete's body were part "hard" and part "soft"
doping substances, the sanction would be determined as if they were first category
substances.[732]
     These infractions included the use of stimulants and narcotic analgesics. The use
of codeine, dextromethorphan, dextropropoxyphene dihydrocodein, diphenoxylate,
ethyl morphine and pholcodine was permitted.

3.1.3. *First offence: suspension of 3 months; second offence: suspension of 1 year; third offence: life-long ban*

International Tennis Federation – ITF

"Class II Prohibited Substances
(a) First Positive/Violation
     A player who is found through the procedures set forth in this Programme to test
     positive for any Class II Prohibited Substance shall be suspended from participa-

---

[730] By Laws of ITF Limited, 8. Tennis Anti-Doping Programme, (M), subsection 3. The ATP and
WTA provisions were identical to those of the ITF.
[731] Rules and Regulations, Division III – Control of Drug Abuse, Art. 60, subsection 2 sub b.
[732] Rules and Regulations, Division III – Control of Drug Abuse, Art. 60, subsection 3.

tion in any and all ITF sanctioned or recognised tournaments or events for a (3) month period.

(b) Second Positive/Violation
A player who commits a second offence under the Programme involving a Class II Prohibited Substance shall be suspended from participation in any and all ITF sanctioned or recognised tournaments or events for a (1) one-year period.

(c) Third Positive/Violation
A player who commits a third offence under the Programme involving a Class II Prohibited Substance shall be permanently disqualified from participation in or association with any ITF sanctioned or recognised tournaments or events."[733]

This offence included the use of stimulants and narcotic analgesics. The use of codeine, dextromethorphan, dextropropoxyphene dihydrocodein, diphenoxylate, ethyl morphine, pholcodine and propoxyphene was allowed.

3.1.4. *First offence: maximum suspension of 3 months; second offence: maximum suspension of 2 years; third offence: possible life-long ban*

International Gymnastics Federation – FIG

"FIG Sanctions
Exclusion for a certain time period from all international competitions (Championships – Cups – Tournaments – Bilateral Competitions, etc.).
If the substance found is Ephedrine, Pseudoephedrine, Caffeine, Strychnine, Cannabis, Phenylpropanolamine, Beta-Blockers, Beta-2 agonists or other related substances or similar substances:
–   1st violation: maximum suspension of 3 months
–   2nd violation: maximum suspension of 2 years
–   3rd violation: possibility of complete exclusion."[734]

This offence included the use of ephedrine, pseudo- ephedrine, caffeine, strychnine, cannabis, phenylpropanolamine, beta-blockers, beta-2 agonists and related substances.

International Amateur Swimming Federation – FINA

"For a doping offence involving ephedrine, pseudoephedrine, phenylpropanolamine, cathine, caffeine, cannabinoids, and all other prohibited substances not otherwise set forth in DC 9.1.1 through DC 9.1.3:
First offence:
01. up to three (3) months' suspension.
Second offence:
02. three (3) months' to two (2) years' suspension.

---

[733] By Laws of ITF Limited, 8. Tennis Anti-Doping Programme, (M), subsection 2. The ATP and WTA provisions were identical to the ITF provisions.
[734] Medical Regulations, Doping Control Regulations, Art. 3.1.

Third offence:
03.   two (2) years' suspension to lifetime expulsion."[735]

This offence included the use of ephedrine, pseudo-ephedrine, phenylpropanolamine, cathine, caffeine, cannabinoids and related substances.

3.1.5. *First offence: maximum suspension of 90 days; second offence: suspension of 2 years*

International Triathlon Union – ITU

"The ITU Penalties for Doping Infractions are:
2.   For Ephedrine, phenylpropanolamine, caffeine, pseudoephedrine, strychnine and related compounds:
–   First Offense: up to a maximum of 90 days suspension.
–   Second Offense: up to a two year suspension."[736]

This offence was understood to include the use of ephedrine, phenylpropanolamine, caffeine, pseudoephedrine, strychnine and related substances.

3.1.6. *First offence: maximum suspension of 3 months and a fine; second offence: suspension of 6 months to 1 year and a fine; third offence: life-long ban and a fine*

International Cycling Union – UCI

"If a rider is found positive with respect to one of the substances in the special section on the list of doping agents referred to in Article 3 (3rd paragraph) above, the following disciplinary measures shall apply:
1)   Elite
MEN
1st offence:
–   disqualification + suspension for three months maximum,
–   fine of SFr. 2,000.S minimum to SFr. 4,000.S maximum.
2nd offence:
–   disqualification + suspension for six months minimum to one year maximum,
–   fine of SFr. 4,000.S minimum to SFr. 6,000.S maximum.
3rd offence:
–   disqualification + permanent debarment,
–   fine of SFr. 8,000.S .
WOMEN
1st offence:
–   disqualification + suspension for three months maximum,
–   fine of SFr. 1,000.S minimum to SFr. 2,000.S maximum.

---

[735] FINA Doping Control Rules, Art. DC 9.1.4.
[736] ITU Doping Control Rules and Procedural Guidelines, 4. ITU Out-of-competition Testing, Art. 7.2.

2... 2nd offence:
- disqualification + suspension for six months minimum to one year maximum,
- fine of SFr. 2,000.S minimum to SFr. 5,000.S maximum.

3rd offence:
- disqualification + permanent debarment,
- a fine of SFr. 8,000.S .

2) Under 23

1st offence:
- disqualification + suspension for three months maximum,
- fine of SFr. 500.S minimum to SFr. 1,000.S maximum.

2nd offence:
- disqualification + suspension for six months minimum to one year maximum,
- fine of SFr. 1,500.S minimum to SFr. 3,000.S maximum.

3rd offence:
- disqualification + permanent debarment,
- a fine of SFr. 8,000.S .

3) Other riders

1st offence:
- disqualification + suspension for three months maximum,

2nd offence:
- disqualification + suspension for six months minimum to one year maximum,

3rd offence:
- disqualification + permanent debarment.
- If, in the case of a second offence, either the first offence or the second offence be an offence referred to in this section, the duration of the suspension to be handed down with respect to the second offence shall be determined according to Article 90, para. 1."[737]

This offence included the use of light stimulants [...], narcotic analgesics, local anaesthetics, beta 2 agonists and marijuana.[738]

3.1.7. *First offence: maximum suspension of 3 months; second offence: suspension of 2 years; third offence: minimum suspension of 3 years*

International Skating Union – ISU

"Ephedrine, phenylpropanolamine, pseudoephedrine, caffeine, strychnine and related substances:
- 3 months for the first offence,
- 2 years for the second offence,
- at least 3 years for the third offence beginning at the day of the sample taking."[739]

This offence included the use of ephedrine, phenylpropanolamine, pseudoephedrine, caffeine, strychnine and related substances.

---

[737] UCI Cycling Regulations, Part XIV, Antidoping Examination Regulations, Chapter VIII, Art. 90(2).
[738] List of categories of doping substances and methods, IV. Substances referred to in Art. 90(2) of the UCI Antidoping Examination Regulations.
[739] General Regulations, I. Doping, Rule 139, subsection 9 sub b).

3.1.8. *First offence: maximum suspension of 3 months; second offence:
        suspension of 2 years (possibly longer); third offence: ban of 5 years
        to life*

International Hockey Federation – FIH

"Doping, no matter what the circumstances, and in particular whether or not the athlete was at fault, shall automatically result in the disqualification of the athlete for the
remainder of the event during which the testing was conducted (provisional suspension). The athlete is still subject to further disciplinary actions under this Doping
Policy.[740]

1st Violation

Athlete

If testing reveals the presence of ephedrine, phenyl-propanolamine, pseudo-ephedrine,
caffeine, strychnine, cannabis or related substances, the FIH Disciplinary Committee
shall pronounce a suspension from all events for a maximum of three months from the
starting date of the provisional suspension; any interruption of this suspension shall be
deducted from the total.

[...]

In either case, the FIH Disciplinary Committee may pronounce a suspension for a
longer period, but which applies only to certain events to be specified.

[...]

2nd Violation

Athlete

If testing reveals the presence of ephedrine, phenyl-propanolamine, pseudo-ephedrine,
caffeine, strychnine, cannabis or related substances, the FIH Disciplinary Committee
shall pronounce a suspension from all events for a maximum of two years from the
starting date of the provisional suspension; any interruption of this suspension shall be
deducted from the total.

[...]

In either case, the FIH Disciplinary Committee may pronounce a suspension for a
longer period, but which applies only to certain events to be specified.

[...]

Further Violations

Upon a third violation, no matter what the substance in question, the FIH Disciplinary
Committee shall pronounce a suspension for a minimum of five years, with the option
of suspension for life."[741]

Although the FIH Doping Policy contained a provision stating that the FIH
recognised the IOC Medical Code, the FIH elected not to adopt the IOC sanctions.[742]

---

[740] FIH Doping Policy, Art. 12.2 Athlete.
[741] FIH Doping Policy, Art. 12.3 Disciplinary Sanctions.
[742] FIH Doping Policy, Art. 3. I.O.C. Medical Code: "The I.O.C. has published a detailed Medical
Code against Doping in Sport setting out testing procedures, dope classes, a national anti-doping
programme, sample analysis, out-of-competition testing, rights and responsibilities of sport organisations

The offence described included the use of ephedrine, phenyl-propanolamine, pseudo-ephedrine, caffeine, strychnine, cannabis and related substances.

3.1.9. *First offence: maximum suspension of 3 months; second offence: suspension of 2 years; third offence: life-long ban*

International Olympic Committee – IOC

> "In cases of a positive result for ephedrine, phenylpropanolamine, pseudoephedrine, caffeine, strychnine and related compounds, a maximum suspension of three months.[743]
> The penalty for a second infraction by a competitor pursuant to the IOC Medical Code shall be disqualification, if the infraction occurred during a competition, plus, [...] in cases referred to in paragraph (2) of Article III, suspension for two years and for any subsequent infraction, a life ban."[744]

In this provision, "soft" doping was understood to include the use of ephedrine, phenylpropanolamine, pseudoephedrine, caffeine, strychnine and related substances.

International Badminton Federation – IBF

> "In accordance with the IBF's declared policy of abhorrence of doping, a player guilty of contravening the IOC requirements shall be liable to a penalty as provided for in Chapter IX of the 1995 IOC Medical Code or any replacement thereof."[745]

International Rowing Federation – FISA

> "The penalty will be determined taking into account the seriousness of the offence according to an established scale as follows:
> Use of any other substance comprising the list of prohibited substances defined in Article 1.3.:
> Maximum suspension of three months for a first offence,
> Suspension for two years for a second offence,
> Life ban for a third offence."[746]

"Soft" doping substances were here considered to be substances described as such in the IOC list.[747]

---

and guidelines for sanction and penalties for breaches thereof. The FIH has adopted this Medical Code and will act in accordance with its directives and recommendations. Amendments, updates, additions and medical control guides relating to the Medical Code and confirmed by the I.O.C. will be similarly adopted."

[743] IOC Medical Code, Chapter IX, Art. III, subsection 2.

[744] IOC Medical Code, Chapter IX, Art. IV.

[745] Competition Regulations, Doping and Femininity Control, Art. 23.1.

[746] By Law to Rules 80 to 83 – Doping, Art. 9.3, sub (b).

[747] By Law to Rules 80 to 83 – Doping, Art. 1.3: "List of Prohibited Substances. The list of prohibited substances is the official list of the IOC valid at the moment of the taking of a sample."

International Baseball Association – IBA

"Only in case of a positive result for ephedrine, phenylpropanolamine, pseudoephedrine, caffeine, strychnine and related compounds the suspension is a maximum of three months.[748]
In case of a second positive result for the above-mentioned substances the suspension will be for two years. For any subsequent infraction, a life ban."[749]

This (minor) doping offence was understood to include the use of ephedrine, phenylpropanolamine, pseudoephedrine, caffeine, strychnine and related substances.

International Basketball Federation – FIBA

With regard to the use of sympathomimetic amines (ephedrine, phenylpropanolamine, pseudoephedrine) and codeine (when given orally for medical reasons together with decongestants and/or antihistamines), the President of the Medical Council of FIBA (or his representative) shall consult with two members of the Medical Council in order to study the possibility of "medical justification." In this case, the player is subject to:
– suspension for a maximum of 3 months for the 1st infraction.
– suspension for 2 years for the 2nd infraction.
– a lifelong ban for the 3rd infraction."[750]

This (minor) doping offence included the use of sympathomimetic amines (ephedrine, phenylpropanolamine, pseudoephedrine) and codeine (when administered for medical reasons). The President of the FIBA Medical Council had to consult two members of the Medical Council to form an opinion on possible "medical justifications."

International Canoe Federation – ICF

"For an offence under Rule 6.1.1. or 6.1.3. above involving substances such as ephedrine, phenylpropanolamine and codeine, administered orally as cough suppressor or painkiller in association with decongestants and/or anti-histamines:
first offence: for maximum three months from the date of the provision of the sample;
second offence: for two years from the date of the sample;
third offence: for life."[751]

This offence included the use of ephedrine, phenylpropanolamine and also codeine in certain circumstances.

International Union for Modern Pentathlon – UIPM

"Sanctions shall be these established by the IOC Rules and adopted by the UIPM Executive Board.[752]

---

[748] Anti Doping Rules, Chapter 13, Art. 13.5.
[749] Anti Doping Rules, Chapter 13, Art. 13.6.
[750] Regulations Governing Doping Control, Art. 6.6.2.
[751] ICF Doping Rules, Art. 2.2.
[752] UIPM Medical Rulebook – Anti-Doping Controls, Rule 7.8.

The penalties are these established by the I.O.C. Rules and adopted by the UIPM Executive Board."[753]

The UIPM could also conduct an alcohol test. If this came up positive (over 0,1g/l) the athlete had to take a compulsory blood test. If the result of this was also positive the athlete would be punished in accordance with Rule 7.8 cited above.[754]

World Taekwondo Federation – WTF

"Ephedrine, Phenylpropanolamine, Pseudoephedrine, Codeine, etc. (when administered orally for medical purposes):
Maximum 3 months for the first offense,
2 years for the second offense,
Life ban for the third offense."[755]

This offence included the use of ephedrine, phenyl-propanolamine, pseudo-ephedrine, caffeine, strychnine or related substances taken for medical purposes.

International Table Tennis Federation – ITTF

"If the following substances are used: ephedrine, phenylpropanolamine, and all other banned substances or practices, then the player shall be banned from entering any competitions organized under the auspices of the ITTF and/or the IOC for a period of three (3) months for the first offence, two (2) years for the second offence, for life for the third offence."[756]

This offence included the use of ephedrine, phenylpropanolamine, and all other prohibited substances and methods.

International Archery Federation – FITA

"Ephedrine, phenylpropanolamime, pseudoephedrine, etc. (when administered orally for medical purposes in association with decongestants)
Maximum 3 months for the first offense;
2 years for the second offense;
Life ban for the third offense."[757]

This offence included the use of among others ephedrine, phenyl-propanolamine, pseudo-ephedrine, again for medical purposes.

An athlete who tested positive for alcohol or cannabinoids would be removed from the competition; a penalty might also be imposed.

---

[753] Modern Pentathlon Competition Rules, Art. 1.38, subsection 9.
[754] UIPM Medical Rulebook – Anti-Doping Controls, Rule 8.2 Alcohol Test.
[755] Regulations For Doping Control, Art. 11.2 sub B.
[756] Anti-Doping Regulations, Art. 7.1.3.
[757] Appendix 4, Doping Control Procedures, Art. 12.2.2.

In accordance with the rules of the international sports federations in some sports, controls could also be held to detect the use of beta-blockers. Positive results could give rise to sanctions.[758]

International Volleyball Federation – FIVB

"A player found positive for ephedrine, phenylpropanolamine, codeine (when administered orally as a cough suppressant or pain-killer in association with decongestants and/or antihistamines) is sanctioned:
maximum 3 months' suspension for the first offence,
2-year suspension for the second offence,
life ban for the third offence."[759]

This offence included the use of ephedrine, phenylpropanolamine and codeine administered for certain ailments together with decongestants and/or antihistamines.
    In accordance with the IFs and the responsible authorities, ethanol tests could also be conducted. Positive results could lead to sanctions.[760]

International Sailing Federation – ISAF

"Sailors in Olympic Classes, when found without doubt to have tested positive for the presence of banned drugs on the ISAF/IOC list, will be subject to the scale of penalties agreed between the IOC and the International Governing Bodies of sport."[761]

World Curling Federation – WCF

"Individual Penalty
1. The penalty for a first infraction by a competitor shall be disqualification for the duration of the WCF Championship, plus:
2. in cases of a positive result for ephedrine phenipropanolamine, pseudo ephedrine caffeine, strychnine and related compounds, a maximum suspension of three months.
3. The penalty for a second infraction by a competitor pursuant to the IOC Medical Code and the present by-law shall be disqualification, if the infraction occurred during a competition, plus, [...] in cases referred to in paragraph (2) of this Article, suspension for two years and, for any subsequent infraction, a life ban."[762]

This offence included the use of ephedrine, pseudoephedrine, caffeine, strychnine and related substances.

---

[758] Appendix 4, Doping Control Procedures, 15 List of Doping Classes and Methods Prohibited by the IOC Medical Commission, III. Classes of drugs subject to certain restrictions.

[759] Medical Regulations. 2. Antidoping Control Regulations, Art. 2.6.3.

[760] Appendix 4 – FIVB Medical Commission: Definition of doping and list of prohibited classes of substances and prohibited methods, Classes of drugs subject to certain restrictions, A).

[761] 1998 ISAF Regulations, Medical Code d 17, Procedures, Art. 3.9.

[762] By Law No. 8 Doping, VI Sanctions and Penalties, Art. 13, sub B).

International Ice Hockey Federation – IIHF

"If a player has tested positive for a doping offense or has refused to submit to doping control tests or if any player or other person has attempted to manipulate or is deemed to have manipulated the results of a test (hereinafter referred to as 'manipulation'), the following shall apply.

A. Players

If the IIHF Directorate or the IIHF Council finds a player tested positive for doping or in the case of refusal of a player to submit to the doping tests, the following sanctions shall apply:

c)   A player with a positive doping test must be sanctioned. Sanctions for the various substances will be as follows and apply to:

   –   Ephedrine, Phenylpropanolamine, pseudoephedrine, caffeine, strychnine, marijuana and related compounds:

At the first infraction of doping regulations – a three month in-season suspension from participating in any competition of a member national association or of the IIHF. The suspension starts from the day of detection of the positive doping test. The applicable playing season shall start on September 1st and end on April 30th, except for the men's World Senior Championship Pool A which ends with the conclusion of that championship. If the suspension spans two seasons the player will also be suspended during the period between these seasons.

At the second infraction of the doping regulations – a two year suspension for all games starting from the day of detection of the positive doping test.

At the third infraction of the doping regulations – a life time ban from all games."[763]

This offence included the use of ephedrine, phenylpropanolamine, pseudoephedrine, caffeine, strychnine, marijuana or related substances.

The three months' suspension for a first offence was an "in-season" suspension, which meant that the suspension would run between 1 September and 30 April, apart from where the men's World Senior Championships Pool A were concerned.

International Luge Federation – FIL

"The penalty for a first infraction by a competitor shall be disqualification, if the infraction occurred during a competition, plus:

2)   in cases of a positive result for ephedrine, phenylpropanolamine, pseudoephedrine, caffeine, strychnine and related compounds, a maximum suspension of three months.[764]

[...]

The penalty for a second infraction by a competitor pursuant to the FIL Medical Code shall be disqualification, if the infraction occurred during a competition, plus, in cases referred to in [...] paragraph (2) of Article III, suspension for two years and for any subsequent infraction, a life ban."[765]

---

[763] By Laws, 1400 Medical Controls (Doping), 1407. Sanctions with Doping.
[764] Supplement 4 – Medical Code, Chapter VII – Penalties for Infractions, Art. III.
[765] Supplement 4 – Medical Code, Chapter VII – Penalties for Infractions, Art. IV.

This offence included the use of ephedrine, phenylpropanolamine, pseudo-ephedrine, caffeine, strychnine and related substances.

3.1.10. *First offence: suspension of 3 months; second offence: suspension of 2 years; third offence: life-long ban*

International Fencing Federation – FIE

"Les sanctions sont obligatoirement les suivantes:
[...]
2. Ephédrine, phénypropanolamine, codéine, etc. (même lorsque administrées oralement comme calmant de la toux ou de la douleur en association avec des décongestionnants et/ou des antihistaminiques):
– 3 mois pour un premier délit,
– 2 ans pour un deuxième délit,
– suspension à vie pour un troisième délit."[766]

This offence included the use of ephedrine, phenylpropanolamine and codeine, taken orally as a cough depressant or painkiller together with decongestants and/or antihistamines.

International Judo Federation – IJF

"In case of a positive check, the sanctions are taken by the IJF Executive Committee; before deciding on sanctions, the Executive Committee must familiarize itself with the defense dossier or with the reality of therapeutic justification.
For a first infraction the incriminated competitor is disqualified from the competition in question. He is removed from the standings. He must return his medal and any other prize received at the prize ceremony, plus
[...]
2) in case of a positive result for ephedrine, phenylpropanolamine, pseudoephedrine, caffeine, strychnine and related compounds he will be suspended for three months.
The sanction is the same if therapeutic justification is not firmly established, or if it is doubtful or incomplete.[767]
The penalty for a second infraction, in cases referred to in paragraph 2 of Article 16, will be a suspension for two years and for any subsequent infraction, a life ban."[768]

This offence included the use of ephedrine, phenylpropanolamine, pseudo-ephedrine, caffeine, strychnine and related substances.

---

[766] Reglement Technique, Titre Cinquieme, Code Disciplinaire Des Epreuves, Chapitre 6 – Dopage, "1. Regles Generales, t.129 sub p) Sanctions."
[767] Regulations and Procedure Concerning Drug Tests, Art. 16. Sanctions.
[768] Regulations and Procedure Concerning Drug Tests, Art. 18. Repeat offenders.

International Bobsleigh and Tobogganing Federation – FIBT

> "The F.I.B.T. Executive Committee shall impose the following penalties in case of a positive result according to items 1 and 3 of the F.I.B.T. Doping Control Regulations.
> [...]
> If the use of ephedrine and its derivates has been proved, the athlete becomes ineligible:
> –   for three months in the case of a first-time contravention,
> –   for two years in the case of a second contravention and,
> –   lifelong after a further and imposed second punishment.
> The athlete concerned and the other members of the crew shall be disqualified from the sports event concerned."[769]

This offence included the use of ephedrine and its derivatives.

International Biathlon Union – IBU

> "A ban of a maximum of three months shall be imposed on athletes who are found guilty, under the application of the IBU Anti-doping, Blood Test and Gender Verification Rules to have been doped with ephedrine, phenylpropanolamine, pseudoephedrine, caffeine, strychnine or equivalent substances during or out of competition. Competitors who are found guilty a second time of having used one of the substances will be banned for a two years period."[770]

This offence included the use of ephedrine, phenyl-propanolamine, pseudo-ephedrine, caffeine, strychnine or related substances.

3.1.11.   *First offence: suspension of 6 months; second offence: suspension of 2 years; third offence: life-long ban*

International Weightlifting Federation – IWF

> "Subject to other provisions in this section, sanctions will apply for the following periods:
> b)   a six (6) months suspension for a first offence involving a substance of the IOC Medical Code's Prohibited Classes of Substances and Prohibited Methods, other than those listed above in (a), a second offence is a two (2) years suspension and a third offence is a life suspension."[771]

For every doping offence which came to light in a doping control carried out by the IWF the national federation had to pay to the IWF a fine of US$ 1000 besides the costs of the control.[772]

---

[769] Doping Control Regulations, Arts. 9.1 en 9.2.
[770] IBU Disciplinary Rules, Art. 5.7.1.
[771] IWF Anti-Doping Policy, Art. 14.2.
[772] IWF Anti-Doping Policy, Art. 14.5.

In accordance with the procedure of the International Sports Federations and the responsible authorities tests could be carried out for ethanol. Ethanol use could lead to sanctions. Beta-blockers could also be tested for in certain sports, in accordance with the rules of the International Sports Federations, and again, the results could give rise to sanctions.

3.1.12. *First offence: maximum suspension of 3 months; second offence: minimum suspension of 3 years; third offence: life-long ban*

International Softball Federation – ISF

> "Penalties for testing positive:
> 1. A minimum of two years disqualification from all ISF competition for the first offense.
> EXCEPTION: In cases of a positive result for ephedrine, phenylpropanolamine, pseudoephedrine, caffeine, strychnine and related compounds, a maximum suspension of three (3) months.
> 2. A minimum of three years for a second offense.
> 3. Life ban for third a offense."[773]

3.1.13. *First offence: suspension of 3 months; second offence: suspension of 4 years; third offence: life-long ban*

International Paralympic Committee – IPC

> "An athlete who has committed a minor doping infraction will be ineligible to participate in activities organized, convened, held or sanctioned by IPC, an International Federation or member thereof for the following time periods:
> –   1st infraction   - 3 months
> –   2nd infraction   - 4 years
> –   3rd infraction   - life"[774]

This (minor) doping offence was understood to include the use of ephedrine, phenylpropanalomine, codeine etc. when administered orally for medical purposes together with decongestants and/or antihistamines, as they are occasionally defined by the International Paralympic Committee.[775]
An athlete who committed a minor doping infraction after a major doping infraction would be punished as if he had committed a second major doping infraction. An athlete who committed a major doping infraction after a minor doping infraction would be punished in accordance with the penalty provisions for a first major doping infraction.[776] Athletes were in any event always disqualified.[777]

---

[773] ISF Code, Art. 15 – International competition and world championships, 15.11.
[774] Doping, 8.2 Penalties For Doping Infractions, Art. 2.1, sub c.
[775] Doping, 8.2 Penalties For Doping Infractions, Art. 1.2 sub 2.
[776] Doping, 8.2 Penalties For Doping Infractions, Art. 2.1, sub d en e.
[777] Doping, 8.2 Penalties For Doping Infractions, Art. 2.2.

3.1.14.   *First offence: possible suspension of 2 years; second offence: possible disqualification for life*

International Amateur Boxing Association – AIBA

> "If in the investigation into a doping offence officials are also found guilty, sanctions may be: temporary suspension for a period of not less than one year, or, suspension for lifetime."[778]

The AIBA did not distinguish between "hard" and "soft" doping offences. Any boxer violating the AIBA anti-doping rules would be disqualified and suspended.[779] Codeine, dextromethorphan, dihydrocodein, diphenoxylate and pholcodine were permitted substances.[780]

3.1.15.   *Malice: suspension of 3 months to 2 years and a fine; no malice: suspension of 1 month to 3 months and a fine*

International Equestrian Federation – FEI

> "The finding on analysis of a Prohibited Substance as defined in Art. 146.2. will always entail the disqualification of the horse and competitor from the event and the forfeiture of any prize money won in the same event.[781]
> The finding on analysis of a Prohibited Substance as defined in Art. 146.2 is presumed to be a deliberate attempt of the Person Responsible to affect the performance of the horse and will entail the suspension of the Person Responsible from 3 to 24 months. A fine of CHF 1,000.- to 15,000.- can also be imposed.[782]
> If the Person Responsible can prove that it was not a deliberate attempt to affect the performance of the horse or that the findings are the results of legitimate treatment of the horse or of one or several parts of his body, the sanction may entail a fine up to CHF 15,000.-, but a suspension from 1 to 3 months may also be imposed.
> In the case of repeated violations of Art. 146.2, paragraph 5.2 will always be applied."[783]

---

[778] Articles of Association and Rules for International Competitions and Tournaments, Art. XXVIII – Disciplinary Action, C. Doping, sub 3.

[779] Articles of Association and Rules for International Competitions and Tournaments, Rule XXII, sub B.

[780] Doping Regulations of AIBA, Art. I, sub B.

[781] General Regulations, Art. 174 sub 5.1. Art. 146, subsection 2: "Any horse found to have a Prohibited Substance in any of its tissues, body fluids or excreta at an event as the result of a Medication Test, is automatically disqualified, together with the competitor, from all competitions at that event and the classification adjusted accordingly, unless the Ground Jury has authorised the horse to continue in the event in accordance with paragraph 3. below. If the disqualified horse and competitor are members of a team, the rest of the team is not disqualified."

[782] General Regulations, Art. 174 sub 5.2.

[783] General Regulations, Art. 174 sub 5.3.

3.1.16. *Discretionary determination of the sanction*

International Association Football Federation – FIFA

> "If specimen 'B' proves positive, the case shall be submitted to the relevant FIFA organising committee. This committee shall investigate the case if necessary with the help of specialists and shall determine the degree of responsibility of the player and/or persons belonging to the national association. The results of their investigation shall be the basis for determining appropriate sanctions."[784]

The FIFA organising committee established the degree of responsibility of the player. The result of the committee's investigation constituted the basis for imposing a proportionate sanction.

The use of cocaine could be allowed to relieve pain. Corticosteroids could only be used if applied locally (otologic, ophthalmologic or dermatologic), by inhalation (asthma, allergic rhinitis) or in local or intra-articular injections.[785]

International Sport Shooting Federation – ISSF

> "At the conclusion of the inquiry, the members of the Commission of Investigation and Inquiry, who heard the shooter, shall forward a detailed and objective report to the Executive Committee of the UIT.
>
> The Executive Committee of the UIT shall study the report and related documents and may again give the shooter the opportunity to submit his point of view orally or in writing, if he requests to do so, at his own cost.
>
> The Executive Committee will decide any penalty to be imposed at its next meeting.
>
> Penalties can apply to:
>
> The shooter
>
> The penalty will be determined, taking into account the seriousness of the offense by applying the IOC Medical Code.
>
> Apart from the penalties applied according to the IOC Medical Code, the shooter shall be disqualified from the competition, even if no fault or negligence is established on the shooter's part."[786]

International Ski Federation – FIS

> "If an athlete is found to have committed a doping offence, and this is confirmed after a hearing or the athlete waives his right to a hearing, then he shall be sanctioned. In addition, where testing was conducted in a competition, the athlete shall be disqualified from that competition and the result amended accordingly.[787]
>
> [...]
>
> When a doping offence is proved (after the mandatory hearing), the FIS Council will be informed and will decide the appropriate sanction(s)."[788]

---

[784] Doping Control Regulations for FIFA Competitions (Except for FIFA World Cup), II. Doping Control Organisation, 8. Procedure If Specimen "B" Proves Positive, Art. 39.

[785] Doping Control Regulations for FIFA Competitions (Except for FIFA World Cup), Ch. I.

[786] Anti-Doping Regulations, 8. Disciplinary measures.

[787] FIS Doping Rules, Rule 5, subsection 3.

[788] FIS Doping Rules, Rule 6.

The use of alcohol was prohibited in all skiing competitions. The FIS Medical Committee could decide to carry out breath and blood tests. The FIS required a zero level of alcohol during competitions; positive results could give rise to sanctions.

Marijuana was also prohibited in all skiing events. The FIS considered findings below the threshold value of 15 ng/ml acceptable; above this level, sanctions would be imposed.[789]

3.1.17. *First offence: suspension of 2 years; second offence: suspension of 4 years*

International Handball Federation – IHF

> "In case of a proven doping offence, the players concerned are disqualified from all further tournament matches. The players are also banned from national and international matches for a period of up to two years.
>
> Should a player be in violation of the Anti-Doping Regulations for the second time, the player is banned from national and international matches for a period of four years."[790]

In the Regulations Concerning Penalties and Fines it was again provided that doping offenders would be disqualified and excluded from participation in national and international competitions for a period of two years. Here, no provision was given for a second offence.

3.1.18. *First offence: suspension of 2 years; second offence: life-long ban*

International Amateur Wrestling Federation – FILA

> "In accordance with Article 10 of the Constitution, any wrestler who refuses to submit to the doping test shall be considered as having tested positive and will be banned from the entire competition, as well as being banned from participating in international events for a period of two years. Moreover, if the examinations or tests carried out under the conditions laid down in the FILA Medical Regulations give a positive result, the doped wrestler shall be disqualified for the entire competition, and shall have his results cancelled, without prejudice to any penalty banning him from international contests for a period of two years. If he offends again, the wrestler at fault shall be banned for life."[791]

Codeine phosphate and medication containing codeine phosphate were considered prohibited substances.

---

[789] List of Banned Doping Classes and Methods, Examples and Explanations, 1. Doping Classes, 1.6 and 1.7.

[790] Anti-Doping Regulations, 11. Sanctions.

[791] Disciplinary Regulations, Art. 13 – Doping Test.

3.1.19. *Doping: warning, ban, fine and suspension of 1 to 3 months; intentional*
         doping: ban, fine and suspension of 2 to 8 years

International Olympic Committee – IOC

"In a case of doping, the penalties for a first offence are as follows:
a)   if the Prohibited Substance used is ephedrine, phenylpropanolamine, pseudoephe-
     drine, caffeine, strychnine or related substances:
     i)   a warning;
     ii)   a ban on participation in one or several sports competitions in any capacity
           whatsoever;
     iii) a fine of up to US$ 100,000;
     iv)   suspension from any competition for a period of one to six months.[792]
In case of
a)   intentional doping;
[...]
The sanctions are as follows:
a)   if the Prohibited Substance used is ephedrine, phenylpropanolamine, pseudoephe-
     drine, caffeine or strychnine and related substances:
     i)   a ban on participation in one or several sports competitions in any capacity
           whatsoever;
     ii)   a fine of up to US$ 100,000;
     iii) suspension from any competition for a period of two to eight years."[793]

This offence included the use of ephedrine, phenylpropanolamine, pseudoephedrine, caffeine, strychnine and related substances.

3.2.   **Table of "soft-doping" sanctions**

Internat. federations	Sanctions		
	1st offence	2nd offence	3rd offence
ITF	advice	suspension of 3 months	suspension of 1 year
IAAF	public warning	minimum suspension of 2 years	life-long suspension
ITF	suspension of 3 months	suspension of 1 year	life-long suspension
FIG, FINA	maximum suspension of 3 months	maximum suspension of 2 years	possible life-long ban
ITU	maximum suspension of 90 days	suspension of 2 years	
UCI	maximum suspension of 3 monthts + fine	suspension of 6 months to 1 year + fine	life-long suspension + fine
ISU	maximum suspension of 3 months	suspension of 2 years	minimum suspension of 3 years

---

[792] OMADC, Chapter II, The Offence of Doping and its Punishment, Art. 3, subsection 1.
[793] OMADC, Chapter II, The Offence of Doping and its Punishment, Art. 3, subsection 2.

Internat. federations	Sanctions		
FIH	maximum suspension of 3 months	suspension of 2 years (possibly longer)	suspension of 5 years to life
IOC (MC), IBF, FISA, IBA, FIBA, ICF, UIPM, WTF, ITTF, FITA, FIVB, ISAF, WCF, IIHF, FIL	maximum suspension of 3 months	suspension of 2 years	life-long ban
FIE, IJF, FIBT, IBU	suspension of 3 months	suspension of 2 years	life-long ban
IWF	suspension of 6 months	suspension of 2 years	life-long ban
ISF	maximum suspension of 3 months	minimum suspension of 3 years	life-long ban
IPC	suspension of 3 months	suspension of 4 years	life-long ban
AIBA	possible suspension of 2 years	possible life-long disqualification	
FEI	malice: suspension of 3 months to 2 years + fine no malice: suspension of 1 month and 3 months + fine		
FIFA, ISSF, FIS	discretionary determination of tha sanction		
IHF	suspension of 2 years	suspension of 4 years	
FILA	suspension of 2 years	life-long ban	
IOC (OMADC)	doping: warning + ban + fine + suspension of 1 to 3 months Intentional doping: ban + fine + suspension of 2 to 8 years		

3.3. Sanctions according to the WADC

Article 10.3 of the WADC concerning specified substances provides that:

> "The Prohibited List may identify specified substances which are particularly suscep-
> tible to unintentional anti-doping rules violations because of their general availability
> in medicinal products or which are less likely to be successfully abused as doping
> agents. Where an Athlete can establish that the use of such a specified substance was
> not intended to enhance sport performance, the period of Ineligibility found in Article
> 10.2 shall be replaced with the following:
> First violation: at a minimum, a warning and reprimand and no period of ineligibil-
>   ity from future events, and at a maximum, one (1) year's ineligibil-
>   ity.
> Second violation: two (2) years ineligibility.
> Third violation: lifetime ineligibility."

Article 10.3 further provides that the athlete shall have the opportunity in each case,
before a period of ineligibility is imposed, to establish the basis for eliminating or
reducing (in the case of a second or third violation) this sanction as provided in
Article 10.5. By this rule, which was already laid down in the OMADC, a measure
of flexibility is introduced in the punishment of athletes who have tested positive as
a result of their negligent use of ordinary medication containing a prohibited stimulant. Reduction of the penalty is only possible in the case of a second or third violation, because the penalty for a first offence already leaves sufficient room to take
the athlete's degree of fault into account.

With the adoption of the WADC, consensus was finally reached on the question of which substances should be considered as "soft doping." Pursuant to the WADA Prohibited List 2005 these are ephedrine, L-methylamphetamine, methylephedrine, cannabinoids, all inhaled Beta-2 agonists except clenbuterol, probenecid, all glucocorticosteroids, all beta blockers and alcohol.

4. SANCTIONS FOR SOME ANCILLARY DOPING INFRACTIONS

Failure to report for in-competition doping control or failure to cooperate in the control is considered a doping offence. The same is true of failure to inform the proper authorities of one's out-of-competition whereabouts.[794] According to Article 10.4.1 WADC the penalties provided for under Article 10.2 shall apply to in-competition violations. This means that for a first offence a two-year ban may be imposed and for a second offence a life-time ban. The WADC contains a separate provision dealing with whereabouts violations and missed tests out of competition, but despite the fact that the drafters of the WADC considered out-of-competition controls to be a core element of the doping control system, the penalties for frustrating such controls are less severe than for frustrating their in-competition counterparts. The sanction for a first offence is three months' to two years' ineligibility in accordance with the rules of the anti-doping organisation whose test the athlete missed or to which it failed to disclose his/her (correct) whereabouts. The WADC further provides that the ineligibility period for subsequent violations of Article 2.4 is as established in the rules of the relevant anti-doping organisation. From the point of view of harmonisation, the discretion which the WADC allows to the various anti-doping organisations is remarkable, especially considering the comment to Article 10.4.3 that "the whereabouts and missed test policies of different Anti-Doping Organizations may vary considerably, particularly at the outset as these policies are being put into place." Instead of establishing uniform sanctions from the moment of the WADC's entry into force, "[...] considerable flexibility has been provided for sanctioning these anti-doping rule violations." Violations of Article 2.4 are not covered by the provisions of Article 10.5 where these concern the elimination or reduction of the ineligibility based on exceptional circumstances, as that article, according to the comment to Article 10.5 WADC, "[...] applies only to the identified anti-doping rule violations because these violations may be based on conduct that is not intentional or purposeful. Violations under Article 2.4 [...] are not included, because the sanction for violations of Article 2.4 [...] already builds in sufficient discretion to allow consideration of the athlete's degree of fault."

---

[794] See *supra* Chapter 3, Section 2.2.1.

5.   TEAM SANCTIONS

5.1. **Primary team sanctions**

The FIH anti-doping rules allowed for the disqualification of a team whose members had tested positive.[795] Furthermore, the FIH Disciplinary Committee could exclude such a team or a national federation from competition for two years. A second doping offence might give rise to a five-year suspension of the team.[796] These sanctions firmly appeared to be primary team sanctions, as the positive test result of only one team member could not lead to these sanctions. In fact, the sanctions ran parallel to any sanctions imposed on the individual athletes. On the other hand, it does not seem likely that these provisions were drafted for the particular occurrence that all team members were found to have used doping. Perhaps the provisions concerned the situation that all team members refused to submit to doping control.

5.2. **Secondary team sanctions**

Some international federations' doping regulations provided that the use by one or several team members of prohibited substances or methods could have consequences for the team as a whole. The repercussions for the team could be many: the competition could, for example, be declared lost or the entire team could be disqualified.

This type of secondary team sanction affects players differently per sport. First of all, there is the distinction between individual sports and team sports. Team sanctions of course mainly apply to team sports, but is possible that an individual sport has team events, such as relay teams in swimming or athletics. It is also possible in purely individual sports, such as boxing, fencing, judo or wrestling, that national or club teams compete in chosen events. The second distinction is between team sports played in relatively large teams, such as football and field hockey, and those played in teams which may be as small as two, such as curling and beach volleyball.

---

[795] FIH Doping Policy, 12. Sanctions, Art. 12.2.
[796] Disciplinary Sanctions
1st Violation
Team or National Association
The FIH Disciplinary Committee may suspend a team or National Association from participation in any FIH approved event for a maximum of two years from the starting date of the provisional suspension; any interruption of this suspension shall be deducted from the total.
2nd Violation
Team or National Association
The FIH Disciplinary Committee may suspend a team or National Association from participation in any FIH approved event for a maximum of five years from the starting date of the provisional suspension; any interruption of this suspension shall be deducted from the total.
FIH Doping Policy, 12. Sanctions, Art. 12.3.

Some fourteen international federations did not provide for secondary team sanctions,[797] even though some of them represented obvious team sports.[798]

5.2.1. *The match is declared lost*

Declaring a match lost is a typical sports sanction which could be equally imposed on the team mates of the athlete who had committed a doping offence. It did not entail any kind of ban or ineligibility for these team mates.

The penalty was included in the IOC Medical Code which provided that the competition in which a member of a team committed a doping offence should be declared lost for the entire team.[799] The IPC used a similar provision.[800] The ISAF and the FIL had copied the rules from the IOC Medical Code into their own anti-doping regulations.

The IBA added to the sanction by determining that all the games in which the doped player had participated with his team after he/she had been asked to report to doping control had to be considered lost.[801]

The FIBA rule declaring the competition lost for the entire team due to a doping offence of one of its members was worded somewhat unusually. It stated that if a team was found guilty of a second doping offence during the same tournament, the entire team would be disqualified, not be allowed to finish the tournament and the match would be declared lost, as would all matches which had been played already.[802] What was strange about this rule was that, on the one hand, no provisions were made for the occurrence of the first doping offence (which did not seem to affect the team), but, on the other hand, all matches played during the tournament were forfeited, whereas it was entirely possible that the doped players were not part of the team during at least some of them.

---

[797] IAAF, AIBA, FIE, FIFA, IWF, IJF, FILA, ISF, WTF, ITF, ITTF, ITU, ATP, WTA.

[798] The CAS in CAS 2004/A/777, 31-1-2005, *ARcycling AG v. UCI*, decided an exceptional case involving team sanctions, although not secondary team sanctions as described here. Nevertheless, the case is too interesting not to cite. In 2004, Phonak dismissed three cyclists from his team after one had been involved in a confirmed doping case and the two others in cases of adverse analytical findings. Due to these cases of doping, the UCI Licence Commission on 22 November 2004 refused to issue a 2005 ProTour licence to Phonak. The Phonak team appealed to the CAS in an attempt to win back its licence. The CAS subsequently set aside the Licence Commission's decision, despite the fact that it considered that this sequence of events undoubtedly was a circumstance which might have contributed to bringing the sport of cycling into disrepute.

[799] IOC Medical Code, Chapter IX – Penalties for Infractions, Art. III, subsection 2.

[800] Doping, 8.1 Doping Operating Procedure, Art. 2.3.

[801] Anti Doping Rules, Chapter 13 – Disciplinary Sanctions, Art. 13.8.

[802] Regulations Governing Doping Control, 6.6. Sanctions, 6.6.1. During competitions, subsection 2: If, during a tournament, a team is found guilty of a second case of doping, this team shall be disqualified, shall not be allowed to finish the tournament and shall lose the game by forfeit as well as the games that have already been played.

The FIVB did not only stipulate that any game played by a team including one doped player was lost, but also by how much the game was lost, namely by 0-3 (0-15, 0-15, 0-15).[803]

As far as the Olympics and Paralympics were concerned, in the event that after the suspension of one or several athletes it was no longer possible to play as a team, the team mates of the player who had been caught using doping were allowed to continue to play in the Games individually if the rules of the relevant federation permitted it.[804] Under the IOC and IPC rules teams, after the exclusion of one or several of their members, could still continue to compete as teams.

5.2.2. *Disqualification of the entire team*

The consequences of a doping offence committed by a team member under this category were more dramatic for the remaining team members than under the previous category. The relevant rules of the federations in this case allowed the entire team to be disqualified. This was a disciplinary sanction rather than a sports sanction.[805]

The IBF Committee of Management, for example, was competent to disqualify a team at any time during a competition when a member had been caught in the use of doping.[806] The ICF and FIH Doping Rules were equally strict[807] and the IHF doping regulations also stipulated that: "should more than one player in a team be in violation of doping regulations, the team is disqualified for the entire event."[808] If the relevant committee of the IBF still had some discretionary powers in imposing a disqualification, these powers were entirely lacking in the ICF and the FIH rules. The ICF provided that "the athlete and his crew shall be disqualified [...],"

---

[803] Medical Regulations, 2. Antidoping Control Regulations, Art. 2.6. Sanctions. Cf. in a judgment of 31 May 2000 ((2001) *SpuRt*, p. 212) the DFB Bundesgericht considered: "Hat in einem Spiel ein gedopter Spieler [Q. Lanzaat; *JWS*] mitgewirkt und ist dieser Spieler – wie vorliegend durch das Urteil des Bundesgerichtes vom 31. Mei 2000 geschehen – wegen Dopings bei dem Spiel bestraft worden, so wird dieses Spiel für seine Mannschaft mit 0:2 Toren verloren und dem Gegner mit 2:0 Toren gewonnen gewertet (para. 25 Nr. 5, 1. *Halbsatz der DFB-Spielordnung*)."

[804] "In sports in which a team may no longer compete after a member has been excluded, the remaining members of the team may compete in an individual capacity provided that the rules of the International Federation concerned so permit," according to the IOC Medical Code, Chapter IX – Penalties for Infractions, Art. III, subsection 2. "In sports in which a team may no longer compete after a member has been excluded, the remaining members may compete in an individual capacity," according to the IPC Doping, 8.1 Doping Operating Procedure, Art. 2.4.

[805] One decision of the Schiedsgericht of the German rugby federation did not result in the disqualification of the entire team: 'Auf eine Disqualifikation der Mannschaft sind daraus keine Rückschlüsse zu ziehen (given that "in den regeln des IRB [...] eine Mannschaftsbestrafung nicht [ist] vorgesehen') aber es ist hierin zu erkennen, dass die Mannschaft insofern schon bestraft wird, dass sie den Spieler in der Zukunft nicht mehr einsetzen darf."

[806] Regulations for the Thomas and Uber Cups, 15. Disqualification, Art. 15.2; Regulations For The Sudirman Cup, 14. Disqualification, Art. 14.2.

[807] ICF Doping Rules, Rule 5 – Disciplinary Procedures For Doping Offences, subsection 4.

[808] Anti-doping Regulations, 11. Similarly: FIVB: Medical Regulations, 2. Antidoping Control Regulations, sub 2.6.5.

and the FIH that "a team, one of whose athletes tested positive or refused to be tested should be disqualified from the entire event."[809] For some of the ICF rules it is not completely clear whether they also addressed the team members. The rules stated that disciplinary measures could be imposed on a participant or several members of a team if they were discovered to have used doping.[810] This seems to indicate that the only team members affected were the ones who had actually committed the violation. The anti-doping rules of the UCI, the UIMP[811] and the IBU[812] also contained a provision according to which the entire team had to be disqualified due to the use of doping by one team member, although where offences during a team contest in a stage tournament were concerned the UCI was more lenient. In such cases the team would be ranked last and in the general ranking 10 minutes would be added to their time.[813]

In one branch of sport, swimming, the response to a team member's doping offence differed in accordance with the particular sport involved. When a FINA doping rule was violated by a member of a water polo team the competition result of the team (or the results of the matches during a given tournament) would be struck off the ranking list and further disciplinary measures against the team could be considered. If the athlete involved was part of the relay team or of a synchronised swimming or diving duet or team the FINA would disqualify the team concerned.[814] Thus, responses to the use of doping by a team member did not only vary among the different international federations, but also at times within one single federation. One other example is the UIPM, whose rules provided that: "If the athlete guilty is a member of a team, the entire team is to be eliminated for the respective competition."[815] In its Fair Play Cup Competition the IIHF would also disqualify the entire team if one of the team members had committed a doping offence.[816] On other occasions, however, the IIHF was less strict and only disqualified the team as a whole after a third team mate had tested positive,[817] provided that the offence did not involve a team or national federation official, as in that case the team was still disqualified immediately (and the official banned for life).[818] This was also the fate

---

[809] FIH Doping Policy, 12. Sanctions, Art. 12.2.

[810] Slalom Racing Competition Rules, 41. Special Rules Relative to World Championships, 41.13. Anti-Doping; Flatwater Racing Competition Rules, Chapter V – Special Rules for World Championships, 48. Doping, 48.4; Marathon Racing Rules, Chapter IV – Racing Regulations, 32. Doping is strictly prohibited.

[811] Although the UIPM does not mention disqualification, but rather "elimination," the purpose is the same. Anti-Doping Controls, 1. Principle.

[812] IBU Anti-doping, Blood Test and Gender Verification Rules, I. Doping Controls, 1. Principle.

[813] Part XIV – Antidoping Examination Regulations, Chapter VIII – Disciplinary Measures, Art. 97.

[814] FINA Doping Control Rules, DC 9 Sanctions, Art. DC 9.5.

[815] Anti-doping Controls, 1. Principle. See also: IBU: Doping Controls, 1. Principle.

[816] By Laws, 600 Competition By Laws, 618. Fair Play Cup.

[817] This was the FIVB's response after a second team member had been caught. Medical Regulations, 2. Antidoping Control Regulations, Art. 2.6. Sanctions.

[818] By Laws, 1400 Medical Controls (Doping), 1407. Sanctions with Doping.

of a team in the event of "very severe offences against the IIHF Medical Regulations." In such cases, the IIHF Council was entitled to disqualify the entire team. The provision containing this rule also contained a rule offering the team leader a kind of "Hobson's choice." The team leader could allow an athlete whose A-sample had tested positive to continue playing until the outcome of the analysis of his/her B-sample became known. If this was positive as well, the entire team would be disqualified from all matches played after the results of the first analysis had become known.[819]

Pursuant to the rules of the WCF a team would only be disqualified if the doping offence took place during the finals.[820] According to the FIL regulations it seems that the team was only disqualified as a whole when every one of its members had used doping: "The penalty for an infraction by individual competitors and teams during an event is temporary or permanent ineligibility or exclusion (disqualification) from that event."[821] In conclusion, mention has only still to be made of the rules of the ISU and the FIS, which also provided for disqualification of the team as punishment for a doping offence of one of its members.[822]

On one occasion the CAS had to address the question whether a whole team should suffer because of a doping violation by one of its members.

> "The Panel is not unsympathetic with the other members of the USA team, who presumably did not want K to take the Darvocet pill, did not know that he had done so, and most of all had no desire to seek an unfair competitive advantage. Nevertheless they were participating in a sport where international organizers had enacted a strict set of anti-doping rules pursuant to which an entire team may be penalized for a violation committed by one member: for example, the rules of the International Rowing Federation and International Swimming Federation provide for mandatory disqualification of the relevant team, while the rules of the International Ice Hockey Federation, International Basketball Federation and Union Cycliste Internationale provide for penalties which in most cases apply to the team as well as to the individual offender, and in some circumstances may include disqualification of the team."[823]

The team was disqualified in its entirety and the team members had to return their medals.

5.2.3. *Other sport sanctions for the entire team*

In the above, two different measures were discussed: declaring the competition lost, which is a sporting sanction, and disqualification of the team, which is a disciplinary sanction. In this section, a few more sporting sanctions to affect the entire team will be discussed. Some federations stipulated that the team would be re-

---

[819] Doping Regulations, I. IIHF Doping Controls, D Sanctions with doping (By Laws 1105).

[820] By Law No. 8 Doping, I General, VI Sanctions and Penalties, Art. 13.

[821] Supplement 4, Medical Code, Chapter VII, Art. II.

[822] ISU General Regulations, I. Doping, Rule 139, sub 9; FIS Doping Rules, Rule 5 – Disciplinary Procedures for Doping Offences, sub 5.

[823] CAS 95/122, 5-3-1996, *National Wheelchair Basketball Association (NWBA) v. IPC*, Matthieu Reeb, ed., *Digest of CAS Awards 1986-1998* (Berne, Editions Stämpfli 1998) pp. 173-185.

moved from the ranking list while others provided that the trophies won by the team had to be returned. Under certain conditions, the UCI could even use time penalties.

The FISA determined that it was not only the doped crew member who should be disqualified, but that the "entire crew of which a member has been so declared, shall not be ranked [...]."[824] Similar provisions were in place for the event that a sculler tested positive "even if no fault or negligence is established on that athlete's part."[825] The ISSF rules included a similar rule providing for removal from the ranking list even if no fault or negligence could be established.[826] Although it might be considered unfair that rehabilitation was not possible, it would also have been unfair if a team which by the disqualification had moved up in the rankings would be made to again relinquish its position at a later stage. The FIH circumvented the problem by not allowing the lower ranking teams to move up a place. The FIH Doping Policy contained a special team provision: "a team, one of whose athletes tests positive or refuses to be tested shall be disqualified from the entire event during which testing was conducted and all results of matches played by this team during this event shall be invalidated and deleted from the record books. The final ranking of the other participating teams shall not, however, be affected. In case of disqualification, the team and the athletes concerned have to return automatically and immediately all trophies and medals received during the tournament to the FIH, or in case of the Olympic Games, to the IOC."[827] The FITA rules provided that if a player who had tested positive participated in the shooting in a team contest, the team result would be invalid.[828]

Once a team had been disqualified, the team members involved had to return automatically and immediately all trophies and medals won during a tournament.[829] When a team was disqualified in a curling final the medals were divided among the three other teams in accordance with their place in the rankings.[830] In gymnastics, the scores given to doped athletes were declared null and his/her doping offence would affect the entire team. Further, the total score of a Rhythmic Sports Gymnastics Group or of a Mixed Pair or Trio in Sports Aerobics would be declared void when a team member tested positive.[831] As was the case for FINA and UIPM athletes and teams, the FIG also imposed different penalties depending on the particular type of event the team would usually participate in.

---

[824] Rules of Racing and Related By Laws, Part VI – Organisation of Regattas, Section 4 – Duties of the Jury and Rules of Umpiring, Rule 9, sub 9.3.2. and Part VII – Medical Provisions, Rule 82 – Penalties for Doping and Rules of Racing and Related By Laws. Similarly: FIBT: Doping Control Regulations, 9. Penalties, sub 9.3. and FIS: Doping Rules, Rule 5, subsection 5.

[825] By Law to Rules 80 to 83 – Doping, 9. Disciplinary Measures, 9.3 The penalties can affect: 9.3.2.

[826] Anti-Doping Regulations, 8. Disciplinary measures, Art. 8.3.

[827] 12. Sanctions, sub 12.2.

[828] Appendix 4 – Doping Control Procedures, 11 Disciplinary Procedures, Art. 11.11.

[829] FIH Doping Policy, 12. Sanctions, Art. 12.2.

[830] WCF By Law No. 8 Doping, I General, VI Sanctions and Penalties, Art. 13.

[831] FIG Doping Control Regulations, Art. 3.1. FIG Sanctions, sub B.

5.2.4. *No team sanctions*

As noted above not every international federation provided for measures affecting the team as a whole after one or several of its members had tested positive. In some sports it would not make much difference to the results if a doped athlete had been part of the team. For example in football, it would be impossible to verify after the match whether the team would also have been victorious if the doped player had not participated in the match. However, if we consider a relay team in athletics, the results of this team are directly connected with the individual performance of each of its members.

The following federations did not provide team sanctions for doping offences commited by one player: the IAAF, AIBA, FIE, IWF, IJF, FILA, ISF, WTF, ITF, ITTF, ITU, ATP and the WTA. It is true that the majority of these federations do not represent team sports, with a few exceptions. However, as has been explained above, team events are possible in non-team sports. In such cases, however, disqualification of the entire team as punishment for a violation by one member does perhaps seem disproportionate. In such cases, it would be best to disqualify only the team member concerned.

5.3. **Sanctions according to the WADC**

In Appendix 1 of the WADC team sport is defined as "a sport in which the substitution of players is permitted during a competition." If several members of a team are suspected of a possible doping offence in the framework of a series of games (or an event),[832] the entire team will be subject to target testing[833] throughout the event. If multiple players on a team are found to test positive during an event, the entire team may be disqualified and be made subject to disciplinary proceedings. This means that when only one team member is suspected or tests positive, this has no ramifications for the team as a whole. This indicates a departure from the idea of fairness with respect to the team's opponents.[834] In his presentation at the last World Conference on Doping Richard Young wondered "[...] what would happen to a team in the event of one of its athletes testing positive, if there was no clarification as to what was considered a team sport" whereupon he cited the definition given above.

---

[832] Event: A series of individual competitions conducted together under one ruling body (e.g., the Olympic Games, FINA World Championships, or Pan American Games). WADC, Appendix 1, Definitions.

[833] Target testing is defined as: "Selection of athletes for testing where specific athletes or groups of athletes are selected on a non-random basis for testing at a specified time," under Appendix 1 – Definitions – WADC.

[834] "[...] it appears to be a laudable policy objective not to repair an accidental unfairness to an individual by creating an intentional unfairness to the whole body of other competitors. This is what would happen if banned performance-enhancing substances were tolerated when absorbed inadvertently," according to the CAS in CAS 94/129, 23-5-1995, *USA Shooting & Q. v. UIT*, Matthieu Reeb, ed., *Digest of CAS Awards 1986-1998* (Berne, Editions Stämpfli 1998) pp. 187-204, and as cited by the drafters of the WADC in the comment to Art. 2.1.1.

"In tennis doubles or team gymnastics, therefore, how disqualification works is left to the rules of the individual IFs." In such cases, it can be concluded from the text of the WADC neither what the fate will be of one team member who tests positive, nor what the fate of his/her team as a whole will be.

Article 11 WADC reads:

"Consequences to teams
Where more than one team member in a team sport has been notified of a possible anti-doping rule violation under Article 7 in connection with an event, the team shall be subject to target testing for the event. If more than one team member in a team sport is found to have committed an anti-doping rule violation during the event, the team may be subject to disqualification or other disciplinary action. In sports which are not team sports but where awards are given to teams, disqualification or other disciplinary action against the team when one or more team members have committed an anti-doping rule violation shall be as provided in the applicable rules of the international federation."

To summarise, if one or more members of a team had been caught using doping, the sports federations would react in various ways. Generally speaking, a sports penalty would be imposed on the entire team. This meant that the team would be disqualified or that the match would be declared lost. However, a number of international federations did not impose any collective sports sanctions at all. All this was notwithstanding the fact that the actual doping offenders would be involved in individual disciplinary proceedings resulting in disciplinary sanctions. Under the WADC the regime is as follows. If at least two team members are suspected of doping during an event, the remaining team members may be required to undergo doping tests. In addition, the entire team may be subject to sports sanctions.

In the above, the focus has been on the imposition of sanctions by international federations. This Section 5 is intended to illustrate the proliferation of sanctions that existed prior to the entry into force of the WADC. In the next section, the sanctions of national federations in pre-WADC times will be examined.

6.   SANCTIONS AT THE NATIONAL LEVEL

At the national level, the range of sanctions was even wider than at the international level. Discussing each national variety, as has been done above with regard to the sanctions of the international federations, would, of course, be possible, but would lead to a virtually impenetrable text because of the myriad details it would have to include. Therefore, only the most salient aspects of the national sanctioning systems will be discussed.

The IOC Medical Code only included sanctions for first and second offences. A first offence was punishable by a two-year ban and a second offence by a life-long ban. The sanctions used by the international and the national sports federations were for the most part more or less grouped around the sanctions used by the IOC. There was, however, no harmony among them whatsoever.[835] Looking at the sanctions which the national federations used to apply to a first offence, sanctions could be imposed well below to well in excess of two years. The same was true for second offences.[836] The division into two types of offences, which the IOC used, was not followed by all federations, some of which also provided for sanctions for third offences (usually a life-time ban, such as the IOC applied to second offences).[837] The first subsection of this Section 6 will deal with sanctions which differed greatly from the IOC norm (the extreme variations), the second subsection will list sanctions which were mainly only found in the doping regulations of national federations (the "exotic" variations) and the third subsection will discuss the shift from fixed sanctions to sanctions with minimum and maximum durations.

6.1.   Extreme variations

6.1.1. *First offence*

Various national federations were extremely lenient in their punishment of first doping offenders. The Greek football federation penalised such athletes by suspending them for two matches,[838] while the *Nederlandse Hippische Sportbond* (KNHS) only suspended riders for two weeks. German footballers only needed to spend four weeks in the stands after having used doping.[839] Boxers who were members of the *Koninklijke Belgische Boksbond* (BBF)were punished by a suspension of a mere month, and this sanction was even provisional where professional boxers were concerned.[840]

However, the number of federations applying sanctions in excess of those prescribed by the IOC was far greater. The Greek boxing federation followed the

---

[835] The time penalties which the national federations had included in their doping regulations varied widely. There were at least thirty diferent suspensions in force: min. 1 week to max. 2 years, max. 2 weeks, 2 matches, 4 weeks, 1 or several competitions, 1 month provisional, 1 month, 6 games to 6 months, 1 to 12 months, 3 months, min. 3 months, 3 months to 2 years, 3 months to 3 years, 6 months to 1 year, 6 months to 2 years, max. 1 year, 1 year, min. 1 year to max. 2 years, min. 1 year to max. 3 years, max. 2 years, 2 years, min. 2 years, 2 to 4 years, min. 2 years, max. 3 years, 4 years, 4 years to life-long ban, min. 4 years, 5 years, discretionary power, max. life-long ban, life-long ban.

[836] Max. 3 months, 3 months + 1 provisional, 6 months, 6 months to 4 years, 1 year, 15 months to 2 years, 6 months, min. 1 year, min. 1 year to max. 2 years, 1 to 2 years, 1 to 22 years, 1 to 3 years, 2 years, max. 2 years, 2 to 4 years, 2 to 6 years, min. 2 years to life-long ban, 3 years, min. 3 years, 4 years, max. 5 years, min. 6 years, 4 years to max. life-long ban, 20 to 30 years, max. life-long ban, life-long ban.

[837] Min. 2 years to life-long ban, 22 years to life-long ban, min. 4 years, 10 to 20 years, life-long ban.

[838] Hellenic Football Association: Art. 32 – Protection of football players' health – excitation through drugs, 12 a.

[839] Deutscher Fußball-Bund: Rechts- und Verfahrungsordnung des DFB, para. 4 – Strafen gegen Spiel in einzelnen Fällen, 2.

[840] Dopingreglement, 2. Bestraffing.

OMADC in using the concept of "intentional doping." When it had been proven that a boxer playing in the Greek competition had intentionally used doping he was threatened with a sanction of four years to life. The British Judo Association (BJA) applied a fixed sanction of five years' suspension to first offenders.[841] Two national rowing federations were as strict as the FISA and suspended a doped rower for life.[842] Several Irish federations used the life-long ban as a maximum, rather than as a fixed sanction.[843]

6.1.2. Second offence

Given that the norm used by the IOC was a life-long ban, extremes in this category were only to be found in one direction, i.e., considerably less than life. What to think of, for example, the maximum of penalty of three months which the *Nederlandse Hippische Sportbond* imposed on repeat offenders?[844] The *Koninklijke Belgische Boksbond* only imposed three months plus one month provisionally on professional boxers in such cases, while amateur boxers were suspended for six months.[845] This was also the punishment imposed on Irish weightlifters.[846] The Belgian *Decreet inzake Medisch Verantwoorde Sportbeoefening* of 27 March 1991 stipulated that a sanction of six months to four years could be imposed on athletes who committed a second offence within two years after their conviction for the first.[847] Table tennis players in Germany were threatened with a suspension of one to two-and-a-half years.[848]

6.1.3. Third offence

Many national federations provided for third offences, which would often result in an unconditional life-time ban. There were some federations, however, which would not even impose a life-time ban for a third offence. Several German federations applied the life-time ban only as a maximum penalty: the German field hockey

---

[841] By Laws relating to Drug Abuse, Appendix "A" – Recommended Sanctions for Positive Cases in Doping Control.

[842] Both the Irish Amateur Rowing Union and the *Koninklijke Nederlandse Roeibond* applied the doping regulations of the FISA.

[843] Equestrian Federation of Ireland: Doping Control Policy, 2.5 What are the Applicable Sanctions?, sub 2.5.1; The Irish Amateur Wrestling Association: Doping Control Policy and Enforcement Rules, 5. Disciplinary Panel and Appeal Panel, sub 5.1.; Volleyball Association of Ireland: Doping Control Policy of the Volleyball Association of Ireland, 1.5 Sanctions, sub 1.5.1; Irish Sailing Association: Doping Control Policy, 2.5. Applicable sanctions, sub 2.5.1.

[844] Humaan Dopingreglement NHS, Artikel 16 – Straffen, subsection 3.

[845] Dopingreglement, 2. Bestraffing.

[846] The Irish Amateur Weightlifting Association follows the doping regulations of the IWF.

[847] Titel VI – Disciplinaire maatregelen inzake medisch verantwoorde sportbeoefening, Hoofdstuk IV – Disciplinaire maatregelen, Art. 40, 2.

[848] Deutsche Tisch Tennis Bund: Auszug aus der Satzung und der Wettspielordnung des DTTB über die Bestimmungen zum Verbot von Doping: para. 56, (1), a).

federation imposed a minimum of 2 years to life[849] and the *Deutscher Sport Bund*[850] and six other German federations imposed 2 years to life.[851] The doping regulations of the Portuguese sports federations typically included sanctions for third offences ranging from ten to twenty years.[852]

6.2. "Exotic" variations

6.2.1. *Suspension from membership*

The *Nederlandse Handbal Verbond* (NHV) had included in its doping regulations the sanction of "life-long suspension as a member, recommended for expulsion [...] to the general assembly" for a second "hard"-doping and a third "soft"-doping offence.[853] The British Judo Association for a first "hard"-doping offence imposed the sanction of: "Four years suspension from membership of the British Judo Association [...]. This period can be extended depending upon the seriousness of the offence." The second offence was punished by: "A Life Ban from membership of the British Judo Association." A first "soft"-doping offence was punished by a one year suspension from membership; a second offence by two years' suspension and the third by a life-long ban.[854] In the Mis-use of Drugs By Laws of the Amateur Rowing Association (ARA) a provision was to be found which stated that: "The Disciplinary Panel will forward a report to the Executive Committee of the ARA for confirmation of penalties imposed and to the Council for confirmation where suspension of membership and/or ban on participation in rowing and associated activities is recommended."[855] The Doping Control Rules of the British Canoe Union also contained a provision making it possible for a member to be suspended from membership for use of doping. "The BCU's Drug Advisory Committee may: [...] in addition to or instead of any of the above penalties recommend to the BCU Council

---

[849] Deutscher Hockey-Bund: Para. 12 – Anti-Doping-Bestimmungen, 7, sub c). This federation even provided for subsequent doping offences: "im dritten Fall und jedem weiteren Fall eine Sperre von mindestens zwei Jahren bis zu lebenslanger Dauer."

[850] Antidoping-Rahmen-Richtlinien, Anlage 2 – Empfehlungen für Zulassungssperren aufgrund der Verantstalterrechte, 1., sub c).

[851] Deutsche Triathlon Union (DTU): Anti-Doping Ordnung, para. 3 Verbot der Anwendung und Strafmaß, para. 3.2, sub c); Deutscher Ruderverband: Doping-Bestimmungen 2000 des Deutschen Ruderverbandes, Ruder-Wettkampf-Regeln, para. 40 a – Wettkampfsperre wegen Dopingverstoß, 3. sub c); Deutscher Basketball Bund, Deutscher Handball-Bund, Deutschen Ringer-Bund and Deutscher Eishockey Bund: reference to the DSB Rahmen-Richtlinien.

[852] See *inter alia* Federação de Triatlo de Portugal: Regulamento Anti-Dopagem, Título IV – Das Sanções Disciplinares, Art. 34 – Das sanções aplicáveis, subsection 1., 1.1, sub c). "Recusa do praticante a submeter-se ao controlo antidopagem, falta à segunda análise ou caso esta não se realize por facto que lhe seja imputável, será sancionado da seguinte forma: [...] De 10 a 20 anos de suspensão da actividade desportiva, no caso de terceira infracção."

[853] Huishoudelijk reglement NHV, Art. 6.3.7.2, subsection 1. sub b.

[854] By Laws relating to Drug Abuse, Appendix "A" – Recommended Sanctions for Positive Cases in Doping Control.

[855] 5. Disciplinary Measures, 5.1, sub 5.1.1.

of Management that the athlete should be suspended or expelled from BCU membership."[856]

6.2.2. Ban from representation

The doping regulations of various Irish federations contained the sanction of suspension of a person "from selection to represent Ireland in international competition for a specified period of time."[857]

6.2.3. Termination of funding

"Sports Councils may suspend or terminate all Sports Council funding to [...] athletes [...], where a governing body's Review Panel finds there is prima facie evidence that a doping offence has been committed," according to the Statement of Anti-Doping Policy of UK Sport.[858] Many Irish federations' regulations included the rule that the use of doping: "make[s] the person ineligible to receive direct or indirect funding from the Irish Triathlon Association."[859]

6.2.4. Suspension in specific areas only

Apart from suspension from membership, the English Table Tennis Association used a sanction which is as unique as it is hard to understand: the geographically defined suspension.

"A Member or former Member or Affiliated Organisation found to be in breach of the ETTA Disciplinary Code shall be liable to one or several of the following penalties: to be suspended from the privileges of membership or affiliation either indefinitely or for a stated period; suspension may be limited to a specified area of jurisdiction or geographical or other defined area or to a specified type of activity."[860]

---

[856] 5. Penalties. See also British Equestrian Federation: Rule Book, Disciplinary and Doping Control Procedures, Suspensions, 24.

[857] Irish Triathlon Association: Doping Policy, 2.5 What are the Applicable Sanctions?, 2.5.1, sub (a); Equestrian Federation of Ireland: Doping Control Policy, 2.5, 2.5.1, sub (a); The Irish Amateur Wrestling Association: Doping Control Policy and Enforcement Rules, 5. Disciplinary Panel and Appeal Panel, 5.1 (a); Volleyball Association of Ireland: Doping Control Policy of the Volleyball Association of Ireland, 1.5 Sanctions, 1.5.1, a; Irish Sailing Association: Doping Control Policy, 2.5. Applicable sanctions, 2.5.1, sub 2.5.1.2.

[858] Sanctions, IX. (a).

[859] Irish Triathlon Association: Doping Policy, 2.5 What are the Applicable Sanctions?, 2.5.1, sub (c); Tennis Ireland: Doping Control Policy, 5. Penalties, sub 5.5.; Irish Canoe Union: Doping Control regulations, 10.00 Sanctions, 10.04 (d); Equestrian Federation of Ireland: Doping Control Policy, 2.5 What are the Applicable Sanctions?, 2.5.1 (c); The Irish Amateur Wrestling Association: Doping Control Policy and Enforcement Rules, 5. Disciplinary Panel and Appeal Panel, 5.1 (c); Volleyball Association of Ireland: Doping Control Policy of the Volleyball Association of Ireland, 1.5 Sanctions, 1.5.1 c.; Irish Sailing Association: Doping Control Policy, 2.5. Applicable sanctions, 2.5.1., sub 2.5.1.4.

[860] 33. ETTA Disciplinary Code, 33.3. and 33.3.1.

6.2.5. *Sanctions according to category*

The UCI used (and still uses) different sanctions according to the various categories which cyclists could compete in. There are three main categories: Elite, under 23 years of age and other cyclists; the first category is subdivided into men and women. Several national cycling federations adopted the UCI's division into categories and included it in their doping regulations.[861]

6.3. **Discretionary powers and flexible sanctions**

The focus of considerations in doping proceedings had increasingly shifted to the sentencing stage as a result of the presumption of liability. For this reason, it was important that disciplinary courts retained at least some discretion in determining the sanction. If disciplinary courts would only be only able to impose fixed sanctions, the athlete's procedural rights could not be properly exercised. Only very few doping regulations included fixed sanctions. The discretion allowed by the remaining regulations could be either full discretion, whereby the disciplinary bodies were bound by neither a minimum, nor a maximum, or discretion in the sense that the disciplinary bodies still had to take account of minimum or maximum penalties, as was the case in the majority of regulations.

6.3.1. *Full discretionary powers*

At the level of the international federations, only the FIFA and the FIS allowed for discretionary powers. At the level of the national federations discretion was a more frequent occurrence. The Doping Control Policy of the Equestrian Federation of Ireland (EFI) stipulated that: "Where this Disciplinary Panel or the Appeal Panel determines that a person has committed a Doping Offence, it will apply one or several of the following sanctions; [...] Any other sanction the Disciplinary Panel or the Appeal Panel, as the case may be, thinks fit."[862] Three federations with jurisdiction over the whole of Great Britain had included a provision granting discretionary powers in their doping regulations: the British Canoe Union,[863] the British Eques-

---

[861] Bund Deutscher Radfahrer: Dopingkontroll-Reglement, 7 Vertragsstrafen, sub 7.1; Hellenic Cycling Federation (which used the UCI International Cycling Regulations); Irish Cycling Federation: Anti-Doping Regulations; Koninklijke Nederlandse Wielren Unie (KNWU): Antidoping Controle Reglement, Hoofdstuk VIII: Straffen, Art. 90; Real Federacion Espanola de Ciclismo: 5. Regulamento Nacional del Control del Dopaje, Art. 84 – Sanciones correspondientes a los ciclistas.

[862] 2.5 What are the Applicable Sanctions?, 2.5.1, sub (j). Similarly: Irish Triathlon Association: Doping Policy, 2.5 What are the Applicable Sanctions?, 2.5.1, sub (j); Tennis Ireland: Doping Control Policy, 5. Penalties, sub 5.12.; The Irish Amateur Wrestling Association: Doping Control Policy and Enforcement Rules, 5. Disciplinary Panel and Appeal Panel, 5.1, sub (j); Volleyball Association of Ireland: Doping Control Policy of the Volleyball Association of Ireland, 1.5 Sanctions, 1.5.1., sub j.; Irish Sailing Association: Doping Control Policy, 2.5. Applicable sanctions, 2.5.1, sub 2.5.1.11.

[863] Doping Control Rules, 5. Penalties: "The BCU's BCU Drug Advisory Committee may: decide to warn or reprimand the athlete or impose a period of suspension from any or all BCU competitive

trian Federation[864] and the British Bobsleigh Association.[865] The Football Association of Wales also allowed for a considerable amount of freedom in the establishment of sanctions, given the provision in its doping regulations that: "if the analysis of a sample obtained from a player indicates the presence of a banned substance, [...] the Association shall take such action as it deems appropriate."[866] In England, two federations took a similar position. The English Table Tennis Association, which provided that: "A Member or former Member or Affiliated Organisation found to be in breach of the ETTA Disciplinary Code shall be liable to one or several of the following penalties: [...] to be fined, to be censured, to give an Undertaking in such terms as the Disciplinary Committee may decide,"[867] and the English Basket Ball Association (EBBA): "Any person for whom a positive result has been determined in respect of the use of a prohibited substance (or refusing to take a test for such substance) shall automatically forthwith be suspended until such time as the EBBA Drug Control Committee has fully investigated the matter and determined the appropriate penalty. The maximum penalty, which may be imposed under this regulation, is suspension sine die. [...]."[868] Although it is unclear whether this was a purely discretionary power, the doping regulations of the *Deutscher Leichtathletik Verband* provided that: "die Antidoping Kommission [...] ein Doping-Verfahren ein(leitet) und [...] die Suspendierung eines Athleten aus(spricht), wenn ein hinreichender Tatverdacht für einen Dopingverstoß besteht."[869]

---

events for a stipulated period or impose a period of suspension from any or all BCU Competitive events up to and including a specified major championships or impose a life-time ban on participation in any or all BCU Competitive events."

[864] Rule Book, Disciplinary and Doping Control Procedures, Immediate Suspension, 16.: "A Participant may be summarily suspended from all rights and privileges of participation at Events following conviction in a British Court of Law of any equestrian-related offence, pending a full investigation by the Stewards at an enquiry called under the terms of Rule 12. Such suspension is to be approved by three members of the Stewards panel, in writing, and may take effect from the date of conviction, or such date as the Stewards shall decide and shall remain in force at the Stewards' absolute discretion until a full hearing under Rule 12 and shall notify the Participant forthwith."

[865] Rules for Doping Control, 5. Sanctions, 5.1: "Where a person commits an offence under these Rules, that person will be liable to be declared ineligible for life from participating in any event or activity organised or authorised by or held under the Rules of the Association (or any directly or indirectly affiliated body) wherever held subject to the following provisos: (i) where the Disciplinary Committee or Appeal Committee decide that the offence committed was not a deliberate attempt to enhance performance, the relevant committee may (at its absolute discretion) reduce the period of the period of ineligibility to any period of not less than two years; (ii) where the prohibited substance with which the offence was committed was a stimulant defined in Class A of the list referred to in Appendix A, the relevant committee shall have discretion to impose whatever penalty it considers appropriate."

[866] Memorandum on the use of doping.

[867] 33. ETTA Disciplinary Code, sub 33.3.

[868] Doping Control (EBBA regulation 26), sub 26.4.

[869] Sonderbedingungen des DLV für Dopingkontrollen, Rechts- und Verfahrensordnung (RVO), para. 82 Vorläufige Wettkampfsperre (Suspendierung), (1).

6.3.2. Table of flexible sanctions

1st infraction	
min. 1 week to max. 2 years	Riksidrottsförbundet (minor doping offence)
max. 2 weeks	Nederlandse Hippische Sportbond
1 or several competitions	Greek Boxing Federation (petty doping offence), Badminton Association of England
6 games to 6 months	Union Royale Belge des Sociétés de Football Assoc.
1 to 12 months	Deutscher Volleyball Verband
min. 3 months	Fédération Luxembourgeoise de Tennis de Table, Deutscher Hockey Bund, Fédération Royale Belge de tennis
3 months to 2 years	FEI, Decreet inz. Medisch verantwoorde sportbeoefening
3 months to 3 years	Fédération Luxembourgeoise de Natation/sauvetage, Fédération Luxembourgeoise de Tennis, Hockey Club Luxembourg, Fédération Luxembourgeoise de Basket-Ball
6 months to 1 year	UCI, Federação Portuguesa de Hoquei, Federação Portuguesa de Badminton, Federação Portuguesa de Halterofilismo, Hellenic Cycling Federation, Koninklijke Nederlandse Wielren Unie, Irish Cycling Federation, Bund Deutscher Radfahrer, British Cycling Federation
6 months to 2 years	Federação de Triatlo de Portugal, Federação Portuguesa de Ténis, Federação Portuguesa de Remo, Federação Portuguesa de Basquetebol, Federação Equestre Portuguesa, Federação Portuguesa de Futebol, Federação Portuguesa de Andebol, Federação Portuguesa de Judo, Federação Portuguesa de Tiro com Arco
max. 1 year	Antidoping Rahmen-Richtlinien, Deutsche Triathlon Union, Deutscher Tisch Tennis Bund, Deutscher Ruderverband, Deutscher Basketball Bund, Deutscher Handball Bund, Deutscher Judo Bund, Deutscher Ringer-Bund, Deutscher Eishockey Bund
min. 1 year to max. 2 years	Riksidrottsförbundet (serious doping offence)
min. 1 year to max. 3 years	Fédération Luxembourgeoise de Volley-Ball, Fédération Royale Belge des Sports Equestres
max. 2 years	AIBA, FIG, FIH, IHF, ITTF, Nederlandse Koninklijke Zwembond (betablokkers and social drugs), Koninklijke Nederlandse Atletiek Unie, Nederlandse IJshockey Bond, Nederlandse Ski Vereniging, The Football Association, Deutscher Sport Bund ("Stimulanzien" and "Narkotika"), Verband Österreicher Schwimmvereine (narcotic analgesics), Österreicher Bogensportverband
min. 2 years	FIBA, IAAF, IOC (OMC), WTF Comitato Olimpico Nazionale Italiano (petty offence), Federazione Italiana Nuoto, Federazione Italiana Tennis, Federazione Italiana Scherma, Federazione Italiana Sport Equestri, Federazione Italiana Pallacanestro, Federazione Italiana Canoa Kayak, Federazione Italiana Pallavola, Federazione Italiana Sport Invernali, Federação Portuguesa de Natação (amphetamines), Greek Boxing Federation (petty doping offence), Badminton Association of England, Deutscher Sport Bund, Great Britain Olympic Hockey Board
2 to 4 years	Real Federación Española de Atletismo, Real Federación Española de Ciclismo, Real Federación Española de Futbol, Real Federación Española de Deportes de Invierno
max. 3 years	Triathlon Luxembourg, Fédération Française de Triathlon, Fédération Française de Tennis de Table, Fédération Française de Natation, Fédération Française de Tennis, Fédération Française de Boxe, Fédération Française de Basketball, Fédération Française de Cyclisme, Fédération Française de Handball, Fédération Française de Judo, Jujitsu, Kendo, Fédération Française de Lutte, Fédération Française de Tir à l'Arc, Fédération Française de Voile, Fédération Française de Ski
4 years to life-long ban	Comitato Olimpico Nazionale Italiano (intentional offence), Federazione Italiana Nuoto, Federazione Italiana Tennis, Federazione Italiana Scherma, Federazione Italiana Sport Equestri, Federazione Italiana Pallacanestro, Federazione Italiana Pallavola, Federazione Italiana Sport Invernali
min. 4 years	FINA, IPC, Federazione Italiana di Atletica Leggera (intentional offence), Federação Portuguesa de Natação (anabolica), Nederlandse Koninklijke Zwembond (anabolen), UK Athletics
max. life-long ban	FISA, Equestrian Federation of Ireland, Irish Amateur Wrestling Association, Volleyball Association of Ireland, Irish Sailing Association

2nd infraction	
min. 1 week to max. 2 years	Riksidrottsförbundet (minor doping offence)
max. 3 months	Nederlandse Hippische Sportbond
6 months to 4 years	Decreet inz. Medisch verantwoorde sportbeoefening
min. 1 year	Fédération Royale Belge de tennis
min. 1 year to max. 2 years	Riksidrottsförbundet (serious doping offence), Hellenic Cycling Federation, Koninklijke Nederlandse Wielren Unie, Irish Cycling Federation, Deutscher Hockey Bund, Bund Deutscher Radfahrer ("Elitekategorie" women, under 23, "andere Sportler/innen")
1 to 2 years	Deutsche Triathlon Union, Bund Deutscher Radfahrer ("Elitekategorie" men)
1 to 22 years	Deutscher Tisch Tennis Bund, Deutscher Volleyball Verband, Deutscher Bob- und Schlittensportverband
1 to 3 years	Union Royale Belge des Sociétés de Football Assoc.
15 months to 2 years	Federação Portuguesa de Hoquei, Federação Portuguesa de Badminton
max. 2 years	FIH, UCI, Deutscher Judo Bund
2 to 4 years	Federação de Triatlo de Portugal, Federação Portuguesa de Ténis, Federação Portuguesa de Remo, Federação Portuguesa de Basquetebol, Federação Equestre Portuguesa, Federação Portuguesa de Futebol, Federação Portuguesa de Andebol, Federação Portuguesa de Judo, Federação Portuguesa de Tiro com Arco
2 to 6 years	Federação Portuguesa de Natação (amphetamines)
min. 2 years	Comitato Olimpico Nazionale Italiano (petty offence), Federazione Italiana Nuoto, Federazione Italiana Tennis, Federazione Italiana Scherma, Federazione Italiana Sport Equestri, Federazione Italiana Pallacanestro, Federazione Italiana Canoa Kayak, Federazione Italiana Pallavola, Federazione Italiana Sport Invernali
min. 2 years to life-long ban	Deutscher Sport Bund ("Stimulanzien" and "Narkotika"), Nederlandse Koninklijke Zwembond (betablokkers), Verband Österreicher Schwimmvereine (amphetamine related substances)
min. 3 years	ISU, National Ice Skating Association of UK
max. 5 years	Triathlon Luxembourg, Fédération Française de Triathlon, Fédération Française de Tennis de Table, Fédération Française de Natation, Fédération Française de Tennis, Fédération Française de Boxe, Fédération Française de Basketball, Fédération Française de Cyclisme, Fédération Française de Handball, Fédération Française de Judo, Jujitsu, Kendo, Fédération Française de Lutte, Fédération Française de Tir à l'Arc, Fédération Française de Voile, Fédération Française de Ski
4 years to max. life-long ban	Comitato Olimpico Nazionale Italiano (petty offence), Federazione Italiana Nuoto, Federazione Italiana Tennis, Federazione Italiana Scherma, Federazione Italiana Sport Equestri, Federazione Italiana Pallacanestro, Federazione Italiana Canoa Kayak, Federazione Italiana Pallavola, Federazione Italiana Sport Invernali, Badminton Association of England, Great Britain Olympic Hockey Board
min. 6 years	Federação Portuguesa de Natação (anabolica)
20 to 30 years	Federação Portuguesa de Halterofilismo
max. life-long ban	Nederlandse Koninklijke Zwembond (social drugs), Koninklijke Nederlandse Atletiek Unie, Nederlandse IJshockey Bond, Deutscher Sport Bund ("Narkotika"), Deutscher Sport Bund ("Narkotika")

3rd infraction	
min. 2 years to life-long ban	Deutscher Hockey Bund
22 years to life-lon ban	Antidoping Rahmen-Richtlinien, Deutsche Triathlon Union, Bund Deutscher Radfahrer ("Elitekategorie" men), Deutscher Ruderverband, Deutscher Basketball Bund, Deutscher Handball Bund, Deutscher Ringer-Bund, Deutscher Eishockey Bund
min. 4 years	Fédération Royale Belge de tennis
5 years to life-long ban	FIH
10 to 20 years	Federação de Triatlo de Portugal, Federação Portuguesa de Ténis, Federação Portuguesa de Hoque, Federação Portuguesa de Remo, Federação Portuguesa de Badminton, Federação Portuguesa de Basquetebol, Federação Equestre Portuguesa, Federação Portuguesa de Futebol, Federação Portuguesa de Andebol, Federação Portuguesa de Judo, Federação Portuguesa de Tiro com Arco

7.   PROPORTIONALITY OF SANCTIONS AND RESTRAINT OF TRADE

7.1. Proportionality of sanctions

With the introduction of strict liability a reversal of the burden of proof had also been effected. Previous descriptions of the doping offence targeted the athlete's actions and imposed on sports organisations the gargantuan task of proving guilt or intent. The new descriptions focusing on the presence of a prohibited substance in the athlete's urine or blood had the great advantage for the sports organisations that this time it was the athlete who had to prove that he had not knowingly, negligently or intentionally used doping. However, in the case law of the CAS and other tribunals, the reversed burden of proof remained a dead letter rule as far as disproving liability was concerned. Instead, any degree in which the athlete could not be considered guilty was taken into account in the determination of the sanctions. Again, however, this could not be the case where regulations provided for fixed sanctions. For this reason, it was suggested during the World Doping Conference in February 1999 that a certain degree of flexibility be introduced in the descriptions of the sanctions. Many international and national sport organisations did begin to provide for minimum and maximum sanctions. As the focus in disciplinary proceedings has increasingly come to lie on the sentencing and as such, on the question of proportionality, any sanction to be imposed had to reflect the seriousness of the offence.[870] According to Vieweg:[871] "with respect to the principle of proportionality, it is necessary to weigh up the interests of the athlete, in particular his right of personality, against those of the federation."[872]

---

[870] See *inter alia*: CAS 99/A/234 & CAS 99/A/235, 29-2-2000, *David Meca-Medina v. FINA & Igor Majcen v. FINA*, ground 11.4: "The Doping Control Panel expressed the view that a sanction of 4 years suspension in such a case may no longer be commensurate with the quality of the offence committed. They quoted the case CAS 96/156, 6-10-1997, *Jessica K. Foschi v. FINA* "the general principle that a penalty must not be disproportionate to the source or guilt must also be observed in doping cases." However, they noted that the FINA Congress had on 6th January 1998 decided unanimously to establish the minimum sanction of 4 years suspension. The Panel shares the view of the Doping Control Panel; but is equally constrained by the law. Beloff, Kerr and Demetriou (Beloff 1999 (*supra* nt. 282), p. 12, have argued in what strikes me as a circular line of reasoning that "[...] the principle of proportionality means that a sanction must be proportionate to the offence and that the sanction must be necessary to achieve the result sought by the body imposing it."

[871] Klaus Vieweg, "The definition of doping and the proof of a doping offence," (2002) *ISLJ*, pp. 2-6.

[872] According to Mario Krogmann (Krogmann 1998, *supra* nt. 11, p. 107 et seq.) "kommt es darauf an, daß die entgegenstehenden grundrechtlich geschützten Interessen von Verband und Sportler bei der Bemessung der Strafe in ein ausgewogenes Verhältnis gebracht werden." See also Christoph Vedder (International Athletic Foundation – Symposium on sport and law, session 7, Harmonisation of international rules and regulations, restraint of trade and rights to work, p. 149): "According to legal principles, there should be means of taking the athlete's lack or presence of personal responsibility into consideration. The personal and subjective circumstances should influence the extent of the penalty [...]." See also Anthony T. Polvino, "Arbitration as preventative medicine for olympic ailments: the International Olympic Committee's Court of Arbitration for Sport and the future for the settlement of international sporting disputes," in *Emory International Law Review*, Vol. 8 1994, p. 357.

To give in to the pressure to impose ever stricter penalties for doping would mean to collide with the boundaries of what is considered proportionate within society. But what indeed is considered proportionate? Is it proportionate to impose a fixed penalty of two years on every athlete who tests positive, regardless of the circumstances? Mr Verbruggen,[873] who is the chairman of the UCI, has observed that: "[...] proportionality does not exist only in relation with the individual position of the athlete, but also in relation with the specific realities of each sport." [...] There is a large majority claiming that the minimum sanction for a first offence should be two years in all sports. Why two years? Why not six months or four years? What are the considerations for determining that under all circumstances and in all sports a two year suspension should be the minimum?"[874] On sanctions Simma has remarked that:[875] "[...] sanctions will affect not only the personal sphere but in many cases also the economic or even 'professional' position of the athlete concerned." He further noted that the liberalisation of the ineligibility rule also opened the door for the "intrusion of domestic law and national judges into the domain of sports because of the protection which domestic legal orders grant to the integrity of the person or to the economic/professional sphere of the individual against interferences considered to be unjustified. What national and international sports bodies had to undertake, therefore, is to tailor the substance and procedures of international sports law in a way so as to render its prescriptions and sanctions "justified," more proportional, in the eyes of national judges. Thus, one could imagine that automatic, life-time, exclusion from competitions as a sanction for a first in-

---

[873] Hein Verbruggen was one of the speakers at a Round Table Session on doping at the T.M.C. Asser Institute in The Hague on 2 December 1999.

[874] He illustrated this statement by the following example: "A cyclist is found positive in the Tour de France of 1998 and is eliminated from the race. He is sanctioned with a suspension of 2 years, taking effect on 1 February 1999, after the disciplinary proceedings have come to an end. He will not participate in any race in 1999 and in 2000. If after two years of inactivity he still would be able to compete again – which is far from likely – he may start riding in February 2001. However he will not be in the required shape to participate in a Tour de France in July. They are not all Armstrongs. This rider will have been excluded from four Tours de France, three World Championships and the Olympic Games in 2000. He will have no income for at least two years. From a physical point of view it is more than likely that he will not come back to his former level. There is a real risk that because of that he will no longer be able to find an employer and that his career will be over. On the other hand we have a top pistol shooter who has a full time job as a policeman or regular officer. The most important competition in which he participates are the Olympic Games. He is found positive and is suspended for two years as from January 1st, 1997. He suffers no loss of income, he can continue to train as before and is entitled to participate in competitions one and a half year before the 2000 Olympics. From a formal point of view this might be harmony or unity, but I feel it as injustice."

[875] Bruno Simma, *The Court of Arbitration for Sport*, in Völkerrecht – Recht der Internationalen Organisationen – Weltwirtschaftsrecht – Law of Nations – Law of International Organizations – World's Economic Law, Festschrift für Ignaz Seldl-Hohenveldern, Liber amicorum honouring Ignaz Seldl-Hohenveldern, Herausgegeben von Karl-Heinz Böckstiegel, Hans-Ernst Folz, Jörg Manfred Mössner, Karl Zemanek, Carl Heymanns Verlag KG – Köln – Berlin – Bonn – München, p. 584. E.g. FISA Rules of Racing and Related By Laws, Part VII – Medical Provisions, Bye- Law to rules 80 to 83 – Doping, Art. 9.3.1 sub a: "Use of anabolic agents [...] whatever the circumstances of the testing: Life ban for the first offence."

stance of doping could be considered as untenable, i.c. manifestly disproportional, from the viewpoint of domestic law." In *Krabbe II* the Appeal Court of Munich would not accept the penalty of three years' ineligibility and reduced it to one year. The Court referred to the basic right of an athlete to work as a professional and to the proportionality of sanctions.[876] In the view of the Court the three-year suspension imposed on Katrin Krabbe had to be considered null as suspensions of "more than two years contravene [...] the constitutional principle of proportionality." Udo Steiner[877] has remarked as follows on the effect of the "Verhältnismäßigkeitsprinzip," the principle of proportionality, and the limits it sets for penalties under German law:

"Fairness und Chancengleichheit sind höchste Sportgüter, Doping deshalb eine tödliche Berufskrankheit. Vor diesem Hintergrund kann nicht umstritten sein, dass dopingbegründete Wettkampfsperren auf Zeit oder Lebenszeit grundsätzlich mit Art. 12 Abs. 1 GG[878] vereinbar sind. Allerdings muß das dopingrechtliche Sanktionssystem den Anforderungen des Verhältnismäßigkeitsgrundsatzes genügen. Folgerungen aus einem so allgemeinen Prinzip sind nicht mit Stringenz zu ziehen. Die Sportverbände der Bundesrepublik haben hier ohne Zweifel einen verfassungsrechtlichen Spielraum. Bei der zeitlichen Bemessung von Wettkampfsperren für Berufssportler muß allgemein berücksichtigt werden, dass – gewiß unterschiedlich nach Sportarten – die Gesamtleistungszeit in Jahren und nicht in Jahrzehnten gerechnet werden kann, ein größerer Zeitraum der Wettkampfsperre physisch und psychisch allein durch Training nur schwer zu überbrücken ist und unter Berücksichtigung des Lebensalters des einzelnen Sportlers die Aufgabe des Berufes bedeuten kann. Zudem ist jede Dopingverurteilung über die Wettkampfsperre hinaus mit schweren Nachteilen – Ansehensminderung, Verlust sportbezogener Einnahmen usw. – verbunden.
Immerhin kann man mit der gebotenen Vorsicht wagen, gewisse Linien aus dem Verhältnismäßigkeitsprinzip zu entwickeln: Automatische Wettkampfsperren von einem Jahr erscheinen verfassungsrechtlich nicht zweifelhaft. Die zweijährige Sperre kann in den Statuten als Regel ausgestaltet sein. Individuelle Gesichtspunkte können aber eine Abweichung von der Regel zugunsten des Athleten rechtfertigen: etwa Grad des Verschuldens, Intensität der Leistungsbeeinflussung, Bereitschaft zur Mitwirkung an der Aufklärung des Dopingvergehens. Je stärker sich die Sperre de facto auf den Berufsausschluß hin bewegt, umso höher muß das Gewicht des Dopingverstoßes sein. Wettkampfsperren über zwei Jahre hinaus und insbesondere auf Lebenszeit dürften nur in den Fällen zulässig sein, in denen der Sportler – etwa wegen wiederholten Doping – für die Sportgemeinschaft schlechterdings unerträglich ist und deshalb seine Rückkehr in den Wettkampf ernsthaft nicht mehr in Betracht kommen kann."

---

[876] In 1991, the IAAF decided to increase the ineligibility period for a first offence involving anabolic steroids from two to four years. After the *Krabbe II* decision the IAAF again reduced the period of ineligibility to two years.

[877] *Doping aus verfassungsrechtlicher Sicht, Doping-Forum* (ed. Röhricht/Vieweg) 2000 Köln, pp. 136-137.

[878] Art. 12 (1) GG: "Alle Deutschen haben das Recht, Beruf, Arbeitsplatz und Ausbildungsstätte frei zu wählen. Die Berufsausübung kann durch Gesetz oder auf Grund eines Gesetzes geregelt werden."

Could the CAS play a role in establishing an acceptable link between the serious-ness of the offence and the severity of the sanction? According to Oschütz[879] it could: "In the area of the sanctions, the Panels have shown a great deal of flexibil-ity. The Panels assume the same powers as the competent organ of the respective federation.[880] Relying mostly on the principle of proportionality[881] the arbitrators have tried to adapt the length of each suspension to the particularities of each case taking into account the circumstances of the doping offence as well as the personal-ity and behaviour of the athlete." In a well-known decision of 31 March 1999[882] the Swiss Federal Tribunal questioned the proportionality of a sanction imposed by the CAS, if not, however, with the desired outcome as far as the athlete was concerned.[883]

The proportionality principle means that a balance must be achieved between the seriousness of the offence and the severity of the sanction. In imposing a sanc-tion, it must always be considered that the period of the suspension is not the only penalty, but that it includes related – sometimes far-reaching – effects, such as loss

---

[879] Frank Oschütz, "The Jurisprudence of the CAS in Doping Cases," (2001) *ISLJ*, pp. 22-30.

[880] CAS 2000/A/317, 9-7-2001, *F. Aanes v. FILA*, p. 24.

[881] CAS 95/141, 22-4-1996, *Chagnaud v. FINA*, Matthieu Reeb, ed., *Digest of CAS Awards 1986-1998* (Berne, Editions Stämpfli 1998) pp. 205-224; CAS 2000/A/317, 9-7-2001, *F. Aanes v. FILA*, p. 24.

[882] Swiss Federal Tribunal: Wang Lu Na, 31 March 1999, ref. 5 P. 83/1999.

[883] Pp. 10-12: "The appellants also claim that the contested award constitutes a serious and unjus-tified infringement of their personal liberties and personal rights. They state that personal freedom and the protection of personal rights should be regarded as included among the fundamental legal prin-ciples protected by the negative public policy clause, in particular with regard to suspensions imposed on athletes by international sports federations. In the present case, they substantially maintain that the penalty upheld by the CAS is an extremely serious violation of their personal liberties and personal rights and that it fails to comply with the principle of proportionality, in so far as the penalty is the minimum one provided for by the Rules although the proportion of banned substance found in their urine samples was very low and a two-year suspension may, having regard to the brief careers of top athletes, end their careers permanently and prevent any further achievements by them in their field of sports activity.
As has already been stated [...], the award complained of was made pursuant to a rule which envisages that, if diuretics have been found in the bodily fluids of a competitor, it is for that competitor to show why he should not suffer the maximum penalty of two years' suspension. Under this system, the ques-tion is not to determine the penalty proportionate to a given quantity of banned substance found in the competitor's urine but to establish whether that competitor has produced evidence of circumstances mitigating the maximum penalty allowed by the Rules, for example the absence of the intent to indulge in doping [...]. The issue of the proportionality of the penalty could therefore only arise, from the restricted standpoint of incompatibility with public policy, if the arbitration award were to constitute an attack on personal rights which was extremely serious and totally disproportionate to the behaviour penalized. In the present case, whatever the appellants may say – and they declare in grandiloquent tones that Aonly the most extreme custodial sentences that can be pronounced by the state courts are capable of producing such effects" – the two years' suspension on them involves only a moderate restriction on their freedom of movement, since they can continue their sport freely, apart from partici-pation in international competitions; it is admittedly a serious penalty, liable to restrict their interna-tional careers as top-level athletes, but the fact remains that it is restricted to two years and arises from a proven violation of an anti-doping rule whose application the appellants have accepted as members of a national federation affiliated to the FINA. In this respect, again, their appeal is seen to be un-founded."

of income, cancelled sponsoring contracts, loss of fame as a media figure, interruption of the rhythm of competing and – last but not least – loss of profession, because at the end of the period of ineligibility the athlete is often too old still to achieve a top performance. In some sports a two-year ban will cause no problems whatsoever, but in others, where the professional life-span of athletes is short, two years can mean life. Penalties for doping offences should not be unified, they should be harmonised, which means that their impact in one sport should be the same as in another sport.

7.2. **Restraint of trade**

From the above it has emerged that disciplinary measures and suspensions imposed for doping may clash with the constitutionally protected right to employment.[884] Another effect of lengthy suspensions may be that they restrain trade. Sport is becoming increasingly international in character. This trend has given rise to the international competence of many sports organisations. How does this affect the possibility to interfere with decisions of these organisations even if they restrain trade? Samuel and Gearhart have cautioned[885] that challenges based on illegal restraint of trade "[...] may not often succeed but where an athlete is backed by a management agency with unlimited funds and a major financial interest in the continuing sporting participation of their client, sports federations find themselves involved in costly litigation and not find it easy to recover their costs against an athlete even if they win." According to Bailey:[886] "Pursuant to English common law restraint principles the factors the Court will consider when determining whether a clause of a contract or rule of a sports governing body is in restraint of trade are as follows: – Is the individual sportsman/sportswoman involved in a recognised trade? – Does the relevant clause within the rules or contract restrain the sportsman or woman in their trade? If the answer to the above questions is yes, then the restraint will be unenforceable unless it is reasonable." In this context it should be mentioned that pursuant to English law, the sport organisation must prove reasonableness in the circumstances. The burden of proof is therefore reversed when the athlete is able to show that a certain provision in the doping regulations results in "restraint of trade."[887]

---

[884] Christoph Vedder, International Athletic Foundation – Symposium on sport and law, session seven, Harmonisation of international rules and regulations, restraint of trade and rights to work, p. 145: "They are restraints of trade. This became obvious in the famous Gasser case, which was settled before the English courts."

[885] Adam Samuel and Richard Gearhart, *Sporting Arbitration and the International Olympic Committee's Court of Arbitration for Sport*, pp. 42-43.

[886] "Doping Control in the United Kingdom – The Regulatory and Legal Framework," in: K. Vieweg, ed., *Doping – Realität und Recht* (1998) p. 339.

[887] Darren Bailey, "Doping Control in the United Kingdom," in *Doping – Realität und Recht*, Berlin 1998, p. 340: "In the event that a Court considers that the particular rule goes further than is reasonably necessary to protect the legitimate interests of the sport, the Court may declare a rule void and unenforceable and/or award damages to the complainant."

In *Gasser v. Stinson* the IAAF[888] argued that the restraint-of-trade rule in English law could not be applied to IAAF rules, which aim to regulate the admission of athletes of all nationalities to sports competitions the world over. The IAAF argued that as a rule of policy the English courts were not entitled to apply English public order rules – based on the English view of freedom of economic competition – to the regulation of international athletics. This argument was rejected "on the grounds that authority was against it and because as a matter of principle, [...] [the Court] did not see why English courts should hold their hands in a case such as the present [...] Is it to be said that the IAAF is beyond the reach of the courts and the law? [...] To the extent, therefore, that there is a policy decision to be made, I am of the opinion that the English restraint of trade rules should be applied to the validity of the IAAF's rules."[889] In addition, the laws of the different countries lead to different outcomes in the application of rules, which arguably have the effect of tempting governing bodies to apply double standards. The IAAF rules, for example, require the national federation to suspend the athlete for a period of four years in the event of a positive doping test. This period was, however, not considered to be reasonable in a number of countries, the result being that athletes are treated differently according to their nationality.

British athlete Paul Edwards was expelled from the Commonwealth Games of 1994. His request to return was rejected although two German athletes were re-admitted after two years as German law considers a suspension of four years unreasonable. England does not have this kind of proportionality rule, which means that Edwards remained banned while his German colleagues, who had been found guilty of similar offences, were again taking part in competitions. The IAAF recognised the unfairness of the situation but it could not – of its own admission – go further than to ban the national federations, which comply with the rules of their country, or to rehabilitate athletes from countries, which consider the period of suspension unacceptable.[890] Based on this double standard it was recommend by the IAAF

---

[888] High Court, 15 June 1988, unreported.

[889] "Such challenges (i.e. on the ground of restraint of trade) would be unlikely to succeed before the English courts, unless the penalties provided for were so manifestly excessive and disproportionate as to go beyond all reasons. Automatic life bans for a first offence without possibility of mitigation or exculpation, applying in a case of innocent ingestion without fault or intention to gain, might be regarded as so harsh as to merit being struck down. But strict and severe penalties short of that may be expected to be upheld, for the English courts would be loath to hand down rulings which would undermine the fight against drugs in sport." Beloff 1999 (*supra* nt. 282), 7.96. In O'Leary 2000, (*supra* nt. 4), p. 56 Beloff notes "that there is a live issue as to whether a life ban (or a ban which operated for an athlete's lifetime) might be an unlawful restraint of trade." In a footnote to this remark (no. 65) he cites the Ben Johnson case. "[...] Johnson, stripped of his gold medal for the 100 m at the Seoul Olympics for a doping offence, was reinstated to sports eligibility in Canada. An independent adjudicator concluded that the lifetime ban imposed on Mr Johnson by Athletics Canada was excessive in the circumstances, partly on the basis that he had been misinformed at an earlier stage about his apparent rights." Unfortunately, Beloff does not pursue this point further.

[890] A certain tension exists between aspects of substantive sports law which may result in unfairness towards the individual athlete and those which may result in unfairness towards the other athletes. "Disqualification is mandatory. It would be unfair to other athletes to include in the ranking someone

congress that the IAAF reduce its suspension period to two years, as the rules in force were not enforceable everywhere. Members who voted against this proposal felt that its outcome would be to undermine the position of doping control officials.[891]

In *Gasser v. Stinson* the English High Court denied relief to Gasser. The dictum suggests that if an arbitral award deprives an athlete of his or her livelihood the reasonableness of the award may be reviewable by a court. Such a court might as well be the CAS. The CAS rejected the notion that a one-year suspension constitutes an unreasonable restraint of trade. Under Rule 58 of the CAS rules "the Panel shall decide the dispute according to the applicable regulations and the rules chosen by the parties. The ITC rules were governed by English law. Under English law a four-year suspension for a doping offence in the field of athletics has been upheld: see *Gasser v. Stinson*: unreported (5th June 1988 Scott J). A one-year suspension must a fortiori be valid."[892] The tennis players Wilander and Novacek, who both tested positive at the 1995 French Open, sought an order to stay any proceedings against them based on Rule 53 of the ITF Anti-Doping Programme. They challenged this rule, as in their opinion it constituted an unfair and unreasonable restraint of trade. Bailey[893] reports that the Court[894] "[...] confirmed that he saw nothing approaching unfairness or unreasonableness in the absolute nature of the offence, or the mandatory sentence. He effectively relied upon the reasoning of Scott J. in the *Gasser* case in this regard. However, he went on to focus on what he considered to be the 'real thrust' of the players' argument, namely the so-called reversal of the burden of proof. Under the ITF Programme challenged by the players at a hearing before the Appeals Committee, it was for the player to establish his guilt or innocence." Felix[895] has remarked that: "Neill J found the shifting of the burden of proof 'troublesome' in that the presumption of innocence was the cornerstone of English criminal law." After having reviewed the whole ITF Programme the Court "[...] concluded that the safeguards provided in the procedure were sufficient to ensure that the testing was carried out in a proper manner and according to the proper rules of a competent laboratory. He therefore rejected the argument that Rule 53 was arguably void as being a restraint of trade."[896]

---

who had used artificial means of performance enhancement if the rules are sufficient clear." Beloff 1999 (*supra* nt. 282), 7.127. Procedural sports law has the task of weighing the interests of the athlete and those of the sport; it should not only serve to protect preconceived ideas.

[891] See Gardiner/O'Leary 1998 (*supra* nt. 14), pp. 248-249.

[892] CAS 98/223, 31-8-1999, *Korda v. ITF*, Matthieu Reeb, ed., *Digest of CAS Awards II 1998-2000* (The Hague, Kluwer Law International 2002) pp. 345-360, ground 67.

[893] Darren Bailey, "Doping Control in the United Kingdom," in Klaus Vieweg, ed., *Doping – Realität und Recht* (Berlin, Duncker & Humblot 1998) p. 346.

[894] Wilander and Novacek/Tobin and Jude (the President and Honorary Treasurer respectively of the ITF, (1997) 1 Lloyds Rep. 195. See: Bailey 1998 (*supra* nt. 887), p. 346. Alexandra Felix, in Gardiner/O'Leary 1998 (*supra* nt. 14), p. 236 et seq. used the transcript of 26 March 1996, and mentioned that this was an unreported High Court case.

[895] Alexandra Felix, in Gardiner/O'Leary 1998 (*supra* nt. 14), p. 236 et seq.

[896] *Idem.*

To sum up the issue of proportionality, the severity of the sanctions which could be imposed under the various doping regulations at times collided with views in society on what is proportionate and what is not. A balance must be struck between the severity of the penalty and the seriousness of the offence. Disproportionate sanctions are not considered acceptable.

7.3.   The approach taken in the WADC – exceptional circumstances

According to art. 10.2 WADC first violations are punishable by two years ineligibility and second violations by lifetime ineligibility. In principle those are fixed sanctions, "however, the athlete [...] shall have the opportunity in each case, before a period of ineligibility is imposed, to establish the basis for eliminating or reducing this sanction as provided in Article 10.5 (exceptional circumstances)."

The concept of exceptional circumstances has already been dealt with in Chapter 4, Section 5. By relying on exceptional circumstances it may be possible to reduce the period of ineligibility. For this reason, the concept could easily have been discussed in the present chapter. However, as it is established by weighing the degree of guilt of the athlete it has been dealt with in the part of the book where these matters are examined and to which I here refer.

8.   REDUCTION OF SANCTION FOR COOPERATION IN THE INVESTIGATION

One final possibility to become eligible for a reduced penalty is for the penalised athlete to cooperate with the relevant authorities to expose other doping offenders. This practice is viewed less positively on the Continent than it is in the United States.

If an athlete has substantially assisted an anti-doping organisation in the detection or establishment of violations of the anti-doping rules by athlete support personnel this organisation may – according to Article 10.5.3 WADC – decide to reduce the ineligibility period of the athlete concerned. When the penalty was imposed for a first violation the reduction may be by as much as half the minimum period of exclusion. If the athlete was banned for life, his/her penalty may only be reduced by a maximum of eight years. The provision does not make clear whether it is the disciplinary body which in its decision has to take account of the athlete's assistance, or whether it is the anti-doping organisation that may reduce any penalty that has been imposed by a disciplinary body. Given that the provision is part of Article 10 (sanctions on individuals) it is probable that the disciplinary body has to reduce the sanction.

9.   SPORT SANCTIONS

In this book, sporting sanctions do not play a prominent role as they are not central to the questions dealt with. Still, they cannot be completely ignored. It might in some respects even have a greater impact on an athlete if he/she is disqualified, has his/her medals taken away and is struck off the ranking list than if he/she is suspended for a certain period of time. The media will certainly pay more attention to the sporting sanction than to a possible suspension. In the discussion of team sanctions above sporting sanctions were already briefly mentioned. Below, sporting sanctions affecting individual athletes will be discussed.

9.1. Disqualification

Disqualification is commonly regarded as a sport sanction. Such sanctions can be imposed without having to enter into the question of fault.[897] A footballer who during a match fails to treat an opponent in accordance with the regulations can be shown the red and sent off by the referee. This player will then be disqualified for the duration of that match and will face disciplinary proceedings. The use of doping could be viewed as the mirror image of rough play. Rough play goes against a rule of play and as such as considered as misconduct. The use of doping is a type of misconduct violating the entire image of the sport. A violation of the doping rules goes against the fairness of competition and must therefore be countered by a sport sanction which can reinstate fairness between the teams or players. As has been explained above in the discussion of team sanctions, there is a difference between sport sanctions (disqualification) and disciplinary sanctions (suspension). This distinction has been clearly recognised by the CAS.

> "It seems to the Panel that the decision of a CAS Panel in Sydney in Raducan[898] aptly identified where the innocence [...] of ingestion of a prohibited substance may be relevant and where it is not. It is not relevant in the case of disqualification, because that would be manifestly unfair to other competitors who did not have the advantage of the prohibited substance. It may be relevant [...] to the existence or extent of any suspicion, because of the potential unfairness of suspending an athlete who is without fault."[899]

Many doping regulations mentioned disqualification in connection with the use of doping. The UEFA doping regulations contained a provision that "[...] if a player is shown a red card and sent off during the match because his behaviour is suspiciously uncoordinated or aggressive, he may [...] be ordered to undergo a doping control at the end of the match [...]."[900] This would not be a case of disqualification

---

[897] Cf., Steiner 2000 (*supra* nt. 439), p. 134: "[...] die Anordnung des Verlustes von Vorteilen (Titeln, Medaillen, Anerkennung von Rekorden, Prämien usw.), die der Sportler dopingunterstützt in einem Wettkampf erzielt hat, (ist) ohne Feststellung des Verschuldens zulässig. Sie stellt nachträglich die Chancengleichheit zwischen den Athleten wieder her."

[898] SYD 011 paras 25-28; see also *CAS Awards Sydney 2000*, pp. 121-122.

[899] CAS 2000/A/270, 23-5-2001, *David Meca-Medina v. FINA & Igor Majcen v. FINA*, ground 9.4.

[900] Regulations governing doping controls at UEFA competition matches and list of banned substances and methods, 1999/2000 season and until further notice, Art. 4. Suspicion of doping.

due to the use of doping; a player acting this way is disqualified for the remainder of the game and it might emerge from the doping control that he has used doping. Disqualification for the use of prohibited substances is a retroactive sanction. Only some time after the end of a game can it can be established whether the athlete's body contained prohibited substances, while rough or unfair play of course can be established immediately. When however a competition takes the shape of a tournament, i.e. is played out over several events during a longer period of time, such as the Olympics or world championships, national championships, etc., the results of doping analysis may become known before the end of the tournament. In cases like these, the athlete, just like the footballer who is sent off, can be disqualified for the remainder of the tournament[901] (possibly in addition to retroactive disqualification for any matches already played during the tournament).[902] The IOC Medical Code provided that "the penalty for an infraction by individual competitors [...] during the Olympic Games is temporary or permanent ineligibility or exclusion (disqualification) from the Olympic Games."[903] Incidentally, it appears that under this provision disqualification was actually regarded as an equivalent of a disciplinary sanction. This ISF punished first doping offences by "a minimum of two years disqualification from all ISF competition [...]."[904] The doping regulations of the IPC were a clear example of the retroactivity of the sanction: "An athlete shall be disqualified from the competition in which he or she was tested [...]."[905]

It may be considered entirely acceptable that disqualifications are retroactive as doped athletes probably did not just dope themselves for one event during a tournament. Not to let the disqualification have retroactive effect would be "manifestly unfair to other competitors who did not have the advantage of the prohibited substance." However, the IAAF provided that "the athlete shall be disqualified from that competition [...] His ineligibility shall begin from the date on which the sample was provided."[906] This rule made it possible that an athlete who made it to the finals was only disqualified for those and not for the preceding games in the tournament.

---

[901] IHF: Anti-Doping Regulations, 11. Sanctions: "In case of a proven doping offence, the players concerned are disqualified from all further tournament matches"; FIH: Doping Policy, 12. Sanctions, 12.2: "Doping [...] shall automatically result in the disqualification of the athlete for the remainder of the event during which the testing was conducted (provisional suspension)."

[902] IJF: Regulations concerning Dope Tests, 16. Sanctions: "For a first infraction, the incriminated competitor is disqualified from the competition in question"; FISA: Disciplinary Regulations, Art. 13 – Doping Test: "[...] the doped wrestler shall be disqualified for the entire competition [...]"; IBU: Disciplinary Rules, para. 5 Penalties, 5.5.: "A competitor [...] shall be disqualified for: [...] taking part in a competition when doped [...]."

[903] Chapter IX – Penalties for infractions, Art. II.

[904] Code, Art. 15, 15.11, sub 1 and Doping Control and Testing as established by the ISF Medical and Doping Commission, 4.0 Penalties, sub 4.1.1.

[905] Doping, 8.2 – Penalties for Doping Infractions, 2.0 – Penalties – Use-Infractions (Athletes), 2.2. See also: FISA: Rules of Racing and Related By Laws, Part. VI – Organisation of Regattas, Section 4 – Duties of the Jury and Rules of Umpiring, Rule 82 – Penalties for Doping; FIBA: Regulations Governing Doping Control, 6.6. Sanctions, 6.6.1. sub 2.

[906] Rules and Regulations, Constitution, Division III – Control of Drug Abuse, Rule 59 – Disciplinary Procedures for Doping Offences, subsection 4.

One may wonder what would have happened if the doping control did not take place until the day after the finals.

The boundaries between the concepts of "disqualification" and "disciplinary sanction" were quite often blurred in the different regulations. The IBA regulations contained the rule that "the penalty for a first infraction by a player shall be disqualification if the infractions occurred during the competition."[907] A further example were the regulations of the AIBA: "A boxer who has been found guilty of doping may be punished by suspension from any competition for a period of up to two years and, in case of recurrence, disqualification for lifetime."[908]

The period of disqualification also varied, both between the different sports organisations and at times also within a single sports organisation, where the time of commencement of the sanction could vary. Several regulations further distinguished between temporary and definitive disqualification. The ICF, for example, among other things provided that: "if an athlete is found to have committed a doping offence [...] the athlete shall be disqualified from the competition [...]"[909] In another rule this federation had established that: "if a competitor [...] (is) found doped, disciplinary measures can be taken by the Board of Directors, e.g. temporary or definitive disqualification."[910]

Disqualification as a result of the use of doping is commonly considered in the world of sport to be a sanction against which no appeal lies; nevertheless, the Russian athlete Korneev and his compatriot, the wrestler Gouliev, appealed against their disqualification from the Olympic Games by the IOC Executive. The IOC had disqualified them for the use of Bromantan. In the appellate ruling against this decision of the IOC the CAS considered that: "in order to justify the disqualification of an athlete for the use of Bromantan it must be established that Bromantan is a stimulant within the meaning of the Medical Code. The burden of establishing that fact, if disputed, is on the suspending body." Given the fact that the IOC Medical Committee was unable to prove that Bromantan, which was not on the IOC list of prohibited substances and methods, was in fact a banned substance, the CAS decided that: "On the basis of the foregoing facts and legal determinations, the ad hoc Division of the Court of Arbitration for Sport decides that the appeals of the athletes Andrei Korneev and Zakhar Gouliev against the decisions of the International Olympic Committee Executive Board disqualifying them for the Games of the XXVI Olympiad for the use of Bromantan be allowed and those decisions be set aside."

As opposed to the doping regulations of the international federations and the interpretation of the concept in practice, the dictionary is clear on the meaning of "to

---

[907] Anti-Doping Rules, Chapter 13 – Disciplinary Sanctions, sub 13.1.
[908] Articles of Association and Rules for International Competitions and Tournaments, Art. XXVII: Disciplinary Action, C. Doping, sub 2.
[909] ICF: Doping Rules, Rule 5, subsection 4.
[910] ICF: Slalom Racing Competition Rules, 41, 41.13. Anti-Doping, sub 41.13.2.

disqualify": "Unfit, disable; incapacitate legally, pronounce unqualified; debar from competition because of infringement of rules."[911] The sports organisations regarded doping primarily as a violation of the rules of play. However, anti-doping regulations are of a completely different character than rules of play.

9.2. Return of prizes, medals, etc.

A sporting sanction closely connected with disqualification is the forced return of prizes, trophies, medals, etc. This is by definition a retroactive sanction. The IOC Medical Code[912] provided that: "In the case of exclusion, any medals or diplomas obtained shall be returned to the IOC Executive Board." The ICF also wanted its medals back: "[S]hould the disqualification take place after the delivery of the medals, the position obtained by the competitor [...] will pass on to the one finishing immediately after. All other competitors will move forward one position. The medals should be returned and presented to the winning competitor(s), according to the new classification."[913] The IPC provided that disqualified athletes: "shall forfeit all records and medals."[914] Finally, pursuant to the FISA doping rules a rower who had tested positive "shall not be ranked in any circumstances"[915] while basketball players who were disqualified for doping "shall lose the game by forfeit as well as the games that have already been played."[916]

9.3. Sport sanctions according to the WADC

The WADC provides for sport sanctions and disciplinary sanctions. The sport sanctions consist of "[...] disqualification of all of the athlete's individual results obtained in that event with all consequences, including forfeiture of all medals, points and prizes."[917] Two particular sets of circumstances can trigger automatic disqualification. Under Article 9 this may happen when the violation of the doping rule takes place "[...] in connection with an in-competition test," and under Article 10.1 when the violation takes place "[...] during or in connection with an event [...], upon the decision of the ruling body of the event." Article 9 is a separate article, while Article 10.1 is part of an Article concerning "Sanctions on individuals." The reason as to why Article 10.1 has not been accorded the status of a separate article as well or has not been joined to Article 9 remains unclear. The only difference between the situations described is that in one the game in question is an individual game and in

---

[911] *The Concise Oxford Dictionary of Current English*, fifth edition 1964.

[912] Chapter IX, Art. II.

[913] Slalom Racing Competition Rules, 41, Special Rules relative to World Championships, 41.13 Anti-Doping, sub 41.13.2.

[914] Doping, 8.2, 2.0, sub 2.2.

[915] Rules of Racing and related By Laws, Part VI, Section 4, rule 9, sub 9.3.2.

[916] FIBA: Regulations governing Doping Control, 6.6., sub 6.6.1., subsection 2.

[917] Art. 9 WADC – Automatic disqualification of individual results and Art. 10.1 WADC – Disqualification of results in event during which an Anti-Doping rule violation occurs.

the other it is part of a series. Article 10.1.1 provides that if the athlete "[...] bears no fault or negligence for the violation, the athlete's individual results in the other competitions shall not be disqualified unless the athlete's results in competitions other than the competition in which the anti-doping rule violation occurred were likely to have been affected by the athlete's anti-doping rule violation." Strangely enough, it seems that this is an exception to the strict liability rule.

10. CONCLUSION

In the first place, it is undisputed that by nature penalties under doping law bear a strong resemblance to penalties under criminal law. After all, the sanctions in doping rules do not aim to re-establish the situation that would have existed if the offence had not taken place, as would be the case under private law, but are instead intended to punish. Being excluded from competition for two years for a first doping offence and for life for a second offence cannot be considered anything other than punishment. In sports, other misconduct is also punished, but not as severely as doping offences. Indeed, from the severity of doping offences it can be concluded that they are considered to be in a completely different league. The FISA, for example, would impose a life-time ban for a first doping offence. This is an expression of fear; a fear that does not exist in the case of other misconduct. There is a strong wish to be rid of the athlete who was caught using doping once and for all, but this desire is not in keeping with what society considers fair. The call for "tougher sanctions" for doping offences here collides with society's views concerning the punishment of similar offences. One example of this struggle is the fact that the FINA began by increasing the suspension period for a first doping offence from two to four years but then had to again reduce it to two. It can be concluded from the wide range of sanctions that have been described in this chapter that the determination and the severity of the sanctions most probably resulted from some serious haggling in the echelons responsible for drafting the sports organisations' rules. At the World Doping Conference in February 1999 the discussion on unification of sanctions was not handled constructively either. Here too, the "tougher sanctionists" and the "proportionalitists" fought their battle without reaching a compromise. Everyone was in agreements that sanctions had to be harmonised, but in practice, the situation remains unchanged.

"Hard" and "soft" doping

Where sanctions are concerned, the response is different according to the type of doping that was used, i.e. soft doping or hard doping. Hard doping is understood to mean "prohibited classes of substances" and "prohibited methods"; soft doping is understood to mean "classes of drugs subject to certain restrictions." Use of the first category of doping substances and methods is never permitted; the use of second category substances and methods is, albeit on the condition that the competent authorities are informed of and have consented to such use.

Sanctions for individual athletes in cases of "hard" doping

Each sport had different sanctions for hard doping offences. Several federations used fixed sanctions, but others used flexible ones and allowed the seriousness of the offence to be taken into consideration. The margin of discretion allowed between a minimum and a maximum penalty meant that sanctions for the same offence could also vary per case within one single federation. There are arguments to be found in favour of both fixed and flexible sanctions. With fixed sanctions, for example, there is the advantage of predictability, legal certainty and equal treatment; the disadvantage, however, is that they may be disproportionate. The seriousness of the offence could be greatly at odds with the severity of the penalty imposed. Flexible sanctions certainly improve proportionality: the seriousness of the offence is actively assessed and reflected in the sanction. The disadvantage of flexible sanctions is, however, that they may be subjective. Given the fact that doping panels continually change their composition, considerations as to the offence's gravity and the gravity of the sanction might also change. Another possibility is that different countries consider different sanctions reasonable (and may thus be prepared or unprepared in different cases to enforce the sanction). This means that the nationality of the athlete who has been penalised may also play a role. Given all these possible variations, it would be welcome if the CAS fulfilled a regulatory function in this respect.

Sanctions for individual athletes in cases of "soft" doping

"Soft" doping includes the use of ephedrine, phenyl-propanolamine, pseudo-ephedrine, caffeine, strychnine and related substances. If these substances are used for medical reasons and the competent authorities have allowed their use in specific cases this will not be considered to constitute a doping offence. However, a finding of these substances in a sample without prior consent will produce a doping offence. Penalties for unauthorised use of "soft" doping substances are usually less severe than those for "hard" doping.

Team sanctions

Team sanctions can be divided into primary team sanctions and secondary team sanctions. Primary team sanctions are sanctions that are imposed on the team as a whole and run parallel to sanctions imposed on the individual athlete as a twist on the old adage "one for all and all for one." Secondary team sanctions are sanctions that are imposed on the team of which the doped athlete is a member. The consequences of team sanctions could be many: the competition could, for example, be declared lost or the entire team could be disqualified. Some federations stipulated that the team had to be removed from the ranking list while others provided that trophies won by the team had to be returned. Not every international federation provided for measures affecting the team as a whole after one or several of its members had tested positive. In some sports it would not make much difference to the results if a doped athlete had been part of the team. For example in football, it would be impossible to verify after the match whether the team would also have been victorious if the doped player had not participated in the match.

Sanctions at the national level

At the national level, the range of sanctions was even wider than at the international level. Discussing each national variety proved impossible as it would have led to a virtually impenetrable text because of the myriad details it would have had to include. For this reason, only the most salient aspects of the national sanctioning systems were discussed while the details were displayed in a Table.

The IOC Medical Code only included sanctions for first and second offences. A first offence was punishable by a two-year ban and a second offence by a life-long ban. The sanctions used by the international and the national sports federations were for the most part more or less grouped around the sanctions used by the IOC. There was, however, no harmony among them whatsoever. Looking at the sanctions which the national federations used to apply to a first offence, sanctions could be imposed well below to well in excess of two years. The same was true for second offences. The division into two types of offences, which the IOC used, was not followed by all federations, some of which also provided for sanctions for third offences (usually a life-time ban, such as the IOC applied to second offences). In addition there were also sanctions that differed greatly from the IOC norm (the extreme variations) and sanctions which were mainly only found in the doping regulations of national federations (the "exotic" variations) including suspension from membership, ban from representation, termination of funding, suspension in specified areas, and sanctions according to category.

Proportionality of sanctions and restraint of trade

Sanctions to be imposed by sports organisations have to reflect the seriousness of the athlete's offence. In other words: it is essential that in sanctioning the respective fundamental rights of the associations on the one hand and those of the athlete on the other are balanced. Although the imposition of a penalty by a sports organisation on an athlete who is bound by the organisational hierarchy is legitimate in the framework of the law of associations, a lengthy suspension or a ban may interfere with the athlete's fundamental rights. This is especially so where professional athletes are concerned. The principle of proportionality makes it necessary to weigh up the interests of the individual athlete against the interests of the sports organisation. The call for increasingly tougher sanctions for doping offences is limited by what in society is considered proportional. the liberalisation of the ineligibility rule has opened the door for the intrusion of domestic law and national judges into the domain of sports and for protection by them of the individual athlete against interferences in the domestic legal order by the sports organisations. The principle of proportionality means striking a balance between the seriousness of the offence and the seriousness of the sentence. In imposing a sanction, it must always be considered that the period of the suspension is not the only penalty, but that it includes related – sometimes far-reaching – effects, such as loss of income, cancelled sponsoring contracts, loss of media exposure, etc., and – last but not least – loss of profession, because at the end of the period of ineligibility the athlete is often too old still to achieve a top performance. In some sports a two-year ban will cause no problems whatsoever, but in others, where the professional life-span of athletes is short, two years can mean life. The re-introduction of fixed sanctions makes it next to impossible to translate the seriousness of the offence into a proportional sanction. Penalties for doping offences should not be unified, they should be harmonised, which means that their impact in one sport should be the same as in another sport.

Athletes may appeal to the right of free exercise of a profession if punished by exclusion. Disciplinary measures and suspension because of the use of doping can clash with the constitutionally protected right to employment. When doping rules offer the opportunity to suspend an athlete over a considerable period of time, such rules should not lead to an "unreasonable restraint of trade." Pursuant to English common law restraint principles the factors to be taken into consideration when determining whether a rule of a sports governing body is in restraint of trade are as follows: is the individual sportsman/sportswoman involved in a recognised trade? and, does the relevant clause within the rules or contract restrain the sportsman or woman in their trade? If the answer to those questions is positive, then the restraint will be unenforceable unless it is reasonable. The sports organisation must prove reasonableness in the circumstances. The burden of proof is therefore reversed when the athlete is able to show that a certain provision in the doping regulations results in "restraint of trade." The imposition of a life-long ban will only be upheld in extremely exceptional cases before the courts in enforcement order/annulment proceedings. A life-long ban is the most far-reaching intervention possible in an athlete's profession and is actually tantamount to a "Berufsverbot." For this reason, it should be impossible in disciplinary proceedings not to consider the circumstances under which the doping offence was committed. This is particularly true for the four-year ban for a first doping offence. This sanction will in every case result in the inability to freely exercise one's profession. The exceptional severity of such exclusion lies in the fact that it makes it impossible for athletes to compete in the next Olympics. However, the situation is different in sports which allow for longer-running careers, such as football and tennis, so that the four-year ban could in principle be imposed there. A two-year suspension for a first doping offence is normally considered acceptable, although not all international federations were in agreement on this.

Sport sanctions

The sports organisations regarded doping primarily as a violation of the rules of play. However, anti-doping regulations are of a completely different character than rules of play.

Disqualification is commonly regarded as a "sport sanction." Such sanctions can be imposed without having to enter into the question of fault. The use of doping could be viewed as the mirror image of rough play. Rough play goes against a rule of play and as such as considered as misconduct. The use of doping is a type of misconduct violating the entire image of the sport. The boundaries between the concepts of "disqualification" and "disciplinary sanction" were quite often blurred in the different regulations. Disqualification for the use of prohibited substances can be considered as a retroactive sanction. Only some time after the end of a game can it be established whether the athlete's body contained prohibited substances, while rough or unfair play of course can be established immediately. Violations of doping rules may nevertheless also be said to be violations of the fairness of competition which should be countered by a sport sanction. The period of disqualification varies greatly, both between the various sports organisations and within sports organisations, where the time of commencement of the sanction may not always be clear. A sport sanction closely connected with disqualification is the forced return of prizes, trophies, medals, etc. This is by definition a retroactive sanction.

INTERIM CHAPTER

Before the adoption of the WADC an official of the international federation in question would inform the relevant bodies and persons within the IF and within the national federation concerned – as referred to in the regulations – of the positive results of the first analysis. The athlete could either be informed immediately, or the national federation or one of its officials was given the task of informing the athlete. Various regulations required that the athlete make a statement concerning the finding of prohibited substances in his/her sample. The regulations often stipulated whether a countercheck was required or not. Various regulations also provided that a countercheck had to be arranged by the IF. It is possible to distinguish between regulations under which proceedings did not commence until the outcome of the second analysis was known and regulations under which proceedings were to commence immediately, in which case the second analysis results would form part of the evidentiary stage of the proceedings. In most cases the evidence against the athlete would not be considered conclusive until he/she had also tested positive in the countercheck, although under the OMADC the athlete was already found guilty after testing positive the first time. Under most IFs' rules, however, the question of guilt was not debated until after the positive outcome of the second analysis. The disciplinary proceedings that would follow usually allowed for the athlete to be heard and would be decisive as to the athlete's guilt.

After a positive result from the analysis of an A sample, various IFs allowed the athlete concerned to make a statement.[918] This statement could persuade the IF not to prosecute. If no statement was given, the test was considered positive and the athlete would be provisionally suspended. Other IFs would already suspend the athlete after the first positive test, i.e. before the final outcome of the doping control became known, and without hearing the athlete first. In these cases, disciplinary proceedings would usually be started immediately. They would include the service of a summons on the athlete and the national federation, the analysis of the B sample,

---

[918] See IAAF Procedural Guidelines for Doping Control, 2.50-2.59; ITU Doping Control Rules And Procedural Guidelines, 3.32-3.42, 5.2-5.6, 5.8-5.12; ISU Communication No. 956, General Regulations, Rule 139, para. 6; FIS Procedural Guidelines for Doping and Hemoglobin Control, A. Doping and Hemoglobin Control During Competitions, 8.2; FISA Rules of Racing and Related By Laws, Rule 82 and By Laws to Rules 80 to 83; IBA Anti Doping Rules, Ch. 10; FEI General Regulations, Ch. VI, Art. 1023(8) and 1024; IWF Anti-Doping Policy, 12.4., 12.9., 15.2., 15.2., 15.5., 15.8., 15.14-15.16.; IHF Anti-Doping Regulations, 10 and 12; FIH Doping Policy, 9.2., 9.3, 10.2.-10.6, 12, Statutes and By Laws, Art. 21, sub 22.4.; FINA Doping Control Rules, DC 8.3.5., 8.3.6., 8.4., 9.2.5., 9.6., 9.7.; ITF By Laws of ITF Limited, 8. Tennis Anti-Doping Programme, (J); ISSF Anti-Doping Regulations, 5.6., 5.7., 7.2., 7.4., 8.2., 9.

the decision to suspend, a hearing, and the delivery of a sentence. Other IFs after a positive result in the first analysis would invite the athlete to attend a hearing at which all parties were given an opportunity to give their version of events. It would then be decided whether to test the B sample. If a doping offence was established, the athlete would be disqualified.

A third possibility was that the athlete would only be considered to have tested positive if both the A and B sample results were positive or if the athlete after a positive A sample result waived his right to the testing of his/her B sample. The athlete would not be suspended until the competent authorities had established the finding of prohibited substances in both samples. The athlete's national federation would be informed of the test results and disciplinary proceedings would be started. The athlete had the right to be heard before any decisions were made concerning his/her punishment.[919]

This wide variety in procedure was to a certain extent abolished with the introduction of the WADC. Article 7 WADC provides a number of principles concerning "[...] a process for the pre-hearing administration of potential anti-doping rule violations." The anti-doping organisations, including the IFs, have to implement a great number of WADC provisions in their anti-doping rules. Other provisions contain mandatory guidelines which allow for some flexibility in the formulation of

---

[919] Cf., IOC Medical Code, Ch. VI, Art. III, Ch. VI, Art. 3, Appendix C, 5.8. and C, 5.10.; IPC Doping, 8.4.4.- 8.4.7., 9.0 iii., 9.1.1., 9.1.2., 9.2., 9.2.3-9.2.10.; IBF Disciplinary Regulations, 3.1.-3.4.; FIBA Regulations Governing Doping Control, 6.6.2.; AIBA Articles of Association and Rules for International Competitions and Tournaments, Art. XXVIII, C, sub 1. and Sampling Procedures in Doping Controls, 4.8.-4.10.; ICF Procedural Guidelines for Doping Controles, 7.4., 7.6.; ICF Doping Rules, Rule 5, Procedural Guidelines for Doping Controles, 7.7.; UCI Part. XIV, Ch. VII, Arts. 68., 69., 71., 72., 73., 76., 78., 81., 82., 84., 106., Part. XIV, Ch. X, Arts. 110, 113; FIE Reglement Technique, Titre Cinquieme, Chapitre 6, 1. Regles Generales, t.129).; FIFA Doping Control Regulations for FIFA Competitions (Except for FIFA World Cup), 8. Procedure if Specimen "B" Proves Positive, 39; Revised Doping Control Regulations for the FIFA World Cup, France 98, Ch. 8 – Procedure if the analysis of specimen "B" proves positive, 44.; FIG 4. Procedure For Testing During The Competition, 4.2. Sample Taking, 4.2.7.Sample Analysis, Doping Control Regulations, 3. Sanctions, 3.1.; IJF Regulations and Procedure Concerning Drug Tests, 14. In 16, New Anti Doping Rules, 3; FILA Disciplinary Regulations, Art. 13.; UIPM Medical Rulebook, Anti-Doping Controls, 7.5.-7.7., Statutes, Ch. VI, 6.7.2.; IBU Anti-Doping, Blood Test and Gender Verification Rules, 7.5., 7.7.; IBU Disciplinary Rules, 11.2.-11.4, 13.3; ISF Doping Control and Testing as Established by the ISF Medical and Doping Commission, 7.5.3., 7.7.; WTF Regulations for Doping Control, 10.3., 11.1.; FITA Appendix 4, 10.5., 11.1., 11.2., 11.4., 11.7., 11.8., 11.10.; FIVB Medical Regulations, 2. Antidoping Control Regulations, 2.4., 2.6.1., 2.6.6.; ISAF Part One – The Doping Control Rules and Regulations of the ISAF, Racing Rules of Sailing for 1997-2000, Fundamental Rule 5 Drugs, Racing Rules of Sailing for 1997-2000, Appendix L, L6.1.-6.2., 1998 ISAF Regulations, Medical Code (Old 17), 3. Sample Analysis, 3.9., Part One – The Doping Control Rules and Regulations of the ISAF, Racing Rules of Sailing For 1997-2000, Fundamental Rule 5 Drugs, Racing Rules of Sailing For 1997-2000, Appendix L, L6.2.; FIBT Doping Control Regulations, 8. Evaluation of Urine Analyses, 8.4., Doping Control Regulations, 8. Evaluation of Urine Analyses, 9, opening words; WCF Constitution, Art. 34, sub b), By Law No. 5, Ch. 1, Art. 12; WCF Doping Policy, 3, sub i read together with 3, Constitution, Art. 34, sub a); IIHF By Laws, 1400 Medical Controls (Doping), 1406, Doping Regulations, II., Ch. V, 17, Statutes, II., D. Arbitration, 45 and 46.; FIL Supplement 4, Medical Code, Ch. VII, Art. VII, Art. XII, Appendix B, 5.8., 5.9., 5.10., Supplement 4, Medical Code, Ch. VIII – Appeals.

rules by the individual anti-doping organisations or establish requirements which every anti-doping organisation has to fulfil, but which do not have to be implemented in their regulations. Article 7 WADC concerning results management is a rule which does not need to be implemented verbatim. The Code therefore does not require absolute uniformity in results management. It does however require that the different methods used by the signatories are consistent with the principles laid down in the Code.[920]

If the results of the A sample analysis are positive, the responsible anti-doping organisation has to examine whether perhaps a dispensation for therapeutic use was granted for the substance found and whether the international standards for doping control and laboratory analysis were complied with or whether they were departed from to such an extent that the analysis results can no longer be used as evidence. Once these investigations have been concluded and no irregularities have been found, the athlete has to be promptly notified of: "the adverse analytical finding; the anti-doping rule violated [...]; the athlete's right to promptly request the analysis of the B sample or, failing such request, that the B sample analysis may be deemed waived; the right of the athlete and/or the athlete's representative to attend the B sample opening and analysis if such analysis is requested; and the athlete's right to request copies of the A and B sample laboratory documentation package which includes information as required by the International Standard for laboratory analysis." The anti-doping organisation has to conduct any follow-up investigation "as may be required by the Prohibited List." The athlete has to be notified promptly concerning the results of the follow-up investigation and of whether or not he/she is considered to have violated an anti-doping rule. Article 7.5 WADC lists a number of principles that apply to provisional suspensions. A sports organisation may adopt rules concerning provisional suspensions prior to the final hearing referred to in Article 8 WADC.[921]

Provisional suspensions may, however, not be imposed "[...] unless the athlete is given either: (a) an opportunity for a provisional hearing either before imposition of the provisional suspension or on a timely basis after imposition of the Provisional Suspension; or (b) an opportunity for an expedited hearing in accordance with Article 8 [...] on a timely basis after imposition of a Provisional Suspension."[922]

---

[920] On this the comment to Art. 7 remarks that: "Various of the Signatories have created their own approaches to results management for Adverse Analytical Findings. While the various approaches have not been entirely uniform, many have proven to be fair and effective systems for results management. The Code does not supplant each of the Signatories' results management systems. This Article does, however, specify basic principles in order to ensure the fundamental fairness of the results management process which must be observed by each Signatory. The specific anti-doping rules of each signatory shall be consistent with these basic principles."

[921] See e.g. ISSF Anti-Doping Rules, 5.8.4 Provisional Suspensions: "The ISSF is authorized to, and will, Provisionally Suspend a Shooter until the time of a full hearing based on an Adverse Analytical Finding and the review described in 5.8.1.2."

[922] See e.g. FINA Doping Rules – New rules 2002-2005, DC 7.1.12: "The FINA Executive, after consultation with the DCRB, may provisionally suspend a competitor prior to the opportunity for a full hearing based on an adverse analytical finding from the competitor's A sample and the review de-

Pursuant to Article 8 WADC, each anti-doping organisation with responsibility for results management has to organise a hearing at which the accused athlete may respond to the asserted anti-doping rule violation. Under the provisions of doping regulations in force before the adoption of the WADC athletes were also subject to disciplinary proceedings. The words chosen to describe the process were, however, much less diplomatic than those used in the WADC. The IAAF regulations for example provided that "[...] where a doping offence has taken place, disciplinary proceedings will take place [...]."[923] As far as the IAAF was concerned, a positive test was proof of a doping offence which gave rise to disciplinary proceedings resulting in a penalty. IFs like the IAAF attempted to eliminate any discussion of guilt from the proceedings, including from the sentencing stage. The strict liability rule is also included in the WADC, as a guiding principle. However, as has emerged in previous chapters above, the strict liability system was not as strict as amongst others the IAAF believed. Although the WADC also takes as its starting point that an athlete is guilty of doping if he/she tests positive at the doping control, this does not automatically lead to the imposition of the sanction which as a general rule applies to this offence. Under the strict liability system as it developed in the case law of the CAS and as it was later laid down in the WADC where a provision is dedicated to exceptional circumstances the degree of fault of the athlete must first be examined before the penalty may be determined. Article 8 WADC stipulates that at the hearing it has to be examined whether an anti-doping violation was committed and, if so, what the appropriate consequences are. The anti-doping organisations do not have to implement this provision literally, but their doping rules have to be consistent with the principles it sets out.[924]

---

scribed in DC 7.1.2. If a provisional suspension is imposed, either the hearing in accordance with DC 8 shall be advanced to a date, which avoids substantial prejudice to the competitor, or the competitor shall be given an opportunity for a provisional hearing before imposition of the provisional suspension or on a timely basis after imposition of the provisional suspension." ITU Anti-Doping Rules, 7.4 Provisional Suspensions: "The ITU Executive Board, after consultation with the ITU Anti-Doping Administrator, may Provisionally Suspend an Athlete prior to the opportunity for a full hearing based on an adverse analytical finding from the athlete's A sample or A and B samples and the review described in Article 7.1. If a provisional suspension is imposed, either the hearing in accordance with Article 8 shall be advanced to a date which avoids substantial prejudice to the athlete, or the athlete shall be given an opportunity for a provisional hearing before imposition of the provisional suspension or on a timely basis after imposition of the provisional suspension. National Federations may impose provisional suspensions in accordance with the principles set forth in this Article 7.3"; and FEI Anti-Doping Rules for Human Athletes in conjunction with The WADC, 7.4 Provisional Suspensions: "the FEI Executive Board, after consultation with the FEI Anti-Doping Administrator and the FEI Medical Committee, may Provisionally Suspend an Athlete prior to the opportunity for a full hearing based on an Adverse Analytical Finding from the Athlete's A Sample or A and B Samples and the review described in Article 7.1. If a Provisional Suspension is imposed, either the hearing in accordance with Article 8 shall be advanced to a date which avoids substantial prejudice to the Athlete, or the Athlete shall be given an opportunity for a Provisional Hearing before imposition of the Provisional Suspension or on a timely basis after imposition of the Provisional Suspension. National Federations may impose Provisional Suspensions in accordance with the principles set forth in this Article 7.3."

[923] IAAF Rules and Regulations, Division III, Rule 59.

[924] See e.g. FINA Doping Rules, New rules 2002-2005, DC 8.1; ISAF Racing Rules, Appendix 3 – ISAF Anti-Doping Code, 21.8.

The IOC Medical Code, which for a long time served as the model code for many international federations, also provided that athletes who were accused of doping had the right to be heard (audi et alteram partem). Remarkably, such a provision was not included in the MC's successor, the OMADC, despite the fact that its preamble clearly advocated the protection of athletes' rights.[925] This failure to include a provision on athletes' rights in the OMADC was a serious omission, given the OMADC's status as a model text. In the WADC, however, more so than in any of its predecessors, sufficient attention is finally devoted to the rights of the defence in the shape of Article 8 which lays down the basic principles to guarantee a fair hearing for persons accused of a violation of anti-doping rules.

The next chapter examines fair trial rights further. First, however, it discusses the position of doping rules within the framework of the freedom of association and the specific nature of disciplinary doping law.

---

[925] "Whereas in keeping with the desire of the Olympic Movement to act in the best interests of athletes [...] whose rights to justice must be safeguarded, the Olympic Movement Anti-Doping Code shall include provisions to enable appeals to be lodged with the Court of Arbitration for Sport (CAS) against certain decisions rendered in application of such Code."

PART II
PROCEDURAL LAW

CHAPTER 6
THE NATURE OF THE DOPING TRIAL AND THE DUE PROCESS PRINCIPLES

1. INTRODUCTION

Athletes who have violated anti-doping rules are prosecuted and punished in accordance with internal disciplinary regulations. Does the freedom of association also include that the drafters of such regulations are completely free in what they provide under these rules, or are they in any way bound by statutory or treaty provisions? Can sports organisations adopt rules that clash with what are commonly accepted human rights standards in our society? What type of law governs the doping trial? Private law only or do rules from other areas of (punitive) law also play a role? It is argued that an unequivocal choice has to be made in favour of one legal area only. At this point, it is on the one hand recognised that disciplinary doping law may be regarded as quasi-criminal law, but on the other hand the principles that are part of the criminal process do not all equally apply to doping trials. If, however, a clear choice is made to uphold the analogy with criminal law at all stages, this would also finally eliminate the application of private law concepts and principles from doping law. It would make clear once and for all that doping law is punitive law, whose objective is to punish rather than to re-establish a prior situation. This would also prevent doping law from becoming an unwieldy tool forged out of irreconcilable concepts. More specifically, the questions which will be discussed in this chapter are whether sports organisations and their disciplinary bodies have to allow athletes to rely on the fair trial rights provided by Article 6 ECHR and whether they are obliged to consider fundamental principles of criminal law in their decisions. The answer to this last question is particularly pivotal to the issues discussed in this book.

2. THE FREEDOM OF ASSOCIATION

If we take the example of the Dutch Constitution, Article 8 provides that: "The right of association shall be recognised."[926] Article 11 ECHR on the freedom of association provides that: "Everyone has the right to freedom of peaceful assembly and to freedom of association with others, including the right to form and to join trade

---

[926] Under Dutch law, legal persons including associations are governed by Arts. 1-52 of Book 2 of the Civil Code.

unions for the protection of his interests" and "No restrictions shall be placed on the exercise of these rights other than such as are prescribed by law and are necessary in a democratic society in the interests of national security or public safety [...]."[927] The same right has been laid down in Article 12(1) of the Charter of Fundamental Rights of the European Union.[928] Within the limits of the law of association, sports organisations are free to organise themselves and to enact codes of conduct and rules for the enforcement of these codes.[929]

The anti-doping regulations of sports organisations are such codes of conduct. They are governed by the law of associations which in turn is governed by private law. The freedom of organisations to create norms for the interaction of their members is exalted in the possibility to punish any violations of these norms by disciplinary measures. Disciplinary action is therefore also part of the freedom of association as laid down in the Constitution. Associations must be able to require their members to refrain from any behaviour which could harm the association.

Sanctions which associations, *in casu quo*: sports organisations, may apply are thus based on the organisation's own regulations, including rules of play, and on the organisation's jurisdiction over its members as established in the articles of association. The members of the organisation among themselves are free to amend and extend the regulations. The question of whether there are public law restraints on this private law freedom will be dealt with further below. First the position within the framework of law in general of private law organisations' regulations will be dealt with.

3. THE POSITION OF DISCIPLINARY DOPING LAW WITHIN THE LEGAL FRAMEWORK

De Doelder is of the opinion that disciplinary law is positioned precisely where administrative law, private law and criminal law intersect.[930] In order to assess in

---

[927] Convention for the Protection of Human Rights and Fundamental Freedoms, Rome, 4 November 1950, CETS No.: 005.

[928] OJ C 364/1, 18 December 2000, p. 1 et seq. (2000/C 364/01). Ch. II – Freedoms, Art. 12 – Freedom of assembly and of association: 1. Everyone has the right to freedom of peaceful assembly and to freedom of association at all levels [...]. See also Art. 20 of the 1948 Universal Declaration of Human Rights and Art. 5 of the European Social Charter (although this provision lacks direct effect).

[929] "Grundsätzlich soll der Sport seine Angelegenheiten selber regeln und sein Haus selber sauber halten. Für diese Selbstorganisation steht den Verbänden des deutschen Sports – wie anderen im privaten Bereich tätigen Verbänden auch – ein durch Art. 9 GG vor staatlicher Fremdbestimmung weitgehend geschützter, eigenverantwortlich auszufüllender Freiraum zur Verfügung, innerhalb dessen sie ihre internen Angelegenheiten eigenständig auf der Grundlage ihrer eigenen Wertvorstellungen nach von ihnen selbst gewählten und selbst gesetzten Regeln gestalten können. Das gilt sowohl für die Regeln, nach denen der jeweilige Verband seinen inneren Aufbau und seinen Sportbetrieb organisieren will, als auch für seine grundsätzliche Befugnis zur staatsfreien Setzung spezifisch sportethischer Werte und Maßstäbe," Volker Röhricht: "Chancen und Grenzen von Sportgerichtsverfahren nach deutschem Recht," in: *Sportgerichtsbarkeit* (Volker Röhricht ed.) Stuttgart, 1997, pp. 20-21.

[930] De Doelder 1981 (*supra* nt. 352), pp. 25-27 and p. 34.

what category certain rules belong De Doelder[931] uses the criterion of voluntariness. De Doelder rightly observes that it is easier for a stamp collector to decline membership of a stamp collectors' club than it is for a professional football player to remain outside the scope of jurisdiction of a football club. The voluntariness of membership is a determining factor in deciding whether the disciplinary law of the association is of a more private law or a more criminal law nature. Van Staveren[932] views disciplinary law in sport from the same angle. In his opinion, the law of obligations (including contract law and the law of legal persons) deeply influences the disciplinary law of "regular associations, among which sports clubs, and several non-major sport federations." He contrasts this with statutory disciplinary law, which is more influenced by criminal law. "The disciplinary law governing professional groups which have more or less voluntarily united in associations lies somewhere between the two extremes. An example would be the disciplinary law that is applicable to top athletes and professional athletes." At present, however, due to the increasing professionalisation and commercialisation of sport, the standard of "the extent to which" membership is voluntary as used by De Doelder or the "more or less" voluntary membership of Van Staveren have become less apt.[933]

Of course people are free to decide whether to take up a sport or not. Equally evidently, once a particular sport has been chosen, the budding athlete will have to abide by some rules, but until he/she reaches a certain level these are only the rules that apply in his/her particular branch of sport, including however rules of disciplinary law. If the athlete happens to be so talented and dedicated that he/she wishes to make a career out of his/her chosen sport, he/she will also become subject to the general disciplinary law – including doping rules – of the international sports federation. It is true that professional athletes have freely chosen their profession, but, as they start to earn respect and popularity both within and outside the sport as a result of wins and scores and possibly begin to make a fair amount of money because of this, the voluntariness of this choice becomes comparable to the voluntariness of the career choice of other professionals to whom statutory rather than association disciplinary law applies. If such professionals are not comfortable with these rules, they can always emigrate, but even that freedom is not available to the professional athlete because the disciplinary law of the international federation applies in every corner of the world. Professional sport has thus put the embeddedness of sport within the law of association under pressure. If one can still speak of the voluntary subjection by professional athletes to the regulations of sports

---

[931] De Doelder 1981 (*supra* nt. 352), p. 45.

[932] H.T. van Staveren, Syllabus Part II, 1998-1999, Ch. V.

[933] "Da Sportler aber praktisch nie Mitglieder des Verbandes sind, muss die Bindung an die Dopingregelungen der Verbände auf Gesetz, Vertrag oder lückenlose Verweisung in den Satzungen der verschiedenen Vereine und Verbände, die sich zwischen dem Sportler und dem die Dopingnormen erlassenden Verband befinden, beruhen," aldus Margareta Baddeley: "Dopingsperren als Verbandssanktion aus nationaler und internationaler Sicht – Insbesondere am Beispiel des schweizerischen, australischen und amerikanischen Rechts," in Jochen Fritzweiler, ed., *Doping – Sanktionen, Beweise, Ansprüche*, (Berne, Stämpfli 2000) p. 13.

organisations, there is at any rate by now a complete lack of such voluntariness where doping regulations are concerned. Such voluntariness is a legal (dogmatic) presumption which does not correspond to reality. In reality, it is more a matter of being forced. "Da im kommerzialisierten Sport die Sportler existentiell auf die Monopol-Organisation angewiesen sind, können sie der Bindung nicht entgehen; ihnen ist faktisch eine autonome Wahrnehmung ihrer eigenen Interessen nicht möglich; sie sind [...] auf Schutz angewiesen," says Fritzweiler.[934] And Reinhart has claimed that: "Der Profisportler muss sich regelmäßig der Sanktionsgewalt des Verbandes unterwerfen, um seinen Beruf überhaupt ausüben zu können. Von der sonst für das Privatrecht typischen Freiwilligkeit kann daher im Bereich der Sportgerichtsbarkeit kaum die Rede sein."[935] Given how relative the professional athlete's voluntary subjection to the sports organisation is it could be argued that the impact of the fundamental principles of criminal law should not only be substantial but should in fact be predominant.[936] There must be no misunderstanding concerning the fact that disciplinary doping law is not criminal law[937] and will never be criminal law, but in the framework of the law of associations it is a *kind* of criminal law,[938] at least, a punitive system to which criminal law principles and concepts should apply.[939] "Although the punishment of doping is not a criminal punishment, it is a criminal-like punishment and will be estimated mainly according to the same principles," according to Tarasti.[940] It is a pity that he failed to provide any foundation for this claim. Given its criminal-like features disciplinary doping law can be characterised as "quasi-penal law" as did the CAS panel in *Bernhard v. ITU*.[941] In this case, the Panel began one of its considerations with the

---

[934] "As the athletes in commercialised sport are essentially committed to the monopolistic organisation, they cannot escape this tie; it is factually impossible for them to serve their own interests; they are dependent on protection," [Transl. *JwS*]. Jochem Fritzweiler, in Fritzweiler/Pfister/Summerer: *Praxishandbuch Sportrecht*, München 1998 (Fritzweiler 1998), p. 12.

[935] "The professional athlete must regularly submit to the federation's power to penalise in order to at least be able to practice his profession. The element of voluntariness, which is typical for private law, is hardly present at all in the prosecution procedures in the realm of sports law," [Transl. *JwS*], Michael Reinhart, "Sportverbandsgerichtsbarkeit und Doppelbestrafungsverbot," (2001) *SpuRt*, p. 48 (Reinhart 2001).

[936] "Nothing would stand in the way of the use of principles of criminal law in this disciplinary law in a law of associations framework," as was remarked during the 1984 conference of the Dutch Society for Procedural Law, G.W. Kernkamp, "Verslag van de discussies bij de overige onderwerpen," in *Tuchtrecht en Fair Play*, Nederlandse Vereniging voor Procesrecht, 1984, p. 328.

[937] In the preamble to the Olympic Charter against Doping in Sport (item C) it is considered that "doping in sport is part of the problem of drug abuse and misuse in society." This points in the direction of a possible notion which the IOC might have had to subsume disciplinary law under criminal law.

[938] Remmelink 1994 (*supra* nt. 293), p. 30.

[939] Summerer 1990 (*supra* nt. 72), p. 163, Rz. 267, is of the opinion that "das vom Sportverband praktizierte Verfahren [...] zwar kein getreues Abbild des staatlichen Strafprozesses sein [muß], doch ist eine *Kongruenz mit den tragenden staatlichen Verfahrensgrundsätzen* zu fordern. So ist bei bedeutsamen Vorgängen wie etwa einer Dopinguntersuchung [...] eine ins einzelne gehende satzungsmäßige Verankerung der Verfahrensweise unerläßlich."

[940] Tarasti 1999 (*supra* nt. 333).

[941] CAS 98/222, 9-8-1999, *Bernhard v. ITU*, Matthieu Reeb, ed., *Digest of CAS Awards II 1998-2000* (The Hague, Kluwer Law International 2002) pp. 330-344, ground 45, and G.N. Barrie, "Disci-

words: "Having in mind the specific disciplinary ('quasi-penal') character of the anti-doping investigations and sanctions [...]."

The doping rules of sports organisations go further even than criminal law where they provide for a duty to prosecute, whereas most Public Prosecutors have some discretion to decide whether to prosecute or not.[942] Another argument for adopting a criminal law approach towards doping law can be found in Article 4 in conjunction with Article 7(2)(d) of the Council of Europe's Anti-Doping Convention.[943] Article 4 provides that:

> "The Parties shall adopt where appropriate legislation [...] to restrict the availability [...] as well as the use in sport of banned doping agents and doping methods and in particular anabolic steroids."

In other words, the parties to the Convention are, where appropriate, bound to include rules in their legislation concerning, inter alia, the use of doping in sport. The provision does not stipulate the type of legislation to be enacted. However, clues may be found by combining Article 4 with Article 7. Under this provision the contracting parties are, among other things, required to urge their sports organisations to harmonise their disciplinary proceedings,

> "applying agreed international principles of natural justice and ensuring respect for the fundamental rights of suspected sportsmen and sportswomen; these principles will include: [...] ii. the right of such person to a fair hearing and to be assisted or represented [...]"

This rule undeniably aims to endow doping law with criminal law characteristics. If Article 7 requires sports organisations to adopt criminal law orientated disciplinary regulations,[944] the conclusion is justified that the legislation referred to in Article 4 is also criminal law orientated. The Convention is presently in force for 36 coun-

---

plinary Tribunals and Administrative Law, Conference on Sport and the law," *Rand Afrikaans University* 7 & 8 September 2000 (Barrie 2000), p. 3: " 'Disciplinary tribunal' in this work means an authority created by statute or agreement which exercises 'quasi penal' functions outside the normal system of courts."

[942] Private law has a similar type of "prosecutorial" discretion: "Public interest requires that there are private law rules and that these *can* be enforced. It does not require however that they *are* enforced. The citizen, not the state, decides whether to invoke protection of his private law interests. The citizen decides to either leave matters as they are or to exercise his rights. The enforcement of private law is left to the discretion of the interested party itself," Van Apeldoorn 2000 (*supra* nt. 36), p. 65.

[943] Anti-Doping Convention, Strasbourg, 16 November 1989, ETS no. 135.

[944] In the *Gasser* case (*Gasser v. SLV* in SJZ 84 (1988), p. 87) it was considered that: "wer – zudem als Monopolverband – Maßnahmen trifft, die eine Person in derart einschneidender Weise treffen können, wie dies bei der Gesuchstellerin der Fall ist, und die zumindest 'quasiberuflichen' Karriere bedeuten können, hat mindestens für ein korrektes Verfahren in der Entscheidfindung zu sorgen. Dazu gehören als absolutes Minimum die Anhörung eines des Dopingvergehens beschuldigte Athleten, die Einsicht in die Beweismittel, die zum Entscheid führen, die schriftliche Ausfertigung eines Urteils, dessen Begründung und eine korrekte und klare Eröffnung des Entscheides. Al dies ist hier unterlassen worden."

tries (both Council of Europe members and non-members),[945] 23 of which have adopted anti-doping rules in their criminal codes. We should ideally consider doping law to be the "penal law of private law organisations"[946] as opposed to a special branch of public law. In this penal law of private law organisations principles of criminal law should also be given a place. This solution is to be preferred to the complete subsumption of doping law under private law or to it being governed by several fields of law simultaneously.[947]

The structural admission of criminal law principles to doping law would add more to the standing of this body of law than the arbitrary application of criminal law principles one day and private law principles the next.[948] So as to illustrate the confusion which may arise if no clear choice is made concerning the application of criminal law principles in doping law, I will provide a few examples from CAS

---

[945] The Convention is in force in: Armenia (1 May 2004), Australia (1 December 1994), Austria (1 September 1991), Azerbaijan (1 January 2004), Belgium (1 January 2002), Bosnia and Herzegovina (1 February 1995), Bulgaria (1 August 1992), Canada (1 May 1996), Croatia (1 March 1993), Cyprus (1 April 1994), Czech Republic (1 June 1995), Denmark (1 March 1990), Estonia (1 January 1998), Finland (1 June 1990), France (1 March 1991), Georgia (1 July 2003), Germany (1 June 1994), Greece (1 May 1996), Hungary (1 March 1990), Iceland (1 May 1991), Ireland (1 March 2003), Italy (1 April 1996), Latvia (1 March 1997), Liechtenstein (1 July 2000), Lithuania (1 July 1996), Luxembourg (1 August 1996), Monaco (1 January 2004), Netherlands (1 June 1995), Norway (1 March 1990), Poland (1 November 1990), Portugal (1 May 1994), Romania (1 February 1999), Russia (1 April 1991), San Marino (1 March 1990), Serbia and Montenegro (1 April 2001), Slovakia (1 July 1993), Slovenia (1 September 1992), Spain (1 July 1992), Sweden (1 August 1990), Switzerland (1 January 1993), the former Yugoslav Republic of Macedonia (1 May 1994), Tunisia (1 April 2004), Turkey (1 January 1994), Ukraine (1 January 2002), United Kingdom (1 March 1990).

[946] "Das sich die Sportverbandsgerichtigkeit nicht mit Generalklauseln begnügt, sondern klar umschriebene Tatbestände bevorzugt, zeigt bereits, dass es ihr nicht – wie man dies der herkömmlichen Disziplinarstrafgewalt gemeinhin unterstellt – nur um Prävention geht. Sie will den Sportler nicht etwa nur zu einer formelhaft umschriebenen Sportlichkeit erziehen, sondern durchaus (auch) ein stattgehabtes Fehlverhalten vergelten und verdeutlicht so bereits ihre Nähe zum Kriminalstrafrecht," Michael Reinhart (Reinhart 2001 *supra* nt. 935, p. 48). Although this statement is not unassailable, given that under ordinary disciplinary sports law it is also possible to rely on flexible provisions, Reinhart's remarks are quite true for disciplinary doping law.

[947] "The *penal* discourse. This discourse asks what is the appropriate penalty and what is the philosophy behind sporting punishments. The answer is both a punitive one and an educational one. The punitive one talks of exemplary punishments as a deterrent to drug abuse. The educational one says that the drug problem can be cured by educating athletes so that they police themselves. In policy terms, the penal discourse would distinguish between young and experienced athletes, between first offences and others, and between recreational and performance enhancing substances. It also encourages rehabilitation programmes to try and cure athletes of drug abuse. This is reflected in the recent moves to have discretionary reinstatement provisions in doping regulations. This allows the carrot of a return to the sport after successful treatment for drug abuse to be used as an incentive," Ken Foster in: *The discourses of doping: law and regulation in the war against drugs.*

[948] In his contribution to the National Doping Debate, Van Staveren argued in favour of a shift towards criminal law where doping proceedings were concerned: "as the athlete's interest in participating in competition increases, these [disciplinary doping] rules have to include more procedural guarantees like the ones applying in criminal law." However, assuming that it would be possible to establish rules which differ in accordance with the particular interest at stake, these rules would have to include criteria for their application which would probably lead to an interpretational quagmire.

case law where the tribunal generally blurs the boundaries or simply contradicts itself:

F. Aanes v. FILA[949]

"As a preliminary remark the Panel wishes to clarify that the legal relations between an athlete and a federation are of a civil nature and do not leave room for the application of principles of criminal law."

Smith-De Bruin v. FINA[950]

"It seems to us that when, in the criminal sphere, the law discriminates between reasonable and unreasonable doubt, it has precisely this kind of dividing line in mind, and we reiterate that, here, the burden on the Respondent is less than the criminal burden. [...]."

Union Cycliste Internationale (UCI) and Comité National Olympique Italien (CONI)[951]

"In the Panel's opinion, the principle whereby a criminal law applies as soon as it comes into force if it is more favourable to the accused (lex mitior) is a fundamental principle of any democratic regime. It is established, for example, by Swiss law (art. 2 para. 2 of the Penal Code) and by Italian law (art. 2 of the Penal Code).
This principle [lex mitior] applies to anti-doping regulations in view of the penal or at the very least disciplinary nature of the penalties that they allow to be imposed."

Cullwick v. FINA[952]

"This principle (lex mitior) applies to the anti-doping regulations in view of the penal at the very least disciplinary nature of the penalties that they allow to be imposed. [...] It is established, for example, by Swiss law (art. 2 para. 2 of the Penal Code) and by Italian law (art. 2 of the Penal Code)."

Bernhard v. ITU[953]

"The situation in 'quasi-penal' procedures, such as doping in sport, should, on the other hand, be looked at differently, among other reasons also due to the principle 'in dubio pro reo', i.e. the benefit of doubt, which itself is an emanation of one of the most important legal presumptions, the presumption of innocence, deeply enshrined in the general principles of law and justice. This principle has the effect that in criminal

---

[949] CAS 2000/A/317, 9-7-2001, F. Aanes v. FILA, ground III.

[950] CAS 98/211, 7-6-1999, Smith-De Bruin v. FINA, Matthieu Reeb, ed., Digest of CAS Awards II 1998-2000 (The Hague, Kluwer Law International 2002) pp. 255-273, grounds 10.2 and 12.12.

[951] CAS 94/128, 5-1-1995, UCI and Comité National Olympique Italien (CONI), Matthieu Reeb, ed., Digest of CAS Awards 1986-1998 (Berne, Editions Stämpfli 1998) pp. 477-511, ground 33.

[952] CAS 96/149, 13-3-1997, Cullwick v. FINA, Matthieu Reeb, ed., Digest of CAS Awards 1986-1998 (Berne, Editions Stämpfli 1998) pp. 251-263, ground 28.

[953] CAS 98/222, 9-8-1999, Bernhard v. ITU, Matthieu Reeb, ed., Digest of CAS Awards II 1998-2000 (The Hague, Kluwer Law International 2002) pp. 330-344, grounds 45 and 60-62.

and similar proceedings, the two parties do not bear equal burden of proof, while the accusing party must prove the alleged facts with certainty, it is sufficient for the accused to establish reasons for doubt."

Although due to its wording ("criminal charge") Article 7 ECHR[954] lacks direct applicability to disciplinary doping law, that does not mean that the applicability in doping procedures of the *nulla poena* principle contained in that provision or of other criminal law principles must be rejected out of hand. As the CAS has stated, these are fundamental principles of any democratic regime. "Das nichtbeachten der [...] strafrechtlichen oder strafprozessualen Grundsätze bedeutet grundsätzlich einen Eingriff in die Persönlichkeit des Betroffenen," according to Scherrer.[955] The application of fundamental criminal law principles in disciplinary doping proceedings demonstrates compliance with the athlete's personality rights and contributes to a fair trial.

An additional argument in favour of the criminal law approach is that several countries have already included provisions on doping in their criminal laws.[956]

The application of generally and internationally recognised criminal law and criminal procedural law principles and concepts to doping law would not only increase protection for the athlete, but would also make the law more transparent and more predictable for the parties concerned, who would no longer have to grapple with a mixture of principles and concepts from different areas of the law. Any punitive system should make use of the principles and concepts which have developed over the centuries in democratic societies, but to apply these principles to doping law would moreover have a harmonising effect.

The majority of national sports organisations began to conduct anti-doping campaigns under outside pressure. Organised sports was called upon to be the errand

---

[954] "Art. 7 – No punishment without law
1. No one shall be held guilty of any criminal offence on account of any act or omission which did not constitute a criminal offence under national or international law at the time when it was committed. Nor shall a heavier penalty be imposed than the one that was applicable at the time the criminal offence was committed.
2. This article shall not prejudice the trial and punishment of any person for any act or omission which, at the time when it was committed, was criminal according to the general principles of law recognised by civilised nations."

[955] "Disregarding the principles of substantive and procedural criminal law constitutes a fundamental violation of the personality rights of the athlete involved," [Transl. *JwS*], in Fritzweiler (ed.) *Doping Sanktionen, Beweise, Ansprüche* (2000), p. 128.

[956] Belgium: Flanders: Decrees of 21 February 1985, 14 January 1987 and 27 March 1991; Wallonia: Law of 2 April 1965, Decrees of 26 August 1985 and 10 October 1989.
Denmark: Anti-Doping Act 1993.
France: Law no. 89-432 of 28 June 1989; Law no. 99-223 of 23 March 1999.
Greece: Law no. 75 of 16 July 1975 and Law no. 1646 of 18 September 1986.
Italy: Law no. 1099 of 25 October 1971.
Austria: Federal laws 166/1991 and 451/1991.
Portugal: Law no. 1/90 of 13 January 1990 and Law no. 183/97 of 26 July 1997 and Administrative Regulation 816/97 of 5 September 1997.
Spain: Law no. 10/1990 of 15 October 1990 and Royal Decrees nos. 48/1992 and 255/1996.

boy in the fight against this undesirable social phenomenon.[957] According to Simon Boyes[958] "[...] there are areas which are traditionally self-regulatory (in the truest sense of the term) that have become sufficiently important to warrant great concern over the extent to which their regulation is subject to scrutiny and required to adhere to constitutional standards. These sectors of activity, of which sport should be considered a foremost example, have, in effect, changed their nature to the extent that their activities can now be regarded as truly 'public' in practice and thus of constitutional significance." If the ordinary disciplinary law of sports organisations has constitutional significance, that significance is even greater where disciplinary doping law is concerned.

After this argument in favour of considering the disciplinary doping law of the private law-governed sports organisations as "quasi-penal law" or "pseudo-criminal law" we will now return to the freedom of association and the possible restrictions under which this concept operates.

The question of whether criminal law principles are actually applied and if so, which ones, will be dealt with further below.

4. REQUIREMENTS FOR DISCIPLINARY DOPING LAW – FAIR TRIAL

As has been explained above, the freedom of association includes the freedom to formulate disciplinary law rules. The parameters of this freedom are usually outlined by national law. Under Dutch law, for example, the relationship between the association and its members is governed by the principle of good faith and by Article 2:8 of the Civil Code which provides that this relationship shall be governed by the requirements of reasonableness and fairness.[959] The contract law standards of reasonableness and fairness supersede all other rules and may set aside custom-

---

[957] "Es ist zunächst einmal der im gesellschaftlichen Bereich verankerte Sport, der bestimmt, nach welchen Regeln der sportliche Wettbewerb abläuft und unter welchen Voraussetzungen er als 'fair' anzusehen ist. Diese grundgesetzliche Kompetenzlage lastet dem Sport und den Sportführern eine erhebliche Verantwortung auf und entlastet zunächst einmal den Staat, von dem verfassungsrechtlich nicht verlangt werden kann, daß er die sportethischen Vorstellungen von Vereinen und Verbänden mit seinen spezifischen Mitteln durchsetzt oder ihre Durchsetzung fördert," Bernard Pfister and Udo Steiner, *Sportrecht von A-Z – Vereine und Verbande, Sportanlagen, Arbeitsrecht und Besteuerung, Unfallhaftung, Sponsoring, Gerichtsbarkeit* (Munich, Beck 1997).

[958] Simon Boyes, in Simon Gardiner, ed., *Sports Law*, 2nd ed. (Londen/Sydney, Cavendish Publishing 2001) p. 198. Boyes has also remarked that: "sports governing bodies are clearly powerful organisations, they regulate particular niches of everyday life in much the same way as might be expected of the State" (p. 195).

[959] Under Dutch law, "[...] associations enjoy a large degree of freedom in how they choose to organise themselves. For example, they can organise themselves in such a manner as to be best able to achieve their chosen objectives. They are free to choose their own structure and to regulate the relationship between the association and its members. Government interference is limited to the specific provisions of Book 2 [of the Civil Code] which aim to ensure the democratic functioning of associations," F.C. Kollen, *De vereniging in de praktijk* (Deventer, Kluwer 1995) pp. 1-2.

ary rules and statutes, regulations, decisions, etc. whose application in the given case conflicts with them.

In European history many historical precedents are to be found – starting with the Magna Carta in 1215 – of documents asserting the right to a fair trial and a just system of law. One of the most recent of these is the ECHR.[960] It is widely recognised that Western criminal procedural law is based on the principles that guarantee a fair trial.[961] In the literature concepts abound like "fair hearing," "due process (of law)," "procedural due process" and "Natural Justice." Under common law systems these terms are comprehensive and cover all guarantees considered indispensable in the reasonable administration of justice.[962] Article 6 ECHR[963] which serves as the yardstick of the civilisation of European legal systems is headed: "right to a fair trial." Although the rights laid down in this article are only of a procedural character, this is in fact an illustration of the high level of development of the European system of human rights. The rights under Article 6 are intended to protect the citizen against the state and have as their objective to guarantee a fair trial in the broadest meaning of the term to every suspect or accused.

Due to the freedom of association the disciplinary law of sports organisations is not subject to government or parliamentary control as long as it is in conformity with the standard of reasonableness and fairness. This lack of control by the public authorities could argue against the applicability of the European Convention of

---

[960] Rome, 4 November 1950, European Treaties Series no. 5. All the signatories, with the exception of Ireland and Norway, have incorporated the Convention into their own law. This means that domestic courts have to take full account of its provisions. Only when domestic remedies are exhausted can an individual look to Strasbourg for help.

[961] See also Rome Statute for the International Criminal Court, A/CONF.183/9 (1998), 37 ILM, Art. 67 – Rights of the accused

[962] D. Dörr, *Faires Verfahren, Gewährleistung im Grundgesetz der Bundesrepublik Deutschland* (Kehl, Engel Verlag 1984) p. 73.

[963] "Art. 6 – Right to a fair trial.

1. In the determination of his civil rights and obligations or of any criminal charge against him, everyone is entitled to a fair and public hearing within a reasonable time by an independent and impartial tribunal established by law. Judgment shall be pronounced publicly but the press and public may be excluded from all or part of the trial in the interests of morals, public order or national security in a democratic society, where the interests of juveniles or the protection of the private life of the parties so require, or to the extent strictly necessary in the opinion of the court in special circumstances where publicity would prejudice the interests of justice.

2. Everyone charged with a criminal offence shall be presumed innocent until proved guilty according to law.

3. Everyone charged with a criminal offence has the following minimum rights:

a. to be informed promptly, in a language which he understands and in detail, of the nature and cause of the accusation against him;

b. to have adequate time and facilities for the preparation of his defence;

c. to defend himself in person or through legal assistance of his own choosing or, if he has not sufficient means to pay for legal assistance, to be given it free when the interests of justice so require;

d. to examine or have examined witnesses against him and to obtain the attendance and examination of witnesses on his behalf under the same conditions as witnesses against him;

e. to have the free assistance of an interpreter if he cannot understand or speak the language used in court."

Human Rights (ECtHR) to the disciplinary law of associations now that Article 57 provides that: "[...] any High Contracting Party shall furnish an explanation of the manner in which its internal law ensures the effective implementation of any provisions of the Convention." By ratifying the Convention states become bound to ensure the rights and freedoms enshrined in it to everyone within its jurisdiction. The Convention only imposes obligations upon states. The doctrine of horizontal or third-party effect falls outside the scope of the Convention. Although the rights of Article 6 could be given horizontal effect in practice, the Supreme Court of the Netherlands for example has disallowed this in 1990.[964, 965] The ECtHR may however review the application of statutory rules of disciplinary law to prevent states from disregarding their obligations under Article 6 through the placement of certain rules in a disciplinary law framework. However, disciplinary sports law is nonstatutory. This means that in this respect states may fail to fulfil their obligations under the Convention. The ECtHR on 8 June 1976[966] held that in all cases where sanctions are imposed which, given their severity, should be considered to be of a criminal law nature, the statutory disciplinary proceedings must be treated like criminal proceedings in the sense of Article 6. However, although sanctions imposed as a result of doping offences may be severe,[967] they are not on the whole sufficiently severe so as to turn disciplinary proceedings under sports law into criminal proceedings.

Article 6(1) also provides that "in the determination of his civil rights and obligations everyone is entitled to a fair and public hearing within a reasonable time by an independent and impartial tribunal established by law." Does this mean that this rule could apply to disciplinary doping proceedings in which the athlete's civil rights and obligations can be said to be determined? The Dutch Supreme Court, for example, on 9 December 1965[968] decided that it had to be concluded from the wording of Article 6(1) that this provision only applied to "legal disputes" (Cf. Art. 14 of the International (UN) Covenant on Civil and Political Rights which in this context speaks of "a suit at law"). By contrast, De Doelder[969] considers that the

---

[964] Dutch Supreme Court, 29 June 1990, *NJ* 1991, 337 (annotated by E.A.E.); RvdW 1990, 136.

[965] Cf. De Doelder 1981 (*supra* nt. 352), pp. 69-73.

[966] *Engel and others v. The Netherlands*, 23 November 1976, A. 22. Cf. D.J. Harris, M. O'Boyle, C. Warbrick, *Law of the European Convention on Human Rights* (London, Butterworths, 1995) p. 167 et seq.; P. van Dijk, G.J.F. van Hoof, *Theory and Practice of the European Convention on Human Rights* (The Hague, Kluwer Law International 1998) (Van Dijk/Van Hoof 1998) p. 409 et seq.

[967] But: "A four year ban can be a 'functional death penalty' for an athlete," says Ken Foster, "The discourses of doping: law and regulation in the war against drugs," in O'Leary, ed., *Drugs and Doping in Sport* (London, Cavendish 2000) p. 181. See also A.B.Diouf's comments on the Braunskill Case (25 May 1996 – *IAAF v. USA Track & Field (USATF)*): "The sanction pronounced by our jury, will deprive an individual from earning his living for a certain time, or maybe for life, since Mr. Kevin Braunskill is now 27. The liberty to work is a fundamental liberty [...] *Indeed such severe professional bans are provisions contrary to the liberty to work, and consequently, they have a character of penal sanction, which no legitimacy allows us to pronounce.* Maybe, this aspect is the most shocking to Civil Courts when athletes, condemned by Sport Bodies, appeal to them [...]."

[968] *NJ* 1966, 378.

[969] De Doelder 1981 (*supra* nt. 352), p. 51.

strict interpretation of certain words appearing in the provision concerning the determination of civil rights and obligations does not affect the applicability of Article 6 to disciplinary proceeding. To support this view, De Doelder[970] refers to a decision of the ECtHR of 28 June 1978[971] from which he concludes that: "where under a certain body of disciplinary law sanctions may be imposed that result in a period of forced professional inactivity, the procedure by which this is made possible should comply with the provisions of Article 6(1)." If we also apply this reasoning to the non-statutory disciplinary law of sports organisations, any proceedings culminating in an athlete's suspension should also comply with the provisions of Article 6 (1). However, before this argument can be validly advanced, the obstacle of the applicability of the Convention per se to private law organisations" disciplinary law has to be overcome.

At first glance and as opposed to paragraph 1 of Article 6 ECHR, paragraphs 2 and 3 appear exclusively to concern criminal offences. The way in which Article 6 is drafted is not as clear-cut as it would seem with three paragraphs each giving separate guarantees, now that on closer inspection, especially of the case law of the ECtHR it emerges that Article 6 must be considered *in toto*. Its three paragraphs must therefore be interpreted together. The concept of fair trial is further explained in the three paragraphs, but must be considered as one indivisible notion. The terms "notamment" in the French version of paragraph 3 and "minimum rights" in the English text indicate that paragraphs 2 and 3 merely provide examples of fair trial rights. P. van Dijk and G.J. van Hoof[972] have noted that paragraph 3 of Article 6, unlike paragraph 1, does not also relate to proceedings concerning the determination of civil rights and obligations; however, if a party to civil proceedings were denied the rights mentioned in paragraph 3, under certain circumstances this could still mean that there has not been a "fair hearing" as referred to in paragraph 1.

Nevertheless, the applicability of Article 6 ECHR to the disciplinary proceedings conducted by private law associations is still doubtful. For one thing, the European Anti-Doping Convention which was adopted by the Council of Europe in 1980 (i.e. by the same body that adopted the ECHR) clearly indicates that the rights enshrined in the ECHR do not automatically apply in the context of the disciplinary doping procedures of the national sports organisations. The States Parties to the Convention[973] undertake to urge their sports organisations to begin a process of harmonisation of (among other things) their respective disciplinary proceedings "applying agreed international principles of natural justice and ensuring respect for the fundamental rights of suspected sportsmen and sportswomen; these principles will include: [...] The right of such persons to a fair hearing and to be assisted or represented."[974] Judging from one implementation of the Convention, namely the

---

[970] De Doelder 1981 (*supra* nt. 352), p. 58.

[971] *NJ* 1980, 54. De Doelder 1981 (*supra* nt. 352), pp. 55-57.

[972] Van Dijk/Van Hoof 1998 (*supra* nt. 966).

[973] COE Anti-Doping Convention, Strasbourg, 16 November 1989, ETS no. 135.

[974] COE Anti-Doping Convention, Art. 7(2)(d).

Belgian *Decreet houdende erkenning en subsidiëring van Vlaamse sportfederaties,* Article 6 ECHR is in any case presumed to lack direct effect in this field as it expressly provides that a sports federation[975] in order to be and remain recognised as such in its statutes and regulations has to embrace: "the principles and rules of democracy [...] and the European Convention on Human Rights and the International Convention on the Rights of the Child [...]."

Are there any arguments that may be advanced in favour of the applicability of the Convention on Human Rights to the disciplinary proceedings of private law organisations? The Dutch legislator has provided for the possible annulment of arbitral awards if during the proceedings leading up to the award fundamental principles of law have been violated to such an extent that the hearing of the case can no longer be considered to have been fair and impartial. The District Court of Breda in a judgment of 11 September 1990[976] held that an arbitral award whose content goes against public order requirements or awards that are the result of flawed proceedings from the point of view of public order, whereby public order is considered to include Article 6 ECHR, or where good morals have been violated, must be open to annulment.[977] It would be fair to assume that this is also true for decisions of disciplinary bodies. Another argument in favour of direct applicability is that it would be difficult to reconcile with logic if a state which has ratified the Convention nevertheless allows private law organisations to disregard the Convention by creating a self-contained legal regime where standards prevail that depart from the standards that generally apply in that state. A further argument derives from the rationale underlying the ECHR. The decision of the states parties to establish this legal instrument was partly based on the fact that their domestic laws had many legal principles in common. According to international law "gaps in international law may be filled by borrowing principles which are common to all or most national systems of law."[978] One such gap may be found in the ECHR in respect of its scope of application *ratione personae.* It can safely be assumed that the drafters of the Convention did not intend to exclude persons who are responsible for establishing the regulations of private law organisations from this scope. In addition, one would be hard put to find a rule in any national system of law which expressly allows private law organisations to depart from national legislation in force and the principles underlying this legislation. For this reason too, one might assume the direct applicability

---

[975] Ch. II, part 1, Art. 3(1)(6).

[976] *Tijdschrift voor Arbitrage* (TvA) 1991, pp. 28-31.

[977] The District Court based its considerations on the Dutch Supreme Court judgments of 3 December 1971 (*NJ* 1972, 137) and 17 March 1978 (*NJ* 1979, 204) in which the Supreme Court held that the responsibility of the state, including that of the courts, for undue care in the decision-making process leading up to the judgment only becomes an issue if in the preparation of that judgment fundamental principles of law were violated to such an extent that the hearing of the case can no longer be considered to have been fair and impartial.

[978] Michael Akehurst, *A Modern Introduction to International Law* (London, Harper Collins Academic 1987) p. 52.

of the fundamental principles laid down in the ECHR to the disciplinary proceedings of sports organisations.[979]

For a long time it was thought that only the words "in the determination of his civil rights and obligations [...]" in Article 6(1) ECHR could pave the way for the applicability of Article 6 and that no argument could be drawn from the words "criminal charge." However, nowadays it is thought that even the words "criminal charge" do not form an insurmountable obstacle. According to Van Dijk and Van Hoof[980] a punitive sanction always makes the charge "criminal." This is of particular interest to the question at hand, given that several years' suspension can certainly be regarded as a punitive sanction. Van Dijk and Van Hoof urge the Court to end the uncertainty and ambiguity with respect to the term "criminal charge" that has resulted from its case law, especially concerning the nature and severity of the penalty. As to the nature of the penalty, Article 6 should be considered applicable to all proceedings which may result in the imposition of a punitive sanction that as to its nature and/or consequences is so similar to a criminal sanction that there is no justification for excluding it from judicial review. "This would include in particular deprivations of liberty and fines, but also concern restrictions of economic or professional freedom of a punitive character (which, moreover, could affect civil rights and obligations)." The fines imposed on athletes for their use of doping could therefore also be subsumed under this heading. "As far as the severity of the penalty is concerned, it is submitted that, since the Court has adopted the position that Article 6 makes no distinction between serious and less serious offences and that it may even apply to proceedings which lead to no penalty at all, there would seem to be no convincing reason to distinguish between [...] fines of a small and of a large amount for the applicability of Article 6 to disciplinary and administrative proceedings; after all, if the severity of the penalty is not a decisive element for the applicability of Article 6 in case there exists a 'criminal charge' it should also not be determinant for the question whether certain proceedings have criminal features which make Article 6 applicable."[981]

From the above it may be concluded that sports organisations are therefore not completely free as to which provisions to include in their disciplinary doping rules.

---

[979] Cf. E.J. Dommering, *Preadvies NJV* (Zwolle 1983) p. 232. The Hague Court of Appeal in its judgement of 28 May 1975, *NJ* 1976, 210 (Van Duivenbode/KNVB) held that decisions of disciplinary bodies must comply with the requirements of the sound administration of disciplinary justice. See also the judgment of the President of the Breda Court of First Instance of 11 March 1998, KG 1998, 123 (AJFR/NAC). In this case the issue was the violation of fundamental principles of disciplinary law.

[980] Van Dijk/Van Hoof 1998 (*supra* nt. 966), p. 418.

[981] In *Öztürk* (judgment of 21 February 1984, Publ. CEDH, Serie A vol. 73) the ECtHR defined when a criminal charge as referred to in Art. 6 ECHR must be considered to have been brought. It further held that the ECHR has to be interpreted autonomously. According to the autonomous interpretation a criminal charge has been laid if one of the following conditions is met: a. the violation of the law is considered a criminal offence in the legal system involved; b. the penalty is intended as a deterrent and consists of a fine or a custodial sentence. In other words, the penalty is intended to punish the offender; c. the penalty is severe. The fact that the violation in the *Öztürk* case was only minor and would not harm the offender's reputation in the Court's view did not prevent the applicability of Art. 6 ECHR.

They are bound not only by the concepts of reasonableness and fairness but also by the provisions of Article 6 ECHR. The athlete accused of the use of doping "often faces the proceedings much as a tourist would experience a hurricane in Fiji: a frightening and isolated event in his life, and for which he is utterly unprepared," according to a description by Jan Paulsson.[982] In such circumstances athletes should at least be able to rely on the right to a fair trial and on fundamental principles of law.

Below, it will be examined whether the various sports organisations were actually aware of their obligation to fulfil these requirements under national and international law and if so, to what extent they had included relevant provisions in their regulations.

5.   FAIR TRIAL RIGHTS IN SPORTS LAW

Only two international federations expressly recognised the athlete's right to a defence as such. The FIH[983] offered the athlete "every opportunity to defend the charges," while the FITA[984] granted to "the accused person the right to defend him/ herself." Of course, this does not mean that other sports organisations who did not expressly provide the *in toto* right to a defence did not entitle athletes to a fair trial. However, the various fair trial rights were scattered quite randomly over the different regulations and never included the full catalogue as provided in Article 6 ECHR.

   Below, a survey will be given of fair trial rights as and when they appeared in the doping regulations of the different sports organisations, whereby a distinction is made between international federations and national federations. Wherever a right found in the doping regulations has an equivalent in Article 6 ECHR this will be mentioned.

5.1.   The right to appear in person / the right to be heard (cf. Art. 6(1) ECHR)

The term "fair hearing" has a special meaning in common law systems where it is used as a comprehensive concept including every procedural guarantee that is indispensable for the sound administration of justice. The concept has its roots in natural law which besides the *iudex in re sua* principle also provides for the principle of *audi alteram partem*. Such principles are part of a certain universal consciousness, rather than of (positive) legal science.[985] This may also explain why the

---

[982] Paulsson 1993 (*supra* nt. 427), p. 361.
[983] Statutes and By Laws, Art. 22.1(a).
[984] Appendix 4 – Doping Control Procedures, Art. 11.5.
[985] P. Jackson, *Natural Justice* (London, Sweet & Maxwell 1979) p. 7. Barrie 2000 (*supra* nt. 936), p. 8.

right to a fair hearing was given such a prominent place in paragraph 1 of Article 6 ECHR.

In this section, I will first discuss provisions in which the right to a fair and public hearing is laid down in so many words. The right to submit evidence can be considered to derive from this right and will be discussed in subsection 5.2. Another "derived" right, the right to conduct the doping trial in writing, will be considered in subsection 5.3.

5.1.1. *The right to be heard*

At the international level

In principle, one must first be entitled to appear in person before it is possible to be heard. The IOC Medical Code however considered this from the opposite angle and provided the right to appear in person as a corollary of the right to be heard.[986] The exercise of the right to be heard is in turn only meaningful when one has previously been informed of the charges. The IAAF, the ICF, the ITF, the FIS, the ATP and WTA Tour[987] all expressly provided for the right to be informed of the charges. The ITF added that, in case the athlete did not wish to appear in person, this would not prevent the Appeals Committee from proceeding with the case.[988] The principle of *audi et alteram partem* does not only include the right to appear in person or through a representative, but also the right to submit evidence and the right to examine witnesses and experts. If the athlete is unable to appear, he/she should be given the opportunity to conduct his/her defence in writing. The principle must also be interpreted to include the athlete's right to make statements. All these rights were included in the IOC Medical Code.[989]

The IAAF and the ICF entitled athletes to a hearing before a competent panel prior to any decisions about their participation in competitions. This right would be set out in the summons. In case the athlete failed to return the form entitling him/her to a hearing within the allotted time, he/she was considered to have voluntarily forfeited this right.[990] The FINA under a similar rule allowed the swimmer in question 28 days to request a hearing. If he/she failed to respond, he/she would be deemed to have voluntarily foregone this right.[991]

---

[986] IOC MC Ch. IX, Art. VII.

[987] IAAF: Rules and Regulations, Division III, Rule 61 sub 5; ICF: Doping Rules and Procedural Guidelines for Doping Control, Rule 5, sub 3; ITF: By Laws of ITF Limited, 8. Tennis Anti-Doping Programme (L) 4; FIS Doping Rules, Rule 7, 2; ATP/WTA: Official Rulebook, Tennis Anti-Doping Program, L, 5.

[988] By Laws of ITF Limited, 8. Tennis Anti-Doping Programme (L) 4.

[989] IOC MC Ch. IX, Art. VII.

[990] Rules and Regulations, Division III, Rule 59 sub 3 and Procedural Guidelines for Doping Control, 2. Doping Control during Competition, 2.58. The Doping Rules & Procedural Guidelines for Doping Control, I.C.F. Doping Control Regulations, Rule 5 is Rule 59 sub 3 of the IAAF verbatim.

[991] Doping Control, Art. DC 8.7.

Various international federations simply provided for the accused athlete's right to a hearing.[992] The anti-doping regulations of the ITTF only listed this right in the part of its regulations dealing with the "World and Olympic Title Competition."[993] A rower or coxswain suspected of doping also had this right, and the relevant provision of the FISA added thereto that sanctions could only be imposed after the right to be heard had been exercised within the time allotted.[994] The provisions of the ITU and the FIS concerning the right to be heard ran parallel to those of the FISA.[995] The UCI regulations provided that the cyclist's national federation "shall summon the rider to come and present his explanations and arguments." The rider could, however, "waive the right to be heard in which case the investigation shall be conducted in writing."[996] In the proceedings as they were described in the regulations of the IWF "the principles of natural justice will be observed." These principles demanded that: "a. the right to be heard by an unbiased committee, and b. the right to be heard in answer to those charges"[997] would be granted. The FIH also stipulated that the procedure should be conducted fairly for all parties involved and that "those parties' basic rights" were upheld. Among other things, the accused athlete had to be given "every reasonable opportunity to defend the charges and to be heard."[998] Under the FIVB regulations, the right to a hearing was not a firm right that athletes could claim: "The FIVB Medical Commission recommends that, before a final decision is made on a particular case, a fair hearing be granted to the player (and possibly the other persons concerned)." However, if the results of a sample analysis only became known after the competition, there was such a firm right: "In case the result is received after the competition, the players have the right to ask for a hearing to be organised or to send a confidential letter to the President of the FIVB Medical Commission, if they want circumstances and facts to be taken into consideration."[999] The FIVB regulations were quite detailed concerning the contents of the hearing (more so than those of any other IF): "Such hearing should take into consideration the circumstances (extenuating or not) and the known facts of the case. During the hearing, it is also recommended that the head of the accredited laboratory who reported the result be consulted." It might impinge upon the athlete's rights if the hearing was planned at very short notice. The athlete must be given ample opportunity to prepare his/her defence. The right to be heard might

---

[992] IBF Disciplinary Regulations, Art. 3.1; FIBA Regulations Governing Doping Control, Art. 6.6.2., paragraph 4; UCI Cycling Regulations, Part XIV, Ch. I, Art. 5; IBU Disciplinary Rules: Art. 11.3 and Appendix 4 B Doping Control Procedures, Art. 11.4.

[993] ITTF Regulations for World and Olympic Title Competition, Art. 4.3.1.4: A player accused of an infringement of the eligibility regulations shall have the right to request a hearing by the IOC Executive Board, whose decision shall be final.

[994] Rules of Racing and Related By Laws, Part VII, Rule 83.

[995] ITU Doping Control Rules And Procedural Guidelines, Arts. 3.40 and 3.41. See also Art. 5.2 and 5.5.; FIS Doping Rules, Rule 5, paragraph 2.

[996] UCI Cycling Regulations, Part XIV, Ch. VII, Art. 69.

[997] IWF Anti-doping Policy, Hearing Of The Appeal, Art. 15.8.

[998] Statutes and By Laws, Art. 22.1.

[999] Medical Regulations, 2. Antidoping Control Regulations, Art. 2.6.6.

also be impinged upon if the hearing took place at a location that was disadvantageous to the athlete or at a disadvantageous time of day, or the combined time and
place could be right for the athlete, but not for possible witnesses and experts.

At the national level

The right to hear and be heard after a positive B sample result was guaranteed by
most doping regulations of national federations and central organisations, if not
always expressly. For example, the *Anti-Dopingbestimmungen* of the *Österreichische
Bundes-Sportorganisation,*[1000] the Belgian *Decreet inzake medisch verantwoorde
sportbeoefening,*[1001] and the anti-doping rules of the NOC and Sports Federation of
Denmark all included the right to be heard.[1002] The hearing described in the doping
rules of the Finnish Anti-doping Committee[1003] were intended to establish whether
the athlete had in fact committed a doping offence. The French Decree no. 2001-
36[1004] provided that: "l'intéressé, accompagné le cas échéant des personnes investies
de l'autorité parentale, est convoqué devant l'organe disciplinaire [...]." This provision further authorised the representation of athletes who were minors by their par-
ents or guardians. The *Deutscher Leichtathletik Verband* in its *Sonderbedingungen
des DLV für Dopingkontrollen* stipulated that "Der Rechtsausschuß [...] nach Eingang
des Antrages unverzüglich einen Termin zur mündlichen Anhörung (bestimmt),
soweit nicht der Athlet und der DLV auf deren Durchführung verzichten."[1005] The
right to be heard was further implied in the Statement of Anti-Doping Policy of UK
Sport, while UK Athletics provided that: "[...] there will be a disciplinary hearing
before the Disciplinary Committee, at a date to be determined by the Chairman of
the Drug Advisory Committee, after consultation with the parties, and, in the absence of agreement, being a date not less than 21 days from the Notice of the hear-

---

[1000] 10. Bekanntgabe des Analyseergebnisses.

[1001] Title VI – Disciplinaire maatregelen inzake medisch verantwoorde sportbeoefening, Ch. V –
Erkenning van de disciplinaire bevoegdheden van sportverenigingen, Art. 41, para. 2, sub 3° e). See
also: Koninklijke Belgische Wielrenunie: Tuchtreglement, Title V: Tuchtreglement van de KBWB,
Book: nationale rechtspleging, Part II – Rechtspleging, Title 1 – De tuchtrechterlijke procedure, Ch. 3
– De zitting van de tuchtcommissie en de tuchtraad, Part 1 – De oproeping van de partijen.

[1002] Anti-Doping regulations, Art. 9.

[1003] The Finnish Antidoping Committee: Doping regulations for sports organisations, 3. Penalty
procedures., 3.1. Positive test results. A control body set up by the Finnish Antidoping Committee
handled all doping cases under this agreement.

[1004] Decree no. 2001-36 of 11 January 2001, relatif aux dispositions que les fédérations sportives
agreéées doivent adopter dans leur règlement en matière de contrôles et de sanctions contre le dopage
en application de l'article L.3634-1 du code de la santé publique: Title II, Section 2, Art. 18.

[1005] Para. 84, sub (3). See also: Deutscher Kanu Verband e.V.: Anti-Dopingbestimmungen, 3. Teil
– Verfahrensvorschriften, para. 23 – Termin zur mündlichen Verhandlung: "Nach Bekanntgabe des
Ergebnisses der B-Probe wird ein Termin zur mündlichen Verhandlung bestimmt." Bund Deutscher
Radfahrer: Dopingkontroll-Reglement, 6 Verfahrensdurchführung / Rechtfertigungs- und
Einspruchsrecht, 6.1 Anspruch auf Rechtfertigung, (1): "Wenn der Sportler / die Sportlerin nicht
fristgerecht um eine Gegenanalyse nachgesucht hat oder das Ergebnis der Gegenanalyse ebenfalls
positiv ist, muß der Sportler / die Sportlerin von der Geschäftsstelle des BDR in terminlicher Abstimmung
mit dem Bundessportgericht zu einer Anhörung vor dem Bundessportgericht eingeladen werden."

ing being given to the athlete."[1006] The British Judo Association also entitled the athlete to a hearing, albeit at his own expense: "The player concerned will be allowed to attend (at his/her own expense) this meeting of the B.J.A. Board of Directors to make a statement in his/her defence."[1007] In the Model Doping Control Policy of the Irish Sports Council it was provided that: "It is critical to the enforceability of any sanctions that, if a person wishes, they are given an opportunity to be properly heard. The law protects those affected by disciplinary actions by importing rules of natural and constitutional justice and fairness."[1008] Under Italian doping law, the athlete had a duty to appear to answer to charges and questions: "Nei confronti del tesserato alla Federazione Sportiva Nazionale o Disciplina Associata che, convocato dall'Ufficio di Procura Antidoping per l'assunzione di informazione o per la contestazione dell'addebito, non si presenti senza giustificato motivo, si applica la sanzione della sospensione per un periodo da mesi 1 a mesi 6."[1009] The doping regulations of the *Nederlandse Hippische Sportbond* provided that: "the disciplinary commission [...] informs the participant that he may request a hearing within seven days of receipt."[1010] Under the *Huishoudelijk Reglement* of the *Koninklijke Nederlandse Roeibond* (KNRB) all doping cases were to be brought before the FISA and the athlete had to be notified of this. This notice had to include the information that: "the athlete or the association may still request a meeting with the board before proceedings are instituted."[1011] The doping regulations of the *Koninklijke Nederlandse Wielren Unie*, which closely resembled those of the UCI, stipulated that the *Unie* had to summon the athlete "in order to hear his explanation and defence."[1012] Pursuant to most doping regulations of the Dutch sports organisations the initiative for a hearing lay with the organisations themselves and the athlete was duly informed.[1013] In most cases provisional suspensions could be effected without any prior hearing being required.[1014] In the Portuguese Statute Law no. 183/97[1015] it was guaranteed that: "any individual who is suspected of infringing these regulations shall be entitled to a hearing [...]." This rule was further

---

[1006] UK Current Doping Rules and Procedures, Appendix B – Rules and Procedures concerning Doping Control, (B7).

[1007] By Laws relating to Drug Abuse, K. 1.

[1008] 3. Guidance Notes, 3.4. What are the Disciplinary Procedures?

[1009] Italian NOC: Regolamento dell'attività antidoping, Title IV – Adempimenti e sanzioni, Art. 11 – Violazione delle norme antidoping e relative sanzioni, sub 2.

[1010] Art. 15(6).

[1011] Art. 1, sub b.

[1012] Title XIV Antidoping Controle Reglement, Ch. VII, Art. 69.

[1013] See *inter alia*: Koninklijke Nederlandse Gymnastiek Bond: Huishoudelijk Reglement, Ch. 4 – Dopingcontrole, 4.3. Tuchtrechtelijke Behandeling en Strafbepaling, 4.3.02, subsection 1; Koninklijke Nederlandse Hockey Bond: KNHB Dopingreglement, Title VII – Tuchtrechtelijke behandeling, Art. 20, subsection 1; Judo Bond Nederland: Bonds Vademecum, 2.5 Dopingreglement, Art. 17, subsection 1.

[1014] See: Koninklijke Nederlandse Zwembond: KNZB-Reglement Dopingcontrole, Art. P9, sub 9.6; Nederlandse Handboog Bond: Dopingreglement, Title VII, Art. 21, subsection 2.

[1015] Statute Law No. 182/97, 26 July 1997, Art. 10, subsection 1, sub e).

elaborated in the doping regulations of the Portuguese sports federations. The *Federação Portuguesa de Remo* (FPR) for example established that:

> "A verificação de um caso de dopagem au a violação da abrigação de confidencialida-de, nos termos do Artigo 15° determina automaticamente a abertura de inquérito por parte da entidade competente com vista a determinar a natureza, as circunstancias e a gravidade da infracção e a eventual existência de envolvimento e o grau de respensa-bilidade soiidária par parte dos agentes desportivos referidos no Artigo 5°, devendo, nomeadamente, averiguar quanto ao modo de obtenção pelo praticante da substância dopante."[1016]

> "La Comisión Antidopaje de la [...] (Federación Española de Baloncesto) se reunirá en un plazo no superior a los cinco dias hábiles que siguen al término del periodo de alegaciones de que dispone el jugador-a y el club."[1017]

Under the doping regulations of the *Federación Española de Gimnasia* and other Spanish federations the hearing subsequent to a positive test result was not so much a right which the athlete could claim, but rather an automatic occurrence which he/she could make use of:

> "[...] la Comisión Antidopaje de la R.F.E.G., al tener conocimiento de tales hechos, pondrá estos, así como la identidad del gimnasta, en conocimiento del Presidente de la R.F.E.G. y del Comité de Disciplina Deportiva de la R.F.E.G. Asimismo, enviará un documento al Presidente del club y al gimnasta implicado (y/o tutor si es menor de edad), por procedimiento que deje constancia de su rerepción, en el que se le infor-mará del procedimiento a seguir."[1018]

This provision also provided for alternative arrangements in case the defending athlete was a minor. Pursuant to the doping rules of the Swedish *Riksidrotts-forbundet,*[1019] "the disciplinary body shall permit the notified person to comment on the notification." Finally, the British Judo Association allowed the athlete to be present at the hearing (at his own expense).[1020]

[1016] Regulamento do Controlo Antidopagem: Ch. III – Procedimento Disciplinar e Regime Sancionatório, Art. 16 – Abertura de Inquerito.

[1017] Reglamento Control de Dopaje, Title IV – Notificación a los órganos disciplinarios, Art. 23, subsection 2.

[1018] Reglamento Control de Dopaje: De la notificación del expediente, Art. 47, subsection 1.

[1019] Ch. 13 – Doping rules, 12 – Administration.

[1020] By Laws relating to Drug Abuse (1-6-1994), K. 1): "The player concerned will be allowed to attend (at his/her own expense) this meeting of the B.J.A. Board of Directors to make a statement in his/her defence."

5.1.2.   *The right to submit evidence*

At the international level

According to the IOC Medical Code, the right to be heard included the right to submit evidence.[1021] A small number of international federations also expressly provided for this right.[1022] No further instructions were given as to the margin of discretion left to doping panels in the admission and weighing of evidence. This left the question of whether, for example, incidents involving false evidence could be dealt with by the panel itself or whether this had to be decided by a civil court.

At the national level

The *Decreet inzake medisch verantwoorde sportbeoefening*[1023] authorised the athlete "to request additional measures of investigation." The doping regulations of the French sports organisations did not include any rules dealing with the submission of evidence. The *Anti-Dopingbestimmungen* of the *Deutscher Kanu Verband* (DKV) provided that: "Der Sachverhalt [...] durch Anhörung des Sportlers und Aufnahme der Beweise zu erörtern (ist)."[1024] UK Sport had included a provision on the burden of proof: "The burden of proof shall be with the governing body in any hearing before the Disciplinary Committee and with the Appellant in any hearing before the Appeal Panel,"[1025] while most other British sports organisations[1026] entitled the athlete to submit evidence. The Guidelines in anti-doping procedures of the Irish Amateur Boxing Association provided that: "The athlete will also have the

---

[1021] IOC MC Ch. IX, Art. VII.

[1022] UCI Cycling Regulations, Part XIV, Ch. VII, Art. 74; FIH Statutes and By Laws, Art. 22.1(a) sub (iii); FIH Doping Policy, Art. 10.3; FIL IRO – International Luge Regulations, Artificial Track, Supplement 4. Ch. Vii, Art. VII; ATP/WTA Official Rulebook, Tennis' Anti-doping Program, L. Art. 6.

[1023] Title VI – Disciplinaire maatregelen inzake medisch verantwoorde sportbeoefening, Ch. V – Erkenning van de disciplinaire bevoegdheden van sportverenigingen, Art. 41, para. 2, sub e).

[1024] 3. Teil – Verfahrensvorschriften, para. 25 – Mündliche Verhandlung, subsection 4.

[1025] Statement of Anti-Doping Policy, Annex A – Anti-doping policy – Governing body requirements and procedures, General requirements, Conduct of Hearings, 36.

[1026] Amateur Rowing Association: Mis-Use of Drugs By Laws, 4. Enquiry, 4.3 "The person may produce evidence." British Equestrian Federation: Rule Book & Disciplinary and Doping Control Procedures, Rights of Participants at Stewards Meetings, 14.1 "[...] a Participant may submit written evidence [...]." Amateur Swimming Federation of Great Britain: ASFGB Doping Control Rules and Protocols, Doping Control Rules, 8 Judicial Procedures, 8.4 "[...] Each party will be given a reasonable opportunity to give and call evidence [...]." British Bobsleigh Association: Rules for Doping Control, 4. Disciplinary measures and procedure, 4.5: "At any hearing under these Rules the person who is the subject of the hearing [...] shall have the right to give and call evidence [...]." Badminton Association of England Ltd.: Doping Control Rules, Disciplinary Procedure, 5.4 "[...] The person concerned will be asked to submit evidence, in writing, to the disciplinary committee [...]"; Ibidem, 5.6: "any hearing under these Rules the person who is the subject of the hearing [...] shall have the right to call evidence, or give evidence provided that it has been submitted and received by the committee, in writing, at least 7 days prior to that hearing."

right to representation before the committee and all oral evidence will be unsworn."
The Doping Control Regulations of the Irish Canoe Union (ICU) established that:
"[...] At a hearing of the Disciplinary Panel or the Appeal Panel, the athlete or
individual and the Irish Canoe Union [...] will have the right to give and call evidence [...]."[1027] When a "factor of a natural character" was discovered which could
influence the final decision at the level of the national association of the cyclist or
licensee, the doping regulations of the *Koninklijke Nederlandse Wielren Unie* permitted the interested party to petition the national association to reopen the case. On
pain of disallowance such reopening must be requested within a month after the
fact concerned was discovered. The burden of proof rested on the party adducing
the new fact.[1028] The *Regulamento do Controlo Antidopagem* of the *Federação
Portuguesa de Remo* stipulated that: "Após a notificação da nota de culpa, o agente
desportivo arguido como responsável disporá de dez dias para a apresentação
fundamentada da sua defesa, podendo indicar testemunhas ou requerer outros meios
de prova."[1029] The *Federação Portuguesa de Hoquei* (FPH) in Article 22 of its
Regulamento Antidopagem[1030] included a series of provisions relating to evidence:

"1º Com a defesa, o arguido pode indicar testemunhas, juntar documentos ou requerer
diligências. 2º Não podem ser oferecidos mais de trés testemunhas por cada facto. 3º
As testemunhas só podem depor sobre factos para que hajam sido indicados pelo
arguido. 4º O inquiridor poderá recusar a inquirição de testemunhas, quando considere
suficientemente provados os factos alegados pelo arguido. 5º A apresentação das
testemunhas para serem inquiridas está a cargo do arguido. 6º Os depoimentos das
testemunhas podem ser gravadas em fita magnética ou por processo semelhante. 7º A
inquirição das testemunhas realizar-se-á na sede da F.P.H., ou na sede da Associação
do Arguido, quando motivos reievantes o justifiquem."

Finally, the doping regulations of the *Federação de Triatlo de Portugal* (FTP) also
included detailed rules concerning evidence.[1031]

[1027] 9.00 Disciplinary & Appeal Procedures, 9.08.See also: Equestrian Federation of Ireland: Model
Doping Control Policy for National Governing Bodies, 2. How does Doping Control work?, 2.4 What
are the Disciplinary Procedures? 2.4.4.; Tennis Ireland: Doping Control Policy, 4. Disciplinary Procedures, 4.8; Irish Triathlon Association: 2. Doping Control Policy, 2.4 What are the Disciplinary Procedures? 2.4.8; Volleyball Association of Ireland: Doping Control Policy, 1.4 Disciplinary procedures,
1.4.8; Irish Sailing Association: 2. Doping Control Policy, 2.4. Disciplinary Procedures, 2.4.7.

[1028] Title XIV Antidoping Controle Reglement, Ch. VII – Recht van verdediging – Beroep, Art. 83.

[1029] Ch. III – Procedimento Disciplinar e Regime Sancionatório, Art. 20 – Defesa, 1. *Idem*: Federação
Portuguesa de Tiro com Arco: Regulamento do Controlo Antidopagem, Ch. III – Procedimento
Disciplinar e Regime Sancionatório, Art. 18.

[1030] Título II – Do Processo Disciplinar, Ch. III – Da Acusação, Art. 22 – Produção de prova pelo
arguido.

[1031] Regulamento Anti-Dopagem, Title VII – Do Processo Disciplinar, Art. 40 – Da defesa, subsection 2: "No mesmo prazo o arguido pode apresentar documentos el ou testemunhas, até ao número de
3 por cada artigo da nota de culpa e até ao máximo de 10 testemunhas"; Art. 42 – Das testemunhas: "A
prova testemunhal seguirá os trâmites prcvistos no regulamento de discipline da FTP."

5.1.3. *The right to conduct the doping trial in writing*

At the international level

The anti-doping regulations of a large number of international federations used to contain provisions enabling athletes who were accused of doping proceedings to handle their case in writing. "The right to be heard includes the right [...] to submit a defence in writing," according to the IOC Medical Code.[1032] Usually, this right was not considered merely as a corollary of the right to be heard, but as an independent right.[1033] The ITF, ATP and WTA also provided for the possibility to decide a case purely on the basis of the case file. This, however, did not relieve the Appeals Committee of its duty to organise a hearing, although the athlete concerned or his/her representative did not need to be present at it. To reach a verdict, the Committee could consider all and any written statements.[1034]

At the national level

"Proceedings shall be oral," according to the rules of the NOC and Sports Confederation of Denmark.[1035] "However, the chairman may decide that proceedings in cases concerning suspension or formality shall be in writing." Many French sport organisations also provided that the defence was allowed "de présenter lors de la réunion de l'organisme disciplinaire des observations écrites ou orales."[1036] Pursuant to the Mis-Use of Drugs By Laws of the British Amateur Rowing Associa-

---

[1032] IOC Medical Code, Ch. IX, Art. VII.

[1033] IAAF Rules and Regulations, Division II, Rule 23, sub 8; IBF Disciplinary Regulations, Art. 3.3; IBA Anti Doping Rules, Ch. 11, Art. 11.3; FIG Medical Regulations, Doping Control Regulations, Art. 3.1. sub C.; IWF Anti-doping Policy, Hearing of the Appeal, Art. 15.9; FIH Doping Policy, Art. 10.2; FIL IRO – International Luge Regulations, Artificial Track, Supplement 4, Ch. VII, Art. VII.

[1034] By Laws of ITF Limited, 8. Tennis Anti-doping Programme (L), Art. 4; ATP/WTA Official Rulebook, Tennis' Anti-doping Program, L., Art. 5.

[1035] Anti-Doping Regulations, Art. 9, subsection 3.

[1036] Fédération Française des Sociétés d'Aviron: Réglementation anti-dopage de la FFSA, Organisme Disciplinaire, Art. 38; Fédération Française de Basketball: Règlement de lutte contre le dopage, Title IV – Première Instance, Art. 22; Fédération Française de Boxe, Règlement Fédéral de la Lutte contre le Dopage, Title II – Organismes Disciplinaires, Art. 24; Fédération Française de Handball: Lutte contre le dopage, Title 2, Chapitre 1 – Organismes disciplinaires, Art. 29; Fédération Française de Judo, Jujitsu, Kendo: Règlement Intérieur de la FFJDA Annex 4, Règlement Particulier de Lutte contre le Dopage, Art. 25; Fédération Française de Lutte: Lutte contre le dopage, Art. 30; Fédération Française de Natation: Règlement Intérieur, Règlement Particulier de Lutte contre le Dopage, Art. 16 – Procédure en 1ᵉ instance; Fédération Française de Tennis: Règlement relatif à la Lutte contre le dopage, Title III – Organismes Disciplinaires, Ch. II – Organisation de la procédure, Art. 24; Fédération Française Tennis de Table: Title II, Ch. I – Organismes Disciplinaire, Art. 30; Fédération Française de Tir: Règlement Particulier de Lutte contre le Dopage, Title II – Organismes et Procédures Disciplinaires, Art. 17 Fédération Française de Tir à L'arc: Lutte contre le Dopage, Title II, Ch. I – Organismes Disciplinaire, Art. 30; Federation Française de Triathlon: Réglementation Générale, 12. Lutte contre le Dopage, 12.5 – Organismes Disciplinaires, Art. 30; Fédération Française de Ski: Règlement Intérieur Particulier, De Lutte contre le Dopage, Art. 31.

tion[1037] "[...] the Disciplinary Panel must give to the person concerned the opportunity to comment either: – orally before the whole panel or before one of its members which it appoints for that purpose, or – in writing." The Dutch Skiing Federation (NSkiV) permitted the athlete to present a further explanation, either orally or in writing, concerning his/her alleged violation of the doping rules.[1038] In Sweden, the doping rules of the *Riksidrottsforbundet* provided that: "a verbal questioning shall be carried out at the request of the notified person. If it is obvious that such questioning is not of any benefit to the investigation, the disciplinary body may reject this request however."[1039]

In the context of the right to be heard, one final observation has to be made concerning the right to a last word. The UCI was the only international federation to grant this right to the accused athlete: "The rider or license-holder shall be entitled to the last word."[1040] National organisations had also included it in their rules, such as the *Bund Deutscher Radfahrer* (BDR): "Der Sportler / die Sportlerin oder der ansonsten beschuldigte Lizenzinhaber hat das Recht auf das letzte Wort."[1041] Finally, under the French *Décret* no 2001-36 of 11 January 2001[1042] and various doping regulations of the French sport organisations it was provided that: "L'intéressé ci, le cas échéant, ses défenseurs sont invités à prendre la parole en dernier."[1043]

5.2.   Open court (cf. Art. 6(1) ECHR)

The Belgian *Decreet inzake medisch verantwoorde sportbeoefening* established that hearings were to be held in open court, "unless at the request of the athlete it is decided to proceed in camera or a public hearing would threaten public order or morality."[1044] The Code of Conduct of the Flemish Gymnasts' League[1045] provided

---

[1037] 4. Enquiry, 4.2.

[1038] Dopingreglement, Tuchtrechtelijke behandeling, Art. 20, subsection 3.

[1039] Ch. 13, 12 para. Administration.

[1040] UCI Cycling Regulations, Part XIV, Ch. VII, Art. 77.

[1041] 6 Verfahrensdurchführung / Rechtfertigungs- und Einspruchsrecht, 6.2 Anhörung des / der Beschuldigten, Verfahrensdurchführung, sub (8).

[1042] Relatif aux dispositions que les fédérations sportives agreéées doivent adopter dans leur règlement en matière de contrôles et de sanctions contre le dopage en application de l'article L.3634-1 du code de la santé publique: Title II – Organes et procédures disciplinaires, Section 2 – Dispositions relatives aux organes disciplinaires de première instance, Art. 19.

[1043] Fédération Française de Boxe: Règlement Fédéral de la Lutte contre le Dopage, Title II – Organismes Disciplinaires, Art. 26; Fédération Française de Lutte: Lutte contre le dopage, Art. 34; Fédération Française de Natation: Règlement Intérieur, Règlement Particulier de Lutte contre le Dopage, Art. 16 – Procédure en 1ᵉ instance; Fédération Française Tennis de Table: Title II, Chapitre I – Organismes Disciplinaire, Art. 34; Fédération Française de Tir: Règlement Particulier de Lutte contre le Dopage, Title II – Organismes et Procédures Disciplinaires, Art. 19; Fédération Française de Tir à L'arc: Lutte contre le Dopage, Title II, Ch. I – Organismes Disciplinaire, Art. 34; Federation Française de Triathlon: Réglementation Générale, 12. Lutte contre le Dopage, 12.5 – Organismes Disciplinaires, Art. 34.

[1044] Title VI – Disciplinaire maatregelen inzake medisch verantwoorde sportbeoefening, Ch. V – Erkenning van de disciplinaire bevoegdheden van sportverenigingen, Art. 41, para. 2, sub 2. *Idem*: Koninklijke Belgische Wielrenunie, Tuchtreglement, Title V, Book 1, Part II, Title 1, Ch. 3, Part 2.

[1045] Art. 5.

that: "the debates (...) are open to the public except when the defence requests otherwise. The defence may also object to the composition of the disciplinary committee. The committee will itself decide on the validity of such an objection. In case the disciplinary committee is required to rule on medical matters such will take place in camera. Those involved may be assisted by counsel. They likewise have the right to have their medical counsel heard during the session." The relevant provision used by the NOC and Sports Confederation of Denmark read as follows: "Oral proceedings shall be open to the public. Proceedings may not be photographed, filmed or recorded. Under exceptional circumstances, such as clarification of the case or out of consideration for a party to the case, the Doping Tribunal may decide that the case shall be heard in camera."[1046] The *Dopingkontroll-Reglement* of the *Bund Deutscher Radfahrer*[1047] stated that: "Die Anhörung ist öffentlich durchzuführen, sofern kein gegenteiliger Antrag des Sportler / der Sportlerin oder des ansonsten beschuldigten Lizenzinhabers vorliegt. Der Vorsitzende des Bundessportgerichts kann seinerseits der Öffentlichkeit offiziell den Zutritt zum Saal während der gesamten oder Teile der Sitzung im Interesse der öffentlichen Ordnung oder, falls es die Achtung des Privatlebens oder das Arztgeheimnis ein solches Vorgehen rechtfertigt, untersagen." The Amateur Swimming Federation of Great Britain provided that: "the hearing shall be in private."[1048] Title XIV of the *Antidoping Controle Reglement* of the *Koninklijke Nederlandse Wielren Unie*[1049] included the rule that: "the hearing is public, except when the cyclist or licensee requests the opposite. The chairman of the organ may also ex officio decide to hear the case or a part of it in camera in the interest of public order or where the right to privacy or medical privilege so requires." From the viewpoint of confidentiality, it is to be applauded that the identity of the athlete is not revealed until he/she is found guilty, but not many doping regulations provided for this right. Of those who did, the Welsh Badminton Union provided that: "Confidentiality of the individuals identity shall be observed until a positive case of doping has been declared and a penalty awarded"[1050] and Tennis Ireland stipulated that: "Tennis Ireland, the members of the Disciplinary Panel and the members of the Appeal Panel shall use their reasonable endeavours to maintain in confidentiality the results of all testing and the identities of any persons involved in proceedings under this Programme, until such time as (1) proceedings under the Programme up to and including the Disciplinary Panel proceedings, if any, are concluded and (2) it has been determined by the Disciplinary Panel that a Doping Offence has been committed."[1051] In stark contrast appeared the provision laid down in the doping regulations of the NOC and Sports

---

[1046] Anti-Doping Regulations, Art. 9, subsection 3.

[1047] 6 Verfahrensdurchführung / Rechtfertigungs- und Einspruchsrecht, 6.2 Anhörung des / der Beschuldigten, Verfahrensdurchführung (6).

[1048] ASFGB Doping Control Rules and Protocols, Doping Control Rules, 9.8.1.

[1049] Ch. VII – Recht van verdediging – Beroep, Art. 76.

[1050] WBU Protocol to be put into action if positive dope test is reported on a Welsh player, Disciplinary hearing, 2.9.

[1051] Doping Control Policy, 4. Disciplinary Procedures, 4.8.

Confederation of Denmark: "Oral proceedings shall be open to the public." However: "Proceedings may not be photographed, filmed or recorded."[1052]

The fact that any decision must state the reasons upon which it is based may be considered self-evident. Still only a few national doping regulations used to (expressly) mention this fact. The Belgian *Decreet inzake medisch verantwoorde sportbeoefening* provided that disciplinary measures were to be imposed by a reasoned decision.[1053] The *Koninklijke Belgische Wielrenunie* also expressly stated that decisions had to be reasoned.[1054] In the French Decree which has already been mentioned several times above[1055] and in the doping regulations of a few French sports organisations[1056] it was stipulated that "La décision de la "commission antidopage," [...] doit être motivée et signée par le président et le secrétaire." Various German sports organisations did not make express mention of the reasoning of decisions, but here reasoning was considered an inherent element in the decision-making process. The athlete was entitled to a copy of the decision, which would be sent to him. In view of the possibility of appeal, this is a logical step. The *Bund Deutscher Radfahrer* in its doping regulations also expressly stated that "Je ein Exemplar der Entscheiding [...] dem Sportler/der Sportlerin bzw. dem Lizenzhaber [...] per Einschreiben met Empfangsbestätigung zuzustellen (ist)"[1057] The British Amateur Rowing Association stipulated that the decision must be "communicated to all interested parties."[1058] The German Volleyball Federation (DVV) did not even limit the publication of decisions to interested parties: "Entscheidungen, durch die Zulassungssperren oder Maßregeln (ausgenommen vorläufige Sperren) verhängt werden, werden vom DVV bekanntgegeben."[1059] The Equestrian Federation of Ireland (EFI) made use of a similar provision: "The Disciplinary Panel will give notice in writing to the person concerned of its decision when it is reached [...]."[1060]

[1052] Anti-Doping Regulations, Art. 9, subsection 3.

[1053] Title VI – Disciplinaire maatregelen inzake medisch verantwoorde sportbeoefening, Ch. V – Erkenning van de disciplinaire bevoegdheden van sportverenigingen, Art. 41, para. 3, sub 4.

[1054] Tuchtreglement, Title V, Book 1, Part II, Title 2, Ch. 1, Part 4.

[1055] Decree no. 2001-36 of 11 January 2001, relatif aux dispositions que les fédérations sportives agreéées doivent adopter dans leur règlement en matière de contrôles et de sanctions contre le dopage en application de l'article L.3634-1 du code de la santé publique: Title II – Organes et procédures disciplinaires, Section 2 – Dispositions relatives aux organes disciplinaires de première instance, Art. 20.

[1056] Fédération Française de Lutte: Lutte contre le dopage, Art. 35; Fédération Française de Boxe: Règlement Fédéral de la Lutte contre le Dopage, Title II – Organismes Disciplinaires, Art. 27; Fédération Française de Natation: Règlement Intérieur, Règlement Particulier de Lutte contre le Dopage, Art. 17 – Décision de l'Organisme disciplinaire; Fédération Française de Tir: Règlement Particulier de Lutte contre le Dopage, Title II – Organismes et Procédures Disciplinaires, Art. 20.

[1057] Dopingkontroll-Reglement, 6 Verfahrensdurchführung / Rechtfertigungs- und Einspruchsrecht, 6.3 Entscheidung / Verfahrensabschluß / Kostenfestlegung, sub (4). See also: Deutsche Triathlon Union (DTU): D) Antidopingordnung, para. 11 Disziplinarverfahren, para. 11.2.

[1058] Mis-Use of Drugs By Laws, 3. Procedure when a sample is declared positive. sub 3.2.

[1059] Anti-Doping Ordnung, Dritter Abschnitt Verfahren, 17. Veröffentlichung der Entscheidungen.

[1060] Model Doping Control Policy for National Governing Bodies, 2. How does Doping Control work?, sub 2.4.2. *Idem*: Irish Amateur Wrestling Association: 4. Disciplinary procedures, sub 4.5.

The *Regolamento dell'attività antidoping* of the Italian NOC established that: "L'U.C.A.A. provvede a dare communicazione alle Federazioni Sportive Nazionali ed alle Discipline Associate dei provvedimenti disciplinari adottati dell medesime in materia di doping."[1061] A combination of the duty to state reasons and the duty of notification of the decision was to be found in the doping regulations of the Amateur Swimming Federation of Great Britain: "Within 14 days of the conclusion of the hearing the decision, together with the reasons for it shall be sent, in writing to the parties [...]."[1062] The disciplinary committee of the Badminton Association of England (BAE) would only make available a "written summary of its reasons" to the parties involved.[1063] The Swedish *Riksidrottsforbundet* (SRF) provided that: "Discipline cases shall be administered and decisions shall be issued as quickly as possible. The disciplinary body is obliged to send the documents relevant to the case to the person authorized by the Swedish Sports Federation to prosecute discipline cases when requested."[1064]

5.3. Impartiality of the tribunal (cf. Art. 6(1) ECHR)

At the international level

Not many IFs included provisions in their regulations concerning the impartiality of the various disciplinary bodies. The reason might partly have been that most IFs left it to the disciplinary bodies of the national sports organisations to handle doping cases. Nevertheless, the IBA provided that: "no member of this body [Disciplinary Body] shall sit if having a direct or indirect interest on this particular case,"[1065] while under the IWF rules:[1066] "Appeal Committee members should be asked to declare any possible conflict of interest in the case. If a possible conflict of interest is evident, a replacement member shall be appointed." The FINA doping panel would consist of 6 members, of which "no two members may be from the same Country or Sport Country,"[1067] so as to ensure impartiality. The ISSF also provided a means to guarantee impartiality: "No Person who was involved in the process

---

[1061] Title IV, Art. 11, subsection 9. The Co-ordinating Office for Doping Activities informs the National Sports Associations and the Member Institutions of the disciplinary measures, which have been imposed by the Associations in connection with doping.

[1062] ASFGB Doping Control Rules and Protocols, Doping Control Rules, 8 Judicial Procedures, sub 8.6. See also: British Bobsleigh Association: Rules for Doping Control, 4. Disciplinary measures and procedure, sub 4.3: "The Disciplinary Committee will give notice in writing to the person concerned of its decision when it is reached and shall give a written summary of its reason." *Idem*: British Bobsleigh Association: Rules for Doping Control, 4. Disciplinary measures and procedure, sub 4.3.

[1063] Doping Control Rules, Disciplinary Procedure, sub 5.4.

[1064] Ch. 13 – Doping rules, 12 para. – Administration.

[1065] Anti Doping Rules, Ch. 11 – Disciplinary Body and Proceedings, 11.1.

[1066] IWF Anti-doping Policy, 15. Appeal, Appeal Committee.

[1067] Constitution, C 17 Doping Panel, C 17.1. In C 17.2. it is provided that Athey [i.e. the members of the Doping Panel] shall be known for their [...] impartiality [...]."

leading to the application of the penalty may be part of the court hearing the appeal."[1068]

At the national level

The Belgian *Decreet inzake medisch verantwoorde sportbeoefening*[1069] provided that disciplinary bodies had to consist of at least three members, none of whom could be considered to be an interested party in the case at hand and none of whom had been involved in its investigation. If the accused athlete suspected that these requirements were not fulfilled, he/she could challenge the member in question. The Flemish Gymnasts' League had a similar provision allowing athletes to object to the composition of the disciplinary committee, whereupon however the committee would itself decide whether these objections were well founded.[1070] In the UK Current Doping Rules and Procedures of UK Athletics the rule was included that: "The Disciplinary Committee will be appointed by the BAF Management Board from a standing panel of names nominated by BAF Council, which panel will not include any person who is currently a member of the BAF Drug Advisory Committee or who is currently a member of any other BAF Committee or Sub-Committee."[1071] By Law 1 (the doping policy) of the Great Britain Olympic Hockey Board (GBOHB) provided that: "The DRP (Doping Review Panel) will consist of an independent lawyer, an independent medical adviser and an official of another sport. [...] The player will be informed of the members of the DRP at the time of notification of any hearing. Should the player object to any member of the panel in writing such objection shall be considered by the officers of the GBOHB who may appoint alternative members."[1072] The Equestrian Federation of Ireland stipulated that: "the Disciplinary Panel shall consist of Sport Expert, Ned Campion, the Medical Officer of E.F.I. and the Legal Officer of E.F.I., all of whom must be impartial and not have been witness to the dope testing."[1073] Finally, the Anti-Doping Regulations of the Irish Cycling Federation[1074] provided that: "[...] before any athlete is declared guilty he will be allowed to state his case in front of a panel (min. 3 persons) the composition of which is designated by the President." This procedure leaves some doubt as to whether it was sufficient to guarantee the impartiality of the panel.

5.4.   The *in dubio pro reo* principle (cf. Art. 6(2) ECHR)

Under Article 6(2) ECHR "everyone charged with a criminal offence shall be presumed innocent until proved guilty according to law." One concretisation of this

---

[1068] Anti-Doping Regulations, 9. Appeals, 9.4.

[1069] Title VI, Ch. V, Art. 41, ' 2, sub 1.

[1070] Gedragscode, Art. 5.

[1071] Appendix B – Rules and Procedures concerning Doping Control, (B7).

[1072] 4. a) The Great Britain Olympic Hockey Board Doping Review Panel.

[1073] Model Doping Control Policy for National Governing Bodies, 2. How does Doping Control work? 2.4 What are the Disciplinary Procedures? 2.4.1.

[1074] Anti-Doping Regulations, 9.

rule is the principle of *in dubio pro reo*. There are two sides to this principle: it can be considered a fair trial right, but it can also act as a fundamental principle of criminal law.[1075] Under the principle of *in dubio pro reo* any insurmountable ambiguity as to whether the accused committed an offence must be interpreted in his/her favour.[1076] The doping regulations did not include any provisions equivalent to Article 6(2) ECHR or provided for the *in dubio pro reo* principle at all. However, it might be possible still to detect its application in practice by examining the case law.

In the case *S. v. FEI*[1077] it emerged from the facts that the bottles containing the urine samples had not been sealed after the doping control, contrary to the provisions of the FEI anti-doping regulations. This left open the possibility that the samples had been manipulated. Technically, it was impossible to exclude this possibility and thereby the possibility of contamination. This caused the CAS panel to find that: "on this point, doubt exists which must be to the benefit of the appellant." From this early (1992) CAS decision it cannot be concluded whether the panel hereby intended to apply the criminal law principle of *in dubio pro reo* or simply gave the athlete the benefit of the doubt.

In 1993, the Swiss Tribunal Fédéral delivered a judgment in which it expressly rejected the applicability of criminal law principles and of Article 6(2) ECHR to proceedings before the CAS.

> "As for the opinion of the CAS, whereby it is sufficient that the analyses performed reveal the presence of a banned product for there to be presumption of doping and, consequently, a reversal of the burden of proof, this relates not to public policy but to the burden of proof and the assessment of evidence, problems which cannot be resolved, in private law matters, in the light of notions proper to criminal law, such as the presumption of innocence and the principle 'in dubio pro reo', and corresponding guarantees which feature in the European Convention on Human Rights."[1078]

[1075] See e.g. the Tadic case before the ICTY (Press Release, The Hague, 11 November 1999, JL/ P.I.S./447-E). "Finally, the Trial Chamber notes that Count 8 of the Amended Indictment charged Dusko Tadic alternatively with two distinct offences, namely torture or inhuman treatment, and that the Appeals Chamber, in convicting Dusko Tadic on this Count, did not specify in respect of which of the two offences it found him guilty. As a consequence, an ambiguity undoubtedly exists. Under these circumstances, the Trial Chamber has applied the principle of in dubio pro reo (which states that any ambiguity must accrue to the defendant's advantage), and has imposed sentence in respect of the lesser offence of inhuman treatment."

[1076] Summerer 1990 (*supra* nt. 72) p. 162: "als ausprägung des Rechtsstaatsprinzips gilt für Sanktionen im Vereinrecht der Grundsatz der *Unschulzvermutung* nach Art. 6 II EMRK."

[1077] CAS 91/56, 25-6-1992, *S. v. FEI*, Matthieu Reeb, ed., *Digest of CAS Awards 1986-1998* (Berne, Editions Stämpfli 1998) pp. 93-103, ground 7. In CAS 92/70, 13-8-1992, *N. v. FEI*, Matthieu Reeb, ed., *Digest of CAS Awards 1986-1998* (Berne, Editions Stämpfli 1998) p. 54 et seq., the CAS considered that "it has the duty of ensuring that this difficult and indispensable fight [against doping] is conducted with due respect to the applicable law, the 'cardinal principle of the presumption of innocence' and the regulations of the FEI in force."

[1078] Extract of the judgment of 15 March 1993, delivered by the 1st Civil Division of the Swiss Tribunal Fédéral in *G. v. Federation Equestre Internationale and Court of Arbitration for Sport (CAS)*.

This line of reasoning is an example of a *contradictio in adjecto*. Within the framework of private law, the reversal of the burden of proof which is not a private law instrument is allowed, but the application of the presumption of innocence, which is deeply embedded in legal doctrine worldwide, is rejected, in part because it is laid down in the ECHR. However, starting from the applicability of Article 6 to doping proceedings the reversal of the burden of proof must be linked first of all to public order and only secondly to the assessment of evidence. Based on Article 6(2) there is a requirement that the adjudicating body must be convinced of the accused's guilt. The accused must be acquitted if the conviction is there, but not the evidence to support it, but acquittal is also indicated if there is sufficient evidence, but the conviction is lacking.

The CAS panel which decided the case of *Bernhard v. ITU*[1079] was considerably more flexible with regard to the applicability of the principle of *in dubio pro reo* to doping proceedings. It considered among other things that:[1080]

> "The situation in 'quasi-penal' procedures, such as doping in sport, should, on the other hand, be looked at differently, among other reasons also due to the principle *'in dubio pro reo'*, i.e. the benefit of doubt, which itself is an emanation of one of the most important legal presumptions, the presumption of innocence, deeply enshrined in the general principles of law and justice. This principle has the effect that in criminal and similar proceedings, the two parties do not bear an equal burden of proof, while the accusing party must prove the alleged facts with *certainty*, it is sufficient for the accused to establish reasons for doubt.
>
> In spite of the very important requirements of an efficient fight against doping and unfair practices in sport, these requirements cannot prevail over the basic legal and procedural guarantee which the rule of 'in dubio pro reo' offers to an accused person.
>
> While, on one hand, it is appropriate to establish rules for efficient sanctioning of offences where the medical science and experience allow no reasonable doubt about the real cause of the presence of forbidden substances, it should be noted, on the other hand, that the principle 'in dubio pro reo' is not contrary to the spirit of the documents of the IOC Medical Commission addressed to those who apply the Medical Code."

Cf. also Beloff (Beloff 1999 (*supra* nt. 282), p. 191: "[...] disciplinary rules [...] take effect as contractual terms." Cf. Christoph J.M. Safferling, Terror and Law – Is the German Legal System Able to Deal with Terrorism? The Bundesgerichtshof (Federal Court of Justice) decision in the case against El Motassadeq, German Law Journal 2004, Vol. 5 no. 5, p. 522: "The principle *'in dubio pro reo'* comes in as part of the careful weighing." The often misconceived concept of "*in dubio pro reo*" is explained by the BGH as follows: it is not an evidence-rule but a principle pertaining to the decision-making ("[...] *der Zweifelsatz* [ist] *keine Beweis-, sondern eine Entscheidungsregel* [...]."). It comes into play after the weighing of evidence has taken place. If at that stage, the judge is not fully convinced of a fact that is relevant for the decision, he has to presume the fact that has the least impact on the accused. The *in dubio*-principle is therefore not applicable to isolated elements of the evidence, but only after the evidence has been scrutinised in its entirety.

[1079] CAS 98/222, 9-8-1999, *Bernhard v. ITU*, Matthieu Reeb, ed., *Digest of CAS Awards II 1998-2000* (The Hague, Kluwer Law International 2002) pp. 330-344.

[1080] *Idem*, grounds 62 and 63.

The panel consequently found in favour of the athlete.

In *UCI v. Möller, Danmarks Idræts-Vorbund and Danmarks Cykle Union*[1081] the panel also considered the issue of the burden of proof within the context of the *in dubio pro reo* rule, of which it recalled that the CAS had dealt with it before in *Bernhard v. ITU*. In this case, the panel did not deny the applicability of the principle as such, but failed to see the need to apply it in this particular case, as in its view there was no doubt about the athlete's guilt.[1082] The panel emphasised that it was up to the athlete to formulate arguments which could induce the panel to give him the benefit of the doubt, but that the athlete had conspicuously failed to take advantage of this opportunity.

In *F. Aanes v. FILA*[1083] the CAS held that the legal relationship between an athlete and a sports organisation was of a private law character and therefore left no room for "the application of principles of criminal law." This therefore did not allow the application of the *in dubio pro reo* principle either.[1084]

German doctrine is positive that the presumption of innocence plays an important role in the procedural law regulating the doping trial. Summerer[1085] does not speak of a criminal law principle, but of a "Rechtsstaatsprinzip" which also applies within the law of association. "Solange dem Beschuldigten die Tat nicht nachgewiesen ist, gilt er als unschuldig. Es gilt der Grundsatz 'in dubio pro reo,' bei Zweifeln darf der angeschuldigte Sportler also nicht verurteilt werden. Das individuelle Freiheitsinteresse ist höherwertig als jeder Strafausspruch."[1086] German law is strongly in favour of the principle's application, as also emerged from a judgment of the OLG Frankfurt of 18 May 2000 (13 W 29/00, 1 O 198/00).

[1081] CAS 99/A/239, 14-4-2000, *UCI v. Möller, Danmarks Idraets-Vorbund and Danmarks Cykle Union*, ground 11.

[1082] In CAS 2000/A/274, 19-10-2000, *Susin v. FINA*, Matthieu Reeb, ed., *Digest of CAS Awards II 1998-2000* (The Hague, Kluwer Law International 2002) pp. 389-409, grounds 20 and 68) the defendant relied on the *in dubio pro reo* principle, but again the Panel did not need to pronounce on its applicability.

[1083] CAS 2000/A/317, 9-7-2001, *F. Aanes v. FILA*, ground V.2.3.

[1084] "This is particularly true for the principles of *in dubio pro reo* and *nulla poena sine culpa* and the presumption of innocence as enshrined in Art. 6 ECHR (Swiss Federal Tribunal, *ASA Bull.* 1993, p. 398, 409 et seq. [*G. v. FEI*] and Swiss Federal Tribunal judgment of March 31, 1999 [5P. 83/1999], unreported, p. 12, see also Margareta Baddeley, *L'association sportive face au droit* (Basel, Helbing und Lichtenhahn 1994) p. 220; Urs Scherrer, "Strafrechtliche und strafprozessuale Grundsätze bei Verbandssanktionen," in: Fritzweiler, ed., *Doping Sanktionen, Beweise, Ansprüche* (Berne, Stämpfli 2000), p. 127.

[1085] Summerer 1990 (*supra* nt. 72), p. 162.

[1086] Summerer (*supra* nt. 72, p. 162) in support of his argument refers to two judgments. The first reference is as follows: "So hat das Schiedsgericht des Deutschen Swimmverbandes z.B. die Sperre der Europameisterin *Sylvia Gerasch* wegen erhöhten Koffeinwertes aufgehoben, weil ihr kein schuldhaftes Verhalten nachzuweisen war." One may wonder how the absence of guilt is related to the principle of *in dubio pro reo*. If I interpret Summerer correctly, there was no doubt that Gerasch was guilty. The same applies to the second case which Summerer cites: "[...] ein Moskauer Bezirksgericht [hat] im Fall der Hallenweltmeisterin *Naroschilenko* [...] die vierjährige Dopingsperre des russischen Leichtathletikverbandes für rechtswidrig befunden, weil deren Ehemann und Trainer ihr ohne ihr Wissen Dopingmittel verabreicht hatte."

"Auch das Schiedsgericht des Deutschen Schwimmverbandes hat im Beschluß vom 23.08.1994 (SpuRt 1994 S. 210), einen Dopingfall betreffend, mit der Begründung im Bereich der Vereinsstrafe müsse die Frage der Strafbarkeit nach allgemein straf-rechtlichen Kriterien beurteilt werden, das Verschulden zur Voraussetzung einer Bestrafung erhoben. Für diese Betrachtungsweise spricht auch der Grundsatz der Unschuldsvermutung des Art.6 Abs. 2 EMRK."

Assuming that the CAS panel in the *Aanes* case was correct in finding that there is no room for the application of criminal law principles to the relationship between the sports organisation and the athlete, it is still difficult to see why the panel did not even recognise the general principle of law of granting the benefit of the doubt. This principle is not only deeply embedded in western culture, but moreover as a corollary of Article 6(2) ECHR should not be questioned. If there is any possibility that the athlete is right and the other party is unable to show the opposite, the prin-ciple of the benefit of the doubt does not allow this doubt to be interpreted in any other way but to the athlete's advantage. In the Aanes case, however, the panel reached the unfortunate conclusion that the doubts which existed obliged it "to weigh the interests of the federation against those of the athlete." I will recall here the words of Mr Beloff (who is a regular member and president of CAS doping panels) that the CAS had to "balance[e] the twin objectives of aiding the fight against drugs and safeguarding the right to fair treatment." In *Aanes*, offering assistance to the sports organisation in its fight against doping seemed to be the primary objec-tive, at the expense of fair treatment of the athlete. The tension between individual interests on the one hand and group interests on the other is best illustrated by the following consideration:

"[...] in recent times the fight against doping has become sport's most burning prob-lem.
At times, public attention and, in particular, that of the media is focused more on whether the athletes are under the influence of doping substances than on the sporting event itself and its results.
This development is a very serious threat to the entire sporting movement and, indi-rectly, to an industry which accounts for an important percentage of the world economy."

However, it is difficult to imagine that a criminal court would be willing to relin-quish the *in dubio pro reo* principle in order to aid the fight against crime, or to prevent a loss of face of criminal law in general or, worse, to prevent a decrease in world economic growth.

The *in dubio pro reo* principle is of crucial importance to the matters dealt with in this book. The CAS panel in *Bernhard v. ITU* considered that: "[...] the benefit of doubt [...] is an emanation of one of the most important legal presumptions, the presumption of innocence, deeply enshrined in the general principles of law and justice." On the one hand, the principle may be regarded as a fair trial right, but on the other hand, it is also an internationally recognised fundamental principle of law. Although the principle is most visible in criminal law, it should in the first place be regarded as "deeply enshrined in the general principles of law and justice." As can be imagined in the context of the discussion of culpability above, the presumption of innocence of Article 6(2) is of great importance in a strict liability environment. The guarantee which it offers that everyone charged with a criminal offence shall be presumed innocent until proven guilty in accordance with the law is not easily reconciled with a presumption of liability which does not even allow the accused any opportunity to exonerate him/herself.

The presumed applicability of Article 6 ECHR to doping trials opens the door for the application in this field of the entire catalogue of fundamental principles as listed especially in paragraph 3 of Article 6. These rights will be examined more closely below.

5.5.   The right to be informed of the charges (cf. Art. 6(3)(a) ECHR)

At the international level

This right, which is seemingly so obvious, was only contained in a limited number of IF's anti-doping regulations. The new OMADC is completely silent on fundamental rights, but the old IOC Medical Code did stipulate that the athlete accused of doping had "the right to be acquainted with the charges,"[1087] although it did not elaborate this point any further. The provision was intended to create a level playing field for the parties to the proceedings. It did not mention whether the defence was entitled to disclosure from the prosecution.

Of the IFs, the FIL used exactly the same provision as the IOC in the Medical Code,[1088] while the IBF[1089] and the FITA[1090] added that the notification had to be in writing and had to include summary information concerning the evidence that had been collected against the athlete. A number of IFs provided for disclosure more expressly, like the IBA, which granted the right "to consult the report of the preliminary investigations"[1091] and the UCI, which entitled the athlete "to take cognisance of the case file."[1092] This was done by providing paid copies of the file to the parties, who could also inspect the file during the hearing. Pursuant to FIH regulations, an accused athlete must not only be informed of the charges, but must also be given access to "all relevant material in the possession or under the control of the FIH" and must be given "every reasonable opportunity to defend the charges."[1093]

[1087] IOC MC Ch. IX, Art. VI.

[1088] IRO – International Luge Regulations – Artificial Track – Supplement 4 – Medical Code, Ch. VII, Art. VII.

[1089] Disciplinary Regulations, 3.2.

[1090] Appendix 4 – Doping Control Procedures, 11 Disciplinary Procedures, Art. 11.4.

[1091] Anti Doping Rules, Ch. 11, Art. 11.3.

[1092] UCI Cycling Regulations, Part XIV, Ch. VII, Art. 75.

[1093] Statutes and By Laws, Art. 22.1 sub (a).

At the national level

According to the *Anti-Dopingbestimmungen* of the *Österreiche Bundes-Sport-organisation:*[1094] "der Fachverband werde in weitere Folge die Information des Sportlers übernimmen." The Belgian *Decreet inzake medisch verantwoorde sportbeoefening*[1095] stipulated that: "persons charged with an offence must be personally or at the least in writing be informed of these charges." The French Decree of 2001[1096] provided that: "L'intéressé, accompagné le cas échéant des personnes investies de l'autorité parentale, est convoqué devant l'organe disciplinaire, par lettre recommandée avec demande d'avis de réception ou par lettre remise contre récépissé, quinze jours au moins avant la date de la séance." The *Rahmen-Richtlinien des DSB zur Bekämpfung des Doping* did not expressly provide for the right to be informed of the charges, but the *Deutscher Leichtathletik Verband*[1097] had established that: "Die Einleitung eines Dopingverfahrens sowie das Ergebnis einer positiven Kontrolle, sonstige Verdachtsgründe und eine Suspendierung [...] dem Athleten unverzüglich bekanntzugeben (sind)." The right was further included in nearly all other German sports organisations' rules and may therefore be considered to have been standard procedure. The rules of the UK umbrella organisations, the British Olympic Association and UK Sport, did not refer to a right to be informed of charges, but the rules of various other British federations did contain such a provision. UK Athletics[1098] for example provided that: "The athlete will be informed that he/she has breached the Federation rules on Doping and is therefore subject to the disciplinary procedure for doping offences."

Another example was the rule of the British Canoe Union[1099] that: "The BCU Drugs Advisory Committee shall investigate the circumstances at a meeting to be held within 28 days of the notification to the athlete concerned and he or she shall be invited to attend the meeting [...]." The Model Doping Control Policy of the Irish Sports Council[1100] explained that: "The law protects those affected by disciplinary actions by importing rules of natural and constitutional justice and fairness. The person concerned must be properly informed of the charge against them [...]." Pur-

---

[1094] 10. Bekanntgabe des Analyseergebnisses.

[1095] Title VI – Disciplinaire maatregelen inzake medisch verantwoorde sportbeoefening, Ch. V – Erkenning van de disciplinaire bevoegdheden van sportverenigingen, Art. 41, para. 2, sub 3.

[1096] Decree no. 2001-36 of 11 January 2001 relatif aux dispositions que les fédérations sportives agreéées doivent adopter dans leur règlement en matière de contrôles et de sanctions contre le dopage en application de l'article L.3634-1 du code de la santé publique: Title II – Organes et procédures disciplinaires, Section 2, Art. 18.

[1097] Sonderbedingungen des DLV für Dopingkontrollen, para. 83 Verfahren, sub (2).

[1098] BCU Sports Management Committee: Doping Control Rules, 4. Procedures following testing, 4.5.

[1099] Guidance Notes, 3.4. What are the Disciplinary Procedures?

[1100] Irish Canoe Union: Doping Control Regulations, 8.00 Procedures, 8.04: "The Irish Canoe Union will inform an athlete or individual in writing, as soon as is practicable, after the time the Irish Canoe Union becomes aware that an offence as defined by the ICF and/or ICU Doping Control Regulations may have been committed [...]."

suant to the doping regulations of the Italian NOC (CONI)[1101] the Office for the Prosecution of Doping Offences after completing its investigations had to forward the relevant documents to the National Association or member institution involved. It would then in a reasoned decision either dismiss the case or refer it to the relevant authorities. The Office for the Prosecution of Doping Offences had to officially inform the athlete, his/her club, the chairman of the relevant federation and the Coordinating Office for Doping Activities. Most Dutch federations referred to their codes of conduct for the applicable procedure for the settlement of disputes, but the *Nederlandse Hippische Sportbond*[1102] included the procedure in its doping regulations, which provided that: "the disciplinary commission [...] shall inform the participant by registered post, return receipt requested, of the charges laid [...]."[1103] The doping regulations of the Swedish *Riksidrottsforbundet*[1104] stated that: "The disciplinary body shall permit the notified person to comment on the notification," from which it emerges that the athlete evidently had a right to be notified.

5.6. The right to inspection of the file (cf. Art. 6(3)(b) ECHR)

In the Belgian *Decreet inzake medisch verantwoorde sportbeoefening* a provision was included entitling the athlete to inspect all the documents making up his/her file,[1105] while the French Decree no. 2001-36 similarly provided that: "l'intéressé ou son défenseur peut consulter avant la séance le rapport et l'intégralité du dossier."[1106] The *Dopingkontroll-Reglement* of the *Bund Deutscher Radfahrer*[1107] granted "Der Beklagte [...] das Recht, von den offiziellen Verhandlungsmaterialien Kenntnis zu nehmen. Jede Partei kann von diesen auf ihre Kosten eine Kopie erhalten." Pur-

---

[1101] Italian NOC: Regolamento dell'attività antidoping, Title IV – Adempimenti e sanzioni, Art. 10 – Procedimento disciplinare, sub 4.

[1102] Dopingreglement NHS, Art. 15 Aangifte, vervolging en bestraffing, sub 7.

[1103] The *Nederlandse Basketbal Bond* has included such a right in its doping regulations in Art. 19, sub a: "The Disciplinary and Disputes Commission, when applicable, informs the athlete involved in a letter sent through registered post with confirmation of receipt, that proceedings have been instituted." See also: Koninklijke Nederlandsche Roeibond, Huishoudelijk Reglement, 1. a; De Koninklijke Nederlandse Wielren Unie (KNWU): Title XIV Antidoping Controle Reglement, Ch. VII – Recht van verdediging – Beroep, Art. 69.: "When the cyclist has not requested a countercheck within the time limit set or when the result of the countercheck is also positive, the national federation of the cyclist must summon the cyclist to a hearing for an explanation and for his defence. The cyclist is summoned by a letter sent through registered post in which he is notified of the positive result of the countercheck. If no countercheck was requested within the time limit set the cyclist will be summoned within two days after the expiry of the time limit." Koninklijke Nederlands Algemene Schermbond, Dopingreglement, Title VII, Tuchtrechtelijke behandeling, Art. 21, 1. a.

[1104] Ch. 13 – Doping rules, 12 – Administration.

[1105] Title VI, Ch. V, Art. 41, para. 2, sub 3 b). See also: Vlaamse Turnliga: Gedragscode, Art. 4: "The summons to appear [...] shall contain the date and place of the hearing, the charges and the manner of inspection of the file."

[1106] Decree no. 2001-36 of 11 January 2001, relatif aux dispositions que les fédérations sportives agreéées doivent adopter dans leur règlement en matière de contrôles et de sanctions contre le dopage en application de l'article L.3634-1 du code de la santé publique: Title II, Section 2, Art. 18.

[1107] 6 Verfahrensdurchführung / Rechtfertigungs- und Einspruchsrecht, 6.2, sub (5).

suant to the doping rules of the Swedish *Riksidrottsforbundet*[1108] "all parties shall have access to all documents in the case."

5.7. The right to representation (cf. Art. 6(3)(c) ECHR)

At the international level

According to the IOC Medical Code, the right to be heard also included the right to representation.[1109] The FIL rule was identical to that of the IOC.[1110] In fact, a wide variety of anti-doping regulations included a similar provision, whereby in some case it was expressly stipulated by whom and at whose expense the athlete could be represented.[1111]

At the national level

The *Decreet inzake medisch verantwoorde sportbeoefening* among other things gave the accused "the right [...] to be assisted during his court appearance by counsel of his choice."[1112]

The *Tuchtreglement* of the *Koninklijke Belgische Wielrenunie*[1113] stated that: "The parties, with the exception of the prosecuting body of the association involved, shall appear in person and are entitled to legal counsel of their choice." If the defendant was a minor at the time of the hearing, he could be represented by a legal representative. According to the Anti-Doping Regulations of the NOC and Sports Confederation of Denmark: "The Doping Tribunal may assign legal counsel for the defendant."[1114] Under the French Decree no. 2001-36: "L'intéressé peut être assisté d'un ou de plusieurs défenseurs de son choix."[1115] The *Fédération Française des Sociétés d'Aviron* (FFSA) allowed the athlete to be accompanied by both legal counsel and the physician who had prescribed the challenged drug: "Le rameur [...] peut

---

[1108] Ch. 12 – Doping rules, 12 – Administration.

[1109] IOC Medical Code Ch. IX, Art. VII.

[1110] IRO – International Luge Regulations, Artificial Track, Suppl. 4, Ch. VII, Art. VII.

[1111] IBF Disciplinary Regulations, Art. 3.4; IBA Anti Doping Rules, Ch. 11, Art. 11.3; UCI Cycling Regulations, Part XIV, Ch. VII, Art. 77; FIG Medical Regulations, Doping Control Regulations, Art. 3.1 sub C.; IWF Anti-doping Policy, Hearing of the Appeal, Art. 15.10 and Statutes and By Laws, Art. 22.1; ATP/WTA Official Rulebook, Tennis' Anti-doping Program, L., Art. 5.

[1112] Title VI – Disciplinaire maatregelen inzake medisch verantwoorde sportbeoefening, Ch. V – Erkenning van de disciplinaire bevoegdheden van sportverenigingen, Art. 41, para. 2, sub 3· c).

[1113] Title V: Tuchtreglement van de KBWB, Book 1: nationale rechtspleging, Part II – Rechtspleging, Title 1 – De tuchtrechterlijke procedure, Ch. 3 – De zitting van de tuchtcommissie en de tuchtraad, Part 2 – De verschijning van de partijen.

[1114] Art. 9, subsection 2.

[1115] Decree no. 2001-36 of 11 January 2001, relatif aux dispositions que les fédérations sportives agreéées doivent adopter dans leur règlement en matière de contrôles et de sanctions contre le dopage en application de l'article L.3634-1 du code de la santé publique: Title II – Organes et procédures disciplinaires, Section 2 – Dispositions relatives aux organes disciplinaires de première instance, Art. 18.

être accompagné et/ou assisté de la personne de son choix, et en particulier par le médecin prescripteur du produit incriminé."[1116] In the *Rahmen-Richtlinien* of the DSB the right to representation was implied, but the doping provisions of the *Deutscher Kanu Verband* expressly stated that the hearing could be attended by "ein oder mehrere vom Sportler beauftragte Rechtsvertreter."[1117] UK Sport's Statement of Anti-Doping Policy provided that: "At all hearings before the Disciplinary Committee and Appeal Panel, the athlete shall be entitled to legal assistance [...],"[1118] and the Amateur Rowing Association had included the rule that: "The person may produce evidence. He/she may be accompanied and/or assisted by a person of his/ her choice, and in particular if applicable by a doctor who prescribed the incriminating product. The person will be provided with advice and help in preparing his case, should he wish, by a member of the Medical Sub-Committee. There will be a permanently nominated member of the Medical Committee to act in this capacity."[1119] The British Equestrian Federation like the Belgian Cycling Federation also provided expressly for the representation of minors: "A Participant shall, if he so desires, be represented by a third party [...] A Participant under the age of 16 must always be accompanied by a parent, guardian or other responsible adult."[1120] The Drug Testing Programme of the Football Association allowed athletes "[...] to be accompanied by representatives of the club, a legal representative and one representative of the Professional Footballers Association, where the player is a member of the P.F.A."[1121] In the Model Doping Control Policy of the Irish Sports Council it was provided that: "the person [...] may be legally represented (or by anyone else) [...]"[1122] which was further elaborated as follows in the Guidance Notes to the Policy: "legal representation and submissions at a hearing should be permitted to enable the person concerned to present their case as effectively as possible. To refuse legal representation could suggest a lack of fairness and may be contrary to constitutional and natural justice." The doping regulations of the *Koninklijke Nederlandse Wielren Unie* contained a rule that "all parties [...] have the right to be represented by a lawyer or a representative by special written authorisation. They are entitled to counsel by any other person of their choice."[1123] Other Dutch sports organisations did not provide such a right, but, as mentioned above, referred to their disciplinary

---

[1116] Réglementation anti-dopage de la FFSA, Art. 26.

[1117] Anti-Dopiungbestimmungen, para. 25 – Mündliche Verhandlung, subsection 2.See also: Bund Deutscher Radfahrer: Dopingkontroll-Reglement, 6 Verfahrensdurchführung / Rechtfertigungs- und Einspruchsrecht, 6.2, sub (7): "Jede Partei hat das Recht, sich von einem Rechtsanwalt oder von einem mit einer speziellen schriftlichen Vollmacht ausgewiesenen Bevollmächtigten vertreten zu lassen. Sie kann sich von jeder anderen Person ihrer Wahl assistieren lassen."

[1118] Annex A – Anti-doping policy – Governing body requirements and procedures, General requirements, Conduct of Hearings, 36.

[1119] Mis-Use of Drugs By Laws, 4. Enquiry, 4.3 and 4.3.1.

[1120] Rule Book & Disciplinary and Doping Control Procedures, Rights of Participants at Stewards Meetings, sub 14.2.

[1121] Memorandum and procedural guidelines for the conduct of drug testing, 12.

[1122] What are the Disciplinary Procedures?, 2.4.8.

[1123] Title XIV Antidoping Controle Reglement, Ch. VII – Recht van verdediging – Beroep, Art. 77.

rules in which the right to representation was mostly included. The Portuguese Statute Law no. 183/97 provided that the rights of the defence had to be incorporated in the doping regulations of Portuguese sport federations. The *Federação Portuguesa de Remo* duly stipulated that: "Após a notificação da nota de culpa, o agente desportivo arguido como responsável disporá de dez dias para a apresentação fundamentada da sua defesa, [...]."[1124] Finally, the doping rules of the Swedish *Riksidrottsforbundet* contained the provision that: "each party may use a representative. The representative shall prove his or her authorization by showing a power of attorney."[1125]

5.8. The right to call witnesses and/or experts (cf. Art. 6(3)(d) ECHR)

At the international level

The anti-doping regulations of some IFs entitled the athlete to call witnesses and/or experts[1126] which the doping panels had to hear, notwithstanding a possible process of selection, for it is not inconceivable that a panel might have to limit the number of witnesses or experts called for the sake of expediency. The anti-doping regulations usually gave no guidance on how the hearing of witnesses should proceed, with the exception of the regulations of the IWF which provided that on appeal all parties could call witnesses and examine and cross-examine them.[1127] Witnesses and experts called by the defence could be heard by the panel as a whole, or by one panel member only.

The regulations usually did not contain any provisions concerning costs either.

Finally, the FIG anti-doping regulations specified which parties could be heard. These parties by answering questions also provided testimony.[1128]

At the national level

Pursuant to the *Tuchtreglement* of the *Koninklijke Belgische Wielrenunie* the parties were throughout the duration of the oral arguments entitled to request additional measures of investigation, such as the hearing of witnesses and experts.[1129] The

---

[1124] Regulamento do Controlo Antidopagem, Ch. III – Procedimento Disciplinar e Regime Sancionatório, Art. 16 – Defesa, subsection 1.

[1125] Ch. 13 – Doping rules, 12 – Administration.

[1126] IBA Anti Doping Rules, Art. 11.3; UCI Cycling Regulations, Part XIV, Ch. VII, Art. 77; IWF Anti-Doping Policy – Hearing of the Appeal, Art. 15.10; FIL IRO – International Luge Regulations, Artificial Track, Suppl. 4, Ch. VII, Art. VII.

[1127] IWF Anti-Doping Policy, Art. 15.10 sub a.

[1128] Medical Regulations – Doping Control Regulations, Art. 3.1: "The Committee will, if so required by the appealing competitor, hear the parties (the gymnast, a representative of his/her Federation, a representative of the laboratory, a representative of the FIG Medical Commission)."

[1129] Title V: Tuchtreglement van de KBWB, Book 1, Part II, Title 1, Ch. 3, Part 3: AIn hearing witnesses and/or experts the parties may request that the testimony is recorded by the clerk and signed by the witness or expert. The president of the tribunal cannot refuse such a request and if such a request

Fédération Française des Sociétés d'Aviron also granted the athlete the right "d'y faire entendre un ou des experts et un ou des témoins. Dans ce dernier cas, l'intéressé doit en formuler la demande 8 jours au moins avant la réunion."[1130] The doping regulations of the *Fédération Française de Basketball* stipulated that the athlete had to give "dans un délai de huit jours, le nom des témoins et experts dont il demande la convocation."[1131] The *Anti-Dopingbestimmungen* of the *Deutscher Kanu Verband* provided that: "Das Präsidium entscheidet weiter, welche Zeugen zu der mündlichen Verhandlung zu laden sind. Von dem Sportler benannte Zeugen sind nur dann nicht zu laden, wenn das, was sie bekunden sollen, als wahr unterstellt werden kann. Zeugen sind rechtzeitig zu laden."[1132] The *Bund Deutscher Radfahrer* on witnesses provided that: "Auf Forderung des Bundessportgerichts oder auf Forderung einer der an der Anhörung beteiligten Parteien können ebenfalls [...] Zeugen und Sachverständige angehört werden. In diesem Falle hat die interessierte Partei selbst für die Ladung dieses von ihr gewünschten Personenkreises zu sorgen und hierüber gleichzeitig die anderen Parteien einschließlich das Bundessportgericht zu informieren."[1133] UK Sport had included in its Statement of Anti-Doping Policy[1134] that: "At all hearings before the Disciplinary Committee and Appeal Panel, the athlete shall be entitled to [...] call witnesses." Apart from calling witnesses, the Amateur Swimming Federation of Great Britain also gave the athlete the right "to cross-examine witnesses."[1135] The *Koninklijke Nederlandse Wielren Unie* also entitled the athlete upon his/her request to examine witnesses and experts, whereby "The interested party is responsible for calling such persons. At the same time, it shall inform the other parties and the competent organ."[1136]

---

is not made can himself order that the testimony is recorded and signed." See also: Vlaamse Turnliga: Gedragscode, Art. 6.

[1130] Réglementation anti-dopage de la FFSA, Organisme Disciplinaire, Art. 38. *Idem*: Fédération Française de Handball: Lutte contre le dopage, Title 2, Ch. 1 – Organismes disciplinaires, Art. 29; Fédération Française de Lutte: Lutte contre le dopage, Art. 30; Fédération Française de Natation: Règlement Intérieur, Règlement Particulier de Lutte contre le Dopage, Art. 16 – Procédure en 1e instance.

[1131] Règlement de lutte contre le dopage, Title IV – Première Instance, Art. 22. *Idem*: Fédération Française de Judo, Jujitsu, Kendo: Règlement Intérieur de la F.F.J.D.A. Annexe 4, Règlement Particulier de Lutte contre le Dopage, Art. 25.

[1132] Part 3 – Verfahrensvorschriften, para. 24, subsections 2 en 3.

[1133] 6 Verfahrensdurchführung / Rechtfertigungs- und Einspruchsrecht, 6.2 Anhörung des / der Beschuldigten, Verfahrensdurchführung, sub (2).

[1134] Annex A – Anti-doping policy – Governing body requirements and procedures, General requirements, Conduct of Hearings, 36. See also: British Equestrian Federation, Rule Book & Disciplinary and Doping Control Procedures, 14.1; Great Britain Olympic Hockey Board: By Law 1 – Doping Policy, 4.b).

[1135] ASFGB Doping Control Rules and Protocols, Doping Control Rules, 8 Judicial Procedures, 8.4.

[1136] Title XIV Antidoping Controle Reglement, Ch. VII – Recht van verdediging – Beroep, Art. 72. *Idem*: Netherlands Skiing Federation: Dopingreglement, Tuchtrechtelijke behandeling, Art. 20, subsection 4. To this it is added that "the TD [...] may appoint one of its members to hear witnesses or experts."

5.9. The right to be assisted by an interpreter (cf. Art. 6(3)(e) ECHR)

Although one would more readily expect to have encountered the right to an interpreter in the doping regulations of the international federations, it was in fact only found in a number of national rules, such as the Belgian *Decreet inzake medisch verantwoorde sportbeoefening* which provided that the athlete was entitled to the assistance of an interpreter if he was unable to understand or speak Dutch,[1137] and the French Decree no. 2001-36 which stipulated that: "S'il ne parle ou ne comprend pas suffisamment la langue française, il peut bénéficier de l'aide d'un interprète aux frais de la fédération."[1138]

5.10. The granting of fair trial rights in practice

As the decisions in doping cases of disciplinary bodies of sports organisations are rarely published, it is not easy to discover whether and how these bodies took account of the rights of the defence in practice. The case law of the CAS could act as one of the few sources of information in this respect. However, appeals to the CAS against federation decisions based on the alleged violation of fair trial rights are usually decided *de novo* in accordance with the CAS Procedural Rules.[1139] In this way, possible violations of the rights of the athlete are automatically "repaired" in the full review process and are therefore not an issue for consideration.[1140] However, despite the fact that the CAS thus does not need to address such complaints, it has at times reluctantly, but never extensively, discussed the right to a fair trial. Under Articles 182(3) and 190(2)(d) of the Swiss Federal Private International Law Act, the CAS as a Swiss arbitration body must of course itself guarantee the equal treatment of the parties and the right of both parties to be heard in adversarial proceedings. In other words, the Panel must itself act in accordance with the principle of fair trial or due process.[1141]

In *USA Shooting & Quigley v. International Shooting Union (UIT)*[1142] the athlete argued that he had not been heard during the proceedings, that the prosecuting

---

[1137] Title VI, Ch. V, Art. 41, para. 2, sub 3, d).

[1138] Decree no. 2001-36 of 11 January 2001, relatif aux dispositions que les fédérations sportives agreéées doivent adopter dans leur règlement en matière de contrôles et de sanctions contre le dopage en application de l'article L.3634-1 du code de la santé publique: Title II – Organes et procédures disciplinaires, Section 2 – Dispositions relatives aux organes disciplinaires de première instance, Art. 18.

[1139] CAS Procedural Rules, R57 – Scope of Panel's Review, Hearing: "The Panel shall have full power to review the facts and the law. It may issue a new decision which replaces the decision challenged or annul the decision and refer the case back to the previous instance."

[1140] "[...] issues relating to the fairness of the hearing before the tribunal of first instance fade to the periphery," as the CAS remarked in case CAS 98/211, 7-6-1999, *Smith-De Bruin v. FINA*, Matthieu Reeb, ed., *Digest of CAS Awards II 1998-2000* (The Hague, Kluwer Law International 2002) pp. 255-273.

[1141] CAS 2000/A/274, 19-10-2000, *Susin v. FINA*, Matthieu Reeb, ed., *Digest of CAS Awards II 1998-2000* (The Hague, Kluwer Law International 2002) pp. 389-409, ground 180.

[1142] CAS 94/129, 23-5-1995, *USA Shooting & Quigley v. UIT*, Matthieu Reeb, ed., *Digest of CAS Awards 1986-1998* (Berne, Editions Stämpfli 1998) pp. 187-204.

party was the same as the party who had imposed the penalty, that he had not been provided with the full data of the analysis, that he had not been given the possibility of legal representation and that he had not received a report of the UIT meeting at which it had been decided to suspend him. The panel first declared that it was not under any duty to consider these points in order to arrive at a decision. However, having nevertheless examined them the panel subsequently declared that they had to be dismissed and that "it may be useful for this Award to indicate why that is so":[1143]

> "In the first place, the Panel is not convinced that fundamental procedural rights include the right to be heard in the context of a physical meeting. In fact, the Court of Arbitration for Sport has had occasion in the past to consider the issue of an accused person's 'right to be heard'. In the award in Case No. 92/84, rendered on 27 February 1993, the Panel decided that whether an accused had been accorded the right to be heard must be judged on a case-by-case basis, but that an accused can be 'heard' either in person or by way of written submissions.
>
> Moreover, even if the 'hearing' in a given case was insufficient in the first instance – for example, by the UIT's Executive Committee – the fact is that as long as there is a possibility of full appeal to the Court of Arbitration for Sport the deficiency may be cured. (It would obviously be wise to ensure that accused competitors are given a satisfactory opportunity to be heard from the start, so that they do not feel impelled to appeal out of frustration, but that is another matter.) Thus, in this case the appellant's 'due process' argument, assuming it to have been valid, could not have stood alone. Nor indeed could it add anything to any of the other three grounds for reversal, including the one which was accepted."

Despite the panel's warning, several years later another athlete argued that her due process rights had been violated by the federation's disciplinary body. Swimmer Jessica Foschi[1144] contended that the FINA disciplinary body had been prejudiced against her, that only one of its members had examined the evidence and that the federation had denied her access to essential information and documents. The CAS considered that:[1145]

> "This Panel shall refrain from ruling upon the 'set of findings' or declaratory orders requested by Appellant [...] because, in view of the fact that this hearing has been a 'trial de novo' in which the Panel has had 'full power to review the facts and the law' [...] any violations of due process, natural justice and/or the fundamental rights of the Appellant which may have occurred in proceedings on this matter before other courts or bodies are hereby cured (though the Panel should like to make clear that it is not ruling on whether there have been any such violations). This is in accordance with the general principle followed by Swiss courts whereby any violation in the initial proceedings (such as a violation of the right to be heard) is deemed to be cured by the higher court if the higher court has respected all of the appellant's basic rights and had

---

[1143] *Idem*, grounds 58-59.
[1144] CAS 96/156, 6-10-1997, *Jessica K. Foschi v. FINA*.
[1145] *Idem*, ground 16.

the same power of review as the initial court (BGE 116 1 a 94; 116 1 b 37). This was the case here. Consequently any procedural violations have been cured and so the Appellant lacks the *locus standi* to seek the requested declaratory relief."

The Chinese swimmers Wang Lu Na, Cai Hui Jue, Zhgang Yi and Wang Wei[1146] and the Irish swimmer Smith-De Bruin[1147] received the same answer to their similar complaints.

Even if the CAS does not have to examine complaints concerning violations of fair trial rights, the CAS could have undertaken to advise the federations in somewhat stronger terms. In the *Foschi* case it confined itself to the general and rather condescending observation that "it would [...] be wise to ensure that accused competitors are given a satisfactory opportunity to be heard from the start, so that they do not feel impelled to appeal out of frustration." Indeed, such frustrations were vented against the FINA on three separate occasions before the CAS.

The tone was quite different in the *Aanes* case.[1148] Although the complaint was again dismissed based on the *de novo* principle, the panel did add that: "Federations have the obligation to respect the right to be heard as one of the fundamental principles of due process."

There has been only one case in which the CAS has gone into the merits of a complaint that the disciplinary body had violated the right to a fair trial, however, not to the athlete's advantage. In *Dieter Baumann v. International Olympic Committee (IOC), National Olympic Committee of Germany and International Amateur Athletics Federation (IAAF)*[1149] the CAS's reasoning was as follows:

"While it is usual for an IAAF arbitration to be heard in Monaco, it was heard in Sydney where the Athlete was, at the time, as an accredited member of the German NOC Team of athletes for the Olympic Games. Modern modes of communication such as video conferencing, interpreter services were all available in Australia had the Athlete made call upon them to assist in the presentation of evidence had he so elected. We find the Athlete, in all the circumstances, was allowed due process and there cannot, therefore, be a finding based on allegations of procedural irregularities that the IAAF panel's decision is null."

[1146] CAS 98/208, 22-12-1998, *Wang Lu Na, Cai Hui Jue, Zhgang Yi, Wang Wei v. FINA*, Matthieu Reeb, ed., *Digest of CAS Awards II 1998-2000* (The Hague, Kluwer Law International 2002) pp. 234-254, ground 5.4: "The Panel therefore finds it unnecessary to consider the charges made by the Appellants as to FINA's violation of due process. For the avoidance of doubt, however, it stresses that its silence should not be taken as endorsement of those charges; and that it sees no reason to doubt the good faith of the Doping Panel, who, whatever the unorthodoxy of its behaviour, sought to give the Appellants by adjournment and otherwise a full opportunity to make their case."

[1147] CAS 98/211, 7-6-1999, *Smith-De Bruin v. FINA*, Matthieu Reeb, ed., *Digest of CAS Awards II 1998-2000* (The Hague, Kluwer Law International 2002) pp. 255-273, ground 7.3: "The Panel therefore finds it unnecessary to consider the charges made by the Appellant as to the alleged violation of due process and bias on the part of the FINA Doping Panel and /or its chairman."

[1148] CAS 2000/A/317, 9-7-2001, *F. Aanes v. FILA*.

[1149] CAS OG 00/006, 22-9-2000, *Dieter Baumann v. IOC, National Olympic Committee of Germany and IAAF*, Matthieu Reeb, ed., *Digest of CAS Awards II 1998-2000* (The Hague, Kluwer Law International 2002) pp. 633-644, ground 38.

5.11. The doctrine of estoppel

Estoppel precludes a person from denying the truth of some statement made by him/her of the existence of facts whether existing or not which he/she has by words or conduct led another to believe in, especially if such denial harms the other. One form of estoppel is equitable estoppel, which means estoppel by conduct. This was the type of estoppel on which the CAS was asked to pronounce in the *Susin* case.[1150] Viviana Susin, a member of the Italian national swimming team, had to undergo a routine doping control after a match. The analysis of her sample revealed a high concentration of testosterone. At the laboratory an IRMS analysis was performed by comparing the Carbon 13 isotope ratio in testosterone to that of other precursors (e.g. cholesterol), so as to determine whether the extra testosterone was exogenous or endogenous. The disciplinary body of the Italian swimming federation did not impose any penalty on Susin, which prompted the FINA Executive Bureau to start proceedings before the FINA Doping Panel, which proceeded to suspend the swimmer for four years. Susin appealed against this decision to the CAS. In neither of the previous doping proceedings the IRMS analysis had been cited. It was only referred to by the FINA for the first time in the proceedings before the CAS. Susin argued that this constituted a new charge which would significantly alter the nature of the proceedings. This caused the CAS panel to examine whether: "[...] FINA [is] precluded from raising the IRMS analysis for the first time in this appeal, under the doctrine of estoppel?" and whether: "[...] the principles of procedural fairness preclude the Panel from relying upon the IRMS analysis in the circumstances of this case?" The athlete argued that: "the prohibition against *venire contra factum proprium,* often compared to the common law principle of estoppel, is widely recognised under Swiss law. This prohibition is based upon the concept of abuse of right under Article 2 of the Swiss Civil Code. Where a party adopts a position contrary to one it has previously taken, its conduct may constitute an abuse of right when the other party has relied on the initial position to its detriment." The panel recalled that under Rule 57 of the CAS Code panels were expressly authorised to perform a full review of the facts and the law. "It follows from this broad scope of review that the parties are not restricted to the evidence adduced, or bound by the arguments advanced, in the proceedings below. The Panel must examine the case *ab novo* and, accordingly, must consider all of the evidence and arguments before it, including those relating to the IRMS analysis."[1151] The panel further considered that: "[...] there is no evidence to suggest that FINA provided any assurances or made representations to the Appellant, express or implied, to the effect that it would not raise the IRMS analysis; nor is there any evidence that the Appellant relied upon any such assurances or representations. The question at issue therefore, is one of procedural fairness: has the Appellant been given a full opportunity to address

---

[1150] CAS 2000/A/274, 19-10-2000, *Susin v. FINA*, Matthieu Reeb, ed., *Digest of CAS Awards II 1998-2000* (The Hague, Kluwer Law International 2002) pp. 389-409.

[1151] *Idem*, Ground 175.

the IRMS analysis in this appeal?"[1152] The panel reached the conclusion that the principles of procedural fairness had been fully respected in these proceedings and, in particular, that Susin had been given a full opportunity to address all the evidence adduced against her, including the IRMS results. It is a pity that the *de novo* examination of the case prevented the panel from elaborating on the place of the doctrine of estoppel in the *lex sportiva*. This would have been different only if the FINA had introduced the IRMS analysis at a late stage during the CAS proceedings.[1153]

5.12. The approach chosen in the WADC

The WADA was *inter alia* given the task of "[...] promoting harmonised rules, disciplinary procedures, sanctions and other means of combating doping in sport, and contributing to the unification thereof taking into account the rights of athletes."[1154] The WADA drew up a draft proposal for the WADC and in March 2003 during the World Conference on Doping in Copenhagen[1155] where sports organisations, governments and anti-doping agencies from the world over unanimously adopted a final version of the Code. In 2004, on the eve of the Athens Olympics, the sports organisation began their implementation of the Code. Although the starting point for the Code remained strict liability,[1156] its drafters still wished for the importance of the athletes to be expressed in the Code. This was done by among other things introducing a number of rights of the defence in the Code which closely resemble the rights provided in Article 6(1) and (3) ECHR. Unfortunately, compliance with these rights is not formulated as a firm duty, as the relevant Article 8 WADC was not intended to supplant the rules provided by the signatories, but rather to inform them of certain minimum requirements which a hearing must fulfil. These minimum requirements are:

[1152] *Idem*, Grounds 176-177.

[1153] Ken Foster, *Lex Sportiva and Lex Ludica: the Court of Arbitration for Sport's Jurisprudence*, S. Blackshaw, R.C.R. Siekmann and J. Soek, eds., *The Court of Arbitration for Sport 1984-2004* (The Hague, T.M.C. Asser Press 2005), p. 420 briefly refers to CAS 2002/A/401, 10-1-2003, IAAF/United States Track and Field (USATF), Matthieu Reeb, ed., *Digest of CAS Awards III 2001-2003* (The Hague, Kluwer Law International 2004) pp. 36-67: "[...] the Court of Arbitration for Sport decided that, although there was an obligation under the IAAF's rules to disclose the results of domestic doping tests to the international federation, nevertheless on the facts an estoppel operated. The panel decided that the IAAF had led the USATF to believe that it had the discretion to promise athletes that the results of their tests would be confidential."

[1154] Draft Mission Statement, 4.6.

[1155] The purpose of this conference "[...] was to review, discuss and agree upon the Code content and its use as the basis for the fight against doping in sport. The approach had been to highlight the importance of the athletes, and its basis was the integrity of sport." (World Conference on Doping in Sport, plenary sessions, Summary Notes, p. 13).

[1156] "The athlete is strictly liable for the presence of any prohibited substance in his or her body. Although the WADC includes some exceptions to this rule, every participant in the Olympic Games and world championships is tested for doping and, if found positive, automatically disqualified." (World Conference on Doping in Sport, plenary sessions, Summary Notes, p. 1.)

- a timely hearing;
- fair and impartial hearing body;
- the right to be represented by counsel at the person's own expense;
- the right to be fairly and timely informed of the asserted anti-doping rule violation;
- the right to respond to the asserted anti-doping rule violation and resulting consequences;
- the right of each party to present evidence, including the right to call and question witnesses (subject to the hearing body's discretion to accept testimony by telephone or written submission);
- the person's right to an interpreter at the hearing, with the hearing body to determine the identity, and responsibility for the cost, of the interpreter; and
- a timely, written, reasoned decision.[1157]

As has been explained above, the disciplinary bodies operating within the area in which the ECHR applies, including the CAS, have to comply with the human rights enumerated in the ECHR, but this is not the case for sports organisations operating outside that area. To them, Article 8 WADC applies, but this only recommends that certain rights are granted. However, it happens to be the case that the majority of international federations have their seat in the area covered by the ECHR. Due to the hierarchy within the organisational structure of the respective sports the international federations would be competent to make the rights under Article 8 WADC mandatory for national organisations that reside outside Europe but are within the international federations' jurisdiction.

There is no equivalent of Article 6(2) ECHR in the WADC. Obviously, the Code's drafters were fully aware that the presumption of innocence cannot be reconciled with the presumption of liability, but they have overlooked the fact that within the area of application of the ECHR the effect of Article 6(2) ECHR is nevertheless inescapable.

[1157] Art. 13.2.2 WADC provides that national sports organisations may elect to entitle their national-level athletes to appeal directly to the CAS against a decision in the last instance of the disciplinary body of the organisation in question. If they do not provide for direct appeal to the CAS, appeals must be heard by an independent and impartial body in accordance with rules established by the national sports organisations. The rules of such appeal shall "respect the following principles: a timely hearing; a fair, impartial and independent hearing body; the right to be represented by counsel at the Person's own expense; and a timely, written, reasoned decision." Where the WADC is cautious in stipulating the procedural rights of international-level athletes, it is quite adamant with respect to the rights of national-level athletes. From the contextual relationship between these provisions it might be concluded that the minimum guarantees which the WADC makes mandatory for national-level athletes do not apply in the same way to international-level athletes. Conversely, one may wonder whether national-level athletes in proceedings before national sports organisations' disciplinary bodies are not entitled to the rights available to international-level athletes, for example, the right to be informed of the charges, the right to submit evidence, or the right to be assisted by an interpreter (in case of bilingual or multi-lingual countries). The provisions of Art. 13.2.2 are especially important in the case of national sports organisations which fall outside the scope of the ECHR. In the case of sports organisations within the scope of the ECHR, Art. 13.2.2 must be considered overruled by Art. 6 ECHR.

This concludes the discussion of the rights of the defence. In the next section, the possibilities for contesting decisions will be examined: the remedies at law or the means of redress. Although these are not human rights in the narrow sense, they do offer to athletes accused of doping an additional guarantee of the fair treatment of their case.

6.   REMEDIES AT LAW

Remedies at law are usually not placed under the umbrella of the rights to a fair trial.[1158] They are not, for example, included in Article 6 ECHR, although they are provided for in Article 2(1) of Protocol 7[1159] to the ECHR and in various other international legal instruments.[1160] However, in the case of disciplinary doping proceedings in sport legal remedies certainly add to the athlete's chances of receiving a fair trial. Within sports organisations there is often only a limited group of potential arbitrators or panellists available to hear doping cases. These persons are recruited over and over again and this increases the possibility of partiality. It is this risk of partiality which makes it so important to be able to oppose a judgment.[1161] The possibility of remedies at law in that sense can be regarded as a corollary of the right to an impartial tribunal. The right to appeal is often laid down in statutory disciplinary law and also in the doping regulations of various sports organisations.

It could also be argued that Article 2(1) of Protocol 7 applies to disciplinary doping proceedings in the same manner as Article 6 ECHR. After all, Article 2(1) provides for the right to review by a higher tribunal for "everyone convicted of a criminal offence," but such persons must at some point have been persons against whom a "criminal charge" as referred to in Article 6 was brought. This means that Article 2(1) has to apply to the same disciplinary proceedings to which Article 6 applies.[1162]

6.1.   Opposing a judgment

One national sports organisation only, the *Koninklijke Belgische Wielrenunie*, offered to athletes against whom a default judgment had been rendered the opportu-

---

[1158] See De Doelder 1981 (*supra* nt. 352), p. 139.

[1159] "Everyone convicted of a criminal offence by a tribunal shall have the right to have his conviction or sentence reviewed by a higher tribunal. The exercise of this right, including the grounds on which it may be exercised, shall be governed by law."

[1160] Art. 81 of the Rome Statute of the International Criminal Court permits persons convicted by the ICC to appeal to the Appeals Chamber on the grounds that a procedural error, error of fact, error of law or any other ground that affects the fairness or reliability of the proceedings or decision has taken place during the trial. If the appeal is successful, the person will have the right to compensation if new or newly discovered facts show conclusively that there has been a miscarriage of justice, unless the non-disclosure was caused by the accused.

[1161] De Doelder 1981 (*supra* nt. 352), p. 139 and Wassing 1978 (*supra* nt. 168), p. 172 both consider the possibility of appeal to be of fundamental importance.

[1162] Van Dijk/Van Hoof 1998 (*supra* nt. 966), p. 685.

nity to oppose that judgment. On pain of disallowance of the opposition, the athlete had to send a reasoned letter by registered post to the chairman of the tribunal within fourteen calendar days of receipt of the judgment. The opposing athlete also had to deposit a security.[1163] If the opposing party, after having been called in the proper manner, again failed to appear, he/she would not be allowed to oppose a second time.

6.2. Right of appeal

The Flemish *Decreet inzake medisch verantwoorde sportbeoefening* provided that disciplinary measures had to be appealable.[1164] The *Koninklijke Belgische Wielrenunie* allowed for appeal against decisions of the disciplinary committee or of the disputes committee to be instituted by registered post within fourteen days of the decision.[1165] The Anti-Doping Regulations of the NOC and Sports Confederation of Denmark stipulated that: "The Doping Tribunal's verdict, of which a copy shall be forwarded to the NOC Secretariat, may within four weeks of receipt be brought before the Commission for Appeals by the defendant, the member organization concerned or the NOC."[1166] The equivalent rule in Finland provided that: "The athlete in question and his/her organization have to be provably notified about the doping verdict issued by the supervisory group. From the point of receiving notification of the supervisory group's doping verdict, both the athlete and the organization separately have, within two weeks, the opportunity to give additional account on the matter and make a motion to the Finnish Antidoping Committee to convert the statement into a less severe penalty withdrawn."[1167] In the French Decree no. 2001-36 it was stated that athletes who had been sentenced would be informed of the possibility to appeal through the notification of the decision: "La décision est signée par le président et le secrétaire. Elle est aussitôt notifiée par lettre recommendée avec demande d'avis de réception ou par lettre remise à l'intéressé contre récépissé. La notification mentionne les voies et délais d'appel."[1168]

[1163] Tuchtreglement, Part IV – Rechtsmiddelen in tucht- en burgerrechtelijke zaken, Ch. 1 – Verzet.

[1164] Title VI – Disciplinaire maatregelen inzake medisch verantwoorde sportbeoefening, Ch. V – Erkenning van de disciplinaire bevoegdheden van sportverenigingen, Art. 41, para. 2, sub 4.

[1165] Tuchtreglement, Title V, Book 1, Part IV, Ch. 2. See also: Vlaamse Turnliga: Gedragscode, Art. 8: "In cases where there is a possibility of appeal, such appeal may be instituted by means of a notice sent by registered post and addressed to the director of the *Vlaamse Turnliga*. The appeal notice must be sent within 15 days of the date of sending of the decision referred to in Art. 7. A judicial deposit of 5 000 BEF is required which will be returned if the contested decision is amended in full."

[1166] Art. 10, subsection 1.

[1167] Doping regulations for sports organisations, 3. Penalty procedures, 3.4. Appeal.

[1168] Decree no. 2001-36 of 11 January 2001, relatif aux dispositions que les fédérations sportives agreéées doivent adopter dans leur règlement en matière de contrôles et de sanctions contre le dopage en application de l'article L.3634-1 du code de la santé publique, Title II – Organes et procédures disciplinaires, Section 2 – Dispositions relatives aux organes disciplinaires de première instance, Art. 20.

The *Réglementation anti-dopage* of the *Fédération Française des Sociétés d'Aviron* provided that: "Dans le délai de 15 jours à compter de sa notification, la décision de l'organisme disciplinaire peut être frappée d'appel par l'intéressé, par le président de la commission d'enquête et par le président de la FFSA."[1169] Similar provisions were to be found in nearly all of the French sport federations' doping rules, whereby time-limits could differ. The *Fédération Française de Tennis* in its regulations added that: "La décision de l'organisme disciplinaire d'appel doit intervenir dans un délai maximum de six mois à compter du jour où un procès-verbal d'enquête ou de contrôle établi en application de l'article 5 de la loi du 28 juin 1989 a été transmis à la fédération. Elle est immédiatement notifiée à l'intéressé, et dans les huit jours au ministre chargé des sports et à la commission nationale de lutte contre le dopage."[1170] All French doping regulations contained the rule that: "l'appel est suspensif."

The *Dopingkontroll-Reglement* of the *Bund Deutscher Radfahrer* provided that: "gegen die Entscheidung des Bundessportgerichts eine Berufung durch den Bestraften oder durch die UCI zulässig [ist] und zwar bei Entscheidungen nach den a) 'Internationalen Bestimmungen' durch Einleitung eines Schiedsverfahrens vor dem Sportschiedsgerichtshof in Lausanne (TAS); b) 'Nationalen Bestimmungen' beim Bundesrechtsausschuß des BDR. Die Berufung des Bestraften richtet sich gegen den BDR."[1171]

The Appeals Panel of the British Olympic Association would, *inter alia*, be convened if a member of the Great Britain Olympic Team had been found guilty of doping. "The Appeals Panel shall first consider written submissions by or on behalf of the appellant and shall, where possible, render its decision based on those submissions. If the Appeals Panel is not minded to allow an appeal based on written submissions or if requested by an appellant the Appeals Panel shall allow an appellant to appear in person and/or be represented before it. Subject thereto, it shall regulate its own procedure as set out in the BOA's Rules for the Appeal Panel under the BOA By Law (in force at the time any appeal is commenced)."[1172] UK Athletics provided a right to appeal within 21 days of suspension.[1173] Members of the Amateur Rowing Association had a time-limit of 10 days,[1174] of the British

---

[1169] Organisme d'Appel, Art. 45.

[1170] Règlement relatif à la Lutte contre le dopage, Title III – Organismes Disciplinaires, Ch. II – Organisation de la procédure, Art. 30. See also: Fédération Française Tennis de Table: Title II, Chapitre I – Organismes Disciplinaire, Art. 42; Fédération Française de Tir à L'arc: Lutte contre le Dopage, Title II, Ch. I – Organismes Disciplinaires, Art. 42; Federation Française de Triathlon: Réglementation Générale, 12. Lutte contre le Dopage, 12.5 – Organismes Disciplinaires, Art. 42.

[1171] 6 Verfahrensdurchführung / Rechtfertigungs- und Einspruchsrecht, 6.5 Berufung, (1). The Deutsche Reiterliche Vereinigung: Abschnitt C IV: Berufung und Revision, para. 940 – Berufung, 1., merely provides: "gegen die Entscheidung des Schgiedsgerichts einer PS/PLS is Berufung zulässig."

[1172] By Law of the NOC, Eligibility for membership of the Great Britain Olympic Team of persons found guilty of a doping offence, 3.

[1173] UK Current Doping Rules and Procedures, Appendix B – Rules and Procedures concerning Doping Control, B8.

[1174] Mis-Use of Drugs By Laws, 6. Appeals, sub 6.1.1.

Canoe Union: 14 days,[1175] and of the British Equestrian Federation: 28 days.[1176]

The Amateur Swimming Federation of Great Britain in its anti-doping rules provided that: "The Tribunal will not be bound by judicial rules governing procedure or the admissibility of evidence. The chairman shall determine the basis on which the appeal will proceed. He may, in his discretion, rehear the whole or any part of evidence given before the Judicial Tribunal, as he considers appropriate. The Chairman shall have full discretionary power to hear and receive further evidence."[1177] The British Bobsleigh Association added that: "The Appeal Committee shall have the power to vary any decision or sanction under appeal."[1178] A similar provision was included in the doping regulations of the Irish Canoe Union.[1179] In fact, all doping regulations of the Irish sports federations provided for the possibility of appeal, some in greater detail than others.

The *Regolamento dell'attività antidoping* of the Italian NOC did not expressly provide for appeal, but did regulate the right of the parties to appeal to the CAS after exhaustion of the remedies provided by the association's own organs.[1180] The doping regulations of the *Federazione Pugilistica Italiana* provided that: "La Federazione Pugilistica Italiana, ricevuti gli atti dall'Ufficio di Procura Antidoping, attiva il procedimenta disciplinare dinanzi al competente Organo di Giustizia Federale di 1° grado, Giudice Sportivo, se pugile professionista; Corte Federale di Appella. Se pugile dilettante, il quale provvede, nel rispetto delle norme regolamèntari federali, alla eventuale applicazione delle sanzioni previste."[1181] The Italian Equestrian Federation provided that: "L'applicazione delle sanzioni è di competenza esclusiva degli Organi di Giustizia (Commissione di Disciplina e Commissione d'Apello) della Federazione Italiana Sport Equestri o delle Federazione."[1182] The *Koninklijke Nederlandse Wielren Unie* provided that the decision of the highest instance within

---

[1175] B.C.U. Sports Management Committee, Doping Control Rules, 6. Subsequent procedures, 6.1.

[1176] Rule Book & Disciplinary and Doping Control Procedures, Complaints of Misconduct, Notice of Findings, Penalties and Appeals, 17.3. British Judo Association: By Laws relating to Drug Abuse, L.: 21 days; Amateur Swimming Federation of Great Britain: ASFGB Doping Control Rules and Protocols, Doping Control Rules, 9 Appeals, 9.1: 28 days; Royal Yachting Association: The Racing Rules of Sailing, 1.6 Appeal procedure, 1.6.1: 20 days; British Bobsleigh Association: Rules for Doping Control, 4. Disciplinary measures and procedure, 4.4: 30 days; Badminton Association of England Ltd.: Doping Control Rules, Disciplinary Procedure, 5.4: 21 days; Welsh Badminton Union: WBU Protocol to be put into action if a positive dope test is reported on a Welsh player, Positive dope test protocol, Section two – Investigation and disciplinary procedures, Right of appeal, 2.11: 7 days.

[1177] ASFGB Doping Control Rules and Protocols, Doping Control Rules, 9. Appeals, sub 9.5.

[1178] Rules for Doping Control, 4. Disciplinary measures and procedure, sub 4.4.

[1179] Doping Control Regulations, 9.07.

[1180] Title IV – Adempimenti e sanzioni, Art. 11, subsection 8: " 'E' fatta la facoltà delle parti del procedimento disciplinare di recorrere al TAS (Tribunale Arbitrale dello Sport) una volta complato il procedimento di competenza degli Organi Federali."

[1181] Regolamento Federale Antidoping, Title VI – Adempimenti e Sanzioni, Art. 11 – Procedimento disciplinare, 5.

[1182] Regolamento Antidoping Cavalieri 2000, Title IV – Adempimenti e Sanzioni, Art. 11 – Procedimento disciplinare, 1.

the national federation was final, thereby implying that this instance could decide on appeal. However, if national law provided otherwise, the "final" decision would also be appealable before a national court. It was added that: "In that case the cyclist or licensee may renounce his right to appeal to that instance and bring his appeal immediately before the TAS."[1183]

The Portuguese Statute Law of 1997 provided that: "the requirements and procedures governing the inquiry and disciplinary processes intended to penalise those agents who are responsible for doping, together with an indication of the methods and instances of appeal, which also must ensure that the prosecuting body is distinct from the disciplinary body."[1184]

6.3. Right of cassation

The right of cassation was only granted under the doping regulations of two Belgian sports organisations Cassation is essentially different from appeal to a higher instance or to the CAS as the final instance. In the proceedings following the institution of these appeals the case would usually be reviewed anew and in full, including where appropriate a new examination of the facts. However, on cassation, the re-examination of the case is limited to points of law, including procedural law, and the facts are considered to be those as established by the lower instance.

The *Koninklijke Belgische Wielrenunie* provided for the possibility of cassation against decisions of the Disciplinary Committee, rendered in the first and final instance, and against decisions of the disciplinary council and the disputes council:[1185] "Upon cassation of the disputed decision the case is referred to a differently composed chamber of the tribunal whose decision was disputed, which will render judgment within the boundaries laid down by the decision on cassation. This judgment will be final." Mention was also made of cassation in the *Règlement en Matière de Dopage* of the *Fédération Royale Belge de Volleyball*: "Les parties concernées pourront introduire un recours devant la Commission d'Appel et de Cassation en respectant les règles de procédure prévues par les Statuts de l'A.I.F." A further remarkable possibility among the various forms of appeal allowed by this federation was that: "Dans le cas où toutes les procédures sont epuisées au niveau fédéral, il est loisible aux parties concernées de porter l'affaire aux juridictions civiles."

6.4. Right of appeal to the court of arbitration for sport (CAS)

The CAS, although often the highest instance, does not provide for cassation. Quite the opposite in fact, as CAS panels have full powers of review, both as concerns the

---

[1183] Title XIV Antidoping Controle Reglement, Art. 81.
[1184] Statute Law No. 183/97 of 26 July 1997, Art. 10, subsection 2 sub (e).
[1185] Tuchtreglement, Title V, Book 1, Part IV, Ch. 3.

facts and the law.[1186] Nearly all international and national sports organisations allow for appeal to the CAS as the highest instance.[1187]

The regulations of the *Bund Deutscher Radfahrer* stated that: "gegen die Entscheidung des Bundessportgerichts [...] eine Berufung durch den Bestraften oder durch die UCI zulässig (ist) und zwar bei Entscheidungen nach den a) 'Internationalen Bestimmungen' durch Einleitung eines Schiedsverfahrens vor dem Sportschiedsgerichtshof in Lausanne (TAS) [...]."[1188]

The British Bobsleigh Association provided that: "the person may appeal to the Court of Arbitration in Lausanne within 10 days of receipt of notification of the decision of the Appeal Committee. The decision of the Court of Arbitration shall be final and binding upon the person and the Association."[1189]

The doping regulations of the Irish Triathlon Association contained a similar provision:[1190] "The Disciplinary Panel will give notice in writing to the person concerned of its decision when it is reached and of the person's right of appeal to Court of Arbitration (CAS)."

One sports organisation in Italy, the *Federazione Italiana Sport Invernali* (FISI), also provided for appeal to the CAS: "E' fatta la facoltà delle parti del procedimento disciplinare di recorrere al TAS (Tribunale Arbitrale dello Sport) una volta complato il procedimento di competenza degli Organi Federali."[1191]

[1186] CAS Procedural Rules, R 57. The CAS (CAS 98/211, 7-6-1999, *Smith-De Bruin v. FINA*, Matthieu Reeb, ed., *Digest of CAS Awards II 1998-2000* (The Hague, Kluwer Law International 2002) pp. 255-273, ground 2.2) considered that under this rule it was "[...] not limited to consideration of the evidence that was adduced before the FINA Doping Panel, but [could] consider all evidence, oral and written, produced before it. None of the arguments advanced by the parties, discussed below, could or did affect the Panel's responsibility in this regard. In short, the hearing before the Panel constituted a hearing 'de novo'," that is, a rehearing of the merits of the case. Cf. CAS 99/A/252, 28-7-2000, *FCLP v. IWF*. Cf., Beloff 1999 (*supra* nt. 282), 7.106.

[1187] CAS, Guide, Foreword: "On 22nd June 1994 in Paris, no less than 31 international sports federations signed the Agreement to constitute the International Council of Arbitration for Sport and, by their signature, recognized the jurisdiction of the Court of Arbitration for Sport."

[1188] Dopingkontroll-Reglement, 6 Verfahrensdurchführung / Rechtfertigungs- und Einspruchsrecht, 6.2 Anhörung des / der Beschuldigten, Verfahrensdurchführung, 6.5 Berufung, (1) (a).

[1189] Rules for Doping Control, 4. Disciplinary measures and procedure, 4.7.

[1190] 2. Doping Control Policy, 2.4 What are the Disciplinary Procedures? 2.4.6. The Policy further provides that: "2.4.7 The person and Tennis Ireland shall have the right of appeal against a decision of the Disciplinary Panel to the Appeal Panel. The appellant shall give notice in writing of the appeal to the other party and either party may request a hearing before the Appeal Panel. [...] The Appeal Panel will notify in writing the person concerned of its decision when it is reached," and "2.4.8 The person concerned or the Irish Triathlon Association may make written representations to either or both the Disciplinary Panel or the Appeal Panel (CAS). At a hearing of the Disciplinary Panel or the Appeal Panel, the person and the Irish Triatlon Association may be legally represented (or by anyone else) and shall have the right to give and call evidence and to address the Disciplinary Panel and the Appeal Panel (CAS). [...]."

[1191] Nuovo Regolamento Antidoping FISI, Title IV – Adempimenti e Sanzioni, Art. 11 – Violazione delle norme antidoping e relative sanzioni, 8. This provision could also be found in the doping regulations of the CONI and in principle applied to all Italian sports organisations. It provided that the parties were entitled to appeal to the CAS after exhaustion of the remedies provided by the organisation in question.

Two Dutch federations permitted appeal to the CAS: the *Nederlandse Hippische Sportbond* and the *Koninklijke Nederlandse Wielren Unie*.[1192] The regulations of the former provided that: "the participant and the NHS may within 30 days bring an appeal against a decision of the court of appeal [...] before the Court of Arbitration for Sport, which decision shall be binding on all parties."[1193] The procedure used by the *Koninklijke Nederlandse Wielren Unie* as has been described above could also culminate in appeal to the CAS by either the cyclist, the licensee or the UCI. It was further provided that: "When a factor of a natural character is discovered which could influence the final decision at the level of the national association of the cyclist or licensee, the interested party may request the national association to re-open the case, unless the fresh fact may be taken into account in the case pending before the CAS. The fresh fact must have occurred before the final decision and the party adducing it must show that it was unable to take earlier cognisance of this fact before at the latest the session preceding the final decision. On pain of disallowance the reopening must be requested within a month after the fact concerned was discovered. The burden of proof rests upon the party adducing the fresh fact."[1194] The cyclist or licensee or the UCI could also choose to appeal against the national federation's decision not to the CAS, but by instituting arbitration proceedings before an arbitration tribunal which was composed in conformity with the statutes and regulations of the CAS. Any other kind of appeal was excluded.[1195] In case of an appeal to the CAS, the UCI had to be sent all the relevant documents and had the right to intervene in the proceedings.[1196]

Under the WADC, the CAS is designated as the highest instance before which an appeal can be instituted.[1197] This is to prevent the dispute from ending up before

---

[1192] Title XIV Antidoping Controle Reglement, Ch. VII – Recht van verdediging – Beroep, Art. 81.

[1193] Dopingreglement NHS, Art. 15. Aangifte. vervolging en bestraffing, 1.

[1194] *Idem:* Art. 83.

[1195] *Idem:* Art. 84.

[1196] *Idem:* Art. 85. See further: Art. 86: AUnder penalty of disallowance the declaration of appeal must be deposited with the TAS by the punished person within one month of receipt of the decision by the appellant, subject to Art. 94. Under penalty of disallowance the declaration of appeal must be instituted by the UCI before the TAS within one month after receipt of the file of the competent organ of the national federation. If the UCI has not claimed the file within 10 days of receipt of the decision the time limit for appeal will expire a within one month after receipt of the decision."
Art 87: "Appeal to the TAS by the punished person does not suspend the execution of the decision taken, without prejudice to the right to apply to the TAS for suspensive effect."
Art. 88: "The arbitral tribunal hears the entire case, unless these regulations stipulate otherwise. No appeal shall lie against the decision, which is final for the parties."
Art. 89: "The TAS may, at the request of another party, increase the seriousness of the appellant's situation. When the respondent includes a rebuttal in his response, the appellant has the right to submit a surrebuttal within one month after receipt of the response, if the TAS allows an extension of the time limits for this purpose. If the respondent is the punished person he shall have the right to submit a final statement within 15 days of receipt of the surrebuttal, if the TAS allows an extension of the time limits for this purpose."

[1197] Art. 13.2 WADC provides that: "A decision that an anti-doping rule violation was committed, a decision imposing consequences for an anti-doping rule violation, a decision that no anti-doping rule violation was committed, a decision that an anti-doping organization lacks jurisdiction to rule on an

the ordinary courts. However, this rule is an oddity in the sense that it prescribes private law arbitration (whereby the case is heard *de novo*) in respect of a disciplinary law, i.e. pseudo-criminal, decision. This aspect has so far been largely ignored in the literature. The CAS Code of Sports-related Arbitration is the basis for the appellate proceedings. It is tempting to call these proceedings arbitral as this ensures that any decisions resulting from them will fall within the scope of the New York Convention on Arbitration, but can they be properly considered as arbitration? Pinna[1198] in this context refers to a judgment of the *Cour d'Appel de Paris*[1199] concerning a decision of the Disciplinary Committee of a private law organisation. The Court decided that "according to French law, arbitration is only possible for the settlement of a dispute arising out of a contract that includes the arbitration agreement. This is not the case for the dispute between the association and one of its members, which is of a disciplinary nature." Using the word arbitration for decision-making in doping cases not only means using the inappropriate term, but also using it to cover up the true nature of the proceedings. Arbitration would entail that the parties contest the decision on equal terms. However, in doping cases before the CAS it is not so much the previous decision that is the object of the proceedings, but the case as a whole, which is reviewed anew, often for the third time, and again the parties are not equal. The CAS proceedings are simply the third disciplinary proceedings in a row. This may be considered a *testimonium paupertatis* with respect to the previous disciplinary bodies. Arbitration before the CAS is not something which the parties voluntarily agree upon, but is compulsory. If the athlete refuses to sign the arbitration clause, he/she will be excluded from competition and his/her sporting career will be damaged, or, according to Pinna:[1200] "he can only practise his sport in marginality, in his garden, without competitors or partners." Pinna further observed that:

> "Today, in legal systems, which have traditionally widely favoured arbitration and more generally alternative dispute resolution, doctrine begins to question the legitimacy of such a policy. This criticism is noticeable mainly in matters where arbitration

---

alleged anti-doping rule violation or its consequences, and a decision to impose a provisional suspension as a result of a provisional hearing or in violation of Art. 7.5 may be appealed exclusively as provided in this Art. 13.2."

Art. 13.2.1: "Appeals involving international-level athletes – In cases arising from competition in an international event or in cases involving international-level athletes, the decision may be appealed exclusively to the Court of Arbitration for Sport ('CAS') in accordance with the provisions applicable before such court."

Pursuant to Art. 13.2.2 sports organisations may elect to comply with this article by giving its national-level athletes the right to appeal directly to CAS.

[1198] Andrea Pinna, "The Trials and Tribulations of the Court of Arbitration for Sport. Contribution to the Study of the Arbitration of Disputes concerning Disciplinary Sanctions," in I. Blackshaw, R.C.R. Siekmann, J. Soek, eds., *The Court of Arbitration for Sport 1984-2004* (The Hague, T.M.C. Asser Press 2005), p. 386 et seq. (Pinna 2005).

[1199] CA Paris, 3-12-1986, (1987) *Rev. Arb.*, p. 352.

[1200] Compare Andrea Pinna (Pinna 2005, *supra* nt. 1198), who quotes F. Knoepfler ((1994) *RSDIE*, p. 153, annotation of Swiss Federal Court 15-3-1993).

is compulsory for the weaker party in contracts of adhesion. Such is especially the case for consumers, employees, franchisees and subcontractors. In these situations, the appeal to arbitration is often considered a tool of oppression of the weaker party, rather than as an instrument of justice. In United States law, the validity of imposed arbitration clauses for the weaker party has become one of the most controversial issues both in case law and in literature."

Arbitration before the CAS therefore invites critical comment, in the first place because of its disciplinary nature implying the inequality of the parties, which is so obviously not an intended feature of arbitration, and in the second place because of this very inequality, whereby the weaker party is forced to participate in the proceedings, in stark contrast to the voluntary nature of proper arbitration proceedings. Finally, it may be argued that forced arbitration goes against the basic principle of law as enshrined for example in Article 17 of the Dutch Constitution that no one may be prevented against his will from being heard by the courts to which he is entitled to apply under the law.[1201]

To sum up this chapter so far, above it has been demonstrated that the disciplinary doping law of sports organisations, although formally speaking a part of private law, should actually be considered as "pseudo-criminal law." In this context, it has first been examined whether the fair trial standards of Article 6 ECHR should and do apply in doping trials. Next it will be examined whether fundamental principles of criminal law are also applied in disciplinary doping proceedings. Due to a lack of published relevant decisions of the various sports organisations' disciplinary tribunals this will be done by discussing the available CAS decisions.[1202]

7.   FUNDAMENTAL CRIMINAL LAW RIGHTS IN PRACTICE

7.1.   The *nulla poena sine lege scripta* principle (the principle of legality)

The principle of *nullum crimen, nulla poena sine praevia lege poenali* is deeply enshrined in continental European legal thinking. It provides that there can be no crime and no punishment of a crime without this having been laid down in a prior criminal law. The principle has also found its way into international criminal law.[1203]

[1201] Cf. Bernhard König, "Sind Schiedsbreden auf den CAS/TAS wirksam?," (2004) *SpuRt*, pp. 137-138.

[1202] "Der [...] vom Schiedsgericht gefällte Schiedsspruch oder zumindest eine Zusammenfassung dessen wird vom CAS im Normalfall veröffentlicht. Nur wenn das Verfahren vertraulich bleiben soll, wie z.B. wegen persönlicher Gründe [...], unterbleibt eine Veröffentlichung," K. Hofmann: "Das Internationale Sportschiedgericht (CAS) in Lausanne," in (2002) *SpuRt*, p. 9. Cf. Stephan Netzle: "Das Internationale Sport-Schiedsgericht in Lausanne. Zusammensetzung, Zuständigkeit und Verfahren," in V. Röhricht, ed., *Sportgerichtsbarkeit* (Stuttgart, Boorberg 1997) p. 15.

[1203] In the Netherlands, the principle has been laid down in Art. 1 of the Criminal Code which provides that: "No act or omission is punishable which did not constitute a criminal offence under the

Its objective is to promote legal certainty. The principle also applies to doping rules.[1204] Before an act of doping can be prosecuted, it has to be laid down in the rules of the sports organisation in question that such an act constitutes an offence and that it is punishable by certain penalties. The rules in question have to be adopted in a general meeting of the association and may only be amended by a majority. National sports organisations often simply copy or refer to the doping provisions of the international federations to which they belong. If this is the case, however, this has to be expressly mentioned in the association's own rules, as only then the athlete will be subject to the "Vereinsstrafgewalt" of the "higher-ranking" organisation, which would bar him from relying on the principle of legality in any doping proceedings against him.[1205]

The essence of the description of the doping offence is the "Tatbestand" or definition of the offence.[1206] This has to be sufficiently specific. In the first-generation descriptions the definition often lacked specification. One example is the definition as formulated by Deutsche Sportärztebund in 1952:

> "doping is understood to mean the taking of a drug – regardless of whether it is effective or not – with the intention of enhancing the performance during the match."[1207]

As we have seen, later definitions referred to a list of prohibited substances. In this case the principle of legality required that the list in question was sufficiently specific.[1208] As has already been observed above in Chapter 2 the body prosecuting a doping offence was not allowed to rely on rules of custom or rules permitting flex-

---

law at the time it was committed." See also Art. 16 of the Dutch Constitution, Art. 15 ICCPR and Art. 7(1) ECHR and Art. 22 (1) of the Statute of the International Criminal Court: "A person shall not be criminally responsible under this Statute unless the conduct in question constitutes, at the time it takes place, a crime within the jurisdiction of the Court" read together with Art. 23: "A person convicted by the Court may be punished only in accordance with this Statute."

[1204] "Der aus Art. 103 II GG abgeleitete Bestimmtheitsgrundsatz komt auch im Vereinsrecht voll zum Tragen," Summerer (*supra* nt. 72) p. 159.

[1205] Cf. the Ngugi case (*John Ngugi v. the Kenyan Amateur Athletic Association (KAAA) and the IAAF*) of 5 November 1994, in Lauri Tarasti, *Legal Solutions in international doping cases,* (Cernusco, Italy 2000), p. 133 et seq. (Tarasti 2000). In Section 1.4.4.1 of his report on Belgium, Prof. Marc Boes observes that: "if a sport federation disposes of a disciplinary procedure and disciplinary organs that satisfy the requirements laid down in Article 41 of the Flemish Community Act, this federation can institute disciplinary proceedings against its members who are suspected of doping. To date, no sport federation exercises this disciplinary power. The reason is that the Flemish administration provides itself such a disciplinary procedure, and this way it is of course less expensive for the sport federation." This means that in Belgium sports organisation may delegate the "Vereinsstrafgewalt" to public bodies. The procedure to be followed by such a public body is completely governed by criminal law.

[1206] See in particular *supra* Chapter 2.

[1207] "Die Einnahme eines jeden Medikamentes – ob wirksam oder nicht – mit der Absicht der Leistungssteigerung während des Wettkampfes eingenommen, is als Doping zu betrachten," in Bette/Schimank 1998 (*supra* nt. 7), p. 358 as cited by M. Sehling/R. Pollert/D. Hackfort, *Doping im Sport. Medizinische, sozialwissenschaftliche und juristische Aspekte* (Munich, BLV1989) p. 18.

[1208] The doping lists do not completely fulfil this aspect of the requirement of legal certainty as often the categories of expressly listed substances include the words "and related substances."

ible interpretations, for example general rules of disciplinary law providing that the members of the organisation by their actions or omissions may not harm the interests of the organisation. Several disciplinary bodies have nevertheless sentenced athletes for unsportsmanlike behaviour after they found that they were unable to base the athlete's act on the definition of doping or the list of prohibited substance in use for their sport.[1209]

In the case of *Korneev and Goukiev v. IOC*[1210] for example traces of the mysterious substance bromantan[1211] had been found in the urine samples of the two athletes which had been collected during the 1996 Atlanta Olympics. The IOC disqualified both athletes as it considered the substance a class IA stimulant on the list of Prohibited Classes of Substances. The laboratories involved had been unable to identify the substance or its properties. The only available literature on bromantan was in Russian and the ad hoc procedure did not leave enough time to have it translated. The CAS ad hoc panel considered that: "Bromantan is not specifically named in the Medical Code as a prohibited substance. Accordingly, in order to justify the disqualification of an athlete for the use of Bromantan it must be established that Bromantan is a stimulant within the meaning of the Medical Code. The burden of establishing that fact, if disputed, is on the suspending body." The IOC was unable to prove that bromantan was a stimulant listed in the Code, whereupon the CAS ruled that: "On the basis of the foregoing facts and legal determinations, the ad hoc Division of the CAS decides that the appeals of the athletes Andrei Korneev and Zakhar Gouliev against the decisions of the IOC Executive Board disqualifying them for the Games of the XXVI Olympiad for the use of Bromantan be allowed and those decisions be set aside." As bromantan did not appear on the list of prohibited substances, the subjective element of the description of the doping offence, i.e. illegality, was not fulfilled.

The CAS again applied the principle of legality in *Rebagliati v. IOC*.[1212] During the 1998 Olympic Winter Games in Nagano traces of marijuana were found in the urine sample of the snowboarder Rebagliati. Pursuant to Chapter II, Article III(B) of the IOC Medical Code the use of marijuana was punishable, provided that this had been agreed between the IOC and the IF in question. Such an agreement had not been concluded between the IOC and the FIS. The CAS considered that: "The Panel recognizes that from an ethical and medical perspective, cannabis consump-

---

[1209] See the *Krabbe II* (see Tarasti 2000 (*supra* nt. 1205), p. 129 et seq.) and the Lanzaat case (DFB Bundesgericht 31-5-2000 ((2001) *SpuRt*, p. 212). "Ist dem Bestimmtheitserfordernis nicht Genüge getan, darf diese Erfordernis nicht über einen *Auffangtatbestand*, beispielsweise denjenigen des sportwidriges Verhaltens, aufgeweicht werden. Die einname eines Medikaments beispielsweise, das nicht in der Liste der verbotenen Substanzen aufgeführt ist, darf alleine nicht regelmäßig einen verstoß gegen die anerkannten Grundsätze sportlichen Verhaltens [...] bedeuten, wenn nicht erschwerende Umstände hinzutreten," Summerer (Summerer 1990, *supra* nt. 72), p. 157.

[1210] CAS 96/003-4, 04-8-1996, *Andrei Korneev v. IOC & Zakhar Goukiev v. IOC*.

[1211] The substance was intended for the Russian army and was not generally available although it could apparently "be obtained in Moscow."

[1212] CAS AH 98/002, 12-2-1998, *Rebagliati v. IOC*, Matthieu Reeb, ed., *Digest of CAS Awards 1986-1998* (Berne, Editions Stämpfli 1998) pp. 419-434. N.K.

tion is a matter of serious social concern. CAS is not, however, a criminal court and can neither promulgate nor apply penal laws. We must decide within the context of the law of sports, and cannot invent prohibitions or sanctions where none appear." In essence, the CAS held here that the principle of legality, and thus a lack of illegality, prevented the imposition of a penalty. The penalties which may be imposed for doping are so severe that it must be carefully examined whether the offence with which the athlete is charged fully corresponds to the offence as described in the applicable regulations.

It is also possible that the rule in question is clear, but that it has been consistently interpreted to the athletes' advantage. This raises legitimate expectations for the future. The disciplinary body in such cases may not simply revert to the actual rule. This is only acceptable when it is announced publicly beforehand. On one occasion the CAS has referred to recent inconsistencies in the sentencing policy of an IF to reduce a penalty.[1213]

7.2. The *lex certa* principle (the principle of legal certainty)

Inextricably bound up with the *nulla poena* principle is the principle of *lex certa* which stipulates that the description of an offence has to be as precise as possible. Without the *lex certa* principle, it would be possible to fulfil the *nulla poena* principle with a minimum of effort through very broadly worded provisions. The *nulla poena* and the *lex certa* principles do not only address the legislator, but also the courts, which have to match the rules with the acts brought before them. In this sense, they could be said to restrict judicial discretion, given that the decision of whether a criminal offence has been committed in the first place depends on the description of the offence provided. Like the *nulla poena* principle, the *lex certa* principle is also laid down in numerous international instruments.[1214] In sports law, the principle in the first place address the sports organisations' rule-making organs. Concerning the "Bestimmtheitsgrundsatz" Summerer has observed that:[1215] "Jeder Sportler [...] unzweideutig erkennen [muß] können, ob und wie ein Fehlverhalten, sanktioniert wirdt [...]. Die Satzung darf es nicht zum zuständigen Organ überlassen, welche Sanktion dieses verhängen will. [...] In jedem Fall unzureichend ist ein pauschales Dopingverbot." In other words, doping regulations have to designate clearly which substances and methods are prohibited. "Eine nur beispielhafte

---

[1213] CAS 95/141, 22-4-1996, *Chagnaud v. FINA*, Matthieu Reeb, ed., *Digest of CAS Awards 1986-1998* (Berne, Editions Stämpfli 1998) pp. 205-224, See *supra* Chapter 4, Section 3.

[1214] The Court of Human Rights has distinguished a third principle in addition to the *nullem crimen* and *nulla poena* principles of Art. 7 ECHR: "the authority applying criminal law shall interpret it not extensively, i.e. by analogy, unless such an application operates in favour of the accused," Van Dijk/Van Hoof 1998 (*supra* nt. 966), p. 481. See further Art. 22(2) of the Statute of the International Criminal Court: "The definition of a crime shall be strictly construed and shall not be extended by analogy. In case of ambiguity, the definition shall be interpreted in favour of the person being investigated, prosecuted or convicted."

[1215] Summerer 1990 (*supra* nt. 72), p. 159.

Aufzählung einiger Wirkstoffe ist im Zeitalter ausgreifender chemischer Analysetechniken nicht ausreichend. Nicht ausreichend ist ferner, wenn [...] bei den verbotenen Verbindungen auf das Kriterium der 'Verwandtschaft' abgestellt wirdt, weil offenbleibt, ob der chemische Wirkmechanismus oder der ababole Effekt maßgeblich sein soll." Summerer thus rejects non-exhaustive lists, but none of the lists used would have been able to fulfil his criteria. The OMADC and all of the doping regulations used by the federations concluded their lists of prohibited substances with the words "and related substances." Federations wished to keep the lists open-ended so as to be able to prosecute athletes whose urine samples revealed the presence of precursors and metabolites of listed substances. They moreover wished to be able to bring within the scope of their lists all the substances that might be developed by the pharmaceutical industry after the establishment of the lists. During the last Olympics, for example, the doping samples of three athletes were found to contain the substance darbepoetine (brand name Aranesp), which had not been on the market for long and had not yet been placed on the IOC list. The Medical Commission through its member Jordi Segura announced that when a product is related to EPO it automatically belongs in the category of prohibited substances. In the *Korneev* case no relationship could be established with any of the substances appearing on the list and the athletes who had used the suspicious substance could not be prosecuted.

Another form of lack of specification could arise if the sports organisation gave various descriptions of the doping offence which did not match. Taken separately, these descriptions could well be sufficiently specific, but taken together, they were not. A good example of such a "cumulative lack of specification" was the *Aanes v. FILA* case,[1216] where the panel distilled from the rules the following rather confusing list of definitions:

> "According to the Constitution, doping is the 'absorption' of a 'substance intended to artificially improve the performance'. In turn Art. 1 of the FILA Anti-Doping Regulations states that it is sufficient for the substance to 'affect' the performance and the same Article declares that 'the presence in the athlete's organism of forbidden substances' constitutes a doping offence.
>
> The FILA Doping Regulations then confirm that the IOC Anti-Doping Code 'must apply' to all FILA competitions and this very IOC Anti-Doping Code states that 'Doping is [...] the presence in the athlete's body of a Prohibited Substance' and the IOC's Explanatory Memorandum further explains that doping 'exists as soon as the presence of a banned substance has been detected in an athlete's body, independent of any element of intention'.
>
> Finally, according to Annex D of the FILA Anti-Doping Regulations there seems to be a requirement of 'proving responsibility' in order for sanctions to be imposed. The same can be concluded from Art. 17.21 of the same regulations which provides for sanctions of a 'wrestler at fault'.
>
> The Panel observes that this 'cocktail' of definitions and legal principles in connection with the fight against doping certainly falls short of the clarity and certainty desirable

---

[1216] CAS 2000/A/317, 9-7-2001, *F. Aanes v. FILA*.

in an area as sensitive as doping and as demanded by CAS [...]. However, in the opinion of the Panel, the lack of clarity in the FILA Regulations does not go quite far enough to justify rejecting them as a whole as being so unclear that they cannot be applied at all. The Panel will therefore apply these rules as they are but will, if necessary, interpret any uncertainties contra stipulatorem, i.e. against FILA."[1217]

The *Aanes* case was the only case in which the CAS has ever threatened to interpret the federation's rules *contra stipulatorem* in case they proved to be unclear. In other cases, the CAS was usually prepared to interpret the rules in a way which sought to discern the intention of the rule maker, and not to frustrate it.[1218]

7.3. The *ne bis in idem* principle

Under Dutch criminal law as under the criminal laws of many countries[1219] and international law (e.g. the law of extradition)[1220] no one may be prosecuted or punished twice for the same offence. Corstens has called this principle "a rule of justice and reasonableness."[1221, 1222] The *ne bis in idem* principle contributes to efficient law enforcement in that it prevents over-punishment, creates incentives for efficient prosecution, prevents vexatious multiple prosecutions and creates incentives for efficient coordination between prosecutors.

It has to be noted that below the principle will only be examined against the background of multiple disciplinary proceedings. It is not applied to concurrent

---

[1217] Both paragraphs 1 and 2 of Art. 2 in Ch. II of the OMADC provided a definition of doping. The definition in paragraph 1 applied to cases of fault liability and the definition of paragraph 2 applied to cases of strict liability: "1. the use of an expedient (substance or method) which is potentially harmful to the athlete's health and/or capable of enhancing their performance, or 2. the presence in the athlete's body of a Prohibited Substance or evidence of the use thereof or evidence of the use of a Prohibited Method." If we look more closely we will find that there are actually three definitions given here if we consider the evidence of use separately. The General Provisions of Ch. I of the Anti-Doping Code added yet another definition that read as follows: "Intentional doping means doping in circumstances where it is established, or may reasonably be presumed, that any Participant acted knowingly or in circumstances amounting to gross negligence."

[1218] Frank Oschütz, "The Jurisprudence of the CAS in Doping Cases," (2001) *ISLJ*, pp. 22-30. Cf., CAS 96/149, 13-3-1997, *Cullwick v. FINA*, Matthieu Reeb, ed., *Digest of CAS Awards 1986-1998* (Berne, Editions Stämpfli 1998) pp. 251-263.

[1219] In Germany the principle is laid down in Art. 103(2) of the Constitution.

[1220] See e.g. Art. 4 of Protocol No. 7 to the ECHR. According to Van Dijk and Van Hoof (Van Dijk/Van Hoof 1998 *supra* nt. 966), p. 690, "[...] it may be concluded that the notion of 'criminal' in Art. 4 of the Protocol No. 7 is identical to the term 'criminal' in Art. 6 of the Convention." See further Art. 50 of the Charter of Fundamental Rights of the European Union and Art. 54 of the Schengen implementation agreement.

[1221] Corstens 1993 (*supra* nt. 584), p. 189. "Das Verbot der Mehrfachbestrafung ('ne bis in idem') in Art. 103 Abs. 3 GG verbietet es zugunsten der Rechtssicherheit, daß jemand wegen derselben Tat, d.h. wegen desselben einheitlichen Lebensvorganges, mehrfach strafrechtlich zur Verantwortung gezogen wird," in Krogmann 1998 (*supra* nt. 11), p. 179.

[1222] "[Muss ...] innerhalb eines Verbandes, der sich vom Landes-, über Bundes-, Europa- zum Weltverband aufbaut, das Doppelbestrafungsverbot gelten [...]. Dies möchte ich voll bejahen, denn es geht dabei ja um die gleichen sportlichen Werte und Güter," Eike Reschke, (2001) *SpuRt*, p. 184.

disciplinary and criminal prosecution.[1223] As De Doelder has observed, this type of double prosecution is not necessarily prohibited by it.[1224]

The CAS has mostly referred to *ne bis in idem* by its common law name of "double jeopardy."[1225] The principle was part of the questions at issue in the CAS case concerning Jessica Foschi. After Foschi had tested positive for doping, the USS National Board of Review, which was the national federation's disciplinary body, punished her by two years' probation. On appeal, the USS Board of Directors changed the penalty into two years' suspension. The swimmer made use of the right under the USS and USOC regulations to lodge a "final appeal" to the American Arbitration Association (AAA). The AAA held that the penalty that had been imposed by the USS Board did not only violate the rules of "fundamental fairness," but that it was moreover "arbitrary and capricious." The penalty was reversed. In the meantime, the FINA had followed its own procedures which had led to a decision by the FINA Executive[1226] to suspend Foschi for two years. Foschi subsequently appealed against the FINA Executive's decision to the FINA Bureau. The Bureau decided unanimously to confirm the decision by the Executive and to reject the appeal, whereupon the swimmer turned to the CAS. One of the arguments put forward by the swimmer was that the proceedings started by the FINA had been in breach of "principles forbidding double jeopardy." The CAS considered that:[1227]

> "Whilst the FINA proceedings are based on the same facts as the proceedings before the national bodies and tribunals (the USS and AAA), they are not based on the same rules and have a far wider scope. Respondent invoked the FINA Rules whereas the national proceedings were held pursuant to the USS's rules (even if these do largely coincide with the FINA Rules). In addition, the ambit of the USS is to ban a swimmer only from competing in national competitions, whereas the ambit of Respondent is to ban a swimmer from competing in international competitions; it is interesting to note in this context that, following suspension by FINA, Appellant continued to compete in national competitions (because the USS was forced to allow that under the AAA deci-

---

[1223] Cf. Reinhart 2001 (*supra* nt. 935), pp. 45-48; Christian Fahl, *Sportverbandsgerichtsbarkeit und Doppelbestrafungsverbod*, (2001) *SpuRt*, pp. 181-183; Eike Rescke, Erwiderung auf Reinhart, (2001) *SpuRt*, p. 45.

[1224] See De Doelder 1981 (*supra* nt. 352), p. 209.

[1225] Under US criminal law noone for the same offence may Abe twice put in jeopardy of life or limb." This is the double jeopardy clause contained in the Fifth Amendment to the Federal Constitutie. See: Lensing 1996 (*supra* nt. 602), p. 315.

[1226] Wise 2000 (*supra* nt. 395): "I believe that the AAA's decision on the matter (where the US national federation is the opposing party) should be the final decision, and that the IF should have no legal right to bring up the same charge again. The AAA decision should be binding on the IF based on some principle like 'res judicata' or the US legal principle of 'collateral estoppel'." After all, the US national federation is closely tied to the IF. IF's know better than to intervene directly as a party in any USarbitration or court procedure – they want to stay clear of all US litigation. They can just stand back and watch what happens in the US proceedings, and if they don't like the result, then can start their own new procedure in Europe. Very unfair to the athlete. Unfortunately, there appear to be no Swiss legal principles (TAS is in Switzerland) to cause the US arbitral decision in the athlete's favor to be binding on the IF, because the IF and the US federation, even though related, are different parties."

[1227] CAS 96/156, 6-10-1997, *Jessica K. Foschi v. FINA*, ground 11.2.

sion) while she was banned from all international competitions. Whether these facts constitute special circumstances allowing a further 'trial' or whether they mean that the further 'trial' before the international federation simply does not constitute a case of double jeopardy can be left aside. Either way, it is the Panel's view that the fact that Appellant's case was brought before Respondent after the national bodies had decided upon the same facts does not breach the general principle forbidding double jeopardy. Moreover the sanction imposed by Respondent does not breach the prohibition of multiple punishment in that it commenced on 4 August 1995 (the day of the meet at which Appellant tested positive) and so will have run parallel to any national sanctions rather than consecutively."

In this case therefore the CAS concluded that there had been no violation of the *ne bis in idem* principle, as although both proceedings had been based on the same facts they were not based on the same rules. An additional argument according to the CAS was the fact that the American decisions were aimed at the athlete's participation in swimming at the national level, while the FINA decisions concerned participation at the international level. According to this CAS decision it is therefore perfectly alright to prosecute twice for the same offence...[1228]

In a Spanish race of several days called the "Vuelta a Murcia" a Danish cyclist tested positive for doping. The UCI Anti-doping Commission requested the Danmarks Cykle Union (DCU) to institute doping proceedings against him based on the UCI Anti-doping Examination Regulations (AER). The DCU thereupon informed the UCI that it had referred the matter to the Danish NOC as the "ruling body in doping cases for all athletes in Denmark." The Danish NOC's Doping Tribunal suspended the cyclist for two years "barring him from participation in all training and competitive activities under the NOC and Sport Confederation of Denmark." The CAS on appeal considered as follows:[1229]

"The effect of the Danish NOC's stance is that a Danish athlete is liable to sanctions both under Danish regulations and also under international regulations. This is a form of double jeopardy which the Panel views with considerable concerns but which the Danish NOC appears to view with equanimity. It cannot be acceptable or just for a Danish athlete to be punished twice for the same offence: one punishment taking ef-

---

[1228] It is not inconceivable that the decision in the *Foschi* case was ill received, especially in the USA. The US Supreme Court understands the principle of *ne bis in idem*: to include not merely the answer to the question of whether the same offence is involved, but also of whether during the second prosecution "factual issues need to be discussed anew which were already resolved in the first proceedings in the defendant's favour," Lensing 1996 (*supra* nt. 602), p. 325-326. However, if two different public authorities are involved, the *ne bis in idem*: principle is applied differently: "Despite the recognised importance of the *ne bis in idem*: rule, the federal Constitition according to the federal Supreme Court does not oppose this. This is a result of the federal structure of the United States: every system is sovereign and entitled to enforce the law within the limits of its jurisdiction," Lensing (Lensing 1996, *supra* nt. 602), p. 332. This *dual sovereignty doctrine* largely corresponds to the law enforcement by the USS and the AAA on the one hand and by the FINA on the other.

[1229] CAS 99/A/239, 14-4-2000, *UCI v. Möller, Danmarks Idraets-Vorbund and Danmarks Cykle Union*, ground III.A.3.

fect only in Denmark, the other punishment taking effect everywhere else in the world. The Panel would seek to persuade the Danish NOC to adopt the international standard so that Danish athletes do not suffer this double jeopardy. If the Danish NOC were to follow this course, the international punishment would take effect also in Denmark."

As opposed to in its decision in Foschi, the CAS here did reach the conclusion that the double jeopardy principle had to apply, although this case mainly concerned double punishment.

Summerer has observed on double jeopardy that under the German Constitution no one may be punished twice for the same offence under the general criminal laws, to which he added that: "Dieser Grundsatz [...] gilt auch für die Vereinsstrafe."[1230] "So verstieße beispielsweise die separate Bestrafung eines Sportlers durch den Weltverband gegen das Verbot der Doppelbestrafung, wenn bereits durch den nationalen Verband in gleicher Sache eine Sanktion verhängt wurde." This point of view certainly does not coincide with that of the Danish NOC as set out above. Under UCI doping rules, international doping cases have to be dealt with by the cyclist's national federation. If this federation like in the *Möller* case decides the matter according to its own rules, which only apply nationally, instead of according to internationally applicable rules, this would according to Summerer's line of reasoning prevent the possibility of further punishment at the international level. In other words, an international doping case under these circumstances could no longer be punished by an international penalty.[1231]

In a case concerning the Latvian bobsleigher Sandis Prusis[1232] the ad hoc CAS panel prevented the double prosecution and punishment of the athlete. The international bobsleighing federation FIBT had suspended Prusis for three months after he had tested positive for doing. However, according to the IOC, the period of suspension was much too brief and went against the OMADC; the suspension should have been for two years.[1233] The three-month suspension period was set to expire exactly

---

[1230] Summerer 1990 (*supra* nt. 72), p. 160. Cf. Krogmann 1998 (*supra* nt. 11), p. 179. The prohibition of double punishment does not, according to Krogmann, prevent that sports organisations may again, in the particular context of the association, punish behaviour that has already been punished by the public authorities.

[1231] See also the Bevilacqua decision of 25 November 1996, *IAAF v. Federazione Italiana di Atletica Leggera FIDAL*. In this case, the FIDAL "prosecutor" had dismissed the case against Bevilacqua based on its own rules. The case had therefore not yet been tried under IAAF rules. In ground 8 it was considered that: "On FIDAL's point regarding the Prosecutor's decision being final and binding, even on the Arbitration Panel, we find that the IAAF has exercised the right of appeal to this Arbitration Panel. FIDAL's rules do not prevent and neither can validly prevent the IAAF to refer the case to the Arbitration Panel. We are of the view that the proceedings before us are really appellate in nature, so there is no question of Ms. Bevilacqua being subjected to double jeopardy."

[1232] CAS OG 02/001, 5-2-2002, Sandis Prusis & Latvian Olympic Committee/IOC, Matthieu Reeb, ed., *Digest of CAS Awards III 2001-2003* (The Hague, Kluwer Law International 2004) pp. 573-580. See also Dirk-Reiner Martens and Frank Oschütz, "Die Entscheidungen des CAS in Salt Lake City," in (2002) *SpuRt*, p. 90 and Gerry Tucker en Antonio Rigozzi, "Sports Arbitration for the 2008 Beijing Olympic Games," in *Arbitration* vol. 69, no. 3, August 2003, p. 188.

[1233] Christiane Ayot, the director of the Montreal laboratory which analysed Prusis's urine samples, declared that at the time of the control Prusis's body contained a thousand times the permitted amount of nandrolone.

at the beginning of the Salt Lake City Olympics, but the IOC denied Prusis entrance to the Games and banned him from the Olympic Village, which it considered itself entitled to do as the organiser of the Games. Prusis appealed against the decision of the IOC to the CAS. The CAS reversed the ban imposed on Prusis by the IOC, considering that it was not for the IOC to interfere in a sports federation's policy.[1234] Only if the IOC was able to show that the FIBT by imposing too brief a period of suspension had violated the Olympic Charter could the athlete's accreditation be withdrawn. However, in the case at hand the CAS held that such a violation had not occurred.

The normal course of affairs after an A sample tests positive is that the athlete in question is first given a sporting sanction (e.g. disqualification, return of prizes or medals, etc.) and is subsequently, after separate proceedings, punished under disciplinary law. Essentially, this also amounts to double punishment for the same offence, but this cumulative effect of sanctions is seldom connected with the *ne bis in idem* principle. In *Fritz Aanes v. Fédération Internationale de Luttes Associées (FILA)*, however, the athlete attempted to persuade the panel to consider his disqualification as a penalty equivalent to any penalty imposed after disciplinary proceedings.[1235] However, the CAS held that in the case of disqualification the question of fault is not at issue and that disqualification is imposed for entirely different reasons.[1236]

7.4. De *lex mitior* principle

The *lex mitior* principle is laid down in an area of the law that is relevant for the CAS, namely Swiss criminal law.[1237] The principle is also used in international criminal law.[1238] It offers a solution in situations where a penalty by which a certain

---

[1234] "[...] the IOC cannot take any action with regard to a specific sport which could be regarded as prejudicial to the independence and autonomy of the International Federation administering that sport." CAS OG 02/00, 5-2-2002, Sandis Prusis & Latvian Olympic Committee/IOC, Matthieu Reeb, ed., *Digest of CAS Awards III 2001-2003* (The Hague, Kluwer Law International 2004) pp. 573-580, para. 30.

[1235] CAS 2000/A/317, 9-7-2001, *F. Aanes v. FILA*. "Even if the FILA doping rules were considered to contain a strict liability regime the Panel should take into account that there was a case of exceptional circumstances which did not warrant a suspension in addition to disqualification from the Olympic Games," ground II.2.1.

[1236] "[...] the Panel wishes to clarify that this principle [of guilt] does not apply to the disqualification of a 'doped athlete' from the event at which the doping test was conducted. It is therefore perfectly proper for the rules of a sporting federation to establish that the results achieved by a 'doped athlete' at a competition during which he was under the influence of a prohibited substance must be cancelled irrespective of any guilt on the part of the athlete. This conclusion is the natural consequence of sporting fairness against the other competitors. The interests of the athlete concerned in not being punished without being guilty must give way to the fundamental principle of sport that all competitors must have equal chances."

[1237] Art. 2(2) of the Swiss Criminal Code. The principle of *lex mitior* applies only to cases where the commission of a crime and subsequent sentencing take place within one and the same jurisdiction.

[1238] See e.g. Art. 24(2) of the Statute of the International Criminal Court: "In the event of a change in the law applicable to a given case prior to a final judgement, the law more favourable to the person

offence is punishable has been reduced or otherwise changed to the offender's advantage in the period between the time the offence was committed and the date on which the court is due to decide or even after the initial penalty was imposed. In several decisions the CAS has been willing to apply the new – less severe – penalty regime.[1239]

In its Advisory Opinion of 5 January 1995 (CAS 94/128) in the case *Union Cycliste Internationale (UCI) v. Comité National Olympique Italien (CONI)*) the CAS considered that:[1240]

> "[...] In the Panel's opinion, the principle whereby a criminal law applies as soon as it comes into force if it is more favourable to the accused (lex mitior) is a fundamental principle of any democratic regime. It is established, for example, by Swiss law (Art. 2 para. 2 of the Penal Code) and by Italian law (Art. 2 of the Penal Code).
>
> This principle applies to anti-doping regulations in view of the penal or at the very least disciplinary nature of the penalties that they allow to be imposed.
>
> By virtue of this principle, the body responsible for setting the punishment must enable the athlete convicted of doping to benefit from the new provisions, assumed to be less severe, even when the events in question occurred before they came into force.
>
> This must be true, in the Panel's opinion, not only when the penalty has not yet been pronounced or appealed, but also when a penalty has become res judicata, provided that it has not yet been fully executed."

The CAS further added that: "Except in cases where the penalty pronounced is entirely executed, the penalty imposed is, depending on the case, either expunged or replaced by the penalty provided by the new provisions."[1241] In *Cullwick v. FINA* (CAS 96/149 of 13 March 1997) the CAS even unequivocally declared that: "The doctrine of lex mitior [...] is applicable to disciplinary matters such as doping cases."[1242] The outcome of the case of *Jessica K. Foschi v. FINA* (CAS 96/156, 6 October 1997) can also be said to have been the result of the *lex mitior* principle. The CAS found that it "does and must have flexibility to reduce a sanction, because the FINA Rules and FINA Guidelines are not sufficiently clear to an athlete."[1243]

---

being investigated, prosecuted or convicted shall apply." None of the doping regulations contained the *non-retroactivity ratione personae* principle of Art. 24(1) ICC: "No person shall be criminally responsible under this Statute for conduct prior to the entry into force of the Statute."

[1239] In September 2003 the FINA brought its Doping Control Rules in line with the WADC. In a press release (no. 70, http://www.fina.org/press_03_no70.html) of 26 September 2003 the FINA declared that a transitional rule had been adopted allowing FINA as of the entry into force of the new rules to reduce any remaining periods of suspension to comply with the new regime. In doping cases that were as yet undecided, the FINA would apply the new rules with the maximum sanction of two years' ineligibility. FINA further declared that Ain the name of fairness against competitors sanctioned according to the old rules and applying the principle of '*lex mitior*' used by the Court for Arbitration in Sport (CAS) in several awards, reduction of sanctions have been made in a few cases."

[1240] Ground 33.
[1241] *Idem*, ground 34.
[1242] *Idem*, grounds 2 and 27.
[1243] *Idem*, ground 15.1.

The FINA in the *Riley* case had imposed a penalty that was less severe than the penalty provided for in its rules. The curious turn in the CAS's argument is that it does not base its decision in favour of a milder penalty for Foschi directly on the fact that the FINA had imposed a milder penalty on Riley, but on the fact that the FINA rules and guidelines were unclear and only then pointed to the *lex mitior* principle: "[...] the analogous application of the criminal law doctrine of lex mitior would lead to the same result." Despite this ambiguity, however, it is nevertheless clear that the CAS has fully accepted the criminal law doctrine of *lex mitior*.[1244]

Beloff has remarked that the *lex mitior* principle is not familiar to common lawyers. Of course, it must be difficult to accept the application of criminal law principles to disciplinary doping proceedings if these are regarded as purely a private law matter rather than a pseudo-criminal law matter. Still, Beloff is willing to consider the principle, if only because aspects of it resemble principles which were developed in common law:

> "The lex mitior concept is not familiar to common lawyers versed in the practice of the English speaking jurisdictions of the world. Whether our courts might be willing to import it remains to be seen. We see no reason why such a felicitous doctrine should not be allowed to take root here, since it is in harmony with the benevolent common law tradition of leaning in favour of the accused in procedural matters arising from the exercise of punitive power."[1245]

7.5. The proportionality principle[1246]

The proportionality principle is widely recognised and accepted. It prohibits the taking of any measure which in view of its objective must be considered to go beyond what is appropriate and necessary. The application of the principle involves the balancing of the interests of the person or persons affected by the measure and the possibly wider social aim which it is intended to achieve.

Some ten years ago, the IOC and the IPC and the international sports federations used to provide for fixed penalties in their anti-doping regulations. After the first World Doping Conference in 1999, most sports organisations abandoned their pre-

---

[1244] CAS 2000/A/274, 19-10-2000, *Susin v. FINA*, Matthieu Reeb, ed., *Digest of CAS Awards II 1998-2000* (The Hague, Kluwer Law International 2002) pp. 389-409, ground 22: "After summarising the evidence on record, the FINA Doping Panel turned to the applicable rules. It found that the Old Rules were applicable because the doping control at issue took place on 24 January 1999. It further held that the New Rules would only apply according to the principle of *'lex mitior'.*" The CAS decision does not state what the results were of this reasoning of the FINA doping panel. See also CAS 99/A/234 & CAS 99/A/235, 29-2-2000, *David Meca-Medina v. FINA & Igor Majcen v. FINA*, ground 3.5.: "The *lex mitior* [...] not only entitles but obliges the Panel to apply the law as it stands at the time of determination, where more favourable to the Appellants; just as the presumption against retroactivity obliges it to apply the law as it stood at the time of the alleged offence, where more favourable to them."

[1245] Beloff 1999 (*supra* nt. 282), p. 210.

[1246] The term "principle of proportionality" is perhaps less fortunate as it is commonly used in criminal law in the context of the degree of force used by investigating officers. To denote the proportionality of the sentence German lawyers speak of *Verhältnismäßigkeitsgrundsatz* and *Übermaßverbot*.

vious sanctioning policies and established minimum penalties. At present, however, the fixed penalties in the WADA Code apply. Fixed penalties offer various advantages: they are predictable and rule out arbitrary sentencing by disciplinary bodies. One main disadvantage is, however, that in imposing these penalties disciplinary bodies cannot take into account the seriousness of the offence and the degree of fault of the offender.[1247] The flexible penalties to a certain degree appeared to solve this problem, but because they operated through a minimum which was often quite high this advantage in reality did not exist. Only maximum penalties like the ones commonly found in national Criminal Codes would allow a disciplinary body to respond adequately to doping offences.

A rule such as: "Der Richter misst die Strafe nach dem Verschulden des Täters zu; er berücksichtigt die Beweggründe, das Vorleben und die persönlichen Verhältnisse des Schuldigen," like in the Swiss Criminal Code,[1248] does full justice to the proportionality principle. Under Dutch criminal law the principle is not expressly provided for, but Remmelink has explained that: "the offence [..] may not for example give rise to the imposition of a disproportionately severe penalty. This could not be reconciled with the law's system which indicates a certain maximum penalty for every single offence or with the principle that punishment presupposes guilt."[1249]

Proportionality has been discussed fairly regularly in CAS decisions and opinions.[1250] In this respect, O'Leary has remarked that: "For all the Court of Arbitration for Sport's insistence upon a fixed disqualification response upon the detection of a doping product it has been keen to advocate a proportionate response once the issue turns to the issue of fixing the other penalties. In this respect the CAS has been somewhat in advance of certain sports governing bodies which have possibly

---

[1247] If a disciplinary body of an international federation has a discretionary power to determine the sanction, the CAS is also entitled to such discretion: "[...] this Panel in its capacity as an appeals body enjoys the same discretion in fixing the extent of the sanction as the Respondent's internal instances [...]. In fact, the Panel would enjoy this discretion even if there were no exceptional attenuating circumstances."

[1248] Swiss Criminal Code, Book 1: Allgemeine Bestimmungen, Part I: Verbrechen und Vergehen, Title III: Strafen, sichernde und andere Massnahmen, Zweiter Abschnitt: Die Strafzumessung, 1. Allgemeine Regel, Art. 63.

[1249] Remmelink 1994 (*supra* nt. 293), p. 820.

[1250] CAS 93/109, 31-8-1994, Fédération Française de Triathlon (FFTri) and ITU Advisory Opinion, Matthieu Reeb, ed., *Digest of CAS Awards 1986-1998* (Berne, Editions Stämpfli 1998) pp. 457-475; CAS 95/122, 5-3-1996, *National Wheelchair Basketball Association (NWBA) v. IPC*, Matthieu Reeb, ed., *Digest of CAS Awards 1986-1998* (Berne, Editions Stämpfli 1998) pp. 173-185; CAS 95/150, 28-6-1996, *Volker v. FINA*, Matthieu Reeb, ed., *Digest of CAS Awards 1986-1998* (Berne, Editions Stämpfli 1998) pp. 265-274; CAS 95/141, 22-4-1996, *Chagnaud v. FINA*, Matthieu Reeb, ed., *Digest of CAS Awards 1986-1998* (Berne, Editions Stämpfli 1998) pp. 205-224; CAS 96/156, 6-10-1997, *Jessica K. Foschi v. FINA*; CAS 98/214, 8-1-1999, *Bouras v. FIJ*, Matthieu Reeb, ed., *Digest of CAS Awards II 1998-2000* (The Hague, Kluwer Law International 2002) pp. 291-324; CAS 99/A/234 & CAS 99/A/235, 29-2-2000, *David Meca-Medina v. FINA & Igor Majcen v. FINA*, CAS 99/A/239, 14-4-2000, *UCI v. Möller, Danmarks Idraets-Vorbund and Danmarks Cykle Union*; CAS 2000/A/317, 9-7-2001, *F. Aanes v. FILA*.

embraced strictly fixed penalties with more enthusiasm than was truly advisable."[1251] In *National Wheelchair Basketball Association (NWBA) v. International Paralympic Committee (IPC)*[1252] the CAS considered that: "rule 1.1.4 [of the ICC anti-doping regulations] creates a regime that does not accommodate considerations of proportionality. Whether more flexible rules are desirable is a matter for debate within the appropriate governing bodies; they cannot be imposed by this Panel." This statement suggests that the CAS as an arbitration body only remains passive where the determination of the sanction is concerned. This impression is however dispelled in other decisions. In *David Meca-Medina v. FINA & Igor Majcen v. FINA*[1253] the panel reasoned as follows:

"The Panel has considered whether the doctrine of proportionality can be applied in reduction of the penalty. In general, associations such as FINA enjoy broad autonomy according to Swiss law, particularly in relation to disciplinary matters:[1254] see e.g. Article 72 of the Swiss Civil Code allowing such an association to expel a member without providing reasons therefor pursuant to properly drafted rules.

Since the hearing the Appellants have supplied the Panel with an opinion of Professor M. Baddeley of the University of Geneva dated 20th February 2000 which confirms the relevance of the doctrine of proportionality in inter alia the Swiss Law of Sports Associations. However the Panel is already alive to that: moreover her views on the applicability of the principles and on the transfer of the burden of proof to the athlete are inconsistent with the decision of the Swiss Federal Court in *Wang v. FINA* (5P. 83/1999) which vindicates the FINA rules in terms of Swiss law.

The Panel recognizes that (i) a four year ban for an athlete is or may be tantamount to a life ban, given the short span of such a person's sporting career. (ii) Many international sporting federations now stipulate for a two year, not four year minimum suspension.[1255] (iii) These Appellants are first offenders: (iv) there has been no repetition of the offence since its commission (v) the Panel has not been obliged to find that the Appellants were guilty of negligence or worse (although the Appellants have not proved otherwise).

The Panel in those circumstances concludes that the Appellant's sentence can properly be reduced by reference to proportionality considerations. While it bears in mind that in two recent cases[1256] bans of four years by FINA were upheld, these predated the new Olympic Antidoping Code in force as from 1st January 2000. Moreover, each case turns necessarily on its own facts and in those cases the violations were more blatantly culpable."

[1251] Project no. C 116-15, Legal Comparison and Harmonisation of Doping Rules, sub 5.

[1252] CAS 95/122, 5-3-1996, *National Wheelchair Basketball Association (NWBA) v. IPC*, Matthieu Reeb, ed., *Digest of CAS Awards 1986-1998* (Berne, Editions Stämpfli 1998) pp. 173-185, ground 37.

[1253] CAS 2000/A/270, 23-5-2001, *David Meca-Medina v. FINA & Igor Majcen v. FINA*, grounds 9.9-9.12.

[1254] See Perrin, *Droit Civil V, Droit de l'association* (Fribourg Ed. Universitaires 1992).

[1255] IAAF, FIBA, AIBA, ICF, FIH, FIG; see also Antidoping Code of the Olympic Movement, Ch. 2, Art. 3.

[1256] CAS 98/208, 22-12-1998, *Wang Lu Na, Cai Hui Jue, Zhgang Yi, Wang Wei v. FINA*, Matthieu Reeb, ed., *Digest of CAS Awards II 1998-2000* (The Hague, Kluwer Law International 2002) pp. 234-254. CAS 98/211, 7-6-1999, *Smith-De Bruin v. FINA*, Matthieu Reeb, ed., *Digest of CAS Awards II 1998-2000* (The Hague, Kluwer Law International 2002) pp. 255-273.

Initially the panel for legalistic reasons was not prepared to examine the athletes' argument that the principle of proportionality should be considered in their case, now that the Swiss Civil Code allowed associations to expel members without having to state its reasons. However, Ms Baddeley's opinion which was also based on Swiss private law caused the panel to change its mind. The line of reasoning which had its source in the NWBA decision could have been extended by the panel with the support of a ruling of the highest Swiss instance in the case of *Wang et al. v. FINA*. Nevertheless, the panel decided to embrace Ms Baddeley's arguments and found that a four-year suspension for a first offence was disproportionate. This decision shows that the CAS does not consider its previous case law to constitute binding precedent, judging from the fact that no mention whatsoever is made of the Bouras case[1257] in which the CAS held that two years' suspension was disproportionate in the circumstances.[1258] However, in Bouras it was not hinted anywhere that the panel required a basis in the law to found its decision on. It was enough for the panel to point to the athlete's outstanding moral character as confirmed by different French authorities.[1259] Furthermore, all previous controls had had negative results.[1260] Bouras had only ingested doping substances once, and this had been under inexplicable circumstances due to inexplicable causes.[1261] All this led the panel to hold that it would neither be proportionate, nor fair to punish Bouras in the same way as athletes who actively and consistently used prohibited substances.[1262] The IOC Medical Code and the FIJ anti-doping rules provided for fixed penalties; in other words, their disciplinary bodies did not enjoy any margin of discretion by which they could vary the period of suspension in accordance with the circumstances of each particular case. The panel here referred to the relevant considerations in NWBA and Chagnaud.[1263] The panel was not comfortable with fixed sanctions and argued in favour of flexible sanctions:

[1257] CAS 98/214, 8-1-1999, *Bouras v. FIJ*, Matthieu Reeb, ed., *Digest of CAS Awards II 1998-2000* (The Hague, Kluwer Law International 2002) pp. 291-324. The CAS, in CAS 2000/A/270, 23-5-2001, *David Meca-Medina v. FINA & Igor Majcen v. FINA*, does refer to *Bouras v. FIJ* in connection with other aspects unrelated to the proportionality of the sanction.

[1258] Cf. the CAS in Aanes (CAS 2000/A/317, 9-7-2001, *F. Aanes v. FILA*): "Even though it is well established that a two-year suspension for a first time doping offence is legally acceptable, there are several CAS decisions according to which a sanction may not be disproportionate and must always reflect the extent of the athlete's guilt."

[1259] "L'appelant jouit d'une excellente moralité, attestée tant par les différentes autorités française [...]."

[1260] "Enfin, comme déjà indiqué, la Formation tient pour établi que l'appelant ne s'est pas soumis à des prises répétées d'agents anabolisants, ce qui expliquerait que ses tests ont toujours été négatifs avant et après Ie contrôle du 2 octobre 1997."

[1261] "L'appelant doit donc être considéré comme ayant ponctuellement absorbé, dans des circonstances et pour des raisons inexpliquées, des substances prohibées."

[1262] "En pareilles circonstances, il ne serait ni adéquat ni équitable de sanctionner l'appelant de la même manière que l'eût été un autre sportif convaincu de dopage actif, dans Ie cadre d'une cure ou d'un programma structuré et répété."

[1263] CAS 95/141, 22-4-1996, *Chagnaud v. FINA*, Matthieu Reeb, ed., *Digest of CAS Awards 1986-1998* (Berne, Editions Stämpfli 1998) pp. 205-224. In this case the position argued earlier by the FINA

"[...] un système fixe de tarification régissant les sanctions en cas de dopage n'est pas souhaitable et un système plus souple, prévoyant des fourchettes dans la durée des suspensions en fonction de la culpabilité de l'athlète, est préférable. Le TAS a même considéré que le règlement sur le contrôle du dopage d'une fédération internationale, prévoyant un système de sanctions fixes, pouvait être modulé en fonction des circonstances propres à chaque cas, pour autant que cette modulation fasse l'objet d'une motivation spéciale."

The question of whether the panel was bound by the fixed penalty prescribed by the sports organisation was answered in the negative,[1264] as this would have given rise to a real danger of unequal treatment in the future between the case under consideration and other much more serious cases. The panel decided to deviate from the rigid penalties under both the Medical Code and the Fédération Internationale de Judo's (FIJ) anti-doping regulations. The panel eventually imposed 15 months' suspension on Bouras.

"En s'en tenant à la règle stricte des deux ans de suspension, la Formation du TAS donnerait naissance à un risque concret d'aboutir à l'avenir à des inégalités de traitement entre le présent cas et des cas plus graves qui pourraient surgir. Elle considère dès lors qu'il convient de s'écarter de la sanction rigide prévue par le Code médical et par le Règlement antidopage de la FIJ. [...] Sur la base de l'ensemble des circonstances, la Formation estime ainsi qu'une suspension d'une durée de quinze mois est adéquate en l'espèce."

Another salient point in this case was that the amount of nandrolone metabolites found in Bouras's sample was not in fact negligibly low. On the contrary, it was abnormally high, and Bouras could offer no explanation.[1265]

If the application of criminal law principles to disciplinary doping proceedings had been recognised in this case this would have resulted in the direct application of Article 63 of the Swiss Criminal Code, which provides the proportionality prin-

---

in Riley that it was possible under certain circumstances to deviate from the fixed penalty of two years' suspension inspired the imposition upon Chagnaud of a penalty that was less severe than the fixed penalty provided under the rules. "[...] the Panel feels that it can apply art. 4.17.4.1 MED more flexibly, in the same way as FINA did, and examine the severity of the sanction imposed on C. taking into account her degree of fault."

[1264] On 9 February 2002 the following item appeared on the German Sportgericht website [http://www.sportgericht.de]: "CAS erhöht Sperre von Jovanovic auf zwei Jahre – Der US-amerikanische Bobfahrer Pavle Jovanovic wurde vom Internationalen Sportgerichtshof (CAS) für zwei Jahre gesperrt. Jovanovic wurde im Dezember letzten Jahres positiv auf Nandrolon getestet. Der Internationale Bob-Verband (FIBT) hatte ihn daraufhin für neun Monate gesperrt. Der angerufene CAS entschied nun auf die höhere Zwei-Jahres-Sperre, da die Statuten des Verbandes nur diese vorsehen würden. Eine Abweichung ist nicht möglich. Brisanz gewinnt in die Entscheidung, da der CAS im Hinweis auf die Verbandsautonomie eine jüngst die Drei-Monats-Sperre des Bobfahrers Prusis gegenüber dem IOC bestätigte."

[1265] "D'un autre côté, il convient aussi de prendre en compte la présence importante de métabolites de la nandrolone découvertes dans l'organisme de l'appelant, á des taux anormalement élevés, ce que ce dernier ne parvient pas à expliquer."

ciple. The CAS has several times recognised the application of the proportionality principle, but never based on Article 63. If it had applied this provision, however, this would have prevented it from time and again having to change its position concerning the principle due to the fact that it based itself on private law, despite the fact that imposing a penalty for a doping offence cannot but serve a punitive goal. The penalty connects the offence to this goal.

In the words of Remmelink, it should not be forgotten that: "the penalty has to convey a message. It has to convey disapproval and should temper any desire for imitation. Last but not least, persons who have been sentenced must be treated with the necessary fairness and humanity. Any form of justice that ignores these objectives would not be able to function in our culture."[1266]

8. CONCLUSION

Due to the internationally recognised freedom of association, sports organisation in principle are allowed to draft their own rules for disciplinary doping procedures. Bearing this fact in mind, in this section disciplinary doping law's position within the legal framework and the category of law to which it belongs have been discussed. It has been examined whether we should position disciplinary doping law within the field of private law due to its origin in the law of associations. The criterion used in this examination was that of voluntariness. It has been established that professional and especially top athletes are not as free to decline to join an association as for example stamp collectors are to decline membership of the stamp collectors society. Based on the criterion of voluntariness, disciplinary doping law must be recognised as having more in common with criminal law than with private law. This makes it pseudo-criminal law, which means that although disciplinary doping proceedings cannot be called criminal proceedings as such, criminal law principles should still have a perceptible effect on them. The application of generally and internationally recognised criminal law and criminal procedural law principles and concepts to disciplinary doping proceedings does not only contribute to the careful and respectful treatment of the athlete but also renders disciplinary doping law more transparent and increases legal certainty for the parties. This cannot be achieved by the application of a cocktail of principles and concepts from different fields of law, as the case law of the CAS has made clear.

After having come to this conclusion, it was again examined how free the drafters of the associations' doping regulations truly are to include in these rules any provisions that they see fit. Are there limits to their discretionary powers in this respect? This does not seem to be the case. National law interferes only marginally in the regulation of the relationship between associations and their members and between the members themselves. The only visible constraints derive from the ECHR, in particular from Article 6. It was then discussed whether the Convention

---

[1266] Remmelink 1994 (*supra* nt. 293), p. 821.

as such can be said to apply to disciplinary doping proceedings. After this had been established, it had to be examined whether the fair trial rights of Article 6 ECHR could be said to apply to disciplinary doping proceedings. Several arguments for and against can be found in the literature, but one in favour that is most convincing is that paragraph 1 of Article 6 *inter alia* provides that: "in the determination of his civil rights and obligations everyone is entitled to a fair and public hearing within a reasonable time by an independent and impartial tribunal established by law." Although it can be argued based on the wording of this provision that it only applies to legal disputes, this would be too strict an interpretation as this would unacceptably limit the protection which the provision aims to offer. Article 6(1) can thus be considered to apply to disciplinary doping proceedings. It is fixed case law of the ECtHR that the imposition of penalties must be preceded by a procedure in which the rights granted under Article 6 are taken into account. The way in which Article 6 is drafted is not as clear-cut as it would seem with three paragraphs each giving separate guarantees, but on closer inspection, especially of the case law of the ECtHR it emerges that Article 6 must be considered *in toto*. Its three paragraphs must therefore be interpreted together. The concept of fair trial is further explained in the three paragraphs, but must be considered as one indivisible notion. This means that an accused athlete who is denied any of the rights granted in paragraphs 2 and 3 cannot be said to have had a fair hearing in accordance with paragraph 1.

The *in dubio pro reo* principle laid down in paragraph 2 of Article 6 is of particular significance to the present study. In an important decision of the CAS, the tribunal considered that the benefit of the doubt is a manifestation of one of the most important legal presumptions, the presumption of innocence, which is deeply enshrined in the general principles of law and justice. The principle can be regarded as both a fair trial right and an internationally recognised fundamental principle of law. Although the principle is most visible in criminal law, it should in the first place be regarded as "deeply enshrined in the general principles of law and justice." The presumption of innocence of Article 6(2) is of great importance in a strict liability environment. The guarantee which it offers that everyone charged with a criminal offence shall be presumed innocent until proven guilty in accordance with the law is not easily reconciled with a presumption of liability which does not even allow the accused an opportunity to exonerate him/herself.

The survey of the various doping regulations of both national and international sports organisations suggests that organisations' rulemakers were largely unaware that their finished product had to comply with the requirements of Article 6 ECHR. Only two international federations expressly recognised the athlete's right to a defence as such, i.e. to the *in toto* fair trial of Article 6. The remaining organisations had scattered the various fair trial rights quite randomly over the different regulations and never included the full catalogue as provided in Article 6 ECHR. Most regulations did however provide for the right to be heard. This right forms the essence of Article 6, with the other rights serving as examples of how the right to be heard can best be realised. This means that once the right to be heard is laid down, it covers all the other rights that are intended to support it.

The doping cases decided by the various disciplinary bodies of sports organisations are rarely published. However, some CAS judgments delivered on appeal
briefly reveal how lower instances have dealt with fair trial rights. Nevertheless,
even these brief glimpses are rare, given that the CAS deals with each case *de novo*
which means that the panel has full power to review the facts and the law. In this
way, possible violations of the rights of the athlete are automatically "repaired" in
the full review process and are therefore not an issue for consideration. Still,
despite the fact that the CAS has never directly referred to Article 6 ECHR, the
brief glimpses mentioned and the few times that the CAS has pronounced on fair
trial issues are sufficient evidence to conclude that the CAS considers that the sports
organisations must respect the athletes' right to be heard as a fundamental principle
of due process.

Remedies at law are usually not placed under the umbrella of the rights to a fair
trial. However, especially in disciplinary proceedings they can be crucial for cor-
recting possible violations of fair trial rights by lower instances, in particular regarding the issue of impartiality of the tribunal. The majority of doping regulations
provide for some form of appeal, and at times even for cassation. Often, the CAS is
designated as the final instance for appeal.

Apart from fair trial rights a different set of rights deriving more directly from
criminal law should logically also be applied to the pseudo-criminal law doping
proceedings, namely the fundamental principles of criminal law. Due to the lack of
published relevant decisions of the various sports organisations' disciplinary tribunals the available CAS decisions have been discussed to examine which criminal
law principles are applied and how.

The *nulla poena sine lege scripta* principle provides that there can be no punishment of a crime without this having been laid down in a prior criminal law. The
CAS has applied it in cases where the prohibition of certain unlisted or insufficiently listed substances was at issue. Inextricably bound up with the *nulla poena*
principle is the principle of *lex certa* which stipulates that the description of an
offence has to be as precise as possible. Without the *lex certa* principle, it would be
possible to fulfil the *nulla poena* principle with a minimum of effort through very
broadly worded provisions. The *nulla poena* and *lex certa* principles do not only
address the legislator, but also the courts, which have to match the rules with the
acts brought before them. In this sense, they could be said to restrict judicial discretion, given that the decision of whether a criminal offence has been committed in
the first place depends on the description of the offence provided.

The *ne bis in idem* principle is deeply rooted in national and international law
systems. It represents justice as well as fairness. The principle protects against
multiple prosecution and punishment of the same offence. Here, the principle has
only been examined against the background of multiple disciplinary proceedings. It
is not applied to concurrent disciplinary and criminal prosecution. The common
law equivalent of the principle, the prohibition of "double jeopardy," has been discussed by the CAS in several decisions, although it could not always prevent double
prosecution or punishment in all of these cases.

The *lex mitior* principle is an internationally accepted fundamental principle of criminal law. It governs situations where a penalty by which a certain offence is punishable has been reduced or otherwise changed to the offender's advantage in the period between the time the offence was committed and the date on which the court is due to decide and even after the initial penalty was imposed. The CAS has recognised this principle as a fundamental principle of any democratic regime.

The proportionality principle is widely recognised and accepted. It prohibits the taking of any measure which in view of its objective must be considered to go beyond what is appropriate and necessary. The application of the principle involves the balancing of the interests of the person or persons affected by the measure and the possibly wider social aim which it is intended to achieve. The CAS has regularly considered whether the doctrine of proportionality could be applied in reduction of a penalty. The application of fixed penalties for doping offences made it difficult to weigh the severity of the offence against the severity of the penalty. Nevertheless, as the CAS on one occasion concluded, when the circumstances of the case so allowed the appellant's sentence could properly be reduced by reference to proportionality considerations.

The main conclusions to be drawn from this chapter are, first, that the full catalogue of fair trial rights as provided in Article 6 ECHR can be directly applied in disciplinary doping proceedings which take place in the area covered by the Convention and, second, that due to disciplinary doping law's predominantly criminal law characteristics, fundamental principles of criminal law and criminal procedural law must also apply to disciplinary doping proceedings. The application of these principles and concepts to disciplinary doping proceedings does not only contribute to the careful and respectful treatment of the athlete but also renders disciplinary doping law more transparent and increases legal certainty for the parties. This cannot be achieved by the application of a cocktail of principles and concepts from different fields of law.

GENERAL SUMMARY AND CONCLUSIONS

Athletes who achieve extraordinary feats on the pitch stir up the imagination and enjoy a unique position within society. However, laurels received one day, may be just as quickly snatched back the next if it becomes known that the athlete achieved his or her exceptional performance with the aid of doping. Manipulating the body by the use of substances and methods that unnaturally enhance athletic performance is considered a violation of several fundamental principles related to sport. The arguments by which sports organisations have sought to justify their fight against doping have been discussed in Chapter 1. Doping is considered a health risk, but also a threat to both athletes' integrity and that of sport as a whole, and consequently, given the position in society occupied by sport, of that of society itself. None of these arguments, however, is entirely convincing. Perhaps this is why many sports organisations have declined to state reasons for their anti-doping policies in their anti-doping regulations. The fight against doping in sport is considered self-evident and the arguments which are advanced in its favour merely serve to illustrate this fact.

It was only a relatively short time ago that the systematic fight against doping in sport through legal rules began. As a separate body of disciplinary law besides their regular disciplinary rules the sports organisations established special anti-doping regulations for the prosecution and punishment of doping offences. As opposed to under general disciplinary law where unwritten minimum standards usually apply, the disciplinary law of doping uses detailed material rules which define the act of doping and the way in which it is to be punished. As such, the disciplinary law concerning doping resembles the statutory disciplinary rules that exist for certain professions, but is also comparable to public punitive law. What sets disciplinary doping law apart however is that the material rules do not aim to regulate the actual exercise of a profession, but are based on the ideological aspects which prevail in the environment where an athlete's activities take place. In disciplinary doping law, for example, there are hardly any examples of professional error, but rather of acts which undermine the image and ethics of the sport. This is an aspect which it has in common with criminal law. Disciplinary doping law which mainly aims to regulate the relevant offences and their prosecution and punishment should therefore be organised along the same lines as criminal law and entitle athletes to certain rights to counter the demands of the collective. This is necessary, as in sport the interests of the collective are often valued above those of the individual.

It is an illusion to assume that doping in sport can be eliminated by means of anti-doping regulations – an illusion, moreover, which might easily result in fanaticism and inquisition. A more reasonable assumption and indeed objective is that doping may become an unattractive option as a result of regulation. Doping in sport is a very real phenomenon which cannot be eradicated simply by appealing to the athletes' own responsibility and ethics. For this reason, we need rules. Personal responsibility is replaced by a duty to comply with these rules; ethical standards are replaced by legal standards.

Chapter 2 discusses and analyses the material rules in force under the disciplinary law of doping. These rules are the descriptions of the doping offence with the definition of the act of doping at their core. The rules in question can be divided into two categories. Into one category fall the rules which make the use of doping an offence (use offences) and in the other category we find rules that make it an offence to prevent the use of doping from being detected (non-use offences). The category of use offences can be once more divided into use by the athlete and third-party assistance in use by the athlete.

In the case of use offences, the sports organisations initially prohibited the use of unspecified substances which were considered to enhance athletic performance. This produced a definition that went to the "essence" of the act of doping. However, as the interests vested in the business that sport also is began to increase, both from a commercial point of view and from the perspective of athletic prestige, athletes who were accused of doping would more and more often seek legal counsel. The lawyers representing the athletes regularly directed the proceedings in such a way that the prosecuting organisation was given the onus of demonstrating first of all that the substance or method used was indeed capable of enhancing athletic performance and secondly that the athlete had actually intended to enhance his/her performance by his/her use of doping. This was virtually impossible for the sports organisations to prove, which forced many organisations to abandon the "essential" definition of doping. Instead they drew up lists of prohibited substances and methods which were considered capable of enhancing athletic performance and provided that doping was the use of any substance or method on the list. In the course of time, however, it emerged that this definition of doping also failed to meet practical requirements. The fact that the athlete had tested positive was still insufficient to be able to punish him/her as the athlete could always argue that he/she was not to blame, for example, because a third party had administered the substance without his/her knowledge. Again sports organisations faced insurmountable evidentiary problems and again they had to conceive of a new description to make their attempts to prosecute doping offenders more successful. The solution which they arrived at was pragmatic – they shifted the focus from the human act of use to the factual circumstance of detection of such use. Descriptions were now as follows: "the offence of doping takes place when a prohibited substance is found to be present within an athlete's body tissue or fluids." This constitutes a presumption of liability.

Now that disciplinary doping law in contrast to other fields of disciplinary law includes strictly worded material rules, the subjective element of illegality should occupy an important place in that law. An act of doping only becomes a punishable doping offence when it falls within the scope of the offence description and is illegal and culpable. Chapter 3 deals with the illegality of the doping act.

Prosecuting sports organisations are not required to prove every time that a material rule is violated that the challenged act was illegal. Illegality is presumed as soon as the sports organisation has established the objective elements of the offence. If the defence intends to show that illegality was lacking, it can start doing so from the moment the athlete is involved in the proceedings. If the athlete succeeds in this defence, he/she must be acquitted due to a lack of punishability of the act.

The issue of illegality may be divided into two aspects. On the one hand, lack of illegality can be argued based on technical grounds, such as gaps in the chain of custody, while on the other it may be based on legal grounds, such as the use of a substance which does not appear on the doping list. Given the provisions laid down in most doping regulations concerning the chain of custody it was very difficult for the defence to prove that a gap had occurred in the chain and that this gap affected the integrity of the samples. Showing that mistakes had been made at the laboratory was even more difficult than proving that mistakes had been made during the taking of the samples and their transportation. Before the adoption of the WADC, most anti-doping regulations took it as their starting point that laboratory tests and analyses were conducted in accordance with the highest scientific standards, providing for example that: "Laboratories are presumed to have conducted testing and custodial procedures in accordance with prevailing and acceptable standards of care. The presumption can be rebutted by evidence to the contrary but the laboratory shall have no onus in the first instance to show that it conducted the procedures other than in accordance with its customary practices." It should also be noted that the defence was only very rarely given access to the full laboratory report. Any attack on the chain of custody at the laboratory therefore often had the nature of a "fishing expedition."

The athlete could also rely on lack of illegality by basing him/herself on various legal grounds. One example was when he/she was being prosecuted for use of a substance which did not appear on the list or which did appear on the list, but for whose use he/she had been given permission by the competent authorities. It was also possible to invoke lack of illegality in case the athlete's own body produced the substances. The rule that was once so clear and provided that the presence of certain substances in the athlete's sample established an offence became increasingly flexible with the development of new scientific insights concerning these substances. Medical science after some time discovered that various substances could in fact be endogenous. The grey area between the natural production of certain substances and the level at which it could no longer be disputed that they had been administered artificially gave rise to much scientific debate.

As regards disciplinary law in general, it can be debated whether guilt and intent are or can be elements of a disciplinary offence and whether these elements have to be interpreted according to private law or criminal law. Here too, the disciplinary law concerning doping differs from regular disciplinary law in that guilt is not only an element, but a prominent element of the doping offence in a way comparable to the criminal law element of guilt. For the actual punishment of an athlete (or a third party) for the use of doping substances or methods it is not only relevant that his/her actions fall within the limits of the description of the doping offence (the material rule), but also that these actions are culpable. The subjective element in the description of the doping offence, i.e. guilt or intent, is the focus of Chapter 4.

By means of a description resulting in a presumption of liability the burden of proof is reversed as soon as a prohibited substance is found in an athlete's body tissue or fluids. The sports organisations considered that such a description obviated the need to establish any kind of link between the finding of the substance and the athlete's volition to commit the offence. The interpretation of the new offence description gradually shifted from a presumption of guilt to a presumption of liability. If the outcome of the analysis was positive, this had to be taken as proof of the intentional use of a prohibited substance and had to result in the automatic imposition of sanctions. This approach by the sports organisations which exclusively focused on the consequences of the punishable act and established the athlete's strict liability was regularly discussed in the case law of the CAS. In various decisions the tribunal considered that if a sports organisation opted to punish the consequences of a violation of the rules rather than the violation itself the causal link between the violation and its consequences had to be established conclusively and unambiguously. Only when the causal link could be thus shown the burden of proof would be reversed, according to the CAS. It was not difficult for sports organisations to show this link as the CAS interpreted the offence description by which the burden of proof shifted in accordance with the sports organisations' wishes. The burden of proof did not shift during the stage of the proceedings in which it had to be decided whether the athlete had culpably committed a doping offence, but only during the stage of the proceedings in which the penalty was determined. This excluded any possibility for the athlete to exonerate him/herself; all that remained was a possibility to plead for a penalty that was related to the degree of his/her guilt.

A system which for pragmatic reasons and reasons of procedural economics starts from a presumption of liability is not necessarily unfair as long as the accused is given the opportunity to submit evidence by which he/she can show that he/she cannot be held liable. The system of strict liability took this one step further because the athlete was not given any opportunity to exonerate him/herself so as to secure his/her acquittal.

The strict liability system was at times criticised in the legal literature for allegedly violating the fundamental right of the athlete to prove his/her innocence, but the main critic of the system was in fact the CAS itself. In the Aanes case, which was decided by a panel consisting entirely of civil law lawyers as opposed to the panels which had decided previous strict liability cases that had been made up exclusively of common law lawyers, the CAS considered that: "as a matter of principle [...] an athlete cannot be banned from competition for having committed a doping offence unless he is guilty, i.e. he has acted with intent or negligence. Even if the rules and regulations of a sports federation do not expressly provide that the guilt of the athlete has to be taken into account the foregoing principle will have to be read into these rules to make them legally acceptable." The panel members deciding this case realised that the strict liability rule was not compatible with the nulla poena sine culpa principle which was enshrined in their own legal systems. They attempted to do justice to the element of guilt by starting from a rebuttable presumption of liability through the introduction of the "Anscheinsbeweis" (*prima facie* evidence) as applied in Swiss and German law. It seems, however, that the Aanes judgment should be considered a one-off, as subsequent CAS panels counting among their members one or more common law lawyers proved unwilling to follow this theory and resumed the reasoning of panels in previous strict liability decisions.

Apart from using doping or participating in the doping use of others, a number of other acts may also constitute a doping offence (ancillary doping infractions). Under many of the doping regulations, an athlete would commit a doping offence when he/she failed to report for doping control or refused to undergo such a control. Not only was the athlete who refused to cooperate in doping control fully liable for this refusal, it was also assumed that this included full liability for the doping offence itself.

A doping offence may also consist of the fact that an athlete admits to having used doping. Of course, athletes are free to admit to having used a prohibited substance, but they have to be aware of the fact that by doing so they may manoeuvre themselves into the same position as an athlete who has tested positive.

As to the issue of participation, under Dutch criminal law for example participants must be aware of all the elements of the offence. If one takes the position that participants fall within the same strict liability regime as perpetrators by *prima facie* presuming such awareness, this makes the question of the object of the participant's intent irrelevant. In fact, any differentiation as to the nature of the participation (accession, encouragement, incitement, etc.) which under criminal law makes a difference for the punishability of the offence becomes irrelevant when the participant is held strictly liable.

If an athlete's actions fall within the scope of the description of the doping offence, and these actions are illegal and culpable, the sports organisation may proceed to punish the athlete. The different penalties by which this may be done are examined in Chapter 5. This chapter also discusses team sanctions and sanctions that are imposed during play (termed "sport sanctions," such as disqualification or a red card).

Doping lists distinguish between prohibited classes of substances and prohibited methods ("hard doping") on the one hand, and classes of drugs subject to certain restrictions ("soft doping") on the other. Use of the first category of doping substances and methods is never permitted; the use of second category substances and methods is, provided that they have been prescribed by a doctor and the competent authorities have given their consent. The sports organisations apply different penalties for each category. Penalties for the unauthorised use of soft doping are usually less severe than for the use of hard doping. For example, athletes are not banned for life for the use of soft doping until they test positive for the third time, whereas in case of hard doping, athletes may already be excluded for life after testing positive a second time. Prior to the adoption of the WADC each sport imposed different sanctions for similar offences. Several federations used fixed sanctions, but others used flexible ones and allowed the seriousness of the offence to be taken into consideration. The margin of discretion allowed between a minimum and a maximum penalty meant that sanctions for the same offence could also vary per case within one single federation. There are arguments to be found in favour of both fixed and flexible sanctions. With fixed sanctions, for example, there is the advantage of predictability, legal certainty and equal treatment; the disadvantage, however, is that they may be disproportionate. The seriousness of the offence could be greatly at odds with the severity of the penalty imposed. Flexible sanctions certainly improve proportionality: the seriousness of the offence is actively assessed and reflected in the sanction. The disadvantage of flexible sanctions is, however, that they may be subjective. Given the fact that doping panels continually change their composition, considerations as to the offence's gravity and the gravity of the sanction might also change. Another possibility is that different countries consider different sanctions reasonable (and may thus be prepared or unprepared in different cases to enforce the sanction). This means that the nationality of the athlete who has been penalised may also play a role. Given all these possible variations, it would be welcome if the CAS fulfilled a regulatory function in this respect.

Sanctions to be imposed by sports organisations have to reflect the seriousness of the athlete's offence. In other words: it is essential that in sanctioning the respective fundamental rights of the associations on the one hand and those of the athlete on the other are balanced. Although the imposition of a penalty by a sports organisation on an athlete who is bound by the organisational hierarchy is legitimate in the framework of the law of associations, a lengthy suspension or a ban may interfere with the athlete's fundamental rights. This is especially so where professional athletes are concerned. The principle of proportionality makes it necessary to weigh the interests of the individual athlete against the interests of the sports organisation. The call for increasingly tougher sanctions for doping offences is limited by what in society is considered proportional. The liberalisation of the ineligibility rule has opened the door for the intrusion of domestic law and national judges into the domain of sports and for protection by them of the individual athlete against interferences in the domestic legal order by the sports organisations. The principle of proportionality means striking a balance between the seriousness of the offence and the seriousness of the sentence. In imposing a sanction, it must always be considered that the period of the suspension is not the only penalty, but that it includes related – sometimes far-reaching – effects, such as loss of income, cancelled sponsoring contracts, loss of media exposure, etc., and – last but not least – loss of profession, because at the end of the period of ineligibility the athlete is often too old still to achieve a top performance. In some sports a two-year ban will cause no problems whatsoever, but in others, where the professional life-span of athletes is short, two years can mean life. The re-introduction of fixed sanctions makes it next to impossible to translate the seriousness of the offence into a proportional sanction. Penalties for doping offences should not be unified, they should be harmonised, which means that their impact in one sport should be the same as in another sport.

Athletes may appeal to the right of free exercise of a profession if punished by exclusion. Disciplinary measures and suspension because of the use of doping can clash with the constitutionally protected right to employment. When doping rules offer the opportunity to suspend an athlete over a considerable period of time, such rules should not lead to an "unreasonable restraint of trade." Pursuant to English common law restraint principles the factors to be taken into consideration when determining whether a rule of a sports governing body is in restraint of trade are as follows: is the individual sportsman/sportswoman involved in a recognised trade? And, does the relevant clause within the rules or contract restrain the sportsman or woman in their trade? If the answer to those questions is positive, then the restraint will be unenforceable unless it is reasonable. The sports organisation must prove reasonableness in the circumstances. The burden of proof is therefore reversed when the athlete is able to show that a certain provision in the doping regulations results in "restraint of trade." The imposition of a life-long ban will only be upheld in extremely exceptional cases before the courts in enforcement order/annulment proceedings. This is also true for the four-year ban for a first doping offence. This sanction will in every case result in the inability to freely exercise one's profession. The exceptional severity of such exclusion lies in the fact that it makes it impossible for athletes to compete in the next Olympics. However, the situation is different in sports which allow for longer-running careers, such as football and tennis, so that the four-year ban could in principle be imposed there. A two-year suspension for a first doping offence is normally considered acceptable, although not all international federations were in agreement on this.

The WADC provides for sanctions imposable on individual athletes, on teams as a whole and on sports organisations. Doping offences are punishable by two years' exclusion for a first offence and life-long exclusion for a second offence. However, the WADC also provides that periods of ineligibility can be eliminated or reduced based on exceptional circumstances.

In Chapter 6 the framework within which disciplinary doping law operates and the type of law that governs disciplinary doping proceedings is discussed. Disciplinary law originates from associations and is therefore governed by the law of associations, which in turn is part of private law. Within the limits of the law of association, sports organisations are free to organise themselves and to enact codes of conduct and rules for the enforcement of these codes. The anti-doping regulations of sports organisations are such codes of conduct. Does it then follow from this that disciplinary doping law is part of private law? This question is often answered in the affirmative in the literature and in case law, but this is not the conclusion that is reached in this study. In order to assess where exactly a certain body of disciplinary law should be positioned within the framework of the different areas of law the criterion of "voluntary presence in the group" may be used. Given the factual forced subjection of professional athletes to the jurisdiction and rules of sports clubs and federations this criterion alone would be sufficient to decide by that disciplinary doping law bears more resemblance to that other punitive law system, criminal law, than to private law. However, this position can be backed up by further arguments. Misconduct in the form of a doping offence is only punishable if this behaviour has beforehand been expressly qualified as such in doping regulations. Under criminal law, this starting point is known as the principle of legality.

Like criminal law, disciplinary doping law is punitive law in which the rights and duties of the various sports organisations' investigative officers in the enforcement of the material rules are laid down. The description of the doping offence is also strikingly similar to offence descriptions in criminal law. A material rule consisting of a narrowly defined undesirable act (the doping offence) is linked to a particular penalty. As is the case in criminal law, in disciplinary doping law the material rules present guidelines for the athlete's future conduct. In addition, when applied by a disciplinary tribunal they are also standards to retrospectively assess the athlete's behaviour by. Finally, the third function of material rules also applies in disciplinary doping law, namely that they give rise to legitimate expectations concerning the behaviour of the self and especially that of others.

By testing the behaviour of an athlete against the material rule – which thus lies at the root of the description of the offence – it may be established whether this behaviour is illegal. Illegality is one of the conditions for punishability. Couched in criminal law terms, a doping offence is a punishable act, consisting of a human act, which falls within the scope of the description of the doping offence, is illegal and is imputable to guilt. Especially the element of guilt is important in the description of the definitions of doping. In this book the criminal law meaning of guilt and intent is used. Guilt (*culpa*) is understood to mean that the perpetrator should have known, while intent is understood to mean that he knew.

By nature penalties under doping law bear a strong and unmistakable resemblance to penalties under criminal law. After all, the sanctions in doping rules do not aim to re-establish the situation that would have existed if the offence had not taken place, as would be the case under private law, but are instead intended to punish. Being excluded from competition for two years for a first doping offence and for life for a second offence cannot be considered anything other than punishment. In sports, other misconduct is also punished, but not as severely as doping offences. Indeed, from the severity of doping offences it can be concluded that they are considered to be in a league of their own.

The description of the doping offence is the trait-d'union between the substantive (material) law and adjective (procedural) disciplinary law on doping. With the adjective description the focus is on the act; this act is already contrary to the doping prohibition and punishable in itself. Such descriptions lead to a constitutive result. Substantive descriptions, by contrast, declare the result of a certain act prohibited and punishable. On the one hand, the description impacts the practical effect of the principle of illegality. A disciplinary law sanction can only be imposed when the facts in a given case correspond to those which were previously described. On the other hand, the description serves to indicate what evidence is required. The description of the doping offence, like the description of the offence in an indictment, indicates what needs to be lawfully proven in order to be able to arrive at the conclusion of punishability. What is true for criminal law, namely that everything contained in the description of the offence in the indictment (and no more) must be proven in accordance with the rules of the procedural criminal law of evidence, is also true for the description of the doping offence under the disciplinary law on doping.

In disciplinary proceedings following a positive doping test the athlete and the prosecuting body occupy more or less the same position as the accused and the prosecution in criminal cases. The parties are in no way equal.

For all these reasons, disciplinary doping law should be regarded as a kind of "pseudo-criminal law." Another argument in favour of this theory may be found in the new WADC. This Code entitles athletes in doping proceedings to all the rights of the defence that according to the ECHR only serve to protect persons against whom criminal charges have been brought. In a punitive system such as provided by disciplinary doping law which has so many criminal law features, criminal law principles have to play an important role. "The disciplinary law of associations is considered part of the private law body of disciplinary law, [...] but there is nothing to prevent the use in this disciplinary law of principles of criminal law in a law of associations framework." This opinion which was advanced in the Dutch literature almost twenty years ago and concerned disciplinary sports law in general, has since acquired particular significance for disciplinary doping law.

Should principles applying under criminal law also apply in the pseudo-criminal disciplinary doping law? There are convincing arguments in favour of the direct applicability of the ECHR to the disciplinary doping proceedings of private law governed sports organisations. The Dutch legislator for example has provided for the possible annulment of arbitral awards if during the proceedings leading up to the award fundamental principles of law have been violated to such an extent that the hearing of the case can no longer be considered to have been fair and impartial. An arbitral award whose content goes against public order requirements or awards that are the result of flawed proceedings from the point of view of public order, whereby public order is considered to include Article 6 ECHR, or where good morals have been violated, must be open to annulment. It would be fair to assume that this is also true for decisions of disciplinary bodies. Another argument in favour of direct applicability is that it would be difficult to reconcile with logic if a state which has ratified the Convention nevertheless allows private law organisations to disregard the Convention by creating a self-contained legal regime where standards prevail that depart from the standards that generally apply in that state. A further argument derives from the rationale underlying the ECHR. The decision of the states parties to establish this legal instrument was partly based on the fact that their domestic laws had many legal principles in common. According to international law "gaps in international law may be filled by borrowing principles which are common to all or most national systems of law." One such gap may be found in the ECHR in respect of its scope of application ratione personae. It can safely be assumed that the drafters of the Convention did not intend to exclude persons who are responsible for establishing the regulations of private law organisations from this scope. In addition, one would be hard put to find a rule in any national system of law which expressly allows private law organisations to depart from national legislation in force and the principles underlying this legislation. For this reason too, one might assume the direct applicability of the fundamental principles laid down in the ECHR to the disciplinary proceedings of sports organisations.

For a long time it was thought that only the words "in the determination of his civil rights and obligations [...]" in Article 6(1) ECHR could pave the way for the applicability of Article 6 and that no argument could be drawn from the words "criminal charge." However, nowadays it is thought that even the words "criminal charge" do not form an insurmountable obstacle, as a punitive sanction always makes the charge "criminal." This is of particular interest to the question at hand, given that several years' suspension can certainly be regarded as a punitive sanction. Van Dijk and Van Hoof urge the Court to end the uncertainty and ambiguity with respect to the term "criminal charge" that has resulted from its case law, especially concerning the nature and severity of the penalty. As to the nature of the penalty, Article 6 should be considered applicable to all proceedings which may result in the imposition of a punitive sanction that as to its nature and/or consequences is so similar to a criminal sanction that there is no justification for excluding it from judicial review. This would include in particular deprivations of liberty and fines, but also concern restrictions of economic or professional freedom of a punitive character (which, moreover, could affect civil rights and obligations). The fines imposed on athletes for their use of doping could therefore also be subsumed under this heading. As far as the severity of the penalty is concerned, it is submitted that, since the Court has adopted the position that Article 6 makes no distinction between serious and less serious offences and that it may even apply to proceedings which lead to no penalty at all, there would seem to be no convincing reason to distinguish between fines of a small and of a large amount for the applicability of Article 6 to disciplinary and administrative proceedings; after all, if the severity of the penalty is not a decisive element for the applicability of Article 6 in case there exists a "criminal charge" it should also not be determinant for the question whether certain proceedings have criminal features which make Article 6 applicable.

From the above it may be concluded that sports organisations are therefore not completely free as to which provisions to include in their disciplinary doping rules. They are bound not only by the concepts of reasonableness and fairness but also by the provisions of Article 6 ECHR. Athletes should at least be able to rely on the right to a fair trial and on fundamental principles of law.

In Chapter 4 it has been explained that the evolution of the description of the doping offence has for now come to a halt at the strict liability rule. The finding of a prohibited substance in an athlete's sample results in an irrebuttable presumption of liability. If one takes the position that the ECHR is applicable to the criminal law-orientated disciplinary law of doping, it soon becomes clear that the strict liability rule and the provisions of Article 6(2) ECHR are strikingly incompatible. The guarantee which this Article offers that everyone charged with a criminal offence shall be presumed innocent until proven guilty in accordance with the law is not easily reconciled with a presumption of liability which does not even allow the accused an opportunity to exonerate him/herself. It is therefore recommended that all sports organisations, or at least those whose seats are within the territory where the ECHR is applicable, amend their doping offence descriptions in such a way that they incorporate the element of guilt. It is also recommended that the WADA do the same. The descriptions could, for example, be "toned down" by introducing a presumption of guilt similar to the German and Swiss Anscheinsbeweis. This would not conflict with the ECHR as a presumption of guilt only violates Article 6(2) if it cannot be rebutted.

In this study it is argued that the disciplinary law concerning doping as essentially punitive law should be regarded as "pseudo-criminal law." Given the striking resemblance between disciplinary doping law and criminal law, private law connotations should not be allowed to intrude in this field. By accepting the analogy between disciplinary doping law and criminal law as this study has done an opening is also created for the analogous application of relevant principles of criminal law, such as the principles of *nulla poena sine lege scripta*, *lex certa* and *ne bis in idem*.

Final statements

1. The disciplinary law concerning doping violations must be considered as pseudo-criminal law.
2. Article 6 ECHR is applicable to disciplinary doping law. The application of the strict liability principle is contrary to Article 6 and should therefore be replaced by the *Anscheinsbeweis*.
3. In disciplinary proceedings concerning doping violations the athlete who is being prosecuted should be entitled to the same rights as are granted to the suspect and accused in criminal proceedings.
4. The harmonisation of sanctions that are imposable for doping violations gives rise to legal inequality.
5. The *lex sportiva* of the CAS can only fully develop if the *stare decisis* principle and the obligation to publish decisions are included in the tribunal's Procedural Rules.

CAS DECISIONS ON DOPING

CAS 91/53	15-1-1992	G. v. FEI (Oswald (CH), Sutter (CH), Alvarez (CH)), Digest of CAS Awards 1986-1998, pp. 67-91.
CAS 91/56	25-6-1992	S. v. FEI (Rasquin (L), Sutter (CH), Klimke (D)), Digest of CAS Awards 1986-1998, pp. 93-103.
CAS 92/63	10-9-1992	G. v. FEI (Rasquin (L), Sutter (CH), Klimke (D)), Digest of CAS Awards 1986-1998, pp. 93-103.
CAS 92/71	20-10-1992	SJ. V. FEI (Rasquin (L), Klimke (D), Lévy (F)), Digest of CAS Awards 1986-1998, pp. 125-143.
CAS 92/73	10-9-1992	N. v. FEI (Rasquin (L), Klimke (D), Sutter (CH)), Digest of CAS Awards 1986-1998, pp. 145-160.
CAS 92/86	9-4-1993	W. v. FEI (Rasquin (L), Klimke (D), Sutter (CH)), Digest of CAS Awards 1986-1998, pp. 161-171.
CAS 93/109	31-8-1994	Fédération Française de Triathlon (FFTri) and ITU (Advisory Opinion) (Rasquin (L), Alaphilippe (F), B. Hodler (CH)), Digest of CAS Awards 1986-1998, pp. 457-475.
CAS 94/126	9-12-1998	N. v. FEI (Paulsson (F), Dallèves (CH), B. Hodler (CH))
CAS 94/128	5-1-1995	UCI and Comité National Olympique Italien (CONI) (Advisory Opinion) (Mbaye (Senegal), Rasquin (L), Barile (I)), Digest of CAS Awards 1986-1998, pp. 477-511.
CAS 94/129	23-5-1995	USA Shooting & Q. v. UIT (Paulsson (F), Oswald (CH), Argand (CH)), Digest of CAS Awards 1986-1998, pp. 187-204.
CAS 95/122	5-3-1996	National Wheelchair Basketball Association (NWBA) v. IPC (Paulsson (F), Argand (CH), Dixon (GB)), Digest of CAS Awards 1986-1998, pp. 173-185.
CAS 95/141	22-4-1996	Chagnaud v. FINA (Raquin (L), Karaquillo (F), Carrard (CH)), Digest of CAS Awards 1986-1998, pp. 205-224.
CAS 95/142	14-2-1996	Lehtinen v. FINA (Netzle (CH), Seim-Haugen (N), Carrard (CH)), Digest of CAS Awards 1986-1998, pp. 225-244.
CAS 95/144	21-12-1995	European Olympic Committees (EOC) (Advisory Opinion) (Rasquin (L)), Digest of CAS Awards 1986-1998, pp. 513-531.
CAS 95 /147	22-4-1996	FEI (Karaquillo (F), Oswald (CH), Klimke (D)), Digest of CAS Awards 1986-1998, pp. 245-250.
CAS 95/150	28-6-1996	Volker v. FINA (Rao (Kenya), Faylor (USA), Carrard (CH)), Digest of CAS Awards 1986-1998, pp. 265-274.
CAS AH 96/003-4	4-8-1996	Andrei Korneev v. IOC & Zakhar Goukiev v. IOC
CAS 96/149	13-3-1997	Cullwick v. FINA (Beloff (GB), Castle (NZ), Carrard (CH)), Digest of CAS Awards 1986-1998, pp. 251-263.
CAS 96/156	6-10-1997	Jessica K. Foschi v. FINA (Martens (D), Oswald (CH), Campbell (USA))
CAS 97/175	15-4-1998	UCI v. A. (Rasquin (L), Carrard (CH), Mauriac (F))
CAS 97/180	14-1-1998	P. & others v. FINA (Swerts (B), Gay (CH), Oswald (CH))

CAS AH 98/002	12-2-1998	Rebagliati v. IOC (Young (USA), Paulsson (F), Zuchowicz (Poland)), Digest of CAS Awards 1986-1998, pp. 419-434.
CAS 98/181	26-11-1998	UCI v. Nielsen (Faylor (Germany), Carrard (Switzerland) Seim-Haugen (Norway))
CAS 98/184	25-9-1998	Phoebe Hearst Cooke v. FEI (Beloff (GB), Young (USA), Natter (CH)), *Digest of CAS Awards II 1998-2000* (The Hague, Kluwer Law International 2002) pp. 197-204.
CAS 98/192	21-10-1998	UCI v. Skelde (Faylor (D), Carrard (CH), De Croock (B)), *Digest of CAS Awards II 1998-2000* (The Hague, Kluwer Law International 2002) pp. 205-220.
CAS 98/208	22-12-1998	Wang Lu Na, Cai Hui Jue, Zhgang Yi, Wang Wei v. FINA (Beloff (GB), Mingzhong Su (China), Oswald (CH)), *Digest of CAS Awards II 1998-2000* (The Hague, Kluwer Law International 2002) pp. 234-254.
CAS 98/211	7- 6-1999	Smith-De Bruin v. FINA (Fortier (CAN), Beloff (GB), Oswald (CH)), *Digest of CAS Awards II 1998-2000* (The Hague, Kluwer Law International 2002) pp. 255-273.
CAS 98/212	21-1-1999	UCI v. Mason (Netzle (CH), Carrard (CH), Argand (CH)), *Digest of CAS Awards II 1998-2000* (The Hague, Kluwer Law International 2002) pp. 274-282.
CAS 98/214	8-1-1999	Bouras v. FIJ (Rasquin (L), Ndiaye (Senegal), Oswald (CH)), *Digest of CAS Awards II 1998-2000* (The Hague, Kluwer Law International 2002) pp. 291-324.
CAS 98/218	27-5-1999	H. v. FINA (Paulsson (France), Beloff QC (England); Oswald (Switzerland)), *Digest of CAS Awards II 1998-2000* (The Hague, Kluwer Law International 2002) pp. 325-329.
CAS 98/222	9-8-1999	Bernhard v. ITU (Ilesic (Slovenie), Krähe (D), Carrard (CH)), *Digest of CAS Awards II 1998-2000* (The Hague, Kluwer Law International 2002) pp. 330-344.
CAS 98/223	31-8-1999	Korda v. ITF (Nater (CH), McLaren (CAN), Beloff (GB)), *Digest of CAS Awards II 1998-2000* (The Hague, Kluwer Law International 2002) pp. 345-360.
CAS 99/A/230	20-12-1999	B. v. IJF (Rasquin (L), Alaphilippe (F), Oswald (CH)), *Digest of CAS Awards II 1998-2000* (The Hague, Kluwer Law International 2002) pp. 361-376.
CAS 99/A/234 &		
CAS 99/A/235	29-2-2000	David Meca-Medina v. FINA & Igor Majcen v. FINA (Beloff (GB), McLaren (Can), Oswald (CH))
CAS 99/A/239	14-4-2000	UCI v. Moller, Danmarks Idraets-Vorbund and Danmarks Cykle Union (John A. Faylor, Olivier Carard, Peter Leaver, Q.C.))
CAS OG 00/006	22-9-2000	Dieter Baumann v. IOC, National Olympic Committee of Germany and IAAF (Kavanagh (Australia), McLaren (Canada); Young (USA)), *Digest of CAS Awards II 1998-2000* (The Hague, Kluwer Law International 2002) pp. 633-644.
CAS OG 00/010	25-9-2000	Alan Tzagaev v. IWF (Paulsson (France), Netzle (Switzerland); Lee (Malaysia)), *Digest of CAS Awards II 1998-2000* (The Hague, Kluwer Law International 2002) pp. 658-664.
CAS OG 00/011	28-9-2000	Andreea Raducan v. IOC (Kavanagh (AUS), Netzle (CH), Oliveau (USA)), *Digest of CAS Awards II 1998-2000* (The Hague, Kluwer Law International 2002) pp. 665-673.

CAS OG 00/015	29-9-2000	Mihaela Melinte v. IAAF (Young (USA), Lee (Malaysia), McLaren (CAN)), *Digest of CAS Awards II 1998-2000* (The Hague, Kluwer Law International 2002) pp. 691-695.
CAS 2000/C/267	1-5-2000	The Australian Olympic Committee Inc. (AOC) (Advisory opinion) (Richard H. McLaren (Canada))
CAS 2000/A/270	23-5-2001	David Meca-Medina v. FINA & Igor Majcen v. FINA (Beloff (England), McLaren (Canada), Oswald (Switzerland))
CAS 2000/A/274	19-10-2000	Susin v. FINA (Fortier (CAN), Coccia (I), Oswald (CH)), *Digest of CAS Awards II 1998-2000* (The Hague, Kluwer Law International 2002) pp. 389-409.
CAS 2000/A/281	22-12-2000	H. v. Fédération Internationale de Motocyclisme (FIM) (Martens (D), McLaren (CAN), Rochat (CH))
CAS 2000/A/317	9-7-2001	F. Aanes v. FILA (Martens (D), Seim-Haugen (N), Rochat (CH))
CAS OG 02/00	5-2-2002	Sandis Prusis & Latvian Olympic Committee/IOC (Coccia (Italy), Leaver (England), Rauste (Finland)), *Digest of CAS Awards III 2001-2003* (The Hague, Kluwer Law International 2004)
CAS 2002/A/370	29-11-2002	Lazutina v. IOC (Leaver (England), Shycoff (USA), States, Martens (Germany)), *Digest of CAS Awards III 2001-2003* (The Hague, Kluwer Law International 2004) pp. 273-285.
CAS 2002/A/374	24-1-2003	Muehlegg v. IOC (McLaren (Canada), Martens (Germany), Morand (Switzerland)), *Digest of CAS Awards III 2001-2003* (The Hague, Kluwer Law International 2004) pp. 286-307.
CAS 2002/A/376	15-10-2002	G. v. FEI (Rivkin (USA), McLaren (Canada), Martens (Germany)), *Digest of CAS Awards III 2001-2003* (The Hague, Kluwer Law International 2004) pp. 303-310.
CAS 2002/A/383	27-1-2003	IAAF v. Dos Santos (Fortier (Canada), Ellicott (Australia), Hinojosa (Spain))
CAS 2002/A/389 & 390 & 391 & 392 & 393, 20-3-2003	23-5-2001	Mayer v. IOC (Netzle (Switzerland), Martens (Germany), Young (USA)), *Digest of CAS Awards III 2001-2003* (The Hague, Kluwer Law International 2004) pp. 348-365.
CAS 2002/A/399	31-1-2003	Poll v. FINA (Schimke (Gedrmany), McLaren (Canada), Oswald (Switzerland)), *Digest of CAS Awards III 2001-2003* (The Hague, Kluwer Law International 2004) pp. 382-395.
CAS 2002/A/401	10-1-2003	IAAF/United States Track and Field (USATF) (Fortier (Canada), Ellicott (Australia), Paulsson (France)), *Digest of CAS Awards III 2001-2003* (The Hague, Kluwer Law International 2004)
CAS 2002/A/403 & CAS 2002/A/408	12-3-2003	UCI, FCI v. Marco Pantani (Fortier (Canada), Coccia (Italy), Nater (Switzerland))
CAS 2002/A/417	12-5-2003	IAAF v. CADA & S. Witteveen (Byrne-Sutton (Switzerland), Kavanagh (Australia), Ferrari (Argentina))
CAS 2002/A/432	27-5-2003	Demetis v. FINA (Faylor Germany), Dedes (Greece), Oswald (Switzerland)), *Digest of CAS Awards III 2001-2003* (The Hague, Kluwer Law International 2004) pp. 419-430.
CAS 2002/A/464	7-10-2003	UCI v. L., R., Federação Portuguesa de Ciclismo (FPC) (Foucher (France), Carrard (Switzerland), Florez Plaza (Spain))

CAS 2003/A/447	20-1-2004	S. v. FINA (Faylor (Germany), Oswald (Switzerland), Dedes (Greece))
CAS 2003/A/459	20-10-2003	VH v. FINA (Beloff (Great Britain), Blackshaw (Great Britain); Oswald (Switzerland))
CAS 2003/A/477	20-10-2003	B. & S. v. Equestrian Federation of Australia Limited (EFA) (Holmes (Australia))
CAS 2003/A/484	11-3-2004	V. v. United States Anti-Doping Agency (USADA) (Fortier (Canada), Fraser (Canada), Leaver (England))
CAS 2003/A/493	22-3-2004	V. v. FINA (Coccia (Italy), Bernasconi (Switzerland), Oswald (Switzerland))
CAS 2003/A/503	8-10-2003	B. v. Real Federacion Española de Ciclismo (RFEC) (Florez Plaza (Spain))
CAS 2003/A/505	19-12-2003	UCI v. P., USA Cyling Inc. (USA Cycling) & United States Anti-Doping Agency (USADA) (Geistlinger (Austria), Hodler (Switzerland), DeFrantz (USA))
CAS 2003/A/507	9-2-2004	S. v. FINA (Haas (Germany), McLaren (Canada); Oswald (Switzerland))
CAS 2003/A/510	15-1-2004	A. v. Confederaçào Brasiliera de Desportos Aquàticos (CBDA)
CAS 2003/A/514	15-1-2004	FINA v. A. (Leaver QC (United Kingdom), Haas (Germany); Carrard (Switzerland))
CAS 2003/A/517	19-4-2004	IAAF v. Qatar Associations of Athletics Federation (QAAF) & Rashid Shafi Al-Dosari (Leaver QC (England), Lin Kok Loh (Singapore); Carrard (Switzerland))
CAS 2003/A/521	18-3-2004	P. v. Royale Ligue Vélocipédique Belge (RLVB) (Gossin (Switzerland); Carrard (Switzerland); Anderes (Switzerland))
CAS 2003/A/522	5-3-2004	C. v. Royale Ligue Vélocipédique Belge (RLVB) (Rasquin (Luxembourg), De Croock (Belgium), Carrard (Switzerland))
CAS 2003/A/524	1-4-2004	Duda v. Royale Ligue Velocipédique Belge (RLVB) (Barbey (Switzerland), De Croock (Belgium), Carrard (Switzerland))
CAS 2003/O/527	21-4-2004	Hamburger Sport-Vereine. v. Odense Boldklub (Netzle (Switzerland), Eilers (Germany), Evensen (Denmark))
CAS 2003/O/530	27-8-2004	AJ Auxerre v. FC Valencia and Sissoko (Carrard (Switzerland), Klein (France), Pintó (Spain))
CAS OG 04/003	17-8-2004	Torri Edwards v. IAAF and USATF (Nater (Switzerland), Martens (Germany), Holmes (England))
CAS 2004/A/544	13-4-2004	Brazilian Equestrian Confederation (CBH) v. FEI (Alaphilippe (France), Morand (Switzerland), Oswald (Switzerland))
CAS 2004/A/549	27-5-2004	Deferr and Real Federacion Española de Gimnasia (RFEG) v. FIG (Foucher (France), Massimo (Italy), Oswald (Switzerland))
CAS 2004/A/555	6-7-2004	Hellenic Hockey Federation (HHF) v. IHF and South African Hockey Association (SAHA) (Geistlinger (Austria), Georghiades (Cyprus), Netzle (Switzerland))
CAS 2004/A/557	13-4-2004	Iverson v. ISAF and International Star Class Yacht Racing Association (Leaver (England))
CAS 2004/A/558	16-9-2004	Senegalese Football Association (FSF) v. African Football Confederation (CAF) (Rasquin (Luxembourg), Karaquillo (France), Appietto (France))
CAS 2004/A/561	2-7-2004	Finnish Ski Association (FSA) v. FIS (Netzle (Switzerland))

CAS 2004/A/564	14-9-2004	IAAF v. French Athletics Federation (FFA) & Stéphane Desaulty (Rasquin (Luxembourg), Fortier (Canada), Karaquillo (France))
CAS 2004/A/568	6-8-2004	Club AC Perugia Spa v. Club SCS Politehnica Timisoara (Bubnik (Czech Republic), Echeverria Bermudez (Costa Rica), Bernasconi (Switzerland))
CAS 2004/A/569	18-6-2004	Al Kuwari v. Asian Football Confederation (AFC) (Parker (England), Eilers (Germany), Rahman Lootah (Dubai))
CAS 2004/A/593	6-7-2004	Football Association of Wales (FAW) v. UEFA (Geistlinger (Austria), Leaver (England), Coccia, (Italy))
CAS 2004/A/599		Austin v. Australian Canoeing Inc. (AC) (Nicholas (Australia))
CAS 2004/A/607	6-12-2004	Galabin Boevski v. IWF (Nater (Switzerland), H. McLaren (Canada), Engelbrecht (Germany))
CAS 2004/A/628	28-6-2004	IAAF v. USA Track & Field (USATF) & Young (Leaver (England), Loh Lin Kok (Singapore), Hunter (England))
CAS 2004/A/633	2-3-2005	IAAF v. FFA & Mr Chouki (communicated on 5-4-2005) (Barbey (Switzerland), Fortier (Canada), Bertrand (France))
CAS 2004/O/645	13-12-2005	United States Anti-doping Agency v. Tim Montgomery (Fortier (Canada), Campbell (United States), Leaver (United Kingdom))
CAS 2004/O/649	13-12-2005	United States Anti-doping Agency v. Chryste Gaines (Fortier (Canada), Campbell (United States), Leaver (United Kingdom))
CAS 2004/A/651	11-7-2005	Mark French v. Australian Sports Commission and Cycling Australia (Appeal Partial Award) (McLaren, McDonald, Jolson)
CAS 2004/A/704	21-10-2004	Yang Tae Young and Korean Olympic Committee (KOC) v. FIG (Beloff (England), Martens (Germany), Rao (Kenya))
CAS 2004/A/707	17-2-2005	David Millar v. The British Cycling Federation (Byrne-Sutton (Switzerland), Bertrand (France), Beloff (England))
CAS 2000/714	31-3-2005	Robert Fazekas v. IOC (Fumagalli (Italy), Geistlinger, (Austria), Martens (Germany))
CAS 2004/A/718	31-3-2005	Adrian Annus v. IOC (Nater (Switzerland), Leaver (England), Geistlinger (Austria))
CAS 2004/725	20-7-2005	USOC, Michael Johnson, Antonio Pettigrew, Angelo Taylor, Alvin Harrison, and Calvin Harrison v. IOC and IAAF (Hobér (Sweden), Fortier (Canada), Williams (New Zealand))
CAS 2004/A/777	31-1-2005	ARcycling AG v. UCI (Coccia (Italy), Hodler (Switzerland), Meltvedt (Norway))
CAS 2005/A/829	5-9-2005	Ludger Beerbaum v. FEI (Beloff (United Kingdom), Martens (Germany), Oswald (Switzerland))
CAS 2005/830	15-7-2005	Giorgia Squizzato v. FINA (Schimke (Germany), Oswald (Switzerland), Coccia (Italy))
CAS 2005/C/841	26-4-2005	CONI (Advisory Opinion) (Carrard (Switzerland), Coccia (Italy), Fumagalli (Italy))
CAS 2005/A/847	20-7-2005	Hans Knauss v. FIS (Haas (Germany), Netzle (Switzerland), Faylor (Germany))

BIBLIOGRAPHY

Jens Adolphsen, 'Zuständigkeit und anwendbares Recht bei Verfahren gegen nationale und internationale Sportverbände', *IPRax* (2000) p. 81 *et seq.*

Jens Adolphsen, *Internationale Dopingstrafen* (Tübingen, Mohr Siebeck 2003).

A.A.M. van Agt, *Zijn nadere wetgevende voorzieningen op het gebied van het tuchtrecht wenselijk?*, Preadvies voor de Nederlandse Juristen Vereniging 1971.

Rainer Ahlers, *Doping und strafrechtliche Verantwortlichkeit: zum strafrechtlichen Schutz des Sportlers vor Körperschäden durch Doping* (Baden-Baden, Nomos-Verl.-Ges. 1994).

Michael Akehurst, *A Modern Introduction to International Law* (London, Harper Collins Academic 1987) p. 52.

Juan Manuel Alonso, 'The Formulation of an Effective National Anti-Doping Programme', in Istvan Gyulai et al. eds., *International Amateur Athletic Federation: Doping is Cheating. Fight for a Clean Sport.* 1st World Anti-Doping Seminar, Report, Heusenstamm, Germany, March 14-16 1994 (Monaco 1995) p. 38 *et seq.*

Paul M. Anderson, 'Drug Testing in Amateur Sports in the US', in O'Leary, ed., *Drugs and Doping in Sport* (London, Cavendish 2000) p. 205 *et seq.*

Jaime Andreu, 'EU Action in the Fight Against Doping', IEC Scientific Conference: *The Limits of Sport: Doping*, Barcelona, 17 and 18 June, 1999. http://www.blues.uab.es/olympic.studies/doping/andreu.htm.

Jaime Andreu, 'Plan für den Beitrag der Gemeinschaft zur Dopingbekämpfung', in V. Röhricht, K. Vieweg, eds., *Doping-Forum* (Stuttgart, Boorberg 2000) p. 99-108.

C. Christine Ansley, 'International Athletic Dispute Resolution: Tarnishing the Olympic Dream', 12(1) *Arizona Journal of International and Comparative Law* p. 277 *et seq.*

L.J. van Apeldoorn, J.M. Reijntjes, P.J. Boon, R.J.B. Bergamin, *Van Apeldoorn's Inleiding tot de studie van het Nederlandse recht* (Deventer, Kluwer 2000).

Michael J. Asken, *Dying to Win: The Athlete's Guide to Safe and Unsafe Drugs in Sports* (Washington, DC, Acropolis Books, 1988).

Thomas Bach, 'Lausanner Erklärung zum Doping und ihre Folgen', in V. Röhricht, K. Vieweg, eds., *Doping-Forum* (Stuttgart, Boorberg 2000) p. 71 *et seq.*

Margareta Baddeley, 'Athletenrechte und Doping aus der Sicht des schweizerischen Rechts', in Klaus Vieweg, ed., *Doping – Realität und Recht* (Berlin, Duncker & Humblot 1998), p. 307-329.

Margareta Baddeley, 'Dopingsperren als Verbandssanktion aus nationaler und internationaler Sicht. Insbesondere am Beispiel des schweizerischen, australischen und amerikanischen Rechts', in Jochen Fritzweiler, ed., *Doping – Sanktionen, Beweise, Ansprüche* (Berne, Stämpfli 2000) p. 9-38.

Reinhold Baier, *Doping im Sport: eine medizinisch-rechtswissenschaftliche Analyse* (München, Techn. Univ., Diss. 1998)

Darren Bailey, 'Doping Control in the United Kingdom – The Regulatory and Legal Framework', in Klaus Vieweg, ed., *Doping – Realität und Recht* (Berlin, Duncker & Humblot 1998) p. 331 *et seq.*

G.N. Barrie, 'Disciplinary Tribunals and Administrative Law, Conference on Sport and the law', Rand Afrikaans University, 7-8 September 2000, p. 3.

Gottfried Baumgärtel, *Beweislastpraxis im Privatrecht. Die Schwierigkeiten der Beweislastverteilung und die Möglichkeiten ihrer Überwindung* (München, Heymann 1998).

Michael Beloff, 'The Court of Arbitration for Sport at the Olympics', 4 (2) *Sport and The Law Journal* (1996) p. 5.

Michael Beloff, 'Drugs, Laws and Versapaks', in O'Leary, ed., *Drugs and Doping in Sport* (London, Cavendish 2000) p. 39.

Michael Beloff, Tim Kerr, Marie Demetriou, *Sports Law* (Oxford, Hart Publishing 1999).

Brigitte Berendonk, Doping Dokumente: von der Forschung zum Betrug (Berlin, Springer 1991).

A.J. van den Berg, R. van Delden, H.J. Snijders, *Arbitragerecht* (Zwolle, W.E.J. Tjeenk Willink 1992).

Berry Bertels, '"Helicopter-view' met Prof. Giltay Veth over "dopinglandschap"', *Sportzaken* (1998) p. 12-14.

Karl-Heinrich Bette, 'Doping: Studies in the Sociology of Deviance', in K.-H. Bette and A. Rütten, eds., *International Sociology of Sport: Contempory Issues, Festschrift in Honour of Günther Lüschen* (Stuttgart , Naglschmid 1995) p. 241.

Karl-Heinrich Bette, Uwe Schimank, *Doping im Hochleistungssport: Anpassung durch Abweichung* (Frankfurt am Main, Suhrkamp 1995).

Karl-Heinrich Bette, Uwe Schimank, 'Doping und Recht – soziologisch betrachtet', in Klaus Vieweg, ed., *Doping – Realität und Recht* (Berlin, Duncker & Humblot 1998) p. 357-390.

Edward J. Bird, Gert G. Wagner, *The Drug Diary: A Modest Proposal to End Doping in Sport* (Bochum, Fak. für Sozialwiss., Ruhr-Univ., 1996).

Melissa R. Bitting, 'Arbitration of Disputes: Comment, Mandatory, Binding Arbitration for Olympic Athletes', in Timothy Davis, Alfred D. Mathewson, Kenneth L. Shropshire, eds., *Sports and the Law: A Modern Anthology* (Durham, NC, Carolina Academic Press 1999) p. 627-634.

Melissa R. Bitting, 'Mandatory, Binding Arbitration for Olympic Athletes: Is the Process Better or Worse for "Job Security"?', in I. Blackshaw, R.C.R. Siekmann, J. Soek, eds., *The Court of Arbitration for Sport 1984–2004* (The Hague, T.M.C. Asser Press 2006), p. 349 *et seq.*

B. Le Bizec, I. Gaudin, A. Pohu, F. Monteau, F. André, 'Identification of endogenous 19-Norandrosterone in human urine', in W. Schänzer, H. Geyer, A. Gotzmann, U. Mareck-Engelke, eds., *Recent Advances in Doping Analysis* (7) (Köln 1999) p. 109-119.

B. Le Bizec, F. Monteau, I. Gaudin, F. André, 'Evidence for the Presence of Endogenous 19-norandrosterone in Human Urine', 723 *Journal of Chromatography B* (1999) p. 157-172.

B. Le Bizec, I. Gaudin, F. Monteau, F. Andre, S. Impens, K. de Wasch, H. De Brabander, 'Consequences of Boar Edible Tissue Consumption on Urinary Profiles of Nandrolone Metabolites. Rapid Communications in Mass Spectrometry', 14 *RCM* (2000) p. 1058-1065.

David L. Black, 'Doping Control Testing Policies and Procedures: A Critique', in W. Wilson, W., E. Derse, eds., *Doping in Elite Sport. The Politics of Drugs in the Olympic Movement* (Champaign, Illinois 2001) p. 29-42.

Simon Boyes, 'Globalisation, Europe and the Re-regulation of sport', in Andrew Caiger and Simon Gardiner, eds., *Professional Sport in the European Union: Regulation and Re-regulation* (The Hague, T.M.C. Asser Press 2000) p. 65 *et seq.*

Simon Boyes, 'The International Olympic Committee, Transnational Doping Policy and Globalisation', in O'Leary, ed., *Drugs and Doping in Sport* (London, Cavendish 2000) p. 167 *et seq.*

Dieter Bremer, Triathlon: Psychologie, Training, Doping / Internat. Triathlon-Symposium, Nürnberg 1987 (Ahrensburg bei Hamburg, Czwalina 1988).

Markus Buchberger, *Die Überprüfbarkeit sportverbandsrechtlicher Entscheidungen durch die ordentliche Gerichtsbarkeit. Ein Vergleich der Rechtslage in der Bundesrepublik Deutschland und den Vereinigten Staaten von Amerika* (Berlin, Duncker und Humblot 1999).

M. Budzisch, K. Huhn, H. Wuschech, *Doping in de BRD – Ein historischer Überblick zu einer verschleierten Praxis* (Berlin, Spotless-Verl. 1999).

Rainer T. Cherkeh, *Betrug (para. 263 StGB), verübt durch Doping im Sport* (Frankfurt am Main, Lang 2000).

Stewart C. Clark, Drugs and sports, [Alberta], Alberta Alcohol and Drug Abuse Commission 1990.

Dirk Clasing, *Doping – verbotene Arzneimittel im Sport* (Stuttgart, G. Fischer 1992).

Dirk Clasing, *Doping und seine Wirkstoffe: verbotene Arzneimittel im Sport* (Balingen, Spitta-Verl. 2004).

Dirk Clasing, Rudhard Klaus Müller, *Dopingkontrolle. Informationen für Aktive, Betreuer und Ärzte zur Bekämpfung des Medikamentenmissbrauchs im Sport* (Köln, Sport und Buch Strauß 2001).

G.J.M. Corstens, *Het Nederlandse strafprocesrecht* (Arnhem, Gouda Quint 1993).

Andy Curtis, 'Running Scared: An Athlete Lawyer's View of the Doping Regime', in O'Leary, ed., *Drugs and Doping in Sport* (London, Cavendish 2000) p. 109 *et seq.*

L. Dallèves, *Chapitres choisis du droit du sport* (Genève, Éd. Médecine et Hygiène 1993) p. 120.

John A. Daly, 'The Moral Imperative of Olympism and its Implications for Contemporary Sports, International Sociology of Sport', in K.-H. Bette and A. Rütten, eds., *Contempory Issues, Festschrift in Honor of Günther Lüschen* (Stuttgart, Naglschmid 1995) p. 199.

G. Debruyckere, C.H. van Peteghem, R. de Sagher, 'Influence of the Consumption of Meat Contaminated with Anabolic Steroids on Doping Tests', 275 *Analytica Chimica Acta* (1993) p. 49-56.

L. Dehennin, Y. Bonnaire, Ph. Plou, 'Urinary Excretion of 19-norandrosterone of Endogenous Origin in Man', 721 *Journal of Chromatography* (1999) p. 301-307.

R. van Delden, *Internationale handelsarbitrage* (Deventer, Kluwer 1996).

Domenico Di Pietro, 'The Ad Hoc Division of the Court of Arbitration for Sport at the Athens 2004 Olympic Games an Overview', in I. Blackshaw, R.C.R. Siekmann, J. Soek, eds., *The Court of Arbitration for Sport 1984–2004* (The Hague, T.M.C. Asser Press 2006), p. 134 *et seq.*

Erna-Marie Dieckmann, *Pervitin als Dopingmittel bei Pferden und Versuche zu seinem chemischen Nachweis nach dem Doping* (Berlin 1951).

P. van Dijk, G.J.H. van Hoof, *Theory and Practice of the European Convention on Human Rights* (The Hague 1998).

Walter Ditz, *Doping im Pferderennsport: e. kriminolog.-empir. Unters. zur Problematik d. künstl. Leistungsveränderung im Pferderennsport* (Pfaffenweiler, Centaurus-Verlagsgesellschaft 1986).

H. de Doelder, 'Terrein en beginselen van tuchtrecht', Diss. (Alphen aan den Rijn, H.D. Tjeenk Willink 1981).

D. Dörr, *Faires Verfahren, Gewährleistung im Grundgesetz der Bundesrepublik Deutschland* (Kehl, Engel Verlag 1984).

Masato Dogauchi, 'The Activities of the Japan Sports Arbitration Agency', *The International Sports Law Journal* (2005) p. 3-7; in I. Blackshaw, R.C.R. Siekmann, J. Soek, eds., *The Court of Arbitration for Sport 1984–2004* (The Hague, T.M.C. Asser Press 2006), p. 300 *et seq.*

Edward F. Dolan, *Drugs in Sports* (New York, F. Watts 1992).

Gabriel Dollé, 'Doping Control Procedures Past and Present', in Istvan Gyulai et al. eds., *International Amateur Athletic Federation: Doping is Cheating. Fight for a Clean Sport*. 1st World Anti-Doping Seminar, Report, Heusenstamm, Germany, March 14–16, 1994 (Monaco 1995) p. 42 *et seq.*

Manfred Donike, in Wolfgang Schild, Manfred Donike, eds., *Rechtliche Fragen des Dopings* (Heidelberg, Müller, Juristischer Verl. 1986).

Manfred Donike, 'Verfahren und Probleme der Dopingkontrolle', in W. Schild, ed., *Rechtliche Fragen des Dopings* (Heidelberg 1986) p. 1-11.

Manfred Donike, in Dirk Clasing, *Doping – verbotene Arzneimittel im Sport* (Stuttgart, G. Fischer 1992).

Manfred Donike, 'Blood Testing – A Fortification of the Anti-Doping Armoury?', in Istvan Gyulai et al. eds., *International Amateur Athletic Federation: Doping is Cheating. Fight for a Clean Sport.* 1st World Anti-Doping Seminar, Report, Heusenstamm, Germany, March 14–16, 1994 (Monaco 1995) p. 23 *et seq.*

Manfred Donike, 'Gutachten zur Frage des Nachweises von Dopingmitteln im Blut', in *Bundesinstitut für Sportwissenschaft Blut und/oder Urin zur Dopingkontrolle* (Schorndorf 1996) p. 127-134.

Manfred Donike, Ch. Kaiser, *Dopingkontrollen* (Köln, Bundesinst. für Sportwiss. 1980).

Manfred Donike, Susanne Rauth, *Dopingkontrollen* (Köln, Bundesinst. für Sportwiss. 1992).

Tom Donohoe, Neil Johnson, *Foul Play: Drug Abuse in Sports* (Oxford, Blackwell 1986).

Herbert Ehrbar, *Die Notwendigkeit weltweiter Trainingskontrollen: mit der Darstellung eines effektiven Doping-Kontroll- Systems* (Leimen 1998).

Herbert Ehrbar, *Das Netz zum Erfolg muß enger werden!: Konzept eines effektiven, finanzierbaren Doping- Kontroll-Systems* (Leimen 1999)

R.J. Ellicott, 'The Rights of Athletes and the Rule of Law', in *International Athletic Foundation, Supplement to the official Proceedings of the IAF Symposium on Sport and Law*, Monte Carlo, 31 Jan.–2 Feb. 1991 (Monaco 1995) p. 48 *et seq.*

Georg Engelbrecht, 'Adoption, Recognition and Harmonization of Doping Sanctions Between World Sports Organisations', *ISLJ* (2000) p. 3-13.

Ch.J. Enschedé, A. Heijder, *Beginselen van strafrecht* (Deventer, Kluwer 1974).

Allan Erbsen, 'The Substance and Illusion of Lex Sportiva', in I. Blackshaw, R.C.R. Siekmann, J. Soek, eds., *The Court of Arbitration for Sport 1984–2004* (The Hague, T.M.C. Asser Press 2006) p. 441 *et seq.*

Alexander Faber, *Doping als unlauterer Wettbewerb und Spielbetrug* (Zürich, Schulthess 1974).

Christian Fahl, 'Sportverbandsgerichtsbarkeit und Doppelbestrafungsverbod', *SpuRt* (2001) p. 181-183.

Herbert Fenn, Grischka Petri, 'Unschuldsvermutung und Anscheinsbeweis im Verbandsstraf-verfahren', *SpuRt* (2000) p. 232-235.

Hilary Findlay, 'Form Follows Function: Crafting Rules for a Sport-specific Arbitration Process "The Canadian CAS"', in I. Blackshaw, R.C.R. Siekmann, J. Soek, eds., *The Court of Arbitration for Sport 1984–2004* (The Hague, T.M.C. Asser Press 2006) p. 280 *et seq.*

C. N. Foster, J. Boyles, D.L. Crone, G.D. Mundy, R.A. Sams, S.D. Stanley, T. Tobin, 'Response to a Survey Among International Racing Authorities on Therapeutic Medications, Environmental and Dietary Substances in Racehorses', in D.E. Auer, E. Houghton, eds., *Proceedings of the 11th International Conference of Racing Analysts and Veterinarians* (Newmarket, R & W Pub. 1996) p. 46-55.

Ken Foster, 'Can Sport Be Regulated by Europe?: An Analysis of Alternative Models', in Andrew Caiger, Simon Gardiner, eds., *Professional Sport in the European Union: Regulation and Re-regulation* (The Hague, T.M.C. Asser Press 2000) p. 43 *et seq.*

Ken Foster, 'The Discourses of Doping: Law and Regulation in the War Against Drugs', in O'Leary, ed., *Drugs and Doping in Sport* (London, Cavendish 2000) p. 181 *et seq.*

Ken Foster, 'Lex Sportiva and Lex Ludica: The Court of Arbitration for Sport's Jurisprudence', in I. Blackshaw, R.C.R. Siekmann, J. Soek, eds., *The Court of Arbitration for Sport 1984–2004* (The Hague, T.M.C. Asser Press 2006), p. 409 *et seq.*

Jochen Fritzweiler, Gesetzliche Bestimmungen zur Ahndung von Doping', in Jochen Fritzweiler, ed., *Doping. Sanktionen, Beweise, Ansprüche* (Berne, Stämpfli; München, Beck; Wien, Manz 2000) p. 155 *et seq.*

Jochen Fritzweiler, Bernhard Pfister, Thomas Summerer, *Praxishandbuch Sportrecht* (München, Beck 1998).

Peter M. Fuchs, *Diagnosis in Track and Field Performances Past the 1988 Ben Johnson Doping Scandal* (Mainz, Johannes-Gutenberg-Universität 1997).

D. Galluzzi, 'The Doping Crisis in International Athletic Competition: Lessons From the Chinese Doping Scandal in Women's Swimming', 10 *Seton Hall J Sport Law* (2000) p. 65.

Michael Gamper, 'Reden ist wichtiger als Handeln. Eine machtanalytische Betrachtung des Dopingdiskurses', in Michael Gamper, M. J. Mühlethaler, F. Reidhaar, eds., *Doping. Spitzensport als gesellschaftliches Problem* (Zürich, NZZ-Verl. 2000) p. 45- 68.

R. Gardner, 'On Performance-enhancing Substances and the Unfair Advantage Argument', XVI *J Philosophy of Sport* (1989) p. 59.

R. Gareau, M. Audran, R.D. Baynes, C.H. Flowers, A. Duvallet, L. Senecal, G.R. Brisson, 'Erythropoietin Abuse in Athletes', *Nature* (1996) p. 113 *et seq.*

Mark Gay, 'Commentary on the Recent Amendments to the IAAF Procedural Guidelines for Doping Control', in *International Athletic Foundation, Supplement to the official Proceedings of the IAF Symposium on Sport and Law*, Monte Carlo, 31 Jan.–2 Feb. 1991 (Monaco 1995) p. 73 *et seq.*

Mark Gay, 'The Sample Collection Phase – Hope for a Legal Challenge', in Istvan Gyulai et al., eds., *International Amateur Athletic Federation: Doping is Cheating. Fight for a Clean Sport. 1st World Anti-Doping Seminar*, Report, Heusenstamm, Germany, March 14–16, 1994 (Monaco 1995) p. 52 *et seq.*

Mark Gay, 'The Legal Context, Workshop 1', in *Sport Council, Conference Proceedings 4th Permanent World Conference on Anti-Doping in Sport* (London, September 5–8, 1993) p. 184.

S. Gearhart, 'Sporting Arbitration and the International Olympic Committee Court of Arbitration of Sport', 6 *Journal of International Arbitration* (1989) p. 39.

Gunter Gebauer, *Olympische Spiele: die andere Utopie der Moderne; Olympia zwischen Kult und Droge* (Frankfurt am Main, Suhrkamp 1996).

Gunter Gebauer, 'Ethik und Moral als Legitimationsquellen im Kampf gegen das Doping?', in D. Kurz, J. Mester, eds., *Doping im Sport* (Köln, Sport und Buch Strauß 1997) p. 69-75.

H. Geyer, U. Mareck-Engelke, U. Reinhart, M. Thevis, W. Schänzer, 'Positive Dopingfälle mit Norandrosteron durch verunreinigte Nahrungsergänzungsmittel', *Zeitschrift für Sportmedizin* (2000) p. 378-382.

Z. Giacometti, F. Fleiner, *Schweizerisches Bundesstaatsrecht* (Zürich, Schulthess, Polygraphischer Verl. 1969).

N.J.P. Giltay Veth, 'Internationale knelpunten bij de juridische aanpak van doping, onder meer in verband met Olympische Spelen en Europacupvoetbal', in N.J.P. Giltay Veth, ed., Sport en Recht, Deel 1 1992/1993, *Doping: ook een juridisch probleem*, p. 31 *et seq.*

N.J.P. Giltay Veth, 'Tuchtrecht in de sport: enige capita selecta', in N.J.P. Giltay Veth, ed., Sport en Recht, Deel 6, 1998, *Tuchtrecht in de sport*, p. 23-35.

Esteban Gorostiaga, 'Les limits de la medicina esportiva', IEC Scientific Conference: *The Limits of Sport: Doping*, Barcelona, 17 and 18 June, 1999: http://www.blues.uab.es/olympic.studies/ doping/gorostiaga. htm.

Volker Grabow, 'Doping aus der Sicht der Aktiven. Zwischen dem Wunsch zur "sauberen" Leistung und öffentlichen Pressionen', in D. Kurz, J. Mester, eds., *Doping im Sport* (Köln 1997) p. 91-95.

Toni Graf-Baumann, 'Doping – spezielle medizinische Aspekte', in V. Röhricht, K. Vieweg, eds., *Doping-Forum* (Stuttgart, Boorberg 2000) p. 27-30.

A. Gray, 'Doping Control: The National Governing Body Perspective', in O'Leary, ed., *Drugs and Doping in Sport* (London, Cavendish 2000) p. 11 *et seq.*

E. Grayson, *Sport and the Law* (London, Butterworths 1999).

Edward Grayson, Gregory Ioannidis, 'Drugs, Health and Sporting Values', in O'Leary, ed., *Drugs and Doping in Sport* (London, Cavendish 2000) p. 243 *et seq.*

E. Grutterink, 'Belgisch arbitragerecht in sportaangelegenheden', 4 *Tijdschrift voor arbitrage* (1994) p. 201-207.

Eugene D. Gulland, 'The Reynolds & Barnes Cases and the Integrity of International Dispute Resolution', in *International Athletic Foundation, Supplement to the official Proceedings of the IAF Symposium on Sport and Law*, Monte Carlo, 31 Jan.–2 Feb. 1991 (Monaco 1995) p. 5 *et seq.*

Ulrike Gutheil, *Doping: die haftungsrechtliche und sportrechtliche Verantwortung von Sportler, Trainer, Arzt und Sportverband* (Hamburg, Kovac 1996).

Josep Anton Gutiérrez, 'La nova lei de l'esport a Catalunya i el dopaje', IEC Scientific Conference: *The Limits of Sport: Doping*, Barcelona, 17 and 18 June, 1999: http://www.blues.uab.es/olympic.studies/doping/gutierrez.htm.

W.L. Haardt, 'Samenvattend Verslag', in: *Tuchtrecht en Fair Play* (Nederlandse Vereniging voor Procesrecht 1984).

Ulrich Haas, 'Aktuelle Entwicklungen in der Dopingbekämpfung', *SpuRt* (2000) p. 5-8.

Dieter Hackfort, *Doping en sport: over geneesmiddelen, van anabolica tot groeihormonen, contrôle en bewijsvoering, twee gevallen uit de praktijk, arts en ethiek, sociaal wetenschappelijke aspecten, juridische aspecten.* (Rijswijk 1990).

Dirk Hagemann, 'Ich bin clean!: Anti-Doping-Fibel der DLV-Jugend', Deutscher Leichtathletik-Verband Jugend, ed. (Aachen, Meyer und Meyer 1993).

Dominique Hahn, 'Présentation de la jurisprudence du TAS', in *Tribunal Arbitral du Sport, Receuil TAS* (1993).

D.J. Harris, M. O'Boyle, C. Warbrick, *Law of the European Convention on Human Rights* (London, Butterworths 1995).

A.E. Harteveld, H.G.M. Krabbe, *De Wegenverkeerswet 1994. Een strafrechtelijk commentaar* (Arnhem, Gouda Quint 1999).

Hazel J. Hartley, '"An Innocent Abroad": The Diane Modahl Doping Case 1994–2001', *ISLJ* (2004) p. 61-65.

Heidi Hassenmüller, *Die Kehrseite der Medaille: Jugend, Hochleistungssport, Doping* (Recklinghausen, Bitter 1995).

Herwig Hasslacher, 'Sanktionen und Dopingverfahren in Österreich', in Jochen Fritzweiler, ed., *Doping. Sanktionen, Beweise, Ansprüche* (Berne, Stämpfli; München, Beck; Wien, Manz 2000) p. 103 *et seq.*

Tanja Haug, Christian Paul, 'Diskussionsbericht zum Doping-Forum', in V. Röhricht, K. Vieweg, eds., *Doping-Forum* (Stuttgart, Boorberg 2000) p. 139-150.

Klaus Heinemann, 'The Economic Colonialisation of Sport. The Loss of Autonomy, and Doping', IEC Scientific Conference: *The Limits of Sport: Doping*, Barcelona, 17 and 18 June, 1999: http://www.blues.uab.es/olympic.studies/doping/heinemann.htm.

Anton Heini, 'Die gerichtliche Überprüfung von Vereinsstrafen', in Peter Forstmoser, Walter R. Schluep, *Festschr. zum 60. Geburtstag von Arthur Meier-Hayoz* (Berne, Stämpfli 1982), p. 223.

Burkhard Heß, 'Voraussetzungen und Grenzen eines autonomen Sportrechts unter besonderer Berücksichtigung des internationalen Spitzensports', in B. Heß, W.-D. Dressler, eds., *Aktuelle Rechtsfragen des Sports* (Heidelberg, Müller 1999) p. 1-48.

John Hoberman, *Sterbliche Maschinen: Doping und die Unmenschlichkeit des Hochleistungssports* (Aachen, Meyer und Meyer 1994).

Karsten Hofmann, 'Das Internationale Sportschiedgericht (CAS) in Lausanne', *SpuRt* (2002) p. 7 *et seq.*

Edward E. Hollis III, 'The United States Olympic Committee and the Suspension of Athletes: Reforming Grievance Procedures Under the Amateur Sports Act of 1978', 71 *Indiana Law Journal* p. 183.

Wildor Hollmann, 'Zum Doping aus sportmedizinischer Sicht', in Klaus Vieweg, ed., *Doping – Realität und Recht* (Berlin, Duncker & Humblot 1998) p. 37-49.

Joop Holthausen, '"Classical" Doping Tests Are Outdated', *ISLJ* (2000) p. 16.

Wolfgang Holzer, Jochen Fritzweiler, 'Auswirkungen von Dopingverstößen auf Arbeits-, Lizenz- und Sponsorenverträge', in Jochen Fritzweiler, ed., *Doping. Sanktionen, Beweise, Ansprüche* (Berne, Stämpfli; München, Beck; Wien, Manz 2000) p. 57-78.

Barrie Houlihan, 'Anti-Doping Policy in Sport: The Politics of International Policy Coordination', 77 *Public Administration* (1999) p. 311.

Barrie Houlihan, 'Anti-Doping Political Measures: The New Approaches After the Lausanne Meeting on Doping', IEC Scientific Conference: *The Limits of Sport: Doping*, Barcelona, 17 and 18 June, 1999: http://www.blues.uab.es/olympic.studies/doping/houlihan.htm.

Barrie Houlihan, *Dying to Win: Doping in Sport and the Development of Anti-Doping Policy* (Strasbourg: Council of Europe 1999).

Barrie Houlihan, 'The World Anti-Doping Agency: Prospects for Success', in O'Leary, ed., *Drugs and Doping in Sport* (London, Cavendish 2000) p. 125 *et seq.*

Klaus Huhn, *Doping, Doping und kein Ende* (Woltersdorf , Bock und Kübler 1991).

Klaus Huhn, *Die unendliche Doping-Story* (Berlin, Spotless-Verl. 1997).

R. Ingelsey, 'Court Sponsored Mediation: The Case Against Mandatory Participation', 56 *Modern Law Review* (1993) p. 441.

P. Jackson, *Natural Justice* (London, Sweet and Maxwell 1979).

W.H.A. Jonkers, *Inleiding tot de strafrechtsdogmatiek: het schuldbeginsel, het legaliteitsbeginsel, de strafbaarheidsvoorwaarden, de poging en de deelneming*, Studiepockets strafrecht, nr. 12 (Zwolle, Tjeenk Willink 1984).

Matthias Kamber, Primus Mullis, Martial Saugy, 'EPO – vom Medikament zur perfekten Wunderwaffe im Sport', *Neue Zürcher Zeitung* (2000) p. 37.

Matthias Kamber, Norbert Baume, Martial Saugy, Laurent Rivier, 'Nutritional Supplements as a Source for Positive Doping Cases', 11 *International Journal of Sport Nutrition* (2001) p. 258-263.

Matthias Kamber, Nadja Mahler, Simone Bader, *Doping – Dopingkontrolle 2004: Booklet für Athletinnen und Athleten* (Magglingen, BASPO 2004).

Craig Kammerer, 'What is Doping and How is it Detected', in W. Wilson, E. Derse, eds., *Doping in Elite Sport. The Politics of Drugs in the Olympic Movement* (Champaign, Illinois 2001) p. 3-28.

Darren Kane, 'Twenty Years On: An Evaluation of the Court of Arbitration for Sport', in I. Blackshaw, R.C.R. Siekmann, J. Soek, eds., *The Court of Arbitration for Sport 1984–2004* (The Hague, T.M.C. Asser Press 2006), p. 455 *et seq.*

Ousmane Kane, 'The CAS Mediation Rules', in I. Blackshaw, R.C.R. Siekmann, J. Soek, eds., *The Court of Arbitration for Sport 1984–2004* (The Hague, T.M.C. Asser Press 2006), p. 194 *et seq.*

Gabrielle Kaufmann-Kohler, *Arbitration at the Olympics: Issues of Fast-track Dispute Resolution and Sports Law* (The Hague, Kluwer Law International 2001).

Gabrielle Kaufmann-Kohler, 'Arbitration at the Sydney Olympic Games', in I. Blackshaw, R.C.R. Siekmann, J. Soek, eds., *The Court of Arbitration for Sport 1984–2004* (The Hague, T.M.C. Asser Press 2006), p. 105 *et seq.*

Gabrielle Kaufmann-Kohler, Philippe Bärtsch, 'The Ordinary Arbitration Procedure of the Court of Arbitration for Sport', in I. Blackshaw, R.C.R. Siekmann, J. Soek, eds., *The Court of Arbitration for Sport 1984–2004* (The Hague, T.M.C. Asser Press 2006), p. 69 *et seq.*

G.W. Kernkamp, 'Verslag van de discussies bij de overige onderwerpen', in *Tuchtrecht en Fair Play* (Nederlandse Vereniging voor Procesrecht 1984).

Tim Kerr, 'Doped or Duped? The Nandrolone Jurisprudence', 3 *International Sports Law Review* (2001) p. 99.

Joseph Keul, *Doping: Pharmakologische Leistungssteigerung und Sport* (Frankfurt/M., Dt. Sportbund 1970).

Adolf Kimmel, *Die Verfassungen der EG- Mitgliedstaaten* (München Dt. Taschenbuch-Verl.; Beck 1993).

Uwe Klug, 'Doping als strafbare Verletzung der Rechtsgüter Leben und Gesundheit', Diss. (Würzburg, Univ., 1998)

Hans-Georg Koch, 'Straf- und arzneimittelrechtliche Probleme des Dopings aus rechtsvergleichender Sicht', in V. Röhricht, K. Vieweg, eds., *Doping-Forum* (Stuttgart, Boorberg 2000) p. 53.

Imke Köhler, *Ein Kommentar aus praktischer Sicht zu: The Drug Diary: A Modest Proposal to End Doping in Sport* (Ruhr-Universität Bochum, Fak. für Sozialwiss., Ruhr-Univ., 1996).

F.C. Kollen, 'Verenigingsrechtelijke aspecten van de relatie tussen het bestuur van een bond, de topsporters en hun trainer/coach', in N.J.P. Giltay Veth, ed., Sport en Recht, Deel 1 1992/ 1993, *Doping: ook een juridisch probleem*, p. 58 *et seq.*

F.C. Kollen, *De vereniging in de praktijk* (Deventer, Kluwer 1995).

Bernhard König, 'Sind Schiedsbreden auf den CAS/TAS wirksam?', *SpuRt* (2004) p. 137-138.

Christian Krähe, 'Beweislastprobleme im internationalen Sport – am Beispiel des Olympic Movement Anti-Doping-Codes', in Jochen Fritzweiler, ed., *Doping. Sanktionen, Beweise, Ansprüche* (Berne, Stämpfli; München, Beck; Wien, Manz 2000) p. 39-56.

Christian Krähe, 'The Appeals Procedure Before the CAS', in I. Blackshaw, R.C.R. Siekmann, J. Soek, eds., *The Court of Arbitration for Sport 1984–2004* (The Hague, T.M.C. Asser Press 2006), p. 99 *et seq.*

Zbeigniew Krawczyk, 'The Human Body as a Value', in Olin Kalevi, ed., *Contribution of Sociology to the Study of Sport: Festschrift Book in Honour of Professor Kalevi Heinilä* (Jyväskylä 1984).

Wolfgang Kreißig, 'Doping aus Athletensicht', in V. Röhricht, K. Vieweg, eds., *Doping-Forum* (Stuttgart, Boorberg 2000) p. 87-94.

Steffen Krieger, *Vereinsstrafen im deutschen, englischen, französischen und schweizerischen Recht. Insbesondere im Hinblick auf die Sanktionsbefugnisse von Sportverbänden* (Berlin, Duncker & Humblot 2003).

Mario Krogmann, *Grundrechte im Sport* (Berlin, Duncker und Humblot 1998).

Mario Krogmann, 'Zur Dopinggesetzgebung im Ausland' – Teil 1 t/m Teil 5, *SpuRt* (1999) p. 19 *et seq.*; 2/1999, p. 61; 4/1999, p. 148 *et seq.*; 1/2000, p. 13 *et seq.*; 3/2000, p. 106.

Arnd Krüger, 'Weshalb es mit den Dopingkontrollen nicht wie bisher weitergehen kann', *Neue Zürcher Zeitung* (1998) p. 37.

Arnd Krüger, 'Die Paradoxien des Dopings. Ein Überblick', in B. Heß, W.-D. Dressler, eds., *Aktuelle Rechtsfragen des Sports* (Heidelberg, Müller 1999) p. 11-34.

M.J.C. Leijten, *Tuchtrecht getoetst* (Arnhem, Gouda Quint 1991).

J.A.W. Lensing, *Amerikaans Strafrecht* (Arnhem, Gouda Quint 1996).

Ralf Lenz, *Die Verfassungsmäßigkeit von Anti-Doping-Bestimmungen* (Frankfurt am Main, Lang 2000).

J. Linck, 'Doping und staatliches Recht', *NJW* (1987) p, 2547.

Arne Ljungqvist, 'The IAAF Anti-Doping Philosophy', in Istvan Gyulai et al. eds., *International Amateur Athletic Federation: Doping is Cheating. Fight for a Clean Sport*. 1st World Anti-Doping Seminar, Report, Heusenstamm, Germany, March 14–16, 1994 (Monaco 1995) p. 20 *et seq.*

J. Lob, 'Dopage, responsabilité objective ("strict liability") et de quelques autres questions', 95(12) *SJZ* (1999) p. 272.

Frank van Look, *Vereinsstrafen als Vertragsstrafen. Ein Beitrag zum inneren Vereinsrecht* (Berlin, Duncker & Humblot 1990).

Jason Lowther, 'Criminal Law Regulation of Performance Enhancing Drugs: Welcome Formalisation or Knee Jerk Response?', in O'Leary, ed., *Drugs and Doping in Sport* (London, Cavendish 2000) p. 225 *et seq.*

Heinz Lünsch, *Doping im Sport* (Erlangen, perimed-Fachbuch-Verl.-Ges., 1991).

Günther Lüschen, 'Before and After Caracas – Drug Abuse and Doping as Deviant Behavior in Sport', in Olin Kalevi, ed., *Contribution of Sociology to the Study of Sport: Festschrift Book in Honour of Professor Kalevi Heinilä* (Jyväskylä, University of Jyväskylä 1984).

Filip de Ly, 'Internationale sportarbitrage en Olympische Spelen', 4 *Tijdschrift voor arbitrage* (2002) p. 158-162.

John MacAloon, 'Doping and Moral Authority: Sport Organisations Today', in W. Wilson, E. Derse, eds., *Doping in Elite Sport. The Politics of Drugs in the Olympic Movement* (Champaign, Illinois 2001) p. 205-224.

David B. Mack, 'Note, Reynolds v. International Amateur Athletic Federation: The Need for an Independent Tribunal in International Athletic Disputes', 653 *Connecticut Journal International Law* (1995) p. 617-627.

Harald Maniera, 'Doping mit anabolen Steroiden und die Auswirkungen auf das Reproduktionssystem bei 41 Schwerathleten', Diss. (Münster, Westfalen, Univ. 1990).

Joachim Mantey, 'Dopingkontrolle, Zuständigkeit', in *Internationaler Sport-Recht Kongress* (AVRIO Publication 2000), p. 176-181.

U. Mareck-Engelke, H. Geyer, W. Schänzer, '19-Norandrosterone – Criteria for the Decision Making Process', in W. Schänzer, H. Geyer, A. Gotzmann, U. Mareck-Engelke, eds., *Recent Advances in Doping Analysis* (6) (Köln, Institut für Biochemie, Deutsche Sporthochschule Köln 1998) p. 119-125.

U. Mareck-Engelke, H. Geyer, W. Schänzer, 'Tetrahydrocannabinol (THC) in Dope Control', in W. Schänzer, H. Geyer, A. Gotzmann, U. Mareck-Engelke, eds., *Recent Advances in Doping Analysis* (7) (Köln, Institut für Biochemie, Deutsche Sporthochschule Köln 1999) p. 51-60.

Dante Marrazzo, 'Athletes and Drug Testing: Why Do We Care if Athletes Inhale?', *Marquette Sports Law Journal* (1997) p. 75-91.

Dirk-Reiner Martens, Frank Oschütz, 'Die Entscheidungen des TAS in Sydney', *SpuRt* (2001) p. 4-8.

Dirk-Reiner Martens, 'CAS Landmark Decisions', in I. Blackshaw, R.C.R. Siekmann, J. Soek, eds., *The Court of Arbitration for Sport 1984–2004* (The Hague, T.M.C. Asser Press 2006), p. 235 *et seq.*

Achilleas Mavromatis, 'The Fight Against Doping: Overview of the Jurisprudence and the Criminal and Pharmaceutical Law; Problems of Anti-Doping Agencies', *Sports Law Commission 44th Congress*, Buenos Aires 2000, Report for Greece.

Keba Mbaye, 'Une nouvelle institution d'arbitrage: le Tribunal Arbitral du Sport (T.A.S.)', Annuaire français de Droit International XXX (1984); in I. Blackshaw, R.C.R. Siekmann, J. Soek, eds., *The Court of Arbitration for Sport 1984–2004* (The Hague, T.M.C. Asser Press 2006), p. 6 *et seq.*

D. McArdle, '"Say it ain't so, Mo" International performers' perceptions of drug use and the Diane Modahl affair', in O'Leary, ed., *Drugs and Doping in Sport* (London, Cavendish 2000) p. 91 *et seq.*

Peter McIntosh, 'Systems of Value and International Sport', in Olin Kalevi, ed., *Contribution of Sociology to the Study of Sport: Festschrift Book in Honour of Professor Kalevi Heinilä* (Jyväskylä, University of Jyväskylä 1984).

Elizabeth McKnight, 'The European Commission and sport', in *International Athletic Foundation, Supplement to the official Proceedings of the IAF Symposium on Sport and Law*, Monte Carlo, 31 Jan.–2 Feb. 1991 (Monaco 1995) p. 131 *et seq.*

Richard McLaren, 'CAS Advisory Opinions', in I. Blackshaw, R.C.R. Siekmann, J. Soek, eds., *The Court of Arbitration for Sport 1984–2004* (The Hague, T.M.C. Asser Press 2006), p. 180 *et seq.*

Volkmar Mehle, 'Doping und Strafrecht', in *Internationaler Sport-Recht Kongress* (AVRIO Publication 2000), p. 182-194.

Martin Meinberg, Dirk Olzen, Steffen Neumann, 'Gutachten über die rechtliche Möglichkeit zur Verhinderung des Doping-Mißbrauchs', in W. Schild, ed., *Rechtliche Fragen des Dopings* (Heidelberg, Müller, Juristischer Verl. 1986) p. 63-92.

Heiner Melchinger, *Einstellungen junger Menschen zum Doping im Sport: Ergebnisse empirischer Erhebungen und Implikationen für die Konzeption von Anti-Doping-Kampagnen* (Hannover, IES 1997).

Thomas Mestwerdt, *Doping – Sittenwidrigkeit und staatliches Sanktionsbedürfnis?* (Hamburg, Mauke 1997).

H. Moeller, 'Wissenswertes zum Nandrolon', *Zeitschrift für Sportmedizin* (1999) p. 382-383.

Tiberius Mohr, *Medizinische Versorgung im Brieftaubensport: Vorsorge – Therapie – Vitamine – Doping* (Stuttgart, Enke 1998).

Miquel de Moragas, 'Esport mediàtic i espectacle: què ens en queda, de lésport?: IEC Scientific Conference, *The Limits of Sport: Doping'*, Barcelona, 17 and 18 June, 1999: http://www.blues.uab.es/olympic.studies/ doping/moragasc.htm.

P. Morris, P. Spink, 'Court of Arbitration for Sport', in W. Stewart, ed., *Sports Law: The Scots Perspective* (Edinburgh, T&T Clark 2000) p. 61.

Tony Morton-Hooper, 'Have We Created a Monster? – A Brief Look at Some Striking Features of Anti-Doping Rules and Procedures', *Drugs in Sport – A Time for Re-evaluation?* A symposium on Legal and Ethical Issues, Royal College of Physicians, 23 April.

Tony Morton-Hooper, 'Sport's War on Drugs Risks Injustices, Says Tony Morton-Hooper', *Times* (April 11, 2000).

David R. Mottram, *Drugs in Sport* (London, Spon 1996).

Jan Mühlethaler, 'Interview mit Martial Saugy Dopingdiskurses', in Michael Gamper, M. J. Mühlethaler, F. Reidhaar, eds., *Doping. Spitzensport als gesellschaftliches Problem* (Zürich, NZZ-Verl. 2000) p. 219-233.

Anja Müller, *Doping im Sport als strafbare Gesundheitsbeschädigung (paras. 223 Abs. 1, 230 StGB)?* (Baden-Baden, Nomos-Verl.-Ges. 1993).

Caroline Müller, Guido Britz, 'Doping im Sport – Perspektiven für ein deutsches Anti-Doping-Gesetz', 2 *Magazin Forschung* (1999) (Universität des Saarlandes) p. 36 *et seq.*

R. K. Müller, 'Eignung von Blut und/oder Urin zum Doping-Nachweis', in Bundesinstitut für Sportwissenschaft, ed., *Blut und/oder Urin zur Dopingkontrolle* (Schorndorf 1996) p. 165-186.

Ingo von Münch, *Grundgesetz-Kommentar* (München, Beck 2000).

James A.R. Nafziger, 'International Law as a Process of Resolving Disputes', in *International Athletic Foundation, Supplement to the official Proceedings of the IAF Symposium on Sport and Law,* Monte Carlo, 31 Jan.–2 Feb. 1991 (Monaco 1995) p. 20 *et seq.*

James A.R. Nafziger, 'International Law as a Process of Resolving Disputes', 45 *International Comparative Law Quarterly* (1996) p. 130 *et seq.*

James A.R. Nafziger, 'The Court of Arbitration for Sport and the General Process of International Sports Law', in Wybo P. Heere, ed. *International law and The Hague's 750th Anniversary* (The Hague, T.M.C. Asser Press 1999) p. 239-250.

James A.R. Nafziger, 'American Law in a Time of Global Interdependence', in U.S. National Reports to the XVIth International Congress of Comparative Law: Section II, Dispute Resolution in the Arena of International Sports Competition, 50 *Am.J.Comp.L.* (2002) p. 161.

James A.R. Nafziger, 'Lex Sportiva', (1-2) *ISLJ* (2004) p. 3 *et seq.*

James A.R. Nafziger, 'Lex Sportiva and CAS', in I. Blackshaw, R.C.R. Siekmann, J. Soek, eds., *The Court of Arbitration for Sport 1984–2004* (The Hague, T.M.C. Asser Press 2006), p. 420 *et seq.*

Stephan Netzle, 'Das Internationale Sport-Schiedsgericht in Lausanne. Zusammensetzung, Zuständigkeit und Verfahren', in Volker Röhricht, Stephan Netzle, eds., *Sportgerichtsbarkeit* (Stuttgart, Boorberg 1997) p. 9-18.

Stephan Netzle, 'Wie hält es das internationale Schiedsgericht mit dem Doping?', in Klaus Vieweg, ed., *Doping – Realität und Recht* (Berlin, Duncker & Humblot 1998) p. 197-218.

Stephan Netzle, 'Doping als rechtliche Herausforderung Dopingdiskurses', in Michael Gamper, M. J. Mühlethaler, F. Reidhaar, eds., *Doping. Spitzensport als gesellschaftliches Problem* (Zürich, NZZ-Verl. 2000) p. 263-285.

Stephan Netzle, 'Examination of Witnesses and Experts in CAS Hearings. Which Rules Apply to the Examination of Witnesses and Experts in a CAS Hearing?', in I. Blackshaw, R.C.R. Siekmann, J. Soek, eds., *The Court of Arbitration for Sport 1984–2004* (The Hague, T.M.C. Asser Press 2006), p. 210 *et seq.*

Fritz Nicklisch, *Inhaltskontrolle von Verbandsnormen* (Heidelberg, Müller Juristischer Verl. 1982).

W. Nieboer, 'Strafrechtelijke zorgplichten', in *Liber Amicorum Th.W. van Veen – Opstellen aangeboden aan Th.W. van Veen ter gelegenheid van zijn vijfenzestigste verjaardag* (Arnhem, Gouda Quint 1985) p. 259.

John O'Leary, 'The Regulation of Drug Use in Sport', in Simon Gardiner, Alexandra Felix, Mark James, Roger Welch & John O'Leary eds., *Sports Law* (London-Sydney, Cavendish 1998) p. 161 *et seq.*

John O'Leary, 'Doping Solutions and the Problem with Problems', in O'Leary, ed., *Drugs and Doping in Sport* (London, Cavendish 2000) p. 255 *et seq.*

John O'Leary, 'Drugs Update: Nandrolone', 3(2) *Sports Law Bulletin* (2000) p. 11.

John O'Leary, 'The State of the Play', in O'Leary, ed., *Drugs and Doping in Sport* (London, Cavendish 2000) p. 1 *et seq.*

José Odriozola, 'The European Perspective: International Amateur Athletic Federation', in Istvan Gyulai et al., eds., *Doping is Cheating. Fight for a Clean Sport. 1st World Anti-Doping Seminar*, Report, Heusenstamm, Germany, March 14–16, 1994 (Monaco 1995) p. 14 *et seq.*

Frank Oschütz, 'The Jurisprudence of the CAS in Doping Cases', *ISLJ* (2001) p. 22-30.

Frank Oschütz, 'The Arbitrability of Sport Disputes and the Rules of the Game', in I. Blackshaw, R.C.R. Siekmann, J. Soek, eds., *The Court of Arbitration for Sport 1984–2004* (The Hague, T.M.C. Asser Press 2006), p. 200 *et seq.*

Frank Oschütz, 'Doping Cases before the CAS and the World Anti-Doping Code', in I. Blackshaw, R.C.R. Siekmann, J. Soek, eds., *The Court of Arbitration for Sport 1984–2004* (The Hague, T.M.C. Asser Press 2006), p. 246 *et seq.*

Frank Oschütz, *Sportschiedsgerichtsbarkeit: die Schiedsverfahren des Tribunal Arbitral du Sport vor dem Hintergrund des schweizerischen und deutschen Schiedsverfahrensrecht* (Berlin, Duncker & Humblot 2005).

D. Panagiotopulos, 'Court of Arbitration for Sports', 6 *Villanova Sports and Entertainment LJ* (1999) p. 49.

Dimitrios Panagiotopoulos, Gregory Ionnidis, 'The Regulation of Sports Activities in Greece', in Andrew Caiger, Simon Gardiner, eds., *Professional Sport in the European Union: Regulation and Re-regulation* (The Hague, T.M.C. Asser Press 2000) p. 259 *et seq.*

Richard Parrish, 'Reconciling Conflicting Approaches to Sport in the European Union', in Andrew Caiger, Simon Gardiner, eds., *Professional Sport in the European Union: Regulation and Re-regulation* (The Hague, T.M.C. Asser Press 2000) p. 21 *et seq.*

Jim Parry, 'Ethics and Doping', *IEC Scientific Conference: The Limits of Sport: Doping*, Barcelona, 17 and 18 June, 1999. http://www.blues.uab.es/olympic.studies/doping/parry.htm.

Christian Paul, *Grenzwerte im Doping. Naturwissenschaftliche Grundlagen und rechtliche Bedeutung* (Berlin, Duncker & Humblot 2004).

Jan Paulsson, 'Arbitration of International Sport Disputes', 9(4) *Arbitration International* (1993), in I. Blackshaw, R.C.R. Siekmann, J. Soek, eds., *The Court of Arbitration for Sport 1984–2004* (The Hague, T.M.C. Asser Press 2006), p. 40 *et seq.*

Guillermo Pérez, 'The Sporting Calendar. The Effort of Elite Competition and the Endurance of the Human Body', IEC Scientific Conference, *The Limits of Sport: Doping*, Barcelona, 17 and 18 June, 1999, <www.blues.uab.es/olympic.studies/doping/ perez.htm>.

Jean-François Perrin, *Droit Civil V, Droit de l'association* (Fribourg, Switzerland, Ed. Universitaires 1992).

Mario Pescante, 'Different Models of Sports Law in Europe', in *International Athletic Foundation, Supplement to the official Proceedings of the IAF Symposium on Sport and Law*, Monte Carlo, 31 Jan.–2 Feb. 1991 (Monaco 1995) p. 127 *et seq.*

Grischka Petri, *Die Dopingsanktion* (Berlin, Duncker & Humblot 2004).

Gerhard Pfeil, 'Positiv enthemmt', 49 *Der Spiegel* (1998) p. 155.

Bernhard Pfister, 'Die Doping-Rechtsprechung des TAS', *SpuRt* (2000) p. 133-137.

Bernhard Pfister, Udo Steiner, *Sportrecht von A-Z – Vereine und Verbande, Sportanlagen, Arbeitsrecht und Besteuerung, Unfallhaftung, Sponsoring, Gerichtsbarkeit* (München, Dt. Taschenbuch-Verl.; München, Beck 1995).

Bodo Pieroth, Bernhard Schlink, *Grundrechte. Staatsrecht II* (Heidelberg 1999).

Andrea Pinna, 'The Trials and Tribulations of the Court of Arbitration for Sport. Contribution to the Study of the Arbitration of Disputes concerning Disciplinary Sanctions', in I. Blackshaw, R.C.R. Siekmann, J. Soek, eds., *The Court of Arbitration for Sport 1984–2004* (The Hague, T.M.C. Asser Press 2006), p. 386 *et seq.*

Alain Plantey, 'Quelques observations sur l'arbitrage sportif international. A propos d'un récent arrêt du Tribunal fédéral suisse', 130(4) *Journal du Droit International* (2003) p. 1085-1104; in I. Blackshaw, R.C.R. Siekmann, J. Soek, eds., *The Court of Arbitration for Sport 1984–2004* (The Hague, T.M.C. Asser Press 2006), p. 54 *et seq.*

Alain Plantey, 'Independence of the CAS recognised by the Swiss Federal Tribunal (translation)', in I. Blackshaw, R.C.R. Siekmann, J. Soek, eds., *The Court of Arbitration for Sport 1984–2004* (The Hague, T.M.C. Asser Press 2006), p. 50 *et seq.*

Anthony Polvino, 'Arbitration as Preventative Medicine for Olympic Ailments: The International Olympic Committee's Court of Arbitration for Sport and the future for the Settlement of International Sporting Disputes', 8 *Emory International L Rev* (1994) p. 347; in I. Blackshaw, R.C.R. Siekmann, J. Soek, eds., *The Court of Arbitration for Sport 1984–2004* (The Hague, T.M.C. Asser Press 2006), p. 326 *et seq.*

Clemens Prokop, 'The Legal Relationship Between Athlete, National & International Federations. Sporting Law vis à vis National Public Law', in Istvanú Gyulai et al., eds., *International Amateur Athletic Federation: Doping is Cheating. Fight for a Clean Sport.* 1st World Anti-Doping Seminar, Report, Heusenstamm, Germany, March 14–16, 1994 (Monaco 1995) p. 59 *et seq.*

Clemens Prokop, *Die Grenzen der Dopingverbote* (Baden-Baden, Nomos-Verl.-Ges. 2000).

Clemens Prokop, 'Probleme einer Nationalen Anti-Doping-Agentur', in V. Röhricht, K. Vieweg, eds., *Doping-Forum* (Stuttgart, Boorberg 2000) p. 77 *et seq.*

Clemens Prokop, 'Probleme der aktuellen Dopingbekämpfung aus Sicht nationaler/internationaler Verbände', in Jochen Fritzweiler, ed., *Doping. Sanktionen, Beweise, Ansprüche* (Berne, Stämpfli; München, Beck; Wien, Manz 2000) p. 79-93.

Clemens Prokop, 'Vorschläge zur Reform der Doping-Regelungen der IAAF', in Jochen Fritzweiler, ed., *Doping. Sanktionen, Beweise, Ansprüche* (Berne, Stämpfli; München, Beck; Wien, Manz 2000) p. 95-102.

N. Raber, 'Dispute Resolution in Olympic Sport: The Court of Arbitration for Sport', 8 *Seton Hall J Sport Law* (1998) p. 75.

Joachim Rain, *Die Einwilligung des Sportlers beim Doping* (Frankfurt am Main, Lang 1998).

Matthieu Reeb, 'The Court of Arbitration for Sport (CAS)', in Matthieu Reeb, ed., *Digest of CAS Awards 1986-1998* (Berne, Staempfli 1998) p. XXIII-XXXI.

Matthieu Reeb, 'Die CAS-Rechtsprechung in Doping-Fällen', in V. Röhricht, K. Vieweg, eds., *Doping-Forum* (Stuttgart, Boorberg 2000) p. 63-70.

Matthieu Reeb, 'The Court of Arbitration for Sport', 3(4) *Sports Law Bulletin* (2000) p. 10.

Matthieu Reeb, 'The Court of Arbitration for Sport: History and operation', in Matthieu Reeb, ed., *Digest of CAS Awards II 1998-2000* (The Hague, Kluwer Law International 2002) p. XXIII-XXX.

Matthieu Reeb, 'The Court of Arbitration for Sport: History and operation', in Matthieu Reeb, ed., *Digest of CAS Awards III 2001-2003* (The Hague, Kluwer Law International 2004) p. XXVII-XXXV.

Matthieu Reeb, 'The Role and Functions of the Court of Arbitration for Sport (CAS)', in I. Blackshaw, R.C.R. Siekmann, J. Soek, eds., *The Court of Arbitration for Sport 1984–2004* (The Hague, T.M.C. Asser Press 2006), p. 31 *et seq.*

Bernhard Reichert, 'Sponsoring und nationales Sportverbandsrecht', in Klaus Vieweg, ed., *Sponsoring im Sport* (Stuttgart, Boorberg 1996) p. 31 ff.

Michael Reinhart, 'Sportverbandsgerichtsbarkeit und Doppelbestrafungsverbot', *SpuRt* (2001) p. 48.

J. Remmelink, *Mr. D. Hazewinkel-Suringa's Inleiding tot de studie van het Nederlandse Strafrecht* (Arnhem, Gouda Quint 1994).

Eike Reschke, *SpuRt* (2001) p. 184.

Eike Reschke, 'Erwiderung auf Reinhart', *SpuRt* (2001) p. 45.

Dieter Reuter, 'Voraussetzungen und Grenzen der Verbindlichkeit internationalen Sportrechis für Sportvereine und Sportler', Dieter Reuter, ed., *Einbindung des nationalen Sportrechts in internationale Bezüge* (Heidelberg, C.F. Müller Juristischer Verlag 1987), p. 53.

Antonio Rigozzi, 'Provisional Measures in CAS Arbitrations', in I. Blackshaw, R.C.R. Siekmann, J. Soek, eds., *The Court of Arbitration for Sport 1984–2004* (The Hague, T.M.C. Asser Press 2006), p. 216 *et seq.*

Gary R. Roberts, 'Harmonisation of Laws in Sporting Matters Lessons From the Butch Reynolds Case', in *International Athletic Foundation, Supplement to the official Proceedings of the IAF Symposium on Sport and Law,* Monte Carlo, 31 Jan.–2 Feb. 1991 (Monaco 1995) p. 13 *et seq.*

J.P. Rochat, 'The Court of Arbitration for Sport', in *International Athletic Foundation, Supplement to the official Proceedings of the IAF Symposium on Sport and Law*, Monte Carlo, 31 Jan.–2 Feb. 1991 (Monaco 1995) p. 43 *et seq.*

Volker Röhricht, 'Chancen und Grenzen von Sportgerichtsverfahren nach deutschem Recht', in Volker Röhricht, Stephan Netzle', eds., *Sportgerichtsbarkeit* (Stuttgart, Boorberg 1997).

Anne Röthel, 'Neues Doping-Gesetz für Frankreich', *Spurt* (1999) p. 20 *et seq.*

Anne Röthel, 'Das Recht der französischen Sportvereine und Sportverbände – Ein Überblick aus Anlass der jüngsten Änderungen des Sportgesetzes', *Spurt* (2001) p. 89 *et seq.*

Staffan Sahlstrom, 'Out-of-competition testing the IAAF and your athlete', in Istvan Gyulai et al., eds., *International Amateur Athletic Federation: Doping is Cheating. Fight for a Clean Sport.* 1st World Anti-Doping Seminar, Report, Heusenstamm, Germany, March 14–16, 1994 (Monaco 1995) p. 21 *et seq.*

Peter Saladin, *Grundrechte im Wandel. Die Rechtsprechung des schweizerischen Bundesgerichts zu den Grundrechten in einer sich ändernden Umwelt* (Berne, Stämpfli 1982).

Adam Samuel, Richard Gearhart, 'Sporting Arbitration and the International Olympic Committee's Court of Arbitration for Sport', in I. Blackshaw, R.C.R. Siekmann, J. Soek, eds., *The Court of Arbitration for Sport 1984–2004* (The Hague, T.M.C. Asser Press 2006), p. 313 *et seq.*

M. Saugy, N. Robinson, C. Cardis, C. Schweizer, L. Rivier, P. Mangin, C. Ayotte, J. Dvorak, 'Nandrolone Metabolites in Football Players: Utility for In and Out of Competition Testing', in W. Schänzer, H. Geyer, A. Gotzmann, U. Mareck-Engelke, eds., *Recent Advances in Doping Analysis* (7) (Köln 1999) p. 95-108.

Otto Schantz, 'Le sport dans une société dopante', IEC Scientific Conference, *The Limits of Sport: Doping,* Barcelona, 17 and 18 June, 1999, http://www.blues.uab.es/olympic.studies/doping/schantz.htm.

Wilhelm Schänzer, 'Neuere Entwicklungen in der Dopinganalytik', in Klaus Vieweg, ed., *Doping – Realität und Recht* (Berlin, Duncker & Humblot 1998) p. 51-66.

Wilhelm Schänzer, 'Positiver Nandrolon-Nachweis – sind Irrtümer möglich?' *Zeitschrift für Sportmedizin* (1999) p. 382.

Wilhelm Schänzer, 'Die medizinische Revolution. Über die Effizienz von Dopingkontrollen und die Nebenwirkungen verbotener Substanzen Dopingdiskurses', in Michael Gamper, M. J. Mühlethaler, F. Reidhaar, eds., *Doping. Spitzensport als gesellschaftliches Problem* (Zürich, NZZ-Verl. 2000) p. 191-218.

Wilhelm Schänzer, 'Dopinganalytik und Grenzwertproblematik', in V. Röhricht, K. Vieweg, eds., *Doping-Forum* (Stuttgart, Boorberg 2000) p. 17-26.

Wilhelm Schänzer, 'Dopingkontrollen und aktueller Stand der Nachweismethoden', Zeitschrift *für Sportmedizin* (2000) p. 260-266.

Urs Scherrer, 'Strafrechtliche und strafprozesuale Grundsätze bei Verbandssanktionen', in Jochen Fritzweiler, ed., *Doping. Sanktionen, Beweise, Ansprüche* (Berne, Stämpfli; München, Beck; Wien, Manz 2000) p. 119 *et seq.*

Urs Scherrer, *Sportrecht: eine Begriffserläuterung* (Zürich, Orell Füssli Verlag 2001).

Urs Scherrer, 'Anfechtungsklage im Lichte von Monopol-Sportverbänden', *SpuRt* (2002) p. 39.

Wolfgang Schild, 'Doping in strafrechtlicher Sicht', in W. Schild, ed., *Rechtliche Fragen des Dopings* (Heidelberg, Müller, Juristischer Verl. 1986).

Martin Schimke, Christophe DeKepper, Günter Poll, *Sport in der Europäischen Union* (Heidelberg, Müller 1995).

Martin Schimke, *Sportrecht* (Frankfurt am Main, Fischer Taschenbuch Verlag; Cologne, Carl Heymann Verlag 1996).

Angela J. Schneider, Robert B. Butcher, 'An Ethical Analysis of Drug Testing', in W. Wilson, E. Derse, eds., *Doping in Elite Sport. The Politics of Drugs in the Olympic Movement* (Champaign, Illinois 2001) p. 129-152.

Christa Brigitte Schneider-Grohe, *Doping: e. kriminolog. u. kriminalist. Unters. zur Problematik d. künstl. Leistungssteigerung im Sport u. zur rechtl. Handhabung dieser Fälle* (Lübeck, Schmidt-Römhild 1979).

Claudia Schoene, *Doping beim Pferd* (Stuttgart, Enke 1996).

Dieter Schwab, 'Zivilrechtliche Haftung beim Doping', in W. Schild, ed., *Rechtliche Fragen des Dopings* (Heidelberg, Müller, Juristischer Verl. 1986).

Michael Schweizer, 'Die Freizügigkeit des Berufssportlers in der Europaischen Gemeinschaft', in Dieter Reuter, ed., *Einbindung des nationalen Sportrechts in internationale Bezüge* (Heidelberg, C.F. Müller Juristischer Verlag 1987), p. 71.

Jürgen Segerer, *Wirkung der Grundrechte zwischen Sportlern, Sportvereinigung und Staat* (Bayreuth, Verl. PCO 1999).

Jordi Segura, 'Sports Drug Testing', IEC Scientific Conference, *The Limits of Sport: Doping*, Barcelona, 17 and 18 June, 1999, http://www.blues.uab.es/olympic.studies/doping/segura.htm.

Michael Sehling, Reinhold Pollert, Dieter Hackfort, *Doping im Sport: medizinische, sozialwissenschaftliche und juristische Aspekte* (München, BLV 1989).

Robert C. R. Siekmann, Janwillem Soek, eds., *Basic Documents of International Sports Organisations* (The Hague, Kluwer Law International 1998).

Robert C. R. Siekmann, Janwillem Soek, Andrea Bellani, eds., *Doping Rules of International Sports Organisations* (The Hague, T.M.C. Asser Press 1999).

Robert C. R. Siekmann, 'Legal Comparison and the Harmonisation of Doping Rules', *ISLJ* (2001) p. 4.

Robert C. R. Siekmann, Janwillem Soek, eds., *Arbitral and Disciplinary Rules of International Sports Organisations* (The Hague, T.M.C. Asser Press 2001).

Robert C. R. Siekmann, Janwillem Soek, eds., *The European Union and Sport* (The Hague, T.M.C. Asser Press 2005), p. 643-648.

Luc Silance, 'Dopingkontrolle in Belgien', in Klaus Vieweg, ed., *Doping – Realität und Recht* (Berlin, Duncker & Humblot 1998) p. 219 *et seq.*

Luc Silance, 'The Approach to Sports Policy in Belgium', in Andrew Caiger, Simon Gardiner, eds., *Professional Sport in the European Union: Regulation and Re-regulation* (The Hague, T.M.C. Asser Press 2000) p. 267 *et seq.*

Bruno Simma, 'The Court of Arbitration for Sport', in Karl-Heinz Böckstiegel, Hans-Ernst Folz, Jörg Manfred Mössner, Karl Zemanek, Carl Heymanns, eds., *Völkerrecht – Recht der Internationalen Organisationen – Weltwirtschaftsrecht – Law of Nations – Law of International Organizations – World's Economic Law, Festschrift für Ignaz Seldl-Hohenveldern, Liber amicorum honouring Ignaz Seldl-Hohenveldern* (Cologne, Heymann 1988) p. 584.

Bruno Simma, 'The Court of Arbitration for Sport', in I. Blackshaw, R.C.R. Siekmann, J. Soek, eds., *The Court of Arbitration for Sport 1984–2004* (The Hague, T.M.C. Asser Press 2006), p. 21 *et seq.*

Vyv Simson, *Geld, Macht und Doping: das Ende der olympischen Idee* (München, Knaus 1992).

Elies van Sliedregt, *'The Criminal Responsibility of Individuals for Violations of International Humanitarian Law'*, PhD. Tilburg (The Hague, T.M.C. Asser Press 2003).

Michelle Smith-de Bruin, 'Irish CAS', in I. Blackshaw, R.C.R. Siekmann, J. Soek, eds., *The Court of Arbitration for Sport 1984–2004* (The Hague, T.M.C. Asser Press 2006), p. 294 *et seq.*

Janwillem Soek, 'Een zaak met een luchtje', *Sportzaken* (1993) p. 60-62.

Janwillem Soek, 'Drugs in Sport: A Time for Re-evaluation?', *Sportzaken* (1999) p. 75-76.

Janwillem Soek, 'Die prozessualen Garantien des Athleten in einem Dopingverfahren', in V. Röhricht, K. Vieweg, eds., *Doping-Forum* (Stuttgart, Boorberg 2000) p. 35-52.

Janwillem Soek, 'Euro 2000, UEFA en doping', *Sportzaken* (2000) p. 60-64.

Janwillem Soek, 'Doping in de denksport', *Sportzaken* (2000) p. 50 *et seq.*

Janwillem Soek, 'The Fundamental Rights of Athletes in Doping Trials', in O'Leary, ed., *Drugs and Doping in Sport* (London, Cavendish 2000) p. 57 *et seq.*

Janwillem Soek, 'Doping: stimulantia voor de congrescultuur', *Sportzaken* (2000) p. 54-57 .

Janwillem Soek, 'The Legal Nature of Doping Law', *ISLJ* (2002) p. 2-7.

Janwillem Soek, 'The WADA World Anti-Doping Code: The Road to Harmonisation', *ISLJ* (2003) p. 2-11.

Janwillem Soek, Emile N. Vrijman, 'De Olympic Movement Anti-Doping Code: de moed van de herder', *Sportzaken* (2000) p. 76-82.

Jeffrey Spender, 'The Integrity of Sporting Performance at the Olympic Games and at Other Elite Sports Events', *9th Greek Australian Legal and Medical Conference*, Rhodes, Greece 2003, <www.lmconference.com.au/papers/2003/spender.html>.

Barbara Spindler, Jochen Fritzweiler, 'Verbandsregelungen zur Dopingbekämpfung', in Jochen Fritzweiler, ed., *Doping. Sanktionen, Beweise, Ansprüche* (Berne, Stämpfli; München, Beck; Wien, Manz 2000) p. 133 *et seq.*

Giselher Spitzer, *Doping in der DDR: ein historischer Überblick zu einer konspirativen Praxis*; *Genese – Verantwortung – Gefahren* (Cologne, Bundesinstitut für Sportwissenschaft 1998).

H.T. van Staveren, M.J.G. Das, *Aspecten van strafrecht en geneesmiddelenrecht bij dopinggeduide middelen – in het bijzonder anabole steroïden* (Amsterdam, Kluwer 1990).

H.T. van Staveren, *Op de grens van sportregel en rechtsregel* (Deventer, Kluwer 1992).

Udo Steiner, 'Verfassungsfragen des Sports', *NJW* (1991) p. 2729-2736.

Udo Steiner, 'Doping aus verfassungsrechtlicher Sicht', in V. Röhricht, K. Vieweg, eds., *Doping-Forum* (Stuttgart, Boorberg 2000) p. 125-138.

Udo Steiner, 'Doping aus verfassungsrechtlicher Sicht', *ISLJ* (2000) p. 13-16.

Udo Steiner, 'Gegenwartsfragen des Sportrechts', Peter J. Tettinger, Klaus Vieweg, eds., *Ausgewählte Schriften* (Berlin, Duncker & Humblot 2004).

Robert Stinson, 'Harmonisation of Laws as They Relate to Sport', in *International Athletic Foundation, Supplement to the official Proceedings of the IAF Symposium on Sport and Law*, Monte Carlo, 31 Jan.–2 Feb. 1991 (Monaco 1995) p. 180 *et seq.*

Frans Stoele, Rens van Kleij, *Anti-Doping policy in the Netherlands – A report on compiance with the Anti-Doping Convention of the Council of Europe by the Netherlands* (Capelle aan den IJssel, NeCeDo 2001).

Vladislav Stolyarov, 'The Aesthetic Value of Sport', in Olin Kalevi, ed., *Contribution of Sociology to the Study of Sport: Festschrift Book in Honour of Professor Kalevi Heinilä* (Jyväskylä, University of Jyväskylä 1984).

Michael S Straubel, 'Arbitrating Sports Disputes: A World View', 35(2) *Valparaiso University Law Review* (2001) p. 353-355.

Thomas Summerer, *Internationales Sportrecht vor dem staatlichen Richter – in der Bundesrepublik Deutschland, Schweiz, USA und England* (Munich, Verlag V. Florentz GmbH 1990).

Thomas Summerer, *Internationales Sportrecht Kongreß*. 4./5, November 1999.

Andrzej J. Swarc, 'Legislation on Sports in Poland', in Andrew Caiger, Simon Gardiner, eds., *Professional Sport in the European Union: Regulation and Re-regulation* (The Hague, T.M.C. Asser Press 2000) p. 237 *et seq.*

Schweizerischer Landesverband für Sport, *Doping: Weisungen zur Bekämpfung der unerlaubten pharmakologisch-medizinischen Leistungsbeeinflussung* (Berne, SLS 1978).

Jan Tamboer, Johan Steenbergen, *Sportfilosofie* (Leende, Damon 2000).

Lauri Tarasti, 'Practical Problems Arising in Anti-Doping Cases Before Tribunals. How to Make the New Supreme IOC/ASOIF Court Effective', in *International Athletic Foundation, Supplement to the official Proceedings of the IAF Symposium on Sport and Law,* Monte Carlo, 31 Jan.–2 Feb. 1991 (Monaco 1995) p. 83 *et seq.*

Lauri Tarasti, 'When Can an Athlete be Punished for a Doping Offence? Procedural Faults and the Burden of Proof', IEC Scientific Conference: *The Limits of Sport: Doping*, Barcelona, 17 and 18 June, 1999, http://www.blues.uab.es/olympic.studies/doping/tarasti.htm.

Lauri Tarasti, *Legal Solutions in International Doping Cases. Awards by the IAAF Arbitration Panel 1985–1999* (Milan, SEP Editrice 2000).

Peter J. Tettinger, 'Die Dopingproblematik im Lichte der europäischen Grundrechtediskussion', in Klaus Vieweg, ed., *Doping – Realität und Recht* (Berlin, Duncker & Humblot 1998) p. 89-112.

Arthur Thomas, *Hormone im Ausdauersport. EPO, Steroide, Wachstumshormone* (Rosenheim, ASS-Verl. 2000).

Angelika Thönneßen, *Doping in der Schule?: leistungsstimulierende Substanzen als thematische Gegenstände der Gesundheitserziehung im Sportunterricht* (Hamburg, Kovac 1999).

Manfred Tietzel, *The Peculiar Economics of Doping* (Duisburg, Gerhard-Mercator-Universität 1999).

I.T.F. Timmermans, Emile N. Vrijman, *Doping in de sport* (Arnhem, NeCeDo 1992).

Jan Todd, Terry Todd, 'Significant Events in the History of Drug Testing and the Olympic Movement', in W. Wilson, E. Derse, eds., *Doping in Elite Sport. The Politics of Drugs in the Olympic Movement* (Champaign, Illinois 2001) p. 63-128.

Gerry Tucker, Antonio Rigozzi with Wang Wenying and Robert Morgan, 'Sports Arbitration for the 2008 Beijing Olympic Games', 69(3) *Arbitration: the journal of the Chartered Institute of Arbitrators* (2003) p. 184-199; in I. Blackshaw, R.C.R. Siekmann, J. Soek, eds., *The Court of Arbitration for Sport 1984–2004* (The Hague, T.M.C. Asser Press 2006), p. 160 *et seq.*

George Turner, 'Die Einwilligung des Sportlers zum Doping', *NJW* (1991) p. 2943-2945.

Jochen Tyrolt, 'Sportschiedsgerichtsbarkeit und zwingendes staatliches Recht', in Klaus Vieweg, ed., *Spektrum des Sportrechts*: Referate zweier Gemeinschaftagungen der Universitäten Erlangen und Tübingen im Deutschen Olympischen Institut (Berlin, Duncker & Humblot 2003) p. 76-104.

Karl-Josef Ulmen, *Pharmakologische Manipulationen (Doping) im Leistungssport der DDR: eine juristische Untersuchung* (Frankfurt am Main, Lang 2000).

Christoph Vedder, **Walther Tröger**, 'Rechtsqualitat der IOC-Zulassungsregel – Anspruch und Wirklichkeit', Dieter Reuter, ed., *Einbindung des nationalen Sportrechts in internationale Bezüge* (Heidelberg, C.F. Müller Juristischer Verlag 1987), p. 1.

Christoph Vedder, 'The Development of Arbitration in Sports Law', in *International Athletic Foundation, Supplement to the official Proceedings of the IAF Symposium on Sport and Law*, Monte Carlo, 31 Jan.–2 Feb. 1991, Monaco 1995, p. 33 *et seq.*

Christoph Vedder, 'The IAAF Arbitration Panel. The Heritage of Two Decades of Arbitration in Doping-Related Disputes', in I. Blackshaw, R.C.R. Siekmann, J. Soek, eds., *The Court of Arbitration for Sport 1984–2004* (The Hague, T.M.C. Asser Press 2006), p. 266 *et seq.*

Hein Verbruggen, 'Towards Harmonization of Doping Rules: Theory and Practice', *ISLJ* (2000) p. 10-12.

P.C.J. Vergouwen, T. Collée, J. J. M. Marx, 'Hematocrit in Elite Athletes', 20 *International Journal of Sports Medicine* (2001) p. 538-541.

J.W.P. Verheugt, *Inleiding in het Nederlandse recht* (Den Haag, Boom Juridische Uitgevers, 2002)

D.J.P.M. Vermunt, *Onrecht en wederrechtelijkheid in de strafrechtsdogmatiek*, PhD. (Arnhem, Gouda Quint 1984).

M. Verroken, 'A time for Re-evaluation: The Challenge to an Athlete's Reputation', in O'Leary, ed., *Drugs and Doping in Sport* (London, Cavendish 2000) p. 31 *et seq.*

M. Verroken, 'Drug Use and Abuse in Sport', in J. M. Holly, P. E. Mullis, eds., Doping in Sport, Vol. 14, *Clinical Endocinology & Metabolism* (London 2000) p. 1-24.

Klaus Vieweg, *Normsetzung und -anwendung deutscher und internationaler Verbände. Eine rechtstatsächliche und rechtliche Untersuchung unter besonderer Berücksichtigung der Sportverbände* (Berlin, Duncker und Humblot 1990).

Klaus Vieweg, 'Doping und Verbandsrecht', *NJW* 1991, p. 1511-1516.

Klaus Vieweg, 'Teilnahmerechte und -pflichten der Vereine und Verbände', in Erwin Deutsch, Fritz Roth, Klaus Vieweg eds., *Teilnahme am Sport als Rechtsproblem: verbands-, vereins- und deliktsrechtliche Probleme* (Heidelberg, Müller, Jur. Verl. 1993).

Klaus Vieweg, 'Zur Bedeutung der Interessenabwägung bei der gerichtlichen Kontrolle von Verbands- Zulassungsentscheidungen', in Führungs- und Verwaltungsakademie des Deutschen Sportbundes, ed., *Verbandsrecht und Zulassungssperren* (Frankfurt am Main 1994) p. 36-49.

Klaus Vieweg, 'Disziplinargewalt und Inhaltskontrolle – Zum "Reiter-Urteil" des Bundesgerichtshofs', *SpuRt* (1995) p. 97- 101.

Klaus Vieweg, 'Judicial Review of Sport Related Decisions in Germany', in *International Athletic Foundation, Supplement to the official Proceedings of the IAF Symposium on Sport and Law*, Monte Carlo, 31 Jan.–2 Feb. 1991 (Monaco 1995) p. 87 *et seq.*

Klaus Vieweg, 'Zivilrechtliche Beurteilung der Blutentnahme zum Zwecke der Dopingkontrolle', in Bundesinstitut für Sportwissenschaft, ed., *Blut und/oder Urin zur Dopingkontrolle* (Schorndorf 1996) p. 89-130.

Klaus Vieweg, 'Grundinformationen zur Dopingproblematik', in Klaus Vieweg, ed., *Doping – Realität und Recht* (Berlin, Duncker & Humblot 1998) p. 21-35.

Klaus Vieweg, 'Divergence and Harmony in Sports Law - The Example of Anti-Doping Rules and Regulations', in D.C. Umbach, C. Vedder, eds., *Sportgerichtsbarkeit und Sanktionen* (Heidelberg, York 1999)

Klaus Vieweg, 'The Legal Autonomy of Sport Organisations and the Restrictions of European Law', in Andrew Caiger, Simon Gardiner, eds., *Professional Sport in the European Union: Regulation and Re-regulation* (The Hague, T.M.C. Asser Press 2000) p. 83 *et seq.*

Klaus Vieweg, 'Aktuelle Rechtsprobleme des Dopings', in V. Röhricht, K. Vieweg, eds., *Doping-Forum* (Stuttgart, Boorberg 2000) p. 13-16.

Klaus Vieweg, 'The Harmonization of Antidoping Rules and Regulations Different Approaches on the Basis of a Cybernatic Model', in Nathalie Korchia and Christophe Pettiti, eds., *Sport et Garanties Fondamentales* (Paris, Paris Bar Association 2001), p. 433.

Klaus Vieweg, *Spektrum des Sportrechts: Referate zweier Gemeinschaftstagungen der Universitäten Erlangen und Tübingen im Deutschen Olympischen Institut* (Berlin, Duncker und Humblot 2003).

Klaus Vieweg, ed., *Spektrum des Sportrechts. Referate zweier Gemeinschaftstagungen der Universitäten Erlangen und Tübingen im Deutschen Olympischen Institut, Berlin* (Berlin, Duncker und Humblot 2003).

Klaus Vieweg, Christian Paul, 'The Definition of Doping and the Proof of a Doping Offence', ISLJ (2002) p. 2-6.

Oscar Vogel, *Grundriss des Zivilprozessrechts und des internationalen Zivilprozessrechts der Schweiz* (Berne, Stämpfli 1999).

Emile N. Vrijman, 'Dopingbeleid in Nederland', in N.J.P. Giltay Veth, ed., Sport en Recht, Deel 1, *Doping: ook een juridisch probleem* (1992/1993) p. 17 *et seq.*

Emile N. Vrijman, *Blood Sampling and Doping Control* (Rotterdam, NeCeDo 1995).

Emile N. Vrijman, *Harmonisation: Can it Ever Be Really Achieved?* (Rotterdam: NeCeDo. 1995).

Emile N. Vrijman, 'Auf dem Weg zur Harmonisierung: Ein Kommentar zu aktuellen Aspekten und Problemen', in Klaus Vieweg, ed., *Doping – Realität und Recht* (Berlin, Duncker & Humblot 1998) p. 182.

Emile N. Vrijman, 'De IOC Conferentie "on Doping in Sport", doorbraak of mislukking?', in *Sportzaken* (1999) p. 78-80.

Emile N. Vrijman, 'Harmonisation: A Bridge too Far? A Commentary on Current Issues and Problems', in O'Leary, ed., *Drugs and Doping in Sport* (London, Cavendish 2000).

Emile N. Vrijman, 'Towards Harmonization: A Commentary on Current Issues and Problems', *ISLJ* (2000) p. 13-15.

Emile N. Vrijman, 'Experiences with Arbitration Before the CAS: Objective Circumstances of Purely Individual Impressions?', in I. Blackshaw, R.C.R. Siekmann, J. Soek, eds., *The Court of Arbitration for Sport 1984–2004* (The Hague, T.M.C. Asser Press 2006), p. 63 *et seq.*

R. de Waard, 'Schuld en wederrechtelijkheid als elementen van het delict', in *Liber Amicorum Th.W. van Veen – Opstellen aangeboden aan Th.W. van Veen ter gelegenheid van zijn vijfenzestigste verjaardag* (Arnhem, Gouda Quint 1985) p. 382.

Gerd Wagner, *The Triple Doping Dilemma: An Economic Analysis of Anti-Doping Regulations* (Bochum, Fak. für Sozialwiss., Ruhr-Univ. 1993).

Gerd Wagner, 'Eine einfache Möglichkeit zur anreizgesteuerten Dopingbekämpfung im Hochleistungssport. Theoriegeleiteter Vorschlag und empirische Evidenz', in Klaus Vieweg, ed., *Doping – Realität und Recht* (Berlin, Duncker & Humblot 1998) p. 391-400.

Wolf-Dietrich Walker, 'Beweisrechtliche und arbeitsrechtliche Probleme des Dopings', in Klaus Vieweg, ed., *Doping – Realität und Recht* (Berlin, Duncker & Humblot 1998) p. 135-176.

A. Wassing, 'Het tuchtrecht van het publiekvoetbal', PhD. (Leiden 1978).

R. Welch, 'A Snort and a Puff: Recreational Drugs and Discipline in Professional Sport', in O'Leary, ed., *Drugs and Doping in Sport* (London, Cavendish 2000) p. 75 *et seq.*

Michael R. Will, 'Rechtsgrundlagen der Bindung nationaler Verbande an internationale Sportverbandsregeln', Dieter Reuter, ed., *Einbindung des nationalen Sportrechts in internationale Bezüge* (Heidelberg, C.F. Müller Juristischer Verlag 1987), p. 29.

Melvin H. Williams, *Rekorde durch Doping? Wie Athleten legal und illegal ihre Leistung verbessern* (Aachen, Meyer u. Meyer 1990).

Tj.B. van Wimersma Greidanus, 'Doping in de sport; definities en middelen', 3 *TGO/JDR* (1991) p. 4-10.

Tj.B. van Wimersma Greidanus, P.A.G.M. de Smet, 'Geneesmiddelen en doping', in P.A.G.M. de Smet, A.C. van Loenen, L. Offerhaus en E. van der Does, eds., *Medicatiebegeleiding* (Houten, Bohn, Stafleu & Van Loghum 1990) p. 412-419.

A.N. Wise, 'Legal Status and Problems of Foreign Athletes in the United States', Paper presented for the T.M.C. Asser Instituut Round Table 'The Americanization of Sports Law? The American and European Sports Models Compared', Utrecht, The Netherlands, March 9, 2000.

Charles E. Yesalis, Andrea N. Kopstein, Michael S. Bahrke, 'Difficulties in Estimating the Prevalence of Drug Use Among Athletes', in W. Wilson, E. Derse, eds., *Doping in Elite Sport. The Politics of Drugs in the Olympic Movement* (Champaign, Illinois 2001) p. 43-62.

Brigitte Zypries, 'Anti-Doping-Politik des Bundes', in V. Röhricht, K. Vieweg, eds., *Doping-Forum* (Stuttgart, Boorberg 2000) p. 95 *et seq.*

LEGISLATION AND REGULATIONS

ANTI-DOPING CODES

TREATIES AND SUPRA-NATIONAL LEGISLATION

NATIONAL LEGISLATION

OTHER SPORT REGULATIONS

Court of Arbitration for Sport

Regulations of International Federations

TABLE OF CASES

THE COURT OF ARBITRATION FOR SPORT

SWITZERLAND

IAAF ARBITRATION PANEL

SUBJECT INDEX

Previous publications by or in cooperation with the
ASSER International Sports Law Centre
T.M.C. Asser Instituut – The Hague – The Netherlands

Basic Documents of International Sports Organisations, R.C.R. Siekmann and J.W. Soek, eds. (The Hague/Boston/London, Kluwer Law International 1998)

Doping Rules of International Sports Organisations, R.C.R. Siekmann, J.W. Soek and A. Bellani, eds. (The Hague, t.m.c.Asser press 1999)

Arbitral and Disciplinary Rules of International Sports Organisations, R.C.R. Siekmann and J.W. Soek, eds. (The Hague, t.m.c.Asser press 2001)

Professional Sport in the European Union: Regulation and Re-regulation, A. Caiger and S. Gardiner, eds. (The Hague, t.m.c.Asser press 2001)

Mediating Sports Disputes: National and International Perspectives, I.S. Blackshaw (The Hague, t.m.c.Asser press 2002)

The European Union and Sport: Legal and Policy Documents, R.C.R. Siekmann and J.W. Soek, eds. (The Hague, t.m.c.Asser press 2005)

Sports Image Rights in Europe, I.S. Blackshaw and R.C.R. Siekmann, eds. (The Hague, t.m.c.Asser press 2005)

The Court of Arbitration for Sport 1984–2004, I.S. Blackshaw, R.C.R. Siekmann and J.W. Soek, eds. (The Hague, t.m.c.Asser press 2006)